发现中国系列

湖北省公益学术著作出版专项资金

总 主 编
陈建国

副总主编
马荣 周莉萍 赵晓峰

数字中国

（双语版）

主 编：刘 威
副 主 编：徐文波 赵晓峰 程云青

华中科技大学出版社
http://press.hust.edu.cn
中国·武汉

图书在版编目（CIP）数据

数字中国 ：汉英对照 / 刘威主编. -- 武汉 ：华中科技大学出版社，2025.6. --（发现中国系列）.
ISBN 978-7-5772-1358-3

Ⅰ. F492

中国国家版本馆 CIP 数据核字第 2025RL2510 号

数字中国（双语版）　　　　　　　　　　　　　　　　　　　　　　　　　　刘　威　主编
Shuzi Zhongguo（Shuangyu Ban）

总 策 划：阮海洪
策划编辑：杨玉斌
责任编辑：陈　露
封面设计：清格印象
责任校对：谢　源
责任监印：朱　玢
出版发行：华中科技大学出版社（中国·武汉）　　　电话：(027)81321913
　　　　　武汉市东湖新技术开发区华工科技园　　　邮编：430223
录　　排：华中科技大学惠友文印中心
印　　刷：湖北金港彩印有限公司
开　　本：787mm×1092mm　1/16
印　　张：27
字　　数：674 千字
版　　次：2025 年 6 月第 1 版第 1 次印刷
定　　价：238.00 元

总　　序

纵观人类历史,教育兴则国家兴,教育强则国家强。如今,随着经济全球化的深入推进,教育对外开放已成为推动国家发展的重要战略。党的十八大以来,有关高等教育国际化发展的重要文件密集出台,国际交流与合作已被列入高校五大职能之一,华中科技大学积极响应号召,发布一系列纲领性文件,深入推进国际化办学,高度重视来华留学生教育工作。"发现中国系列"正是在这一背景下为来华留学生打造的经典著作,可以说既是时代之需,也是责任之举。

我们身处的时代,是一个交通高度发达、人员往来密切、文化交流日益频繁的时代。在这个时代,如何讲好中国故事,让世界更好地了解中国,成为摆在我们面前的重要课题。我们深知,来华留学生具有"贯通中外"的优势,是中外友好往来的特殊使者,是沟通中国与世界的重要桥梁。向来华留学生全面系统讲述中国经济社会发展情况,有助于赋能来华留学生讲好中国故事,增强中华文明的国际传播力和影响力。

近年来,习近平总书记多次饱含深情给海外学子、留学归国人员、来华留学生回信,认真学习这些回信让我深受启发,倍感鼓舞。一方面,我曾是海外学子,于 1995 年出国留学,先后在德国、美国学习工作 6 年多,这些经历让我更了解来华留学生的学习和生活需求;另一方面,留学归国 20 多年来,我一直在高校从事科研教学和管理工作,在担任华中科技大学副校长期间更是分管国际交流与合作工作多年,来华留学生教育工作是我的重要工作职责之一。我见证和亲历了我国高等教育事业和科技事业的飞速发展,面对日益庞大的来华留学生队伍,深感骄傲和自豪,同时也感到责任重大。

当前,我国社会正处于高质量发展的新阶段,以高水平对外开放促进高质量发展已成为时代要求,在经济领域如是,在教育领域亦然。我相信,高水平的教育对外开放既是推动高校"双一流"建设的动力,也是开辟高校国际合作新领域的契机。因而,在国际化工作中,我们始终坚持从国际维度布局,在国际坐标定位,以国际名校为标杆,大力拓展与国际顶尖大学的实质性合作,在扩大我校来华留学生规模的基础上,进一步提升来华留学生教育质量。

"发现中国系列"选取了中国的经济发展、医疗卫生、数字化建设等民生热点,通过阐述各大领域的发展历程、技术创新、政策演变、深层逻辑、国际合作等内容,全面介绍现代化建设的中国质量和中国速度,不仅是对中国现代化建设的生动记录,更是对中华文明精神标识和文化精髓的提炼展示。

该系列每一本书都由相关领域的权威专家担任主编,在这里,我要特别感谢各位主编的大力支持与辛勤付出。他们既是深耕科研的顶尖专家学者,对我国乃至国际的经济与科技发展态势有敏锐的感知,具有丰富的图书编写经验,对内容的把握高屋建瓴,又是拥有丰富教学经验的一线教师,了解来华留学生的需求,深谙授业之道,在人才培养上有独特的见解。我相信,这样一套契合时代背景、精选热点主题、洞悉读者需求的双语系列图书,能很好地向广大来华留学生展示全面、立体、真实的中国,赋能他们讲好中国故事,当好友谊使者,搭起合作桥梁。

据我所知,"发现中国系列"已与世界知名出版机构施普林格达成英文版出版协议,将面向全世界出版发行。这也意味着,我们将站在一个更为广阔的舞台上讲述中国故事,宣介中国智慧、中国方案,有助于推进对外文化交流、加强国际传播能力建设,构建中国叙事体系。

未来,"发现中国系列"还会陆续编写、出版,为来华留学生的教育工作逐步夯实基础,一步一个脚印、稳扎稳打做好我校国际化建设工作。我很期待来华留学生和海外读者能从"发现中国系列"中认识中国、了解中国、爱上中国,也很希望该系列能够成为中外文化交流的一道亮丽风景线,为推动构建人类命运共同体贡献我们的智慧和力量。

陈建国

华中科技大学原副校长

Series Editor's Preface

Throughout the history of mankind, when education in a country thrives, the country will thrive, and strong education makes a strong nation. Today, as economic globalization continues to deepen, the opening-up of education has become an essential strategy for national development. Since the 18th National Congress of the Communist Party of China, numerous important documents concerning the internationalization of higher education have been issued, with international exchange and cooperation now being one of the five major functions of universities. Huazhong University of Science and Technology (HUST) has actively responded to this call by releasing a series of guiding documents to promote the internationalization of education, and placing significant emphasis on the education of international students in China. The "Introduction to China's S&T Innovation" is a classic collection of works created for international students in China in this context, which can be said to be both a need of the times and a responsibility.

We live in an era characterized by advanced transportation, frequent interpersonal exchanges, and increasingly dynamic cultural interactions. In this era, how to tell China's stories well and let the world understand China better has become an important issue for us. We are fully aware that international students in China possess the unique advantage of being "bridges between China and the world," serving as special envoys of friendship between China and the world and important connectors between China and the world. By providing international students with a comprehensive understanding of China's economic and social development, we can empower them to tell China's stories well, thereby enhancing the international dissemination of Chinese civilization.

In recent years, Xi Jinping, General Secretary of the Central Committee of the Communist Party of China, has written numerous heartfelt letters to overseas students, returning scholars, and international students in China. Studying these letters has deeply inspired and encouraged me. On the one hand, as a former overseas student who studied abroad in Germany and the United States for over six years starting in 1995, I have gained a deep understanding of the academic and living needs of international students in China. On the other hand, since returning from studying abroad over 20 years ago, I have been engaged in research, teaching, and administrative work at universities. During my tenure as Vice President of Huazhong University of Science and Technology, I was responsible for international exchange and cooperation for many years, with international student education being one of my primary responsibilities. I have witnessed and experienced the rapid development of China's higher education and scientific research. As the number of international students in China continues to grow, I feel proud and honored, and at the same time, I also feel a great sense of responsibility.

At present, China is in a new phase of high-quality development, where promoting high-quality development through high-level opening-up has become a requirement of the times, both in the economic and educational fields. I believe that high-level opening-up of education is not only a driving force for the "Double First-Class" initiative in Chinese universities, but also an opportunity to explore new areas of international cooperation for universities. Therefore, in our internationalization efforts, we have consistently adopted an international perspective, positioning ourselves within a global framework, benchmarking against world-class universities, and actively expanding substantial cooperation with top international institutions. While expanding the scale of international students in China, we have also worked to further improve the quality of their education.

The "Introduction to China's S&T Innovation" selects key topics related to China's economic development, medical and health care, digitalization construction and other hot spots of China's livelihood. By explaining the development process, technological innovations, policy evolution, underlying logic, and international cooperation in these fields, the series provides a comprehensive introduction to the quality and speed of China's modernization efforts. It not only serves as a vivid record of China's modernization, but also highlights the spiritual symbols and cultural essence of Chinese civilization.

Each book in this series is edited by authoritative experts in the relevant field. Here, I would like to extend my heartfelt gratitude to the chief editors for their strong support and hard work. They are leading scholars deeply engaged in scientific research, with keen insights into the trends of economic and technological development in China and internationally. They possess rich experience in book compilation and a profound understanding of the content. Furthermore, they are front-line educators with extensive teaching experience, who understand the needs of international students in China, know the ways of teaching, and have unique insights into talent cultivation. I am confident that this series, which fits the background of the times, carefully selects hot topics, and understands readers' needs, will be able to present a comprehensive, multidimensional, and authentic China to international students. It will empower them to tell a good story about China, act as good envoys of friendship, and build bridges of cooperation.

As far as I know, the "Introduction to China's S&T Innovation" has reached an agreement with Springer, a world-renowned publishing house, to publish the English version, which will be distributed worldwide. This also means that we will stand on a broader stage to tell China's stories, promote Chinese wisdom and solutions, and contribute to advancing cultural exchanges, strengthening international communication capabilities, and shaping a Chinese narrative.

Looking ahead, the "Introduction to China's S&T Innovation" will continue to be developed and published, laying a solid foundation for the education of international students in China. We will continue to advance the internationalization of our university step by step. I look forward to seeing international students and overseas readers get to know, understand, and fall in love with China through the "Introduction to China's S&T Innovation." I also hope that this series will become a beautiful landscape of cultural exchange between China and the world, contributing our wisdom and strength to the building of a community with a shared future for mankind.

Chen Jianguo
Former Vice President of Huazhong University of Science and Technology

序　言

在经济全球化与信息数字化深度交融的时代浪潮中,以人工智能、大数据、云计算、区块链等为代表的新一代信息技术,正以前所未有的强劲态势,全方位重塑世界经济格局,革新社会运行模式。这些技术深度渗透到各个产业,催生出全新的商业模式与业态,推动世界经济格局发生深刻变革。世界主要经济体,如美国、俄罗斯、欧盟、日本等,都敏锐洞察到这一发展趋势,纷纷在不同领域制定了面向 2030 年的数字化发展目标。

中国在信息产业发展和信息化基础设施建设等领域成绩斐然,举世瞩目,已然成为全球数字变革的领军者。2023 年 2 月,中国发布《数字中国建设整体布局规划》,明确提出到 2035 年将数字化发展水平提升至世界前列的宏伟目标。当下,新一轮数字化浪潮正席卷中国大地,即将在社会经济、生产生活等诸多方面掀起深刻变革,重塑中国未来发展格局。

在此时代背景下,更新高等院校信息素养类通识课程内容势在必行,这有助于本科生和研究生拓宽数字视野,把握数字发展趋势。然而,与其他通识课程相比,国内缺乏全面介绍数字中国的图书。来华留学的国际学生对中国的数字化发展状况兴趣浓厚,但目前大多通过日常生活中的数字应用管中窥豹。《数字中国(双语版)》正是为满足这一需求而编写的。全书共 8 章,涵盖信息产业概述、数字中国概况、信息技术创新、数字产业化、产业数字化、数字社会、网络空间治理、国际数字合作等内容,旨在为读者呈现数字中国的全景风貌。

第 1 章"信息产业概述"主要普及信息技术与信息产业的基本概念和特征。该章先梳理信息产业的发展脉络,从语言文字的诞生,到邮政、电信、广播的兴起,再到计算机与互联网时代的变革,展现其演进历程;接着深入分析信息产业的特征,包括产业范围、在经济体系中的地位、自身特性及发展规律;随后介绍新一代信息技术和第四次工业革命,探讨它们为信息产业带来的变革与机遇;最后聚焦新型数字经济,解读其涵盖领域和全球数字战略布局。

第 2 章"数字中国概况"介绍中国信息产业的基本背景和现有规划。该章首先以时间为线索,简要回顾中国信息产业从无到有、由弱变强的发展历程;接着阐述数字中国当前的规模与水平,让读者了解其发展现状;随后剖析中国信息产业的宏观战略与产业规划,涵盖国家发展战略、政府规划及政策工具等方面;最后聚焦数字中国的发展目标与建设重点,介绍中国政府在数字基础设施、数字经济、数字社会等方面的发展规划。

第 3 章"信息技术创新"解读中国如何通过统筹规划,推动信息技术和产业创新与国民经济融合发展。该章先介绍中国科技研发体系的构成,以及科技发展计划的组织与实施;然后以案例的形式,介绍超级计算机、量子通信、北斗导航等重大科技基础设施工程,以及超高清视频、移动通信、集成电路等产业攻关科技成就。

第 4 章"数字产业化"阐述"十四五"初期中国传统信息产业的主要成就。该章依次介绍基础电信业、互联网产业、软件和信息技术服务业、电子信息制造业四个数字产业板块:在基础电信业方面,重点介绍中国 5G 移动通信网络、卫星互联网、车联网、算力设施等新型信息基础设施的建设进展;在互联网产业方面,聚焦中国在社交网络、电子商务、移动支付等特色应用上的成果;在软件和信息技术服务业方面,介绍中国近年来云计算、大数据、人工智能、区块链等产业的发展情况;在电子信息制造业方面,重点讲解中国在新型显示器件、集成电路芯片等领域取得的技术突破。

第 5 章"产业数字化"介绍中国以信息化带动工业化,在制造业、农业、能源、交通等行业开展数字化转型升级的代表性成就。该章首先聚焦智能制造,从工业互联网搭建产业互联桥梁,到工业机器人提升生产效率,再到智能工厂实现生产智能化升级,全方位展现制造业的数字化转型;接着关注智慧农业,介绍农业大数据如何助力科学决策,智慧种植和智慧养殖怎样推动农业现代化发展;随后探索智慧能源领域,涵盖智能煤矿、智慧电厂和智能电网的建设成果;最后走近智能交通,展现智慧道路交通、智能轨道交通和智能水运交通的高效便捷。

第 6 章"数字社会"讲述中国利用数字化技术提升城市、乡村公共服务水平,提供更优质教育、医疗等社会服务的实践。该章首先介绍中国在智慧城市方面的探索,从城市交通管控的智能化,到城市大脑的高效运行,再到数字孪生城市的创新构建,展现中国运用数字技术提升城市治理水平的举措;接着介绍中国推进数字乡村建设的各项举措,借助信息网络基础设施建设实施扶贫攻坚行动,建立完善的数字公共服务体系,支持农村电子商务发展,实现乡村振兴;智慧教育部分涵盖数字校园设施建设、数字课程平台搭建、互联网教育等多元应用;智慧医疗板块则呈现数字医疗基础设施的进步,以及互联网医疗和智慧医疗的实际应用成果。

第 7 章"网络空间治理"阐述中国在网络空间治理领域的现状与成就。该章首先阐述网络空间的基本概念,以及安全与治理面临的需求和挑战;接着介绍中国构建的网络空间法律体系,涵盖个人权益保障、数字经济规则、网络信息安全、网络生态规范等多方面的法律建设;然后介绍中国在网络空间安全保护能力建设方面的成果,包括网络安全技术标准、网络安全保护队伍建设和网络安全产业发展等;最后介绍中国在网络空间社会治理方面采取的全方位、多维度举措,涉及公共环境治理、个人隐私保护、数字内容监管、数字经济监管等。

第 8 章"国际数字合作"介绍中国在全球网络空间治理中的贡献。该章首先阐明全球网络空间数字合作面临的挑战与机遇,包括网络安全风险、数字贸易需求等;随后阐述中国提出的构建全球"网络空间命运共同体"的主张,包括其核心思想和深刻内涵;接着介绍中国在数字经济国际合作方面的成果,特别是在全球数字服务供给、跨境电子商务等领域;最后在网络空间治理国际合作部分,介绍中国在网络安全、打击网络犯罪等方面开展的国际合作。

国家主席习近平在致 2022 年世界互联网大会乌镇峰会的贺信中强调:"中国愿同世界各国一道,携手走出一条数字资源共建共享、数字经济活力迸发、数字治理精准高效、数字文化繁荣发展、数字安全保障有力、数字合作互利共赢的全球数字发展道路,加快构建网络空间命运共同体,为世界和平发展和人类文明进步贡献智慧和力量。"《数字中国(双语版)》搭建起中国与世界沟通的桥梁,为国际学生提供深入了解中国数字发展状况的窗口,让他们在学习过程中感受中国数字领域的创新活力与发展成就,为未来国际合作与交流贡献智慧和力量。

本书编写组由华中科技大学国际教育学院、电子信息与通信学院等单位从事来华留学教育的师资组成。刘威、徐文波、程云青等负责组织撰写信息产业概述、数字中国概况、信息技术创新、数字产业化、产业数字化等章节，赵晓峰、马荣等负责组织撰写数字社会、网络空间治理、国际数字合作等章节。在华中科技大学"来华留学大工科教学基地"的支持下，书稿部分内容以课程、讲座等形式进行教学，并根据收集的国际学生意见进行了修改。本书的撰写还获得了中国高等教育学会"数字教育发展推动国际学生教育变革创新研究"重大项目(23LH0102)的支持。

数字中国是当前中国全力推进的数字化全面赋能经济社会高质量发展的宏大工程，其涉及范围广泛、内容繁杂，且建设进展日新月异。本书8章内容仅是当代中国数字化建设的一个缩影。为在有限篇幅内实现全景式介绍，编写组重点参考了"十四五"以来政府部门、行业学会发布的公开资料。编写组虽全力以赴，但受专业水平、时间和精力所限，书中难免存在疏漏之处，诚望广大读者批评指正。

Preface

In the era of deep integration of economic globalization and digital informatization, a new generation of information and communications technology (ICT), represented by artificial intelligence, big data, cloud computing, blockchain, etc., is reshaping the global economic landscape and revolutionizing the social operation modes with unprecedented momentum. These technologies have deeply penetrated into various industries, giving rise to new business models and forms, and driving profound changes in the global economic landscape. Major economies in the world, such as the United States, Russia, the European Union, and Japan, have keenly perceived this development trend and formulated their digital development goals for 2030 across diverse domains.

China has made remarkable achievements in the development of the information industry and information infrastructure construction, attracting worldwide attention and emerging as a global leader in digital transformation. In February 2023, China released the "Overall Layout Plan for Digital China Construction", clearly outlining the ambitious goal of elevating its digital development level to the forefront of the world by 2035. Currently, a new wave of digitization is sweeping across China, which is about to trigger profound changes in society, economy, production, and life, and reshape China's future development pattern.

Against this background, it is imperative to update the content of information literacy general courses in colleges and universities. This is conducive to helping undergraduate and postgraduate students broaden their digital horizons and keep up with the digital development trend. However, compared with other general courses, there is a lack of books in China that comprehensively introduce "Digital China". International students studying in China show great enthusiasm for China's digital development. Yet currently, they mostly get a partial understanding through digital applications in their daily lives. This textbook, *Digital China (Bilingual version)*, is thus written to meet this need. Comprising eight chapters, the book covers topics such as the basics of the ICT industry, overview of "Digital China", ICT innovations, digital industrialization, industrial digitalization, digital society, cyberspace governance, and international digital cooperation, aiming to present readers with a panoramic view of "Digital China".

Chapter 1, "Basics of the ICT Industry", primarily introduces the basic concepts and features of the ICT industry. This chapter first traces the development trajectory of the ICT industry, from the birth of language and writing, the rise of postal services, telecommunications, and broadcasting, to the revolutionary changes in the computer and Internet era. Then it deeply analyzes the features of the ICT industry, including its industrial scope, position in the economic system, inherent features, and development laws. Subsequently, it introduces the new-generation information technologies and the Fourth Industrial Revolution, and explores the changes and opportunities they bring to the ICT industry. Finally, it focuses on the new digital economy, interpreting the covered areas and the related digital strategic layout made by different countries.

Chapter 2, "Overview of Digital China", introduces the basic background and existing plans of China's ICT industry. Firstly, this chapter briefly reviews the development journey of China's ICT industry, from its humble beginnings to its current strength, in chronological order. Then it expounds on the current scale and development level of Digital China, enabling readers to have a clear understanding of its status quo. Subsequently, it analyzes related macro strategies and industrial plans of China's ICT industry, covering national development strategies, government plans, and policy tools. Finally, it focuses on the development goals and construction priorities of "Digital China", introducing the Chinese government's development plans in digital infrastructure, digital economy, digital society, and other aspects.

Chapter 3, "ICT Innovations", interprets how China promotes the integrated development of information technology, and industrial innovation with the national economy through overall planning. This chapter first introduces the composition of China's scientific research and development system, as well as the organization and implementation of scientific and technological development plans. Then, through case studies, it introduces major scientific and technological infrastructure projects such as supercomputers, quantum communications, and BeiDou navigation, along with scientific and technological achievements in industrial research and development such as Ultra-HD video, mobile communications, and integrated circuits.

Chapter 4, "Digital Industrialization", elaborates on the main achievements of China's traditional information industry in the early stage of the "14th Five-Year Plan". This chapter successively introduces four digital industry sectors: basic telecommunications industry, Internet industry, software and information technology services industry, and electronic information manufacturing industry. In the aspect of basic telecommunications industry, it focuses on the construction progress of new-type information infrastructure in China, such as 5G mobile communications networks, satellite Internet, Internet of Vehicles, and computing infrastructure. In the aspect of Internet industry, it focuses on the achievements of China in characteristic applications such as social media, e-commerce, and mobile payments. In the aspect of software and information technology services, it introduces the development of cloud computing, big data, artificial intelligence, and blockchain in recent years. In the aspect of electronic information manufacturing industry, it emphasizes on the technological breakthroughs made by China in fields such as new display devices and integrated circuit chips.

Chapter 5, "Industrial Digitalization", presents China's representative achievements in promoting the digital transformation of industries such as manufacturing, agriculture, energy, and transportation by leveraging informatization to drive industrialization. This chapter first focuses on intelligent manufacturing, showing the digital transformation of the manufacturing industry from the industrial Internet platforms that build industry-wide connections, to the use of industrial robots to improve production efficiency, and then to the intelligent upgrading of production in intelligent factories. Then it pays attention to smart agriculture, introducing how agricultural big data helps with scientific decision-making and how smart cultivation and smart farming promote the modernization of agriculture. Subsequently, it explores the field of smart energy, covering the construction achievements of intelligent coal mines, smart power plants, and smart power grids. Finally, it enters the field of intelligent transportation, showing the high-efficiency and convenience of smart road transportation, intelligent rail transportation, and intelligent water transportation.

Chapter 6, "Digital Society", tells China's practice of using digital technologies to improve the level of public services in cities and rural areas and provide better social services such as education and healthcare. This chapter first introduces China's exploration in smart cities, from the coordination of urban traffic, the efficient operation of the urban brain, to the innovative construction of digital twin cities, showing China's measures to improve urban governance with digital technologies. Then it introduces various measures taken by China to promote the construction of digital villages, such as strengthening the construction of communications infrastructure to assist the "poverty alleviation" campaign, establishing a complete rural digital public service system, and supporting the development of rural e-commerce to achieve rural revitalization. In the section on smart education, it covers diverse applications such as the construction of digital campus facilities, the establishment of digital course platforms, and Internet-based education. The smart healthcare section presents the progress of digital healthcare infrastructure and the practical application results of Internet healthcare services and smart healthcare applications.

Chapter 7, "Cyberspace Governance", elaborates on the current situation and achievements of China in the field of cyberspace governance. This chapter first expounds on the basic concept of cyberspace and the needs and challenges faced in security and governance. Then it introduces the legal framework of cyberspace constructed by China, covering legal construction in multiple aspects, including the protection of personal rights and interests, digital economic rules, network information security, and network ecological norms. Then it introduces the achievements of China in the construction of cyberspace security protection capabilities, including cybersecurity technical standards, the cybersecurity protection forces, and the development of the cybersecurity industry. Finally, it introduces the comprehensive and multi-dimensional governance carried out by China in cyberspace social governance, involving public environment governance, personal privacy protection, digital content supervision, and digital economic regulation.

Chapter 8, "International Digital Cooperation", introduces China's contributions to global cyberspace governance. This chapter first points out the challenges and opportunities faced by global digital cooperation in cyberspace, including cybersecurity risks and digital trade demands. Subsequently, it expounds on China's proposition of building a global "community with a shared future in cyberspace", including its core ideas and profound connotations. Then it introduces China's achievements in the development of the international digital economy, especially in the fields of global digital service supply and cross-border e-commerce. Finally, in the part of international cooperation on cyberspace governance, it introduces the international cooperation carried out by China in cybersecurity cooperation and the fight against cybercrime.

Chinese President Xi Jinping sent congratulations to 2022 World Internet Conference Wuzhen Summit and stressed: "China is willing to work with countries around the world to jointly explore a path of global digital development featuring the joint construction and sharing of digital resources, the vibrant development of the digital economy, well-targeted and efficient digital governance, the prosperous development of digital culture, strong digital security protection, and mutually beneficial digital cooperation. We aim to accelerate the building of a community with a shared future in cyberspace and contribute wisdom and strength to world peace and development and the progress of human civilization." *Digital China (Bilingual version)* serves as a communication bridge between China and the world. It provides a window for international students to gain in-depth knowledge of China's digital development, and enables them to experience the innovative vitality and development achievements of China's digital field, thus contributing wisdom and strength to future international cooperation and exchanges.

The writing team of this book is composed of the faculties engaged in international student education from the School of International Education and the School of Electronic Information and Communications at Huazhong University of Science and Technology (HUST). Liu Wei, Xu Wenbo and Cheng Yunqing are responsible for organizing and writing the chapters of basics of the ICT industry, overview of Digital China, ICT innovations, digital industrialization, and industrial digitalization. Zhao Xiaofeng and Ma Rong are responsible for organizing and writing the chapters of digital society, cyberspace governance, and international digital cooperation. With the support of International Education Base of Engineering at HUST, some of the book's content was taught in the form of courses and lectures and revised based on the opinions collected from international students. This writing process has also received support from the project "Promoting International Student Education Innovation through Digital Education Development"

(23LH0102) by China Association of Higher Education.

Digital China is a grand project of comprehensively empowering the high-quality development of the economy and society through digitalization that China is currently vigorously promoting. It covers a wide range of areas, involves complex content, and its construction progress is changing rapidly. The eight-chapter content of this book is only a microcosm of contemporary China's digital construction. In order to provide a panoramic introduction within a limited space, the writing team mainly referred to publicly available materials released by government departments and industry associations since the "14th Five-Year Plan". Although the writing team has gone all out, due to limitations in professional expertise, time, and energy, there are bound to be some oversights in this book. We sincerely welcome readers to offer their criticisms and suggestions.

目录

Contents

1 信息产业概述

1.1 发 展 简 史

信息是事物运动变化的表征。从古人产生和发展语言到发明文字进行书写交流，再到今天人们利用电子技术处理和传播信息，人类的信息交流史跨越了数千年。人类经历了 5 次信息技术创新，并在技术的推广应用中形成了相应的信息产业。

1.1.1 语言与文字

语言和文字的产生与使用通常被认为是人类信息技术创新的开始，促进了远古农业、手工业和商业的发展。人类语言是最原始也是最持久的信息载体。语言是人类最重要的交流工具，是人类沟通交流的表达符号。文字是承载语言的书写符号，是人类用以传递信息的工具，也使得信息可以突破时间、空间的限制而流传。

现代智人依靠较强的语言沟通能力走出非洲，进入欧亚大陆。在漫长的岁月中，世界上不同的民族形成了自己的语言，其中四大古文明都拥有自己的文字，如表 1-1 所示。

表 1-1　人类四大古文明概况

文明名称	文明出现时间	地域	文字	示例
古埃及文明	约公元前 3000 年	非洲尼罗河流域	象形文字	
古印度文明	约公元前 2500 年	亚洲印度河流域	印章文字	

续表

文明名称	文明出现时间	地域	文字	示例
中华文明	约公元前 2070 年	亚洲黄河、长江流域	甲骨文	
古巴比伦文明	约公元前 1800 年	亚洲底格里斯河、幼发拉底河流域	楔形文字	

文字的形态与书写方式、记录载体密切相关,并随着社会生产力的发展逐步演变。下面以中国的文字为例进行说明。目前可以追溯的具有文字符号特征的最早的中国文字,是出现于公元前 2500 年左右龙山文化遗存中的刻在兽骨上的文字符号,这种文字符号具备象形文字的特征。出现于约公元前 1400 年中国商朝的甲骨文被视为中国文字的第一种形式,甲骨文是以占卜为目的刻写在龟甲和兽骨上的文字。中国周朝出现了毛笔,使用毛笔可以将文字书写在竹简或纺织物(例如帛)上,不同诸侯国有自己的文字符号,这显然阻碍了文化交流。

公元前 221 年,秦始皇统一中国,宣布以"小篆"为全国统一的文字,首次规范了中国文字的书写形式。在中国东汉时期,约公元 105 年,造纸术得到改良,纸开始被作为主要的书写材料;同时代出现了隶书、楷书,更加简单且易于辨识。经过汉朝的发展,中国文字体系趋近于成熟,字形基本固定,因此中国文字也称为"汉字"。汉字的数量随着时间的推移而增长,至清朝,《康熙字典》收录的汉字已有 47 035 个。

传统汉字笔画较多,不便于认读和速记。1956 年,中华人民共和国国务院公布《汉字简化方案》。1964 年,中国文字改革委员会正式编印《简化字总表》,该表共收录了 2 238 个简化汉字,即目前通行的汉字形态。表 1-2 列出了 3 个典型中国文字的字形演变过程。

表 1-2 中国文字字形演变示例

字体	出现时期	记录方式	示例 1(马)	示例 2(鱼)	示例 3(册)
甲骨文	约公元前 1400 年	刻写在龟甲或者兽骨上			
金文	约公元前 1300 年	铸或刻在青铜器上			
小篆	公元前 221 年	书写在竹简上			

续表

字体	出现时期	记录方式	示例 1（马）	示例 2（鱼）	示例 3（册）
隶书	约公元 150 年	书写在纸张上	馬	魚	冊
楷书	约公元 220 年	书写在纸张上	馬	魚	冊
简化字	1955 年	书写或者印刷在纸张上	马	鱼	册

　　文字的出现为知识和历史的记录提供了可能。中国历朝历代都十分重视历史的记录，约公元前 104 年—前 91 年撰成的《史记》记录了从上古时代到汉朝的中华历史。在四大古文明中，中华文明是唯一延续至今没有中断且有完整文字历史记录的文明。

1.1.2　印刷与邮政

　　人类历史上出现过多种记录文字的载体，纸张是其中最方便和应用最广泛的载体。在印刷术出现之前，人类以手写抄录的方式书写文字，应用范围和规模有限。在中国北宋时期，约公元 1040 年，出现了活字印刷术，使得规模化复制书籍成为可能（见图 1-1）。活字印刷术先后传到朝鲜、日本和中亚地区，并经过阿拉伯等地传入欧洲，促进了世界文明的发展。

图 1-1　采用活字印刷的古籍残页（北宋，约公元 1100 年）[①]

图片来源：温州博物馆

[①]　北宋《佛说观无量寿佛经》活字印刷残页，现藏于中国温州博物馆，是迄今发现存世最早的活字印刷品。

古代信息的交流与传播主要依赖于纸质载体的运输。中国古代建立了专用于信息载体和物资运输的系统，称为邮驿，其中"邮"是专职传递官方文书的机构，而"驿"是传递文书的马和车中转的处所。古代王朝通常会在主要交通市镇设立专用的机构"驿站"，往来文书一站一站接力传递，汉朝急件每日可以传递400里（约200千米）。图1-2为丝绸之路上的嘉峪关出土的魏晋彩绘驿使图砖。中国古代的邮驿系统主要为官方服务，直到1896年清朝建立邮政系统才废止，存在了约2 000年。

图1-2　古代邮驿驿使形象（魏晋时期，约公元220—420年）

图片来源：甘肃省博物馆

随着社会的发展，出现了专门提供书信、包裹运输服务的行业，即邮政业。在中国明清时期出现了为百姓提供邮寄服务的"信局"，各信局的投递业务并不互通。现代邮政业诞生在英国，1840年英国发行了世界上第一枚邮票"黑便士"，通过邮资预付推动邮政业的发展。1874年"邮政总联盟"（现为万国邮政联盟）成立，通过邮政系统寄送书信成为当时世界各国进行信息交流的主要方式。

1.1.3　电信与广播

19世纪中叶到20世纪中叶，电磁学理论逐步成熟，以电信号为载体进行通信成为可能。人类通信领域发生了根本性的巨大变革，信息传递可以脱离常规的视听方式，利用金属导线来传递信息，甚至通过看不见、摸不着的电磁波来通信。

美国科学家莫尔斯发明了电报机，将英文字母等文本表达为点和线的组合，通过发送不同时长电信号的组合传递信息，实现了文本信息通过电磁信号的传递。美国人贝尔发明的电话通过麦克风和扬声器将语音转换为电信号，实现了语言信息通过电缆的传递。意大利科学家马可尼发明了无线电报机，实现了以空气为介质的通信。英美科学家研制的收音机、电视机，可以接收电台和电视台的广播信号，解调、恢复并播放语音和视频信号。电报、电话和广播电视的诞生，改变了人们通过纸质媒介交流信息的方式，实现了跨越地域的远距离通信。表1-3列举了电信与广播领域的主要发明。

表 1-3　电信与广播领域的主要发明

领域	发明	代表性事件
电信	有线电报	1837 年,美国科学家莫尔斯成功研制基于有线电缆的电磁电报机;1858 年,横跨大西洋连接欧美两洲的海底电报电缆铺设成功
	无线电报	1896 年,意大利科学家马可尼成功研制了无线电报机;1901 年,跨大西洋无线电通信得以实现
	有线电话	1876 年,美国人贝尔为自己发明的电话申请了专利;1878 年,在波士顿和纽约之间进行的长途电话通话实验获得成功
	电话交换机	1926 年,世界上第一个大型纵横制自动电话交换机在瑞典投入使用;1938 年,美国开通了纵横制自动电话交换系统
广播	电子管	1904 年,英国科学家弗莱明发明了真空二极管;1906 年,美国发明家李·德福雷斯特发明了真空三极管;20 世纪 30 年代末,电子管成为主流的电子元件
	收音机	1906 年,美国科学家费森登进行了用调制的无线电波发送音乐和讲话的广播实验;1910 年,美国人邓伍迪和皮卡德成功研制了基于电子管的矿石收音机
	电视机	1933 年,美国科学家佐利金成功研制了电视映像用的摄像管和映像管;1954 年,美国成功研制了世界上第一台彩色电视机

电报、电话等通信技术也催生了现代电信服务业,代表公司有美国电话电报公司等。无线电广播、电视催生了现代媒体服务业,代表公司有英国广播公司等。联合国于 1949 年首次制定《所有经济活动的国际标准行业分类》,用编码 73 指代通信业,其中既包括传统的邮政业,也包括基于有线电和无线电等技术提供的信息传输服务,以及相关的信息交换、存储和记录服务等。

1.1.4　计算机与互联网

20 世纪中叶到 21 世纪初的 50 余年间,半导体、计算机、互联网、移动通信等技术获得突破,掀起了信息技术革命的浪潮。

微电子学的发展为电子元件、器件和电路的技术升级提供了理论基础。1958 年,集成电路的发明更使得半导体技术的发展进入了快车道。1965 年,戈登·摩尔预测,未来一个芯片上的晶体管数每 18 个月翻一番。半导体工业和技术的迅速发展,为各类电子信息产品的生产和制造奠定了物质基础。表 1-4 列举了微电子领域的主要技术进展。

表 1-4　微电子领域的主要技术进展

成果	代表性事件
晶体管	1948 年 6 月,美国贝尔实验室固体物理研究小组发明了晶体管;1953 年,该研究小组的肖克利等人成功研制出硅结型场效应晶体管;晶体管体积小、性能稳定,开始替代电子管成为电子信息产品的基础器件

续表

成果	代表性事件
集成电路	1958 年 9 月,美国德州仪器公司的基尔比研制出了世界上第一块包含晶体管、电阻器和电容器的锗集成电路板;1959 年,美国仙童半导体公司的诺伊斯用平面工艺制作出硅集成电路,真正实现了单片集成电路
大规模集成电路	1967 年,美国贝尔实验室制成了世界上第一块大规模集成电路(单个芯片上集成 1 000 个元件),并很快推广到工业生产和实际应用中

现代计算机原理和架构获得理论上的突破。1945 年,科学家约翰·冯·诺依曼提出了二进制存储程序通用电子计算机方案。1946 年,第一台电子计算机在美国研制成功。伴随着微电子学的发展,计算机从电子管、晶体管的时代步入集成电路的时代,计算能力随着中央处理器生产工艺的改良获得巨大提升。计算机从少数机构才有机会使用的大型设备,变成了走进千家万户的消费电子设备。表 1-5 列举了计算机领域的主要技术进展。

表 1-5　计算机领域的主要技术进展

成果	代表性事件
电子管计算机	1946 年 2 月,美国宾夕法尼亚大学教授莫契利和埃克特共同成功研制出计算机 ENIAC,该计算机是世界上第一台通用计算机,共使用了约 18 000 个电子管,被用于国防和科学计算;1951 年,美国雷明顿兰德公司研制出的计算机 UNIVAC 被应用于美国人口普查,计算机开始民用服务
晶体管计算机	1954 年,美国贝尔实验室研制了世界上第一台晶体管计算机 TRADIC,同一时期,操作系统和算法语言诞生,COBOL、LISP 等高级语言进入实用阶段
集成电路计算机	1964 年 4 月,美国国际商业机器公司(IBM 公司)推出世界上首个使用集成电路的计算机系列 IBM System/360;1968 年,IBM 公司发布世界上首个商用数据库系统——信息管理系统(IMS);1981 年,IBM 公司推出世界上首部个人计算机 IBM 5150,提出了采用微处理器的架构标准
计算机中央处理器	1971 年,美国英特尔公司发布世界上第一款 4 位微处理器 4004(内含 2 000 多个晶体管,10 微米制程生产);1979 年,英特尔公司推出 8 位微处理器 Intel 8088(内含约 2.9 万个晶体管);1985 年,英特尔公司推出 32 位微处理器 80386(内含约 27.5 万个晶体管);1993 年,英特尔公司推出奔腾处理器(内含约 300 万个晶体管,0.8 微米制程生产);1999 年,英特尔公司推出奔腾Ⅲ处理器(内含约 950 万个晶体管,0.25 微米制程生产);2006 年,英特尔公司推出安腾处理器(内含约 17.2 亿个晶体管,90 纳米制程生产)

续表

成果	代表性事件
计算机软件	1970年,美国贝尔实验室推出了 Unix 操作系统;1970年,IBM 公司的埃德加·弗兰克·科德提出了关系数据库理论;1984年,美国苹果电脑公司推出计算机 Macintosh(简称 Mac),提供了图形化的操作系统界面;1991年,芬兰大学生林纳斯·托瓦兹开发了开源系统 Linux 操作系统;1995年,美国微软公司发布了 Windows 95 操作系统和办公软件 Microsoft Office 95,成为主流的计算机软件

面向计算机互联的全球互联网得到验证和应用。在美国国防部高级研究计划局的资助下,美国的主要科研机构在 20 年间逐步接入阿帕网(又称"高级研究计划局网络"),并且探索出了适用于大规模异构网络互联的方案。1995年,互联网开始商业化运营后,迅速在全球普及,并且成为目前最主流的通信网络。万维网、搜索引擎、在线电子商务、社交网络等互联网信息服务将全民带入了网络时代。表 1-6 列举了互联网领域的主要技术进展。

表 1-6 互联网领域的主要技术进展

技术	代表性事件
阿帕网	1966年,美国国防部高级研究计划局启动了阿帕网的研究计划;1969年,美国加利福尼亚大学洛杉矶分校和斯坦福研究所实现了首次分组交换网络的远程通信;1974年,面向异构网络计算机联网通信的传输控制协议(TCP)首个版本正式发布;1983年,TCP 分解为 TCP/IP 协议族,并获阿帕网使用
互联网	1989年,基于超文本标记语言(HTML)和超文本传送协议(HTTP)的 Web 服务发布;1995年,美国商务部从国防部接管了互联网数字分配机构的职能,互联网开启了商业化进程;1998年,互联网名称与数字地址分配机构(ICANN)成立
互联网服务	1994年,雅虎公司成立并提供搜索引擎服务,亚马逊公司成立并提供在线图书销售服务;1998年,谷歌公司成立并提供搜索引擎服务;2004年,脸书公司(后改为 Meta)成立并提供社交网络服务

公共蜂窝移动通信网络提供全球漫游无线服务。20 世纪 80 年代,全球开始部署基于蜂窝基站的个人移动通信网络。移动通信的需求从语音业务逐步转向数据业务,手机收发短信、电子邮件得到普遍应用。2007年,苹果公司推出 iPhone 手机,标志着基于触控操作的智能手机时代的到来。手机开始逐步取代个人计算机成为个人上网的主要电子设备,手机上运行的应用程序成为个人软件的主要形式。表 1-7 列举了移动通信领域的主要技术进展。

表 1-7 移动通信领域的主要技术进展

技术	代表性事件
第一代移动通信技术 1G	1978年,美国贝尔实验室成功研制出先进移动电话系统(AMPS),标志着以模拟式蜂窝网为主要特征的 1G 系统正式登上历史舞台;1G 模拟蜂窝系统容量十分有限,仅支持语音通话,不能提供数据和漫游服务

续表

技术	代表性事件
第二代移动通信技术 2G	1990年,以数字化为特征的2G系统在全球范围内开始广泛部署;2G系统主要包括欧洲提出的全球移动通信系统(GSM)和美国提出的临时标准-95(IS-95)系统;2G系统在性能和容量上得到了显著提升,改善了语音质量和保密性,传输速率接近1 Mbps(兆比特/秒)
第三代移动通信技术 3G	2000年左右,3G系统开始大规模商用;3G系统以数据业务为中心,实现了真正意义上的移动多媒体通信,传输速率约为3 Mbps;中国提出的时分同步码分多址(TD-SCDMA)系统被列为3G的三大国际标准之一
第四代移动通信技术 4G	2010年左右,4G系统开始投入商用;4G系统在传输速度上有着非常大的提升,可以满足游戏、高清移动电视、视频会议等应用需求,传输速率最大可达100 Mbps;中国提出的时分同步码分多址长期演进技术增强版(TD-LTE-Advanced)被列为4G的国际标准之一

信息通信技术以半导体、计算机、互联网、移动通信等技术为代表,以微电子和光电子学为基础,以计算机和通信技术为支撑,覆盖了信息的获取、传递、存储、处理、显示、分发等方面。这些技术相互影响、快速迭代,对人类社会产生了巨大的影响,带来了第四次信息技术革命。

围绕着信息的处理和加工,产生了很多新的产业和门类。2006年,联合国公布《所有经济活动的国际标准行业分类》修订本第4版,新设门类J"信息和通信",包括"出版活动"(58类)、"电影、录像和电视节目的制作,录音及音乐作品出版活动"(59类)、"电台和电视广播"(60类)、"电信"(61类)、"计算机程序设计、咨询及相关活动"(62类)、"信息服务活动"(63类)等多个子类。此外,在门类C"制造业"中,设立了"计算机、电子产品和光学产品的制造"(26类)。

1.2 信息产业特征

1.2.1 信息产业的范围

中国将整个社会的产业分为三大产业。第一产业,包括农业、种植业、畜牧业和渔业等。第二产业,包括采矿业、建筑业、机械制造业等。第三产业,包括教育、卫生、金融、交通等服务业。虽然信息产业的经济活动早就出现了,但是这些经济活动还附属于其他产业,比如信息设备制造业起初是属于第二产业的,咨询服务业起初是属于第三产业的。随着信息技术在经济、社会各领域的广泛应用,信息产业的经济活动过程逐渐从其他产业的相应过程中分离出来,形成了一个独立的产业。美国商务部按照美国1987年发布的"标准产业分类"(SIC),在《数字经济2000年》中给出了信息产业的定义:信息产业应该由硬件业、软件业、服务业、通信设备制造业以及通信服务业等内容组成。表1-8列出了信息产业的基本分类。

表 1-8　信息产业的基本分类

子类名称	范围
基础电信业	为大众提供基础通信和传输服务,包括传统的电报、电话等业务,面向互联网的有线宽带数据通信服务,面向个人的移动通信服务等
信息服务业	包括传统信息服务业和新型信息服务业,其中传统信息服务业包括出版业、邮政业、文献信息业、广播电视业等;新型信息服务业又称电子信息服务业,是以计算机和现代通信等电子信息技术为主要处理手段的信息服务业,提供信息生产与供给、信息咨询、网络运营与网络增值服务等服务
信息开发业	包括软件产业、数据库开发业、电子出版(含游戏、动漫等)业、应用程序开发和其他信息开发业务等
信息制造业	以电子计算机和通信设备制造为主要内容的信息制造业,包括电子工业(电子元件、器件、整机制造)、通信与网络设备制造业、其他信息设备制造业等

1.2.2　信息产业的地位

信息产业是基础产业。基础产业是指对国民经济和社会发展具有支撑和承载作用的产业,其发展规模和水平制约着整个国民经济的发展速度和质量。世界银行的研究报告表明,一个经济体的信息通信技术发展水平越高,其经济增长速度就越快。数据统计规律表明,高速宽带互联网普及率每提高 10%,发展中经济体的人均 GDP(国内生产总值)就增加约 1.38%,移动电话普及率每提高 10%,发展中经济体的人均 GDP 就增加约 0.81%。

信息产业是主导产业。主导产业是指对国民经济中的其他产业的发展具有导向性和较大促进作用的产业。信息技术在传统产业改造中的投入产出比在发达国家可以达到 1∶10 以上。信息技术与机械、能源、交通、建筑、纺织、冶金等产业的结合不断催生新的产业门类和更广阔的技术领域。信息产业催生和带动新兴产业的发展,例如网络出版、在线游戏、数字音乐、手机媒体等数字内容产业,以及电子商务、现代物流、软件和服务外包等新型互联网服务业。

信息产业是战略性产业。信息产业已经成为各国争夺科技、经济、人才以及军事主导权和制高点的战略性产业。在信息通信技术领域,技术标准竞争的激烈程度远超其他行业。一个国家或一家企业能够控制标准,就具备了其他国家或企业难以超越的竞争优势。同时,电子信息产品制造业和软件业,也是关系到国家安全的战略性产业,关系到国家网络与信息安全的根本保障。

1.2.3　信息产业的特征

信息产业是智力密集型产业。信息产业本是收集信息、生产和经营信息的产业,其特点是以脑力劳动为重点的大量知识、技术的开发。信息产业是国际专利技术竞争最为集中和激烈的产业。美国排名前三位的高专利密集度产业为计算机产业、通信产业和电子产业。

例如,为了抢占移动互联网和大数据源头与入口,围绕智能终端展开专利收购,谷歌公司以125亿美元的价格收购了摩托罗拉移动的1.7万件专利。

信息产业是高创新性产业。信息产业以科研为先导,具有高创新性和高更新频率等特征。信息产业的创新速度也是其他产业无法比拟的:信息技术每3年增加一倍,全球信息技术专利每年新增超过30万件,科研资料的有效寿命平均只有5年。信息技术的飞速发展导致信息产品的生命周期缩短,产品更新换代越来越快。微软公司前任总裁比尔·盖茨总是告诫员工:微软离破产永远只有18个月。

信息产业是高风险与高收益并存的产业。研究和开发信息产品需要巨额的资金,并且由于创造发明成功率的不确定性,巨额投资有可能血本无归。信息产品的研究和开发,具有高固定成本和低边际成本的特点,而批量化规模生产阶段的投资成本相对较低。信息产品往往具有规模经济效应,厂商一旦打开销路,利润率比传统产品高得多。

1.2.4 信息产业的发展规律

与传统产业相比,信息产业有其自身的发展规律、发展路径和发展模式。信息产业发展规律中,较有名、影响较深远的有摩尔定律、梅特卡夫定律、微笑曲线等。

1.2.4.1 摩尔定律

摩尔定律是由英特尔创始人之一戈登·摩尔提出来的。1965年,摩尔应邀为《电子学》杂志35周年专刊写了一篇观察评论报告,标题是《让集成电路填满更多元件》。摩尔分析数据时发现:每一代芯片可容纳晶体管的数量大约是上一代芯片的2倍,两代芯片的时间间隔在18~24个月。如果芯片容量按这个趋势发展,计算能力相对于时间周期将呈指数式上升。

摩尔定律归纳了信息技术发展速度的规律。摩尔定律指明,30年来,集成电路芯片的性能的确得到了大幅度的提高。展望集成电路芯片的未来时,信息技术专家认为,摩尔定律在未来可能依旧适用。但随着晶体管电路逐渐接近性能极限,摩尔定律将走到尽头。

1.2.4.2 梅特卡夫定律

梅特卡夫定律是由美国网络设备公司3Com公司的创始人罗伯特·梅特卡夫提出的,其基本内容是网络的价值等于网络节点数的平方,即网络的商业价值与联网用户数量的平方成正比。梅特卡夫定律揭示了网络的商业价值随着联网用户数量的增长而呈平方级增长的规律。

梅特卡夫定律表明,当一项技术已建立必要的用户规模,它的价值将会呈爆炸式增长。20世纪90年代以来,互联网不仅呈现出这种超乎寻常的增长趋势,而且向经济和社会的各个领域进行了广泛的渗透和扩张。随着联网用户数量的增长,网络资源呈指数级增长。当前,随着移动互联网、社交媒体的广泛应用,梅特卡夫定律得到了充分证实。

1.2.4.3 微笑曲线

宏碁集团创始人施振荣先生在1992年为了"再造宏碁"提出了有名的"微笑曲线"理论(见图1-3)。"微笑曲线"将制造行业的产业链划分为三个环节,分别为研发、制造、营销,认为产业的附加价值更多地体现在两端,即研发环节和营销环节,而处于中间的制造环节附加价值最低。有关现代产业价值链的研究也表明,处在产业链两端的企业利润率在20%~25%,而处在中间的制造企业的利润率只有5%左右。这种两端朝上、中间朝下的形态,就如一个微笑标识。

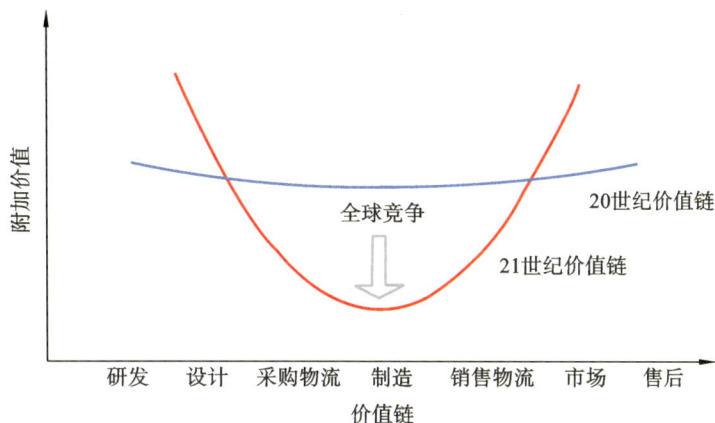

图 1-3 微笑曲线

图片来源:施振荣,《宏碁的世纪变革》,2005 年

从全球范围看,发达国家和地区主导着信息产业发展的趋势和格局,处于价值链的高端。美国凭借其雄厚的经济实力、大规模基础研究、完善的风险投资机制,致力于信息技术的研究、开发与应用,不断推出新的技术,处于世界领先地位。英国、德国等欧洲国家也致力于信息产业部分领域的研发、标准制定,处于价值链的高端。韩国、新加坡等国家和地区处于产业链中以生产技术为主的中端。

1.3 技术产业革命

1.3.1 新一代信息技术

2010 年以后,信息技术迎来了新一轮发展热潮。人工智能、物联网、新一代移动通信技术等被认为是信息产业的又一轮重大变革。这些新技术将颠覆传统通信、计算模式,带动信息产业向更高层面跃进。这些新技术互为支撑、群体演变、加速突破,并得到了广泛应用。具有代表性的新一代信息技术如表 1-9 所示。

表 1-9 具有代表性的新一代信息技术

领域	技术内容
第五代移动通信技术	第五代移动通信技术简称 5G,是一种具有高速率、低时延和大连接等特点的新一代移动通信技术,国际电信联盟定义的 5G 三大类应用场景为增强移动宽带(eMBB)、超高可靠低时延通信(uRLLC)和海量机器类通信(mMTC)
工业互联网	工业互联网是新一代信息通信技术与工业经济深度融合的新型基础设施、应用模式和工业生态,通过对人、机、物、系统等的全面连接,构建起覆盖全产业链、全价值链的全新制造和服务体系,其网络体系包括网络互联、数据互通、标识解析三个部分

续表

领域	技术内容
物联网	物联网是以各种传感设备为节点的网络及其应用系统，它可以实现对物理世界物品的识别、环境的感知、设备的控制等，提高生产生活中的自动化水平，代表性技术包括射频识别（RFID）、传感器网络、机器到机器（M2M）等
云计算	云计算是通过网络为用户按需提供计算资源（服务器、数据库、存储等）和软件服务（平台、架构、应用等）的模式，云计算服务提供商通过分布式计算、虚拟化等技术实现计算资源的自动化管理、共享与分配
大数据	大数据技术是处理、存储、分析与管理高速、大量、多样化的数据集的技术，伴随互联网技术积累的巨量数据，大数据技术需要处理大量的结构化、半结构化和非结构化数据，往往依托云计算来实现
区块链	区块链是一种基于互联网实现的分布式存储系统，其采用了点对点传输、共识机制、加密算法等技术，具有匿名性、不可篡改性，提供了安全可信的去中心化的存储方案
元宇宙	元宇宙是利用科技手段进行链接与创造的和现实世界映射与交互的虚拟世界系统，它涉及虚拟现实、增强现实、数字孪生、人机交互等技术，可以构成具备新型社会体系的数字生活空间
人工智能	人工智能是使用计算机来模拟人的某些思维过程和智能行为（如学习、推理、思考、规划等）的技术，涉及机器人、语言识别、图像识别、自然语言处理、计算机视觉、机器学习和专家系统等领域，近年来，人工智能大模型采用超大规模参数（通常在10亿个以上）、超强计算资源的机器学习模型，在自然语言处理、图像处理等方面具有优异的性能

新一代信息技术加速向其他经济部门横向扩散，与物理世界相互渗透融合。信息技术在高科技产业中发挥的基础性、主导性、牵引性作用越来越显著。具体表现为：

第一，信息空间的内涵不断丰富、深化，已成为实现对物质、能量进行控制的重要载体。信息物理的深度融合极大地改变了传统控制回路中的感知、分析决策和执行过程，控制系统向智能化迈出实质性步伐。人工智能技术可以实现自主认识、学习，从而优化、重构生产和产业运行方式，创造更大的增量价值。

第二，信息技术的体系化发展成为电子信息领域技术竞争的重要形态。感知、传输、存储、计算等关键环节的技术不断交叉融合，体系化发展模式日益明显。互联网和大数据催生了基于数据驱动的工程技术发展新范式，引发了科研方法、组织方式的深刻变化。

第三，信息技术作为一种通用技术，与各领域相结合并产生新的技术方向。例如，信息技术与制造、材料、能源、生物等技术加速交叉融合,催生了智能制造、新型材料、生物信息等新的技术方向,创造了工业互联网、"互联网＋"、共享经济等新的产业形态以及商业模式。

1.3.2　第四次工业革命

科学技术是推动社会经济发展的主要动力,经济的每一次快速增长都与一次大规模的工业革命紧密相连。产业革命是以新的科学发现为基础,以技术革命爆发为标志,新技术广泛应用于人类的生产、生活,从而引发产业结构、经济形势、社会分工体系、全球政治经济格局的变化,并改变社会文化价值观、社会成员心理状态的过程。

第一次工业革命以蒸汽机的发明为标志,由英国引领,表现为以机械动力替代人力、畜力,促成了大规模工厂化生产,引发了纺织业的机械化和冶金工业的变革。第二次工业革命以内燃机和电力技术的发明与应用为主要标志,由美国和德国引领,以电力为动力实现了生产生活的电气化,催生了汽车制造业和石化工业,推动了铁路运输业、造船工业等创新产业的发展。第三次工业革命是信息技术革命,以电子计算机技术的发展和应用为代表,继续由美国引领,实现了生产生活的自动化、信息化和现代化。

当前,以人工智能、大数据、物联网、太空技术、生物技术、量子科技为代表的新技术革命正在进行。《工业4.0:即将来袭的第四次工业革命》一书的作者乌尔里希·森德勒将这次技术革命称为第四次工业革命。本次技术革命所采纳的多种新技术对人类的影响具有系统性、整体性。各项新兴技术高度融合,相互渗透,形成了一个完整的技术系统,对人类社会的改造有同步性、系统性和整体性等特点,创造出了跨越传统产业边界的新产品、新业态、新模式。第四次工业革命是智能化革命,以基因工程、量子计算、新材料技术、新能源技术、虚拟现实等为代表,实现生产生活系统的全面智能化,使经济社会的发展方式出现重大变革。例如,互联网在逐步趋向物联网,传统企业也纷纷演变成数字企业,传统制造业正在向"智造业"转变,智能机器人将出现在人类生产生活的各个领域。图1-4展示了技术浪潮与工业革命的历史。

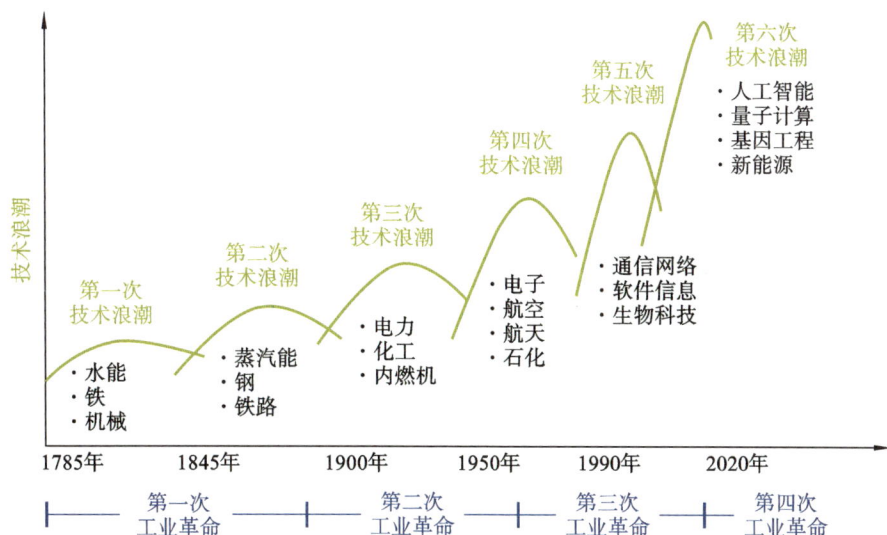

图1-4　技术浪潮与工业革命

1.4　新型数字经济

1.4.1　数字经济的范围

从产业革命史的角度看,数字经济可以上溯到20世纪50年代电子计算机的出现。数字经济的早期表现形式即互联网经济。1994年,"数字经济"这个概念出现了。著名经济学家唐·塔普斯科特的著作《数字经济》在这一年出版,这是第一本关于数字经济的书,预测了互联网时代经济发展的新形态,比如预测了"电子商务社区"的出现。尼古拉·尼葛洛庞帝在其著作《数字化生存》中描述了数字时代的社会生活场景。

随着互联网和各类信息技术的推广应用,数据成为一种关键生产要素全面嵌入经济体系中。由于具有可复制、易传播、跨时空等特性,数据在各个部门呈现出前所未有的应用潜力,数据资源被称为"21世纪的新石油"。数据能够有效驱动劳动力、资本、技术等要素网络共享、协作开发以及高效利用,提升全要素生产率,为经济社会发展提供新动能。

数字经济是继农业经济、工业经济之后的主要经济形态,数字化转型正在驱动生产方式、生活方式和治理方式发生重大变革,对世界经济、政治和科技格局产生深远影响。关于数字经济的定义,许多国际机构和组织进行了概括,以2016年二十国集团领导人峰会在杭州发布的《二十国集团数字经济发展与合作倡议》中的定义最具代表性:"数字经济是指以使用数字化的知识和信息作为关键生产要素、以现代信息网络作为重要载体、以信息通信技术的有效使用作为效率提升和经济结构优化的重要推动力的一系列经济活动。"数字经济代表了围绕数据这种关键生产要素所进行的一系列生产、流通和消费的经济活动的总和。

在数字经济时代,传统的信息产业逐步转变为以数字为主要生产要素的数字产业而推进新一代信息产业发展的过程被称为"数字产业化",指数据要素的产业化、商业化和市场化。而传统产业的信息化以及数字化转型被称为"产业数字化",即利用现代数字信息技术、先进互联网和人工智能技术对传统产业进行全方位、全角度、全链条改造,使数字技术与实体经济各行各业深度融合发展。

2021年5月,中国国家统计局公布了《数字经济及其核心产业统计分类(2021)》,首次确定了数字经济的产业范围:数字产品制造业、数字产品服务业、数字技术应用业、数字要素驱动业、数字化效率提升业等5个大类。这5个大类可以划分为数字产业化和产业数字化两个部分。

数字产业化:前4个大类为数字产业化部分,即数字经济核心产业,是指为产业数字化发展提供数字技术、产品、服务、基础设施和解决方案,以及完全依赖于数字技术、数据要素的各类经济活动,对应《国民经济行业分类》中的26个大类、68个中类、126个小类,是数字经济发展的基础。数字产业化的范围与传统的信息产业范围基本一致,包括基础电信业、互联网产业、信息服务业以及电子信息制造业。

产业数字化:第5个大类"数字化效率提升业",即产业数字化部分,是指应用数字技术和数据资源为传统产业带来的产出增加和效率提升,是数字技术与实体经济的融合。该部分涵盖智能制造、智慧农业、智能交通等数字化应用场景,对应《国民经济行业分类》中的91个大类、431个中类、1 256个小类,体现了数字技术已经并将进一步与国民经济各行业深度融合。

1.4.2　全球数字战略

数据对经济的促进作用正在不断凸显,利用信息技术推动传统产业的数字化转型,已经成为各国的共识。近年来,欧盟、英国、美国、巴西、日本等国家和地区的数据要素价值不断释放,数据市场价值不断提高,数据专业人员、数据企业等相关数据指标都获得了较快提升。2020年,欧盟27国数据经济价值达约3 551亿欧元,比2019年增长了9.3%。为了进一步促进信息产业、数字经济的发展,越来越多的国家采取各种积极措施,保护和发展本国的信息产业。经济合作与发展组织(OECD)发布的《经济合作与发展组织数字经济展望2020》显示,在对37个国家开展的数字经济政策调查中,有34个国家制定了国家总体数字战略。

美国为维护其在电子信息领域的全球绝对领导地位,不断加强政府对信息技术发展方向的引导,及时发布相关发展计划或战略。1998年,美国商务部便发布了《浮现中的数字经济》系列报告;近年来又先后发布了《美国数字经济议程》《联邦数据战略2020年行动计划》《2021年美国创新与竞争法》,一再强调数字经济在国家经济发展中的重要作用。2020年10月,美国发布《关键与新兴技术国家战略》,重新定义20项关键与新兴技术,提出全力维护美国在量子物理学、人工智能等尖端技术领域的全球领导地位。

欧盟为重建欧洲在信息通信技术领域的国际竞争优势,积极布局信息技术创新发展。"地平线2020"科研计划的实施时间为2014—2020年,强化信息技术的创新与应用,其中信息通信技术领域的投资占该计划总投资的46%。欧盟在2014年提出"数据价值链战略计划"后,又陆续推出《欧洲工业数字化战略》《欧盟人工智能法案》等文件,并于2020年2月发布了《塑造欧洲数字未来》,于2021年3月发布了《2030数字指南针:欧洲数字十年之路》,全面规划了2021—2030年欧盟的数字化发展路径。

1.5　小　　结

信息科技水平对社会经济生活具有重要的影响。古代中国的造纸术和印刷术为传统信息的记录和交流提供了载体,促进了古代世界文明的发展和交流。受益于现代科学技术的发展,基于电子器件和无线电波的电报、电话、电视得以发明,将人类社会带入全球化通信与交流的时代。近半个世纪以来,集成电路、计算机、互联网、移动通信等信息技术迅速发展,带动人类社会快速进步和发展,深刻影响了人们的工作和生活。信息产业的发展历史表明,信息技术作为通用技术,对其他产业和社会的发展有很强的带动作用和辐射效应,是经济增长"倍增器"、发展方式"转换器"和产业升级"助推器"。

当前,以云计算、大数据、5G、工业互联网、人工智能、区块链等为代表的新一轮信息技术正在迅速发展,同时也在推动全球范围内的第四次工业革命。信息技术在各行各业的广泛应用,加快了数字化社会的到来。数据成为重要的生产要素和战略资源,是优化资源配置、推动传统产业不断升级、提高社会劳动生产率的新动力。发展以数据为核心要素的数字经济已经成为各国的共识,制定相应的信息科技发展规划、数字经济发展战略已经成为主要工业化国家的共识。

2　数字中国概况

2.1　发 展 历 程

2.1.1　自力更生——中国信息产业的初步建立(1949—1978 年)

1949 年 10 月 1 日,毛泽东主席在北京天安门宣布中华人民共和国成立。中国结束了 100 多年被压迫、被侵略的苦难历史,终于获得了独立自主发展的机会。彼时的中国刚刚结束数十年战乱,满目疮痍,百废待兴,是一个连铁皮汽油桶都无法生产的落后农业国,工业基础几乎为零,电子产品主要依赖进口。当时的中国仅有少数大城市有电话,全国电话用户只有 26 万户,有线电话普及率只有 0.05%。全国从事科学技术工作的人员不超过 5 万人,电子技术方面的人才更是寥寥无几。

中国从无到有建立了自主的电子工业。从 1952 年开始,中国通过改造、新建等方式建立了一批电子工业制造企业(见表 2-1)。其中,南京无线电厂于 1953 年成功研制出中国第一台全国产化电子管收音机"红星牌"502 型,结束了只能依靠国外元器件装配收音机的历史。北京电子管厂在苏联的援助下建立了电子管生产线,该厂是 20 世纪 60 年代亚洲生产规模最大的电子管厂。1963 年,第四机械工业部(1982 年改称电子工业部)成立,统筹全国电子工业,标志着中国信息产业成为独立的工业部门。

中国从无到有组建了电子工业的科研队伍和人才培养体系。1949 年 11 月,中国科学院成立,形成了中国的战略科技力量。在电子工业相关领域,中国科学院先后设立了应用物理研究所(1950 年)、电子学研究所(1956 年)、计算技术研究所(1959 年)、半导体研究所(1960 年)等,初步形成了覆盖电子信息相关领域的科研国家队。1952 年,中国开始调整全国高等教育体系,以满足国民经济发展需求。中国在综合性高等学校新开设了电子通信相关院系,例如 1952 年在清华大学设立无线电工程系、1958 年在北京大学设立无线电电子学系;还组建了电子通信领域的专业工科院校,如 1955 年组建了北京邮电学院(现北京邮电大学)、1956 年组建了成都电讯工程学院(现电子科技大学)。

在复杂多变的国际形势下,中国长期处于自力更生、艰苦创业的阶段,在近 30 年组建了发展电子技术、通信技术、半导体技术的科研队伍,建立了独立自主的电子工业体系,具备了生产简单电子管、晶体管等基础电子器件的能力,以及研制电子产品、计算机的能力。

表 2-1　中国电子制造发展历程(20 世纪 50—70 年代)

领域	发展历程
半导体	1952 年,南京电工厂成功研制出中国第一套收音机用电子管; 1956 年,中国科学院应用物理研究所研制出中国第一个晶体三极管; 1957 年,北京电子管厂拉制出中国第一根锗单晶; 1968 年,上海无线电十四厂制成 PMOS 集成电路
电子产品	1953 年,南京无线电厂成功研制出第一台全国产化电子管收音机; 1958 年,中国第一台黑白电视机诞生,被命名为"北京"; 1960 年,中国自主研制出第一套 1 000 门纵横制自动电话交换设备; 1970 年,中国第一颗人造地球卫星"东方红一号"发射成功
计算机	1958 年,中国科学院计算技术研究所成功研制出中国第一台小型电子管通用计算机 103 机; 1965 年,中国科学院计算技术研究所成功研制出第一台大型晶体管计算机 109 乙机; 1974 年,清华大学等单位联合成功研制出采用集成电路的 DJS-130 小型多用计算机

　　然而,受限于当时的整体国力,此阶段中国的电信服务基础设施还比较薄弱。到 1978 年,全国的电话网络尚未部署自动交换机,很多县城和农村地区的电话网络依靠人工交换,长途传输主要靠明线和模拟微波,全国电话容量 359 万门,用户 214 万户,电话普及率仅为 0.38%,每 200 人拥有的话机还不到 1 部,不及当时世界水平的 1/10。

2.1.2　改革开放——中国信息产业的快速发展(1978—2010 年)

　　20 世纪 70 年代后期,国际形势发生了巨大变化。20 世纪 80 年代,和平与发展逐渐成为时代主题。1978 年底,中国开始施行"改革开放"①国策,集中精力开展经济建设,中国的信息产业迎来了快速发展。从 1986 年开始,中国以五年规划的形式对邮电通信业、电子工业的发展进行了规划。1993 年,中国设立了国家经济信息化联席会议,对中国的信息化建设,特别是国家信息网络基础设施建设进行部署。1998 年,国务院将邮电部、电子工业部合并重组为信息产业部。2006 年,中国制定了为期 15 年的《2006—2020 年国家信息化发展战略》,贯彻落实"以信息化带动工业化,以工业化促进信息化"的新型工业化道路的指导思想。2008 年,信息产业部和国务院信息化工作办公室整合重组,成立了工业和信息化部。

　　在历次五年规划中,电子工业、信息产业都是工业发展的重点,而推动全国电话网络、数据通信网络的普及都是信息基础设施布局的重点。随着中国信息产业的迅速发展和信息基础设施的不断完善,信息产业逐步成为推动国家工业升级、促进整体国民经济发展的重要动力。表 2-2 列举了 1986—2010 年中国信息产业发展规划。

---

　　①　1978 年底,中国开始实行对内改革、对外开放的国策,将计划经济体制改革成社会主义市场经济体制,积极参与经济全球化条件下的国际经济合作和竞争。

表 2-2　中国信息产业发展规划（1986—2010 年）

规划期	重点规划内容
"七五"时期 （1986—1990 年）	1986 年 12 月，国务院办公厅转发电子振兴领导小组《关于搞好我国计算机推广应用工作的汇报提纲》，该提纲提出电子工业要迅速转移到以微电子技术为基础、以计算机和通信装备为主体的轨道上来； 1986 年 3 月，《中华人民共和国国民经济和社会发展第七个五年计划》提出，把交通运输和通信的发展放到优先地位
"八五"时期 （1991—1995 年）	1991 年 4 月，《中华人民共和国国民经济和社会发展十年规划和第八个五年计划纲要》提出，把发展电子工业放在突出位置，使之成为促进产业结构和整个国民经济现代化的带头产业
"九五"时期 （1996—2000 年）	1996 年 3 月，《中华人民共和国国民经济和社会发展"九五"计划和 2010 年远景目标纲要》提出，要重点发展邮电通信业，形成全国统一的通信网络体系； 1997 年 4 月，全国信息化工作会议通过《国家信息化"九五"规划和 2010 年远景目标（纲要）》，提出建立国家互联网信息中心和互联网交换中心，并将互联网列入国家信息基础设施
"十五"时期 （2001—2005 年）	2001 年 3 月，《中华人民共和国国民经济和社会发展第十个五年计划纲要》提出，以信息化带动工业化，加速推进信息化，提高信息产业在国民经济中的比重； 2002 年 10 月，《国民经济和社会发展第十个五年计划信息化发展重点专项规划》提出，推广信息技术应用，提高信息化水平，加强现代信息基础设施建设
"十一五"时期 （2006—2010 年）	2006 年 3 月，《中华人民共和国国民经济和社会发展第十一个五年规划纲要》提出，在电子信息制造业大力发展集成电路、软件和新型元器件等核心产业，重点培育光电通信、无线通信、高性能计算及网络设备等信息产业群； 2006 年 5 月，《2006—2020 年国家信息化发展战略》发布，进一步强调"以信息化促进工业化，以工业化带动信息化"，提出关键信息技术自主创新计划等战略行动

　　信息产业逐步成为中国国民经济的支柱产业。2010 年，中国规模以上电子信息制造业销售收入达 63 945 亿元，较 2005 年（31 010 亿元）翻一番，5 年间年均增速超过 15%；电子信息产品出口占全国外贸出口的比重一直保持在 30% 以上；彩电、微型计算机、手机等主要整机产品产量分别达 1.2 亿台、2.5 亿台和 10 亿部，均占全球总产量的 40% 以上。产业集中度明显提高，以百强企业为代表的骨干企业竞争力显著增强。2005—2010 年，电子信息百强企业主营业务收入由 9 643 亿元增长到 15 354 亿元，出现了华为、联想、海尔等销售收入过千亿元的企业。

　　企业为主体的创新体系逐步形成。薄膜晶体管液晶显示屏（TFT-LCD）和等离子显示屏（PDP）面板规模化生产技术取得重大进展。中央处理器（CPU）、移动通信芯片等一批中高端集成电路产品取得突破，65 纳米先进工艺和高压工艺等特色技术实现量产，三维封装等新型封装技术均得到开发和生产应用。TD-SCDMA 技术形成完整的产业链体系，40 Gbps 超大容量光传输系统领域取得技术突破。数字电视地面传输技术及数字音视频编解码技术达到国际先进水平。表 2-3 列举了 1978—2010 年中国在通信基础设施方面的成就。

表 2-3 中国在通信基础设施方面的成就(1978—2010 年)

领域	代表性成就
光纤通信	1982 年,中国建成第一个光纤通信系统工程,全长 13.3 千米,速率 8.448 Mbps,传输 120 路电话,开创了中国数字化通信新纪元; 1998 年,中国"八纵八横"格状光缆骨干网提前 2 年建成,网络覆盖全国省会以上城市和 70% 地市,全国长途光缆达到 20 万千米,中国形成以光缆为主、卫星和数字微波为辅的长途骨干通信网络; 2006 年,中国和美国之间首个兆兆级、10 Gbps 波长的海底光缆系统——跨太平洋直达光缆系统建成
移动通信	1993 年,中国第一个 GSM 数字移动电话通信网(2G)开通; 2001 年,中国的移动通信用户数超过了 1.2 亿,中国超过美国跃居为第一手机用户大国; 2003 年,中国固定电话用户数达到 2.55 亿户,移动电话用户数达到 2.57 亿户,移动电话用户数首次超过固定电话用户数; 2009 年,中国发放 3 张 3G 牌照(CDMA2000、WCDMA 和 TD-SCDMA)
卫星通信	1984 年,中国第一颗静止轨道试验通信卫星"东方红二号"发射成功,开启了中国进行卫星通信的历史; 1986 年,中国国内卫星通信网正式建成,包括 5 颗通信卫星; 1997 年,中国成功发射"东方红三号"卫星,该卫星装有 24 个 C 频段转发器,达到了国际同类通信卫星的先进水平; 2000 年,中国成功发射北斗一号卫星导航系统首批 2 颗地球静止轨道卫星,为中国提供定位服务
互联网	1994 年,中国国家计算机与网络设施工程通过 64 Kbps(千比特/秒)国际专线正式接入国际互联网,开启了中国的互联网时代; 1997 年,中国将互联网列入国家信息基础设施建设计划,逐步建成了具有国际出口能力的四大骨干网,并建立了中国国家顶级域名(.CN)运行管理体系; 2008 年,中国网民规模达到 2.98 亿,互联网普及率超过全球平均水平

在基础通信设施方面,中国加快推进光纤通信、移动通信、卫星通信等基础网络的建设,并先后组建了中国电信、中国移动、中国联通、中国卫通等国有通信运营商。2010 年,中国基础电信企业光缆线路长度达到 996.2 万千米,互联网宽带接入端口达到 1.88 亿个,国际通信业务出口总带宽达到 1.6 Tbps(太比特/秒),拥有 7 条登陆海缆、20 条陆缆,累计建成 3G 网络基站 62 万个。2010 年,中国电话用户总数达到 11.53 亿户,普及率为 86.5 部/百人;网民规模达到 4.57 亿人,普及率为 34.3%。继固定电话和移动电话之后,中国网民和宽带接入用户总数于 2008 年跃升全球首位。

在互联网方面,中国互联网网站数量由 2005 年底的 69.4 万个增长至 2010 年的 191 万个,容量接近 1 800 TB。2010 年,中国互联网服务市场规模超过 2 000 亿元,形成了一批初具国际影响力的骨干企业;2010 年,中国网上零售用户规模达 1.61 亿,交易额达到 5 131 亿元,占社会消费品零售总额的比重达到 3.3%,网上零售交易额增速是同期社会消费品零售额增速的 5.7 倍。网上支付、移动支付、电话支付等新兴支付服务发展迅猛,第三方电子支付规模增长迅速,2010 年达到 1.01 万亿元。现代物流业快速发展,网上零售带动了快递服务业的迅速发展,2010 年中国规模以上快递服务企业业务量达 23.4 亿件,业务收入达574.6 亿元。

2.1.3 迈向新时代——中国信息产业的跨越提升(2011 年至今)

2010 年以后,全球再次掀起加快信息化发展的浪潮,以互联网为代表的信息技术快速普及,对国际政治、经济、社会和文化产生了深刻影响。各个国家纷纷加快推进信息技术研发和应用,综合信息网络向宽带、融合、泛在方向演进,信息技术、产品、内容、网络和平台等加速融合发展。

2017 年,中国共产党第十九次全国代表大会(简称"中共十九大")报告明确提出建设网络强国、数字中国、智慧社会的发展战略。从"十二五"开始,中国逐步形成了覆盖面广泛、层次丰富的信息化规划体系,在每 5 年的常规规划之外,提出了专门针对国家信息基础设施建设、经济转型升级、新技术发展等方面的规划。2011—2020 年中国信息产业发展规划见表2-4。

表 2-4 中国信息产业发展规划(2011—2020 年)

规划时期	规划内容
"十二五"时期 2011—2015 年	2011 年 3 月,《中华人民共和国国民经济和社会发展第十二个五年规划纲要》发布,提出培育发展"新一代信息技术产业"等战略性新兴产业; 2013 年 8 月,国务院发布《"宽带中国"战略及实施方案》,提出到 2020 年固定宽带家庭普及率达到 70%,行政村通宽带比例超过 98%,城市和农村家庭宽带接入能力分别达到 50 Mbps 和 12 Mbps; 2015 年 3 月,《国务院关于积极推进"互联网+"行动的指导意见》发布,提出推动"互联网+"创业创新、协同制造、现代农业、智慧能源、普惠金融、益民服务、高效物流、电子商务、便捷交通、绿色生态、人工智能等十一项重点行动,支撑中国经济转型
"十三五"时期 2016—2020 年	2016 年 3 月,《中华人民共和国国民经济和社会发展第十三个五年规划纲要》发布,再次强调支持战略性新兴产业发展,提出拓展网络经济空间、发展现代互联网产业体系、实施国家大数据战略、强化信息安全保障; 2016 年 7 月,中共中央办公厅、国务院办公厅印发《国家信息化发展战略纲要》,提出建设网络强国,到 2025 年,固定宽带家庭普及率接近国际先进水平,建成国际领先的移动通信网络,实现宽带网络无缝覆盖; 2017 年 3 月,国务院印发《新一代人工智能发展规划》,指出人工智能产业成为新的重要经济增长点,提出到 2030 年成为世界主要人工智能创新中心,智能经济、智能社会取得明显成效

数字经济规模持续快速增长。2017—2021 年,中国数字经济规模从 27.2 万亿元增至 45.5 万亿元,总量稳居世界第二,复合年均增长率达 13.6%,占 GDP 比重从 32.9% 提升至 39.8%,成为推动经济增长的主要引擎之一(见图 2-1)。

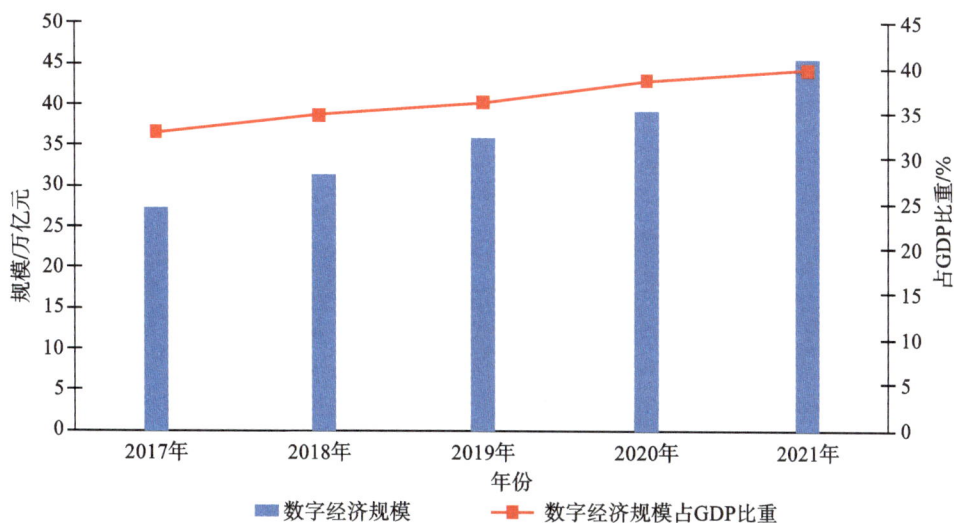

图 2-1   2017—2021 年中国数字经济规模及占 GDP 比重

数据来源:中国信息通信研究院

数字产业规模快速壮大。2017—2021 年,规模以上计算机、通信和其他电子设备制造业营业收入由 10.6 万亿元增长至 14.1 万亿元;规模以上软件业营业收入由 5.5 万亿元增长至 9.5 万亿元;规模以上互联网和相关服务业营业收入由 0.7 万亿元增长至 1.6 万亿元(见图 2-2)。2015—2020 年,中国电子商务交易额由 21.8 万亿元增长到 37.2 万亿元。2015—2020 年,中国信息消费蓬勃发展,信息消费规模由 3.4 万亿元增长到 5.8 万亿元。2016 年,大数据产业规模为 0.34 万亿元,到 2020 年已超过 1 万亿元。

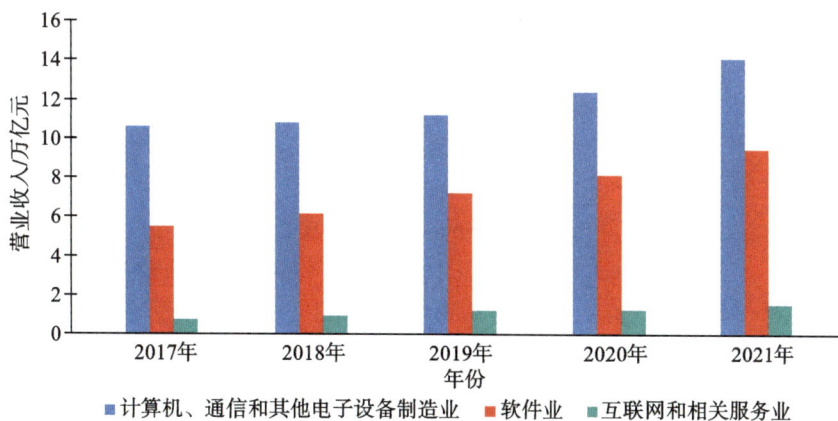

图 2-2   2017—2021 年中国数字产业营业收入增长情况

数据来源:工业和信息化部

网络基础设施全球领先。到 2020 年,中国所有地级市均建成光网城市,光纤网络接入带宽实现从十兆到百兆再到千兆的指数级增长;移动网络实现从"3G 突破"到"4G 同步"再到"5G 引领"的跨越。截至 2022 年 8 月末,中国 5G 基站总数达到 210.2 万个,所有地级市和县城城区实现 5G 全覆盖,历史性实现全国行政村"村村通宽带",为全面完成脱贫攻坚[①]目标做出了贡献。网络基础设施全面支持第 6 版互联网协议(IPv6)。国家级互联网骨干直联点增加至 19 个,数据中心规模超过 520 万标准机架。北斗三号全球卫星导航系统(GNSS)开通,全球范围定位精度优于 10 米。2011 年至今中国网络基础设施建设成果见表 2-5。

表 2-5　中国网络基础设施建设成果(2011 年至今)

领域	发展历程
光纤通信	2015 年,固定宽带用户数超过 2 亿户,宽带用户规模居全球首位; 2021 年,光纤宽带千兆光网覆盖家庭超过了 1.2 亿户,宽带端到端用户体验速度达到 51.2 Mbps,在全球 176 个国家和地区排名第十八位
移动通信	2013 年,发放 4G 商用牌照,从此开启了中国的 4G 时代; 2015 年,4G 用户突破 3.8 亿户,移动宽带用户(3G/4G)占移动用户总数的比重达到 60.1%; 2019 年,发放 5G 商用牌照,从此开启了中国的 5G 时代
卫星通信	2012 年,建成北斗二号卫星导航系统,包括 14 颗卫星(5 颗地球静止轨道卫星、5 颗倾斜地球同步轨道卫星、4 颗中圆地球轨道卫星),实现对亚太地区的定位服务; 2017 年,发射中星 16 号,采用 Ka 频段多波束宽带通信系统,总容量达到 20 Gbps(吉比特/秒); 2020 年,建成北斗三号全球卫星导航系统,共计 55 颗卫星,提供全球定位服务
互联网	2012 年,手机超越台式电脑成为中国网民接入互联网的首选终端; 2015 年,网民规模达到 6.88 亿人,90.1% 的网民通过手机上网,手机网民规模达 6.2 亿人; 2015 年,网上零售交易额跃居全球第一,达 3.88 万亿元; 2020 年,电子商务交易额达到 37.2 万亿元

中国网民规模由 2015 年底的 6.88 亿人增长到 2020 年底的 9.89 亿人,互联网普及率由 50.3% 提升到 70.4%,移动电话用户规模从 11.1 亿户增长到 16.43 亿户,其中 5G 电话用户从无到有,达到 3.55 亿户。网络提速降费力度不断加大,2020 年固定宽带和手机流量平均资费水平相比 2015 年下降幅度超过 95%,平均网络速率提升 7 倍以上。固定宽带家庭普及率由 2015 年底的 52.6% 提升到 2020 年底的 96%,移动宽带用户普及率由 2015 年底的 57.4% 提升到 2020 年底的 108%,全国行政村通光纤和通 4G 比例均超过 98%。从宽带成本支出占人均 GDP 的比重来看,中国固定宽带价格指数全球排名从 2017 年全球第七十一上升至 2021 年的第三,移动宽带价格指数连续 5 年低于全球平均水平。图 2-3 展示了 2017—2021 年中国网民规模及互联网普及率变化趋势。

---

① "脱贫攻坚"是中国为改善贫困地区和贫困人口生活条件、促进经济发展和社会进步而实施的一项大规模、系统性的战略行动。2021 年 2 月 25 日,中共中央总书记习近平宣布,中国完成了消除绝对贫困的艰巨任务。这是人类历史上的一项伟大成就。

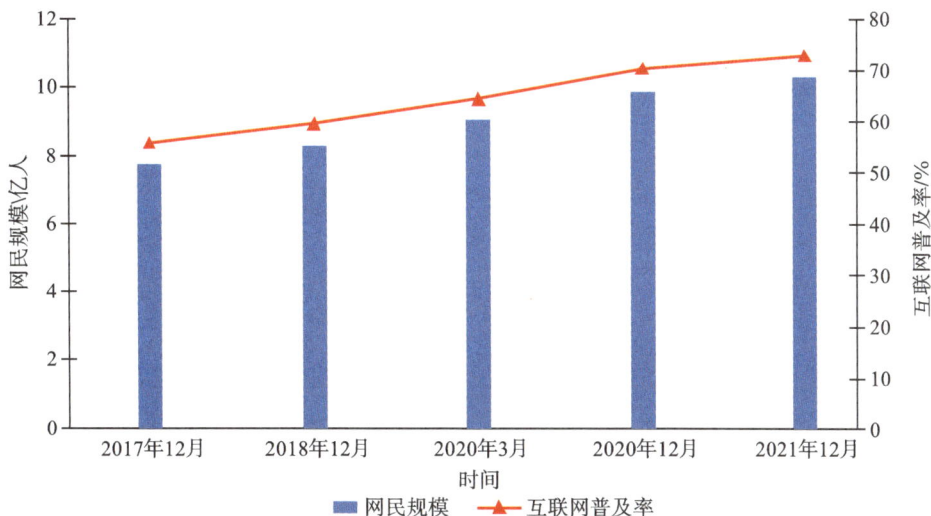

图 2-3   2017—2021 年中国网民规模及互联网普及率变化趋势

数据来源：中国互联网络信息中心

2.2   当前规模与水平

经过 40 多年的改革开放，中国在传统经济领域已经取得了巨大的成就。从 2012 年到 2021 年，中国制造业增加值从 16.98 万亿元增加到 31.4 万亿元，占全球比重从 22.5％提高到近 30％，持续保持世界第一制造大国地位。2012—2021 年，以不变价计算，中国全部工业增加值年均增长 6.3％，远高于同期全球工业增加值 2％左右的年均增速。在 500 种主要工业产品中，中国有四成以上产品的产量居世界第一，个人计算机、空调、太阳能电池板、手机等重要产品产量占全球一半以上。

在数字经济方面，中国也在全球数字经济发展浪潮中占据突出位置，数字经济增长显著高于其他主要经济体。2020 年，美中德日英数字经济规模占全球的 79％。美国数字经济世界第一，规模达到 13.6 万亿美元，占全球比重为 41.7％；中国数字经济位居世界第二，规模为 5.4 万亿美元；德国、日本、英国分列第三至第五，规模分别为 2.54 万亿美元、2.48 万亿美元和 1.79 万亿美元。2020 年，中国数字经济核心产业增加值占 GDP 比重达到 7.8％。上海社会科学院发布的《全球数字经济竞争力发展报告（2020）》显示，中国数字经济竞争力位居全球第三，仅次于美国、新加坡，且与美国的差距呈逐年缩小的态势。在各项分指标中，中国在数字产业上的得分位居全球首位，且领先优势逐年扩大。2020 年全球数字经济国家竞争力评价结果与排名见表 2-6。

表 2-6   2020 年全球数字经济竞争力评价结果与排名

排名	国家	数字产业	数字创新	数字设施	数字治理	总得分
1	美国	46.76	80.18	69.89	86.54	70.84
2	新加坡	27.55	82.18	50.53	67.43	56.92

续表

排名	国家	数字产业	数字创新	数字设施	数字治理	总得分
3	中国	65.31	51.52	46.07	49.65	53.14
4	韩国	12.85	68.48	46.33	65.40	48.27
5	英国	20.32	65.37	33.42	72.80	47.98
6	日本	12.66	73.45	39.09	63.40	47.15
7	芬兰	3.07	85.54	33.51	63.77	46.47
8	瑞典	9.32	69.71	38.18	62.82	45.01

　　在数字基础设施方面，目前中国已经建成了全球规模最大、普及率高、技术先进的信息基础设施。网络设施方面，移动通信网络和光纤网络全球规模最大、覆盖广泛、技术领先。算力设施方面，互联网数据中心规模持续快速增长，一批专用于人工智能的高性能公共算力开放平台、智能计算中心等正在逐步形成。感知设施方面，形成窄带物联网（NB-IoT）、4G和5G多网协同发展的格局，网络覆盖能力持续提升。近年中国信息基础设施规模与水平见表2-7。

表 2-7　近年中国信息基础设施规模与水平

类型	指标	规模与水平
网络设施	宽带固定网络覆盖水平	所有地级市全面建成光网城市，截至 2022 年 10 月底，百兆及以上接入速率用户占比达 93.8%，千兆接入速率用户突破 8 000 万户
	移动通信网络覆盖水平	建成全球最大规模 5G 网络，截至 2022 年 9 月底，中国 5G 基站数达 222 万个，5G 基站占全球总量的一半以上，5G 移动电话用户达 5.1 亿户
	卫星定位导航服务覆盖水平	2020 年 7 月，北斗三号全球卫星导航系统正式开通，1 年后，在 20 多个国家开通高精度服务，总用户数超 20 亿
	IPv6 地址资源规模	网络基础设施全面向 IPv6 演进升级，截至 2022 年 6 月，IPv6 地址资源总量位居世界第一，IPv6 活跃用户数达 6.83 亿人
	居民用户互联网接入水平	截至 2022 年 6 月，中国网民规模 10.51 亿人，互联网普及率 74.4%，特别是农村地区互联网普及率提升到 58.8%
	中小学校园互联网接入水平	截至 2021 年底，中小学互联网接入率达到 100%，出口带宽 100 Mbps 以上的学校比例达到 99.95%，接入无线网的学校超过 21 万所

续表

类型	指标	规模与水平
算力设施	数据中心服务器规模	截至 2020 年底,中国在用数据中心标准机架数约为 440 万架,云计算规模接近 4 300 万核,平均上架率约 50％,存储容量达到 800 EB(艾字节)
	数据中心算力水平	截至 2021 年底,中国算力总规模超过 140 EFLOPS(每秒百亿亿次浮点数运算),近 5 年年均增速超过 30％,算力规模排名全球第二
感知设施	窄带物联网覆盖规模	建成全球最大的窄带物联网,部署百万规模的窄带物联网基站,基本实现县城以上连续覆盖,截至 2022 年 12 月,移动物联网连接数达到 18.45亿户,蜂窝物联网终端用户规模快速接近移动电话用户规模
	物联网应用数量	截至 2022 年底,已形成水表、气表、烟感、追踪类 4 个千万级应用,白色家电、路灯、停车、农业等 7 个百万级应用

中国电商在网上零售额、网购人数等方面稳居世界第一。2013—2022 年,中国网上零售市场规模连续 9 年居世界首位。以电商销售额占全国整个零售市场的比例测算,2022 年中国达到 55.6％,排名世界第一,而排名第二的韩国为 31.6％,排名第三的英国为 28.5％,美国仅为 16.3％,西欧国家平均为 14.8％(见图 2-4)。中国网上零售额从 2012 年的1.31万亿元增长到 2021 年的 13.1 万亿元,年均增长率达 29.15％;电子商务交易额由 2012 年的 8 万亿元增长至 2021 年的 42.3 万亿元,年均增长率达 20.3％。依托线上电子商务和移动支付,网约车、网上外卖、数字文化、智慧旅游等行业的市场规模不断扩大。

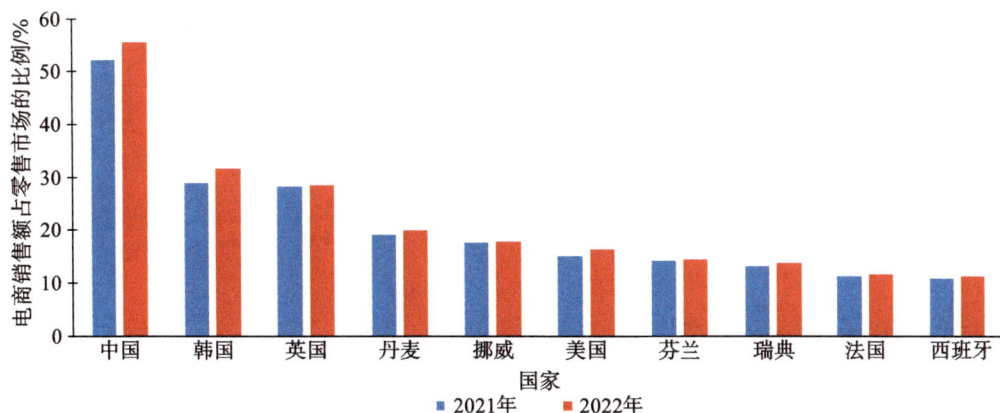

图 2-4 2021—2022 年各国电商销售额占零售市场的比例

数据来源:eMarketer

2.3   宏观战略与产业规划

2.3.1   国家发展战略

中国共产党是领导中国改革和发展的核心力量。在中国共产党的重要会议中形成的整体战略,经过全国人民代表大会讨论后,由各级政府指定相应的规划进行落实。中共十九大(2017年)和中共二十大(2022年)形成了整体国家信息化战略,包括面向信息产业发展的"网络强国"战略,面向民生服务和社会治理的"智慧社会"战略,以及面向国民经济和社会整体数字化的"数字中国"战略等。

2.3.1.1   网络强国

2014年2月,中共中央总书记习近平强调,要从国际国内大势出发,总体布局,统筹各方,创新发展,努力把我国建设成为网络强国。2017年,中共十九大报告明确提出建设"网络强国"。2022年,中共二十大报告再次提出建设"网络强国"。建设"网络强国"的战略部署要与"两个一百年"①奋斗目标同步推进,向着网络基础设施基本普及、自主创新能力显著增强、信息经济全面发展、网络安全保障有力、网络攻防实力均衡的方向不断前进。主要任务包括:

(1)在与互联网相关的信息化基础设施方面达到世界领先水平。网络规模和宽带普及率、与网络相关的信息产业的竞争力、网络安全能力等达到世界领先水平,云计算、移动互联网、大数据以及物联网的建设和应用等也要达到世界领先水平。

(2)在与互联网相关的关键技术方面实现自主可控。从根本上改变关键技术受制于人的局面,需要在芯片技术、操作系统以及CPU技术等关键技术领域实现大的突破。

(3)在互联网应用方面达到世界领先水平。产业互联网、消费互联网整体上要达到比较高的水平,电子商务、电子政务等得到较为广泛的普及与应用。

2.3.1.2   智慧社会

"智慧社会"一词最初是由欧盟提出来的,旨在探究如何利用当代技术趋势解决现代社会面临的挑战。国际电信联盟电信发展部门认为,智慧社会是指利用技术的力量和潜力提高人类的生产力,将资源聚焦于重要的活动和关系,并最终改善健康、福祉和生活质量。

2017年,中共十九大报告明确提出建设"智慧社会"。"智慧社会"建设以民生保障为目标,充分依托信息化、智能化手段,为群众提供多样化、普惠化、均等化的公共服务。主要任务包括:

(1)基础设施智能化。对涉及广大人民群众生活的公共社会基础设施,包括交通、电网、水务、物流等,进行智慧化改造。

(2)规划管理信息化。通过城市信息模型、地理信息系统等技术的综合运用,推进城乡规划、国土利用、城乡管网、园林绿化、环境保护等城乡基础设施管理的数字化和精准化。

---

①   "两个一百年"奋斗目标是,到中国共产党建党100周年(2021年)时在中国全面建成小康社会,到中华人民共和国成立100周年(2049年)时将中国建设成富强民主文明和谐美丽的社会主义现代化强国。

（3）公共服务普惠化。推进医疗、教育、文化、旅游等领域的信息化和智能化，推动优质医疗资源、教育资源的共享和流动，促进图书馆、博物馆等公益场馆的数字化。

2.3.1.3　数字中国

随着经济社会各领域数字化进程的持续加快，数据要素将对经济运行效率和全要素生产率跃升产生更大的推动作用。世界各国都将数字化作为经济发展重点，纷纷制定政策、加大投入。

2017年，中共十九大报告明确提出建设"数字中国"。2022年，中共二十大报告进一步指出要建设"数字中国"，加快发展数字经济，促进数字经济和实体经济深度融合，打造具有国际竞争力的数字产业集群。主要任务包括：

（1）打造数字经济新优势。一是加强关键数字技术创新应用。加快推进高端芯片、操作系统、人工智能关键算法、传感器、通用处理器等技术的研发突破和迭代应用。二是加快推动数字产业化。培育壮大新兴数字产业，提升通信设备、核心电子元器件、关键软件等产业水平。三是推进产业数字化转型。实施"上云用数赋智"行动，推动数据赋能全产业链协同转型。深入推进服务业数字化转型，培育众包设计、智慧物流、新零售等新增长点。

（2）加快数字社会建设新步伐。一是提供智慧便捷的公共服务。推进学校、医院、养老院等公共服务机构资源数字化，加大资源开放共享服务力度。积极发展在线课堂、互联网医院、智慧图书馆等。二是建设智慧城市和数字乡村。分级分类推进新型智慧城市建设，将物联网感知设施、通信系统等纳入公共基础设施统一规划建设，推进市政公共设施智能化改造，推进城市数据大脑建设。三是构筑美好数字生活新图景。推进智慧社区建设，发展线上线下融合的社区生活服务、社区治理等。

（3）营造数字化发展新生态。一是建立健全数据要素市场规则。培育规范的数据交易平台和市场主体，推进数据安全、个人信息保护等领域基础性立法，推动数据跨境安全有序流动。二是营造规范有序的政策环境。健全共享经济、平台经济和新个体经济管理规范，健全数字经济统计监测体系。三是加强网络安全防护。建立健全关键信息基础设施保护体系，加强网络安全风险评估和审查。四是推动构建网络空间命运共同体。推动以联合国为主渠道、以联合国宪章为基础原则制定数字和网络空间国际规则，推动建立多边、民主、透明的全球互联网治理体系。

2.3.2　政府规划层次

目前，中国已经建立了遍及各级政府部门、覆盖各类行业的信息产业和信息化规划体系（见表2-8）。其中，全国性的规划主要包括：

（1）中长期发展规划。对于国家信息化发展的远景进行15年左右的中长期规划，其中既包括宏观的整体规划，例如2006年发布的《2006—2020年国家信息化发展战略》、2016年发布的《国家信息化发展战略纲要》，又包括某个方面的专项规划，例如大数据、人工智能、5G等专项规划。

（2）五年规划。结合国民经济和社会发展五年规划，分行业给出信息化要求，涉及战略性新兴产业、电子信息制造业、传统产业数字化转型、社会信息化等多个领域；各行业主管部门再依据五年规划，制定各领域的信息化分项五年规划。

（3）短期规划。国家有关部委针对某个领域发展的时代需求，提出3年左右的行动计划，组织协调本领域的全国性重大项目、重点工程等，对相关配套政策、措施、环境等进行专项调整和改进。

表 2-8　中国"十四五"期间信息产业和信息化相关规划

规划类型	细分类型	发文机关	信息产业和信息化相关的主要规划
中长期规划	宏观规划	中共中央办公厅 国务院办公厅	《国家信息化发展战略纲要》
			《中华人民共和国国民经济和社会发展第十四个五年规划和 2035 年远景目标纲要》
	专项规划	国务院	《新一代人工智能发展规划》
五年规划	宏观专项规划	中央网络安全和信息化委员会	《"十四五"国家信息化规划》
		国务院	《"十四五"数字经济发展规划》
		国务院办公厅	《"十四五"现代物流发展规划》
	信息产业规划	工业和信息化部	《"十四五"信息通信行业发展规划》 《"十四五"大数据产业发展规划》 《"十四五"软件和信息技术服务业发展规划》
	行业信息化规划	工业和信息化部等	《"十四五"智能制造发展规划》 《"十四五"信息化和工业化深度融合发展规划》
		农业农村部	《"十四五"全国农业农村信息化发展规划》
		国家广播电视总局	《广播电视和网络视听"十四五"发展规划》
		商务部等	《"十四五"电子商务发展规划》
		交通运输部	《数字交通"十四五"发展规划》
		住房和城乡建设部等	《"十四五"全国城市基础设施建设规划》
		民政部	《"十四五"民政信息化发展规划》
		国家卫生健康委等	《"十四五"全民健康信息化规划》
		国家发展改革委	《"十四五"推进国家政务信息化规划》

续表

规划类型	细分类型	发文机关	信息产业和信息化相关的主要规划
短期规划	信息产业规划	工业和信息化部等	《物联网新型基础设施建设三年行动计划（2021—2023 年）》 《"双千兆"网络协同发展行动计划（2021—2023 年）》 《新型数据中心发展三年行动计划（2021—2023 年）》 《信息通信行业绿色低碳发展行动计划（2022—2025 年）》 《基础电子元器件产业发展行动计划（2021—2023 年）》
		工业互联网专项工作组	《工业互联网创新发展行动计划(2021—2023 年)》
	信息化应用规划	工业和信息化部等	《虚拟现实与行业应用融合发展行动计划（2022—2026 年）》 《5G 应用"扬帆"行动计划(2021—2023 年)》
		中央网信办等	《数字乡村发展行动计划(2022—2025 年)》

中国形成了完善的"调研—规划—执行—评估"的规划体系。中央政府和部委在研制规划的过程中，会征求相关行业机构和专家的意见，确保规划的科学性和可实施性。国家级的重大规划，例如国民经济和社会发展五年规划，需要由全国人民代表大会等机关审查。国家级规划发布后，各级政府根据其精神，结合当地的实际，研制本级的相应规划，并提交本级人民代表大会审查。各级政府将规划中的目标列为每年工作汇报和总结的部分，向相关层级的人民代表大会报告执行进展，并接受监督。

中国分层分级的规划体系，可以确保中央政府的政策和规划可以在全国得到落实。如表 2-9 所示，以湖北省、武汉市为例，在国务院制定国家五年规划之后，湖北省和武汉市也会分别制定本级政府的相关规划；在国家部委制定本行业（例如大数据行业）五年规划后，湖北省相关行业主管部门进一步制定本省该行业五年规划。

表 2-9　中国信息产业规划的分解层次（以湖北省武汉市为例）

类型	发文机关	层级	规划	发布时间
宏观发展规划分解		国家级	《中华人民共和国国民经济和社会发展第十四个五年规划和 2035 年远景目标纲要》	2021 年 3 月
		省级	《湖北省国民经济和社会发展第十四个五年规划和 2035 年远景目标纲要》	2021 年 4 月
		市级	《武汉市国民经济和社会发展第十四个五年规划和 2035 年远景目标纲要》	2021 年 4 月

续表

类型	发文机关	层级	规划	发布时间
行业发展规划分解	工业和信息化部	国家级	《"十四五"大数据产业发展规划》	2021年10月
	湖北省经济和信息化厅	省级	《湖北省大数据产业"十四五"发展规划》	2022年3月

2.3.3　规划政策工具

中国政府综合运用各种政策工具,推动和促进相关信息产业行业的发展。以2011—2020年发布的信息产业相关规划为例,分析所采用的政策工具,共收集国务院办公厅、工业和信息化部、国家发展和改革委员会(简称"国家发展改革委")、科学技术部(简称"科技部")等部门发布的90份政策文献,按照供给、环境、需求三个方面对常用的政策工具进行分类统计,结果见表2-10。

表2-10　2011—2020年中国信息技术产业规划政策工具统计

工具类型	具体工具名称	举例	政策工具数量	占全部工具比例
供给型	人才培养	在信息技术等重点领域培养研发急需紧缺专门人才	36	13.8%
	基础设施建设	支持建设电子信息产业工程研究中心、工程实验室、企业技术中心	5	2.0%
	公共服务	支持电子信息产业创新知识中心、数据中心、检验检测、质量认证等公共研发服务平台建设	32	12.3%
	科技资金投入	充分利用国家集成电路产业投资基金等政策性资金,引导社会资金投入,支持重大产业化项目发展	26	10.0%
环境型	目标规划	中国软件名城、国家新型工业化产业示范基地(软件和信息服务)建设迈向更高水平,产业收入超千亿元的城市达20个以上	47	18.0%
	法规管制	加快建立有利于新一代信息技术产业发展的行业标准和重要产品技术标准体系,优化市场准入的审批管理程序	24	9.2%
	对外开放	鼓励境内集成电路企业扩大国际合作,整合国际资源,拓展国际市场	16	6.1%
	金融支持	积极支持符合条件的软件企业和集成电路企业采取发行股票、债券等多种方式筹集资金,拓宽直接融资渠道	11	4.2%
	税收优惠	对相关集成电路企业因购进设备形成的增值税期末留抵税额准予退还	15	5.7%
	知识产权保护	积极开发和应用正版软件网络版权保护技术,有效保护软件和集成电路知识产权	17	6.5%

续表

工具类型	具体工具名称	举例	政策工具数量	占全部工具比例
需求型	政府采购	实施新一代信息技术产业创新产品和服务推广计划,加大政府对软件等产品的首购、订购力度	6	2.3%
	科技成果转化	建立企业、科研院所、高校良性互动机制,为促进新一代信息技术产业技术转移和成果转化提供全过程服务	23	8.8%
	贸易管制	通过出口补助等方式支持软件出口、服务外包	3	1.1%

政府对新一代信息技术产业的政策支持主要以供给型和环境型政策工具为主。"十二五"期间,有一些细分政策工具还未启用,如供给型中的基础设施建设、需求型中的贸易管制。"十三五"以来,各类型政策工具得到了一定的丰富与扩展。在供给型政策工具中,人才培养、公共服务、科技资金投入作为主要支持工具,支持力度在 2016 年大幅增加,而基础设施建设支持力度相对较低;在环境型政策工具中,政府主要通过制定发展目标和规划等引导性政策来促进产业发展,其次为知识产权保护相关政策及金融支持相关政策;在需求型政策工具中,科技成果转化的支持力度最高,在 2015 年之后迅速增长,并且和供给型政策主要支持工具相比差距甚大。中国政府正在积极探索不同类型的产业激励和促进手段的应用方法,结合各行业的痛点和缺点,推进产业的发展和进步。

2.4　发展目标与建设重点

2023 年 2 月,中共中央、国务院印发《数字中国建设整体布局规划》。该规划指出,建设数字中国是数字时代推进中国式现代化的重要引擎,是构筑国家竞争新优势的有力支撑。数字中国建设按照"2522"的整体框架进行布局,即夯实数字基础设施和数据资源体系"两大基础",推进数字技术与经济、政治、文化、社会、生态文明建设"五位一体"深度融合,强化数字技术创新体系和数字安全屏障"两大能力",优化数字化发展国内国际"两个环境"(见图 2-5)。

中国建设数字中国的整体目标为:到 2025 年,数字中国建设取得决定性进展,信息化发展水平大幅跃升,数字基础设施全面夯实,数字技术创新能力显著增强,数据要素价值充分发挥,数字经济高质量发展,数字治理效能整体提升。

2.4.1　数字基础设施

2020 年 3 月,中共中央政治局常务委员会明确提出加快 5G 网络、数据中心等新型基础设施建设(简称"新基建")进度。新基建是结合新一轮科技革命和产业变革特征,面向国家战略需求,为经济社会的创新、协调、绿色、开放、共享发展提供底层支撑的具有乘数效应的战略性、网络型基础设施。新型基础设施主要包括三大类:一是信息基础设施,主要指新一数字中国建设"两个环境"

国内：数字治理生态　　　国际：数字领域国际合作

数字中国建设"两大能力"

数字技术与"五位一体"深度融合

| 数字经济 | 数字政务 | 数字文化 | 数字社会 | 数字生态文明 |

数字中国建设"两大基础"

数字基础设施　　　　　　数据资源体系

（左侧：数字技术创新体系　右侧：数字安全屏障）

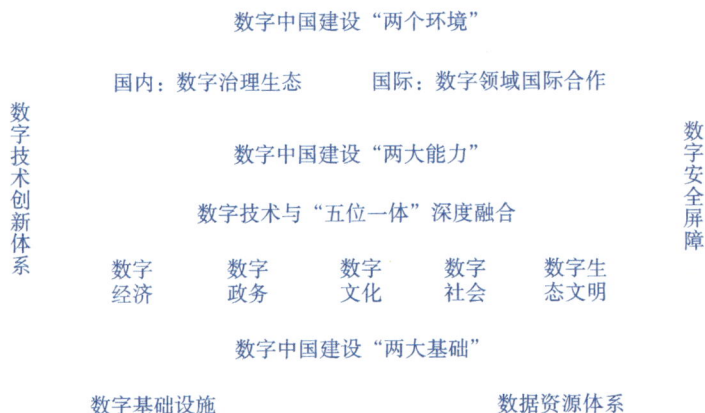

图 2-5　《数字中国建设整体布局规划》内容框架（2023 年 2 月）

图片来源：中国网信网

代信息技术演化生成的基础设施,例如,以 5G、物联网、工业互联网、卫星互联网为代表的通信网络基础设施,以数据中心、智能计算中心为代表的算力基础设施,以人工智能、云计算、区块链为代表的新技术基础设施等。二是融合基础设施,主要指深度应用互联网、大数据、人工智能等技术,支撑传统基础设施转型升级,进而形成的融合基础设施,比如智能交通基础设施、智慧能源基础设施等。三是创新基础设施,主要指支撑科学研究、技术开发、产品研制的具有公益属性的基础设施,比如重大科技基础设施、科教基础设施、产业技术创新基础设施等。伴随技术革命和产业变革,新型基础设施的内涵、外延并非一成不变,而是会持续发展变化。中国新基建主要内容见表 2-11。

表 2-11　中国新基建主要内容

领域	细分领域	范围
信息基础设施	通信网络基础设施	5G、物联网、工业互联网、卫星互联网等
	算力基础设施	数据中心、智能计算中心等
	新技术基础设施	人工智能、云计算、区块链等
融合基础设施	智能交通基础设施	城际高速铁路、城市轨道交通
	智慧能源基础设施	特高压输变电网络、新能源汽车充电桩
创新基础设施	支撑科技发展的公益基础设施	重大科技基础设施、科教基础设施、产业技术创新基础设施等

2023 年 2 月印发的《数字中国建设整体布局规划》将"新基建"中的"信息基础设施"称为"数字基础设施",并且给出了近期的建设重点。在网络基础设施方面,加快 5G 网络与千兆光网协同建设,深入推进 IPv6 的规模部署与应用,推进移动物联网全面发展,大力推进北斗规模应用;在算力基础设施方面,系统优化算力基础设施布局,促进东西部算力高效互补和协同联动,引导通用数据中心、超算中心、智能计算中心、边缘数据中心等合理梯次布局;在应用基础设施方面,加强传统基础设施的数字化、智能化改造,提升电力、交通、物流等社会通用基础设施的智能化水平。中国通信网络基础设施的"十四五"建设目标见表 2-12。

表 2-12　中国通信网络基础设施的"十四五"建设目标

指标	2020 年	2025 年
网民规模	9.89 亿人	12 亿人
5G 用户普及率	15％	56％
千兆及以上速率的光纤接入用户	640 万户	6 000 万户
IPv6 活跃用户数	4.62 亿人	8 亿人

2.4.2　数字经济

进入"十四五"时期以来，中国密集发布了数字经济相关的多项重要规划，包括《中华人民共和国国民经济和社会发展第十四个五年规划和 2035 年远景目标纲要》《"十四五"数字经济发展规划》《"十四五"信息化和工业化深度融合发展规划》等。国家"十四五"规划纲要构建了推动数字化发展的系统性框架，在整体目标方面，提出到 2025 年，中国数字经济核心产业增加值占 GDP 的比重从 2020 年的 7.8％提升到 10％。中国数字经济"十四五"建设目标见表 2-13。

表 2-13　中国数字经济"十四五"建设目标

指标	2020 年	2025 年
数字经济核心产业增加值占 GDP 的比重	7.8％	10％
数字产业化方面，信息消费规模	5.8 万亿元	7.5 万亿元
数字产业化方面，网上零售额	11.76 万亿元	17 万亿元
产业数字化方面，企业工业设备上云率	13.1％	30％
产业数字化方面，关键业务环节全面数字化的企业比例	48.3％	60％

2.4.2.1　数字产业化

加快推动数字产业化。培育壮大人工智能、大数据、区块链、云计算、网络安全等新兴数字产业，提升通信设备、核心电子元器件、关键软件等产业水平；鼓励企业开放搜索、电商、社交等数据，发展第三方大数据服务产业；促进共享经济、平台经济健康发展。中国"十四五"期间数字产业化的重点产业及其发展目标见表 2-14。

表 2-14　中国"十四五"期间数字产业化的重点产业及其发展目标

数字化产业	产业发展目标
云计算	加快云操作系统迭代升级，推动超大规模分布式存储、弹性计算、数据虚拟隔离等技术创新，提高云安全水平；以混合云为重点培育行业解决方案、系统集成、运维管理等云服务产业
大数据	推动大数据采集、清洗、存储、挖掘、分析、可视化算法等技术创新，培育数据采集、标注、存储、传输、管理、应用等全生命周期产业体系，完善大数据标准体系

数字化产业	产业发展目标
物联网	推动传感器、网络切片、高精度定位等技术创新，协同发展云服务与边缘计算服务，培育车联网、医疗物联网、家居物联网产业
工业互联网	打造自主可控的标识解析体系、标准体系、安全管理体系，加强工业软件研发应用，培育形成具有国际影响力的工业互联网平台，推进"工业互联网＋智能制造"产业生态建设
区块链	推动智能合约、共识算法、加密算法、分布式系统等区块链技术创新，以联盟链为重点发展区块链服务平台和金融科技、供应链管理、政务服务等领域应用方案，完善监管机制
人工智能	建设重点行业人工智能数据集，发展算法推理训练场景，推进智能医疗装备、智能运载工具、智能识别系统等智能产品设计与制造，推动通用化和行业性人工智能开放平台建设

2.4.2.2　产业数字化

推进产业数字化转型。加快新一代信息技术与实体经济融合应用，实施"上云用数赋智"行动，打造大数据支撑、网络化共享、智能化协作的智慧供应链体系。建设智慧农业，加快农业生产、加工、销售、物流等产业链各环节数字化、智能化升级，构建农业基础数据资源体系，加快农业科技服务信息化建设。加快制造业数字化转型，发展多层次系统化工业互联网平台体系和创新应用，强化两化（信息化和工业化）融合标准体系建设，深入实施智能制造工程。深入推进服务业数字化转型，培育众包设计、智慧物流、新零售等新增长点。中国"十四五"期间产业数字化的典型行业发展目标见表 2-15。

表 2-15　中国"十四五"期间产业数字化的典型行业发展目标

典型行业	发展目标
智能制造	促进设备联网、生产环节数字化连接和供应链协同响应，推进生产数据贯通化、制造柔性化、产品个性化、管理智能化
智慧农业	推广大田作物精准播种、精准施肥施药、精准收获，推动设施园艺、畜禽水产养殖智能化应用；构建智慧水利体系，以流域为单元提升水情测报和智能调度能力
智慧能源	推动煤矿、油气田、电厂等智能化升级，开展用能信息广泛采集、能效在线分析，实现源网荷储互动、多能协同互补、用能需求智能调控
智能交通	发展自动驾驶和车路协同的出行服务，推广公路智能管理、交通信号联动、公交优先通行控制，建设智能铁路、智慧民航、智慧港口、数字航道、智慧停车场

2.4.3 数字社会

《"十四五"国家信息化规划》提出,稳步推进数字社会建设。培育数字技术、数据资源驱动的新业态新模式。鼓励出行、餐饮、住宿、文化、旅游、体育、物流、家政等领域智能化升级和商业模式创新,促进品牌消费、品质消费,培育高质量的数字生活服务市场。公共服务体系更加便捷惠民,信息化对基本民生保障、基本社会服务的支撑作用有效发挥,数字公共服务均等化水平明显提高,城乡区域间服务水平差距明显缩小。中国"十四五"期间数字公共服务的典型领域发展目标见表2-16。

表 2-16　中国"十四五"期间数字公共服务的典型领域发展目标

典型领域	发展目标
智慧教育	推动社会化高质量在线课程资源纳入公共教学体系,推进优质教育资源在线辐射农村和边远地区薄弱学校,发展场景式、体验式学习和智能化教育管理评价
智慧医疗	完善电子健康档案和病历、电子处方等数据库,加快医疗卫生机构数据共享;推广远程医疗,推进医学影像辅助判读、临床辅助诊断等应用;运用大数据提升对医疗机构和医疗行为的监管能力
智慧文旅	推动景区、博物馆等发展线上数字化体验产品,建设景区监测设施和大数据平台,发展沉浸式体验、虚拟展厅、高清直播等新型文旅服务
智慧社区	推动政务服务平台、社区感知设施和家庭终端联通,发展智能预警、应急救援救护和智慧养老等社区惠民服务,建立无人物流配送体系
智慧家居	应用感应控制、语音控制、远程控制等技术手段,发展智能家电、智能照明、智能安防监控、智能音箱、可穿戴设备、服务机器人等

2.5　小　　结

在中国共产党的领导下,中国经过70余年的发展,从一个贫穷落后的农业国发展成了一个富强进步的工业国。中国大地发生了翻天覆地的变化,中国人民正享受着富足安康的生活。

中国不但建成了全球领先的信息基础设施,而且打造了技术领先、覆盖全面的产业链,在移动互联网、电子商务、移动支付等多个应用领域处于全球领先的地位。目前,中国的数字经济规模稳居世界第二,数字经济核心产业增加值占GDP比重还在逐步提升。中国在信息技术领域的自主创新能力显著增强,科技实力与国际竞争力与日俱增。

作为社会主义国家,中国在产业规划和发展方面彰显出制度优势。政府构建了覆盖全行业的信息产业和信息化规划体系,涵盖中长期规划、五年规划、短期规划等多层级布局,并综合运用供给型、环境型、需求型等政策工具,精准推动信息产业发展。目前,中国确立了网络强国、智慧社会、数字中国等宏观战略。网络强国聚焦基础设施、关键技术与应用创新;智慧社会推动基础设施智能化与公共服务普惠化;数字中国强调打造数字经济新优势、营造数字化发展新生态。

中国政府高度重视信息技术对产业与社会的变革作用,多次五年规划将电信基础设施建设列为重点,并以此为根基推动全行业数字化转型与产业升级。中国正以稳健的步伐向数字中国目标迈进,在全球信息化浪潮中展现出强劲动力与光明前景。

3　信息技术创新

中国改革开放的总设计师邓小平指出,科学技术是第一生产力。信息科技创新是发展信息产业的核心要素。由于信息产业所具有的高创新性、高风险特征,开展有组织的科学研究成为中国赶超世界先进科技水平的特色之路。本章首先对中国现有的科技研发体系、科技发展计划进行介绍,然后重点介绍中国近年来在信息技术领域的重大科技工程、产业技术攻关成果。

3.1　科技研发体系

1949 年中华人民共和国成立时,全国专门从事科技研究的机构仅有 30 多家,专项从事信息技术研究的科研队伍几乎空白。此后,中国从零开始逐步建立信息技术方面的教学、研究、生产基地。经过 70 年左右的发展,目前中国已经建立了相对完备的信息技术研发体系,包括院校、科研机构、产业集群等。

3.1.1　战略科研力量

20 世纪 50 年代,中国初步建立了独立自主的信息技术研发队伍。1956 年教育部将 5 所大学的师生集中到北京大学物理系,创办了中国第一个半导体专业。1956 年中国科学院计算技术研究所成立,1960 年中国科学院半导体研究所成立。改革开放以后,国家战略科技力量体系逐步完善,涵盖了面向基础研究的国家重点实验室,面向市场应用的国家工程研究中心、国家技术创新中心等创新基地。

3.1.1.1　国家重点实验室

国家重点实验室是中国组织开展基础研究、应用基础研究与前沿技术研究,凝聚培养创新领军人才、开展高水平创新合作、产出重大原创成果的重要科技创新基地。1984 年开始组建的国家重点实验室,截止到 2021 年总数达到 265 个,主要依托单位是中国的重点大学和相关领域的主要科研机构。国家重点实验室积极参与国际大科学计划和大科学工程,推动中国在基础理论研究、重大关键技术等方面的突破。至 2021 年,信息技术领域的国家重点实验室有 26 个,涉及半导体、电磁学、通信、计算机、网络等多个领域。

根据《中华人民共和国国民经济和社会发展第十四个五年规划和 2035 年远景目标纲要》,中国将强化国家战略科技力量,以国家战略性需求为导向推进创新体系优化组合,加快构建以国家实验室为引领的战略科技力量。聚焦量子信息、光子与微纳电子、网络通信、人工智能等重大创新领域组建一批国家实验室,重组国家重点实验室,形成结构合理、运行高效的实验室体系。优化提升国家工程研究中心、国家技术创新中心等创新基地,开展产学研深度合作,推动基础理论、关键技术对产业的辐射和带动作用。

2022年1月开始施行的《中华人民共和国科学技术进步法》中提出,"建立健全以国家实验室为引领、全国重点实验室为支撑的实验室体系"。全国重点实验室接替国家重点实验室,成为重要战略科技力量。2022年7月,科技部组织召开国家重点实验室优化重组工作推进会,经过重组、推荐和评议,遴选出首批20个标杆全国重点实验室批准建设。其中,信息技术领域的全国重点实验室有9个,覆盖人工智能、集成电路、微纳电子等细分领域(见表3-1)。

表 3-1　中国在信息技术领域的标杆全国重点实验室(2022 年 7 月)

全国重点实验室	依托单位
微纳电子器件与集成技术全国重点实验室	北京大学
虚拟现实技术与系统全国重点实验室	北京航空航天大学
集成芯片与系统全国重点实验室	复旦大学
脑机智能全国重点实验室	浙江大学
自主智能无人系统全国重点实验室	北京理工大学、同济大学
认知智能全国重点实验室	科大讯飞股份有限公司、中国科学技术大学
处理器芯片全国重点实验室	中国科学院计算技术研究所
集成电路材料全国重点实验室	中国科学院上海微系统与信息技术研究所
多模态人工智能系统全国重点实验室	中国科学院自动化研究所

3.1.1.2　国家工程研究中心

国家工程研究中心是国家发展改革委组织具有较强研发能力和综合实力的高等院校、科研机构、企业等建设的研究开发实体,是国家创新体系的重要组成部分。面向国家重大战略任务和重点工程建设需求,开展关键技术攻关和试验研究、重大装备研制、重大科技成果的工程化实验验证,突破关键技术和核心装备制约。

截至2022年末,纳入新序列管理的国家工程研究中心共191个,其中信息技术领域的国家工程研究中心有50个,建设单位的覆盖范围较广,既包括知名的高等院校和科研机构,又包括主要电信企业(如中国电信、中国移动、中国联通等)、主要信息科技公司(如百度、科大讯飞等)、主要电子制造公司(如京东方、海尔等),还包括在各行业开展信息化的主要科技力量(如中国银联、中国石油等)。表3-2列出了中国在信息技术领域的12个国家工程研究中心。

表 3-2　中国在信息技术领域的国家工程研究中心

国家工程研究中心	牵头建设单位
下一代互联网核心技术国家工程研究中心	清华大学
移动专用网络国家工程研究中心	北京交通大学
移动互联网安全技术国家工程研究中心	北京邮电大学
下一代互联网接入系统国家工程研究中心	华中科技大学

国家工程研究中心	牵头建设单位
光纤传感技术与网络国家工程研究中心	武汉理工大学
新一代移动通信测试验证国家工程研究中心	中国信息通信研究院
国家网络安全应急工程技术研究中心	国家计算机网络与信息安全管理中心
云网基础设施安全国家工程研究中心	中国电信集团有限公司
下一代互联网宽带业务应用国家工程研究中心	中国联通网络技术研究院
新一代移动信息通信技术国家工程研究中心	中国移动通信集团有限公司
移动通信及车联网国家工程研究中心	大唐电信科技股份有限公司
数字家庭网络国家工程研究中心	海尔集团公司

根据《中华人民共和国国民经济和社会发展第十四个五年规划和 2035 年远景目标纲要》,中国将集中力量整合提升一批关键共性技术平台,支持行业龙头企业高等院校、科研院所和行业上下游企业共建国家产业创新中心,承担国家重大科技项目;支持有条件的企业联合转制科研院所组建行业研究院,提供公益性共性技术服务;打造新型共性技术平台,解决跨行业跨领域关键共性技术问题。

3.1.2　高新技术产业开发区

高新技术产业开发区(以下简称"高新区")是经各级政府批准建立的以发展高新技术为目的而设置的特定区域,主要依靠知识密集、技术密集、区域经济实力、地理位置以及对外开放等优势,集中发展国家政策支持和鼓励的高新技术产业。入驻高新区的企业可以享受所得税优惠税率、免征出口关税、免征厂房建设税等优惠政策。截至 2020 年底,国家高新技术产业开发区(以下简称"国家高新区")总数达 169 家,其中东部 70 家、中部 44 家、西部 39 家、东北 16 家,建设了 21 家国家自主创新示范区,成为实施创新驱动发展战略的重要载体。21 家国家自主创新示范区和 169 家国家高新区已成为地方创新发展"领头雁"。2015—2020 年国家高新区生产总值从 8.1 万亿元增长到 12.2 万亿元,5 年增长超过 50%;高新技术企业从 7.9 万家增长到 22.5 万家。

高新区已成为突破关键核心技术、增强原始创新能力的重要科技力量。2021 年,国家高新区聚集了全国 84% 的国家重点实验室、78% 的国家技术创新中心;企业研发经费支出是 2012 年的 3.3 倍,占全国研发经费总支出的 50%;《专利合作条约》(PCT)国际专利申请数量约占全国的 50%。截至 2022 年底,国家高新区建有 128 个创新型产业集群,北京中关村的信息技术产业规模占全国的 17%,武汉东湖高新区的光电子信息产业规模占全国的 50%,上海张江高新区的集成电路产业规模占全国的 35%。高新区培育和集聚了全国 36.2% 的高新技术企业、67.1% 的科创板上市企业、35.9% 的科技型中小企业,还涌现了一批世界一流企业。

3.1.3　创新型产业集群

1949 年以来,中国初步建立了独立自主的电子信息产业链,涵盖从原材料到器件、仪器仪表、系统设备的制造等上下游环节,形成了以国家信息安全产业基地、国家信息安全产业园为主体的区域产业集群,主要集中在环渤海地区(北京、天津)、长江三角洲(上海、杭州)、珠江三角洲(广州、深圳)三大区域。

近年来,中国将信息产业作为战略性新兴产业之一,结合产业集群政策进行推广。2010年,《国务院关于加快培育和发展战略性新兴产业的决定》发布,新一代信息技术被列为战略性新兴产业之一。2019年,《国家发展改革委关于加快推进战略性新兴产业集群建设有关工作的通知》发布,在12个重点领域公布了第一批国家级战略性新兴产业集群建设名单,共涉及22个省(区、市)的66个集群,其中新一代信息技术领域共设立产业集群23个,如表3-3所示。为了促进各地区信息技术产业的均衡发展,位于东部的上海和位于中部地区的武汉、合肥各有3个产业集群进入名单,成为新一代信息技术领域战略性新兴产业集群最多的城市。

表 3-3 中国在新一代信息技术领域设立的产业集群

分领域	名称
集成电路	上海浦东新区集成电路产业集群
	西安市集成电路产业集群
	北京经济技术开发区集成电路产业集群
	武汉市集成电路产业集群
	合肥市集成电路产业集群
新型显示器件	合肥市新型显示器件产业集群
	深圳市新型显示器件产业集群
	武汉市新型显示器件产业集群
下一代信息网络	武汉市下一代信息网络产业集群
	鹰潭市下一代信息网络产业集群
	郑州市下一代信息网络产业集群
信息技术服务	杭州市信息技术服务产业集群
	济南市信息技术服务产业集群
	贵阳市信息技术服务产业集群
	大连市信息技术服务产业集群
	上海杨浦区信息技术服务产业集群
	澄迈县信息技术服务产业集群
	郑州市信息技术服务产业集群
网络信息安全产品和服务	天津滨海高新区网络信息安全产品和服务产业集群
人工智能	北京海淀区人工智能产业集群
	合肥市人工智能产业集群
	上海徐汇区人工智能产业集群
	深圳市人工智能产业集群

产业集群具有网络化组织、柔性制造等特征,有利于实现持续科技创新,推动区域经济

发展。《中华人民共和国国民经济和社会发展第十四个五年规划和 2035 年远景目标纲要》和《"十四五"数字经济发展规划》中明确提出,鼓励有条件地方依托产业集群创办混合所有制产业技术研究院,服务区域关键共性技术研发;积极探索平台企业与产业园区联合运营模式,探索建立各类产业集群跨区域、跨平台协同新机制。

3.1.4　科技创新能力

世界知识产权组织发布的《2021 年全球创新指数报告》显示,中国位居全球第十二,较 2020 年上升两位,是全球前三十位中唯一的中等收入经济体,排名超过日本、以色列、加拿大等发达经济体。在全球"最佳科技集群"排名中,中国有 19 个集群入榜,仅比美国少 5 个,位列第二。其中,深圳—香港—广州稳居第二,北京上升至第三。2021 年,中国 PCT 国际专利申请总数量为 69 540 件,连续 3 年位列全球第一;信息技术领域 PCT 国际专利申请数量超过 30 000 件,比 2017 年提升 60%,占全球比重达 37.80%(见图 3-1)。

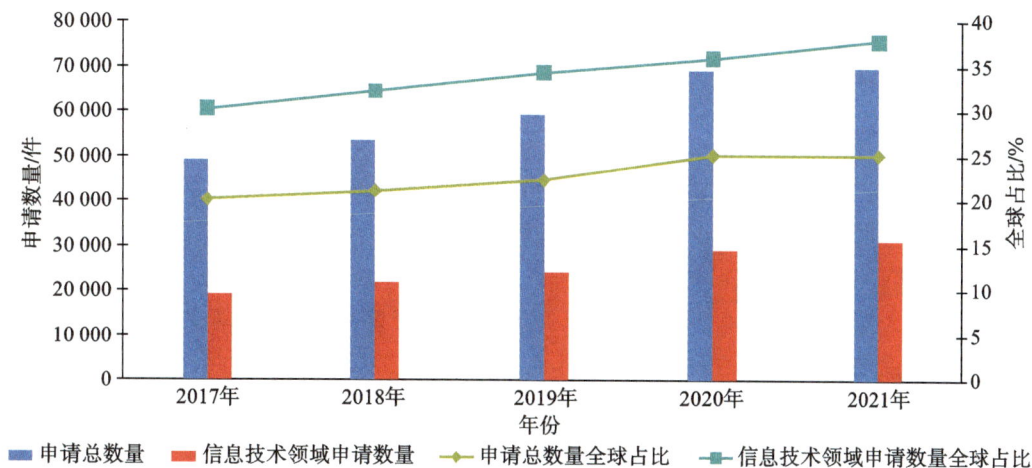

图 3-1　2017—2021 年中国 PCT 国际专利申请数量增长情况

数据来源:世界知识产权组织

2021 年,中国在计算机技术、数字通信领域 PCT 国际专利申请数量均位列全球第一,全球占比均超过 1/3;中国国内发明专利有效量增长最快的两大领域分别是信息技术管理方法和计算机技术,分别同比增长 100.3% 和 32.7%;企业创新活力进一步激发,中国 13 家企业进入全球 PCT 国际专利申请人排行榜前 50 位,华为连续 5 年位居榜首。数字技术领域高水平论文数量进一步提升,截至 2021 年 9 月,中国高被引论文数量为 4.29 万篇,占全球 24.8% 的份额,其中计算机科学领域论文国际被引次数提升至世界第一。

中国在 5G 移动通信、人工智能等技术领域取得了长足的进步。截至 2020 年 10 月,中国共计声明 13 282 件 5G 标准必要专利,占全球总量的 37%。华为、中兴在欧洲电信标准化协会公布的 5G 标准必要专利声明排名中位居世界前三。中国成为仅次于美国的全球第二大人工智能创新中心。2015—2020 年的全球前 100 篇人工智能方向高被引论文中,中国产出 21 篇,居世界第二。2011—2020 年,中国人工智能领域专利申请数量占全球总量的 74.7%,是美国的 8.2 倍。

此外,中国在信息技术领域的很多核心技术方面取得了新进展。关键基础软件加速发展,桌面操作系统生态兼容性持续提高,面向全场景的分布式操作系统进入产业化阶段,云数据库部分技术指标全球领先。部分领域芯片设计水平跻身国际一流行列,3D NAND 闪存、DRAM 内存等存储器工艺加速发展,千万门级现场可编程门阵列(FPGA)产品成功量产。新型显示产业取得新突破,2020 年中国大陆地区 TFT-LCD 产能规模跃居全球第一,国产柔性有源矩阵有机发光二极管(AMOLED)进入国际一线品牌供应链。光通信关键技术能力持续提升,部分 25 G 以上激光器芯片、探测器芯片、配套电芯片等高端光电芯片实现批量生产。

3.2　科技发展计划

3.2.1　国家科技计划

中国自 1982 年出台第一个国家科技计划以来,已经有 30 多个科技计划从不同角度支撑着国民经济和社会发展以及科技自身的发展。这些计划相互补充,形成了一个有机整体。当前中国的国家科技计划体系可分为五大类,即国家自然科学基金、国家科技重大专项、国家重点研发计划、技术创新引导专项(基金)、基地和人才专项。其中前三类是科技创新的主要牵引计划。

(1)国家自然科学基金:为推动国家科技体制改革、变革科研经费拨款方式而设立的面向全国的自然科学基金,旨在支持国家基础研究。国家自然科学基金在发展中逐渐形成了由研究项目、人才项目和环境条件项目三大系列组成的资助格局,在推动中国自然科学基础研究的发展,促进基础学科建设,发现、培养优秀科技人才等方面取得了巨大成绩。

(2)国家科技重大专项:为了实现国家目标,通过核心技术突破和资源集成,在一定时限内完成的重大战略产品、关键共性技术和重大工程。国家科技重大专项通过充分发挥社会主义制度集中力量办大事的优势和市场机制的作用,力争取得突破,努力实现以科技发展的局部跃升带动生产力的跨越发展,并填补国家战略空白。

(3)国家重点研发计划:面向世界科技前沿、面向经济主战场、面向国家重大需求,重点资助事关国计民生的农业、能源、生态环境、健康等领域中需要长期演进的重大社会公益性研究,以及事关产业核心竞争力、整体自主创新能力和国家安全的战略性、基础性、前瞻性重大科学问题、重大共性关键技术和产品、重大国际科技合作等。

信息技术领域是国家科技计划重点支持的领域之一,目前在研的国家自然科学基金、国家科技重大专项、国家重点研发计划项目如表 3-4 所示。

表 3-4　中国信息技术领域的代表性国家科技计划项目(2020—2022 年)

国家科技计划	代表性项目
国家自然科学基金	"共融机器人基础理论与关键技术研究"重大研究计划、"未来工业互联网基础理论与关键技术"重大研究计划、"第二代量子体系的构筑和操控"重大研究计划
国家科技重大专项	核心电子器件、高端通用芯片及基础软件产品,极大规模集成电路制造技术及成套工艺,新一代宽带无线移动通信

续表

国家科技计划	代表性项目
国家重点研发计划	新一代人工智能、先进计算与新兴软件、社会治理与智慧社会科技支撑、智能传感器、智能机器人、网络空间安全治理、信息光子技术、微纳电子技术、多模态网络与通信、区块链、新型显示与战略性电子材料、量子调控与量子信息

3.2.2　国家数字化工程

根据《"十四五"国家信息化规划》,中国将数字中国的建设目标分解为多个建设目标,具体包括数字基础设施体系、数据要素资源体系、数字生产力创新发展体系、数字产业体系、产业数字化转型发展体系、数字社会治理体系等。该规划共设立 17 个国家信息化重点工程,如表 3-5 所示。

表 3-5　"十四五"期间国家信息化重点工程

领域	工程名称
数字基础设施	5G 创新应用工程
	"智能网联"设施建设和应用推广工程
	全国一体化大数据中心体系建设工程
	空天地海立体化网络建设和应用示范工程
数字技术创新体系	信息领域核心技术突破工程
	信息技术知识产权与标准化创新工程
数字经济	数据要素市场培育工程
	大数据应用提升工程
	信息技术产业生态培育工程
	制造业数字化转型工程
	信息消费扩容提质工程
数字社会	智慧公安建设提升工程
	人工智能社会治理实验工程
	应急管理现代化能力提升工程
数字政府	全国一体化政务服务提升工程
数字民生	数字公共服务优化升级工程
数字领域国际合作	"数字丝绸之路"共建共享工程

3.2.3　研发经费投入

自 2009 年超越日本、2013 年超越欧盟后,中国一直是仅次于美国的世界第二大研究与试验发展(简称"研发")经费支出大国。2019 年中国研发经费投入首次突破 2 万亿元大关；2020 年研发经费投入达 2.4 万亿元，研发经费投入强度(与国内生产总值之比)为 2.4％。按 2019 年购买力平价美元计算,中国研发经费支出占经济合作与发展组织统计的 37 个国家研发经费支出总和的 25％左右,仅次于美国(30％左右)。根据《中华人民共和国国民经济和社会发展第十四个五年规划和 2035 年远景目标纲要》,在"十四五"期间,中国将加大基础研究财政投入力度、优化支出结构,对企业投入基础研究实行税收优惠,鼓励社会以捐赠和建立基金等方式多渠道投入,形成持续稳定投入机制,基础研究经费投入占研发经费投入比重提高到 8％以上。

除了国家在基础研究、公共信息设施方面的投入之外,行业企业也投入了巨量的研发资金。信息产业是典型的技术密集型产业,产业技术迭代迅速,市场变化较快。企业往往需要投入较高的研发成本,才能快速迭代相关技术,进而抢占技术先机和制高点。2017—2021 年,中国上市互联网企业研发经费投入增长 227％。在欧盟委员会发布的 2021 年全球产业研发经费投入 2 500 强企业中,中国企业入选 597 家,其中信息技术软件服务、硬件设备领域企业数量达 210 家。例如,华为 2012 年的研发经费投入为 301 亿元,强度为 13.7％,2021 年的研发经费投入则增长至 1 427 亿元,强度为 22.4％;中兴通讯 2012 年的研发经费投入为 88.29 亿元,强度为 10.5％,2021 年的研发经费投入为 188 亿元,强度高达 16.4％。这些企业的整体研发经费投入远远高于传统企业及一般制造业企业,为信息技术的快速发展奠定了基础。

3.3　重大科技工程

在国家发展面临重大机遇和挑战时,有必要以国家利益为核心,以国家意志为主导,在准确把握国家目标的基础上,集中全国最优秀的科技人才、管理人才,开展基础性的重大科技工程建设。这种举国体制在科技创新领域被世界各国广泛采用,如美国的曼哈顿计划、阿波罗计划,日本的第五代计算机计划、超大规模集成电路计划等。本节以超级计算机、量子通信与量子计算机、北斗卫星导航系统为例,介绍中国在基础研究和重大工程方面的进展。

3.3.1　超级计算机

超级计算机(简称"超算")是指能够执行一般性的个人计算机无法处理的大量高速运算的计算机。高性能计算成为影响高能核物理、空间科学、材料科学、生命科学与人工智能等数据密集型研究学科的演进方向,支撑产业规模增长与应用模式创新的核心基础设施,是世界主要发达国家竞相争夺的战略制高点,美国、欧盟、日本相继制订了开放科学网络、高性能基础设施、高级计算合作伙伴等最高级计划。

中国"超算"事业于 20 世纪 70 年代起步。1972 年 10 月,超级计算机的研制被列为国家重点工程。1983 年 12 月,中国研制出第一台亿次超级计算机"银河"。"银河"亿次计算机成为当时中国运算速度最快、存储容量最大、功能最强的计算机,打破了发达国家在该领域的技术垄断。中国成为继美、日、法、英、德之后能够独立设计、制造超级计算机的国家。在"银河-Ⅰ"之后,中国又研制出不同量级的"银河"系列超级计算机。

2006 年,科技部将高性能计算机作为国家科技计划内容予以实施。"天河一号"作为高技术研究发展计划(863 计划)的一个重大项目,是在国防科技大学"银河"系列超级计算机的基础上研制而成的。2009 年 10 月 29 日,国防科技大学成功研制出峰值性能为每秒 1 206 万亿次的"天河一号"超级计算机,使中国成为继美国之后,全世界第二个能够研制千万亿次算力超级计算机的国家。2016 年 6 月 20 日,国际超算大会在德国法兰克福召开,会议期间国际 TOP 500 组织第 47 期榜单正式发布,中国的"神威·太湖之光"取代"天河二号"登上榜首(见图 3-2)。2022 年国际 TOP 500 榜单前十中,中国有 2 台超级计算机入选,分别是排名第六的"神威·太湖之光"和排名第九的"天河二号",前者峰值运算能力达到每秒 125.44 千万亿次,后者峰值运算能力达到每秒 100.68 千万亿次。在 2022 年国际 TOP 500 榜单中,中国以 186 台超级计算机继续领先全球,美国以 123 台超级计算机排名世界第二。

图 3-2 "神威·太湖之光"超级计算机(2016 年)
图片来源:《深圳特区报》

"神威·太湖之光"使用的是中国自主知识产权的芯片,运算速度更快、更节能。一块 5 平方厘米左右的"芯片"集成 260 个运算核心、数十亿晶体管,拥有每秒 3 万亿次以上的运算能力。"神威·太湖之光"超级计算机 1 分钟的计算能力,大约是全球 70 多亿人同时用计算器不间断计算 32 年。目前,中国超级计算机的整机应用涉及天气气候、地球科学、海洋环境、材料设计、生物制药、航空航天、图计算、量子计算、生命科学、天体物理等众多领域(见图 3-3)。例如,利用超级计算机进行高分辨率中国海区域大气-海洋耦合模式的演算,在 25 分钟内就可以完成未来 10 天的三维海流、海浪、海温、盐度、海面高度等海洋环境要素预报。

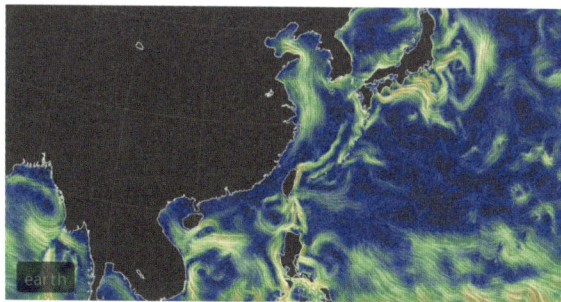

图 3-3 利用超级计算机开展海洋环境要素预报
图片来源:国家超级计算广州中心

3.3.2 量子通信与量子计算机

量子计算机的概念最早由美国物理学家费曼在 1982 年提出。它是利用量子力学原理,进行高速数学和逻辑运算、存储及处理量子信息的物理装置。量子计算的天然并行特性在处理某些大规模并行运算时将发挥巨大作用,在海量信息处理、重大科学问题研究等领域发挥关键作用,对国家的经济、科技、军事和信息安全等方面产生巨大影响,已成为全球人类共同关注和探索的科技焦点之一。2018 年,谷歌公司发布了 72 位超导量子芯片。2019 年,美国 IBM 公司发布了 IBM Q System One 量子计算机。2020 年,美国宣布建设"下一代量子科学与工程"(Q-NEXT)国家量子信息科学研究中心等 5 个量子科学联合研究中心,持续推动量子技术的发展。

2005 年,中国在《国家中长期科学和技术发展规划纲要(2006—2020 年)》中将"量子调控研究"列为国家重大科学研究计划之一。2017 年,中国将"量子通信与量子计算机"列入"科技创新 2030－重大项目",给予大力支持。2016 年 8 月,中国在酒泉卫星发射中心用长征二号丁运载火箭成功将世界首颗量子科学实验卫星"墨子号"发射升空。中国科学技术大学研究团队通过"墨子号"卫星在相距超过 1 120 千米的两个地面站之间建立了量子纠缠和安全通信(见图 3-4),并于 2020 年 6 月在国际著名学术期刊《自然》上在线发表了题为《基于纠缠的千公里级安全量子加密》的研究论文。根据中国量子通信发展规划,量子卫星发射以后,中国将建成"量子通信京沪干线",国内初步形成广域量子通信体系。到 2030 年左右,中国将率先建成全球化的量子通信网络。

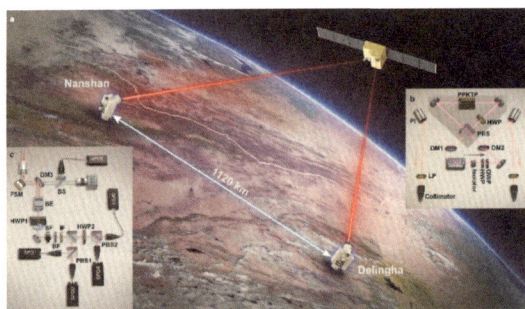

图 3-4　中国量子科学实验卫星"墨子号"实现远距离地面量子通信

图片来源:中国科学技术大学

2017 年,中国科学技术大学潘建伟团队构建了世界首台超越早期经典计算机的光量子计算原型机,通过实验逐步展示了量子计算的优越性。2020 年,该团队成功构建了 76 个光子、100 个模式的高斯玻色取样量子计算原型机"九章",输出量子态空间规模达到了 10^{30},处理高斯玻色取样的速度比超级计算机"富岳"快 100 万亿倍。2021 年,"九章二号"(见图3-5)探测到的光子数增加到了 113 个,输出态空间维度达到了 10^{43},完成了对用于演示"量子计算优越性"的高斯玻色取样任务的快速求解,处理速度比目前最快的超级计算机快 10^{24} 倍。

3.3.3　北斗卫星导航系统

全球卫星导航系统能在地球表面或近地空间的任何地点为用户提供全天候的三维坐标、速度、时间信息的空基无线电导航定位服务。20 世纪 70 年代,美国国防部开始研制"导航卫星定时和测距全球定位系统",简称"全球定位系统"。全球定位系统在军事、防灾减灾、测绘等方面发挥着重要的基础作用。

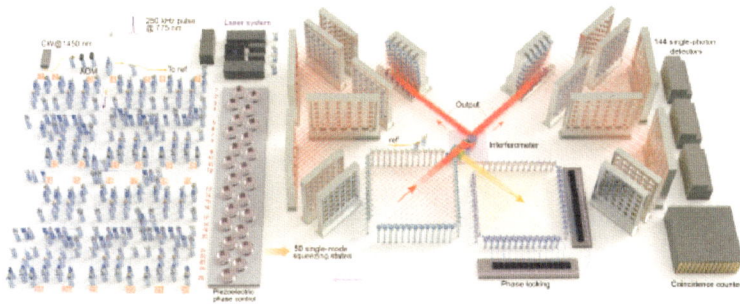

图 3-5 中国量子计算原型机"九章二号"研制成功
图片来源:中国科学技术大学

1994年,中国启动北斗卫星导航试验系统的建设。2003年建成的北斗一号卫星导航系统由3颗地球静止轨道卫星和相关地面系统组成,解决了中国卫星导航系统的有无问题,实现了中国及周边区域的有源定位。中国也成为世界上继美国、俄罗斯之后第三个拥有独立卫星导航系统的国家。

2004年,中国启动北斗二号卫星工程,目标是建立区域性的卫星导航系统。2011年12月,北斗卫星导航系统开通试运行服务,此后逐步向中国及其他亚太地区提供服务。北斗卫星导航系统采用了地球静止轨道、倾斜地球同步轨道、中圆地球轨道卫星混合星座组网的方案,实现了有源与无源导航多功能服务融合的卫星方案。

2012年,中国启动北斗三号全球卫星导航系统的建设。研究团队攻克了星座星间链路技术,采取星间、星地传输功能一体化设计,实现了卫星与卫星、卫星与地面站的链路互通。2020年6月23日,第55颗北斗导航卫星成功发射,北斗三号全球卫星导航系统星座部署全面完成。2020年7月31日,中国国家主席习近平宣布北斗三号全球卫星导航系统正式开通。北斗卫星导航系统如图3-6所示。

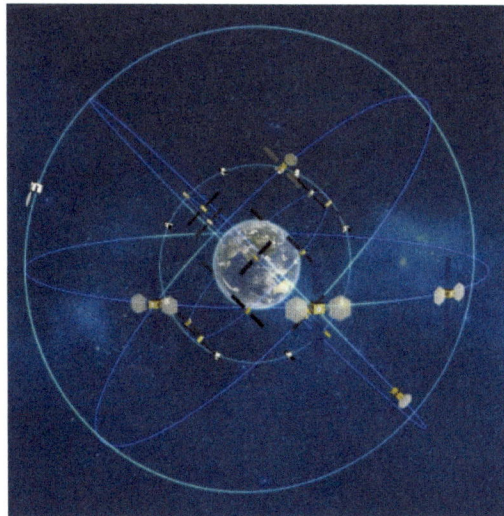

图 3-6 北斗卫星导航系统示意图
图片来源:《光明日报》

《2022 中国卫星导航与位置服务产业发展白皮书》显示,2021 年中国与卫星导航技术研发和应用直接相关的芯片、器件、算法等在内的产业核心产值达 1 454 亿元,由卫星导航应用和服务带动形成的关联产值达 3 236 亿元,卫星导航与位置服务领域企事业单位总数量达1.4万家,从业人员数量超 50 万。截至 2023 年 1 月,北斗时空智能服务的全球累计接入智能设备超 15 亿台;北斗高精度时空服务月调用次数超过 1 700 亿次,服务覆盖全球超 230 个国家和地区;北斗成为中国国产智能手机等的"标配",高德地图调用北斗卫星日定位量超 3 000 亿次。

3.4　产业技术攻关

信息产业的许多关键技术的研发不但需要巨量的资金投入,还需要明确的市场回报。中国通过多种方式整合高等院校、科研机构和企业的力量,共同突破行业技术瓶颈,推动产业进步和发展。本节以超高清视频产业、移动通信产业、集成电路产业等产业为例,介绍中国在信息产业技术攻关方面的进展。

3.4.1　超高清视频产业

高清晰度电视(HDTV,简称"高清电视")最早的试验性工作开始于 1968 年。日本放送协会(NHK)于 1980 年前后完成了高清晰度电视系统与 MUSE 卫星传播制式的研发,发布了第一个 HDTV 视频信号标准——1125/60 制式。1996 年,美国先进电视制式委员会(ATSC)发布了基于全数字系统地面传输的高清电视标准。

中国对高清电视的关注始于"八五"时期,1993 年国家科学技术委员会组织成立了"高清晰度电视发展战略专家组"。1998 年,中国首台高清电视地面数字样机研制成功。2003 年 10 月,国家发展改革委设立地面数字电视传输标准研发项目,清华大学、上海交通大学、广播电视科学研究院等 11 家高校及科研单位成立数字电视地面传输国家标准特别工作组,旨在在清华大学 DMB-T、上海交通大学 ADTB-T、广播电视科学研究院 TiMi 三个标准方案的基础上研发形成新方案。2006 年 8 月,《数字电视地面广播传输系统帧结构、信道编码和调制》成为强制性国家标准,标准编号"GB 20600－2006",于 2007 年 8 月 1 日正式实施。

2008 年 1 月 1 日上午 9 时整,中国中央电视台免费地面数字高清电视正式开播,标志着中国地面数字电视国家标准实质性启动。2008 年 5 月 1 日,北京电视台奥运高清频道开播(见图 3-7)。这批高清频道播出采用的核心设备全部国产化,基本全部采用地面数字电视单载波模式及相关设备。高清电视在中国的发展借助了奥运会的契机,收到了良好的效果。截至 2008 年底,中国数字电视用户达 4 528 万户,较 2007 年同比增长近 70%,其中高清电视用户突破 50 万户,北京用户占比超过 60%。截至 2009 年 3 月,中国已有 229 个城市进行了有线电视数字化整体转换。

高清电视技术标准推动了电视产业的升级换代。2012 年 6 月,"十二五"863 计划项目"新一代数字电视关键技术研究及验证"启动会议在北京召开,推进"内容与网络的协同""广播网与互联网的互动""新型无线覆盖网设计"等方面的技术突破。2019 年 2 月,工业和信息化部、国家广播电视总局、中央广播电视总台联合印发《超高清视频产业发展行动计划

图 3-7　2008 年北京奥运会期间北京电视台高清转播机房

图片来源:央视网

(2019—2022 年)》,明确了超高清视频产业发展总体要求、发展目标、重点任务和保障措施等。2019 年,中国的超高清视频显示技术逐步成熟,主要包括存储芯片、高性能显示驱动芯片、电视主控芯片、超高清机顶盒芯片、4K/8K 画质图像处理芯片等领域的技术。中国 4K电视销量逐步增长,在超高清视频产业中占据主导地位。

4K 电视产业发展促进 4K 超高清视频产业生态逐渐走向成熟。中国知名企业(例如TCL、海信、创维等)的市场占有率和国际影响力不断提高。2019 年,中国三大运营商的新增机顶盒全面支持 4K 60 帧/HDR/BT.2020/10bit 的视频解码能力。2020 年,全球 4K 机顶盒出货量超过 1.2 亿台,中国成为全球最大的 4K 机顶盒需求市场。

3.4.2　移动通信产业

移动通信技术涉及各国的信息基础设施,新一代 5G 移动通信技术竞争激烈。在国际上,韩国于 2017 年启动韩国国家 5G 标准的制定,2019 年启动 5G 商用服务;欧盟于 2016 年发布《5G 行动计划》,2017 年公布将在"地平线 2020"科研规划中划拨 7 亿欧元支持 5G 发展;美国于 2016 年 7 月发布 5G 的 24 GHz 高频频段,计划投入 4 亿美元支持 5G 试验及研发。

中国移动通信经历了 2G 跟随、3G 突破、4G 同步的发展历程,正在争取实现 5G 引领的新目标。在 2G 时代,中国引进了全球移动通信系统(GSM)、码分多址(CDMA)等国外 2G技术标准,逐步实现设备和产品的自主研发。在 3G 时代,中国的时分同步码分多址(TD-SCDMA)标准技术在 2000 年 5 月被国际电信联盟批准成为 3G 国际标准之一,并于 2009 年成功实现商用。在 4G 时代,中国主导的时分同步码分多址长期演进(TD-LTE)标准于2012 年 1 月成为 4G 国际标准。

借助 3G、4G 的技术积累和产业化发展成果,中国全面启动了 5G 研发和标准化工作。2013 年 2 月,工业和信息化部、国家发展改革委和科技部联合推动成立 IMT-2020(5G)推进组,统筹中国 5G 技术研究、标准制定、研发试验、产业推进等工作。2015 年 10 月,国际电信联盟 2015 年世界无线电通信大会在瑞士日内瓦召开。在此次大会上,中国提出的"5G 之花"9 个技术指标中的 8 个被国际电信联盟采纳(见图 3-8)。此后,中国通信企业提出的灵活系统设计、极化码、大规模天线和新型网络架构等关键技术成为国际标准的重点内容,中国的技术专家开始在国际电信联盟、第三代合作伙伴计划(3GPP)等国际标准组织担任多个重要职务,并主持关键项目的相关工作。

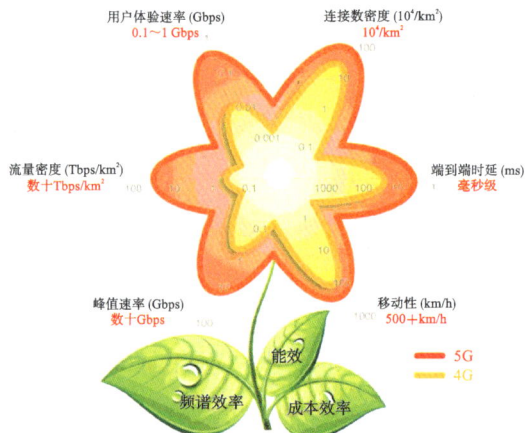

图 3-8　中国提出的"5G 之花"标准

图片来源：IMT-2020(5G)推进组，《5G 愿景与需求白皮书》，2014 年

在 5G 技术研发方面，中国的科研团队和企业取得了突破性进展。在 5G 基带芯片方面，华为推出的多模商用 5G 基带芯片巴龙 5000（Balong 5000）同时支持 2G/3G/4G/5G 网络、Sub-6 GHz、毫米波、5G 非独立组网（NSA）和 5G 独立组网（SA）。在 5G 空中接口技术领域，华为和中兴是大规模天线技术的领导者，华为发布全球首款 5G 基站核心芯片。在信道编码领域，华为等公司推出的极化码是目前能够被严格证明达到香农极限的信道编码方法，确定了增强移动宽带场景的信道编码技术方案。在核心网领域，中国移动牵头，联合全球 14 家运营商及华为等 12 家网络设备商提出服务化架构，被 3GPP 正式确认为 5G 核心网的唯一基础架构标准。

5G 标准的部分核心技术也受到专利的保护，相关的专利被称为 5G 标准必要专利。5G 标准必要专利技术方向包括无线资源管理、接入技术、多载波传输、信道编码、核心网、下一代接入网。当前 5G 通信标准的 R15、R16 和 R17 都已经完成"冻版"，对应的标准必要专利布局基本已成定局。德国专利数据库公司 IPlytics 的数据库检索结果显示，截至 2022 年 2 月，中国企业所拥有的 5G 标准必要专利数量在全球有关国家/地区中排名第二，占比38.4％（见图 3-9）。截至 2022 年 12 月，全球声明的 5G 标准必要专利超过 8.49 万件，其中排名前十的企业贡献了全部专利族数量的 75％；中国企业华为的有效全球专利族数量占比为 14.6％，在全球企业中位列第一，中国企业中兴、大唐、OPPO、小米等的有效全球专利族数量也位居全球前十。

在 5G 商用方面，中国在 2016 年启动了面向商用的 5G 技术研发试验。2018 年 12 月工业和信息化部向中国电信、中国移动、中国联通发放了 5G 系统中低频段试验频率使用许可。为了降低 5G 建设的投入，在政府的牵头组织下，通过中国铁塔公司实现了中国电信与中国联通 5G 网络基站的共建共享，共享 5G 基站超 30 万个，节省建设投资超 600 亿元。截至 2023 年底，中国已经建成开通 5G 基站 337.7 万余个，实现全国地级以上城市全覆盖，5G 移动电话用户达 8.05 亿户，5G 网络接入流量占比达 47％。2023 年 1—12 月，中国国内 5G 手机出货量 2.4 亿部，同比增长 11.9％，占同期手机出货量的 82.8％。中国已经成为全球 5G 应用规模最大的国家。

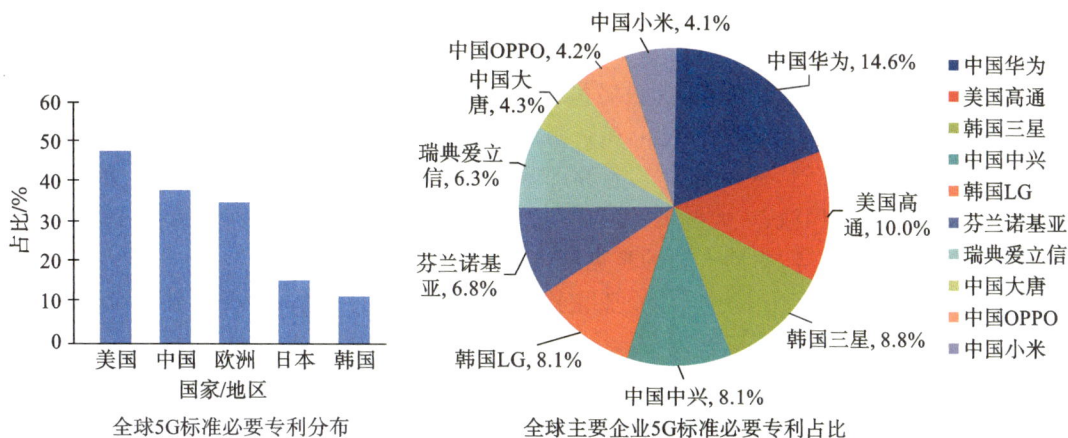

图 3-9　2022 年 2 月全球 5G 标准必要专利分布情况

数据来源：国家知识产权局，中国信息通信研究院

随着商用的推进，5G 这个数字经济时代的发展新引擎不仅将为信息产业开启新的发展空间，还将与实体经济深度融合；商用的 5G 专业模组也已推出，可以支持 5G 8K 电视、5G 工业生产线、智能交通等多个行业应用。中国信息通信研究院的相关报告预测，2025 年，5G 将拉动中国经济增加值约 1.1 万亿元，对当年 GDP 增长的贡献率达 3.2％，间接拉动的 GDP 将达到 2.1 万亿元；2030 年，预计 5G 对中国经济增加值的贡献将超过 2.9 万亿元，10 年间的复合年均增长率将达到 41％。

3.4.3　集成电路产业

集成电路被誉为信息产业的根基。集成电路产业是影响国家经济、政治、国防综合竞争力的战略性产业，其技术水平和产业规模已成为衡量一个国家产业竞争力和综合国力的重要标志。

集成电路包括多个领域，较有代表性的是存储芯片领域。数据显示，2022 年全球半导体市场规模超过 1 800 亿美元，存储芯片占 35％左右。存储芯片市场以 DRAM 内存和 NAND 闪存为主，其中 DRAM 内存市场规模约占全球储存市场规模的 61％，而 NAND 闪存市场规模约占 36％。几年前的国际半导体存储器领域主要被美、韩、日等国的几家企业所垄断，如韩国三星和海力士、美国镁光、日本东芝等。中国每年的芯片进口额近 2.8 万亿元，其中存储芯片的进口额约为 7 000 亿元。

为了解决集成电路产业的共性技术问题，中国于 2008 年启动了国家科技重大专项"极大规模集成电路制造装备及成套工艺"。该专项的总体目标是开展集成电路制造装备、成套工艺和材料技术攻关，掌握核心技术。该专项实施以来，共有 200 多家企事业单位，2 万多名科研人员参与技术攻关。2008 年以前，中国集成电路制造最先进的量产工艺是 130 纳米，研发的工艺水平为 90 纳米；经过该专项的实施，到 2017 年主流工艺水平提升了 5 代，55 纳米、40 纳米、28 纳米三代成套工艺研发成功，并且实现量产，22 纳米、14 纳米先导技术研发取得突破，形成了自主知识产权。中国已经研制成功 14 纳米刻蚀机、薄膜沉积等 30 多种高端装备和靶材、抛光液等上百种材料产品，性能达到国际先进水平。

为了解决集成电路产业的融资扶持问题，中国国务院于 2014 年 6 月印发《国家集成电路产业发展推进纲要》，同年国家集成电路产业投资基金股份有限公司（简称"国家大基金"）成立，2019年国家集成电路产业投资基金二期股份有限公司（简称"国家大基金二期"）成立。截至2021年12月，国家大基金一期和二期完成对83家集成电路实体公司的投资，覆盖了产业链环节中的骨干企业。例如，晶圆制造业的中芯国际、华虹集团、华润微等，存储产业的长江存储、长鑫存储、兆易创新等，封测产业的长电科技、通富微电、华天科技等，电子设计自动化工具产业的国微、华大九天，设计产业的紫光展锐、智芯微等，装备和零部件产业的北方华创、中微半导体等，材料产业的雅克科技、安集科技等。

通过采取上述措施，中国半导体企业在技术、资金等方面的许多问题得到了解决，国内企业在多个半导体领域获得了突破。

在内存芯片方面。长鑫存储于2016年5月在合肥由合肥市政府、兆易创新、国家大基金等共同组建，项目总投资超过2 000亿元，是中国首个内存芯片自主制造项目。长鑫存储采购了德国企业奇梦达的内存技术，完成了原始技术积累，后来长鑫存储投入25亿美元的研发费用进行更新换代。2018年第一季度，长鑫存储完成第一座12英寸（30.48厘米）晶圆厂的设备安装，同年研发出中国首个8 Gb DDR4芯片。2019年第三季度，长鑫存储成功量产19纳米工艺的DDR4内存（见图3-10）和LPDDR4内存，良率在70%～75%，最高速率可达3 200 Mbps，成为全球第四家可以量产20纳米以下内存芯片的厂商。长鑫存储在2021年已经实现6万片/月的内存芯片产能，未来的目标是实现30万片/月的产能。

图3-10　长鑫存储推出的DDR4内存模组

图片来源：长鑫存储

在闪存芯片方面。长江存储于2016年7月在武汉成立，投资方包括紫光集团、湖北省集成电路产业投资基金、国开发展基金、国家大基金等。长江存储和飞索半导体合作完成了基础技术的积累，此后与中国科学院微电子研究所共同研发。2017年2月，中国科学院微电子研究所宣布，国产32层3D NAND闪存芯片通过电学特性等各项测试。2018年8月，长江存储在全球闪存峰会（FMW）发布Xtacking技术。该技术将存储单元和逻辑电路在两片晶圆上分别加工，然后将两片晶圆通过数百万根金属通道连接在一起；该技术将闪存芯片的最高存取速度提升至DDR4内存的水平。2019年9月，长江存储打造出世界首款基于Xtacking架构的64层TLC 3D NAND闪存芯片并实现量产（见图3-11）。2020年4月，长江存储推出全球首款128层QLC 3D NAND闪存芯片，做到了存储容量最大、I/O接口传输速度最高。2021年底，长江存储达到了每月生产10万片晶圆的产能。2022年11月，长江存储实现232层3D NAND闪存芯片的量产，在世界NAND存储厂商中率先实现200层以上NAND闪存芯片的量产，NAND闪存X3-9070的I/O速度达到2400 MT/s（每秒百万次传输），性能提升50%而功耗降低25%。

经过近 6 年的时间,以长鑫存储和长江存储为代表的中国半导体存储企业整合中国科技项目的成果,积极进取、创新突破,完成了存储领域"零"的突破。据统计,2015 年中国厂商在全球存储芯片市场的市场占有率还是 0%,但到了 2022 年,中国厂商在全球 DRAM 内存＋NAND 闪存芯片市场的市场占有率合计接近于 5%。这些企业的快速成长,离不开国家政策的支持、国有科研院所的科技成果分享、国家大基金的扶持。

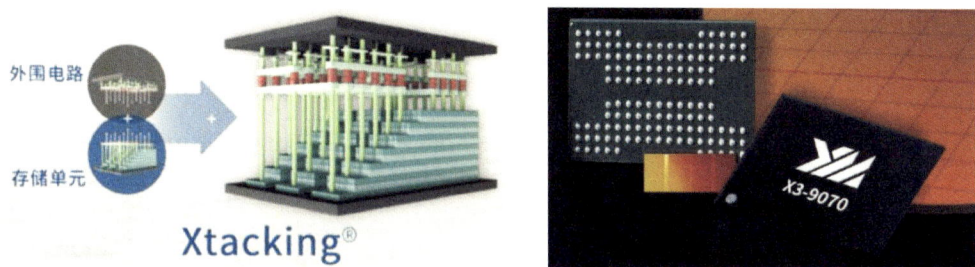

图 3-11   长江存储推出的 Xtacking 架构的 NAND 闪存芯片
图片来源:长江存储

3.5   小   结

新中国成立之初,信息技术研发基础十分薄弱。经过 70 多年的发展,中国逐步构建了完备的科学研究和技术研发体系。中国建立了高效的战略科技力量体系,其中全国重点实验室、国家工程研究中心等机构承担起了基础理论和关键技术方面的研究。同时,中国建立了高新技术产业开发区、创新型产业集群等多类型的产业创新基地,鼓励企业开展技术攻关和创新,目前已经在集成电路、新型显示等领域获得了突破性的进展。

中国构建了全面的科技发展计划体系。中国通过国家自然科学基金、国家科技重大专项、国家重点研发计划等不同层次的科技规划,引导国内科研机构和企业在关键领域开展研究。中国也为数字中国建设部署了多项国家级重点工程,涉及数字基础设施、数字经济等领域,为中国各行业的数字化转型升级奠定了基础。中国建立了多维度的科技研发投入机制,国家在基础理论方面的研发投入不断加大,企业在产品研发方面的经费投入也逐步加大。

在重大科技工程方面,中国取得了多项举世瞩目的成就。超级计算机的发展成绩斐然,从"银河"系列到"天河"系列,再到"神威·太湖之光",计算能力不断攀升,并应用于科学计算等多个领域。量子通信与量子计算机领域成果突出,"墨子号"卫星实现远距离量子通信,"九章"量子计算原型机展现出超强计算能力,相关技术走在世界前列。北斗导航工程历经三轮建设,已经实现了全球组网,提供了先进的民用全球导航服务。

在信息产业技术攻关方面,中国也取得了长足的进步。超高清视频产业形成了数字电视标准,产业生态逐渐完善,引领了 4K 超高清技术的发展。移动通信产业实现了从跟跑到引领的跨越,在 5G 基带芯片、空中接口技术等方面取得突破性进展,新一代移动通信的 5G 标准必要专利数量领先,商用规模全球最大。集成电路产业通过国家专项和基金支持,在存储芯片领域取得重大突破,逐步克服了"卡脖子"技术难题。

在信息技术创新方面,中国取得了全方位的发展和进步。中国多年来建立的国民教育体系为信息产业培养了健全的工程师队伍。中国构建的战略科研力量为攻克信息科学的理论难题提供了重要支撑。中国建立了科技发展计划体系，形成了高效的科研组织模式，完成了超级计算机、量子计算机等重大科技工程。中国政府通过建立高新技术产业开发区、创新型产业集群，以及设立产业发展基金等措施，鼓励企业开展技术创新，实现了多项产业技术的突破。

4 数字产业化

数字产业化,即数字技术的产业化,是将数字技术转化为可在市场上交易的商品和服务,形成具有经济规模和市场竞争力的产业。数字产业化的内容涉及数字产品制造、数字产品服务、数字技术应用等方面,其范围包括传统信息产业和新兴的数字应用产业。为便于读者对照,本章节采用传统信息产业分类(基础电信业、互联网产业、软件和信息技术服务业、电子信息制造业)来组织内容,介绍近年来中国取得的发展成就。

4.1 基础电信业

2012—2021 年,中国信息通信行业充分把握全球化发展机遇,快速融入国际产业分工体系,以电信为代表的现代信息通信业务快速崛起。10 年间,中国的电信业务总量规模平均增长率达到 20% 以上,远超同期 GDP 平均增长速度,尤其在 2017 年和 2018 年,电信业务总量增长率分别高达 76.7% 和 137.5%。2021 年,中国的电信业务总量完成 1.7 万亿元。

4.1.1 互联网设施

4.1.1.1 光纤骨干网络

中国在 1994 年形成了覆盖全国所有城市的多张高性能骨干网。2000 年以后,又逐步建立了以北京、上海、广州三个骨干直联点为主、交换中心为辅的骨干网网间互联顶层架构。2013 年,新增成都、武汉、西安、沈阳、南京、重庆、郑州 7 个骨干直联点。新增骨干直联点开通后,互联性能提升 60% 以上,骨干网网间互通效率明显改善,区域均衡格局基本形成。

光纤骨干网建设成绩斐然。中国已建成世界上最大的光纤宽带网络,自 2014 年以来长期占据世界光缆市场需求的一半左右。2021 年底,中国光缆线路总长度已达 5 481 万千米,相较于 2012 年长度增加约 2.7 倍。与此同时,骨干传输向超高速大容量演进,已全面建成覆盖全国的单波 100 Gbps 骨干网;骨干网传输速率进入 200 Gbps 时代,400 Gbps 传输系统已经在部分城市开展试点。2016 年—2021 年 6 月中国光缆线路总长度及干线长度变化情况如图 4-1 所示。

网络综合承载能力不断提升。截至 2021 年 6 月,中国骨干直联点累计建成 14 个,以国家(杭州)新型互联网交换中心为例,其接入总带宽达 2 Tbps,全方位、多层次、立体化的网络互联架构进一步优化,网间通信性能持续提升。截至 2021 年 6 月底,中国互联网国际出入口带宽达 8.6 Tbps,同比提升 31.6%。

网络基础设施全面支持 IPv6。中国已建成全球规模最大的 IPv6 网络基础设施。截至

图 4-1　2016 年—2021 年 6 月中国光缆线路总长度及干线长度变化情况

数据来源：工业和信息化部

2021 年 12 月，中国已申请 IPv6 地址资源总量达 60 059 块（/32），地址资源位居世界第一；中国 IPv6 活跃用户数达 6.08 亿人，占中国网民总数的 60.11%；IPv6 网络流量增长较快，移动网络 IPv6 流量占比达 35.15%。

国际互联设施进一步升级。海底光缆、跨境陆缆等国际信息通信基础设施建设步伐加快，与共建"一带一路"国家的互联互通水平稳步提升。截至 2021 年 6 月底，中国互联网国际出入口带宽达 8.6 Tbps，同比提升 31.6%。截至 2020 年底，中国电信、中国移动、中国联通累计建设海外因特网接入点（POP）超 400 个。

4.1.1.2　光纤接入网络

宽带接入网络持续升级。2021 年 3 月，工业和信息化部印发《"双千兆"网络协同发展行动计划（2021—2023 年）》。以千兆光网和 5G 网络为代表的"双千兆"网络，能向单个用户提供固定和移动网络千兆接入能力，具有超大带宽、超低时延、先进可靠等特征，是新型基础设施的重要组成和承载底座。

千兆光纤已覆盖中国 1/3 的家庭。截至 2021 年 6 月底，中国光纤接入（FTTH/O）端口总计达 9.2 亿个，在所有宽带接入端口中占比 93.5%，较 2020 年同期提升 1.4 个百分点。中国光纤接入能力普遍超过百兆，并进一步向千兆以上速率升级。截至 2021 年 6 月，中国 36 家省级运营商发布光纤到房间（FTTR）套餐，试点基本覆盖全国，家庭、企业超高速局域网组网方案将逐步推广应用。2021 年 12 月，中国 29 个城市成为首批"千兆城市"，建成万兆无源光网络（10G-PON）端口 786 万个，千兆光网具备覆盖超过 3 亿户家庭的能力。2016 年—2021 年 6 月中国光纤接入端口数量及其占比变化趋势如图 4-2 所示。

用户上网实际体验速率大幅提升。2012 年中国的平均接入网速仅为 2 Mbps 左右，在全球主要国家中处于中下水平。2021 年，中国移动网络平均下载速率达到了 59.34 Mbps，固定网络平均下载速率达到了 62.55 Mbps，已居世界前列；农村光纤平均下载速率也超过了 100 Mbps，基础设施建设实现了网络覆盖及网络速率的双提升。网速测试统计公司 Ookla 发布的监测数据显示，2021 年 9 月，中国固定宽带平均下载速率在 181 个国家中排名第十五。

4.1.1.3　移动通信网络

2012—2021 年的 10 年间，中国移动通信成功实现了从 3G 突破、4G 同步到 5G 引领的

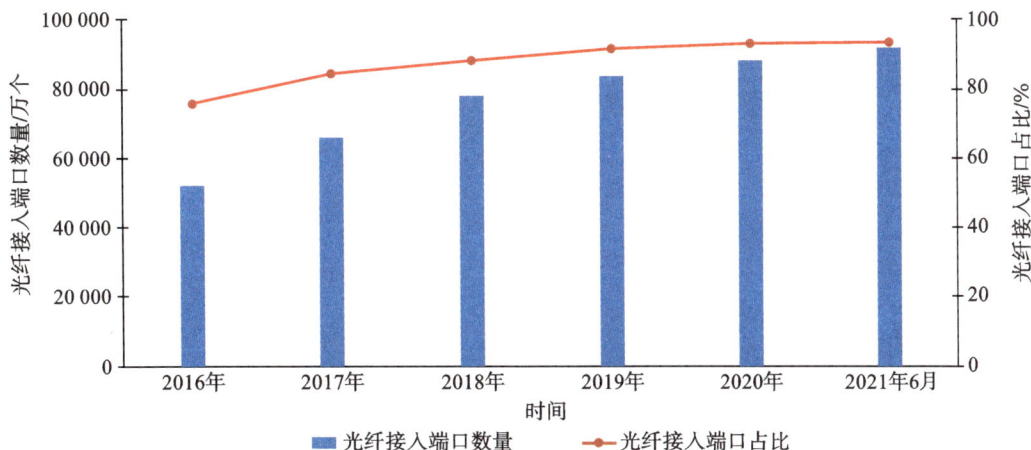

图 4-2　2016 年—2021 年 6 月中国光纤接入端口数量及其占比变化趋势

数据来源:工业和信息化部

技术逆袭之路。2013 年中国实现 4G 商业化,2019 年中国实现 5G 商业化。2021 年,中国
5G 专利申请数量呈爆炸式增长,移动通信专利数量已占全球总量的 30% 以上。中国已成为
全球 5G 专利的首要产出国和标准的制定国,实现了移动通信技术的引领。

　　与技术突破同步,中国基站建设水平也在快速提高。截至 2019 年底,中国移动通信基
站总数已达 841 万个,其中 4G 基站总数达到 544 万个;截至 2021 年底,中国迈入 5G 时代已
超 2 年,移动通信基站总数已达 996 万个,较 2019 年再增 18.4%,其中 4G 基站数量达 590
万个,5G 基站数量达 142.5 万个,5G 网络已覆盖中国所有地级市城区、超过 98% 的县城城
区和 80% 的乡镇镇区,中国行政村通 4G 比例超过 99%。从国际比较来看,5G 时代中国基
站建设领先全球,全球超过 60% 的 5G 基站建于中国,中国已成为全球 5G 网络建设强国。
2020 年 3 月至 2021 年 6 月中国 5G 基站数量及其占比变化趋势如图 4-3 所示。

　　移动终端日益普及。根据中国工业和信息化部及全球移动通信系统协会(GSMA)的统
计,截至 2021 年,中国移动电话用户数量达 16.43 亿户,普及率为 116.3 部/百人;5G 手机
终端连接数量快速增长,已超过 4.9 亿户。随着 4G 用户逐步向 5G 迁转,2021 年中国 4G
用户数较 2020 年下降 12%,约为 11.3 亿户,渗透率为 68.8%。2021 年,中国移动数据流量
继续保持增长态势,10 月户均移动互联网接入流量(DOU)为 14.32 GB,比全球平均水平高
出约 23.7%。

　　移动资费持续下降。2021 年上半年,中国移动数据流量平均资费降至 3.2 元/GB,同比
下降 24.6%,用户月均移动数据使用量为 12.6 GB,同比增长 32.6%。由于移动数据流量消
费大幅增长,移动通信用户月均支出(ARPU)同比提升 4.8%,达到 49.9 元。从国际对比
看,根据 GSMA 的统计,2020 年第四季度,中国移动通信资费在全球处于偏低水平,移动通
信用户月均支出在 237 个国家和地区中按价格由低至高排名第九十三,排名远低于美国、加
拿大、韩国等国家。2020 年 3 月—2021 年 6 月中国移动数据流量平均资费和累计用户月均
移动数据使用量情况如图 4-4 所示。

4.1.2　卫星互联网

　　卫星通信是解决未来泛在通信的有效手段,卫星根据轨道类型分为低地球轨道(LEO)、

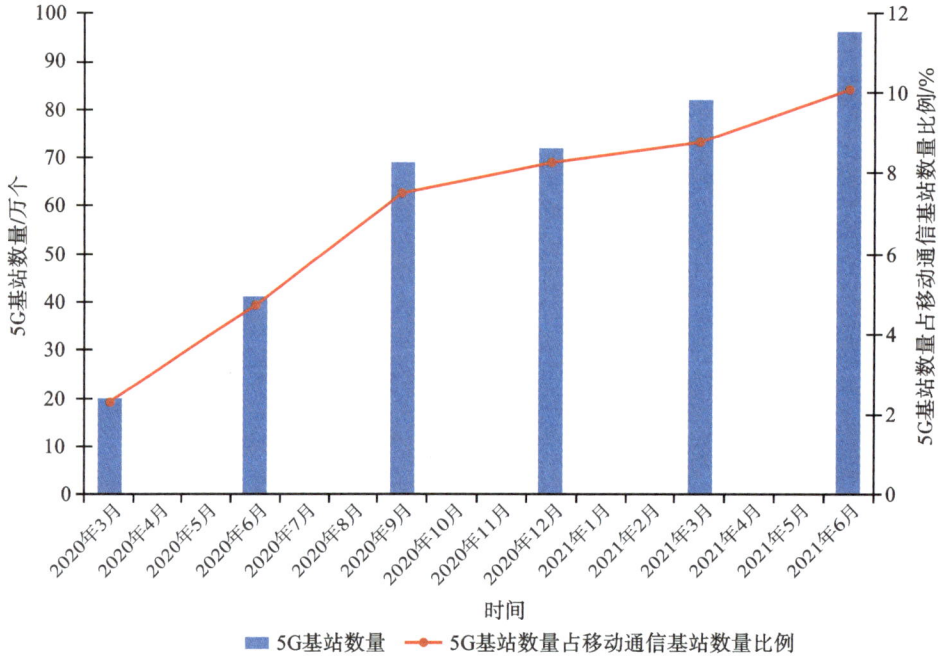

图 4-3　2020 年 3 月—2021 年 6 月中国 5G 基站数量及其占比变化趋势

数据来源：工业和信息化部

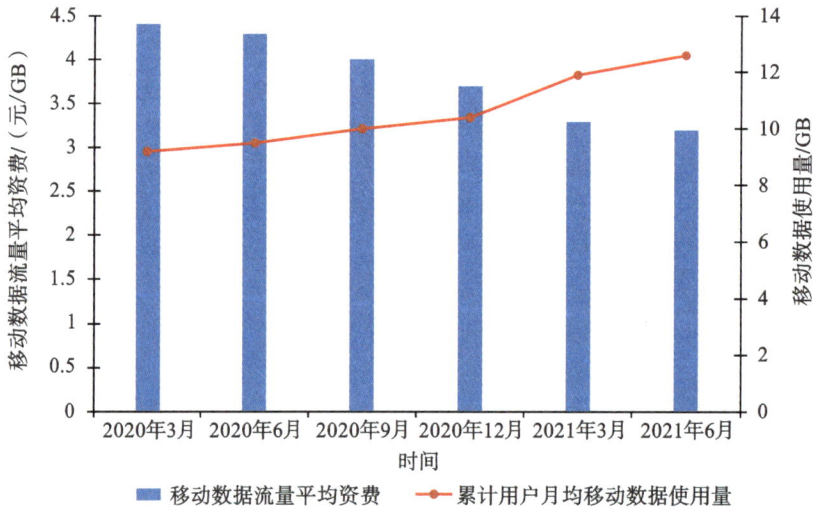

图 4-4　2020 年 3 月—2021 年 6 月中国移动数据流量平均资费和累计用户月均移动数据使用量情况

数据来源：工业和信息化部

中地球轨道（MEO）、地球静止轨道（GEO）、太阳同步轨道（SSO）、倾斜地球同步轨道（IGSO）
5 种。由于空间环境的特殊要求，每颗卫星仍面临着数十倍甚至百倍于无线基站的建设和
运维成本，卫星通信的资费高于地面移动通信。现阶段卫星通信的定位是对传统光纤、5G
覆盖能力的补充，主要着眼于光纤无法覆盖的偏远地区，以及海洋、沙漠、极地等特定地区，
将网络覆盖能力由人口覆盖转向国土覆盖。

近年来,低轨宽带通信卫星日益受到业界关注。低轨宽带通信卫星具有发射成本较低、往返时间较短等优势,被认为是实现卫星互联网的主要途径,也被下一代移动通信6G标准所关注。低轨宽带通信卫星之间需要采用星间链路技术,通过激光或微波链路建立空间骨干网;卫星通信终端可以通过轨道卫星星座,经空间骨干网传输或直接通过信关站落地,形成国际互联网通信。目前,SpaceX公司的星链计划已经发射了大量的低轨宽带通信卫星,2021年8月已覆盖除南极和北极外地球上所有地区,相关服务已落地美国、加拿大以及欧洲地区,到2027年将完成1.2万颗卫星部署。

在高通量卫星方面,中国已经建成了由3颗高通量卫星构成的卫星网络。2017年4月,中国发射了首颗高通量卫星——中星16号卫星,该卫星Ka频段多波束宽带通信总容量达20 Gbps,覆盖中国大部分地区,并于2020年7月通过了商用航班联网测试,接入速率达150 Mbps以上。2022年11月,中国发射了高通量卫星中星19号卫星,覆盖太平洋地区。2023年2月,中国发射了高通量卫星中星26号卫星,覆盖中国国土及周边地区。中星26号卫星是目前中国最先进的民商用通信卫星,通信容量超100 Gbps,配置94个用户波束和11个信关波束,终端通信速率最高达450 Mbps。这3颗高通量卫星共同组网,为用户提供高速组网通信服务以及卫星互联网接入等服务。

在地球静止轨道卫星移动通信系统方面,中国发射了3颗"天通一号"卫星。2016年8月,中国发射了天通一号01星,这是中国卫星移动通信系统首发星;之后,中国分别于2020年11月、2021年1月发射了天通一号02星和天通一号03星。这些卫星已经与中国的地面移动通信系统共同构成天地一体化移动通信网络,为中国及周边的亚洲其他地区、太平洋和印度洋的部分海域用户提供全天候、全天时、稳定可靠的移动通信服务。2023年8月,华为Mate 60 Pro上市,该手机支持接入天通一号卫星移动通信系统,是全球首款支持卫星移动通信的普通商用手机,持有者可以在高山、荒漠、海岛等移动通信网络难以覆盖的地方拨打、接听卫星电话。

在低地球轨道卫星通信网络方面,中国两大航天集团(中国航天科技集团有限公司和中国航天科工集团有限公司)分别启动了各自的低轨网络项目,即"鸿雁星座"(计划发射300颗小卫星)和"虹云工程"(计划发射156颗卫星),并都于2018年完成了首颗星的发射。2020年4月,卫星互联网被中国纳入"新基建"信息基础设施之一,标志着2020年成为中国卫星互联网建设元年。2021年3月,《中华人民共和国国民经济和社会发展第十四个五年规划和2035年远景目标纲要》明确提出要建设高速泛在、天地一体、集成互联、安全高效的信息基础设施。2021年4月,中国卫星网络集团有限公司(中国星网)揭牌成立,专项从事卫星互联网的设计、建设和运营。中国已经向国际电信联盟提交了低地球轨道星座轨道和频率的网络申请资料,总计卫星数量为12 992颗,分布在距地面590~1 145千米的低地球轨道。中国星网计划5年内发射其中约10%的卫星,将为2035年前部署6G移动通信网络提供帮助。

4.1.3　物联网

物联网是以多网协同的蜂窝移动通信网络为载体,实现万物互联、连接泛在的数字信息基础设施。国际通信标准化组织陆续完成了从窄带低速到高速低时延的各类物联网相关技术标准,其中,窄带物联网(NB-IoT)满足大部分低速物联需求,4G Cat.1(即速率类别1的4G网络,含LTE-Cat.1)满足中等物联需求和语音需求,5G RedCap满足中高速率需求,5G

NR满足高速率、低时延物联需求。

在覆盖广、时延不敏感、低速率等场景，例如智能表具、追踪定位、智能烟感、智慧停车等，适合采用NB-IoT技术。在对速率要求不高，对功耗和传输稳定性有一定要求的场景，例如扫码支付、充电桩等，适合采用4G Cat.1技术。在对速率要求较高，对尺寸、成本、耗电有一定要求的场景，例如视频监控、工业传感、医疗监测、高端可穿戴设备等，适合采用5G RedCap技术。在有超高带宽、低时延、移动性要求高等需求的极致场景，例如工业互联、智慧医疗、智能交通、文体娱乐等，适合采用5G NR技术。

中国高度重视移动物联网，持续推动移动物联网发展。2020年5月，《工业和信息化部办公厅关于深入推进移动物联网全面发展的通知》发布并提出，推动2G/3G物联网业务迁移转网，建立NB-IoT、4G和5G协同发展的移动物联网综合生态体系。中国电信运营商通过补贴等方式推动NB-IoT终端的普及。据2021年发布的《中国窄带物联网NB-IoT行业市场研究》，自2017年起，中国移动NB-IoT模组专项补贴达10亿元，单个模组的最高补贴率达80％；中国电信对单个模组的补贴率提高到了50％，最高补贴30元；NB-IoT模组进入15元时代，已经开始和2G物联网模组价格趋于持平。NB-IoT已在多个行业实现百万量级连接，规模化示范效应助力减小收益和连接之间的剪刀差。

目前，中国已经建成全球规模最大的移动物联网，连接数达到18.45亿户，占全球总连接数的70％以上，成为全球主要经济体中率先实现"物超人"的国家。目前，NB-IoT在水务、燃气、消防、跟踪定位、门锁、电动车防盗等领域形成百万乃至千万级连接。移动物联网在数字城市建设、智能制造、智慧交通、移动支付等领域实现了较大规模应用，深刻地改变了我们的生活方式。

4.1.4　车联网

车联网借助新一代信息通信技术，实现车内、车与车、车与路、车与人、车与服务平台的全方位网络连接。车联网可以提升汽车智能化水平和自动驾驶能力，构建汽车和交通服务新业态。在车与车连接组网标准和技术方面，2015年初3GPP启动长期演进车联万物（LTE-V2X）的标准化工作，中国在相关国际标准化工作中发挥着引领作用。

中国已建成基于LTE-V2X技术的完备产业链，芯片、模组、车载电子标签（OBU）、路侧单元（RSU）等都已成熟且经过大规模测试，满足了商用部署条件。在基于5G蜂窝网络的车联网标准和技术方面，5G汽车联盟（5GAA）和欧洲的5GCroCo项目均开展了远程遥控驾驶相关应用场景研究，2019年中国IMT-2020（5G）推进组支持创建了首批移动边缘计算与蜂窝车联万物（C-V2X）的融合测试床。

2018年10月，工业和信息化部在全球率先发布《车联网（智能网联汽车）直连通信使用5905-5925MHz频段管理规定（暂行）》，规划5905-5925MHz频段作为基于LTE-V2X的车联网（智能网联汽车）直连通信的工作频段。2020年2月，国家发展改革委等11部委联合发布《智能汽车创新发展战略》，提出到2025年，车用无线通信网络（LTE-V2X等）实现区域覆盖，新一代车用无线通信网络（5G-V2X）在部分城市、高速公路逐步开展应用，高精度时空基准服务网络实现全覆盖。2020年3月，工业和信息化部印发《关于推动5G加快发展的通知》，提出促进"5G＋车联网"协同发展。2020年11月，国务院印发了《新能源汽车产业发展规划（2021—2035年）》，进一步要求促进新能源汽车与能源、交通、信息通信深度融合，协调推动智能路网设施建设。

中国车联网新型基础设施快速落地并初见成效。2019—2023年,工业和信息化部先后批复江苏(无锡)、天津(西青)、湖南(长沙)、重庆(两江新区)、湖北(襄阳)、浙江(德清)、广西(柳州)7个国家级车联网先导区,积极推进车联网基础设施建设、互联互通验证、规模化试点示范等。

2021年,住房城乡建设部、工业和信息化部确定了16个城市为智慧城市基础设施与智能网联汽车协同发展试点城市,开展不同等级智能网联汽车在特定场景下的示范应用。截至2021年10月,中国20余个城市和多条高速公路共计部署4 000余台支持直连通信的RSU,其中城市道路部署3 500余台,高速公路部署500余台,覆盖道路总长度3 500多千米。

4.1.5　算力设施

在数字经济时代,算力正在成为一种新的生产力,为千行百业的数字化转型提供基础动力。数据中心是算力的物理承载,是数字化发展的关键基础设施。随着中国互联网和信息化应用的普及、深入,数据中心和服务器的规模迅速增加。2021年,中国在用数据中心机架规模达到520万架。其中,大型以上数据中心机架规模为420万架,占总量的比重约为80%;在用数据中心服务器规模1 900万台,存储容量达到800 EB。2017—2023年中国在用数据中心机架规模如图4-5所示。

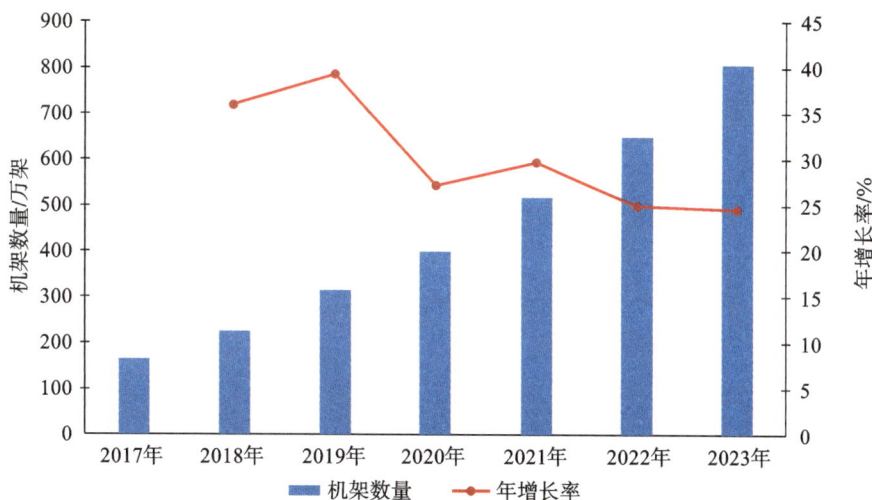

图4-5　2017—2023年中国在用数据中心机架规模
数据来源:工业和信息化部

然而,大型数据中心的高能耗问题日益突出。以2020年为例,当年中国在用的数据中心机架总规模超300万架,所产生的年耗电量突破2 000亿千瓦时(功率密度按标准机架2.5千瓦计),几乎相当于2个三峡水电站[①]的发电量,能耗占全国总用电量的2.7%。为此,数据中心的节能降耗问题成为数据中心企业关注的重点。中国企业进行了积极的探索。以阿里云为例,阿里云是阿里巴巴集团下运营云服务的公司。阿里云在中国已经建成了杭州、南

---

① 三峡水电站位于中国湖北省宜昌市,是世界上最大的水电站,也是中国有史以来最大的工程项目。它于1994年正式开工建设,2009年竣工。2023年,它已经完成了8 027.1亿千瓦时的发电。

通、张北、乌兰察布、河源 5 个超级数据中心,应用了自研的数据中心技术降低数据中心能耗。例如,杭州数据中心采用了全球最大的全浸没式液冷服务器集群,乌兰察布数据中心大规模使用风能、太阳能等绿色能源并采用自然风冷散热,河源数据中心采用深层湖水自然冷却等。

从更大范围来看,中国各地的算力需求与能源供给的矛盾日益突出。中国东部沿海经济发达地区的算力需求旺盛,但用电缺口较大;西部地区的各类清洁发电能源丰富,但经济发展相对滞后且算力需求较少。通过构建全国一体化大数据中心体系,可以建设数据中心、云计算、大数据一体化的新型算力网络体系,将东部算力需求有序引导到西部,就近消纳西部绿色能源,解决数据中心能耗高、数据资源利用效率低等长期存在的问题。

《中华人民共和国国民经济和社会发展第十四个五年规划和 2035 年远景目标纲要》中明确提出要"加快构建全国一体化大数据中心体系,强化算力统筹智能调度,建设若干国家枢纽节点和大数据中心集群"。2021 年 5 月,国家发展改革委、工业和信息化部等单位联合印发《全国一体化大数据中心协同创新体系算力枢纽实施方案》,提出支持开展"东数西算"示范工程。东数西算是从国家角度出发的一体化布局超级工程,对全国算力资源进行调整配置。该工程包括八大算力枢纽节点、十大国家数据中心集群,以及其间的全光互联高速网络。在京津冀、长三角、粤港澳大湾区、成渝这 4 个经济大区打造数据中心集群,在内蒙古、贵州、甘肃、宁夏这 4 个西部地区建设算力枢纽节点,后者承接前者的算力需求,实施国家体系内算力一体化调度,实现"东数西算"。

"东数西算"工程不但可以缓解中国每年迅速增长的算力需求压力,还可以缓解东西部之间经济发展不均衡的问题。该工程每年投资体量会达到几千亿元,对相关产业的拉动作用会达到 1∶8。数据中心产业链既包括传统的土建工程,又涉及信息技术设备制造、信息通信、基础软件、绿色能源供给等产业,产业链条长、覆盖门类广、带动效应大。算力枢纽和数据中心集群的建设将有力带动中国西部地区产业上下游投资,促进社会经济增长。

4.2 互联网产业

中国的互联网产业从无到有、从弱到强,目前中国已经成为世界上的互联网强国。中国的互联网头部企业包括阿里、腾讯、蚂蚁、抖音、拼多多、京东等(见表 4-1)。截至 2022 年 7 月,中国电信业务持证企业超过 13 万家,是 2012 年的 4.9 倍,市场主体更加多元;10 家企业跻身全球互联网企业市值前 30 强,核心竞争力不断提升。

表 4-1　2022 年中国互联网代表企业

简称	全称	业务和品牌	所在地
腾讯	深圳市腾讯计算机系统有限公司	微信、QQ、腾讯云	广东省
阿里	阿里巴巴(中国)有限公司	淘宝、阿里云、优酷、饿了么	浙江省
美团	北京三快在线科技有限公司	美团、大众点评、美团外卖	北京市
蚂蚁	蚂蚁科技集团股份有限公司	支付宝、蚂蚁链、OceanBase 数据库	浙江省
抖音	北京抖音信息服务有限公司	抖音、今日头条、西瓜视频	北京市
京东	京东集团股份有限公司	京东商城、京东物流、京东科技	北京市

简称	全称	业务和品牌	所在地
百度	百度在线网络技术（北京）有限公司	百度搜索、百度云、百度 Apollo	北京市
拼多多	上海寻梦信息技术有限公司	拼多多	上海市
快手	北京快手科技有限公司	快手、快手极速版、AC-Fun	北京市
携程	携程集团有限公司	携程旅行、去哪儿、天巡	上海市

数据来源：中国互联网协会

在以电子商务、社交、娱乐媒体、金融为代表的互联网应用领域，中国的各类应用领先全球。在电子商务方面，中国的交易额和市场规模常年保持全球第一；在社交领域，中国的社交工具微信、QQ 的月活跃用户数接近 10 亿人；在娱乐媒体领域，中国企业开发的 TikTok 等应用程序风靡全球；在金融领域，中国的支付宝、微信等第三方支付工具的应用规模居全球第一。

2022 年上半年，中国各类个人互联网应用持续发展。其中，短视频的用户规模增长最为明显，较 2021 年 12 月增长 2 805 万人，增长率达 3.0%，带动网络视频的使用率增长至94.6%；即时通信的用户规模保持第一，较 2021 年 12 月增长 2 042 万人，使用率达 97.7%；网络新闻、网络直播的用户规模分别较 2021 年 12 月增长 1 698 万人、1 290 万人，增长率分别为2.2%、1.8%。2022 年上半年中国各类互联网应用用户规模和网民使用率如表 4-2 所示。

表 4-2　2022 年上半年中国各类互联网应用用户规模和网民使用率

应用类型	应用名称	2021 年 12 月		2022 年 6 月		增长率/%
		用户规模/万人	网民使用率/%	用户规模/万人	网民使用率/%	
即时通信	即时通信	100 666	97.5	102 708	97.7	2.0
内容服务	网络视频（含短视频）	97 471	94.5	99 488	94.6	2.1
	短视频	93 415	90.5	96 220	91.5	3.0
	搜索引擎	82 884	80.3	82 147	78.2	−0.9
	网络新闻	77 109	74.7	78 807	75.0	2.2
	网络音乐	72 946	70.7	72 789	69.2	−0.2
	网络直播	70 337	68.2	71 627	68.1	1.8
	网络游戏	55 354	53.6	55 239	52.6	−0.2
	网络文学	50 159	48.6	49 322	46.9	−1.7
电子商务	网络支付	90 363	87.6	90 444	86.0	0.1
	网络购物	84 210	81.6	84 057	80.0	−0.2
线上线下商务（O2O）服务	在线办公	46 884	45.4	46 066	43.8	−1.7
	网约车	45 261	43.9	40 507	38.5	−10.5
	在线旅行预订	39 710	38.5	33 250	31.6	−16.3
	在线医疗	29 788	28.9	29 984	28.5	0.7

4.2.1　即时通信

1994—2009 年,互联网的载体主要以个人计算机终端为主。2009 年 12 月,中国手机网民占比首次超 50%;2012 年 6 月,通过手机接入互联网的网民数量达到 3.88 亿人,手机成了中国网民的第一大上网终端。2010 年以后,伴随移动互联网的飞速发展,中国手机网民占整体网民的比例从 2010 年 12 月的 66.2% 跃升到 2022 年 6 月的 99.6%。2002 年 6 月—2022 年 6 月中国互联网各类终端的用户规模如图 4-6 所示。

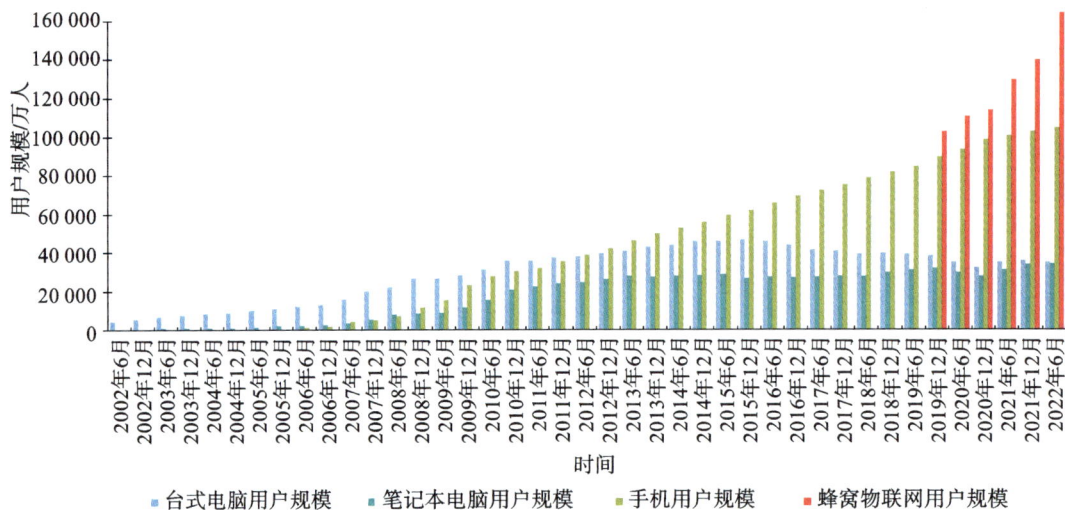

图 4-6　2002 年 6 月—2022 年 6 月中国互联网各类终端的用户规模

数据来源:中国互联网络信息中心

即时通信是中国互联网用户日常生活中最常使用的互联网应用类型,典型的即时通信应用程序包括微信、QQ 等。截至 2022 年 6 月,中国即时通信用户规模达 10.27 亿人,较 2021 年 12 月增长 2 042 万人,占互联网用户整体的 97.7%。移动互联网流量快速增长。2022 年上半年,移动互联网接入流量达 1 241 亿 GB,同比增长 20.2%。

微信成为中国互联网用户必备的即时通信工具。与传统的即时通信软件不同,微信通过公众号、小程序等方式允许微信调用或者跳转到第三方移动应用程序,形成了巨大的应用程序生态圈。微信已经成为中国互联网用户访问各类移动应用程序的主要入口,月活跃用户常年保持在 10 亿量级。据统计,2021 年 8 月月活跃用户超 1 亿人的微信小程序应用类型,涉及城市服务(含健康码)、生活缴费、办公文档、网络购物、网约出行等方面,覆盖了中国普通互联网用户日常生活的主要应用领域。2020—2021 年微信月活跃用户规模及微信小程序渗透率如图 4-7 所示。

4.2.2　电子商务

电子商务是通过互联网等信息网络销售商品或者提供服务的经营活动,是数字经济和实体经济的重要组成部分。在电子商务方面,中国的交易额和市场规模常年保持全球第一。中国电子商务已深度融入生产生活各领域,在经济社会数字化转型方面发挥了举足轻重的作用。

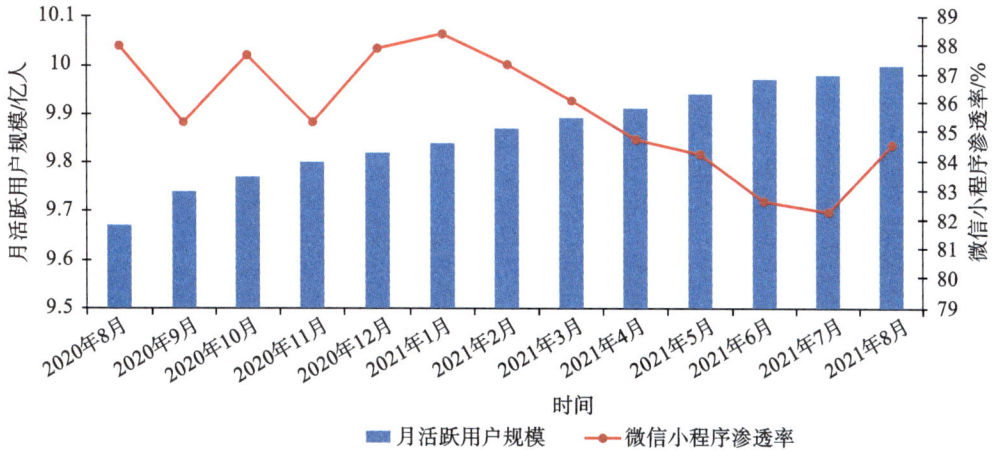

图 4-7　2020—2021 年微信月活跃用户规模及微信小程序渗透率

数据来源:北京贵士信息科技有限公司

中国国家统计局数据显示,2021 年全国电子商务交易额达 42.3 万亿元,同比增长 19.6%。按交易对象分,商品类交易额 31.3 万亿元,同比增长 16.6%;服务类交易额 11 万亿元,同比增长 28.9%。按地区分,东部地区电子商务交易额 27.4 万亿元,同比增长 18.2%;中部地区电子商务交易额 7.1 万亿元,同比增长 22.6%;西部地区电子商务交易额 6.5 万亿元,同比增长 24.2%;东北地区电子商务交易额 1.3 万亿元,同比增长 11.8%。2011—2021 年中国电子商务交易额及年增长率如图 4-8 所示。

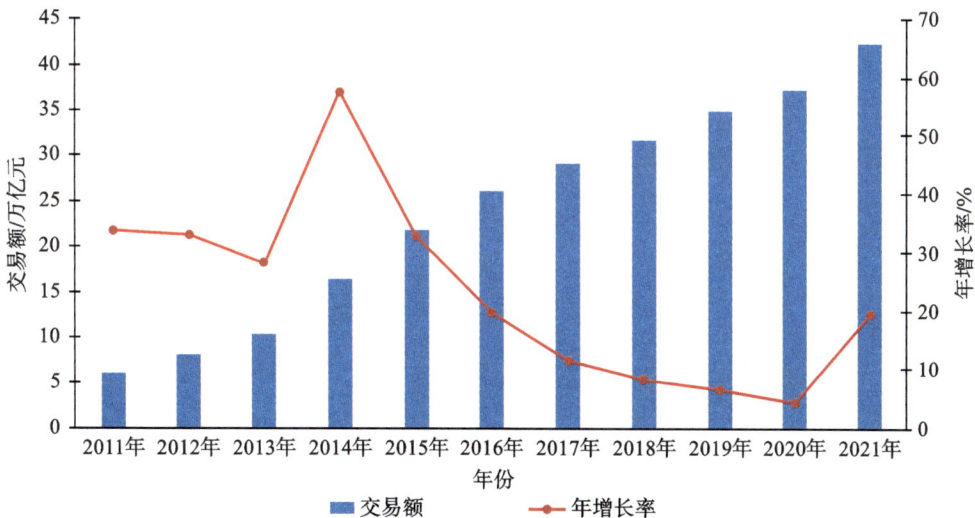

图 4-8　2011—2021 年中国电子商务交易额及年增长率

数据来源:国家统计局

直播带货、社区团购等各类电子商务新业态快速发展,电子商务与实体经济的加速融合带动更多人从事电子商务行业。据电子商务交易技术国家工程实验室测算,2021 年,中国电子商务从业人员达到了 6 727.8 万人,同比增长 11.8%。其中,电子商务直接吸纳就业和创业人数达 4 126.32 万人，电子商务带动信息技术、相关服务及支撑行业从业人数 2 601.48 万人。2014—2021 年中国电子商务就业规模及年增长率如图 4-9 所示。

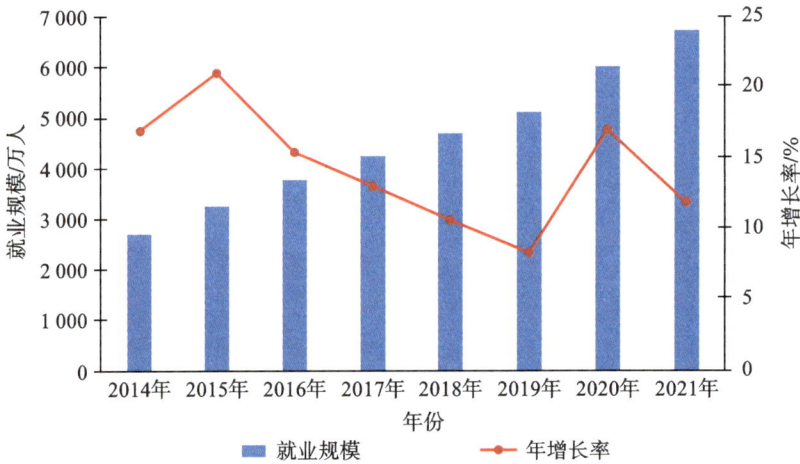

图 4-9　2014—2021 年中国电子商务就业规模及年增长率

数据来源：电子商务交易技术国家工程实验室

4.2.2.1　产业电商

产业电商指企业之间通过第三方及自营 B2B 平台在企业间进行的交易，包括提供大宗商品贸易服务的大宗电商、提供企业非生产性物料（MRO）及生产性资料（BOM）服务的工业品电商、提供消费品在线批发服务的批发电商、提供办公用品及商务服务等的企业采购电商以及相关服务商等业态。产业电商产业链中的综合类企业包括阿里巴巴、国联股份、网盛生意宝、慧聪集团、焦点科技、网库集团、义乌购等。据统计，中国产业电商市场规模从 2012 年的 6.25 万亿元增长到 2021 年的 25.19 万亿元，10 年增长约 3.03 倍。2015—2023 年中国产业电商市场规模及年增长率如图 4-10 所示。

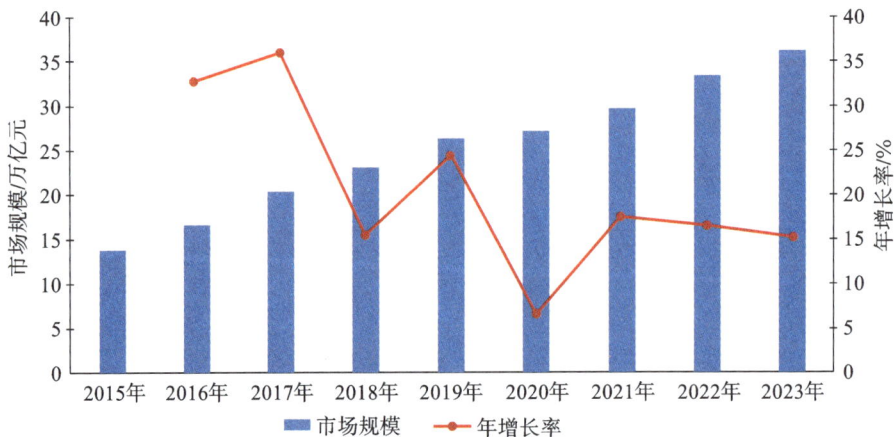

图 4-10　2015—2023 年中国产业电商市场规模及年增长率

数据来源：智研咨询

4.2.2.2　网上零售

中国互联网络信息中心的数据显示，截至 2021 年 12 月，中国网上购物用户规模达 8.42 亿人，占互联网用户整体的 81.6%。国家统计局数据显示，2021 年中国网上零售额达 13.09 万亿元，同比增长 14.1%，连续 9 年保持全球最大网上零售市场地位；实物商品网上零售额 10.8 万亿元，同比增长 12.0%，占社会消费品零售总额的比重为 24.5%；在实物商品网上零售额中，吃类、穿类和用类商品分别增长 17.8%、8.3% 和 12.5%。从商品品类看，服装鞋帽针纺织品、日用品、家用电器和音像器材网上零售额排名前三，分别占实物商品网上零售额的 22.94%、15.23% 和 10.43%。2011—2021 年中国网上零售额及年增长率如图 4-11 所示。

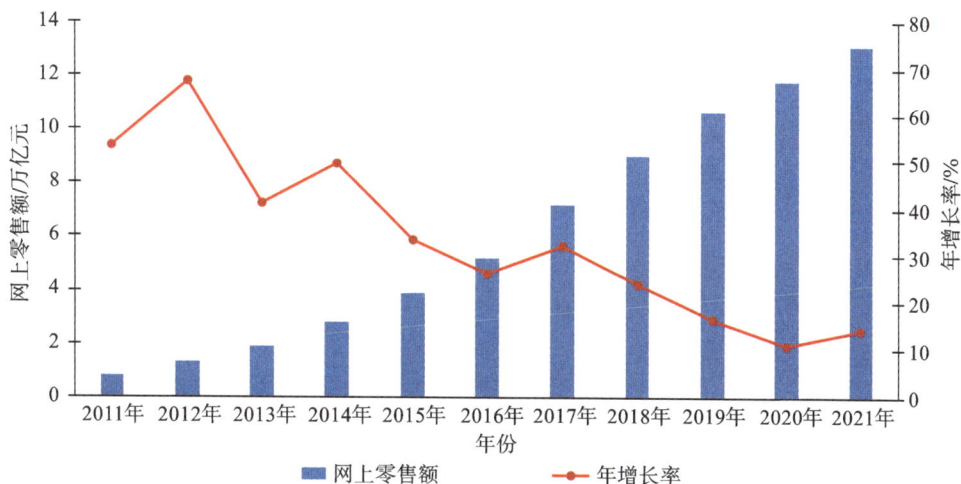

图 4-11　2011—2021 年中国网上零售额及年增长率

数据来源：国家统计局

"双十一"购物节是中国网上零售市场的一大特色。2009 年 11 月，淘宝商城依托"光棍节"赋予了"双十一"这个日子特殊地位，"双十一"购物节活动应运而生。2019 年天猫"双十一"购物节的销售额是 2 684 亿元，是当年西方"黑色星期五"购物节的 5 倍。

如今，"双十一"购物节不但成了中国主流电商平台（淘宝、天猫、京东等）参与的销售节，也成为全球消费者和生产商每年一度的集体节日，许多国外品牌也通过国家馆、海外淘、品牌直营等方式积极参与。数据显示，2009—2021 年中国电商平台"双十一"购物节成交总额呈逐年上升趋势，由 2009 年的 0.52 亿元增至 2021 年的 9 651.20 亿元。2013—2021 年"双十一"购物节中国电商平台交易额及年增长率如图 4-12 所示。

随着越来越多的互联网平台涉足电商业务，网购用户的线上消费渠道逐步从淘宝、京东等传统电商平台向短视频、社区团购、社交平台扩散。据估算，2022 年 1—6 月，只在传统电商平台消费的用户占网购用户的比例为 27.3%，在短视频直播、生鲜电商、社区团购及微信等平台进行网购消费的用户比例分别为 49.7%、37.2%、32.4% 和 19.6%。

4.2.2.3　快递物流

网络购物成为中国居民的重要消费渠道，带动相关市场加快发展。2021 年中国快递

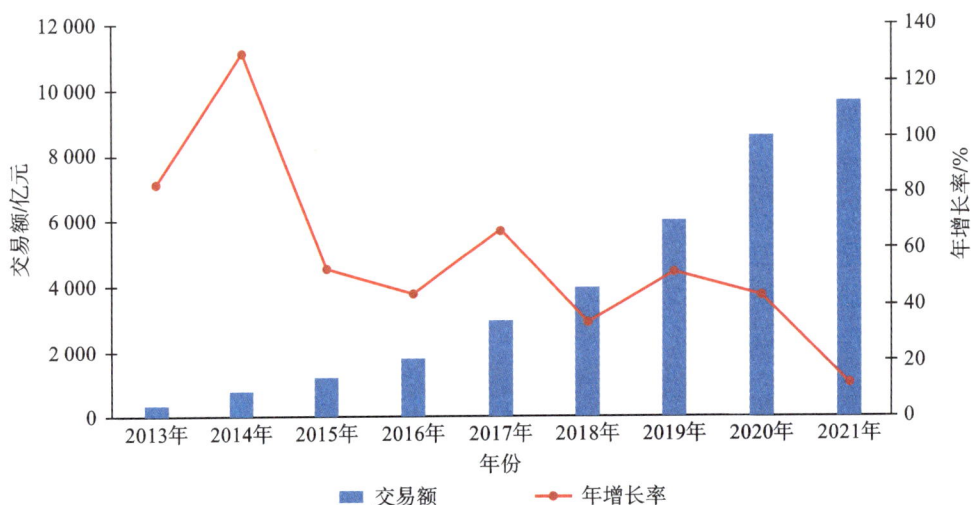

图 4-12   2013—2021 年"双十一"购物节中国电商平台交易额及年增长率

数据来源:艾媒数据中心

业业务量与业务收入均保持快速增长。中国国家邮政局统计数据显示,2021 年中国快递服务企业业务量累计 1 083.0 亿件,同比增长 29.9%;业务收入累计 10 332.3 亿元,同比增长17.5%。其中,同城业务量累计 141.1 亿件,同比增长 16.0%;异地业务量累计 920.8亿件,同比增长 32.8%。2011—2021 年中国快递服务企业业务量及年增长率如图 4-13所示。

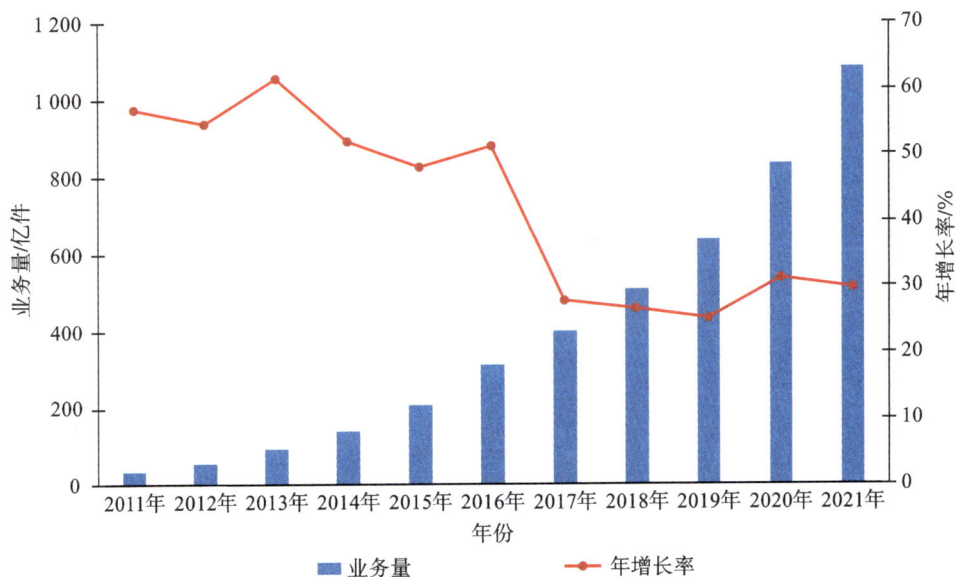

图 4-13   2011—2021 年中国快递服务企业业务量及年增长率

数据来源:国家邮政局

各类自动化、无人系统被引入物流环节。在无人仓储方面,2016 年 11 月,南京苏宁超级云仓已建成投产,建筑面积约 20 万平方米,是亚洲最大的智慧物流基地之一。2019 年,超级云仓迭代升级为"新一代无人仓",已整合无人车、全自动搬运机器人、机械臂、自动包装机等众多技术设备,实现了全流程无人化运作。2018 年,菜鸟与圆通联合打造的超级机器人分拨中心在圆通速递杭州转运中心正式启用,内置 350 台机器人,每天可分拣超过 50 万个包裹。2019 年,中国智能快递柜投放量达到 40.6 万组,同比增长 49.3%;与 2014 年相比增长近 26 倍。2020 年 1 月,京东启动全球首个消费品无人机送货实验。

4.2.3　内容服务

内容服务是互联网的主要应用之一。早期互联网内容服务以搜索引擎为主;近年来,面向移动互联网碎片化、多场景的阅读需求,出现了以"算法编辑＋智能分发"模式推送新闻的应用程序,例如今日头条。截至 2022 年 6 月,中国搜索引擎用户规模达 8.21 亿人,较 2021 年 12 月减少 737 万人,占互联网用户整体的 78.2%;中国网络新闻用户规模达 7.88 亿人,较 2021 年 12 月增长 1 698 万人,占互联网用户整体的 75.0%。

以音乐、视频、直播、游戏等内容为主的娱乐产业也是互联网内容服务的重要组成部分。截至 2022 年 6 月,中国网络视频用户规模为 9.95 亿人,较 2021 年 12 月增长 2 017 万人,占互联网用户整体的 94.6%。各大网络视频平台通过深耕垂直类别市场,发力自制剧、定制剧等视频类型,吸引、沉淀付费会员,提升会员收入。会员收入已经成为各主要视频平台除广告之外的主要收入来源,例如 2022 年第一季度哔哩哔哩付费会员数量达到 2 010 万人,同比增长 25%,其中近 80% 是年度付费会员或自动续费会员;爱奇艺会员服务营收 45 亿元,同比增长 4%。2020 年 12 月与 2021 年 12 月中国网络内容(娱乐行业)各分类用户规模以及网民使用率如图 4-14 所示。

4.2.3.1　短视频

短视频行业萌芽于 2011 年,初期以个人用户加工和分享自制视频为主。这种新的传播形式顺应了移动互联网碎片化、去中心化传播的特点,以其丰富的内容类型和逐渐增强的社交属性,满足了用户多样化的内容和社交需求,成为互联网行业蓬勃发展的重要产业。

据中国互联网络信息中心统计,2021 年 12 月中国短视频用户规模达到 9.34 亿人,同比增长 7%,占整体互联网用户比例达到 90.5%。据北京贵士信息科技有限公司统计,2021年 12 月抖音[①]、快手两大短视频平台月活跃用户数分别为 6.72 亿人、4.11 亿人。2021 年12 月短视频行业月人均使用时长增长至 53.2 小时,总时长占全网总时长的比例达 25.7%,超过即时通信成为用户使用时长最长的行业。短视频的用户规模远超音乐、直播、游戏等其他泛娱乐方式,网民使用率仍在提升,短视频已经成为人们非常重要的线上社交和娱乐方式。2020 年 12 月与 2021 年 12 月中国主要短视频平台用户规模如图 4-15 所示。

短视频用户规模和活跃渗透率高,用户使用时间长,积累大量用户数据,一方面使广告投放具有广泛的受众,另一方面使个性化推荐算法能向受众精准推送广告,提高转化率。短视频广告占据网络广告市场首位,成为数字营销的重要渠道。在中国互联网广告市场细分结构里,短视频于 2020 年以 17.4% 的市场份额超越搜索引擎广告,成为仅次于电商广告的第二大广告类型。

---

① 　TikTok 移动应用(2017 年发布)是抖音应用(2016 年发布)的英文国际版。

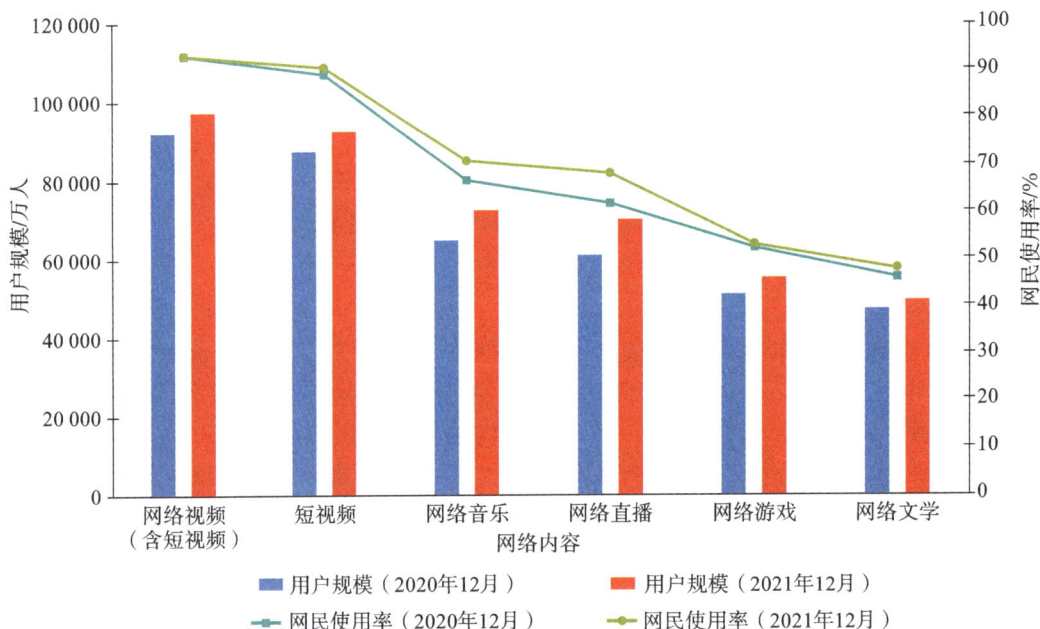

图 4-14 2020 年 12 月与 2021 年 12 月中国网络内容(娱乐行业)各分类用户规模以及网民使用率

数据来源:中国互联网络信息中心

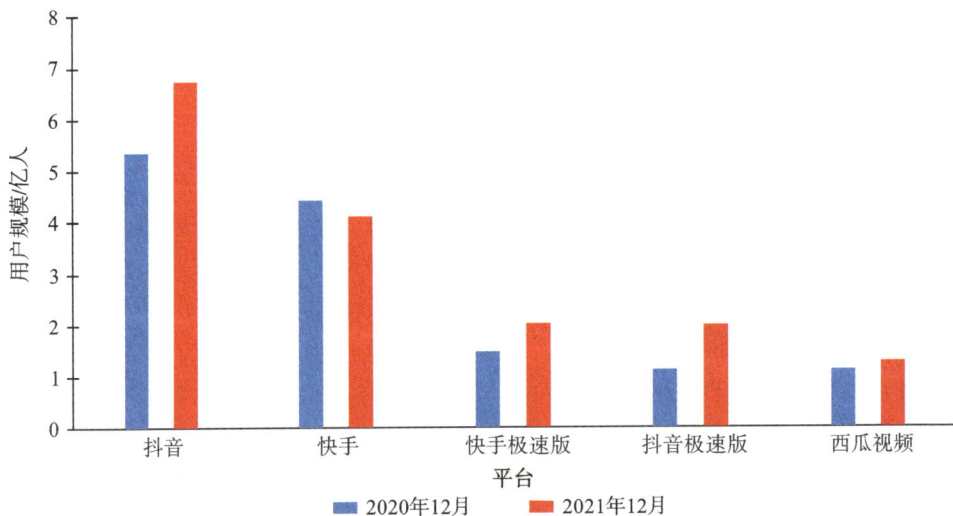

图 4-15 2020 年 12 月与 2021 年 12 月中国主要短视频平台用户规模

数据来源:北京贵士信息科技有限公司

短视频促使中国电子商务用户的消费行为从搜索型消费逐渐向推荐型消费转变。传统的网络消费行为主要基于对产品及服务的信息搜索展开,而随着大数据、人工智能技术的发展,基于算法的个性化推荐逐渐成为主流。2021 年 5 月至 2022 年 4 月,抖音电商售出超过 100 亿件商品,交易总额同比增长 2.2 倍;平台上每月有超 900 万场直播。

4.2.3.2 直播

直播行业起源于 2005 年,初期以垂直品类、泛娱乐品类为主,目前主要拓展为电商直播、游戏赛事、泛娱乐直播、教育直播和旅游直播等。2016 年女性电商平台蘑菇街与大型综合电商平台淘宝首次打造直播间,进行直播带货;2016—2018 年两大短视频平台抖音和快手也迅速试水,加码直播电商。截至 2022 年 6 月,中国网络直播用户规模达 7.16 亿人,较 2021 年 12 月增长 1 290 万人,占互联网用户整体的 68.1%。

直播电商为消费者提供身临其境般的沉浸式用户体验,同时增添实时互动功能,让主播随时掌握观看用户的选择倾向,微调营销策略。大量网红主播、明星、行业管理人员等加入电商直播大军,出现了万物可播、人人可播的景象。网络直播、网络社交推动社交媒体营销兴起,利用人与人之间的口口相传拉动消费增长,形成网红经济、信任经济等新经济模式。

2020 年 6 月至 2022 年 6 月,中国电商直播用户规模从 3.09 亿人增长至 4.69 亿人,复合年均增长率达 23.2%;网民使用率从 32.9% 提升到 44.6%,两年增长 11.7 个百分点。据中国互联网络信息中心统计,截至 2022 年 6 月,中国电商直播用户规模为 4.69 亿人,较 2021 年 12 月增长 533 万人,占互联网用户整体的 44.6%。2020 年 4 月,中国消费者协会发布的《直播电商购物消费者满意度在线调查报告》调查数据显示,使用淘宝直播的消费者占比为 68.5%,经常使用淘宝直播的消费者占比为 46.3%。2020 年 1—3 月中国直播电商购物平台消费者占有率如图 4-16 所示。

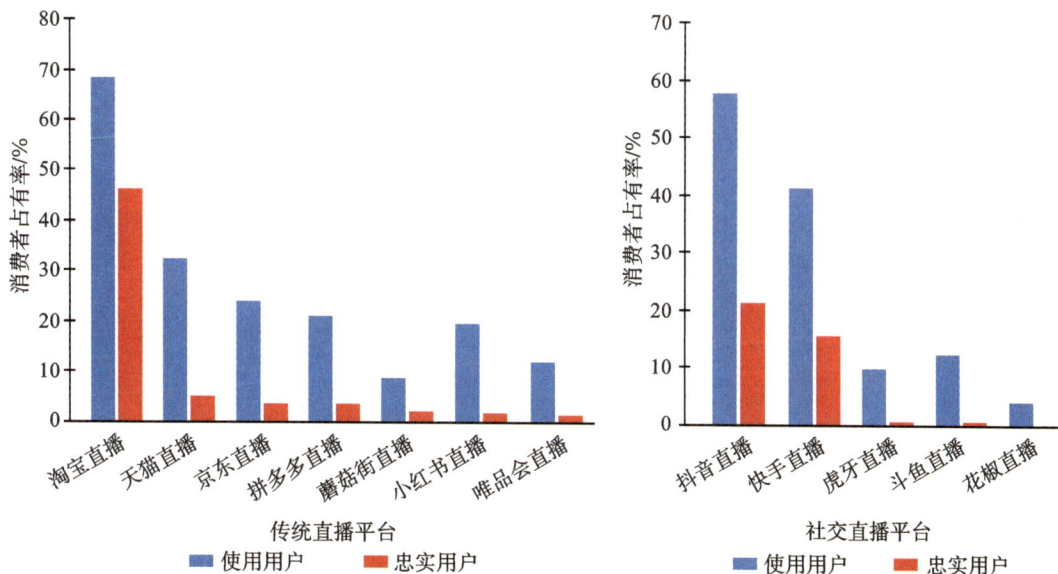

图 4-16　2020 年 1—3 月中国直播电商购物平台消费者占有率

数据来源:中国消费者协会

4.2.4　生活服务

服务业数字化进程加快,O2O 互动模式活力显现,引领互联网与服务业融合创新。以移动互联网为代表的新技术不断驱动线上线下互动融合,为消费者提供了更多服务选择和交付便利,基于用户数据的深度挖掘进一步增强了商品服务与用户需求的匹配度,促进了产业链资源整合、实体店转型、运营效率提升和商业模式创新。目前,O2O 已成为大众创业、万众创新最活跃的领域之一,旅游、租车约车、餐饮外卖、家政服务、美容保健、教育培训、车辆维保等服务业领域,基于O2O模式的产品种类和服务形态日益丰富。

数字技术与各行业加速融合,带动消费市场持续回暖,餐饮、旅游、购物等线下优势场景不断向线上转移。截至2021年12月,中国在线办公、在线医疗、网上外卖用户规模分别达4.69亿人、2.98亿人、5.44亿人,同比分别增长35.7%、38.7%、29.9%。在线旅游、认养农业、创意民宿等新业态新模式蓬勃发展。截至2022年6月,中国在线旅行预订用户规模达3.33亿人,较2021年12月减少6 460万人,占互联网用户整体的31.6%;中国在线医疗用户规模达3.00亿人,较2021年12月增长196万人,占互联网用户整体的28.5%。

4.2.5　支付服务

4.2.5.1　网络支付

中国是网络支付的大国。截至2015年12月,中国网络支付用户规模达4.16亿人,首次超过网络购物用户规模,表明互联网逐步深入线下消费场景,出门"无钱包"、消费"无纸币"习惯初步养成。截至2022年6月,中国网络支付用户规模达9.04亿人,较2021年12月增长81万人,占互联网用户整体的86.0%。

2020年以来,网络支付与无接触支付等方式深度结合,成为继即时通信、网络视频(含短视频)后的第三大网络应用,线上线下融合消费基本成型。中国支付清算协会发布的《2020年移动支付用户问卷调查报告》显示,近75%的用户每天使用移动支付。数据显示,2022年第一季度银行共处理网上支付业务235.70亿笔,金额585.16万亿元,同比分别增长4.60%和5.72%;移动支付业务346.53亿笔,金额131.58万亿元,同比分别增长6.24%和1.11%。

支付宝在2007年启动全球化业务。截至2019年6月,支付宝及其境外合作伙伴为全球超过12亿名用户提供移动支付和普惠金融服务,支付宝已经成为全球最大的非社交类应用程序。支付宝致力于为全球商户和消费者提供三种金融服务,包括全球付网上支付通路、出境游线下支付和全球数字普惠金融服务。

全球付是指支付宝联合全球金融机构及第三方合作伙伴,打通世界各地的网上支付渠道,支持全球消费者用本地化的方式完成跨境付款。目前,支付宝已与全球250多个金融机构建立合作,打通了全球220多个国家和地区的网上支付业务,支持27个币种交易,全球付让全球买、全球卖成为可能。2007年6月—2022年6月中国网络购物与网络支付用户规模如图4-17所示。

4.2.5.2　无人经济

无人经济是信息技术高度发展的产物,其以互联网为基础,借助大数据、射频识别、物联网等传感技术,减少劳务输出。无人超市、无人售货机、无人货架等是目前有代表性的无人经济终端形式。中国无人零售经济整体发展迅速,2014年市场规模约为17亿元。自2017年行业"起飞"后,市场规模高速增长,2018年约为198亿元,2023年超过400亿元,预计2026年将超过800亿元,在零售渠道中表现突出。其中,自助售货机仍是主流渠道,占据大部分的市场份额。2015年,中国自动售货机行业销售规模达到12.82万台,分布在北京、上海、广州、深圳等经济发达地区。在服务类型上,从传统的餐饮类售货机,逐步扩展到自助咖啡机、饮料机、KTV唱吧等多种类型。2016—2022年中国无人零售市场规模及年增长率如图4-18所示。

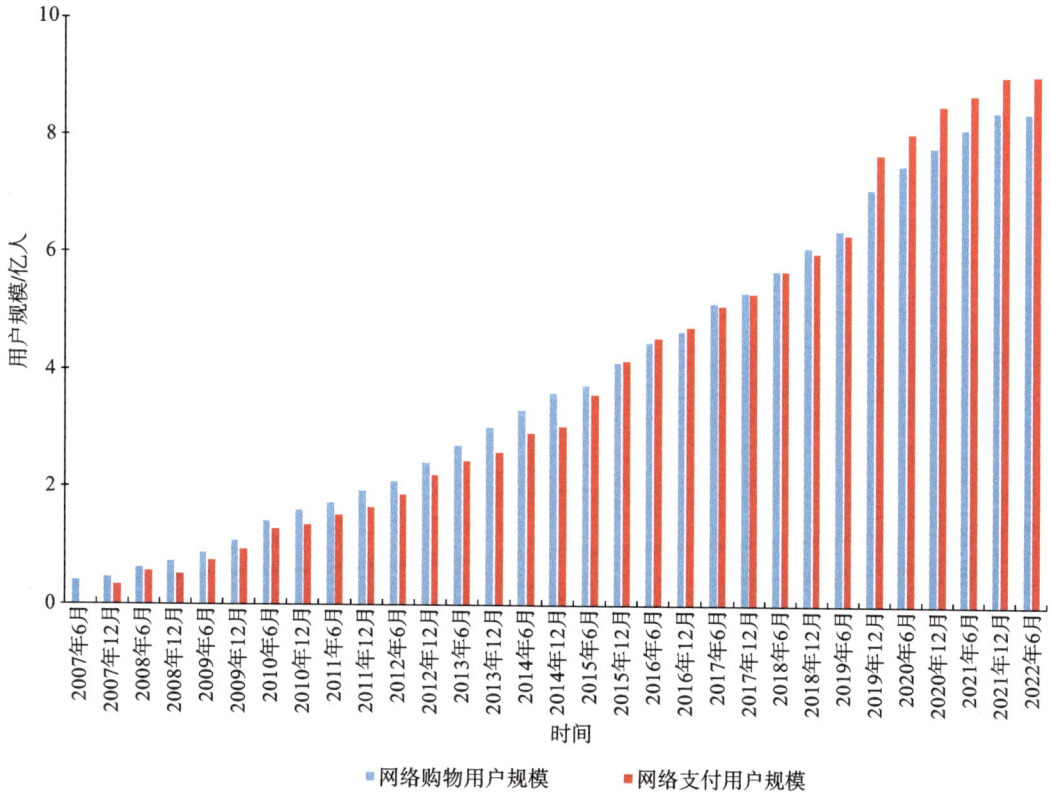

图 4-17 2007 年 6 月—2022 年 6 月中国网络购物与网络支付用户规模

数据来源：中国互联网络信息中心

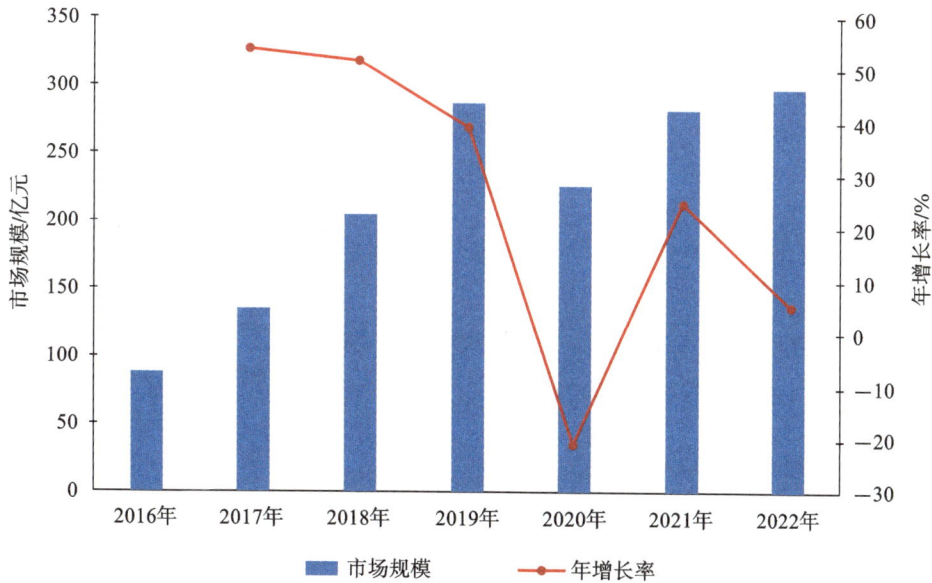

图 4-18 2016—2022 年中国无人零售市场规模及年增长率

数据来源：观研天下整理

4.3　软件和信息技术服务业

中国软件和信息技术服务业快速发展，产业规模效益快速增长。2012—2021年的10年间，中国软件产业规模增长了约2.8倍，从2012年的24 794亿元增长至2021年的94 994亿元，复合年均增长率达16.1%，位居国民经济各行业前列。中国软件和信息技术服务业产业规模占电子信息产业的比重从2012年的23.4%升至2021年的33.0%，成为提升电子信息产业规模的重要驱动因素。2013—2020年中国软件和信息技术服务业营业收入增长情况如图4-19所示。

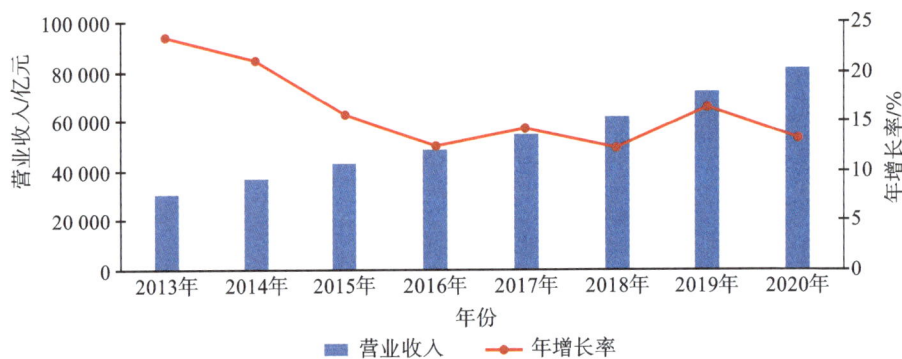

图4-19　2013—2020年中国软件和信息技术服务业营业收入增长情况

数据来源：工业和信息化部

软件和信息技术服务业创新体系基本建立，操作系统、数据库、中间件、办公软件等基础软件实现突破，取得一系列标志性成果。远程办公、协同研发等软件创新应用，有力支撑各行业发展。2022年，中国共登记计算机软件著作权183.5万件，登记数量连续5年保持在100万件以上。与2012年相比，年度登记软件数量已增长了12倍。

融合应用日益深化，赋能作用显著提升。2022年，中国人工智能、大数据类软件的登记数量均超过3.5万件。截至2020年底，建成具有一定影响力的工业互联网平台近100个，设备连接数量超过7 000万台，工业应用程序数量突破35万个，有力推动制造业转型升级；上云企业数量超百万家，软件和信息技术服务消费在信息消费中的占比超过50%。

骨干企业实力提升，国际竞争力明显增强。2020年，中国软件和信息技术服务业规模以上企业超4万家，从业人数达704.7万人；百强企业收入占全行业比重超过25%，较2015年提升5个百分点，研发投入占全行业比重达27.9%；收入超千亿元的企业达10家，2家企业跻身全球企业市值前10强。

产业集聚效应凸显，服务体系更加完善。2020年，中国268家软件园区贡献了75%以上的软件业务收入，13家中国软件名城业务收入占比达77.5%。"十三五"期间，共制定269项软件国家标准、43项行业标准，税收等惠企政策更加健全，投融资、知识产权、人才培养等公共服务体系持续优化。

4.3.1　基础软件

4.3.1.1　操作系统

操作系统是计算机最重要、最核心的基础软件,其位于 CPU、内存等硬件之上,各类应用软件之下,是最接近硬件层的基础软件。根据内核代码来说,操作系统分为开源操作系统与闭源操作系统,其中开源操作系统主要有 Linux,闭源操作系统主要有 Windows 和 MacOS 等。从终端设备来看,操作系统可以分为桌面操作系统、服务器操作系统与移动端操作系统。全球服务器操作系统主要由 Linux 与 Windows 构成。2021 年全球 1 354 万台服务器出货中,63.47% 安装了 Linux 系统,36.25% 安装了 Windows 系统,只有 0.28% 安装了 Unix 等其他操作系统。2022 年,中国服务器操作系统市场中 Linux 以 79.1% 的市场占有率排在第一,其次为 Windows,市场占有率为 20.1%。

2018 年的"中兴事件"[①]说明了发展中国自主数字化生态系统的重要性。国产操作系统作为最基础、最底层的计算机软件,是构建安全自主的数字化生态系统的重要一环,发展国产操作系统势在必行。中国的国产操作系统从"可用"到"好用",已经有了很大的飞跃。

在桌面主机方面,中国已经出现了 30 余个国产操作系统产品。这些国产操作系统多为基于 Linux 内核二次开发的操作系统,主要有麒麟、统信、普华、欧拉等。从应用领域来看,国产操作系统已在党政、金融、交通、能源、电信等多个行业领域涌现出应用落地的实例,并逐渐向核心业务领域渗透。

在服务器方面,华为研发了面向数字基础设施的欧拉开源操作系统(openEuler)。欧拉开源操作系统面向企业级数据库、大数据、云计算、人工智能等应用场景,支持鲲鹏及其他多种处理器;截至 2022 年 11 月,欧拉开源操作系统的累计装机量达到 245 万套,欧拉社区已经有超过 75 万名社区用户,贡献者超过 1.2 万名。

在移动终端方面,华为研发了鸿蒙操作系统(HarmonyOS),可以在智能手机、电脑、平板、电视、智能手表等消费电子设备和家用电器上运行。据全球著名的市场研究机构——策略分析的统计,华为鸿蒙操作系统在 2022 年占全球移动操作系统 2% 的市场份额,排名在 iOS 和 Android 之外的世界第三;此外,截至 2022 年 7 月,鸿蒙智联已有超过 2 000 家合作伙伴,搭载 HarmonyOS 的华为设备超过 3.2 亿台。

4.3.1.2　数据库

数据库是有关联关系的数据的集合。数据库管理系统是负责数据库搭建、使用和维护的系统软件,通过组织、索引、查询、修改数据库文件,实现数据定义、组织、存储、管理以及数据库操作、运行、维护等主要功能。根据部署方式,可以分为部署于企业或者平台内部的传统数据库和部署于公共云上的云数据库。据艾瑞咨询统计,2021 年中国数据库市场总规模达 286.8 亿元,较 2020 年增长 16.1%,2021—2026 年复合年均增长率预计可达 13.4%。

在传统私有数据库方面,中国国产阵营中以达梦、人大金仓、南大通用、神舟通用为代表。这些传统数据库也可以通过云部署而为用户提供服务。随着云计算的发展,出现了为云环境设计的云原生数据库,这些数据库在利用云计算环境方面更有优势,例如阿里云的

---

①　2018 年 4 月 16 日晚,美国商务部宣布,美国政府将禁止中兴通讯在未来 7 年内从美国公司购买敏感产品。从那时起,越来越多的中国高科技公司,如华为,被禁止从美国购买电子产品和零部件。

PolarDB，华为云的 GaussDB 等。据艾瑞咨询统计，2020 年中国公有云部署模式的数据库市场份额（按营业收入）占比达 32.7%。2021 年，阿里云分布式数据库 PolarDB 首次进入国际研究机构高德纳的全球数据库领导者象限，市场份额位居全球云数据库第三。

随着数据量爆发式的增长以及应用负载的快速增加，分布式成为提升数据库访问性能的热门解决方案。目前，中国完全自研的数据库产品中具有代表性的有 OceanBase、TiDB 等。OceanBase 数据库原来是阿里巴巴公司内部研制的自主分布式数据库，2014 年取代传统国外数据库厂商甲骨文支撑支付宝核心交易系统；2015 年承担"双十一"购物节 100% 的交易流量；2016 年上线支付宝核心账务、核心支付系统，支撑 12 万笔/秒的支付峰值、17.5 万笔/秒的交易峰值；2019 年在数据库产品公开测试 TPC-C 测试中获得 6 088 万 tpmC（每分钟内系统处理的新订单个数）的成绩，打破了甲骨文保持 9 年的世界纪录，"双十一"购物节期间创造 6 100 万次/秒的数据库处理峰值纪录；2020 年在 TPC-C 测试中获得 7.07 亿 tpmC 的成绩。

4.3.2　云计算

云计算是一种按使用量付费的模式，用户可通过其提供的可用的、便捷的、按需的网络访问，进入可配置的计算资源共享池（资源包括网络、服务器、存储、应用软件、服务等）。2006 年，谷歌公司正式对外介绍主打数据服务与服务器基建的"云计算"概念，之后越来越多的开发者与企业开始使用云计算，以 IaaS（基础设施即服务）、PaaS（平台即服务）、SaaS（软件即服务）三类交付为主的云服务行业渐成。

2015 年是中国云计算政策元年，中国先后出台了三项与云计算密切相关的政策文件，分别从产业发展、行业推广、应用基础、安全管理等多个重要环节进行调控。2022 年 4 月，工业和信息化部启动《上云用云实施指南（2022）》编制工作，持续深化企业上云行动，进一步提升应用云计算的能力和效果，推动企业高质量上云用云。

中国云计算市场持续高速增长。2021 年，中国云计算总体处于快速发展阶段，市场规模达 3 229 亿元，较 2020 年增长 54.4%。其中，公有云市场继续高歌猛进，市场规模增长 70.8%，达到 2 181 亿元，有望成为未来几年中国云计算市场增长的主要动力；与此同时，私有云市场突破千亿元大关，同比增长 28.7%，达到 1 048 亿元。中国公有云 IaaS 及 PaaS 保持高速增长，SaaS 稳步发展。2021 年，公有云 IaaS 市场规模达 1 614.7 亿元，同比增长 80.4%，占总体规模的比例接近 75%；PaaS 依然保持着各细分市场中最高的增长速度，同比增长 90.7%，达到 196 亿元；SaaS 市场继续稳步发展，规模达到 370.4 亿元。2017—2021 年中国公有云市场规模及年增长率如图 4-20 所示。

中国企业所提供的云服务发展迅速。截至 2021 年，阿里云已经在全球 25 个地理区域部署了上百个云数据中心，总计 80 个可用区。阿里云采用自研的云操作系统飞天管理全球数百万台服务器，覆盖东南亚、日本、澳大利亚、美国、欧洲、中东等主要海外市场。据国际数据公司（IDC）统计，2020 年阿里云在全球的公有云 IaaS 市场上排名第三，仅次于亚马逊和微软。高德纳的数据显示，2020 年阿里云在亚太地区公有云 IaaS 市场排名第一，份额是亚马逊和微软的总和。

4.3.3　大数据

大数据是大量数据的集合，具备海量、异构、高速、价值四大特性。大数据产业是以数据

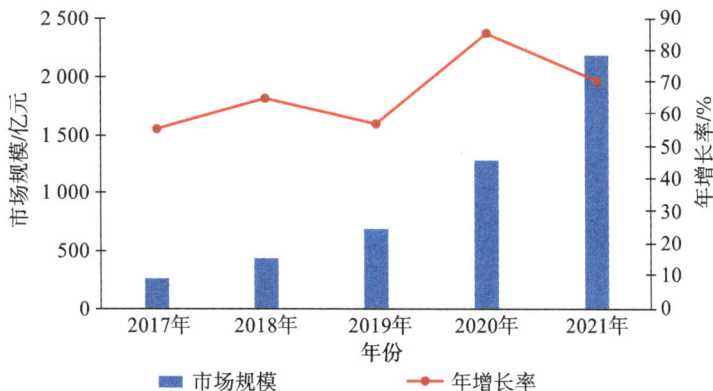

图 4-20 2017—2021 年中国公有云市场规模及年增长率

数据来源:中国信息通信研究院

生成、采集、存储、加工、分析、服务为主的战略性新兴产业。2015 年 8 月,国务院印发《促进大数据发展行动纲要》,大数据正式上升为国家发展战略。2016 年,工业和信息化部发布《大数据产业发展规划(2016—2020 年)》,迎来大数据产业建设高峰。近年来,中国政府围绕数字经济、数据要素市场、国家一体化大数据中心布局等作出一系列战略部署,有关部委出台了 20 余份大数据政策文件,各地方出台了 300 余项相关政策,23 个省区市、14 个计划单列市和副省级城市设立了大数据管理机构,央地协同、区域联动的大数据发展推进体系逐步形成。

需要特别指出的是,中国政府积极探索信息产业与区域经济的融合发展。以贵州为例,贵州是中国西南地区的经济欠发达省份之一。该省地处云贵高原,92.5% 的土地为山地和丘陵,人均耕地面积仅为 1.35 亩(1 亩≈666.67 平方米),是中国政府脱贫攻坚的重点省份。贵州的高山地貌提供了气候凉爽、电力充足、远离地震的条件,适合发展大型的数据中心等算力基础设施。为此,中国提出了发展贵州的大扶贫、大数据战略,推进国家大数据产业向贵州迁移。

国家大数据综合试验区在大数据制度创新、公共数据开放共享、大数据创新应用、大数据产业聚集等方面进行试验探索。2015 年 9 月,贵州启动中国首个国家级大数据综合试验区建设工作,截至 2022 年已有 11 个超大型数据中心。2017 年,贵州省政府与苹果公司签订协议,苹果公司中国内地 iCloud 服务由云上贵州公司运营,同期华为、腾讯、苹果的数据中心相继开工建设。其中,贵州贵安新区成为全球集聚超大型数据中心最多的地区之一。大数据已经成为贵州经济发展的重要抓手。2021 年,贵州软件和信息技术服务业收入同比增长59.3%,增速全国第一,其中云服务成为贵州名副其实的“首位产业”,占软件和信息技术服务业收入的比重从 2020 年的 23.1% 升至 2021 年的 46.4%。2021 年,贵州数字经济增速达20.6%,高出全国平均数字经济增速 4.4 个百分点。截至 2022 年,贵州聚集了超过 9 000 家大数据企业,产值超过 1 000 亿元,每年吸引上万名大数据人才。

2016 年 10 月,第二批大数据综合试验区获得批复,包括 2 个跨区类综合试验区(京津冀、珠江三角洲)、4 个区域示范类综合试验区(上海、河南、重庆、沈阳)、1 个大数据基础设施统筹发展类综合试验区(内蒙古),组织建设了 11 个大数据领域国家新型工业化产业示范基地。此外,各地政府和企业也在积极推进大数据产业的发展,陆续设立大数据产业园区,累计建成大数据产业园 100 多个。

2017—2021 年,中国数据产量从 2.3 ZB 增长至 6.6 ZB,2021 年全球占比 10.5%,数据产量位居全球第二。中国大数据产业规模快速增长,从 2016 年的 3 400 亿元增长至 2022 年的 1.57 万亿元,复合年均增长率将近 30%。2017—2021 年,中国省级公共数据开放平台由 5 个增至 24 个,开放的有效数据集由 8 398 个增至近 25 万个。截至 2022 年,中国已有 208 个省级和市级地方政府上线政府数据开放平台,全国一体化政务数据共享枢纽发布各类数据资源共计 1.5 万类,累计支撑共享调用超过 5 000 亿次。中国大数据应用范围加速拓展,产业规模实现快速增长。2016—2022 年中国大数据产业规模及年增长率如图 4-21 所示。

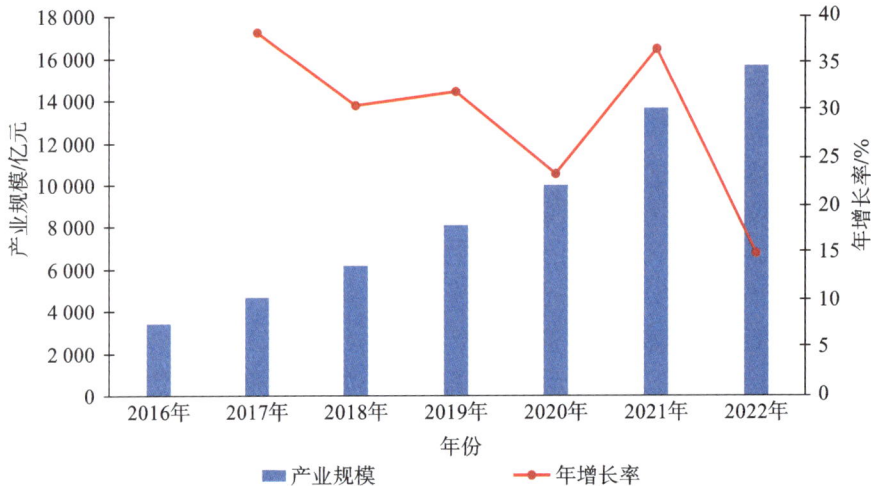

图 4-21　2016—2022 年中国大数据产业规模及年增长率

数据来源:国家互联网信息办公室,国家数据局

4.3.4　人工智能

人工智能是引领未来的新兴战略性技术,是驱动新一轮科技革命和产业变革的重要力量。2015 年 7 月中国出台的《国务院关于积极推进"互联网十"行动的指导意见》首次将人工智能的发展纳入重点任务之一;2017 年 7 月国务院印发《新一代人工智能发展规划》,将其上升至国家战略。2019 年,中央全面深化改革委员会第七次会议审议通过了《关于促进人工智能和实体经济深度融合的指导意见》,旨在充分发挥人工智能产业融合性的特点,推进国家新一轮的产业升级。工业和信息化部出台《促进新一代人工智能产业发展三年行动计划(2018—2020 年)》等多项政策文件,各地方超过 20 个省、自治区、直辖市相继出台人工智能专项规划 60 余项。

人工智能技术创新能力持续提升。中国在计算机视觉、语音等智能任务全球比赛的入榜率较高,多次在对话式问答、阅读理解、人脸识别等全球比赛中刷新智能任务的 SOTA 模型(某项任务上水平最好的模型)准确率。中国的人工智能论文数量、高被引论文数量和发明专利授权量处在第一梯队。中国人工智能专利从 2012 年的 7 968 件增长至 2021 年的 80 785 件,占全球比重 70.9%,位列全球第一。2012—2021 年,中国人工智能论文数量已从 3 423 篇增长到 2.6 万篇,占全球比重上升至 26.5%,位列全球第一。从论文细分领域来看,中国人工智能论文主题主要集中在决策系统、计算机视觉、深度学习、智能机器人、专家系统、故障诊断和神经网络等领域。

人工智能产业规模不断发展壮大。产业生态基本形成,产业整体实力显著增强。截至2020年,中国人工智能产业规模、核心企业数量,包括独角兽企业数量,均仅次于美国,位居全球第二,建立了比较完备的产业链。

从人工智能算力基础设施网络布局来看,中国已构建全球规模最大的人工智能算力网络集群,已建成并投运的人工智能计算中心有鹏城云脑Ⅱ、横琴先进智能计算平台、武汉人工智能计算中心、南京人工智能计算中心、南京鲲鹏·昇腾人工智能计算中心、西安未来人工智能计算中心、中原人工智能计算中心和成都人工智能计算中心等。其中,2019年在广东省珠海市建成的横琴先进智能计算平台规划建成全球最大的人工智能算力中心;2022年6月由鹏城实验室联合华为打造的中国算力网一期工程核心板块之一"智算网络"则是中国首个人工智能算力网络,标志着"中国算力网"计划的全面开展,全球规模最大的一体化人工智能算力网络版图已初步形成。

从核心技术研发方面来看,中国的多个互联网企业开展了人工智能技术的研究。例如先后成立深度学习研究院、人工智能实验室和智能驾驶团队,开展机器学习、深度学习、图像识别、语音识别、自动驾驶等各人工智能领域核心技术研究。近10年来,百度先后推出了"智能云""百度大脑"等产品。阿里巴巴在2012年开始构建人工智能研究院,2015年推出集成阿里巴巴核心AI算法库的可视化AI平台DT-PAI。同时,阿里巴巴还推出了虚拟助手"阿里小蜜"和ET机器人。此外,近10年来阿里巴巴尝试将人工智能与电子商务、大数据、云计算等原有业务相融合,推出了仓储机器人、城市大脑、电商大脑、工业大脑、阿里绿网和医疗大脑等智能生态产品。

从产业创新发展来看,截至2022年,中国已经完成建设8个国家新一代人工智能创新应用先导区和18个国家新一代人工智能创新发展试验区。中国人工智能产业发展不断深入,与一、二、三产业融合成效初显,正在从部分先导领域如医疗、交通、教育等服务领域向制造业、农业等产业领域拓展;智能金融、智能医疗、智能安防、智能交通等领域已经成为企业加速人工智能产业化落地的热点应用场景,智能化新产品、新业态、新模式不断涌现。2020—2023年中国人工智能产业规模及2023年人工智能产业模态占比如图4-22所示。

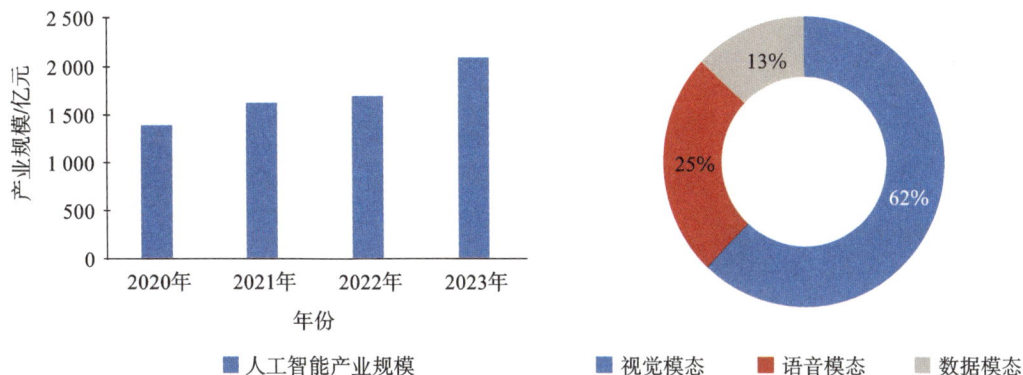

图 4-22 2020—2023 年中国人工智能产业规模及 2023 年人工智能产业模态占比

数据来源:艾瑞咨询

4.3.5　区块链

区块链是记录信息和数据的分布式数字账本,该账本存储于对等网络的多个参与者之间,参与者可以使用加密签名将新的交易添加到现有交易链中,形成安全、连续、不变的链式数据结构。区块链实现了多节点共识、公开透明和不可篡改,被视为保护数据资产的重要技术。发展区块链技术,可以推动数据要素确权,创新数据共享和开放方式,构建数据监管治理体系。

自2016年中国将区块链写入"十三五"规划以来,国家不断出台支持区块链行业发展的各项政策,鼓励区块链技术在各行业进行应用,在"十四五"规划中将区块链列为七大数字经济重点产业之一。中国的区块链技术研发在世界上处于前列。据硅谷洞察研究院发布的2018年区块链顶尖论文及学者50强榜单,上榜学者中30%来自美国,28%来自中国。2018年全球区块链专利申请数量已经达到2 966个,其中中国区块链专利申请数量达到2 435个,占全球的比重为82.1%。

区块链产业规模呈稳步提升态势。2020年后,中国各地省级政府部门积极推进区块链技术应用落地,启动区块链项目超过90个,项目主要集中在政务服务、司法、溯源和贸易金融等领域,应用规模持续扩大。2021年,中国区块链产业规模持续上升,全年产业规模约65亿元,同比增长34.9%。例如,海南省区块链"财政电子票据"应用平台利用区块链技术使得财政电子票据具有可信可验证、数据隐私安全、全局可监管等能力。基于区块链的财政电子票据,能够提升各公共服务领域财政支出的追踪、审计水平,杜绝重复报销现象。截至2021年10月,海南省已开具区块链财政电子票据2 661万份,金额超过400亿元,上线单位数量达2 795家,涵盖司法、不动产、教育、医疗等14个领域。2018—2021年中国区块链产业规模及年增长率如图4-23所示。

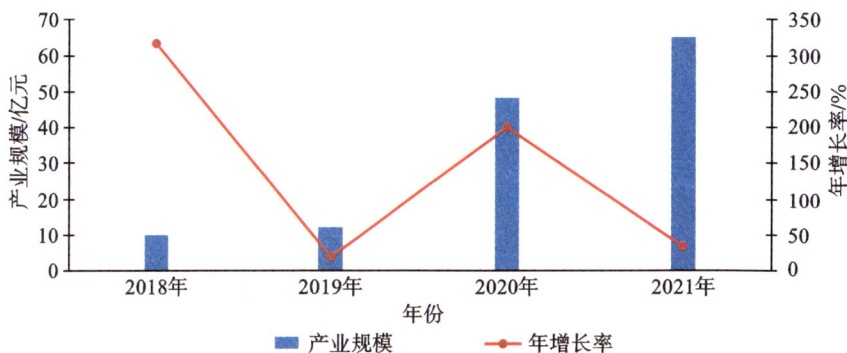

图4-23　2018—2021年中国区块链产业规模及年增长率
来源:中国电子信息产业发展研究院

4.4　电子信息制造业

2012—2021年,中国电子信息制造业企业利润在10年内实现了突飞猛进,年增长率从2012年的7.9%增长至2021年的38.9%;中国规模以上电子信息制造业营业收入从10.7

万亿元增长至 14.1 万亿元,增速高于中国工业的平均增速,电子信息制造业对中国工业生产的拉动作用在明显增强。

从产品研发来看,中国电子信息制造业关键环节和核心技术不断突破,部分领域已达业界先进水平。芯片领域,龙芯 3A5000 性能已经逼近市场主流桌面 CPU 水平;存储领域,已建成了与国际主流 DRAM 产品同步的 10 纳米级第一代 8 GB DDR4 产品生产线;打印机领域,已经逐步实现了激光打印引擎核心技术的突破,目前基于龙芯、飞腾等芯片的打印设备已经量产并得到广泛应用。

从专利数来看,电子信息制造业发明专利申请数量提升迅速,远超其他制造行业。2020年占全国发明专利申请数量的 27.4%,比排名第二的电气机械和器材制造业发明专利占比高 14 个百分点。在世界知识产权组织公布的 2021 年全球国际专利申请企业前 10 榜单中,中国企业华为、OPPO 和京东方上榜,三家企业均为电子信息制造企业。

从平台建设来看,新型显示、集成电路等创新平台在核心技术攻关等方面发挥重要作用。目前,中国已建成了国家印刷及柔性显示创新中心、国家集成电路创新中心、国家智能传感器创新中心、国家新型显示技术创新中心、国家第三代半导体技术创新中心等机构,凝聚起了产业重点环节的"中国力量",推动了中国集成电路设计核心关键技术的创新。

4.4.1　半导体产业

2015 年以来,中国加大对半导体行业的支持,相应政策与资金也在逐步落实。《国家集成电路产业发展推进纲要》对半导体产业市场规模、材料与设备、设计、制造、封装等各环节都提出了政策目标,并给予了相应的政策支持、财税优惠。"十四五"规划中提出高端芯片是"国家急迫需要和长远需求",集成电路是"事关发展全局和国家安全的基础核心领域"。

根据中国国家统计局发布的数据,2021 年中国半导体集成电路产量为 3 594 亿块,比上年增长 33.3%。根据美国半导体行业协会的数据,2021 年中国企业在全球半导体市场的份额为 15%。2021 年,中国半导体行业市场规模为 1 925 亿美元(合 1.39 万亿元),同比增长27.1%。2015—2021 年中国半导体行业市场规模及年增长率如图 4-24 所示。

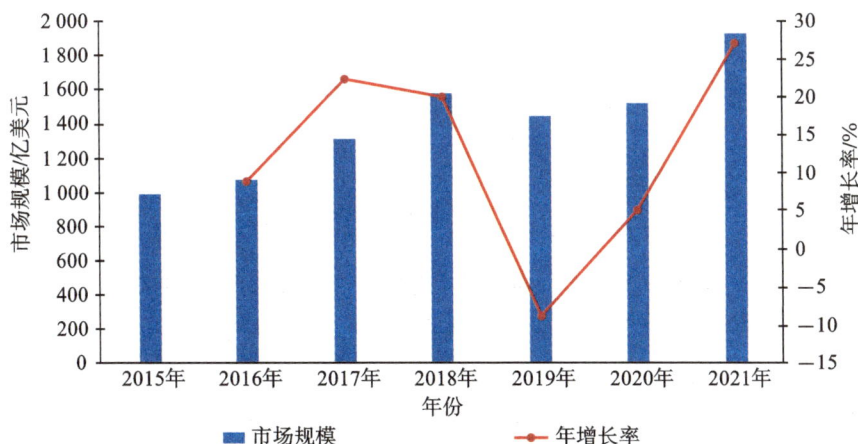

图 4-24　2015—2021 年中国半导体行业市场规模及年增长率

数据来源:观研报告网

4.4.1.1　半导体材料

半导体材料指用于电子元器件、组件及系统制备的专用电子功能材料、互联与封装材料、工艺及辅助材料。在半导体制造过程中，材料的应用贯穿始终。在晶圆制造工艺中，硅片、电子特气、光掩膜版、抛光材料等用量较大；在封装测试中，封装基板、引线框架等是较为主要的材料。半导体材料在电子信息产品的生产加工过程中发挥着重要的作用，其工艺水平和产品质量直接决定了元器件的性能。

2020 年，国家发展改革委等部门发布了《关于扩大战略性新兴产业投资 培育壮大新增长点增长极的指导意见》，提出加快在高强高导耐热材料、耐腐蚀材料、大尺寸硅片、电子封装材料等领域实现突破。从中国半导体材料市场规模占全球比重的变化情况来看，2012—2019 年比重逐年增长，从 2012 年的 12.28％增长至 2019 年的 16.67％，排名全球第三。据国家统计局统计，2018—2020 年中国电子专用材料制造行业收入稳定增长，2020 年中国电子专用材料制造行业收入 1 609.4 亿元，同比增长 39.39％。

半导体硅片是晶圆制造的主要材料之一，成品被称为"硅晶圆"，硅晶圆主要应用于集成电路等半导体产品的制造。2016—2018 年，中国大陆半导体硅片产业的市场规模从 5 亿美元增长至 9.96 亿美元。目前，中国已经成为中小尺寸硅单晶的最大生产国，印刷电路板、覆铜板、磁性材料、有机薄膜等材料的产量位居世界前列。2017—2020 年，中国多地投建硅片生产项目并扩大硅片产能，晶圆厂产能以 13％的复合年均增长率增长。中国晶圆生产从 2015 年的每月 230 万片增长到 2020 年的 471.7 万片，预计在 2035 年能够达到 858.3 万片。调研机构 Knometa Research 的数据显示，2021 年中国大陆晶圆产能占全球的 16％，中国大陆晶圆厂扩产速度显著高于其他国家和地区。2015—2021 年中国半导体材料市场规模及年增长率如图 4-25 所示。

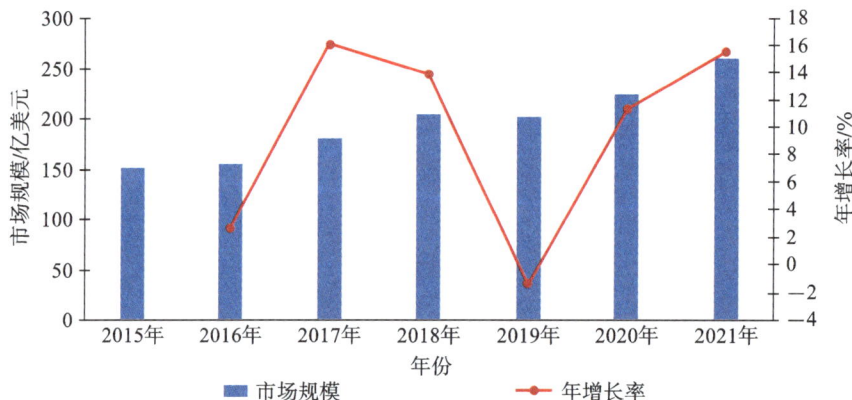

图 4-25　2015—2021 年中国半导体材料市场规模及年增长率

数据来源：国际半导体产业协会，前瞻产业研究院

4.4.1.2　半导体设备

半导体设备，即在芯片制造和封测流程中应用到的设备，涉及的设备种类主要包括光刻机、刻蚀机、薄膜沉积设备、离子注入机、测试机、分选机、探针台等。半导体设备要超前半导体产品制造开发；新一代产品每更新一代工艺制程，则需更新一代更为先进的制程设备。目前全球半导体设备市场集中度较高，以美国、荷兰、日本为代表的前 10 名企业垄断了全球半

导体设备市场 90％以上的份额。

中国高度重视半导体设备的研制,科技部组织了重大科技攻关项目"极大规模集成电路制造装备及成套工艺",集合产业链上制造工艺、装备、相关零部件和材料等上下游企业、相关研究机构和高等院校达 200 多家单位共同开展产学研协同攻关。从国内半导体设备的整体类别而言,国产设备基本可以覆盖到半导体制造的各阶段所需,尤其在刻蚀、清洗、薄膜等设备方面表现突出。中国企业北方华创位列全球半导体设备企业前十。国际半导体产业协会的数据显示,2021 年中国大陆半导体设备市场规模为 296 亿美元,占全球的 29％,是全球第一大市场。中国半导体设备国产化率从 2020 年的 17％提升至 2021 年的 20％,中国电子专用设备工业协会数据显示,2021 年中国大陆主要国产半导体设备市场规模为 386 亿元,国产化率达到 20.2％。2016—2022 年中国半导体装备市场规模及年增长率如图 4-26 所示。

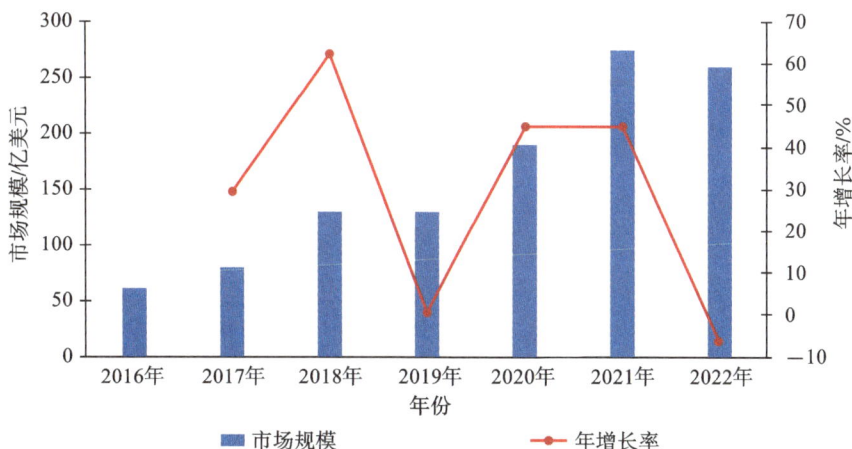

图 4-26　2016—2022 年中国半导体装备市场规模及年增长率

数据来源:华经产业研究院

4.4.1.3　电子元器件

电子元器件是电子元件和小型的机器、仪器的组成部分,是电容、晶体管、游丝、发条等电子器件的总称。电子元器件是支撑信息技术产业发展的基石,也是保障产业链供应链安全稳定的关键。以多层片式陶瓷电容器(MLCC)为例,每台智能手机平均使用数量超过 1 000 只,每辆新能源汽车使用量超过 10 000 只。

中国已经形成世界上产销规模最大、门类较为齐全、产业链基本完整的电子元器件工业体系,电声器件、磁性材料元件、光电线缆等多个门类电子元器件的产量居全球第一,电子元器件产业整体规模已突破 2 万亿元。2019 年 12 月,中国电子元件及电子专用材料制造业增加值同比增长 20.7％,出口交货值同比下降 2.3％,主要产品中,电子元件产量同比增长 26.9％。2019 年,中国电子元件及电子专用材料制造业营业收入同比增长 0.3％,利润同比下降 2.1％。2015—2020 年中国半导体分立器件产量及年增长率如图 4-27 所示。

4.4.1.4　集成电路与芯片

半导体按照其功能结构分类,通常可以分为集成电路、分立器件、光电器件及传感器四大类。集成电路是指经过一定的电路设计,利用半导体加工工艺,集成于一小块半导体晶片

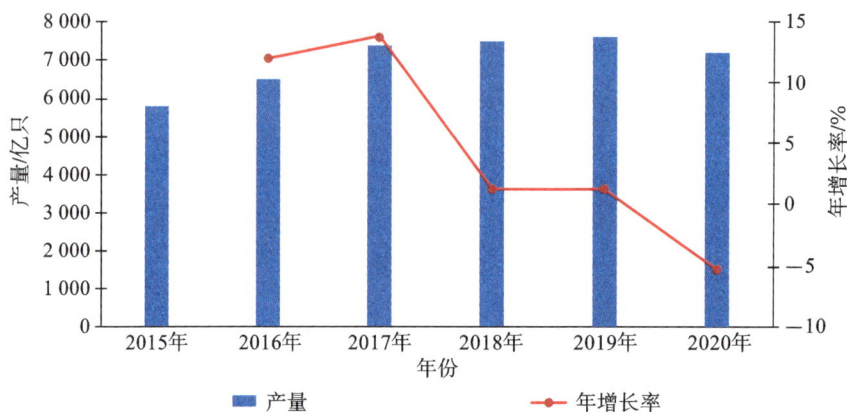

图 4-27　2015—2020 年中国半导体分立器件产量及年增长率

数据来源:国家统计局,前瞻产业研究院

上的一组微型电子电路。集成电路的销售额通常占全球半导体销售额的 80％左右,被誉为
"工业粮食",是现代信息技术产业的核心。集成电路产业主要包括设计业、制造业和封装测
试业。

2014 年,国务院印发《国家集成电路产业发展推进纲要》,将集成电路产业的发展上升
为国家战略。同年 9 月,国家集成电路产业投资基金设立,首期总金额超 1 300 亿元。2020
年,国务院印发《新时期促进集成电路产业和软件产业高质量发展的若干政策》。

中国集成电路产业起步较晚,但已经在全球集成电路市场中占有举足轻重的地位。根
据中国半导体行业协会的数据,截至 2020 年上半年,中国集成电路产业销售额达到 3 539 亿
元,同比增长 16.1％;2018—2021 年复合年均增长率为 17％,是同期全球增速的 3 倍多。
2020 年,中国集成电路产量达 2 612.6 亿块,同比增长 29.45％。2015—2021 年中国集成电
路产量及年增长率如图 4-28 所示。

图 4-28　2015—2021 年中国集成电路产量及年增长率

数据来源:国家统计局,前瞻产业研究院

自主能力实现新突破。在国家科技重大专项的实施带动下,中国面向主流工艺节点的
关键集成电路设备国产化验证效率提升 4 倍,化学机械抛光设备、介质刻蚀设备、清洗机等

主要设备进入先进工艺节点验证阶段,国产先进封装设备采购比例达到79%,节约设备采购资金30%以上,七大类别数百种关键工艺材料的品种覆盖率超过25%,国产化率达到20%以上。

中国芯片设计水平和创新能力也在不断提升。截至2021年12月,中国(不含港澳台)芯片设计企业已经由2020年的2 218家增长至2 810家,同比增长26.7%。2020年,高性能处理器产品全面服务于党政军用市场,中国的大容量高密度3D NAND闪存芯片和DDR4内存芯片实现从无到有的突破。

高端芯片领域取得长足发展。经过10年的发展,中国的国产通用CPU从"基本不可用"到"完全可用"。国产嵌入式CPU已经实现了与国外产品同台竞争,年销售量达到数亿颗。国产三维闪存和动态随机存取存储器进入量产,技术接近国际先进水平。国产FPGA芯片全面进入通信和整机市场。国产电子设计自动化工具领域在模拟、数字电路流程上形成了一系列重要的单点工具。

中低端芯片实现了进口替代。中国的国产半导体中低端芯片已经可以完全替代欧美半导体产品。以江苏润石为例,经过4~5年的沉淀,该企业在模拟芯片方面有了很多积累,其运算放大器、比较器、模拟开关、电平转换等产品可以替换德州仪器、亚德诺半导体、微芯科技、安森美对应的产品。

4.4.2　新型显示产业

新型显示是先导性、基础性产业,《"十二五"国家战略性新兴产业发展规划》首次将新型显示产业提升到国家战略性产业的高度。国家发展改革委、科技部、工业和信息化部等部委通过制定一系列专项规划,明确了产业发展重点和技术突破方向,促进新型显示产业的发展。同时,中国作为全球最大的消费电子产品市场,也为该产业的发展提供了动力。2012—2021的10年间,中国新型显示产业实现了从"跟跑""并跑"到"领跑"的华丽蜕变,曾经困扰多年的"少屏"难题得到彻底解决,新型显示产业规模、TFT-LCD产能规模实现全球"双第一"。2017—2022年中国新型显示产业规模及年增长率如图4-29所示。

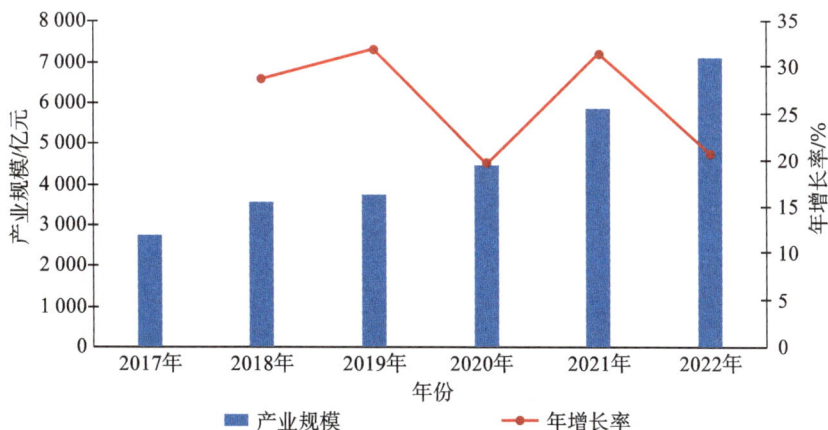

图4-29　2017—2022年中国新型显示产业规模及年增长率

数据来源:中国光学光电子行业协会

中国已形成了以面板制造为核心的完整新型显示产业链。中国的新型显示全产业营业收入由 2012 年的 740 亿元增至 2021 年的约 5 100 亿元,近 10 年以超过 20％的复合年均增长率高速增长。2021 年中国显示配套领域整体营业收入规模突破 1 000 亿元,保障了中国新型显示产业供应链的安全稳定。中国的手机、电视、平板电脑、笔记本电脑、显示器等五大类面板应用市场规模均居全球第一。2013—2022 年,中国智能手机、平板电脑、电视的年均出货量分别达到 3.91 亿部、2 203 万台、4 595 万台。

新型显示各技术路线都形成创新突破。在知识产权方面,中国已经成为面板技术第一大来源国,截至 2021 年,中国面板专利申请数量占全球面板专利总申请数量的 35％,其中京东方、武汉华星光电、深圳华星光电是 2021 年进入全球国际专利申请人排行榜前 50 的中国企业。在技术创新方面,mini-LED、Dual Cell 等背光调节技术,以及量子点彩色化解决方案等已经在 LCD 大尺寸产品生产中实现大规模量产,低功耗自适应调频、屏下指纹、屏下摄像头、无偏光片(Pol-less)等技术已经成功导入 OLED 中小尺寸产品,国产柔性 OLED 屏幕成功打入多款全球高端旗舰品牌供应链体系。

4.4.3　电子制造产业

4.4.3.1　电子计算机

电子计算机制造业是生产各种计算机系统、外围设备、终端设备以及其他有关装置的产业。随着物理元器件的变化,不仅计算机主机经历了更新换代,它的外部设备也在不断地变革。

中国计算机类产品的产量居世界第一。2021 年,中国电子计算机产量为 48 546.4 万台,同比增长 19.8％。2021 年,中国西南地区电子计算机产量为 21 922.21 万台,占全国电子计算机总产量的 45.05％。2021 年,中国各分类计算机产品中,笔记本电脑约 2.3 亿台,台式机 7 000 万台,其他为平板电脑、工作站、工控终端等。据国际数据公司统计,2021 年中国电子计算机市场前五大厂商及其市场份额为:联想 32.8％、惠普 15.6％、戴尔 14.0％、华为 10.4％、苹果 7.3％。2016—2021 年中国电子计算机产量及年增长率如图 4-30 所示。

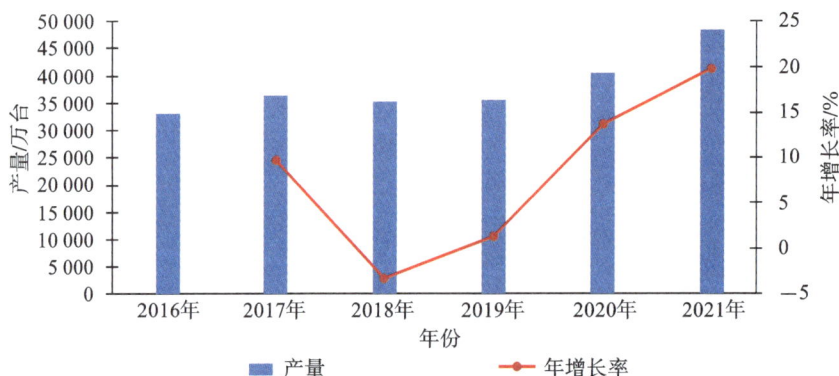

图 4-30　2016—2021 年中国电子计算机产量及年增长率

数据来源:国家统计局

在服务器市场方面,中国服务器的出货量持续增加,2021 年达到 391.1 万台,占世界出货量的 28.9％,同比增长 11.7％,浪潮、联想、华为是中国服务器出货量最大的 3 家企业。

其中,浪潮已成为全球三大开放计算组织开放数据中心委员会(ODCC)、开放计算项目(OCP)、OPEN19 基金会的核心成员和标准倡导者,其业务范围遍及全球 120 个国家和地区,2021 年全球服务器市场占有率达 9.4%,排名全球第二。

4.4.3.2 通信设备

通信系统设备制造业是指固定或移动通信接入、传输、交换设备等通信系统建设所需设备的制造,包括为运营商及企业客户提供传输网、接入网、承载网等解决方案。通信终端设备包括音频通信终端、图形图像通信终端、视频通信终端、数据通信终端、多媒体通信终端等。

在通信系统设备方面,近年来多部门陆续印发了支持、规范通信设备制造业的发展政策文件,内容涉及 5G 网络建设、终端 IPv6 升级改造、"双千兆"网络基础设施建设、工业互联网建设等内容。根据《中国电子信息产业统计年鉴 2019》,2014—2019 年中国规模以上通信设备制造业营业收入持续增长。据工业和信息化部统计,2020 年中国通信设备制造业营业收入同比增长 4.7%。

在通信终端方面,中国是全球手机产业链最为完善的市场。2012—2021 的 10 年间,中国民族企业深耕产业链终端设备制造,国产手机品牌竞相崛起。2012 年中国手机年生产量为 11.8 亿台,主打低价策略;到了 2021 年,中国手机终端年产量增长至 16.6 亿台,成为世界第一大信息通信终端生产国。市场调查机构 Counterpoint Research 发布报告称,2021 年,中国贡献了全球手机产量的 67%。小米以 190.3 万台的出货量位居全球智能手机市场第三,占全球市场份额超过 14%,与 OPPO、Vivo 共同占据全球智能手机市场前 5 名中的 3 个席位。据国际数据公司统计,2021 年全年中国智能手机出货量达到 3.4 亿台,同比增长 13.33%。据中国信息通信研究院统计,2021 年中国国产品牌手机出货量累计 3.04 亿台,同比增长 12.6%;5G 手机出货量 2.66 亿部,同比增长 63.5%,占同期手机出货量的 75.9%。2011—2021 年中国智能手机出货量及年增长率如图 4-31 所示。

图 4-31　2011—2021 年中国智能手机出货量及年增长率
数据来源:工业和信息化部,国际数据公司

华为(包含荣耀)手机市场占有率一度达到 46%,但美国在 2018 年发动贸易战,华为智能手机的市场份额受到较大影响,子品牌荣耀被迫独立。中国国产手机厂商受到美国断供芯片的影响,纷纷开始加强科技创新并自研芯片,Vivo 推出了 V1 影像芯片,OPPO 推出了 6 纳米的影像专用 NPU 芯片,小米也推出了澎湃 C1 和澎湃 P1,以提升手机的影像和充电性能。国际数据公司统计数据显示,2021年全年中国智能手机市场出货量前5名的厂商分别为 Vivo、OPPO、小米、苹果和荣耀。

4.4.3.3　消费电子产品

2017—2022年,中国连续6年保持世界货物贸易第一大国地位,百余种产品产量位居全球首位。2021年,中国家电行业主营业务收入为1.73万亿元,同比增长15.5%;利润为1 218亿元,同比增长4.5%。从细分行业看,制冷产品、空调、厨电等传统大家电行业的主营业务收入增速都达到两位数。2021年,中国的家电行业出口额突破了1 000亿美元,中国的家电产品畅销全球160多个国家和地区,全世界有20多亿家庭在使用中国的家电产品。冰箱、空调、洗衣机、电视,以及广大年轻人非常喜爱的小家电,在全世界的产品产量占有率都在50%以上。

家电行业公认的发展趋势从单品智能向全屋智能靠拢。2012—2021年,中国智能小家电市场规模由2 621亿元增长到3 793亿元,提升了45%;可穿戴设备出货量由230万台提升至1.4亿台,增长了60倍。2020年,中国智能家居设备市场出货量约为2.01亿台,而在2021年上半年,中国智能家居设备市场出货量约为1亿台,同比增长13.7%。国际数据公司预计,未来中国智能家居设备市场出货量将持续增长,至2025年出货量将达到5.4亿台。2012—2021年中国家电市场全品类零售额及年增长率如图4-32所示。

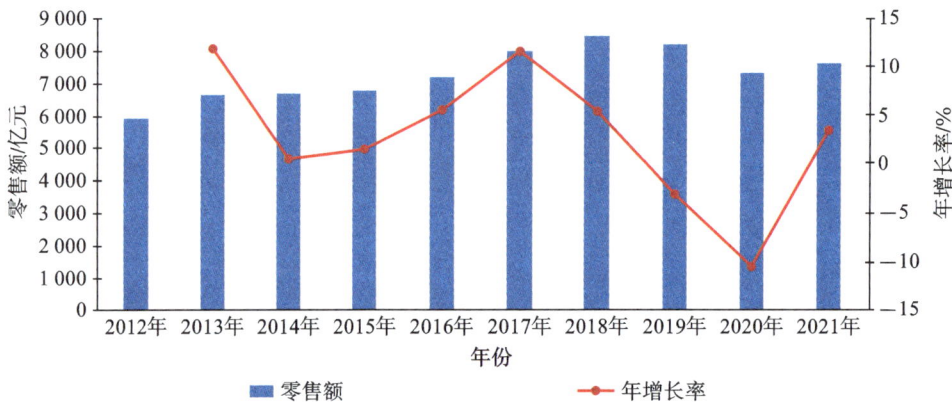

图4-32　2012—2021年中国家电市场全品类零售额及年增长率

数据来源:奥维云网

中国拥有全球最大的家电制造基地。2020年,海尔在全球运营14个研发中心、122个制造中心、108个营销中心,形成了遍布全球的研发资源共享网络,共享通用模块和复用技术,并共享部分专利;在2020年"全球智慧家庭发明专利排行榜"中,海尔智家以2 034件排名榜首,连续4次排名全球第一。2020年,美的在全球设有约200家子公司、28个研发中心和34个主要生产基地,其中在海外设有18个研发中心,研发人员超过15 000人。截至2020年底,美的累计专利申请数量突破16万件,授权维持数量超过6.2万件。

4.5　小　　结

在数字经济蓬勃发展的时代,传统信息与通信产业加速转型升级,深度融入数字经济浪潮,逐步发展成为涵盖新型数字产品及前沿数字技术的关键产业。中国以"数字产业化"这一概念,概括数字经济新形势下信息与通信产业的发展内涵,涉及基础电信业、互联网产业、软件和信息技术服务业、电子信息制造业等多个领域。

在基础电信业领域,中国充分发挥政策引领和国有企业的示范带动作用,持续推动全国通信网络设施的优化升级。在互联网基础设施建设方面,中国构建起全球规模最大的光纤宽带网络,IPv6 地址数量和活跃用户数均位居世界首位。在移动通信方面,中国成绩斐然,率先实现 5G 技术突破并建成全球最大的 5G 移动通信网络,5G 基站数量占全球总量的 60% 以上。卫星互联网建设稳步推进,多种卫星成功发射组网,低轨卫星网络项目有序开展。同时,中国在物联网和车联网领域也取得了重大进展,建成全球规模最大的移动物联网,并设立多个车联网应用示范基地。先进且性价比高的通信网络基础设施不仅极大地提升了人民群众的生活品质,还为各类信息化应用的广泛普及与深入推广筑牢了坚实基础。

互联网产业被中国视为推动经济高质量发展和转型升级的重要引擎。中国政府积极营造良好的政策环境,鼓励各类市场主体开展互联网创新活动,大力推进"互联网+"战略在各领域的深度应用。在互联网应用层面,中国在电子商务、社交娱乐、金融科技等领域展现出强大的竞争力。中国网上零售额连续多年蝉联全球第一;即时通信用户规模庞大,已超过 10 亿人;短视频行业发展迅猛,用户规模超过 10 亿人,短视频平台成为数字营销的新兴重要渠道。此外,中国的在线支付应用规模全球领先,移动支付凭借其便捷性和高效性,深刻改变了人们的支付习惯。支付宝积极拓展全球业务,为全球超过 12 亿用户提供了优质的金融服务。依托蓬勃发展的互联网产业,共享经济、短视频、直播带货等新业态、新模式不断涌现,有力地促进了中国实体经济的繁荣发展。

软件和信息技术服务业作为战略性新兴产业,受到中国政府的高度重视和大力扶持。中国通过一系列产业政策,全力推动软件和信息技术服务业自主可控发展,不断完善软件创新体系。在基础软件领域,中国取得了一系列关键突破,成功研发出多款具有自主知识产权的基础软件产品,涵盖服务器、个人计算机、移动终端操作系统以及分布式数据库等,并在众多行业实现了规模化应用。在云计算、大数据、人工智能、区块链等新兴信息技术领域,中国企业积极创新,推出了一系列先进的技术和产品。云计算市场保持高速增长,公共云服务在国际市场上的竞争力不断增强;大数据产业蓬勃兴起,数据开放共享水平处于世界前列;人工智能领域创新成果丰硕,产业规模持续扩大;区块链技术研发处于世界领先地位,并在金融等多个领域开始规模化应用。新兴软件和信息技术服务业的快速发展为各行业的信息化建设注入了源源不断的创新活力。

电子信息制造业是中国制造业的重要支柱,中国凭借完备的产业体系,生产了全球大量的电子器件和产品,同时积极推动集成电路等高端制造业的产业升级。在半导体领域,中国企业迎难而上,持续攻克关键技术"卡脖子"问题,在半导体材料、装备、集成电路等方面取得了显著突破,实现了大部分中低端产品的进口替代。在新型显示领域,中国企业实现了从技术跟跑到技术领跑的跨越,构建了完备的产业链,产业规模和技术专利数量均位居全球前列。在计算机、通信设备、消费电子设备等产品制造领域,中国不仅具备强大的制造优势,而且技术创新能力不断提升。中国的电子信息产品和技术广泛出口到世界各地,为全球消费者提供了丰富多样的产品选择。

近年来,中国在基础电信业、互联网产业、软件和信息技术服务业、电子信息制造业等领域取得了举世瞩目的发展成就。先进的网络基础设施覆盖广泛,为信息流通搭建了高速通道;互联网领域的创新应用层出不穷,塑造了便捷高效的生活和消费模式;软件和信息技术服务业的技术突破与产品创新,为各行业数字化转型提供了有力支撑;电子信息制造业的产业升级和技术进步,提升了中国在全球产业链中的地位。这些成就显著改善了中国的社会面貌:便捷的网络通信让人们随时随地畅享信息,移动支付、电子商务等应用简化了消费流程,短视频、即时通信丰富了社交和娱乐生活。同时,这些成就也对中国整体经济发展起到了关键的推动作用。它们催生了大量新业态、新模式,创造了众多就业机会,促进了实体经济的转型升级,带动了相关产业的协同发展,成为推动中国经济高质量发展的重要引擎,为中国在全球数字经济竞争中赢得了优势地位。

5 产业数字化

产业数字化,即应用信息技术和数据资源为传统产业带来的产出增加和效率提升。近10年来,中国积极推动各产业的数字化进程,通过数字化转型促进产业升级。本章重点介绍中国在制造业、农业、能源、交通等行业的数字化发展现状与成就。

5.1 智 能 制 造

中国是制造业大国,具有"世界工厂"的称号。2012—2021年,中国制造业增加值从16.98万亿元增加到31.4万亿元,占全球比重从22.5%提高到近30%,持续保持世界第一制造大国地位;入围世界品牌500强的工业和信息化领域品牌数量从10个增加到24个。

中国制造业有31个大类、179个中类和609个小类,是全球产业门类最齐全、产业体系最完整的制造业。2015年5月,国务院印发《中国制造2025》,提出通过"互联网+"推动工业化和信息化的融合发展。2021年4月,工业和信息化部发布《"十四五"智能制造发展规划》,提出到2035年规模以上制造业企业全面普及数字化网络化,重点行业骨干企业基本实现智能化。

5.1.1 工业互联网

工业互联网作为新一代信息技术与制造业深度融合形成的新兴业态和应用模式,是实现工业数字化转型的关键基础。随着信息技术与工业领域的融合,工业装备逐步网络化,工业软件逐步智能化,工业制造逐步协同化,推动各类新型的工业制造应用的出现。2017年11月,国务院印发《关于深化"互联网+先进制造业"发展工业互联网的指导意见》;2020年12月,工业和信息化部印发《工业互联网创新发展行动计划(2021—2023年)》,提出了5个方面、11项重点行动和10个重点工程,着力解决工业互联网发展中的深层次问题。

工业互联网平台体系纵深范围不断扩大。当前,中国"综合性+特色性+专业性"的工业互联网平台体系不断完善。截至2021年12月,有全国影响力的工业互联网平台已经超过150个,接入设备总量超过7 600万台(套);综合型工业互联网平台标杆引领效用显著,15家企业加快建设跨行业跨领域平台,为工业企业的发展提供支撑;特色型工业互联网平台进行行业深耕,不断形成差异化发展格局;专业型工业互联网平台加速发展,覆盖数字孪生、工业智能、工业大数据分析、边缘计算、远程监控等多个特定领域。

在工业互联网标识解析体系方面,2020年6月,中国信息通信研究院获得国际自动识别与移动技术协会授权,成为与国际物品编码协会、美国电气电子工程师学会、万国邮政联盟等大型国际组织并列的国际发码机构,代码为"VAA",具备全球标识编码分配能力。2021年1月,数据标识符列表的全球唯一管理机构数据标识符管理委员会正式批准工业互联网标识专属国际数据标识符"15N"并授予中国信息通信研究院管理和维护权限,对工业互联网标识的国际化推广具有重要意义。

深入实施制造业数字化转型行动和智能制造工程,打造信息化和工业化融合贯标升级版。截至2022年10月,中国开展信息化和工业化融合管理体系贯标的企业累计超过5.7万家,制造业数字化网络化智能化试点示范类项目超过1 500个,工业应用程序数量达到28.32万个,发布智能制造国家标准300余项、国际标准42项,培育出主营业务收入超10亿元的供应商近百家,服务范围覆盖汽车、纺织、医药等90%以上的制造业领域。

5.1.2 工业机器人

机器人产业蓬勃发展,为经济社会发展注入强劲动能。"十三五"期间,通过持续创新、深化应用,中国机器人产业呈现良好发展势头,产业规模快速增长,复合年均增长率约为15%;2020年机器人产业营业收入突破1 000亿元,工业机器人产量达21.2万台(套);2020年制造业机器人密度达到246台/万人,是全球平均水平的近2倍。

机器人产业核心竞争力持续提升。中国攻克了减速器、控制器、伺服系统等关键核心零部件领域的部分难题,核心零部件逐步实现国产化。以减速器为例,绿的谐波研发的基于三次谐波减速原理的Y系列谐波减速器产品,扭转刚度、传动精度大幅度提升。机器视觉技术的应用大幅提高了工业生产中的柔性和自动化程度。例如,中科新松有限公司将机器视觉与协作机器人相结合,为协作机器人作业提供稳定持续的3D视觉柔性化定位。

工业机器人向复杂精密场景渗透。工业机器人在融入了柔顺力控特性后更加柔性化,可实现更高精度、更强灵敏性的应用,在装配、研磨、铆接等复杂精密场景加快普及应用。重庆华数机器人有限公司针对计算机类、通信类和消费类电子产品(3C产品)推出精密加工机器人,该工业机器人配备自主研发的高性能伺服电机和控制技术,重点突破笔记本电脑全制程典型工序应用,实现全制程机器人生产及立体库全套自动化工厂应用。

5.1.3 智能工厂

5.1.3.1 电子设备制造业

实现柔性生产制造,提高生产能力。华为与中国移动合作,在广东省松山湖的华为南方工厂利用5G技术实现了柔性生产制造场景的应用(见图5-1)。原有手机生产车间需要布线9万米,每条生产线平均拥有186台设备,生产线每半年随新手机机型的更新进行升级和调整,对车间所有网线重新布放,每次调整需要停工2周,而通过5G与工业互联网的融合应用,华为南方工厂将生产线现有的贴片机、回流炉、点胶机等通过5G网络实现无线连接,每次生产线调整时间从2周缩短到2天。

现场辅助装配,加快装配效率。海尔与中国移动合作,在山东省青岛市利用5G技术实现了精密工业装备的现场辅助装配。海尔青岛洗衣机互联工厂打造基于5G MEC(移动边缘计算)的互联工厂,开展了基于AR眼镜的5G远程辅助装配。工人通过佩戴AR眼镜采集关键工业装备的现场视频,同时从后台系统调取产品安装指导推送到AR眼镜上,实现高效装配。工人还可以通过5G网络联系专家,实现远程指导。

图 5-1 华为:松山湖手机生产基地

图片来源:华为

部署机器视觉质检,增强自动检测。格力与中国联通合作,在广东省利用 5G 技术实现了机器视觉质检。格力在总装车间建立了工业虚拟专网,实现生产控制网与生产管理网融合,利用 5G 网络自动拍摄待检内容,并将照片视频流上传至部署在 MEC 平台的机器视觉质检应用,运用 GPU 算力资源与数据模型做实时比对分析检测,实现设备自动识别,质检系统做出不良品分离操作(见图 5-2)。

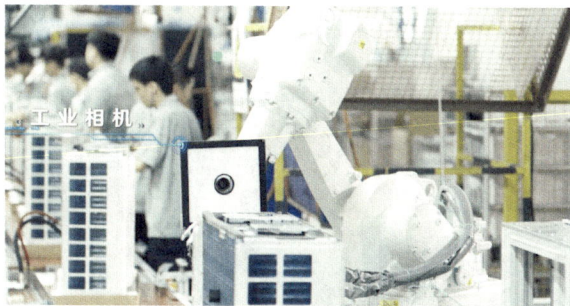

图 5-2 格力:机器视觉质检应用

图片来源:格力

5.1.3.2 装备制造业

打造厂区智慧物流,增强物流发展水平。福田汽车与中国联通合作,在山东省潍坊市诸城市打造超级卡车工厂,利用 5G 网络实现了厂区智慧物流。在入厂车辆调度环节,开发集虚拟电子围栏、车辆自动识别、车辆探测等多种技术于一体的入厂协同系统,利用 5G 技术将厂区车辆泊位状态等信息实时传递到各种智能显示终端及信息系统,实现无纸化收货。

协同研发设计,加快研发进程。中国商用飞机有限责任公司(简称"中国商飞")与中国联通合作,在上海市浦东新区开展了"5G+工业互联网赋能大飞机智能制造"项目建设。中国商飞基于 5G 网络服务,通过 AR 数据实时上传,支持产品研发实验阶段的跨地区实时在线协同与远程诊断(见图 5-3),实现了研发设计环节的问题定位,压缩了研发实验的时间成本。

实现设备协同作业,提高调度效率。三一重工与中国电信、华为合作,在北京市开展了"5G+工业互联网"项目建设,5G 技术与机械制造生产工艺流程深度结合,实现了设备协同作业。通过 5G 技术搭建车间自组网,基于大带宽低时延的 5G 网络传输自动导引车的 3D 图像和状态信息;利用 5G MEC 平台和 GPU 算力集成能力,降低自动导引车单机功能复杂度和成本,提高生产调度效率。

图 5-3　中国商飞：AR 眼镜辅助装配远程诊断

图片来源：新华社

5.1.3.3　钢铁行业

实现远程设备操控，提高作业效率。湖南华菱钢铁股份有限公司（简称"华菱钢铁"）与中国移动合作，在湖南省依托 5G 技术实现了天车、加渣机械臂的远程设备操控场景的应用（见图5-4）。利用 5G 超大上行与下载速率，操作人员可在远程操控室实时操控天车卸车、吊运装槽、配合检修等作业，保障远程操控的精准度和实时性，提高了作业效率。

图 5-4　华菱钢铁：远程操控天车和机械臂

图片来源：中国新闻网

开展机器视觉质检，提升监测效率。鞍山钢铁集团有限公司（简称"鞍钢"）与中国移动合作，在辽宁省开展了"基于 5G 的机器视觉带钢表面检测平台研发与应用"项目建设（见图 5-5）。利用 5G 网络将采集到的冷轧现场高清图像数据传至操作室平台，通过平台的视觉 AI 分析能力对图像进行处理分析，完成带钢表面缺陷的实时检测。方案部署完成后，提升了带钢常规缺陷检出率，减少了带钢缺陷造成的断带和伤辊换辊停机时间。

图 5-5　鞍钢：机器视觉带钢表面缺陷检测

图片来源：《鞍钢日报》

进行设备故障诊断,提高预测准确率。宝山钢铁股份有限公司(简称"宝钢")与中国联通合作,在广东省湛江市开展"流程行业 5G＋工业互联网高质量网络和公共服务平台"项目建设,利用 5G 技术实现了连铸辊、风机等设备故障诊断(见图 5-6)。通过 5G 网络实时传输设备数据到设备故障诊断等相关系统,采用人工智能和大数据技术对设备寿命进行预测,减少了现场布线的工作量,提高了设备寿命预测的准确率。

图 5-6　宝钢:远程工业控制

图片来源:《湛江日报》

5.2　智　慧　农　业

中国是农业大国,虽然农业产量位居世界前列,但是人均农业资源较为紧缺。2019 年底,中国耕地面积 19.18 亿亩,人均耕地面积只有 1.36 亩,不足世界平均水平的 40％。同时,中国耕地资源空间分布不均衡,总体质量不高,超过一半的耕地靠天收。

1949 年以来,中国通过科学育种、兴修水利、推广农机等多种手段提升国内的农业发展水平,实现了三大主粮的自给自足。中国用不足世界 9％的耕地实现了约占世界 25％的粮食产量,保障了世界近 20％人口的粮食需求,创造了举世瞩目的成就。

为了促进农业科技现代化,中国近年来先后出台了《"十四五"全国农业农村信息化发展规划》《"十三五"农业科技发展规划》《数字农业农村发展规划(2019—2025 年)》等政策文件。从 2011 年起,中国政府安排中央预算内投资资金,支持地方实施国家物联网应用示范工程智能农业项目。

2021 年 2 月,《中共中央 国务院关于全面推进乡村振兴　加快农业农村现代化的意见》印发,提出发展智慧农业。智慧农业是通过将互联网、物联网、大数据、云计算、人工智能等现代信息技术与农业深度融合,实现农业信息感知、定量决策、智能控制、精准投入、个性化服务的全新的农业生产方式。智慧农业依靠信息技术的支撑,利用高新技术和科学管理来达到资源最大化节约利用。

5.2.1　农业大数据

建成中国农业地理大数据平台。中国农业农村部建成地理信息公共服务平台、政务服务平台、农业农村大数据平台等应用平台。中国自然资源三维立体"一张图"持续完善,耕地和永久基本农田、生态保护红线、城镇开发边界（"三线"）划定成果已上图入库（见图 5-7）。通过建设农业农村各类业务数据图层，形成"1 张底图＋N 个农业专题应用图"，实现数据精细化、可视化的分级展现、直观对比和动态跟踪。"空、天、地"立体化新型农作物对地调查体系初步建立，可以准确获取主要农作物的播种面积、空间分布、作物长势等数据。

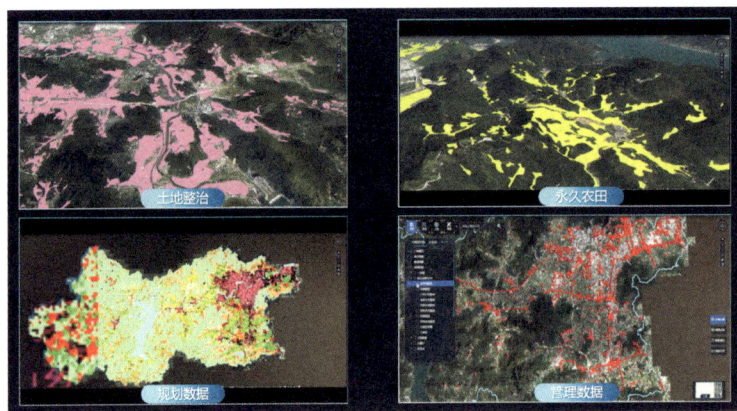

图 5-7   自然资源三维立体展示（土地整治、永久农田、规划数据等）

图片来源：台州市自然资源和规划局

开展农业重大自然灾害预警与监测。气象信息预警系统和农情信息调度系统在应对 2021 年秋冬种期间洪涝灾害、2022 年长江流域气象干旱中发挥了重要作用。农业面源污染和灌溉用水监测得到全面加强，截至 2022 年 6 月，中国共监测 3 882 个农业面源污染控制断面。中国农作物重大病虫害数字化监测预警系统不断完善，已对接省级平台 22 个、物联网设备 4 000 多台，为有效发现和防治小麦条锈病、稻飞虱、草地贪夜蛾等重大病虫害提供了有力支撑。

开展农产品市场监测预警。建立一批重要农产品单品种全产业链大数据分析应用中心。加强农业监测预警体系建设，完善农产品供需平衡分析制度，引导各类市场主体对农业农村大数据进行挖掘和创新应用。大豆、苹果等 8 类 15 个品种的全产业链大数据建设试点稳步推进，生猪产品信息数据平台上线运行，发布生猪全产业链数据。农业农村部网站开设了数据频道，编制发布"农产品批发价格 200 指数"，农产品市场分析研判能力明显提升。

开展农产品/农资质量安全追溯。2022 年，中国的国家农产品质量安全追溯管理信息平台已实现与 31 个省级平台及农垦平台的对接互通，推广应用"承诺达标合格证＋追溯码"模式，实现从田间到餐桌的全程可追溯。截至 2022 年 6 月，国家农产品质量安全追溯管理信息平台已有 46.5 万家生产经营主体完成注册，"阳光农安"在 5 个省份开展试点，农产品质量安全追溯体系日益完善。农药、兽药和化肥等农资信息化管理全面深入推进，截至 2022 年 8 月，中国农药数字监督管理平台实现全国农药产品"一瓶一码"100％可追溯。

5.2.2   智慧种植

在农业农村部的指导下，现代信息技术在种植业生产中加快应用，精准播种、变量施肥、智慧灌溉、环境控制、农业无人机等技术和装备开始大面积推广。截至 2021 年，中国累计设立 9 个农业物联网示范省份，建设 100 个数字农业试点项目，征集发布 426 项节本增效农业物联网应用成果和模式。

农业无人机获得大规模应用。与人工或者传统机械相比,无人机在农作物的播种(授粉)、洒药、施肥,以及长势和病虫害的监测等方面具有明显优势。中国已经成为全球最大的农业无人机应用国。2020 年,中国约有 1.5 亿亩耕地使用了植保无人机和遥感无人机作业,占全国耕地面积的 8.3%,超过日本无人机作业面积的 100 倍。中国农业农村部的数据显示,2021 年春耕期间有超过 3 万台无人机投入使用。截至 2022 年,中国植保无人机保有量为 12.1 万架,年作业 10.7 亿亩次。图 5-8 展示了重庆市农业科学院研制的 5G 网联植保无人机的应用。

图 5-8　重庆市农业科学院研制的 5G 网联植保无人机
图片来源:红星新闻(左),新华网(右)

无人农机装备获得大范围应用。截至 2022 年,农机北斗终端的精度提升到了 2 米;已有超过 60 万台拖拉机、联合收割机配置了基于北斗定位的作业监测和智能控制终端,其中安装有辅助自动驾驶系统的拖拉机超 10 万台;数据平台汇集了 49 万台农机北斗终端的 200 亿条农机综合数据,实现了中国全域农机作业数据的实时采集、动态展示。2021 年,中国装备北斗导航设备的作业面积超过 6 000 万亩。其中,黑龙江垦区建成 6 个智慧(无人化)农场群,累计改装升级水旱田无人驾驶及辅助驾驶机具 6 288 台,示范作业面积 608 万亩,亩均增产 3%~5%。图 5-9 展示了北大荒集团红卫农场使用北斗无人插秧机和无人收割机的场景。

图 5-9　北大荒集团红卫农场使用的北斗无人插秧机和无人收割机
图片来源:《黑龙江日报》

物联网辅助精细化种植也取得规模化应用。安徽省智慧"芜湖大米"生产示范基地将水稻生产过程划分为播种、插秧、分蘖等 13 个环节,并细化出品种选择、土地平整、氮肥用量等 49 个智慧决策点,构建起"智慧农艺+智能农机"双轮驱动技术体系,实现了耕种管收全过程信息感知、定量决策、智能作业(见图 5-10),2022 年试验面积已扩大到 15 万亩,试验结果显示亩均增产 14.3%、节约氮肥 32.5%、节约磷肥 16.8%、减药 38.0%、亩均增收 500 元左右。据统计,2021 年,中国大田种植信息化率为 21.8%,其中,小麦、稻谷、棉花、玉米的生产信息化率分别为 39.6%、37.7%、36.3% 和 26.9%。

图 5-10　安徽省智慧"芜湖大米"生产示范基地使用的稻田传感器和自动灌溉系统

图片来源:芜湖新闻网(左),皖江明珠网(右)

5.2.3　智慧养殖

现代信息技术在畜禽养殖全过程得到广泛应用。2021 年,中国畜禽养殖信息化率达 34.0%,其中,生猪和家禽养殖信息化率分别为 36.9% 和 36.4%。畜牧业综合信息平台、饲料和生鲜乳质量安全监管系统已实现对全国 18 万余个规模猪场、4 200 多个生鲜乳收购站、5 800 多辆运输车、300 余个牧场、1.3 万家左右持有饲料生产许可证企业的全面监管。各类养殖场通过应用无人环控平台、自动巡检报警系统、智能饲喂系统等,劳动生产率提高 30% 以上,每头出栏生猪成本降低 150 元左右。

智慧养殖场实现了养殖环境智能监控、畜禽个体行为监测。例如,在全自动化无人养殖"未来猪场",移动 5G 巡栏机器人对着猪圈来回扫描,猪的体温、猪圈温度等数据都在后方的大屏上实时显示。"未来猪场"做到了生猪饲养管理全程智能化、数字化、无人化,平均每头母猪年提供商品猪从常规养殖方式的 18.5 头提高到了 26.5 头,增效达 43.2%;每饲养 2 500 头生猪的用工量从 4 人下降到 0.8 人,用工节省 80%;牧场总用水量节省 60%。图 5-11 展示了浙江省桐乡市石门镇的"未来猪场"。

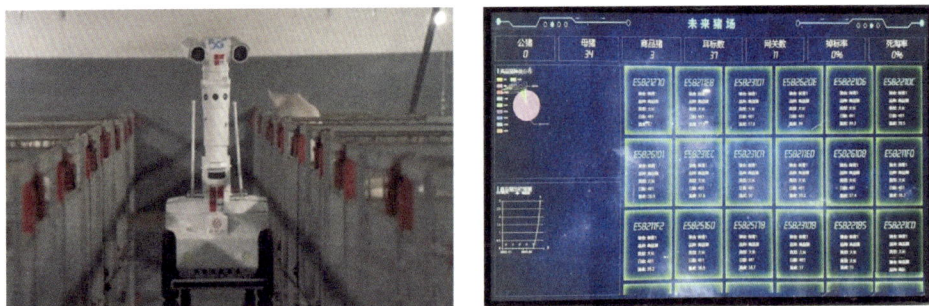

图 5-11　浙江省桐乡市石门镇的"未来猪场"

图片来源:光明网

渔业行业推广基于数字技术的工厂化养殖、稻虾养殖、鱼菜共生模式。2021 年,中国水产养殖信息化率为 16.6%,其中,蟹类、虾类、鱼类和贝类的生产信息化率分别为 23.6%、21.6%、20.9% 和 6.0%。沿海省份持续开展海洋渔船北斗和天通卫星终端等装备建设。依托渔船动态监控管理系统,中国建成海洋渔船动态船位信息全国"一张图",形成了完备的"渔船+船港+船员、近海+远洋"捕捞业数据库,伏季休渔管理、渔船监管等工作得到有力支撑。

江苏省南京市浦口区通过生产、流通、消费全环节数字化,打造青虾订单生产、透明供应、信任消费的产业体系,构建青虾数字化养殖系统,实现养殖环境在线感知、水体溶氧实时调控和饲料精细投喂;改善水体环境,养殖密度由每亩 10 万尾提升到 12 万尾,产量提高 20%;人工成本投入减少 150 元/亩,投入品节约 200 元/亩;青虾储运存活时间由 1 小时提高到 10 小时,存活率达 98% 以上。全系统节省养殖人工成本 15% 以上,节约仓储加工物流配送成本 20% 以上,养殖收益增加 15% 以上。图 5-12 展示了江苏省南京市浦口区的"数字渔场"。

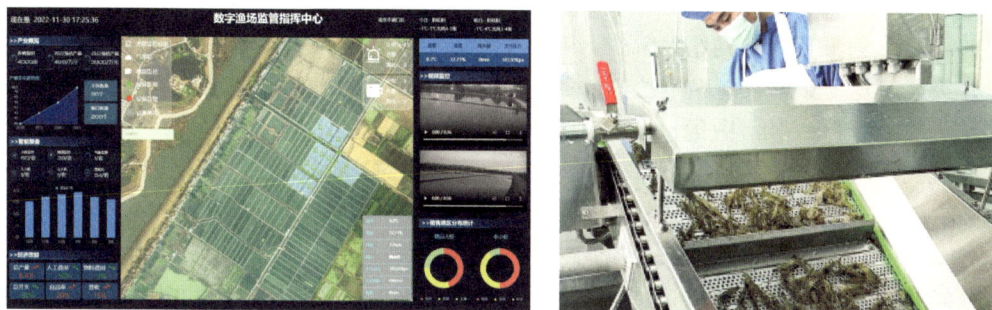

图 5-12   江苏省南京市浦口区的"数字渔场"

图片来源:南报网(左),浦口区融媒体中心(右)

5.3 智慧能源

中国是能源生产和消费大国。中国基本形成了煤、油、气、电、核、新能源和可再生能源多轮驱动的能源生产体系。2019 年,中国一次能源生产总量达 39.7 亿吨标准煤,为世界能源生产第一大国,水电、风电、光伏发电累计装机容量均居世界首位,在运在建核电装机容量居世界第二。"十三五"期间,中国能源结构持续优化,低碳转型成效显著,煤炭消费比重下降至 56.8%,常规水电、风电、太阳能发电、核电装机容量分别达到 3.4 亿千瓦、2.8 亿千瓦、2.5 亿千瓦、0.5 亿千瓦。

为了应对全球变暖等环境挑战,2016 年全球 178 个缔约方签署了共同应对气候变化的《巴黎协定》。2020 年 9 月 22 日,在第七十五届联合国大会一般性辩论上,中国国家主席习近平向全世界郑重宣布,中国将提高国家自主贡献力度,采取更加有力的政策和措施,二氧化碳排放力争于 2030 年前达到峰值,努力争取 2060 年前实现碳中和。推动能源行业的数字化和智能化是保障中国提出的碳达峰、碳中和目标的重要手段。2020 年,中国提出了新基建建设计划,将特高压输电线、新能源充电桩等能源基础设施列入新基建内容,并提出建立智慧能源基础设施。2022 年 1 月,国家发展改革委、国家能源局印发《"十四五"现代能源体系规划》,提出推动能源基础设施数字化,推动能源产业数字化升级,加强新一代信息技术、人工智能、云计算、区块链、物联网、大数据等新技术在能源领域的推广应用。

5.3.1 智能煤矿

2020 年 2 月,中国政府八部委联合印发《关于加快煤矿智能化发展的指导意见》,要求利用信息通信技术形成全面感知、实时互联、分析决策、自主学习、动态预测、协同控制的智能系统,实现煤矿开拓、采掘(剥)、运输、通风、洗选、安全保障、经营管理等过程的智能化运行,提升煤矿安全生产水平、保障煤炭稳定供应。到 2035 年,各类煤矿基本实现智能化,构建多产业链、多系统集成的煤矿智能化系统,建成智能感知、智能决策、自动执行的煤矿智能化体系。

煤炭行业的信息基础设施水平显著提高。厂区作业网络从百兆、千兆工业以太环网升级到万兆甚至 10 万兆以上。井下无线通信系统从原来的 3G、4G 网络部署升级到以 5G、Wi-Fi 6、F5G(第五代固定网络)等融合组网通信为主。井下人员定位系统从射频识别区间定位升级至超宽带亚米级精准定位等。2020 年 6 月,中国首座 5G 智能煤矿在山西省新元煤矿正式落成。2023 年,中国已有百余座煤矿实施了 5G 组网和应用,采煤和掘进工作面远程操控、全景视频拼接、露天煤矿自动驾驶、AR 智能巡检以及远程诊断等应用持续深化。

自动驾驶技术在露天煤矿获得应用。内蒙古大雁矿业集团有限责任公司开展"极寒型复杂气候环境露天煤矿 5G+无人驾驶卡车编组安全示范工程",运行速度达到业内最高的 40 千米/时,无人驾驶系统可动率大于 96.7%,无人驾驶运输综合效率不低于有人驾驶。该示范工程是中国首个 5G 独立组网露天煤矿无人驾驶项目、首个 200 吨级以上无人化改造项目、首个实现全天候三班无人化编组运行项目。截至 2021 年末,中国露天煤矿无人驾驶车辆达 146 台。图 5-13 展示了内蒙古大雁矿业集团有限责任公司的"无人矿车"。

图 5-13 内蒙古大雁矿业集团有限责任公司的"无人矿车"

图片来源:中国煤炭网

矿业装备的联网改造取得进展。2021 年,国家能源投资集团有限责任公司(简称"国家能源集团")与华为公司在北京发布矿山领域首个工业互联网操作系统——矿鸿,截至 2022 年 11 月,已经在 13 座煤矿和 1 家洗煤厂部署 3 300 多套设备,支持的应用包括装备智能控制、固定场所无人巡检、设备在线升级等。矿鸿系统利用 5G+人工智能视频拼接技术实现远程操控;利用 5G 实时回传主运皮带的画面,人工智能算法识别煤块、锚杆等异常,实现全时段监测,可减少 20％的井下巡检人员。图 5-14 展示了矿鸿系统辅助煤矿实现智能巡检的场景。

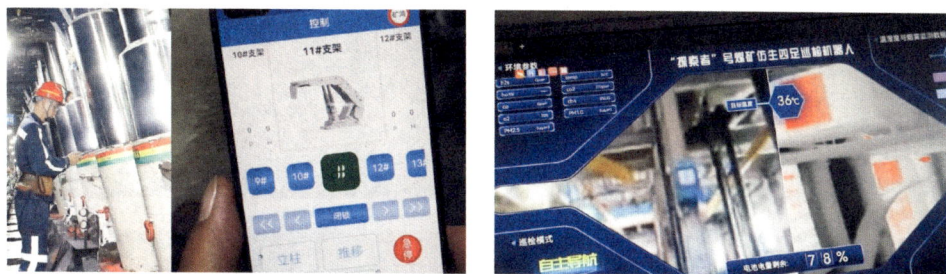

图 5-14　华为工业互联网操作系统"矿鸿"辅助煤矿实现智能巡检

图片来源:华为

5.3.2　智慧电厂

2023 年 3 月,《国家能源局关于加快推进能源数字化智能化发展的若干意见》发布,提出以数字化智能化技术加速发电清洁低碳转型;加快火电、水电等传统电源数字化设计建造和智能化升级,推进智能分散控制系统发展和应用。智慧电厂是以物理电厂为基础,将各个系统与信息技术、智能控制技术、发电行业技术结合而形成的新型电厂。

火电厂智能化改造取得显著进展。依靠煤炭的传统火电仍是中国发电的主力军,2021年中国火力发电量约占全社会发电量的 71.13％,发电量同比增长 8.4％。国电内蒙古东胜热电有限公司在 2019 年 7 月部署了盘煤机器人。煤仓顶棚柔性导轨式 3D 激光无人盘煤机器人可绘制出煤场煤堆的三维立体图形,实现无人干预、智能巡护的三维激光无人盘煤,盘点一个煤场只需要 5 分钟。2020 年,东胜热电构建了厂级 5G 自组织网络,实现了火电厂区范围内下行速率 350 Mbps、上行速率 160 Mbps,网络双向时延小于 15 毫秒,借助无人机器人实现生产现场、高危现场全覆盖,多业务、多操作模式功能的全能巡检操作。图 5-15 展示了东胜热电的"智能火电厂"。

海上风电场的数字化取得重大进展。海上风电站场通常在距离陆地 20～120 千米的位置,仅依托陆上移动通信基站无法实现对风电站场的覆盖。过去的近海通信以卫星和窄带专网通信为主,仅能满足基础的语音和简单的数据采集业务需求。2022 年 12 月,国家电投揭阳神泉二海上风电项目在广东省揭阳市顺利实现全容量并网发电,该项目是全球批量应用单机容量最大的海上风电项目,总装机容量达 502 兆瓦。广东移动携手华为,在距离海岸线 25 海里的海上升压站部署开通了 2 座 5G 基站,实现对周围 20～50 千米海域总计超1 000平方千米的区域的网络覆盖,下载速率超 100 Mbps,网络时延低于 40 毫秒。5G 助力实现了海上风电场的高清视频监控、海上巡检、智能调度等应用。图 5-16 展示了广东省揭阳市的 5G 海上风电场。

5.3.3　智能电网

中国的能源资源与能源负荷在地理分布上十分不均衡。80％以上的能源资源分布在西部和北部地区,70％以上的能源消费集中在东中部地区,需要大规模、远距离、高效率的电力

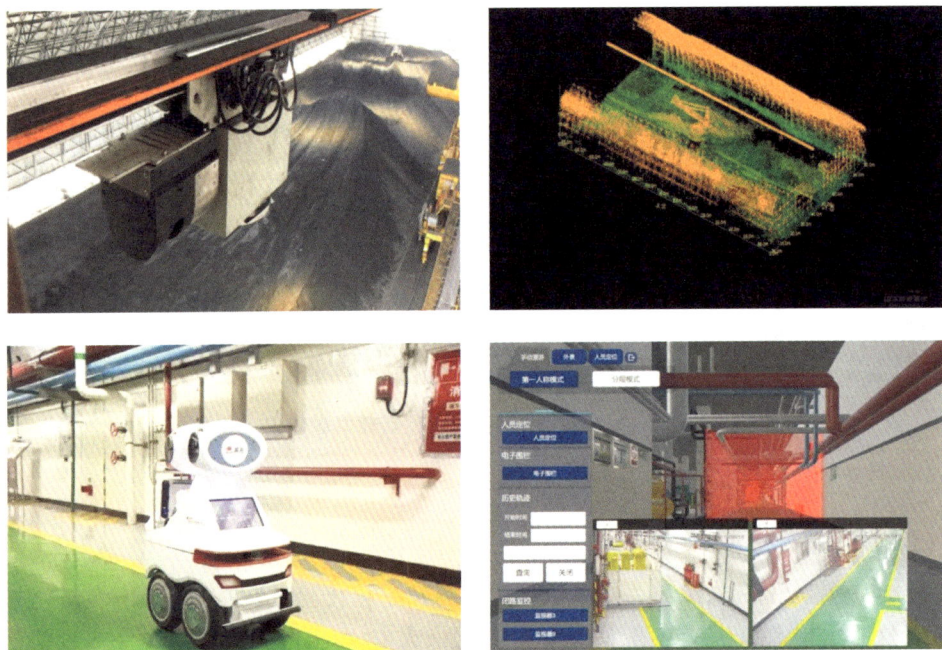

图 5-15　东胜热电的"智能火电厂"

图片来源：国家能源集团（上），国家能源之声（下）

图 5-16　广东省揭阳市的 5G 海上风电场

图片来源：《中国日报》（左），华为（右）

输送。长线路、跨区域传输电力需要对电网进行精细调控。中国于 2009 年 5 月提出了"坚强智能电网"的发展规划。该网络以特高压电网为骨干网架，各级电网协调发展，具有信息化、自动化、互动化特征。2017 年底，"四交四直"特高压工程全部投运。这些特高压工程起点多位于能源资源丰富的西部、北部地区，落点多在东中部地区，满足了负荷中心日益增长的用电需求。2020 年末，中国已基本全面建成统一的坚强智能电网，技术和装备达到国际先进水平。

2023 年 3 月，《国家能源局关于加快推进能源数字化智能化发展的若干意见》发布，提出以数字化智能化电网支撑新型电力系统建设，推动实体电网数字呈现、仿真和决策，探索人工智能及数字孪生在电网智能辅助决策和调控方面的应用，提升电力系统多能互补联合调度智能化水平。目前，中国正在加速推动从电网数字化转型向能源互联网演进升级。

规划建设可视化。国家电网有限公司(简称"国家电网")聚焦生产、运营、服务等重点领域,融汇各类业务系统和数据,实现电网问题图上诊断、规划智能生成、项目在线审查、计划智能优选、报表自动生成。截至 2022 年,中国南方电网有限责任公司(简称"南方电网")生产领域数字化覆盖发电、输电、变电、配电 4 个专业 68 个应用场景 933 个应用环节(见图5-17),输电方面,完成超 130 万千米的三维数字孪生构建,实现超 25 万千米的自动驾驶航线,积累了超 40 万张显卡的人工智能训练样本库,缺陷分析时间由原来的 15～30 天压缩到了目前的小时级;变电方面,实现对变电站的远程自动控制,做到了变电站"无人值守、远程操作",变电站设备操作效率提升了 30%。

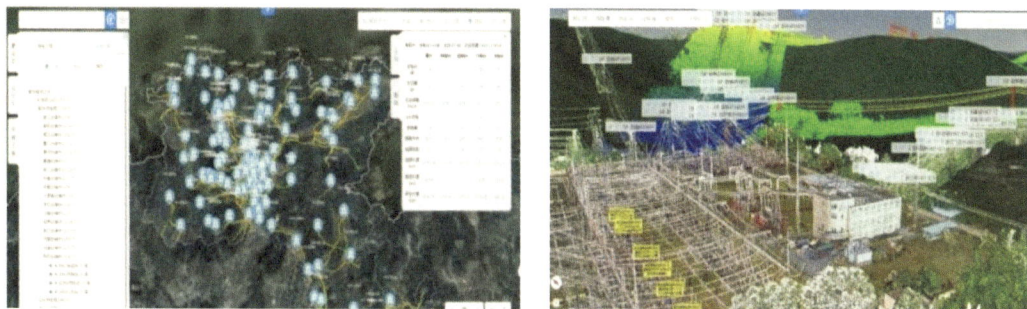

图 5-17　南方电网:110 kV 及以上传输主网的数字孪生

图片来源:南方电网

生产运行智能化。国家电网强化电网调度运行、生产检修等环节的数字化管控,打造了新一代调度技术支持系统,实现了电网运行状态全息感知、源荷资源可观可控和调度业务高效运转,支撑大电网安全运行。国家电网在运检领域推广无人机自主巡检,实现设备巡检图像自动识别,部分地方实现了采用喷火无人机清理电线异物等功能;实施变电站(换流站)智能巡检,在运特高压变电站(换流站)平均巡检时间从人巡的 120 分钟缩短至机巡的 40 分钟,初步形成"机巡为主、人巡为辅"的"机器代人"巡检模式(见图 5-18)。

图 5-18　国家电网:无人机、无人车参与设施运维

图片来源:澎湃新闻(左),国家电网(右)

电力设备自主化。电力芯片为电力行业的发展提供底层核心支撑,是电力控制系统中最关键的部件。目前,中国输电、变电、配电设备中的核心芯片国产化率仍然偏低,但 2013年以来,中国的电力硬件层面的芯片国产化水平不断提升。2019 年底,南方电网研制的"伏羲"芯片样片顺利交付,完全基于国产指令架构和国产内核,综合性能是进口同类产品的

1.5 倍。"伏羲"芯片先后在变电、配电、新能源、边缘计算等领域的近 30 类装置成功应用(见图5-19)。2021 年,深圳有充电桩、电能表、集中器等 8 类共 340 台电力装备使用"伏羲"芯片。

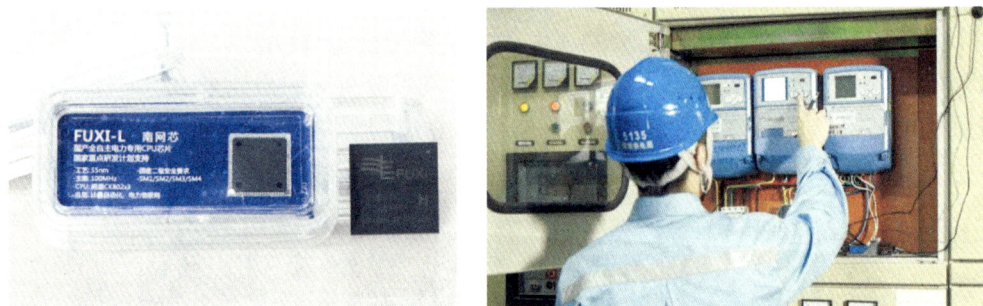

图 5-19　南方电网在电网中应用国产电力专用主控芯片"伏羲"

图片来源:《人民日报》(左),《羊城晚报》(右)

用电服务数字化。国家电网建成全球规模最大的新能源云平台,为新能源规划建设、交易结算等提供一站式服务;建成全球覆盖范围最广、接入充电桩最多、车桩网协同发展的智慧车联网平台,为新能源车主出行提供便捷智能的充换电服务;依托"网上国网"APP、新能源云等线上平台,打造户用光伏建站、并网、结算全流程一站式服务,提升服务客户的能力(见图 5-20)。

图 5-20　"网上国网"APP 可以办理居民光伏发电、新能源电表等业务

图片来源:国家电网(左),宁波发布(中),浙江新闻(右)

5.4　智能交通

1949 年以来,中国一直将交通基础设施列为国家经济建设的基础和重点,建成了全世界规模最大的交通基础设施。截至 2021 年底,中国公路总里程达到 528 万千米,国家高速公路已建成 11.7 万千米,高速公路①里程位居世界第一。截至 2022 年 7 月,以国家高速公路为主体的中国公路网络已经覆盖了 98.8% 的城区人口 20 万以上城市及地级行政中心,连接了全国约 88% 的县级行政区和约 95% 的人口。截至 2022 年底,中国铁路营业里程达到

---

①　高速公路指的是专供汽车分方向、分车道行驶,全部控制出入的多车道公路,限速 60~120 千米/时。

15.5万千米,其中高铁①4.2万千米,高铁里程排名世界第一;累计有53个城市开通了城市轨道交通项目,运营总里程达到9 584千米,其中地铁8 000多千米,地铁里程位居世界第一;内河航道通航里程12.8万千米。2022年,中国水路完成货运量约85.5亿吨,其中长江干线货运量超过30亿吨,连续10余年位居内河航运世界第一;港口完成货物吞吐量156.8亿吨,全球十大港口、十大集装箱港口中中国港口分别占8席、7席。

同时,中国交通基础设施的信息化发展迅速。据《数字中国发展报告(2020年)》,截至2020年底,中国21个省(区、市)开展了公路水路建设和运输市场信用信息服务系统建设,实现了全国高速公路电子不停车收费(ETC)系统联网运行,建成了42个船舶交通管理系统(VTMS)和覆盖沿海、长江干线及其他内河通航水域的船舶自动识别系统(AIS);实现303个地级以上城市交通一卡通互联互通,城市轨道交通大力推动智慧地铁服务,服务人口规模超过3.9亿,全国日均客运量超过4 500万人次;网约车"一键叫车"功能覆盖近300个城市,网约车监管信息交互平台接入超过200家网约车平台,日均订单量达到2 100万单。

2021年12月,交通部印发《数字交通"十四五"发展规划》,提出到2025年实现"交通设施数字感知、信息网络广泛覆盖、运输服务便捷智能、行业治理在线协同、技术应用创新活跃、网络安全保障有力"等六大发展目标。2021年12月,国务院印发《"十四五"现代综合交通运输体系发展规划》,提出到2035年建成便捷顺畅、经济高效、安全可靠、绿色集约、智能先进的现代化高质量国家综合立体交通网。

5.4.1　智慧道路交通

5.4.1.1　公路运营管理

公路是中国道路交通体系中的基础组成部分,是国民经济健康运行的大动脉。据《数字中国发展报告(2020年)》,中国的交通基础设施数字化程度显著提升,公路建筑信息模型广泛应用,智能养护系统加速推广,高速公路实现了收费、通信、监控系统的全覆盖,为高速公路运营管理和车辆安全服务提供全面保障,50%的国省干线公路重点路段、特大桥梁、特长隧道运行状况实现动态监测。截至2021年底,中国公路网密度达到每百平方千米55千米。

道路管理方面。2019年,中国高速公路取消省界收费站,ETC系统实现了全国联网。截至2020年底,中国高速公路电子ETC车道达到6.6万条,ETC用户累计达2.27亿;客车ETC使用率超过70%,货车ETC使用率超过56%;全国高速公路已经拥有2.8万个ETC门架、25万套天线和车牌识别装置,超过1 PB(拍字节)的记录数据积累。2022年,交通运输部路网监测与应急处理中心正在建设全国高速交通路网"交通守望者"综合系统,通过公路监控视频感知交通事件后,回传给路网监测指挥中心,通告临近的ETC门架和交通情报板,及时疏导交通流量。

车辆信息管理方面。交通运输部利用北斗定位增强对特种车辆的管理,2011年8月后新出厂的"两客一危"车辆("两客"是指旅游包车、三类以上班线客车,"一危"指危险化学品运输车)在车辆出厂前应安装北斗卫星定位装置,建成了覆盖全国的"两客一危"重点运营车辆智能化监测平台,对重点车辆运行状态进行动态监测和管理,截至2021年底,已有超过790万辆道路营运车辆安装使用北斗系统。

---

① 高速铁路,简称高铁,指的是支持高速列车运行的封闭式轨道交通系统,运行时速通常在250~350千米/时。

以广东省为例,2021 年 2 月广东省"两客一危一重货"重点车辆智能监控预警融合平台(见图 5-21)正式上线,在全省 40.5 万辆重点车辆上免费安装智能视频监控系统,对驾驶者驾驶行为及车辆运行轨迹(车速、地理位置等)进行监控,识别、预警各类交通危险或者违法行为。2021 年,广东省涉"两客一危"交通事故起数和死亡人数与 2020 年同期相比分别下降了 62.87％和 59.26％。

图 5-21　广东省"两客一危一重货"重点车辆智能监控预警融合平台应用场景
图片来源:《羊城晚报》(左),南方新闻网(右)

5.4.1.2　智能网联汽车

中国从 20 世纪 80 年代开始进行无人驾驶汽车的研究。根据自动化程度,自动驾驶分为 L1—L5 共 5 个级别。L2 级别在驾驶者监视下可以实现部分功能自动化(例如自适应巡航、车道保持、自动刹车辅助、自动泊车)。L4 级别为高度自动驾驶,系统完成所有驾驶操作,特定环境下系统会向驾驶者提出响应请求,驾驶者可以对系统请求不进行响应。

到 2022 年 11 月,中国具备 L2 级别智能辅助驾驶功能的车辆的销售量已经超过了 800 万辆,渗透率达到 33％左右;L4 级别自动驾驶的实际道路测试里程超过 4 000 万千米。2013 年,百度开始研发无人驾驶汽车。百度无人驾驶汽车依托交通场景物体识别技术和环境感知技术,实现高精度车辆探测、识别、跟踪、距离和速度估计、路面分割、车道线检测。2015 年 12 月,百度无人驾驶汽车在中国首次实现城市、环路及高速道路混合路况下的全自动驾驶。2019 年,百度和中国第一汽车集团有限公司(简称"中国一汽")联手打造的中国首批量产 L4 级别自动驾驶乘用车,车辆顶端搭载一个激光雷达采集车身周围的数据,其有效探测距离可以达到 240 米。2020 年 10 月,百度自动驾驶出租车服务在北京全面开放。

智能网联汽车利用现代通信和网络技术,在车上装载传感器,从而实现对复杂环境的感知,若路端也加装相应的传感器及通信设备,则可以实现车端和路端的信息共享;车上的计算单元实现信息融合、智能决策,执行器按照计算单元发出的指令执行相应动作,使汽车在高效节能的情况下安全行驶,实现汽车的智能化操控。

2021 年 7 月,工业和信息化部、公安部、交通运输部联合印发《智能网联汽车道路测试与示范应用管理规范(试行)》。截至 2021 年 8 月,中国建成 16 个智能网联汽车测试示范区,开放 3 500 多千米测试道路,发放 700 余张测试牌照,道路测试总里程超过 700 万千米。以武汉市为例,国家智能网联汽车(武汉)测试示范区(见图 5-22)于 2019 年 9 月揭牌,规划测试道路 159 千米,覆盖居住区、商业区、物流区、旅游风景区和工业区,采用"5G＋北斗"车路协同网络,建成中国最先进的 V2X 车路协同测试区域,时延达到毫秒级、定位精度达到厘米级,在道路沿线开通自动驾驶公交示范运营线路,并布设物流末端无人派送、无人清扫、智慧停车等示范应用场景。

图 5-22　国家智能网联汽车(武汉)测试示范区

图片来源:《湖北日报》

5.4.2　智能轨道交通

5.4.2.1　智慧高铁

中国政府将高铁作为重要的国家公共交通基础设施进行建设。中国幅员辽阔,在改革开放的过程中沿海地区率先发展起来,但是各地经济发展不均衡,尤其是中部、西部、东北等地区的经济发展相对滞后。高铁作为大运力、长距离的交通工具,可以缩短各地的时空距离,有利于将分散于各地的禀赋资源进行有效链接,加速物流、人流、信息流、资金流的整合。

目前,中国已建成"四纵四横"的庞大高铁网络,高铁里程居世界第一,高铁通达约95%的50万人口以上城市,在多个大城市周边形成了"小时经济圈"。2016年7月,国家发展改革委印发《中长期铁路网规划》,明确提出构筑"八纵八横"高速铁路主通道。预计到2026年左右,"八纵八横"通道将基本建成。2020年,中国提出新基建计划,将城市高速铁路、城市轨道交通等交通基础设施列入新基建内容,并提出建设智能交通基础设施。伴随着中国高铁网络的建设,中国在路网建设、高铁列车智能化方面也取得了显著进展。

在高铁建设方面,京张高铁是世界上第一条按照智能化理念进行设计的高铁(见图5-23)。京张高铁工程面向2020年北京冬奥会的需求,连接北京市和张家口市。该工程于2016年4月开工建设,2019年12月开通运营,正线全长174千米,最高设计速度为350千米/时。京张高铁是一项庞大复杂的系统性工程,参与专业多,协调难度大。为此,京张高铁采用了建筑信息模型(BIM)、大数据、人工智能、北斗卫星导航、5G等新一代信息技术,对京张高铁建造、装备和运营技术进行智能化创新,构建了基于BIM的多专业协同设计平台,自主开发了测绘、线路、桥梁、隧道、路基、接触网、信号等多个专业BIM协同设计软件,节省了约8%的协调联络时间和3%的材料费用。

在高铁列车智能化方面,京张高铁实现了动车组的智能化。新型动车系统集成了智能复合传感器、车地信息实时传输、大数据挖掘与分析、自动化控制、信息智能处理、故障预测与健康管理等技术,实现了智能行车、智能运维(监控点多达2 718个)、智能服务、安全监测(新增走行部振动监测点168个)。通过在CTCS-3级列控系统的基础上增加列车自动驾驶(ATO)相关设备实现列车自动驾驶(见图5-24),在车站股道增加地面精确定位应答器实现列车自动精确对标停车,实现了车站自动发车、区间自动运行、自动停车、自动开门、车门与站台门联动。京张高铁创造了世界上首次350千米/时的动车组自动驾驶纪录。

图 5-23　京张高铁：高铁工程的智能建造

图片来源：WANG TJ，The intelligent Beijing-Zhangjiakou high-speed railway，
Engineering，2021，7(12)：1665-1672

图 5-24　京张高铁：高铁列车的自动驾驶

图片来源：央视网

5.4.2.2　智慧地铁

伴随着城市化的发展，中国城市人口不断增加，城市交通压力日益显著。根据 2021 年第七次全国人口普查结果，中国常住人口超过 500 万的特大城市有 21 个，其中北京、上海、广州等 7 个城市的人口超过 1 000 万。中国人口密度高的城市主要集中在长三角、珠三角、京津等地区，其中排名前八的城市的人口密度均超过 2 000 人/平方千米。地铁是城市综合立体交通体系的重要组成部分，也是缓解大城市交通压力的重要手段。根据交通运输部的数据，截至 2022 年底，中国有 53 个城市开通运营了城市轨道交通 290 条，运营总里程约 9 584 千米。伴随着地铁建设与发展，中国各地开始探索综合运用各类信息技术改善地铁运营和管理的数字化水平。

传统地铁采用单线运营、人工管理的模式。智慧车站则可以打通地铁各专业之间的壁垒，实现设备之间的联动，并在地铁车站构建智能综控平台。以北京地铁国家重点研发计划项目"超大城市轨道交通系统高效运输与安全服务关键技术"示范应用工程为例，项目将依托北斗、5G、空间数字化等新兴技术,将北京首都国际机场线打造成为中国首条全场景化的智慧地铁示范线路。站内系统数据接入了气象数据,可以实时接收天气预警信息,车站的智能监测设备可以对站外雨量和水位进行监测(见图 5-25),遇到险情时,还能够自动启动相应设备,应对现场突发情况。通过北斗定位+多制式导航系统验证,乘客未来可以通过北京地铁 APP、小程序等,在北京首都国际机场线享受精准的位置查询、路径规划等服务,缩短进站时间,提高出行效率。

图 5-25 北京地铁实现天气感知和客户流量调度

图片来源:《北京青年报》

5.4.3 智能水运交通

与公路和铁路等陆地运输相比,水运具有运量大、成本低、能耗少、污染小的比较优势,是中国加快运输结构调整、推进交通运输绿色低碳转型的主攻方向。港口与航道作为水运这种交通方式的重要组成部分,是国家综合立体交通网的重要枢纽和重要通道。

中国构建了以沿海运输通道、长江干线、西江航运干线、京杭运河、淮河干流等为水运主要通道,以主要港口为枢纽,衔接铁路、公路、管道等方式,连通世界、干支衔接的水运基础设施体系。水运承担了大量的中国境内跨区域货物运输和约 95% 的外贸物资运输。

5.4.3.1 数字航道

截至 2021 年底,中国港口拥有生产用码头泊位 20 867 个,万吨级及以上泊位 2 659 个,内河航道通航里程 12.76 万千米,其中三级及以上航道通航里程 1.45 万千米,拥有水上运输船舶 12.59 万艘。长江是中国水上交通最繁忙的航道,长江货运量已连续多年位居世界内河之首。

"数字长江"建设不断推进,成效初显。2019 年 9 月 30 日,长江干道数字航道全面联通,正式运行,实现了对长江 2 687.8 千米干线航道的航标、水情、控制河段、航道尺度等信息的动态监测。以长江航运综合信息(公共服务)平台移动端长江电子航道图、长江航道综合服务信息系统(门户网站)为载体的航道维护管理平台、航道动态监测平台、航道应急指挥平台"一图一站三平台"先后建立(见图 5-26)。长江航道管理服务方式正在由传统人工模式向数字化模式转型,实现了"远程看、精细管、走着用"。

5.4.3.2 智慧港口

中国是全球海运连接度最高的国家(已与 100 多个国家和地区的主要港口建立了海运航线联系),在全球航运、物流体系中的枢纽地位不断提升。在全球港口货物吞吐量、集装箱

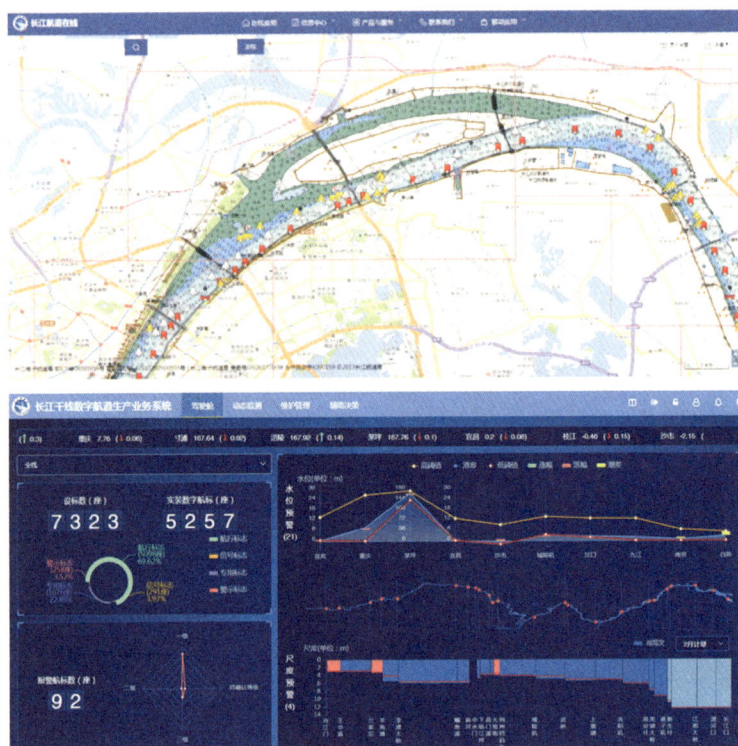

图 5-26　长江干线数字航道的水情与航运监测

图片来源:长江航道局(上),长江航道(下)

吞吐量前十名的港口当中,中国分别占了 8 席和 7 席。上海港、宁波舟山港、深圳港的集装箱吞吐量连续多年位居前列。2021 年,中国港口完成货物吞吐量 155.5 亿吨,比 2020 年增长 6.8%,确保了"出口货物出得去、进口货物进得来"。

港口物流信息化持续深入。经过多年的建设发展,中国沿海专业化码头装卸作业效率、百米岸线完成集装箱吞吐量均处于世界领先水平。中国基本形成"货运一单制、信息一网通"的港口物流运作体系,区块链电子放货平台加快应用。中、日、韩三国 19 个主要港口间实现集装箱船舶和集装箱动态信息交换。海上国际集装箱运输全部实现电子数据交换(EDI),并纳入国际贸易"单一窗口"体系。

集装箱自动化码头建设成效显著。中国已建成了厦门远海、青岛前湾等多个全自动化集装箱码头,其中上海洋山深水港四期自动化码头(见图 5-27)是世界上智能化程度最高的集装箱码头。上海国际港务(集团)股份有限公司自主研发的全自动化码头智能生产管控系统和上海振华重工(集团)股份有限公司自主研发的设备管理控制系统组成了这个全新码头的"大脑"与"神经"。由锂电池驱动的自动导引车实现了无人驾驶、自动导航、路径优化等功能。上海洋山深水港四期自动化码头的 100 多台轨道吊和 160 多部自动导引车,可以在无人干预的情况下每天 24 小时不间歇地装货、卸货,吊装精度达毫米级,显著提升了港口的运作效率。上海洋山深水港四期自动化码头的昼夜吞吐量可达到 20 823.25 标准箱,人均劳动生产率为传统码头的 213%。

图 5-27　上海洋山深水港四期自动化码头的监控室和无人自动导引车

图片来源：上观新闻（左），新华社（右）

5.5　小　　结

长期以来，中国高度重视发挥信息技术对传统产业发展的推动效能，先后提出"以信息化带动工业化""推动信息化和工业化深度融合"等发展理念。自"十三五"时期以来，中国依据国情和时代发展需求，精心制定科学的发展规划与战略，积极推动制造业、农业、能源和交通等重点产业的数字化转型与升级发展。

制造业领域，中国作为拥有完备工业体系的"世界工厂"，在全球制造业版图中占据重要位置。当前，中国正积极应对向环境友好型高端制造业转型的挑战，大力推动工业互联网、工业机器人、5G等新技术在制造业的落地应用。在电子设备制造、装备制造、钢铁冶炼等行业，智能工厂不断涌现，有效提升了生产效率，优化了产品质量，为全球制造业的转型升级提供了中国范例。

农业领域，中国已实现主粮自给自足，有力保障了国家粮食安全。然而，人均农业资源相对不足仍是中国面临的难题。为此，中国构建了多个面向农业的大数据系统，实现了灾害预警、市场监测、产品追溯等功能。在农业种植领域，无人机、无人农机和物联网技术广泛应用，既提升了大型农场的作业效率，又提高了小型农场的作业精度。在畜牧和渔业领域，机器人、物联网技术的应用实现了智能化监测和数字化管理，为农业现代化发展注入新动力。

能源领域，中国是全球最大的能源生产国和消费国，积极践行应对气候变化的责任，向世界宣告碳达峰、碳中和目标。中国加速能源产业数字化、智能化发展。在智能煤矿领域，实现信息基础设施升级，自动驾驶和设备互联取得突破；智慧电厂建设推动火电、风电等领域智能化转型；智能电网建设有效缓解了能源供需地域不平衡问题，在电网可视化、智能化运营以及电力设备国产化等方面取得了显著成效。

交通领域，中国构建起世界上规模最大的交通基础设施网络。为进一步提升交通运输质量和效率，中国大力发展智能交通。在智能公路交通方面，道路设施数字化管理水平显著提升，ETC系统全面普及，智能网联汽车、自动驾驶等技术实现了规模化应用，处于全球领先方阵。在智能轨道交通方面，高铁智能化建设成果显著，地铁运营管理数字化持续推进。在智能水运交通方面，数字航道建设和港口智能化发展成效显著，提升了水运效率和服务质量。

　　实现传统产业数字化转型与升级,是世界各国面临的共同挑战。在产业数字化进程中,中国充分发挥国有企业的引领带动作用,通过开展示范项目,促进新技术广泛应用;持续加强产业数字基础设施建设,搭建行业平台,完善监管体系。中国传统产业数字化转型成果,不仅推动了自身经济高质量发展,更为全球产业数字化发展贡献了中国智慧和中国方案。

6 数 字 社 会

数字社会是以数字化技术深度融入社会运行和生活方式为特征的新型社会形态。根据 2023 年发布的《数字中国建设整体布局规划》,数字社会的建设内容包括数字公共服务普惠化、数字社会治理精准化、数字生活智能化等。本章介绍中国近年来在智慧城市、数字乡村、智慧教育、智慧医疗等方面取得的成就。

6.1 智 慧 城 市

中国是世界上的人口大国,目前中国人口主要集中在城市。中国的城镇化率从 2003 年开始进入 40％区位,2011 年达到 51.27％,这标志着中国开始进入以城市型社会为主体的时代。目前,中国 100 万人口以上的城市有 300 多个,按照 1.2％的年均增速,2030 年中国城镇化率将达 70％。密集人口在城市的聚集,对于城市交通、市政、水电等各项基础设施提出了巨大的挑战,通过数字化、信息化建设智慧城市是破解上述问题的重要手段。

中国将智慧城市视为城市信息化建设的高级阶段。2013 年 1 月,科技部和国家标准化管理委员会下发通知,将在 20 个城市开展智慧城市试点示范工作;住房城乡建设部公布了90 个首批国家智慧城市试点名单。2014 年,《关于促进智慧城市健康发展的指导意见》发布;2017 年,《智慧城市技术参考模型》《智慧城市评价模型及基础评价指标体系》等国家标准发布。截至 2018 年 8 月,中国 100％的副省级以上城市[①]、76％以上的地级市和 32％以上的县级市,总计大约 500 个城市已经明确提出或者正在建设新型智慧城市。

6.1.1 城市交通管控

城市交通是城市运营管理的主要内容之一。中国 400 多个城市建成了集接处警、信息采集、交通控制等功能于一体的智能化交通指挥控制中心,建设了交通信号控制、交通诱导、交通监控、电子警察等重点系统。北京、上海、广州、深圳等特大城市建成了交通运行协调指挥中心(TOCC),对综合交通运行状态进行智能化监测、运行协调和指挥调度,实现了城市道路交通、轨道、民航以及城市停车、公交等的综合协调管理与服务。

公共交通综合监测平台成果显著。以深圳市为例,改革开放以来,深圳从一个 3 万多人的边陲小镇,发展成为面积 1 997 平方千米、常住人口 1 756.01 万、车辆密度全国第一(每千

---

① 在统计时,常把中国的城市划分为 4 类,包括直辖市(例如北京、上海)、副省级城市(例如广州、深圳、武汉等)、地级市、县级市。

米道路车辆密度超 500 辆)、港口集装箱吞吐量全国第三的超大规模超高密度城市。深圳建成全国首个涵盖海陆空铁全领域的综合交通运行指挥中心(见图 6-1),全市 2 700 多个灯控路口信号灯,联网率达 98%,实现配时优化人员投入减少 70%,人工巡查工作量降低 30% 以上,超过 700 个路口大规模部署智能信控,交通运行管控效能大幅提升。2020 年,深圳早高峰道路运行车速达 27.1 千米/时,交通运行效率在一线城市保持最优,万车死亡率降至 0.62 人/万车。

面向个人的公共交通数据服务日益普及。基于海量移动终端定位信息,手机导航应用程序可以估计实时交通状态。例如,百度地图慧眼融合了位置增强数据、实时卫星轨道数据、道路数据、卫星信号、手机传感器数据五大数据源,实现全国超 380 个城市交通动态数据的分钟级实时更新,位置精度可达车道级别(见图 6-2)。截至 2021 年底,百度地图日均位置服务请求突破 1 300 亿次,道路覆盖里程超 1 100 万千米,服务超过 60 万个移动应用程序。

图 6-1　深圳城市交通管理:综合交通运行指挥中心

图片来源:深圳市综合交通运行指挥中心

图 6-2　百度地图慧眼:城市通勤大数据与车流迁徙态势感知

图片来源:百度地图

6.1.2　城市大脑

城市大脑的概念由中国首次创新提出,是中国为全世界城市发展做出的有益探索。城市大脑是互联网大脑架构与智慧城市建设相结合的产物,是城市级的类脑复杂智能巨系统。2016 年 3 月在杭州市政府主导下,城市大脑启动;2016 年 10 月,在杭州云栖大会上,城市大脑 1.0 版发布。城市大脑可以提高城市运行效率,解决城市运行中面临的复杂问题。目前产业界、学术界,以及经济社会发展各个领域对城市大脑的认识尚未统一,例如有的从城市交通角度着手,有的从城市安防角度展开,有的从城市人工智能中枢角度切入,还有的从城市类脑结构角度进行分析,对城市大脑的研究和应用角度不一,成果各异。

2020年11月,国家信息中心信息化和产业发展部在"全球智慧城市大会"提出"城市大脑的核心是基于万物感知、全面互联、数字孪生而形成数据驱动的人工智能中枢平台"。2020年12月,城市大脑全球标准研究组、中国科学院虚拟经济与数据科学研究中心、中国国家创新与发展战略研究会数字治理研究中心联合发布《城市大脑全球标准研究报告》,提出了城市大脑全球标准的9个研究方向,关于城市大脑的研究不断深入。截至2020年,城市大脑已经覆盖了杭州、苏州、海口等10余个城市,中国近500个城市启动了城市大脑建设计划,建设资金达数百亿元。

杭州作为首个尝鲜的城市,自2016年10月开始与阿里云合作,率先将城市大脑应用于城市交通、应急救援和公共安全领域(见图6-3)。截至2017年,城市大脑接管了杭州128个信号灯路口,试点区域通行时间缩短15.3%,主城区高架道路出行时间节省4.6分钟;在杭州主城区,城市大脑日均事件报警500次以上,准确率达92%;在杭州萧山区,120救护车到达现场用时缩短一半。

图6-3　杭州城市大脑:城市交通与公共安全领域
图片来源:人民政协网

6.1.3　数字孪生城市

数字孪生指将物理实体镜像映射到虚拟空间,生成一个"数字双胞胎"。数字孪生城市利用物联网技术、地理信息技术以及智能建筑城市模型等,将物理城市转化为虚拟数字城市模型,通过模型模拟运营,实现预测、分析、优化等功能。数字孪生城市将虚拟和现实结合起来,在数字化、信息化的基础上将物理实体与对应孪生体重叠,实现虚实互动。

2021年6月,住房和城乡建设部印发《城市信息模型(CIM)基础平台技术导则》(修订版),从技术实施层面加强数字孪生城市"三维数字底板"建设规范指引。上海、浙江、河北雄安新区等地加快打造城市级CIM基础平台,探索部署数字孪生应用试点。

上海试运营了基于数字孪生技术的城市综合管理系统,初步实现"一网统管"(见图6-4)。上海的"一网统管"系统整合接入公共安全、绿化市容、住房和城乡建设、交通、应急、生态环境、卫生健康等领域,支持跨部门、跨系统的联勤联动、增效赋能。截至2022年,上海市城市运行中心已经接入72个部门(单位)的220个系统和一批数字孪生应用场景,并不断总结提升,积极推广数字孪生在基础设施、历史建筑、社区、文旅、教育、医疗、应急、消防等领域的应用,在城市安全、城市运行、创新引领等方面打造一批独具特色的数字孪生应用场景。上海以一栋楼为城市最小管理单元,提出城市智能体的概念,探索城市数字化治理转型创新实践。

图 6-4 上海数字孪生城市：基于城市智能体的数字化治理
图片来源：网信上海

6.2 数字乡村

从世界各国的现代化历史来看，伴随着工业化和城市化的发展，很多国家的乡村人口下滑、乡村经济衰落，导致了社会动荡。乡村地区往往地广人稀，建设公共交通、信息网络、医疗保健等基础设施的成本高、收益慢。中国作为社会主义国家，十分重视现代化进程中的城乡关系问题，吸取和借鉴西方国家在城乡发展过程中的经验，提出"乡村振兴"的战略。

中国在"十四五"规划中提出"强化以工补农、以城带乡，推动形成工农互促、城乡互补、协调发展、共同繁荣的新型工农城乡关系，加快农业农村现代化"。中国将建设数字乡村作为推进乡村振兴、促进城乡融合发展的重要途径。

6.2.1 农村网络基础设施

6.2.1.1 "村村通"工程

改革开放以来，中国信息通信业大踏步、跨越式发展，但是农村尤其是"老少边穷"地区通信发展矛盾日益突出。2003 年，中国 69.5 万个行政村中还有近 8 万个没有通电话。为解决农村通信发展难题，2004 年 1 月，信息产业部出台《农村通信普遍服务——村通工程实施方案》(简称"村村通"工程)，要求基础电信运营企业采取分片包干、自筹资金、自行经营维护的方式，承担农村及偏远地区的通信网络建设。"村村通"工程分为三个阶段实施：第一阶段(2004—2005 年)实现全国 95％以上的行政村通电话；第二阶段(2006—2010 年)基本实现全国"村村通电话，乡乡能上网"；第三阶段(2011—2015 年)基本实现行政村"村村通宽带"。

在偏远农村地区进行通信网络建设，面临很多困难。一方面，偏远农村地区大多地理位置偏僻、气候条件严酷、自然灾害频发，工程施工难度非常大，时常遇到工程建设极端难题和人类工作极限问题。另一方面，农村地区整体经济相对落后，地广人稀，无论光纤网络还是移动通信基站，建设投资和后续运营成本都非常高，而且用户数量较少，市场收益很低。根据估算，在"三区三州"①每个行政村通光纤的成本平均是东中部地区的 4 倍，每个基站的建设成本平均是东中部地区的 3.3 倍，在部分偏远地区，建设成本达到了东中部地区的约 10 倍。

---

① "三区"是指西藏自治区、新疆维吾尔自治区南疆四地州和四川省、云南省、甘肃省、青海省涉藏州县；"三州"是指四川省凉山彝族自治州、云南省怒江傈僳族自治州和甘肃省临夏回族自治州。这些地区地理条件恶劣，经济发展滞后，被列为国家级贫困地区。

作为全球人口数量最多的发展中国家,中国发挥集中力量办大事的制度优势,举国攻坚、政企联动,由国有电信运营企业采用"分片包干"的方法推进"村村通"工程,将电信普遍服务需要的资金分摊给当年的中国电信、中国网通、中国移动、中国联通、中国卫通、中国铁通这6家电信运营企业。各企业分摊的比例,与其收入和利润分别占所有电信运营企业收入与利润的比例一致,利润和收入的权重各为50%。

经过10余年的推进,"村村通"工程阶段性目标基本完成,农村通信能力建设和服务水平显著改善,通信普遍服务内容逐步从话音业务扩展到互联网业务。2014年底,"村村通"工程年度任务超额完成,电信普遍服务取得新进展,全国通宽带行政村比例达到93.5%,20户以上自然村通电话比例达到95.8%,完成3 000余个乡镇和15万多个行政村宽带建设,1.8万个特困村实现互联网覆盖,6 400所农村学校和公益机构通宽带。

6.2.1.2 网络扶贫行动计划

2012年,中国开始实施脱贫攻坚工程,拟解决全国约1.22亿农村人口的贫困问题。继"村村通"工程之后,一场世所未见、席卷神州的网络扶贫攻坚战全面打响。网络扶贫的目标是,把最先进的光纤宽带、4G网络通到贫困村,实现农村城市同网同速。

2015年10月14日,国务院常务会议决定,加大中央财政投入,引导地方强化政策和资金支持,鼓励基础电信企业、广电企业和民间资本通过竞争性招标等公平参与农村宽带建设和运行维护,同时探索PPP、委托运营等市场化方式调动各类主体参与积极性。

2016年中央网信办、国家发展改革委、国务院扶贫开发领导小组办公室联合印发的《网络扶贫行动计划》中提出,网络扶贫工程包括网络覆盖工程、农村电商工程、网络扶智工程、信息服务工程、网络公益工程五大工程。其中,网络覆盖工程,也就是电信普遍服务试点工程,涉及的建设任务大多是"村村通"工程剩下的最难啃的"硬骨头",主要分布在高山峡谷人迹罕至的偏远地区(见图6-5)。

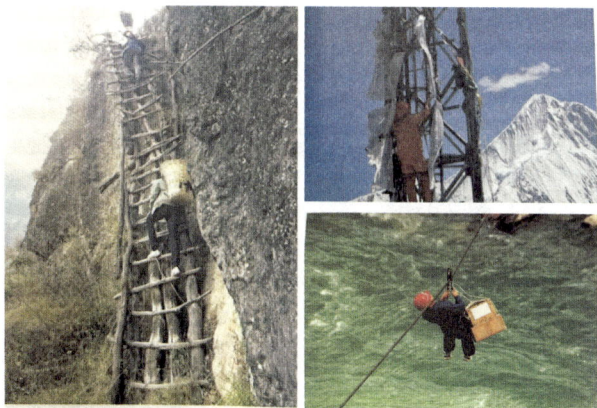

图6-5 网络扶贫:通信网络铺设的恶劣条件

图片来源:倪光南主编,《中国科技之路·信息卷·智联万物》,2021年

电信运营企业等行业中坚全力以赴,上百万通信人日夜奋战,创造了农村通信覆盖的世界奇迹——截至2020年,中国连续实施了6批电信普遍服务试点工程,覆盖全国27个省(区、市),完成了13万个行政村的光纤网络和5万个农村的4G基站建设任务,其中包括4.3万个贫困村的光纤网络和1.5万个贫困村的4G基站建设,中国行政村通光纤、通4G的比

例均超过 98%,农村光纤宽带平均下载速率超过 100 Mbps,基本实现农村、城市"同网同速",提前超额完成《"十三五"脱贫攻坚规划》提出的"宽带网络覆盖 90% 以上的贫困村"的目标。曾经与世隔绝的大山深处建起了比肩城市的信息高速路,越来越多偏远地区的群众共享到了信息时代的数字红利,走上了脱贫致富奔小康的幸福大道。

在网络扶贫行动计划实施过程中,中国国有电信运营商投入巨大。截至 2019 年,中国电信累计在农村地区投入超过 1 000 亿元,实现了全国乡镇 4G 网络覆盖率 100%,91% 以上的行政村通宽带,全国乡镇光纤宽带覆盖率 90%;中国移动累计投入超 800 亿元,实现了 12.2 万个自然村通电话、84 万个行政村通宽带,全国行政村 4G 覆盖率超过 98%;中国联通对全国超 9 万个乡镇实现网络 100% 覆盖,行政村覆盖总量已超 46 万个。

中国电信、中国移动、中国联通推出了大规模让利行动,让偏远地区的群众不仅用得上宽带网络,还用得起、用得好。2020 年,中国电信在全国 3.5 万个营业点上线扶贫套餐,2019 年以来累计让利超 19 亿元,建设精准扶贫大数据管理平台,服务 17 个省(区、市)3 900 万贫困群众;中国移动面向贫困群众推出大幅优惠的专享"扶贫套餐"和购机补贴,累计惠及建档立卡贫困户 1 400 余万人,让利 30 亿元,并向贫困地区群众捐赠自有品牌手机等终端设备;中国联通为贫困地区提供资费优惠,推出专属优惠套餐超过 150 款,累计减免通信费用 3.67 亿元,帮助超过 40 万贫困户成功脱贫。2016—2020 年中国行政村光纤网络和 4G 网络覆盖情况如图 6-6 所示。

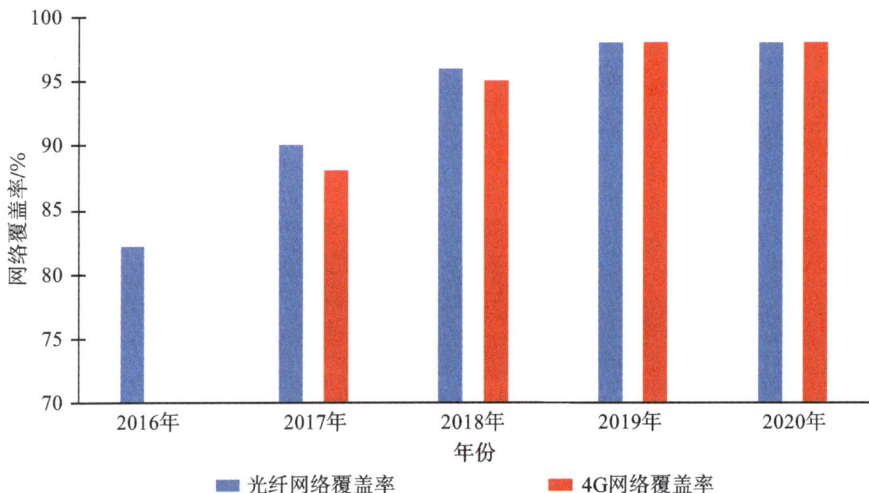

图 6-6　2016—2020 年中国行政村光纤网络和 4G 网络覆盖情况

数据来源:工业和信息化部

通过系列农村网络基础设施建设,中国城乡之间的数字鸿沟逐步缩小。2021 年中国行政村实现"村村通宽带",全国行政村通宽带比例达到 100%,通光纤、通 4G 的比例均超过 99%,基本实现农村城市同网同速。5G 加速向农村延伸,截至 2022 年,中国已累计建成并开通 5G 基站 196.8 万个,5G 网络覆盖所有地级市城区、县城城区和 96% 的乡镇镇区,实现"县县通 5G"。截至 2021 年,中国农村居民平均每百户接入互联网移动电话 229 部,比 2020 年增长 4.4%。截至 2022 年 6 月,中国农村互联网用户规模达 2.93 亿人,农村互联网普及率达到 58.8%,与"十三五"初期相比,城乡互联网普及率差距缩小近 15 个百分点。

6.2.2 农村电子商务

中国政府将发展农村电商作为发展农村数字经济的主要手段。各级政府发起和组织了不同类型的农村电商促进活动,例如"互联网＋"农产品出村进城工程、"数商兴农"工程、"大国农匠"全国农民技能大赛等。近年来,商务部等部门持续推进电子商务进农村工作,取得了显著成效,截至 2023 年,安排中央财政资金 200 多亿元,累计支持 1 489 个县,建设 2 600 多个县级电商公共服务中心和物流配送中心,超过 15 万个乡村电商和快递服务站点。中国快递服务不断向乡村基层延伸,2021 年,"快递进村"比例超过 80%,农村地区收投快递包裹总量达 370 亿件。

截至 2021 年底,中国 36.3% 的市级以上重点农业龙头企业通过电商开展销售,利用电商销售的农产品加工企业营业收入比上年增长 10.8%。电子商务助力脱贫地区农产品销售,为防止规模性返贫发挥着重要作用。2022 年,中国农村网上零售额达 2.17 万亿元,比2021 年增长 3.6%。2016—2022 年中国农村网上零售额如图 6-7 所示。

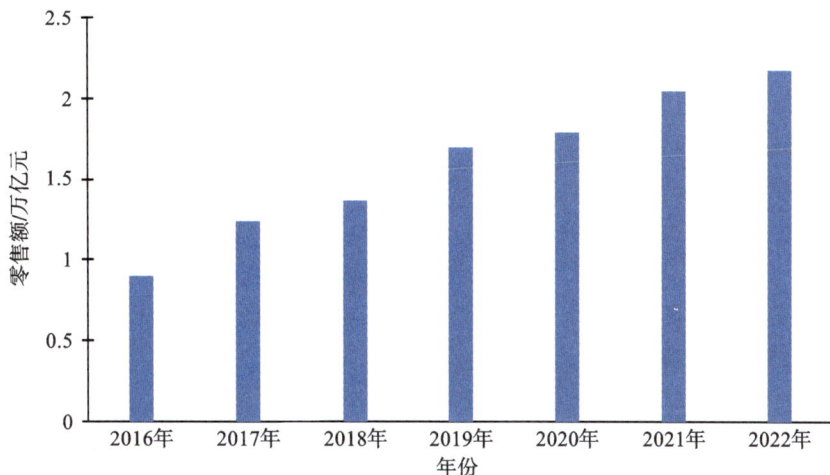

图 6-7 2016—2022 年中国农村网上零售额
数据来源:商务部

直播带货成为农村电子商务的靓丽风景线。2019 年,在国家发展改革委地区振兴司、国家广播电视总局公共服务司等有关部委的组织下,阿里巴巴集团的淘宝平台推出了"村播计划",针对农民在线直播、线上流量管理等技能进行培训。至 2021 年 9 月,该计划累计孵化农民主播 11 万余人,助农直播超 230 万场,覆盖全国 31 个省(区、市)的 2 000 多个县域,带动农产品销售超 50 亿,带动 20 多万人就业。

"淘宝村"发展迅速,它是对农村电商区域性集聚现象的一种指称。淘宝村的统计标准有三个:(1)经营场所。在农村地区,以行政村为单元。(2)销售规模。全村电子商务年销售额达到 1 000 万元。(3)网商规模。本村活跃网店数量达到 100 家,或活跃网店数量达到当地家庭户数的 10%。从 2009 年首批 3 个淘宝村出现至今,淘宝村实现了裂变式增长。截至2022 年淘宝村已经覆盖全国 28 个省(区、市)和 180 个市(地区),数量达到 7 780 个(见图6-8)。淘宝村的出现及其数量的增加,代表着以行政村为单元的基层电子商务规模化经营水平不断提升,吸引越来越多的人才扎根农村沃土,促进农村产业兴旺。

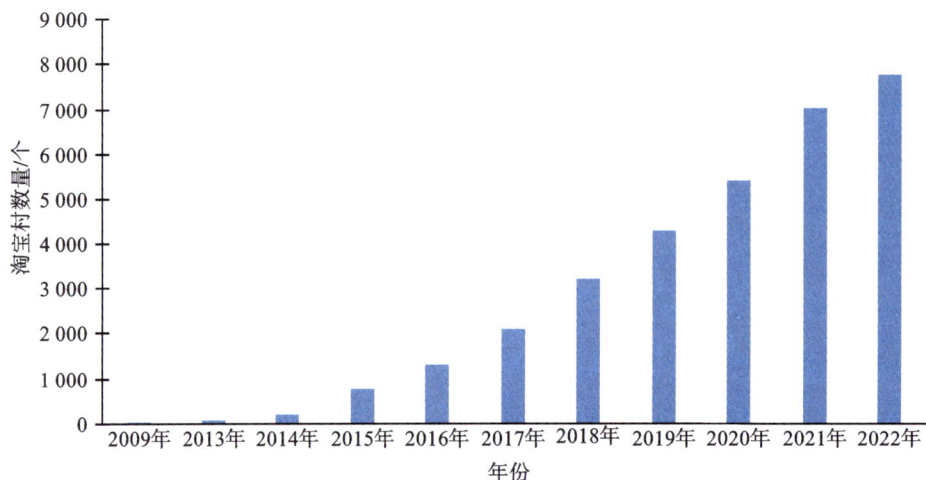

图 6-8　2009—2022 年中国淘宝村数量变化
数据来源:商务部

以淘宝村为代表的农村电子商务也成了中国政府在农村地区消除贫困的重要方式之一。以山东省菏泽市为例,推广"电商扶贫"模式,与阿里、京东等电商平台深化合作,开展淘宝店铺运营技巧提升、新媒体运营、直播带货等精准培训。截至 2018 年 11 月,菏泽市在 563个贫困村发展电商,受益贫困群众 2.5 万余人,其中 43 个贫困村发展为淘宝村并实现整村脱贫。2019 年 10 月,菏泽市扶贫开发办公室荣获 2019 年全国脱贫攻坚奖组织创新奖。2019 年 11 月,世界银行、阿里巴巴集团及中国国际发展知识中心发布《电子商务发展:来自中国的经验》。该报告肯定了网商首创精神是淘宝村发展最基本、最根本的动力,希望淘宝村的经验在中部和西部地区得到更广泛的传播和应用,从而能够改变更多落后村镇的状况,也希望能够在广大发展中国家复制、扩散淘宝村的经验。

互联网技术和信息化手段助力乡村旅游、休闲农业、民宿经济加快发展。截至 2022 年 9月,农业农村部通过官方网站发布推介乡村休闲旅游精品景点线路 70 余次,覆盖全国 31 个省(区、市)148 个县(市、区)的 211 条乡村休闲旅游线路;利用"想去乡游"小程序推介乡村休闲旅游精品线路 681 条,涵盖 2 500 多个精品景点等优质资源。返乡入乡创业就业快速增长,2021 年中国返乡入乡创业人员达到 1 120 万人,较 2020 年增长 10.9%。

6.2.3　农村公共服务

农村基层综合治理水平不断提高。"互联网＋基层社会治理"行动深入实施,各地积极推进基层社会治理数据资源建设和开放共享,截至 2021 年底,中国利用信息化手段开展基本公共服务和公共事业服务的村级综合服务站点共 48.3 万个,行政村覆盖率达到 86.0%。2021 年,公共安全视频图像应用系统行政村覆盖率达到 80.4%,特别是在农村水域安装水位临界报警监控和全景监控,防范溺水意外事故成效明显。依托儿童福利管理信息系统,摸清农村地区关爱服务对象底数,2021 年 7 月至 2022 年 6 月共采集 75.5 万留守儿童信息,农村地区儿童福利和未成年人保护工作精准化程度进一步提升。

"三农"信息服务更加便捷深化。截至 2021 年底,中国共建成运营益农信息社 46.7 万个,累计提供各类信息服务 9.8 亿人次。农技服务从田间地头走到云端线上,12316 热线电话、全国农业科教云平台等为农服务方式不断创新。截至 2022 年 8 月，全国农业科教云平台注册用户超过 1 300 万人，累计访问超过 35 亿次，日均服务超过 400 万人次，在线提问解答率保持在 92％以上。据监测，2021 年中国接受信息化农技推广服务的新型农业经营主体（包括农民合作社和家庭农场）共计 223.3 万个。

农村网络文化生活精彩纷呈。互联网成为大家参与、体验中国农民丰收节的重要渠道。2022 年，中央广播电视总台打造首台沉浸式网络丰收节晚会《2022 网络丰晚》。"互联网＋"群众文化活动蓬勃兴起，2022 年元旦、春节期间，国家公共文化云平台推出线上"村晚"专题，直播各地精选"村晚"127 场，线上参与达 1.48 亿人次。贵州省台江县台盘村村民自发组织的"六月六"苗族吃新节篮球赛火爆出圈，被网友们亲切地称为"村 BA"，相关网络直播及短视频全网传播，线上观众超过 1 亿人次（见图 6-9）。

图 6-9　贵州省台江县台盘村"村 BA"直播
图片来源：天眼新闻，新华社，央视新闻，央视频

数字技术促进农耕文明的文化价值、社会价值、经济价值得到持续挖掘和释放。中国传统村落非遗资源数字化持续推进，将具有重要价值和鲜明特色的乡村文化形态纳入国家级文化生态保护（实验）区整体性保护范围，2021 年和 2022 年重点支持了 364 个中国传统村落的非遗资源保护数字化工作。截至 2022 年 6 月，中国传统村落数字博物馆已收集整理6 819 个传统村落的基本信息，建设完成 658 个村落单馆，形成了涵盖全景漫游、图文、影音、实景模型等多种数据类型的传统村落数据库。

6.3　智　慧　教　育

中国在国民教育方面取得了巨大的成就。首先，教育普及水平实现历史性跨越。截至2021 年底，中国共有各级各类学校 52.93 万所，在校生 2.91 亿人；义务教育[①]阶段学校 20.7万所，在校生 1.58 亿人，已实现义务教育全面普及；高中阶段教育学校 2.2 万所，在校生3 916.84 万人，毛入学率 91.4％；高等教育学校 3 012 所，在学总规模 4 430 万人，毛入学率57.8％。其次，教育公平取得新成效。截至 2022 年，中国 2 895 个县实现义务教育基本均衡发展，建成覆盖"所有学段、所有学校、所有家庭经济困难学生"的学生资助政策体系，确保

---

① 自 1986 年《中华人民共和国义务教育法》颁布以来，中国确立了九年义务教育制度，覆盖小学和初中阶段，保障所有适龄儿童、少年接受义务教育的权利。

"不让一个学生因家庭经济困难而失学"。

教育信息化有助于推动优质教育资源的共享,促进教育公平、提高教育质量。中国教育部高度重视教育信息化,开展了长期而持续的教育信息化建设。2012 年,教育部印发《教育信息化十年发展规划(2011—2020 年)》,将"三通两平台"作为目标,实现"宽带网络校校通、优质资源班班通、网络学习空间人人通",建设学校接入网络、教育资源公共服务平台和教育管理公共服务平台。2018 年,教育部发布《教育信息化 2.0 行动计划》,提出"三全两高一大"的发展目标,即"教学应用覆盖全体教师、学习应用覆盖全体适龄学生、数字校园建设覆盖全体学校,信息化应用水平和师生信息素养普遍提高,建成'互联网+教育'大平台"。

经过多年的教育信息化建设,目前中国的教育信息化发展阶段已经从应用普及转向了融合创新。利用信息技术促进中国教育数字化转型、实现高质量发展成为新时代的发展任务。2019 年 2 月,中国发布《中国教育现代化 2035》,这是首个以教育现代化为主题的中长期战略规划,其中提出"加快信息化时代教育变革",重点任务聚焦在智能化校园建设,利用现代技术加快推动人才培养模式改革。2021 年 7 月,教育部等六部门印发《关于推进教育新型基础设施建设　构建高质量教育支撑体系的指导意见》,提出了信息网络、平台体系、数字资源、智慧校园、创新应用、可信安全等六位一体的教育新型基础设施体系。

6.3.1　数字校园设施

各级各类学校的网络条件显著改善。2012 年,教育部提出了"宽带网络校校通"的建设目标。截至 2022 年,中国中小学(含教学点[①])互联网接入率已达 100%(见图 6-10),比 2012年提高了 75 个百分点;超 75% 的学校覆盖了无线网络,99.5% 的学校拥有多媒体教室,总数量超过 400 万间,学校配备的师生终端数量超过 2 800 万台;中国小学、初中每百名学生拥有的数字终端数量分别为 14.9 台、21.0 台,较 10 年前分别增加 8.4 台和 10.6 台;中小学数字化教学条件全面提档升级,基本形成了网络覆盖完全、线下多媒体教学空间和网络教学空间融合的泛在化学习环境。

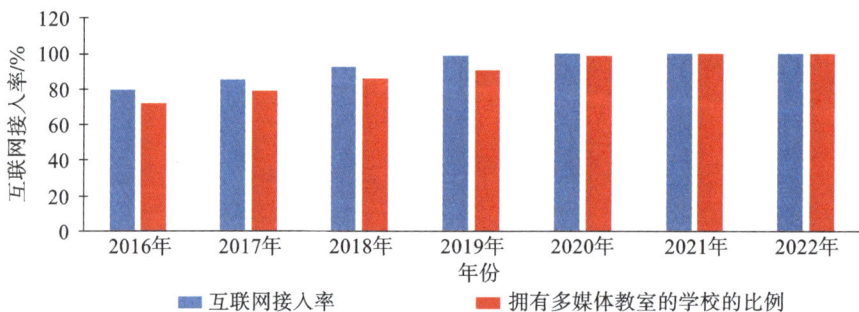

图 6-10　2016—2022 年中国中小学(含教学点)校园网络建设情况

数据来源:教育部

依托校园网络条件的改善,优质教育信息资源可以有效共享。以宁夏回族自治区为例,该省区地处中国西北腹地,教育发展不平衡、不充分的问题相对突出。2018 年宁夏获批建

---

①　教学点是在偏远及课程资源不足地区设立的,以多年级混合编班为主的小规模非完全小学学校,通常仅覆盖低年级且学生人数不足 20 人。

设全国"互联网＋教育"示范区,全区实现学校 200M 网络宽带接入,建成数字化教室 2.9 万间。借助高速完善的网络基础设施,宁夏 500 多所学校与北京、福建等地优质学校网上结对①,所有乡村中小学校与城镇学校线上牵手,通过跨校联教、在线支教,有效缓解薄弱学校缺师少教的难题。宁夏基础教育信息化发展综合指数排名从 2017 年的全国第十五位上升至 2020 年的第六位。截至 2023 年,宁夏用户在国家中小学智慧教育平台的注册量达 125 万,涵盖全区中小学 100％ 的教师和 64.9％ 的学生。

目前,中国已经建立了完善的数字校园标准体系,涵盖中小学、职业院校、高等院校等不同类型学校的数字化建设标准。数字校园的建设内容覆盖网络教育、教育管理、教育评价、应用服务、网络安全等方面。2012 年,教育部启动"百所数字校园示范校"评比等活动,进一步落实相关标准的实施;各省级教育主管部门也定期开展数字校园建设方面的评比和考核工作。中国目前的校园信息化建设重点已经从"数字校园"向"智慧校园"转变。例如,2023 年北京市教育委员会发布《北京市中小学智慧校园建设规范(试行)》,提出智慧校园建设内容包含智能环境、应用融合创新、学校教育数据及应用、互联网服务及应用、数字素养与技能、保障及运行服务等内容,重点突出共建共享和智慧应用。

6.3.2　数字课程平台

中国建成了面向中小学的国家数字教育资源公共服务体系。截至 2020 年 11 月,国家数字教育资源公共服务体系已接入省级、市级各类教育资源平台 84 个,为师生提供教育教学和教育管理服务,应用访问总数累计超 3 亿人次,资源共享总数超过 3.2 亿次,月活跃用户达 6 000 多万人;全国师生网络学习空间开通数量超过 1 亿个,将近半数的教师应用网络学习空间开展教学和教研;实施农村教学点数字教育资源全覆盖项目,整合开发英语、音乐、美术等学科数字资源 6 948 学时,与基础教育阶段所有学科教材配套的资源达 5 000 万条。

中国形成了面向高等教育的系列在线课程平台。慕课,即英文 MOOC 的中文翻译,代表大规模在线开放教育。2013 年,中国的大学开始自发建设慕课。跨校跨区域在线教学、"1(门慕课)＋M(所大学)＋N(个学生)"协同教学、线上线下混合式教学、"MOOC＋SPOC②＋翻转课堂"正在越来越多地走进高校课堂。2019 年教育部高等教育司发出"慕课西部行"号召,累计向西部高校提供 17.29 万门慕课及定制化课程服务,帮助西部地区开展混合式教学 327.24 万门次,学生参与学习达 3.76 亿人次,西部地区教师参加应用培训 171.4 万人次。

2020 年初,突如其来的新冠肺炎疫情引发了一次史无前例的大规模在线教学实践。教育部启动"停课不停学"工作,开通国家中小学网络云平台,通过空中课堂(电视版)保障没有网络或网速较慢地区学生的居家学习。依托已有的教育信息平台和资源,各级各类学校的教师积极开展教学活动(见图 6-11)。2020 年 2 月,教育部国家中小学网络云平台顺利开通,累计协调 7 000 个服务器,90 T 带宽,可供 5 000 万学生同时在线使用。至 2020 年 5 月,国家中小学网络云平台浏览次数达 20.73 亿次,访问量达 17.11 亿人次。27 个省份开通了

---

①　网上结对是对口支援的具体形式。中国通过组织发达省份与欠发达省份建立"对口支援"机制,以跨区域协作形式进行资金、技术、资源等方面的定向帮扶,缩小区域发展差距。这一举措依托中国特色社会主义制度优势,通过政府主导的资源横向调配实现了不同区域协同发展。

②　私授课,一种结合了实体课堂和在线学习的混合式教学模式。

省级网络学习平台,并指导确有条件的部分市县和学校用好本地本校资源。

图 6-11   疫情期间学生通过多种方式学习线上课程
图片来源:武汉广播电视台

疫情期间,中国 1 454 所高校开展在线教学,103 万教师在线开出了 107 万门课程,在线学习的大学生共计 1 775 万人。依托世界慕课与在线教育联盟秘书处,中国大学组织了超过 10 场全球在线教育对话活动,开设了 168 门全球融合式课程,与 11 个国家的 13 所世界著名大学实行了互认学分,推出了 8 门英文全球公开课,吸引全球学习者 730 万人,国际在线教育合作交流不断深入。2020 年 3 月 13 日,联合国教科文组织向全球发布了远程教学解决方案,推荐了世界范围内可免费获取的 27 个学习应用程序和平台,爱课程网、阿里钉钉入选(见图 6-12)。

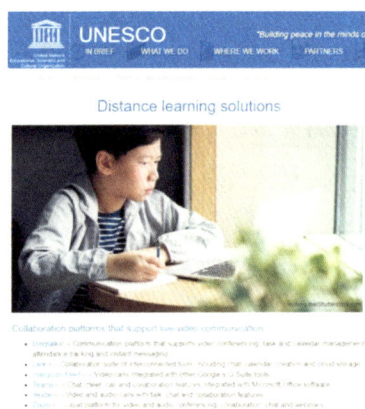

图 6-12   中国在线课程平台被列入联合国教科文组织推荐的远程学习解决方案
图片来源:联合国教科文组织

近年来,中国进一步整合国家数字教育资源公共服务体系、国家中小学网络云平台等在线数字教育资源和平台。2022 年 3 月,面向在校学生的国家智慧教育公共服务平台正式上线,覆盖中小学教育、职业教育、高等教育三大资源平台,提供 26 项政务服务。平台汇集了基础教育课程资源 4.4 万节、职业教育在线精品课 6 628 门、高等教育优质课程 2.7 万门。同时,面向社会开放的公共在线课程平台也蓬勃发展。截至 2022 年 11 月,上线慕课超过 6.19 万门,注册用户 4.02 亿,学习人数达 9.79 亿人次,中国慕课数量和学习人数均居世界第一,并保持快速增长的态势。部分慕课平台开设了面向海外的国际版,已免费向世界各国学习者提供 900 余门多语种课程资源和必要的教学服务。向全世界大学生和学习者开放近千门、14 个语种的在线课程,全球累计学习人数达 67 万人次。

6.3.3　互联网教育应用

"三个课堂"是中国教育部针对教学薄弱地区中小学提出的三类网络协同教学形式,具体包括"专递课堂""名师课堂"和"名校网络课堂"(见表6-1)。

表6-1　中国教育部针对教学薄弱地区推行的三类网络协同教学形式

应用名称	目标	服务对象	建设内容	设施条件
专递课堂	解决农村薄弱学校和教学点缺少师资、开不出开不足开不好国家规定课程的问题	农村薄弱学校和教学点的学生	采用网上专门开课或同步上课等形式,帮助其开齐开足开好国家规定课程	直播录播系统、远端多媒体显示设备等
名师课堂	辅助农村地区教师技能培训	农村薄弱学校的教师	组建网络研修共同体,以优秀教师带动普通教师水平提升	互动录播系统、网络教师研修平台等
名校网络课堂	缩小区域、城乡、校际教育质量的差异	农村薄弱学校的教师和学生	以优质学校为主体,通过网络学校、网络课程等形式推动优质教育资源在区域内共享	智慧教室、跨学校的教学平台等

2012年,在教育部"教育信息化试点工作座谈会"上,教育部首次提出了要发展"三个课堂",提升偏远地区教育质量,促进优质教学资源共享。2014年,《构建利用信息化手段扩大优质教育资源覆盖面有效机制的实施方案》中,教育部指出,要通过"三个课堂"等多种形式,促进教育公平,提高教育质量。2016年,在《教育信息化"十三五"规划》中提出,要积极推动"专递课堂"建设,巩固深化"教学点数字教学资源全覆盖"项目成果。2020年3月,教育部发布了《关于加强"三个课堂"应用的指导意见》,要求到2022年,全面实现"三个课堂"。2022年4月,中央电化教育馆发布"三个课堂"应用的创新案例及入围案例,推广典型经验做法,发挥示范带动作用。"三个课堂"的应用如图6-13至图6-15所示。

图6-13　"专递课堂"的应用:江西省赣州经济技术开发区教学点学生与授课端学生互动

图片来源:《中国教育报》

图 6-14 "名师课堂"的应用：浙江省三门县心湖小学教共体开展教研活动

图片来源：《中国教育报》

图 6-15 "名校网络课堂"的应用：赣浙三校联盟"名校网络课堂"交流培训

图片来源：《中国教育报》

6.3.4 智慧教育应用

人工智能时代对教育提出了全方位的挑战，中国高度重视人工智能技术对教育的影响。2017 年 7 月，国务院发布了《新一代人工智能发展规划》，明确提出发展智能教育。2018 年 4 月，教育部发布《高等学校人工智能创新行动计划》和《教育信息化 2.0 行动计划》，进一步明确了人工智能与教育融合发展，并启动了人工智能助推教师队伍建设行动试点工作。

人工智能教育正在逐步进入学校课堂。教育部所编的《普通高中信息技术课程标准（2017 年版 2020 年修订）》的必修模块中增加了人工智能基础知识的内容。各地中小学积极探索向低年级学生逐步普及信息技术、人工智能技术。基于智能机器人开展创客教育和 STEAM 教育，各学校以信息技术课和校本选修课等形式开设智能机器人编程课程、组建课余活动兴趣小组，在部分年级开设基于智能机器人编程的人工智能普及课程，让人工智能课程进入中小学生课堂（见图 6-16）。

人工智能技术正在成为辅助教学的重要手段。2016 年，科大讯飞与教育部考试中心（现教育考试院）共建联合实验室，探索研发面向中高考英语口语、作文等环节的智能阅卷技术。2017 年上半年，智能阅卷技术被应用于全国大学英语四、六级考试笔试及 25 个地区的中考、高考、学考中，覆盖近 700 万名考生，可对空白试卷、疑似雷同试卷等问题试卷进行检测，减少 20% 的工作量。根据华东师范大学、中国教育科学研究院、腾讯研究院、腾讯教育联合发布的《2022 年人工智能教育蓝皮书》显示，在全国 25 个省份 2.8 万个教师样本中，有

图 6-16 中学开展人工智能课程教学与竞赛活动
图片来源:《中国教育报》

58％的教师在所教授学科中使用过人工智能技术,有 72％的教师运用计算机视觉技术进行图谱识别,超过半数教师使用智能作业布置、智慧课堂、智能学情分析等相关工具。各地小学还开展了将人形机器人引入课堂辅助教学过程的教学探索,如图 6-17 所示。

图 6-17 小学引入人形机器人辅助课堂教学
图片来源:《中国教育报》(左),人民网(右)

6.4 智 慧 医 疗

中国在国民卫生健康事业方面取得了巨大的成就。2019 年,中国居民人均预期寿命达到 77.3 岁,孕产妇死亡率、婴儿死亡率、5 岁以下儿童死亡率分别降至 17.8/10 万、5.6‰、7.8‰,主要健康指标总体上优于中高收入国家平均水平。中国特色基本医疗卫生制度框架基本建立,医疗卫生服务可及性不断提高,截至 2020 年,每千人口医疗卫生机构床位数达到6.46 张,84％的县级医院达到二级及以上医院水平[①],近 90％的家庭 15 分钟内能够到达最近的医疗点。中国的基本公共卫生服务均等化水平进一步提高,免费向全体城乡居民提供14 大类国家基本公共卫生服务项目。

---

① 根据中国国家卫生健康委员会的标准,中国的医院根据其规模、设施条件、服务范围等分为 3 级 10 等。一般来说,一级医院为当地社区居民提供医疗服务;二级医院是服务于多个社区的区域性医院;三级医院是跨区域的医疗中心,可以为来自当地城市、当地省份甚至全国的患者提供服务。

随着中国经济和社会的发展,新时代中国的卫生健康事业的重点已经从疾病治疗转变为全民健康。2016 年 10 月,中共中央、国务院颁布《"健康中国 2030"规划纲要》,确立了"把以治病为中心"转变为"以人民健康为中心"的新主旨。但是,中国面临医疗资源分布不均、服务水平差异大、医疗卫生服务供需缺口持续扩大的基本国情。《2020 中国卫生健康统计年鉴》显示,无论是医院数量、三级医院数量,还是卫生技术人员数量、执业医师数量,东部地区明显多于中部、西部地区。推动医疗卫生服务体系的信息化、智能化升级是摆脱医疗资源分布不均衡困境的重要举措。2022 年 11 月,国家卫生健康委、国家中医药局、国家疾控局联合颁布了《"十四五"全民健康信息化规划》,提出面对数字化变革带来的机遇与挑战,必须进一步夯实全民健康信息化新基建,培育卫生健康服务新业态,提升卫生健康行业发展新动能。

6.4.1 数字医疗基础设施

中国的医院信息化经历了多个阶段。20 世纪 90 年代进入起步阶段,这一时期的信息化重点是医院管理信息化,将传统的业务管理模式计算机化(包括医院财务管理、收费管理系统等),实现计算机技术在医疗卫生系统的应用。2010 年进入深度应用阶段,医院信息化的重点是实现以电子病历系统为核心的各类临床信息系统,包括临床检验信息管理系统、医学影像信息管理系统等(见图 6-18)。2015 年后进入医院集成平台化阶段,即实现院内的信息交换,推动电子病历的深度应用。

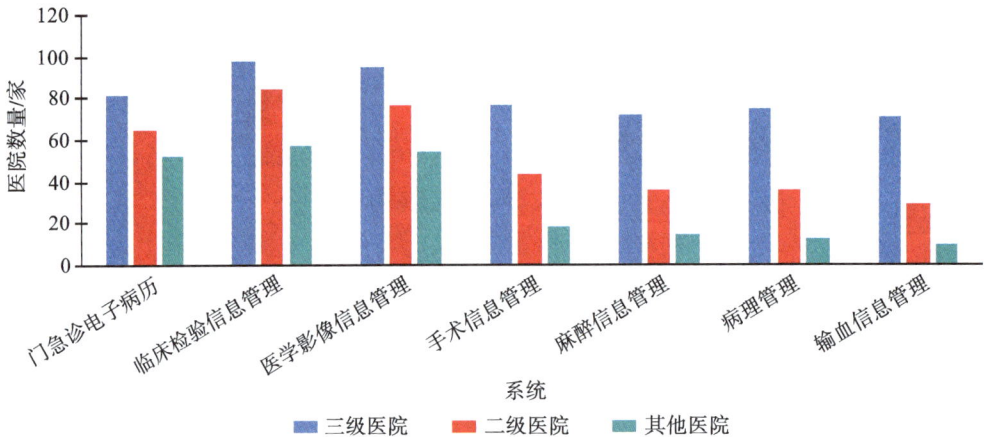

图 6-18 中国各级医院临床医疗应用开展情况

数据来源:国家卫生健康委统计信息中心编著,《全民健康信息化调查报告——区域卫生信息化与
医院信息化(2021)》,2021 年

中国制定了全国医疗卫生机构信息化建设系列标准。2018—2019 年,国家卫生健康委先后发布《全国医院信息化建设标准与规范(试行)》《电子病历系统应用水平分级评价管理办法(试行)》《电子病历系统应用水平分级评价标准(试行)》《全国基层医疗卫生机构信息化建设标准与规范(试行)》,针对不同等级医院、社区卫生服务中心(站)、乡镇卫生院(村卫生室)等基层医疗卫生机构,明确了其各项业务流程的信息化服务标准建设内容。国家卫生健康委将电子病历系统应用水平分级评价作为医疗卫生机构信息化的标志性指标之一。截至2021 年 7 月,中国共有 118 家医院参加电子病历评价并获评五级及以上医疗卫生机构;153

个区域主管单位、503 家二级及以上医院通过互联互通等级测评。

目前,中国正在积极推进区域医疗卫生信息化,利用分级诊疗和数据共享,在一定地域范围内为医疗服务提供者、卫生管理机构、患者、医疗支付方以及医药产品供应商等机构和个人提供数据共享服务。例如,江苏省建设了覆盖全省的全民健康信息平台,截至 2022 年 5 月,已对接全省 13 个市级、96 个县(区)级区域全民健康信息平台,联通 2 万余家医疗卫生机构,制定并发布近 40 项地方卫生信息化标准,实现数据标准化采集,汇聚数据 418 亿条。基于全民健康信息平台,江苏省建设了"江苏健康通"一站式惠民服务系统,已提供全省居民健康档案调阅 1 000 多万人次;开展了医疗服务综合监管、基层卫生监管、妇幼保健管理、传染病监测预警等 10 多项业务应用。

同时,中国也在推进医疗保险支付服务信息化。2022 年,中国全面建成全国统一的医保信息平台,接入约 40 万家定点医疗机构和 40 万家定点零售药店,有效覆盖全体参保人。国家医保服务平台实名用户达 2.8 亿,涵盖 100 余项服务功能。数字技术在辅助诊断、康复、配送转运、医疗机器人等方面的新应用快速普及,互联网直播互动式家庭育儿、线上婴幼儿养育课程、父母课堂等新形式不断涌现。

6.4.2 互联网医疗应用

互联网医疗加速应用,线下线上医疗呈现协同发展趋势。截至 2020 年 10 月,全国已有 900 多家互联网医院,远程医疗协作网覆盖所有地级市,5 500 多家二级以上的医院可以提供线上服务。截至 2021 年底,二级以上公立医院中,能够提供远程医疗的达 64.6%,开通预约诊疗服务的达 54.5%。中医馆健康信息平台服务能力持续提升,累计接入 1.62 万家中医馆,截至 2020 年 12 月底,平台累计接诊病人 1 300 万人次,填写中医电子病历近 100 万份,辨证论治开方 87 万多张,查询知识库 103 万多次。"互联网+"防疫科普、在线咨询、远程会诊、药品配送等健康服务新业态快速普及。

2020 年 2 月新冠肺炎疫情期间,全国各地有 4.2 万余名医护人员驰援湖北。与此同时,更多医生借助信息技术优势,在网上开辟"第二战场",突破了医疗服务供给瓶颈,有力支援了湖北主战场。比如,广东省对口支援①湖北荆州医疗队联合荆州市建设互联网医院,广东 15 家医疗机构、1 300 多名医生自愿参加,上线 18 天总访问量就突破 10 万人次,为当地留下了一支带不走的医疗队。"互联网+医疗健康"打破了医疗资源分布的时空局限,通过创新服务模式,提高服务效率,降低服务成本,在新冠肺炎疫情防控阻击战中发挥了积极作用。

5G 智慧急救提升救治效率。2020 年 3 月,海南省在琼海市人民医院和博鳌市中心医院开展 5G 智慧急救平台建设。从急救人员接到患者的第一刻起,将患者的基本体征数据、病情评估图像、急症病情记录通过 5G 网络实时传输到指挥中心和急救站,院内专家可查看到患者检测、监护信息和急救车内视频,通过远程会诊系统对随车医护人员进行远程指导并提前制定抢救方案(见图 6-19)。2020 年海南省"基于 5G 物联网的基层医疗卫生机构能力提升工程"启动建设,至 2021 年 4 月,该项目实现了对全省 7 家三甲医院、18 个市县的县级医院、340 家乡镇级医疗机构和 2 693 家村卫生室进行 5G 智慧化升级。

---

① 中国在 2020 年新冠肺炎疫情初期启动"对口支援"机制,由国务院联防联控机制统筹,指定 16 个省份以"一省包一市"方式,一对一支援湖北省除武汉外的地级市,通过医疗资源调配缓解当地救治压力。

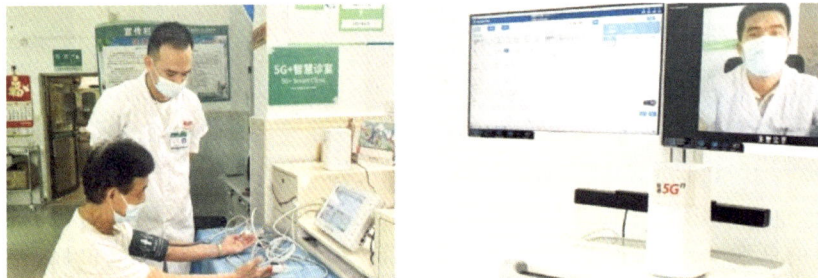

图 6-19   5G 远程急救:海南省 5G 智慧急救平台

图片来源:《人民日报》

5G 远程手术开始营业。5G 高带宽、低时延特性能够将网络时延缩短至 10 毫秒,使得远程手术成为可能(见图 6-20)。2019 年 1 月,全球首例基于 5G 网络的远程动物手术在福建省福州市实施成功。医生与"患者"(小猪)相隔 50 千米,通过福建联通搭建的 5G 网络环境,医生远程操控手术机器人,将小猪的肝小叶顺利切除。2019 年 3 月,全国首例基于 5G 的远程人体手术——帕金森病"脑起搏器"植入手术在北京完成。本次手术通过 5G 网络,跨越近 3 000 千米,成功实现了位于北京的中国人民解放军总医院第一医学中心与海南医院间的帕金森病"脑起搏器"植入手术,实现 5G 远程手术操控。

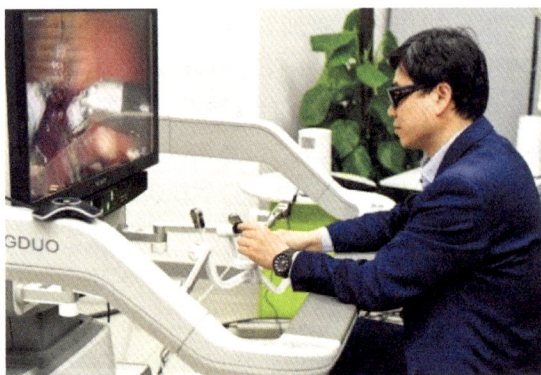

图 6-20   5G 远程手术

图片来源:人民网

6.4.3   智慧医疗应用

人工智能开始在辅助诊断中发挥作用。长期以来,中国农村基层医疗资源较为薄弱,利用人工智能技术,可以为基层医生提供辅助诊断建议,提升基层医生诊疗水平。"智医助理"是安徽省卫生健康委员会推广的一款适用于医疗卫生机构的人工智能应用。该应用基于医学知识图谱,通过提取并分析就诊患者电子病历信息,为医生提供电子病历信息对应的疑似疾病列表。"智医助理"已经具备对全部 40 种法定传染病、15 种重点传染病、6 个症候群的监测和预警能力。2017 年,"智医助理"成为通过国家医师资格考试医学综合笔试的人工智能辅助诊断系统。"智医助理"还支持批量语音外呼功能,能帮助基层医生完成签约居民慢性病随访、妇保随访、通知、宣教、体检预约等工作。截至 2022 年 10 月,"智医助理"已在安徽省实现了104个区县全覆盖和常态化应用,累计服务超过3万名基层医生,累计协助医生完成超过1.6亿份电子病历,提供4.3亿余次辅助诊断建议,合理用药质检处方达1.3亿余张。

人工智能在病理诊断中发挥着越来越重要的作用。目前,中国要求每100张床位配备1~2名病理医生,以此计算中国病理医生岗位有8万~10万的缺口;此外,一般病理医生人工阅片每张需要30~40分钟,但看片正确率仅有六成。人工智能技术可以帮助医生提高诊断的可重复性、准确率、效率,从一定程度上缓解病理医生不足的状况。2017年11月,科技部公布首批国家新一代人工智能开放创新平台名单,并明确依托腾讯建设"医疗影像国家新一代人工智能开放创新平台"。2018年,腾讯成立了AI医疗中心,申请了超过1 500项专利,在顶级学术会议上也发表了超过300篇论文。截至2019年,腾讯与中国超过100家三甲医院达成合作,医疗影像方面累计处理超过2.7亿张影像图片,开发了早期食管癌筛查、早期肺癌筛查、糖尿病性视网膜病变检测、结直肠癌筛查、早期乳腺癌筛查和早期宫颈癌筛查等AI影像产品,AI辅/导诊系统导入了300家医院,进行了470万例精确导诊。

6.5　小　　　结

中国政府高度重视提高国民生活水平和质量。近年来,中国充分发挥信息化优势,构建起全方位、多层次的数字社会服务体系,极大地拓展了公共服务的覆盖范围,显著提升了基本公共服务均等化水平。通过智慧城市和数字乡村建设,城乡公共服务实现协同优化,人民群众的生活更加便捷美好;智慧教育和智慧医疗深入推进,有力促进了教育公平和医疗资源的合理分配。

中国将智慧城市视为城市信息化建设的高级阶段,积极通过信息化手段解决人口密集城市在发展中面临的诸多挑战。在城市交通管控方面,多个城市构建了智能化交通指挥控制中心,例如深圳市综合交通运行指挥中心,极大地提升了交通效率。在城市综合治理方面,中国首创"城市大脑"概念,杭州等地的实践成果丰硕,有效解决了城市运行难题。在城市数字化治理方面,上海等地探索了数字孪生城市系统的建设,使得城市管理更加高效、智能。

中国重视城乡协调发展,将数字乡村建设作为乡村振兴的关键途径。在乡村网络基础设施建设方面,政府多年来持续投入,通过"村村通""网络扶贫"等工程,克服重重困难,实现乡村网络基础设施全覆盖,大幅缩小城乡"数字鸿沟"。在乡村数字经济方面,政府积极推动农村电子商务发展,通过淘宝村等创新模式,带动农产品销售和农民就业,为全球乡村经济发展和减贫事业提供了新思路。此外,中国还借助数字化手段提升了乡村公共服务水平和乡村基层综合治理水平,丰富了农民的文化生活。

中国将教育信息化视为解决教育资源分布不均的重要途径,并积极推动教育的数字化转型。在数字校园设施建设方面,学校网络条件显著改善,优质教育资源得以共享,数字校园标准体系得以建立。数字课程平台不断完善,涵盖中小学教育和高等教育,在疫情期间发挥了重要作用,实现了停课不停学。以"三个课堂"为代表的互联网教育应用,促进了基础教育阶段的教育公平,有效解决了农村偏远地区教育资源不足的问题。以信息技术教育、机器人科创等为代表的人工智能通识教育在中小学逐步推广，为培养中国未来的科研人才队伍提供了支撑。

中国将医疗信息化作为解决医疗资源分布不均的重要抓手。在数字医疗基础设施方面，中国建立了覆盖全民的基本医疗保障体系，制定了医院信息化标准，显著提升了各级各类医疗机构的现代化水平。在互联网医疗应用方面，通过 5G 等信息技术的应用，在远程急救和远程手术方面实现了突破，缩小了地区之间医疗水平的发展差距。在新技术应用方面，人工智能在辅助诊断和病理诊断中的应用日趋成熟，提升了基层医疗水平，缓解了医疗人力资源不足的问题，为全球医疗发展贡献了中国智慧。

值得一提的是，在智慧社会建设过程中的诸多难点和挑战面前，中国特色社会主义制度优势发挥了关键作用。以乡村网络建设为例，尽管面临建设投入大、维护成本高、投资收益低等难题，中国国有企业依然从国家战略和人民利益出发，勇挑重担，持续投入，成功将网络基础设施铺设到每一个偏远乡村，建成了全球覆盖最广的信息网络，为中国全面打赢脱贫攻坚战提供了坚实支撑，彰显了中国特色社会主义制度集中力量办大事的强大优势，也为全球数字社会建设提供了可资借鉴的成功范例。

7 网络空间治理

7.1 需求与挑战

7.1.1 网络空间概述

网络空间的概念由西方学者提出,随后在全球范围内逐步得到认可。1984 年,美国科幻作家威廉·吉布森在其长篇小说《神经漫游者》中首次提出"网络空间"这一概念,意指全球计算机网络构成的空间。全球主要国家对网络空间的定义并不相同,例如:美国将网络空间描述为"由信息技术基础设施构成的相互信赖的网络,包括互联网、电信网、计算机系统等,以及信息与人交互的虚拟环境";德国将网络空间定义为"包括所有可以跨越领土边界通过互联网访问的信息基础设施";英国将网络空间明确为"由数字网络构成并用于储存、修改和传递信息的人机交互领域,包含互联网和其他用于支持商业、基础设施与服务的信息系统";中国的《国家网络空间安全战略》指出,网络空间由"互联网、通信网、计算机系统、自动化控制系统、数字设备及其承载的应用、服务和数据等组成"。

网络空间已经成为由信息和网络技术、产品构建的数字社会的总称。互联网无处不在,一个安全、稳定、繁荣的网络空间,对一国乃至世界和平与发展越来越具有重大意义。网络空间治理主要包括网络空间信息安全、网络空间法治建设、数字经济监管等多个方面。相比于传统人类社会的治理,网络空间的治理具有 4 个特征。

首先,网络空间治理具有基础性。随着全球信息化的飞速发展,网络信息系统已经成为国家政治、经济、文化、社会的关键平台和神经中枢。无论是社会生产和生活中的各种活动,还是国家机关、各种企事业组织履行社会管理职责、提供社会服务以及维持自身的正常运转,都越来越离不开网络信息系统。

其次,网络空间治理具有开放性。互联网是开放的,网络空间的信息交流跨越了地理上的界限,不受空间约束。这种特性也导致网络空间安全不具备明显的边界。从这个意义上说,网络空间安全不仅仅是一个国家的责任,也是国际社会的共同责任。

再次,网络空间治理具有系统性。网络安全小到组网的硬件、管理控制网络的软件,大到网络服务、网络应用,信息化程度越高,所分布的节点越多。网络中不管哪个节点都可以影响网络空间安全,好比木桶效应,越是复杂的网络系统越要注重最薄弱环节的安全水平。

最后,网络空间治理具有战略性。随着网络安全和信息化在国家安全与发展中的地位和作用不断提升,网络安全和信息化已经上升为国家的重大战略,中国正需要加强顶层设计和战略统筹。网络空间安全是网络时代的一种战略思维和部署。

7.1.2　网络空间安全与治理

网络空间安全是一种全新的社会结构形态安全，主要涵盖了全球范围之内的政府、社会组织及个体的安全。网络空间安全主要包括计算机系统安全、系统内程序和数据安全、网络连接安全三个方面。计算机系统安全作为网络空间安全的物理基础，既为网络正常运行提供支撑，同时接受服务，是网络体系正常操作和安全运行的重要保障。系统内程序和数据安全是应用程序稳定可靠运行以及软件数据不受损坏和窃取的重要保障。网络连接安全则是网络连接过程中的信息安全保障，比如对信息传播路径和具体内容的保护，保障传递过程中的信息不被恶意篡改，防御木马病毒的入侵，等等。

网络空间逐步成为社会生活、经济交往、政治博弈、文化交融的重要场域，但是并未从根本上改变人类社会的基本法治秩序。个人和团体在实际物理空间和虚拟网络空间的行为，构成了其在人类社会的完整行为，都需要受到法治的保护和监督。人类在虚拟网络空间中的持续性交互与协作行为，推动着网络社会的形成。网络社会治理的概念和范畴仍在不断发展和演化之中，其中代表性的问题包括用户数字权利保护、网络行为治理、技术算法治理、数字经济监管等，具体而言：

第一，用户数字权利内涵比较广泛，通常包括每个公民享有的正常接入互联网的权利、在互联网上开展相关行为的权利、保护个人数字化信息隐私的权利等。网络接入服务已经成为如同普通邮政服务一样的公共服务，个人在互联网上开展民事行为同样具有法律效力，例如支付、签名等，需要有健全的个人身份认证体系进行保障。个人在参与网络行为，例如线上购物、线上问诊等的过程中也会涉及个人隐私等信息，需要有完善的个人信息保护机制。

第二，网络空间中也存在着多种不良活动和违法行为，需要结合已有的法律法规与时俱进进行治理。典型的违法网络行为是传播违法内容，包括编辑传播侵权的数字内容、传递暴力反动等内容、传递虚假消息等。此外，利用互联网从事违法活动也会令广大群众权益受损，例如网络诈骗、网络赌博、网络传销、网络非法集资等违法活动，更会给受害人财产造成重大损失，影响正常生活秩序。

第三，网络空间的技术和算法治理面临多维度挑战。以机器学习算法为主导的人工智能技术已成为各大网络平台的核心驱动力，但其在公平性、透明性和安全性层面的结构性缺陷，导致算法应用失范现象频发。这些技术风险逐步演变为网络社会治理的复合性挑战，影响到社会公平公正、互联网用户合法权益及虚拟财产安全等诸多方面。

第四，数字经济时代网络市场竞争带来许多新的问题。例如超级平台已经成为高度数字市场化环境下形成的数字经济基础设施，平台的运行监管难以通过传统的市场监管手段进行管理。又例如网络商品交易不仅涉及买卖、售后服务等线上环节，还涉及快递物流等线下环节，难以通过传统渠道进行跟踪和监管。

网络空间不是法外之地。保障个人和团体在网络空间的合法权利，维护网络空间的正常运行，是每个政府面临的新挑战。各国纷纷采取措施，通过立法等方式对网络社会行为进行治理。以 2020 年为例，2020 年 1 月，美国白宫发布了《人工智能应用规范指南》，提出各主管机关采取弹性监管方法，避免因为严格监管对创新产生阻碍；2020 年 2 月，欧盟委员会发布《人工智能白皮书——通往卓越和信任的欧洲路径》,提出建立"可信赖的人工智能框架";2020 年 6 月,欧盟发布《通用数据保护条例》,确定了"原则上禁止,有合法授权时允许"的个人数据使用模式;2020 年 12 月,欧盟委员会对外公布《数字服务法案》和《数字市场法案》草案,要求科技公司不能利用其竞争对手的数据与对手竞争,也不能在自己的平台上优先展示本公司的产品。

7.2　网络空间法律体系

　　中国网络立法随着互联网发展经历了从无到有、从少到多、由点到面、由面到体的发展过程。

　　第一阶段是从 1994 年到 1999 年,是互联网的接入普及阶段。上网用户和设备数量稳步增加。这一阶段的网络立法主要聚焦于网络基础设施安全,即计算机系统安全和联网安全。

　　第二阶段是从 2000 年到 2011 年,是互联网的广泛应用阶段,在此阶段个人计算机是访问互联网的主要终端设备。随着计算机数量逐步增加、上网资费逐步降低,用户上网日益普遍,网络信息服务迅猛发展。这一阶段的网络立法转向侧重网络服务管理和内容管理。

　　第三阶段是从 2012 年至今,是移动互联网的广泛应用阶段,在此阶段智能手机成为访问互联网的主要终端设备。这一阶段的网络立法逐步趋向全面涵盖网络信息服务、信息化发展、网络安全保护等在内的网络综合治理。

　　截至 2023 年,中国已经制定出台网络领域立法 140 余部,基本形成了以宪法为根本,以法律、行政法规、部门规章和地方性法规、地方政府规章为依托,以传统立法为基础,以网络内容建设与管理、网络安全和信息化等网络专门立法为主干的网络法律体系,为网络强国建设提供了坚实的制度保障(见表 7-1)。

表 7-1　中国网络立法概况

类型	示例
法律	《中华人民共和国电子商务法》《中华人民共和国电子签名法》《中华人民共和国网络安全法》《中华人民共和国数据安全法》《中华人民共和国个人信息保护法》《中华人民共和国反电信网络诈骗法》
行政法规	《中华人民共和国计算机信息系统安全保护条例》《计算机软件保护条例》《互联网信息服务管理办法》《中华人民共和国电信条例》《外商投资电信企业管理规定》《信息网络传播权保护条例》《关键信息基础设施安全保护条例》
部门规章	《儿童个人信息网络保护规定》《互联网域名管理办法》《网络交易监督管理办法》《互联网新闻信息服务管理规定》《网络信息内容生态治理规定》《互联网信息服务算法推荐管理规定》
地方性法规	《广东省数字经济促进条例》《浙江省数字经济促进条例》《河北省信息化条例》《贵州省政府数据共享开放条例》《上海市数据条例》

续表

类型	示例
地方政府规章	《广东省公共数据管理办法》《安徽省政务数据资源管理办法》《江西省计算机信息系统安全保护办法》《杭州市网络交易管理暂行办法》

7.2.1　个人权益保障

保障公民通信自由和通信秘密。通信自由和通信秘密的保护是确保公民能够自主地在网络空间表达诉求和思想的前提。早在 1997 年,国务院就制定了《计算机信息网络国际联网安全保护管理办法》,落实宪法对通信自由和通信秘密基本权利的保护;2000 年公布的《中华人民共和国电信条例》规定,电信用户依法使用电信的自由和通信秘密受法律保护;2016 年修订的《中华人民共和国无线电管理条例》进一步强化无线电领域对通信秘密的保护,实现对这一基本权利在网络空间的全方位保障。

保护个人信息权益。通过民法、刑法和专门立法,构建个人信息权益全链条保护的法律屏障。2015 年通过的《中华人民共和国刑法修正案(九)》对非法获取公民个人信息罪进行了更加细致的规定,强化了个人信息的刑法保护。在网络专门立法中,2012 年通过的《全国人民代表大会常务委员会关于加强网络信息保护的决定》明确保护能够识别公民个人身份和涉及公民个人隐私的电子信息;2016 年颁布的《中华人民共和国网络安全法》进一步完善了个人信息保护规则;2021 年颁布的《中华人民共和国个人信息保护法》细化完善了个人信息保护原则和个人信息处理规则,依法规范国家机关处理个人信息的活动,赋予个人信息主体多项权利,强化个人信息处理者义务。

守护公民财产安全。中国持续加大立法保护力度,遏制利用网络侵犯财产权益的行为。2018 年出台的《中华人民共和国电子商务法》规定,“电子商务经营者销售的商品或者提供的服务应当符合保障人身、财产安全的要求和环境保护要求,不得销售或者提供法律、行政法规禁止交易的商品或者服务。”《中华人民共和国民法典》明确利用网络侵害他人财产权益的行为应当承担相应的法律责任。2022 年出台的《中华人民共和国反电信网络诈骗法》为打击电信网络诈骗活动提供有力的法律支撑,切实维护人民群众的财产权益。

保障特殊群体的数字权利。通过多层次、多维度立法,弥合未成年人、老年人、残疾人等特殊群体的数字鸿沟,使其能够更加平等广泛地融入数字社会,享受数字时代的红利。《中华人民共和国网络安全法》规定,“国家支持研究开发有利于未成年人健康成长的网络产品和服务,依法惩治利用网络从事危害未成年人身心健康的活动,为未成年人提供安全、健康的网络环境。”2019 年发布的《儿童个人信息网络保护规定》对儿童个人信息权益予以重点保护。2020 年修订的《中华人民共和国未成年人保护法》对加强未成年人网络素养教育、强化未成年人网络内容监管、加强未成年人个人信息保护和网络沉迷防治等做出专门规定,保护未成年人的网络合法权益。2021 年出台的《中华人民共和国数据安全法》要求智能化公共服务应当充分考虑老年人、残疾人的需求,避免对老年人、残疾人的日常生活造成障碍。

7.2.2　数字经济规则

中国不断完善数据基础制度,维护数字市场秩序,规范数字经济新业态新模式,为数字经济健康发展提供良好制度基础,助力经济由高速增长转向高质量发展。中国注重发挥数据的基础资源作用和创新引擎作用,《中华人民共和国数据安全法》对实施大数据战略、支持数据相关技术研发和商业创新、推进数据相关标准体系建设、培育数据交易市场等做出相关规定,提升数据开发利用水平,促进以数据为关键要素的数字经济发展。

明晰数字市场运行制度。中国坚持依法规范发展数字市场,坚决反对垄断和不正当竞争,健全数字规则,有力维护公平竞争的市场环境。《中华人民共和国电子商务法》全面规范电子商务经营行为,明确电子商务平台经营者和平台内经营者责任,要求具有市场支配地位的电子商务经营者不得滥用市场支配地位排除、限制竞争,维护公平市场竞争秩序。2013年修订的《中华人民共和国消费者权益保护法》建立网络购物"七日无理由退货"等制度,强化网络经营者消费维权主体责任。2017年修订的《中华人民共和国反不正当竞争法》增加互联网专条,禁止利用技术手段进行不正当竞争。2021年制定的《网络交易监督管理办法》细化《中华人民共和国电子商务法》的有关规定,进一步完善了网络交易监管制度体系。

规范数字经济新业态、新模式。中国的数字经济新业态、新模式快速涌现,在为经济社会发展带来巨大动力和潜能的同时,也对社会治理、产业发展等提出了新的挑战。《中华人民共和国民法典》完善了电子合同订立和履行规则,将数据和网络虚拟财产纳入法律的保护范围,促进数字经济发展。《网络预约出租汽车经营服务管理暂行办法》《互联网信息服务算法推荐管理规定》《区块链信息服务管理规定》《网络借贷信息中介机构业务活动管理暂行办法》《在线旅游经营服务管理暂行规定》等规范网约车、算法、区块链、互联网金融、在线旅游等新技术新业态,丰富"互联网＋"各领域治理的法律依据。

7.2.3 网络信息安全

确立网络安全规则。中国于1994年出台《中华人民共和国计算机信息系统安全保护条例》,确立计算机信息系统安全保护制度和安全监督制度;2000年通过《全国人民代表大会常务委员会关于维护互联网安全的决定》,将互联网安全划分为互联网运行安全和互联网信息安全,确立民事责任、行政责任和刑事责任三位一体的网络安全责任体系框架;2016年11月7日通过《中华人民共和国网络安全法》,这是中国第一部全面规范网络安全管理方面问题的基础性法律。《中华人民共和国网络安全法》明确维护网络运行安全、网络产品和服务安全、网络数据安全、网络信息安全等方面的制度。《网络安全审查办法》《网络产品安全漏洞管理规定》等法律法规进一步细化《中华人民共和国网络安全法》的相关制度。2019年5月,《信息安全技术——网络安全等级保护基本要求》正式发布,中国网络安全等级保护工作正式进入"2.0时代"。

保障关键信息基础设施安全。关键信息基础设施是经济社会运行的神经中枢,对于维护国家网络主权和国家安全、保障经济社会健康发展、维护公共利益和公民合法权益具有重大意义。2021年通过的《关键信息基础设施安全保护条例》完善了关键信息基础设施认定机制,对关键信息基础设施运营者落实网络安全责任、建立健全网络安全保护制度、设置专门安全管理机构、开展安全监测和风险评估、规范网络产品和服务采购活动等做出了具体规定,为加快提升关键信息基础设施安全保护能力提供了法律依据。

构建数据安全管理法律制度。中国立足数据安全工作实际,着眼数据安全领域突出问题,通过立法加强数据安全保护,提升国家数据安全保障能力。《中华人民共和国数据安全法》于 2021 年 6 月正式出台，实现了数据治理制度从无到有的"突破"，成为中国数据安全领域的基础性法律。《中华人民共和国数据安全法》明确了建立健全数据分类分级保护、风险监测预警和应急处置、数据安全审查等制度，对支持促进数据安全与发展的措施、推进政务数据安全与开放等做出规定。

7.2.4   网络生态规范

网络空间是亿万民众共同的精神家园，网络空间天朗气清、生态良好，是人民对网上家园的美好向往。中国本着对社会负责、对人民负责的态度，以网络信息内容为主要规制对象，建立健全网络综合治理法律规范，持续净化网络空间。

规范网络信息传播秩序。面对网络信息治理这一世界性难题，中国出台了《中华人民共和国民法典》《中华人民共和国网络安全法》《互联网信息服务管理办法》等法律法规，明确网络信息内容传播规范和相关主体的责任，为治理危害国家安全、损害公共利益、侵害他人合法权益的违法行为提供了法律依据。

打造网络反恐法律利器。中国坚决依法遏制恐怖主义在网络空间的威胁，《中华人民共和国刑法》《中华人民共和国刑事诉讼法》《中华人民共和国反洗钱法》等法律对恐怖活动犯罪的刑事责任、惩治恐怖活动犯罪的诉讼程序、涉恐资金监控等做出了规定。2015 年通过的《中华人民共和国反恐怖主义法》对网络反恐的对象、措施和机制等做出了专门规定。

7.3   网络安全保护

7.3.1   网络安全技术标准

中国加强新技术研究，研发和部署了一系列安全产品和系统平台，攻克了一批信息安全重大技术难题。中国自主研发了加密强度与国际主流密码算法相当的祖冲之[①]序列密码算法，安全可靠的基础软硬件联合攻关取得重大进展，自主安全操作系统等已从"基本可用"迈向"可用"，国产数据库在国家机关和重要领域广泛应用，基于国产基础软硬件的国产整机在部分党政机关得到试用，工业控制系统的安全防护系统产业化取得积极进展。2010 年 8 月，中国提出的三元对等鉴别协议获国际标准化组织正式批准，成为在网络安全基础共性技术领域获得通过的第一个国际标准。

中国积极推动网络安全标准化工作，建设完善的网络安全国家标准体系。2020 年，全国信息安全标准化技术委员会推动发布了 53 项网络安全国家标准，推动发布 10 余项中国主导和参与的国际标准。2021 年，中国商用密码国际标准化工作取得新突破，中国自主研发的 SM9 标识密码算法正式发布为 ISO/IEC（国际标准化组织/国际电工委员会）国际标准，SM4 分组密码算法进入 ISO/IEC 正式发布阶段。截至 2021 年 6 月，中国已累计发布 323 项网络安全国家标准，这些标准在支撑国家网络安全工作、维护广大互联网用户切身利益等方面发挥了基础性、规范性、引领性作用。

---

① 　祖冲之是公元 5 世纪中国著名数学家、天文学家。

7.3.2 网络安全保护队伍

中国先后建立了多个网络安全专业机构,有效提升了网络安全监测和应急处置能力。1996年,国家计算机病毒应急处理中心成立,调动国内防病毒力量,快速发现、处置计算机病毒疫情与网络攻击,为国家制定计算机病毒防治政策、法规和标准提供了重要技术支持。1998年,中国信息安全测评中心成立,开展信息技术产品、系统的安全漏洞分析与信息通报。2001年,国家计算机网络应急技术处理协调中心(CNCERT/CC)成立,开展互联网网络安全事件的预防、发现、预警和协调处置工作。2004年,国家网络与信息安全信息通报中心成立,作为国家级网络和信息安全信息通报出口,对中国网络信息安全方面的信息进行报告和通报。2005年,国家信息技术安全研究中心成立,主要承担信息技术产品和系统的安全性分析与研究、国家基础信息网络和重要信息系统的信息安全保障任务。

目前,中国具备了网络有害信息甄别、突发事件早期发现等信息内容监管技术能力,网络安全事件应急响应与协同处置、信息系统纵深防护等网络空间整体对抗技术能力,政府部门网络集中接入、网络身份认证管理等信息资源保障技术能力,云计算、物联网等新技术、新应用安全支撑技术能力,形成了比较健全的网络安全防护能力体系。

2020年,国家计算机网络应急技术处理协调中心协调处置各类网络安全事件约10.3万起,同比减少4.2%。2016—2020年,中国感染计算机恶意程序的主机数量持续下降,并保持在较低感染水平,年均减少率为25.1%。通过中国互联网网络安全威胁治理联盟,联合国内10家浏览器厂商通过协同防御试点方式,在用户访问钓鱼网站时进行提示拦截,2020年提示拦截次数达到3.9亿次。国家计算机网络应急技术处理协调中心对被用于进行分布式拒绝服务(DDoS)攻击的网络资源持续开展治理工作,中国境内可被利用的攻击资源不断减少,DDoS攻击事件从源头上得到遏制。据统计,2020年中国境内DDoS攻击次数同比减少了16.16%,攻击总流量下降了19.67%,僵尸网络控制端数量在全球的占比稳步下降至2.05%。

7.3.3 网络安全产业发展

中国网络安全产业实现了从无到有、从小到大的发展,产业结构逐渐齐全,产业集聚效应开始显现,在促进互联网健康发展方面发挥了重要作用。国家发展改革委"信息安全专项"、科技部"国家科技支撑计划"、工业和信息化部"电子信息产业发展基金项目"等项目有力推进了网络安全产业化。2019年9月,工业和信息化部《关于促进网络安全产业发展的指导意见(征求意见稿)》公开征求意见,致力于加强对网络安全的重视,提高网络安全产品的应用规模,积极创新网络安全服务模式。

中国自主研发的网络安全产品涵盖了物理安全、通信安全、数据安全、应用安全、安全管理平台以及新技术、新应用安全等领域,形成了从安全芯片、网络与边界安全产品、数据安全产品、应用安全产品到安全服务较为完善的信息安全产业链。从基础软硬件到应用软件的自主研发、生产、升级、维护全程可控体系基本形成。在基础硬件方面,处理器、交换芯片、显示芯片等国产芯片产品已接近国外主流产品水平,具备系统性应用的条件。在基础软件方面,国产操作系统、国产数据库技术趋于成熟,已覆盖服务器、桌面、移动和嵌入式等领域。在应用软件方面,中国自主可控的办公自动化、企业管理及行业应用系统等软件,已在通信、军事、航空、航天等高精尖技术及实时性要求高的领域得到应用。

2019年,中国网络安全产业规模达到1 563.59亿元,较2018年增长17.1％,明显高于国际9.11％的平均增速,保持健康的发展态势。截至2019年11月底,中国国内上市的网络安全企业达到了23家,有100多家创投机构在网络安全领域进行投资布局,汇集超过了150家创新创业的企业。根据2020年6月中国网络空间安全协会发布的《2020年中国网络安全产业统计报告》,2019年中国网络安全技术、产品与服务总收入约为523.09亿元,同比增长25.37％;网络安全企业从业人员约为10万人。

7.4　网络空间治理

7.4.1　公共环境治理

中国建立和完善了互联网基础性法治环境,先后出台了一系列与互联网相关的法律法规,涉及互联网基础资源管理、信息传播规范、市场秩序规范、信息安全保障等多个方面,对互联网接入服务提供者、互联网信息服务提供者、政府管理部门及互联网用户等行为主体的责任和义务做出了规定。有关部门根据职责,在互联网新闻信息服务、新闻出版、视听节目、网络游戏、网络文化、网络药品、网络版权、网络交易、电子认证、互联网域名、互联网接入、系统安全和保密等领域分别出台了一系列部门规章和规范性文件。

互联网基础资源管理方面,中国依法加强对域名、IP地址和网站登记备案、接入服务等互联网基础资源管理。2004年12月20日,《中国互联网域名管理办法》正式施行,保障了中国互联网域名系统安全、可靠地运行,规范了中国互联网域名系统管理和域名注册服务。2005年2月,中国信息产业部开展全国互联网站集中备案工作,逐步建立ICP(网络内容服务商)备案信息、IP地址使用信息、域名信息等3个基础数据库。截至2015年,中国网站备案率提升至99.98％,备案主体信息准确率达84.7％。

用户账号名称管理方面,中国于2002年9月出台《互联网上网服务营业场所管理条例》,以加强对互联网上网服务营业场所的管理,规范经营者经营行为。2012年,中国开始对互联网信息服务使用者注册账号进行真实身份信息认证;自2013年9月1日起,新增固定电话、移动电话(含无线上网卡)用户实施真实身份信息登记。2021年1月22日,国家互联网信息办公室(国家网信办)发布修订的《互联网用户公众账号信息服务管理规定》,对公众账号的管理更加精细化和精准化。

7.4.2　个人隐私保护

数据安全关系个人安全。一旦大量涉及个人身份、家庭、经济状况、兴趣爱好等公民个人隐私,以及人脸、指纹、DNA等不可逆转的生物特征信息被恶意泄露,安全隐患不容小觑。基于此,中国已先后制定了《中华人民共和国网络安全法》《中华人民共和国电子商务法》《中华人民共和国民法典》等法律法规,2021年9月起施行的《中华人民共和国数据安全法》和2021年11月起施行的《中华人民共和国个人信息保护法》则构成了中国不断加强个人信息安全和隐私保护的另两大支柱。

2020 年开始,中国广泛推广用于流行病学调查、保护公共卫生安全的应用程序,保护其中的个人隐私数据尤为重要。2020 年 3 月 6 日,中国发布了新版《信息安全技术　个人信息安全规范》,规范明确了"行踪轨迹"属于"个人敏感信息",在收集此类信息时,需满足"最小必要原则"和"合法性原则",只有在"与公共安全、公共卫生、重大公共利益直接相关"等 11 种例外情形下才不必征得授权同意。

7.4.3　个体权益保障

移动互联网应用程序成为个人信息保护重点领域。2021 年 3 月,国家网信办等部门联合印发《常见类型移动互联网应用程序必要个人信息范围规定》,明确了 39 种基础类型应用程序的基本功能及保障其正常运行所需收集的个人信息的具体类型、使用要求。2021 年 4 月,工业和信息化部会同公安部、国家市场监督管理总局起草并公布《移动互联网应用程序个人信息保护管理暂行规定(征求意见稿)》,细化了"知情同意""最小必要"的认定标准,推动有效解决在实践中对用户个人信息收集使用规则、目的、方式和范围不明确的问题。

在未成年人网络内容保护方面,修订的《中华人民共和国未成年人保护法》于 2021 年 6 月 1 日正式生效,开启未成年人网络保护新篇章。有关部门陆续发布规范性文件,部署未成年人网络保护相关专项行动。在全国联合开展打击互联网和手机媒体淫秽色情、整治互联网低俗之风、整治网络欺凌暴力、"黑网吧"治理、清理整治网络游戏等一系列专项行动,组织新闻网站和商业网站自查自纠清理各类违法有害信息,网络环境得到持续净化。

在老年人使用互联网支撑方面,2020 年 12 月,工业和信息化部印发《互联网应用适老化及无障碍改造专项行动方案》,部署相关产品和服务措施。2021 年 4 月,工业和信息化部发布《移动互联网应用(APP)适老化通用设计规范》《互联网网站适老化通用设计规范》,明确在适老版界面中严禁出现广告内容及插件,禁止出现诱导下载、诱导付款等诱导式按键。2021 年 6 月,工业和信息化部正式发布《移动终端适老化技术要求》《移动终端适老化测试方法》《智能电视适老化设计技术要求》三项标准,侧重于解决老年人在使用智能终端产品的过程中遇到的各种困难。

在数字经济劳动者权益保护方面,中国注重保护广大劳动者、消费者等群体的利益,维护社会公平、正义,确保数字经济持续稳定健康发展。2021 年 7 月 26 日,国家市场监督管理总局、国家网信办等七部门以规范性文件的形式,联合印发《关于落实网络餐饮平台责任　切实维护外卖送餐员权益的指导意见》,对保障外卖送餐员的正当权益提出全面具体要求,从劳动收入、考核制度、派单机制、劳动安全等 10 个方面,要求切实维护外卖送餐员的正当权益。

7.4.4　数字内容监管

为保护著作权人、表演者、录音录像作者的信息网络传播权,2001 年 10 月,信息网络传播权正式列入修订后的《中华人民共和国著作权法》;2006 年 5 月,《信息网络传播权保护条例》正式颁布。2014 年 6 月,国家版权局联合国家网信办、工业和信息化部、公安部启动"剑网 2014"专项行动,持续开展网络侵权盗版专项治理,侦破一批重点网络侵权盗版案件,依法关闭 200 个涉嫌侵权盗版的网站。

中国依法严厉打击电信网络诈骗、侵犯公民个人信息等违法犯罪,组织开展"净网"专项行动。"清朗"专项行动深入实施,有效抑制网络乱象滋生蔓延。2019—2022年,中国通过近30项专项治理,清理违法和不良信息204.93亿条、账号13.89亿个,下架违法违规应用程序6.7万余款,关闭违法网站4.2万余家。中国不断加强网络信息内容建设,积极营造良好网络生态,推动形成风清气正的网络空间。

7.4.5 信息技术治理

制定人工智能算法管理的专门法律规则。2021年8月,中国印发《国家新一代人工智能标准体系建设指南》,规范人工智能服务,满足传统道德伦理和法律秩序的要求。2021年8月27日,国家网信办发布了关于《互联网信息服务算法推荐管理规定(征求意见稿)》公开征求意见的通知,对算法推荐技术进行专门管理规定。2021年9月,国家网信办等九部委联合印发《关于加强互联网信息服务算法综合治理的指导意见》,明确要求使用算法的企业对算法应用结果负主体责任,并建立算法安全责任制度和科技伦理审查制度,健全算法安全管理组织机构,加强风险防控和隐患排查治理,提升应对算法安全突发事件的能力和水平。

制定车联网和汽车数据安全的相关规范。2021年8月,国家网信办等部门联合发布了《汽车数据安全管理若干规定(试行)》,倡导坚持"车内处理""默认不收集""精度范围适用""脱敏处理"等原则,减少对汽车数据的无序收集和违规滥用。2021年9月13日,工业和信息化部发布《工业和信息化部关于加强车联网卡实名登记管理的通知》,明确不同销售阶段对车联网卡实名登记的要求,防范车联网中的安全风险。2021年9月15日,工业和信息化部发布《工业和信息化部关于加强车联网网络安全和数据安全工作的通知》,对车联网的网络安全和数据安全提出了基本要求。

7.4.6 数字经济监管

在数字经济的平台经济发展初期,中国采取"包容审慎"的发展理念,不过多过早干预企业行为,但在平台企业已具有相当规模、行业发展日趋成熟的阶段,强化监管就成了维护市场竞争、促进优胜劣汰的必要之举。

中国积极构建数字化发展治理体系,打造健康有序的发展环境,制定实施《中华人民共和国电子商务法》《中华人民共和国反不正当竞争法》《中华人民共和国反垄断法》《优化营商环境条例》,发布《国务院办公厅关于促进平台经济规范健康发展的指导意见》,推动平台经济规范健康发展,有效维护市场主体和人民群众合法权益。2021年2月,国务院反垄断委员会发布《国务院反垄断委员会关于平台经济领域的反垄断指南》,明确平台经济领域反垄断执法原则。2021年3月,国家市场监督管理总局出台《网络交易监督管理办法》,进一步规范网络交易活动,维护网络交易秩序,保障网络交易各方主体合法权益。

中国针对新型网络营销方式,与时俱进制定了相关规范。针对网络直播和营销领域,2020年底,《市场监管总局关于加强网络直播营销活动监管的指导意见》《国家广播电视总局关于加强网络秀场直播和电商直播管理的通知》等相关规范性文件相继出台。2021年4月16日,中央网信办、公安部、商务部等七部委联合印发《网络直播营销管理办法(试行)》,通过发布规范性文件的形式系统、全面地解决电商网络直播营销问题。

7.4.7 协同治理模式

中国政府发挥统筹引领作用,统筹协调各方积极参与互联网治理。政府综合采用法律规制、行政管理、产业政策、技术标准、宣传教育等多种措施,调动各方力量共同推进互联网发展,建立了既符合互联网规律又具有中国特色的互联网治理模式。

互联网企业认真履行主体责任。2004 年 11 月,新浪、搜狐、网易公布中国互联网行业"诚信自律同盟"的自律细则,标志着中国互联网信息服务企业主动承担维护市场秩序的主体责任。2013 年 6 月,阿里巴巴、腾讯、百度、新浪、盛大、网易等 21 家互联网企业成立了"互联网反欺诈委员会",推进全网联合打击网络诈骗,共建交易安全生态圈。2013 年,百度、奇虎 360 等搜索引擎服务企业先后发布互联网用户权益保障计划,承担起更大的社会责任。

行业组织有力促进互联网健康发展。中国高度重视社会组织在互联网治理中的重要作用,大力支持各类行业协会和社会组织建设,积极参与互联网治理。2001 年 5 月,全国性行业组织中国互联网协会成立,制定发布了《中国互联网行业自律公约》《互联网站禁止传播淫秽色情等不良信息自律规范》《抵制恶意软件自律公约》《中国互联网行业版权自律宣言》等一系列自律规范。2002 年 11 月,中国互联网协会设立了反垃圾邮件协调小组,为治理垃圾邮件做出了突出贡献。

7.5　小　　结

互联网及其所衍生的网络空间,是人类文明发展进程中的璀璨结晶。在网络空间,个人与团体的各类行为活动均须在人类社会法治的框架下接受保护与监督。网络社会治理的概念和范畴始终处于动态发展与演进之中,世界各国政府都肩负着保障个人和团体在网络空间的合法权益、维护网络空间正常秩序的重要使命。

中国构建了完备的网络空间法律体系。从最初接入互联网,到成长为引领移动互联网应用创新潮流的世界大国,中国网络立法实现了从空白到逐步健全、从单一规范到全面覆盖的历史性跨越。截至 2024 年 6 月,中国已制定出台网络领域立法 150 余部,其内容涵盖个人数字权益保障、数字经济规则完善、网络信息安全维护、网络生态规范优化等多个关键领域。中国的网络空间法律体系不仅保障了中国网络空间的有序发展,也为全球网络立法提供了丰富的参考范例。

中国打造了强大的网络空间安全保护力量。中国坚持自主研发网络安全系列技术,攻克了多项关键安全技术难题,研发出一系列先进的安全技术与算法,构建起科学完备的安全技术标准体系。中国组建了覆盖关键安全领域的专业保护机构和高素质队伍,具备了常态化网络监测与高效应急处理能力,能够及时、妥善应对各类网络安全威胁。中国网络安全产业呈现出蓬勃发展的良好态势,产业规模持续稳定增长,产品广泛覆盖多个关键领域,形成了完整且成熟的产业链。中国的网络安全技术和产业不但保障了本国网络与信息系统的健康运行,而且可以为其他国家提供专业的安全保障服务。

中国开展了全方位、多维度的网络社会治理实践。在公共环境治理领域,不断优化互联网法治环境,强化互联网基础资源管理,严格规范用户账号管理,维护了良好的网络空间秩序。在个人权益保障领域,通过规范数据收集流程、加强个人隐私保护,全力保障青少年、老年人等群体平等便捷地接入网络,切实维护数字经济劳动者的合法权益。此外,中国在数字内容监管、信息技术治理、数字经济监管等方面持续发力。中国政府发挥统筹引领作用,协调互联网产业相关各方参与网络空间治理,形成了协同高效、可持续发展的治理模式。

　　互联网的蓬勃发展为全球带来了难得的机遇,也带来了诸多挑战,而法治无疑是互联网治理的核心要素。中国自接入国际互联网后,全面推进网络空间法治化,构建了完善的法治体系,有力促进了网络安全与发展的良性互动。中国走出的依法治网之路,不仅显著提升了本国互联网治理水平,还为世界其他国家提供了全面的、系统的、具有借鉴意义的治理样本,为推动全球互联网治理体系的完善与发展贡献了中国智慧。

8 国际数字合作

8.1 需求与挑战

进入 21 世纪以来,信息与通信技术的发展拓展了人类的生存空间,也变革了社会生产方式,但是并未从根本上改变国际政治秩序。网络空间全球治理中存在各种问题,比如东西方矛盾和南北差距,迫切要求世界各国携起手来,共同面对。

8.1.1 互联网时代数字鸿沟

互联网是人类的共同生存空间,互联网的发展体现了一个国家的经济和科技发展水平。当然,全球互联网发展存在着国家之间和地区之间的差距,这种差距即"数字鸿沟"。

全球的数字鸿沟依然存在,而且日益扩大。国际电信联盟的数据显示,2021 年底,全球网民达到 49 亿,大约占全球人口的 63%,其中发展中国家的网民年增长率达到 13.3%。2015—2021 年,全球 4G 网络覆盖率增长了 1 倍,覆盖全球人口的 88%。在亚太地区、欧洲和美洲,90% 的人口可以使用移动宽带网络(3G 或以上)。2020—2021 年,非洲 4G 网络覆盖率增长了 21 个百分点,但截至 2021 年仍有 18% 的人口无法接入移动宽带网络,与其他地区的覆盖率差距仍然较大。2021 年,全球依然还有 29 亿人无法上网,其中 96% 处于发展中国家,约 3.9 亿人甚至生活在没有移动宽带信号覆盖的地区。2022 年全球无法上网人口的分布及数量如图 8-1 所示。

发达国家利用其技术先发优势,掌握了互联网的规则制定权和网络话语权。网络发展中国家无法平等参与全球网络空间治理的各项事务,技术上受制于人,经济上受到遏制和盘剥。这反映了网络空间存在着发展不平衡、不充分的问题,需要在全球网络空间建立公正合理的规则和机制,维护发展中国家平等参与全球网络空间事务的权利,实现网络空间可持续发展。

8.1.2 全球网络安全风险

近年来,全球网络安全态势日趋严峻,出现了很多重大的网络公共安全事件,例如 DDoS 攻击、勒索软件攻击、电信诈骗、移动终端恶意代码攻击等。世界经济论坛发布的《2024 年全球风险报告》显示,网络不安全是未来 10 年最受关注的全球十大风险之一。2021 年,网络攻击事件多次引发网络服务中断、工厂停产等严重后果,对社会稳定运行和民众生产生活产生恶劣影响。

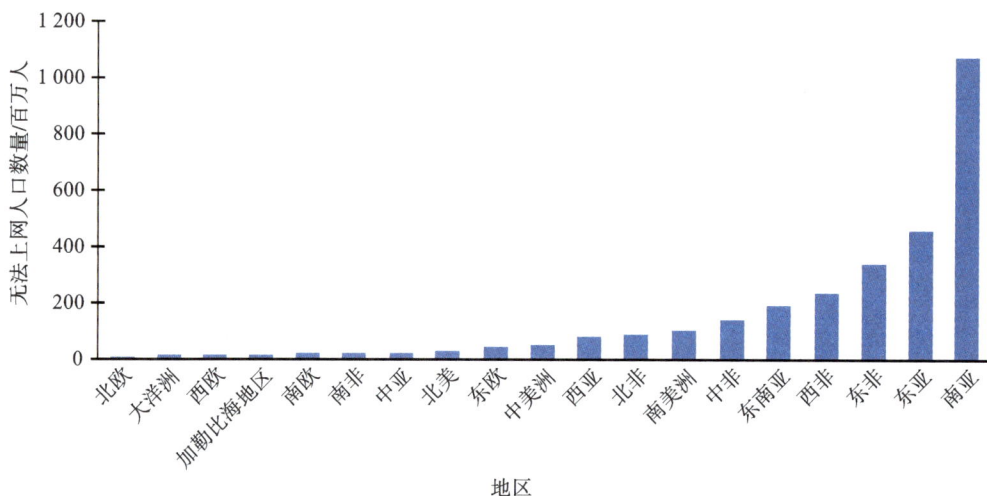

图 8-1　2022 年全球无法上网人口的分布及数量

数据来源：Digital 2022：Global Overview Report

例如，2021 年 5 月，美国最大成品油管道运营商科洛尼尔管道运输公司遭黑客组织"黑暗面"的勒索软件攻击，严重影响美国东海岸成品油供应。2021 年 7 月，英国北方铁路公司的自动售票系统遭勒索软件攻击，导致售票网络瘫痪。2021 年 9 月，新西兰基础电信企业 Vocus 遭 DDoS 攻击，导致奥克兰、惠灵顿等城市网络服务中断。

网络恐怖主义在网络空间肆意蔓延，传统刑事犯罪网络化也呈现高发的态势。为此，很多国家已将网络安全的重要性提高到国家战略的高度。2014 年，美国国家标准与技术研究院（NIST）发布了《美国增强关键基础设施网络安全框架》，将网络安全解释为"通过预防、检测和响应攻击以保护信息的过程"。2014 年，俄罗斯联邦在《俄罗斯联邦网络安全战略构想》中将网络安全解释为"所有网络空间组成部分处在避免潜在威胁及其后果影响的各种条件的总和"。2020 年，欧盟发布《欧盟数字十年的网络安全战略》，包含法规、投资和政策工具方面的相关建议。

新技术的不断迭代及其社会应用的普及，也为国际社会带来了新的治理难题与挑战。随着大数据、人工智能等新技术的出现和推广，网络安全面临更多的前所未有的技术挑战。2020 年 11 月，世界经济论坛发布题为《未来系列：网络安全、新兴技术与系统性风险》的报告。该报告称，随着新兴技术的发展，网络空间的规模、速度和互联性正在发生重大变化，这些变化将带来一系列新的系统性风险和挑战。因此，有必要建立各国普遍认同的网络空间安全规范，将跨国网络犯罪问题纳入法治化的轨道，保障各国网络行为主体的合法权益。

8.1.3　全球数字贸易需求

新一代信息技术加速向国际经贸领域延伸，数字贸易应运而生，对贸易方式、贸易对象、贸易规则、贸易格局产生深远影响。2011—2020 年，全球数字贸易快速发展，数字服务贸易复合年均增长率达 4.4%，显著高于传统的国际服务贸易（1.19%）和货物贸易（－0.4%）。数字贸易占全球贸易的比重日益增加。2012 年开始，超过 90% 的服务贸易协定中开始包含数字贸易（电子商务）的相关条款或专章。与此同时，国际数字贸易也面临许多挑战，例如贸易对象和方式的数字化使得诸多新兴规则空白亟待健全,原有贸易规则体系和谈判机制需要修改和更新。

随着信息技术的发展,越来越多的货物贸易转变为数字化、虚拟的服务贸易。虽然数字技术可以通过降低贸易成本和进入门槛使发展中国家中小企业受益,但是受到技术产业发展规律和超级平台的影响,发展中国家在开展数字贸易方面面临更大挑战。例如,发展中国家中小企业通过在线平台开展国际贸易时,可能遭遇到在线平台服务提供商的不公平待遇。发展中国家在数据基础设施、数据管理经验等方面的短板也可能导致其蒙受损失。例如,由于缺乏合适的技术监管手段,发展中国家数字贸易的关税收入面临侵蚀风险。

8.2　网络空间命运共同体

网络空间命运共同体,是人类命运共同体的概念在网络空间的延伸。2013 年 3 月,中国国家主席习近平在访问俄罗斯时,首次提出人类命运共同体的重要理念。2020 年 11 月 23 日,世界互联网大会·互联网发展论坛在浙江乌镇开幕,习近平主席向论坛致贺信,在贺信中指出:中国愿同世界各国一道,把握信息革命历史机遇,培育创新发展新动能,开创数字合作新局面,打造网络安全新格局,构建网络空间命运共同体,携手创造人类更加美好的未来。

8.2.1　网络治理的中国声音

2014 年以来,中国连续 11 年在浙江乌镇举办世界互联网大会,搭建中国与世界互联互通的国际平台和国际互联网共享共治的中国平台,各国政府、国际组织、互联网企业、智库、行业协会、技术社群等各界代表应邀参会交流。

大会组委会先后发布《携手构建网络空间命运共同体》概念文件、《携手构建网络空间命运共同体行动倡议》,举办案例发布展示活动,深入阐释落实构建网络空间命运共同体理念。大会的成功举办极大地促进了各国互联网领域的紧密联系与深入交流,有力推动了构建网络空间命运共同体的中国经验、中国方案、中国智慧日益从理念共识走向具体实践,推动全球互联网治理体系向着更加公正合理的方向迈进。

2021 年 8 月,以"共谋发展　共享安全　携手构建网络空间命运共同体"为主题的中非互联网发展与合作论坛以视频连线的方式举办。来自 14 个非洲国家及非盟委员会的代表出席论坛,围绕共享数字技术红利、携手维护网络安全等议题开展深入交流。中方发起"中非携手构建网络空间命运共同体倡议",呼吁中国与非洲国家政府、互联网企业、技术社群、社会组织、公民个人共同参与,携手构建更加紧密的网络空间命运共同体。

中国持续深入推进网络空间国际交流合作进程。以联合国为主渠道、以《联合国宪章》为基本原则,中国积极参与制定数字和网络空间国际规则。中国还向欠发达国家提供技术、设备、服务等数字援助,使各国共享数字时代红利,推动落实联合国 2030 年可持续发展议程。

8.2.2　构建网络空间命运共同体

中国推出的网络空间命运共同体的主张,内涵较为丰富。中国坚持共商、共建、共享的全球治理观,推动构建多边、民主、透明的国际互联网治理体系。中国主张未来的国际网络空间应该创新发展、安全有序、平等尊重、开放共享。世界各国在网络空间方面应做到发展共同推进、安全共同维护、治理共同参与、成果共同分享。网络空间命运共同体就可以解读为发展共同体、安全共同体、责任共同体、利益共同体。

构建发展共同体。不同国家和地区在互联网普及、基础设施建设、技术创新创造、数字经济发展、数字素养与技能等方面的发展水平不平衡,影响和限制世界各国特别是发展中国家的信息化建设与数字化转型。构建发展共同体,就是采取更加积极、包容、协调、普惠的政策,推动全球信息基础设施加快普及,为广大发展中国家提供用得上、用得起、用得好的网络服务,充分发挥数字经济在全球经济发展中的引擎作用,积极推进数字产业化发展和产业数字化转型。

构建安全共同体。安全是发展的前提,一个安全稳定繁荣的网络空间,对世界各国都具有重大意义。网络安全是全球性挑战,没有哪个国家能够置身事外、独善其身,维护网络安全是国际社会的共同责任。构建安全共同体,就是倡导开放合作的网络安全理念,坚持安全与发展并重、鼓励与规范并举。加强关键信息基础设施保护和数据安全国际合作,维护信息技术中立和产业全球化,共同遏制信息技术滥用。进一步增强战略互信,及时共享网络威胁信息,有效协调处置重大网络安全事件,合作打击网络恐怖主义和网络犯罪,共同维护网络空间和平与安全。

构建责任共同体。网络空间是人类共同的活动空间,网络空间前途命运应由世界各国共同掌握。构建责任共同体,就是坚持多边参与、多方参与,积极推进全球互联网治理体系改革和建设。发挥联合国在网络空间国际治理中的主渠道作用,发挥政府、国际组织、互联网企业、技术社群、社会组织、公民个人等各主体的作用,建立相互信任、协调有序的合作。完善对话协商机制,共同研究制定网络空间治理规范,更加平衡地反映各方利益关切,特别是广大发展中国家的利益,使治理体系更加公正、合理。

构建利益共同体。互联网发展治理成果应由世界各国共同分享,确保不同国家、不同民族、不同人群平等享有互联网发展红利。帮助中小微企业利用新一代信息技术促进产品、服务、流程、组织和商业模式的创新,让中小微企业更多地从数字经济的发展中分享机遇。注重对弱势群体的网络保护,加强网络伦理和网络文明建设,在全球范围内促进普惠式发展,提升广大发展中国家网络发展能力,弥合数字鸿沟。

8.3　数字经济国际合作

中国积极参与数字经济国际合作。中国参与各地区的互联网信息基础设施建设,推动各类互联网新技术及其应用的国际化,促进提升全球数字互联互通水平。中国也与各国积极开展数字贸易方面的合作,促进全球数字经济与实体经济融合发展。

8.3.1　国际信息基础设施建设

8.3.1.1　互联网基础资源管理

互联网的公共基础资源包括 IP 地址、域名等。中国高度重视与互联网名称与数字地址分配机构(ICANN)、亚太互联网络信息中心(APNIC)、万维网联盟(W3C)、国际互联网协会(ISOC)、互联网架构委员会(IAB)、国际互联网工程任务组(IETF)等国际互联网行业组织的交流合作,推动互联网关键资源的合理分配以及互联网基础服务(例如域名服务)的互联互通。

2002年,ICANN会议首次在中国上海举办。2003年,中国科学院研究员钱华林当选ICANN理事。2020年11月,中国互联网络信息中心(CNNIC)的技术专家姚健康当选国家和地区名称支持组织(ccNSO)新一届理事,在该组织相关政策制定、议题设置和国际交流合作等方面发挥积极作用,提升中国在国际技术社群的活跃度和认可度。

亚太顶级域名联合会(APTLD)是国家和地区顶级域名(ccTLD)在亚太地区的组织机构,其宗旨是促进会员之间互联网域名应用技术发展信息交流,提升会员在全球互联网领域的影响力。截至2021年,APTLD有50个正式机构会员、19个准会员。2021年2月,CNNIC代表当选APTLD新一届董事,为进一步维护国际社群关系、深化区域交流合作做出了重要贡献。

APNIC是全球五大区域级互联网IP地址注册管理机构之一,负责亚太地区IP地址的分配管理,中国所有的IP地址资源均从APNIC申请获得。2021年3月,CNNIC代表当选APNIC执行委员会委员,中国借此深化与APNIC的合作与交流,促进与周边国家及"一带一路"国家和地区在互联网基础资源方面的合作。

8.3.1.2　非洲信息基础设施建设

长期以来,中国积极参与非洲的基础设施建设,帮助非洲国家实施了大量基础设施和民生项目。自2000年中非合作论坛成立至2021年,中国为非洲新增和升级铁路网超过了1万千米,公路近10万千米,电力装机容量1.2亿千瓦,通信骨干网达15万千米。截至2019年6月,非洲约80%的骨干网络基础设施是中资企业投融资建设的;在非洲54国中,有40多个国家在通信网络设施方面采用了中国的产品和技术。

2018年在北京举行的中非合作论坛北京峰会发布了《中非合作论坛——北京行动计划(2019—2021年)》。中国和非洲国家鼓励、支持各自企业合作参与非洲国家光缆骨干网、跨境互联互通、国际海底光缆、新一代移动通信网络、数据中心等通信基础设施建设,双方将积极探讨和促进云计算、大数据、移动互联网等新技术应用,提升信息通信技术在维护社会治安、反恐和打击犯罪等方面的作用。

在中资企业的参与下,部分非洲国家的宽带网络基础设施的水平获得显著改善。例如,中资企业承建尼日利亚电信运营商Globacom的Glo-2海底光缆系统。该系统将沿尼日利亚海岸进行铺设,连接拉各斯阿尔法海滩到南部地区,全长850千米,提供12 Tbps的传输容量。

在中资企业的参与下,非洲地区也在加速进入5G商用时代。2020年7月,南非电信运营商Rain在华为的技术支持下顺利发布了非洲首个5G独立组网商用网络。2022年11月,赞比亚移动通信运营商MTN在华为的支持下启动该国首个5G商用网络服务。2023年4月,中资企业与乌干达电信运营商MTN及HIMA水泥公司等合作伙伴在乌干达首都坎帕拉共同发布了由该中资企业支持的该国首个5G数字水泥工厂项目,实现生产区域的数据实时传输。

8.3.2　全球数字服务供给

除了网络基础设施之外，中国也积极参与各国的数字产业化进程，向世界各国提供了全球化的信息技术服务，包括北斗卫星导航服务、云服务等。

北斗成为全球重要的时空基础设施。中国与阿拉伯国家联盟（简称"阿盟"）、东南亚国家联盟（简称"东盟"）、中亚、非洲等地区、国家和区域组织持续开展卫星导航合作与交流，北斗相关产品已出口至全球一半以上国家和地区。2021年，在北京举办的第一届中非北斗合作论坛上，《北斗卫星导航系统在非十大应用场景》正式发布，展示了北斗在非洲道路运输、车辆管理、铁路行业、精准农业等领域的应用案例、应用解决方案。

中阿北斗/GNSS中心坐落于突尼斯首都突尼斯城，是中国第一个海外北斗中心，为非洲与阿拉伯国家提供卫星导航培训、测试评估和技术研究。该中心的中心屏幕上实时显示采集的数据，突尼斯平均可以收到12颗以上北斗卫星发出的信号。在莫桑比克，中非赛赛农业合作项目将北斗定位的无人机广泛应用于农田测绘、水稻播种、农药喷洒等田间植保作业。与传统人工喷洒每小时仅3～4亩相比，植保无人机每小时能为上百亩田地喷洒农药，累计作业已超过3万亩。

此外，中国的云计算平台也开始提供国际化服务，特别是为非洲、中东、东南亚国家以及共建"一带一路"国家提供云服务支持。由中国引领构建的全球微生物大数据平台基础设施"全球微生物资源数据共享平台"，截至2021年已汇聚了来自51个国家141家合作伙伴的52万株微生物实物资源数据，形成了互联互通的微生物数据信息化合作网络，建立了全球微生物菌种保藏目录，促进了全球微生物数据资源的有效利用。

8.3.3　数字经济交流合作

中国积极参与国际和区域性多边机制下的数字经济治理合作，推动发起多个倡议、宣言，提出多项符合大多数国家利益和诉求的提案，加强同专业性国际组织合作，为全球数字经济治理贡献力量。

推进亚太经济合作组织（简称"亚太经合组织"）数字经济合作进程。2014年，中国作为亚太经合组织东道主首次将互联网经济引入亚太经合组织合作框架，发起并推动通过《亚太经合组织促进互联网经济合作倡议》。2019年，亚太经合组织数字经济指导组成立后，中国积极推动全面平衡落实《亚太经合组织互联网和数字经济路线图》。2020年以来，中国先后提出"优化数字营商环境　激活市场主体活力"等倡议，均获亚太经合组织协商一致通过。

积极参与二十国集团框架下的数字经济合作。2016年，二十国集团领导人第十一次峰会在中国举行。在中国的推动下，此次会议首次将"数字经济"列为二十国集团创新增长蓝图中的一项重要议题，并通过了《二十国集团数字经济发展与合作倡议》，这是全球首个由多国领导人共同签署的数字经济政策文件，此后，数字经济成为二十国集团的核心议题之一。近年来，中国积极参加二十国集团数字经济部长会议和数字经济任务组相关磋商，推动数字经济任务组升级为工作组，推动数字经济发展成果惠及世界人民。

不断拓展金砖国家数字经济交流合作。2017年，金砖国家领导人第九次会晤在中国举行，会上通过的《金砖国家领导人厦门宣言》明确提出深化信息通信技术、电子商务、互联网空间领域的务实合作。2019年，金砖国家未来网络研究院中国分院正式在深圳揭牌成立。

2022 年,金砖国家领导人第十四次会晤通过了《金砖国家数字经济伙伴关系框架》。此外,中国举办了金砖国家数字经济对话会等重要活动,开启了金砖国家数字经济合作新进程。

深化同东盟数字经济合作。2020 年,中国—东盟数字经济合作年举行,主题为"集智聚力共战疫　互利共赢同发展",举行网络事务对话,第二十三次中国—东盟领导人会议发表《中国—东盟关于建立数字经济合作伙伴关系的倡议》,同意进一步加深数字经济领域合作。

积极推动世界贸易组织数字经济合作。2017 年,中国正式宣布加入世界贸易组织"电子商务发展之友",协同发展中成员共同支持世界贸易组织电子商务议题磋商。2019 年,中国与美国、欧盟、俄罗斯、巴西、新加坡、尼日利亚、缅甸等 76 个世贸组织成员共同发表《关于电子商务的联合声明》,启动与贸易有关的电子商务议题谈判。2022 年,中国与其他世贸组织成员共同发表《电子商务工作计划》部长决定,支持电子传输免征关税,助力全球数字经济发展。

8.3.4　国际跨境电子商务

中国是跨境电商出口大国,也是全球跨境电商最大进口市场。伴随着跨境电商的蓬勃发展,中国正积极与其他国家在跨境电商国际法律和规则领域加强协调互动,深化与其他发展中国家以及经济落后国家在电子商务领域的合作,帮助各国中小企业缩小数字鸿沟,形成国际合作共赢的发展格局。中国跨境电商的发展从买全球、卖全球,现在已经发展到了国际生态合作阶段。跨境电商的发展不仅将产品出售给海外市场的终端消费者,还融入了国内和国外的各种资源,整合不同国家的市场主体,形成跨国界的跨境电商生态服务体系,促进全球数字贸易的发展。

2021 年 10 月,商务部、中央网信办、发展改革委联合发布《"十四五"电子商务发展规划》,在跨境电商相关部分提出了发展目标,即到 2025 年将跨境电子商务的交易额从 2020 年的 1.69 万亿元提升到 2.5 万亿元。2023 年,中国跨境电商进出口总额 2.38 万亿元,增长 15.6%;其中,出口 1.83 万亿元,增长 19.6%;进口 5 483 亿元,增长 3.9%。中国参与跨境电商进口的消费者数量逐年增加,2023 年已达到 1.63 亿。

8.3.4.1　跨境电商合作政策

中国积极推动跨境电商方面的国际合作,参与世界贸易组织、二十国集团、亚太经济合作组织、金砖国家、上海合作组织(简称"上合组织")等多边和区域贸易机制下的电子商务议题磋商,与自贸伙伴共同构建区域高水平数字经济规则,电子商务国际规则构建取得突破。《区域全面经济伙伴关系协定》中的电子商务章节成为目前覆盖区域较广、内容较全面、水平较高的电子商务国际规则。2022 年,中国跨境电商出口额前十的国家分别为美国、马来西亚、新加坡、澳大利亚、越南、韩国、泰国、菲律宾、印度、日本;跨境电商进口额排名前十的国家(地区)分别为中国香港、韩国、日本、美国、澳大利亚、荷兰、新西兰、德国、法国、英国。

配合"一带一路"倡议,中国提出了"丝路电商"双边国际合作机制。通过签署双边电子商务合作备忘录,中国针对合作国的经济发展特点制定跨境电子商务策略,发挥中国电子商务技术应用、模式创新和市场规模等优势。2022 年 11 月 4 日,习近平总书记在第五届中国国际进口博览会开幕式致辞中提出,创建"丝路电商"合作先行区,推进高质量共建"一带一路"。截至 2023 年 9 月,中国已与 30 个国家签署了双边电子商务合作备忘录,"丝路电商"成为国际经贸合作的新渠道和新亮点,合作伙伴国遍及全球五大洲。2023 年,中国与"丝路电商"伙伴国的跨境电商进出口额占中国跨境电商进出口总额的30%以上。

"丝路电商"的合作机制有利于各国共享中国市场机遇。历届中国国际进口博览会上,"丝路电商"伙伴国以进博会为窗口,专门设立国家馆,展示自身最具特色和高科技含量的产品,迅速上线跨境电商平台,获得了巨额的中国订单。虹桥品汇是上海进口商品展示交易中心,也是中国国际进口博览会的常年展示中心。2022年,虹桥品汇建成上海国际友城港和直播电商基地两个重要子平台,吸引36个共建国家近5 000种商品入驻。2023年,虹桥品汇开设"丝路电商"线上国家馆,为"丝路电商"伙伴国优质企业与商品进入中国市场创造便利,仅2023年上半年就引进共建国家的供应商42家。

8.3.4.2 跨境电商发展措施

跨境电子商务的管理涉及交易、支付、物流、通关、退税、结汇等多个环节的管理。为了促进跨境电商产业发展,中国积极探索更加高效的跨境电商管理机制。中国在多个城市和地区设立了跨境电子商务综合试验区,旨在推动跨境电子商务技术标准、业务流程、监管模式和信息化建设等方面先行先试。以2015年3月国务院同意设立中国(杭州)跨境电子商务综合试验区为起点,截至2022年11月,中国跨境电子商务综合试验区数量达到165个,覆盖31个省份。以中国(杭州)跨境电子商务综合试验区为例,该区域开展了跨境电子商务"小包出口""直邮进口""网购保税进口",以及跨境B2B出口、保税出口等业务试点,率先探索跨境电商退换货中心、"全球中心仓"、定点配送、"保税进口+零售加工"等举措。截至2023年6月,中国(杭州)跨境电子商务综合试验区实现跨境电商进出口规模由成立初期的1.2亿元扩大到1 200多亿元,跨境电商企业由200多家跃升至5.5万余家,集聚全国2/3的跨境电商平台,在杭跨境支付机构服务全国150万卖家,交易额占全国跨境支付交易额的70%。

跨境电子商务的实施离不开跨境国际物流体系建设。"中欧班列"和"丝路海运"是中国促进国际综合物流服务的重要平台。中欧班列是往来于中国与欧洲以及"一带一路"沿线各国的集装箱国际铁路联运班列。2011年3月,首趟中欧班列从中国重庆发出开往德国杜伊斯堡。经过10余年发展,中欧班列已经开通70多条运行线路,可以通达欧洲22个国家的160多个城市,成为国际物流陆路的运输骨干。截至2023年11月,中欧班列累计开行7.7万列,行驶总里程逾7亿千米。丝路海运是中国发起的连接全球港口航运的国际航运综合服务平台,可以实现港口、航运、物流、贸易等企业的数据共享、信息互通。2018年12月首条以"丝路海运"命名的集装箱航线从中国厦门开行,至2024年4月"丝路海运"命名航线已达122条,通达全球46个国家和地区的135座港口,包括37个共建"一带一路"国家和地区的106座港口。通过海铁联运,可以将港口功能延伸到内陆货源腹地,江西、湖南等地的跨境电商货品通过"一箱到底"模式,抵达港口后直接上船出海,缩短了运输时间。中国企业还在加快建设海外服务网络,特别是海外仓。所谓海外仓,是指国内企业将商品通过海运、陆运、空运等运输形式运往目标国家,在当地自建仓库或跟平台仓、第三方海外仓合作,根据销售订单在当地的仓库进行分拣、发货等操作,与国内直发相比效率提高了不少。截至2024年5月,中国企业建设的海外仓超2 500个、面积超3 000万平方米,其中专注于服务跨境电商的海外仓超1 800个,面积超2 200万平方米。

依托跨境电子商务综合试验区、跨境物流平台等产业促进措施,中国各地着力发展特色跨境电子商务产业。以中国陕西西安为例,该城市位于中国内陆,是西北地区中欧班列的重要站点。西安国际港站占地约 500 个足球场大小,年设计集装箱吞吐量是 540 万标箱,铁路货运量是 6 600 万吨,常态化开行西安至哈萨克斯坦阿拉木图、乌兹别克斯坦塔什干、德国汉堡及跨里海等 18 条国际干线,覆盖亚欧大陆全境。平均每 100 分钟,就有一列中欧班列从西安国际港站启程或到达。2015 年,西安国际港务区获批国家级电子商务示范基地以来,大力发展跨境电商产业,先后获批了"跨境电子商务综合试验区""进口贸易促进创新示范区"等 15 个国家试点,逐步构建起以阿里巴巴、京东、亚马逊、易趣、抖音等各类电子商务龙头企业为引领的完整跨境电商产业生态。截至 2023 年底,西安国际港务区汇聚了跨境电商及上下游企业 322 家,年跨境电商交易额突破 40 亿元。

8.3.4.3 跨境电商出口

中国制造业规模位居世界首位,2023 年中国出口了 23.51 万亿元的制造业产品,其中跨境电子商务交易额在逐年增加。中国的大型电商平台纷纷在海外布局分支机构,例如京东建立面向全球消费者的电商平台京东全球售,商家可以通过该平台将产品销往 200 多个国家和地区。京东已经在美国、印度尼西亚、拉丁美洲、欧洲等国家和地区设立了分公司,还建立了俄语、西语、英语等多个子网站,并在五大洲设立超过 110 个海外物流仓,降低全球购不必要的物流成本。跨境电商规模扩大的同时,一批新一代跨境电商平台在海外市场快速发展,成为不容忽视的"中国力量"。如今,这些跨境电商平台在全球市场的份额不断变大,成为全球消费者购物的新选择。众多跨境电商平台中,以 Shein(希音)、拼多多旗下 Temu、AliExpress(全球速卖通)以及字节跳动旗下 TikTok 推出的 TikTok Shop 最为引人注目。据上海浦东国际机场海关统计,Temu、TikTok、Shein 这三家电商平台 2023 年的出口申报量同比增长超 10 倍。

新型跨境电商平台依靠电子商务成功经验,整合中国国内的供应链,迅速占领了多个国家的电子商务市场。2022 年 9 月 Temu 在美国上线,提出了"像亿万富翁一样购物"的宣传语。一方面,Temu 在美国复制了拼多多在中国发展用户的营销模式,集聚了大量的用户订单;另一方面,Temu 面向中国的中小企业推出了"全托管""柔性供应"等服务,对于入驻的商家和企业,Temu 推出 0 佣金、0 保证金的扶持政策,并提供仓储、物流、售后等基础设施服务。"多多出海扶持计划"专项团队先后深入中国 10 余个省份的 100 多个小商品产业带,组织具有高性价比的商品输出至海外。相关数据显示,Temu 上的鞋服、日用百货等用品价格通常比竞争对手低 30%～50%。多多跨境每天出口包裹量超过 40 万个,日均货重达 600 吨左右。截至 2023 年 12 月,Temu 的全球独立访客数量达 4.67 亿,在跨境电商中位居全球第二,仅次于亚马逊;约有 18% 的美国家庭在 Temu 上购物过。2023 年,Temu 为拼多多带来的营收超过 250 亿元。

同时,中国创业者拓展了海外市场。Kilimall 于 2014 年创立于肯尼亚,是较早进入非洲市场并占据和保持领先地位的电商平台。该平台参考中国发展电子商务的经验,本着扎根非洲、与非洲当地合作伙伴共生共荣的理念,逐步打造了 Kilimall 电商交易服务、LipaPay 支付服务、KiliExpress 物流服务、KiliShop 社区服务小店、KiliWarehouse 仓储服务、KiliClick 营销服务等六大服务体系。Kilimall 在非洲的市场占有率处于领先地位,尤其是东非市场份额保持在 50% 以上。截至 2022 年底,平台注册用户数已超 1 000 万,年度活跃用户逾 720 万,年复购率超 50%,是目前在非洲具有显著影响力的电子商务平台。Kilimall 服务超过 8 000 家企业、开通 1.2 万多个店铺、商品超 100 万种、创造 5 000 余个工作岗位,不但为非洲民众带去了质优价廉的中国商品,也促进了非洲当地中小企业产品的在线销售。

8.3.4.4　跨境电商进口

中国拥有较大规模的中等收入群体,也是全球最具潜力的市场之一。2023年,中国进口超过5万亿元的大宗商品、近3万亿元的电子元件和近2万亿元的消费品,为各国企业提供了广阔的市场空间和合作机遇。2023年,中国进口1.95万亿元的特色食品、母婴用品、数码家电等消费品,增长1.2%;其中,跨境电商进口5 483亿元,增长3.9%。尼尔森IQ发布的《2024年中国跨境进口消费趋势白皮书》显示,2018—2023年中国跨境进口电商规模从4 441亿元提升至5 483亿元,2017—2023年中国跨境进口电商使用人数以近两成的增速逐年攀升,在2023年达到1.88亿人。

中国的主要电子商务平台如天猫、京东等都开辟了国际频道,专项从事跨境电商进口。以天猫国际为例,其在2014年2月正式上线,从最初与100个海外品牌合作,逐步成长至囊括来自全球90多个国家和地区的46 000多个全球品牌,涵盖7 000多个商品类别,服务超过1亿消费群体的跨境电商平台。天猫国际率先启动保税仓网络和相关基础设施建设,海外商品可以暂存在保税区,由海关、检验检疫部门监管,产生订单后商品从保税区发出,1~3天就可以送达消费者。截至2023年底,天猫国际在海外地区建设了六大采购中心,供应链物流网络涵盖100多个海外仓、500条海陆空国际运输干线、40个核心港口及超过100个保税仓。天猫国际保税仓发货商品中80%支持送货上门服务,覆盖中国260多个城市,全中国一半以上的订单可实现"次日达";海外直邮商品中,超过一半订单可实现7日内送达。

中国跨境电商的发展,也带动了货源国相关产业的快速发展,较有代表性的案例是智利车厘子产业。智利地处南半球,其水果供应期恰好对应中国水果稀缺的冬季市场;过去智利车厘子运抵中国的成本较高,大宗运输的路线、存储、保鲜都是难题。在中国冬季水果市场需求的驱动下,中国的跨境电商、物流平台积极调整应对。中国远洋海运集团有限公司等货运企业开设了连接智利圣安东尼奥港与中国上海的"樱桃快航",将原先的32天航程压缩到了23天,海运车厘子的供应量提高了1.8倍。京东、天猫等跨境电商平台在智利布局直采,监测全流程供应链,最大限度地缩短车厘子从产地到用户的时间。多方举措之下,智利车厘子逐步成为中国电商平台的冬季热销水果。据智利水果出口商协会统计,2016—2023年智利车厘子对华出口量年均增长约29%,每年11月底到次年2月有高达92%的车厘子发往中国。智利农业研究和政策办公室公布的数据显示,智利车厘子种植面积已经从2000年的3 241公顷快速增长到2023年的67 570公顷,车厘子在中国市场的热销反向推动了智利原产地的农业增产。

中国跨境电商的发展,也为通过跨国贸易消除贫困探索出了新路,较为典型的案例是埃塞俄比亚的咖啡。过去,埃塞俄比亚的咖啡豆以一般贸易出口生豆为主,加之传统贸易规则的限制,贸易成本较高,咖啡种植加工环节的收益占产业链收益的比例不到10%,绝大多数利润在流通销售环节。阿里巴巴倡议建立的世界电子贸易平台与马来西亚、埃塞俄比亚、卢旺达等国展开通关、支付、物流等合作创新。借助世界电子贸易平台,通过天猫国际销售,能够有效降低贸易成本,让本土咖农获益的同时,也让中国消费者以更优惠的价格品尝到原产于埃塞俄比亚的精品咖啡豆。同时,中国市场的迅速扩大也增进了埃塞俄比亚咖啡厂商从中国采购全自动咖啡烘焙包装设备的意愿,在当地生产咖啡熟豆产品,进一步拓展市场。2022年1月,埃塞俄比亚驻华大使在中国电商平台直播销售咖啡,4吨埃塞俄比亚咖啡豆5

秒售罄。近年来,埃塞俄比亚咖啡豆在中国市场的销量以每年 27% 的速度快速增长。中国海关数据显示,仅 2023 年 1—11 月,中国就从埃塞俄比亚进口了 2 万吨咖啡生豆。2023 年世界互联网大会上,"阿里巴巴数字乡村携手联合国国际贸易中心助力非洲发展中国家数字减贫"项目入选 2023 年"携手构建网络空间命运共同体精品案例",联合国国际贸易中心执行主任帕梅拉·科克-汉密尔顿表示,发展电子商务是中小企业实现增长的重要渠道,该项目为非洲发展中国家提供了新的发展机会。

8.4　网络空间治理国际合作

维护网络安全是国际社会的共同责任。中国坚定维护以联合国为核心的国际体系、以国际法为基础的国际秩序、以《联合国宪章》宗旨和原则为基础的国际关系基本准则,并在此基础上制定各方普遍接受的网络空间国际规则。中国深化网络安全应急响应国际合作,与国际社会携手提高数据安全和个人信息保护合作水平,共同打击网络犯罪和网络恐怖主义。

8.4.1　互联网治理国际协作

中国始终恪守《联合国宪章》确立的主权平等、不得使用或威胁使用武力、和平解决争端等原则,尊重各国自主选择网络发展道路、网络管理模式、互联网公共政策和平等参与网络空间国际治理的权利。中国始终认为,国家不分大小、强弱、贫富,都是平等成员,都有权平等参与国际规则与秩序建构,确保网络空间未来发展由各国人民共同掌握。2020 年 9 月,《中国关于联合国成立 75 周年立场文件》发布,呼吁国际社会在相互尊重、平等互利基础上,加强对话合作,把网络空间用于促进经济社会发展、国际和平与稳定和人类福祉,反对网络战和网络军备竞赛,共同建立和平、安全、开放、合作、有序的网络空间。

中国支持发挥联合国在网络空间国际治理中的主渠道作用。支持联合国制定打击网络犯罪全球性公约,共提并推动联合国大会通过决议,设立政府间特设专家委员会,呼吁尽早共同达成具有权威性、普遍性的公约,为国际社会合作应对网络犯罪挑战提供法律基础。注重发挥联合国在应对国际信息安全威胁领域的关键作用,与上海合作组织其他成员国共同向联合国提交"信息安全国际行为准则"更新草案。中国拓展与联合国专门机构的网络事务合作,参与联合国教育、科学及文化组织《人工智能伦理建议书》的制定,并与世界知识产权组织在域名规则制定和域名争议解决领域开展广泛合作。

2017 年 3 月,中国发布首份《网络空间国际合作战略》,就推动网络空间国际交流合作首次全面系统提出中国主张,向世界发出了中国致力于网络空间和平发展、合作共赢的积极信号。中国积极参与形成区域性网络治理规则。中国签署《区域全面经济伙伴关系协定》,其电子商务章节是目前全球覆盖区域最广、内容全面、水平较高的电子商务国际规则。中国积极推动加入《全面与进步跨太平洋伙伴关系协定》和《数字经济伙伴关系协定》进程,参与数字经济领域高标准规则制定。

中国以平等和相互尊重的态度与美国开展对话交流。中国致力于在尊重彼此核心关切、妥善管控分歧的基础上,与美国开展互联网领域对话交流,为包括美国在内的世界各国企业在华发展创造良好市场环境,推进中美网信领域的合作。但一段时间以来,美国采取错误对华政策，致使中美关系遭遇严重困难，但中国将坚持独立自主，坚定不移地维护在网络空间的国家主权、安全、发展利益。

中国深化与俄罗斯在网信领域的高水平合作。2015年，中俄两国签署《中华人民共和国政府和俄罗斯联邦政府关于在保障国际信息安全领域合作协定》，为两国信息安全领域合作规划方向。2021年，在《中华人民共和国和俄罗斯联邦睦邻友好合作条约》签署20周年之际，中俄发布联合声明，双方重申将巩固国际信息安全领域的双、多边合作，继续推动构建以防止信息空间冲突、鼓励和平使用信息技术为原则的全球国际信息安全体系。

中国坚持以开放包容的态度推进中欧网信领域合作。与欧盟委员会共同成立中欧数字经济和网络安全专家工作组，先后召开多次会议；2012年建立中欧网络工作组机制，双方在工作组框架下不断加强网络领域对话合作；与德国共同发布《2019中德互联网经济对话成果文件》。与英国联合主办多届中英互联网圆桌会议，在数字经济、网络安全、儿童在线保护、数据和人工智能等领域达成多项合作共识。

中国加强与周边和广大发展中国家网信领域合作。中国—东盟信息港论坛连续成功举办，持续推动中国与东盟国家在数字领域的合作，建立中国—东盟网络事务对话机制；建立中、日、韩三方网络磋商机制；与韩国联合主办中韩互联网圆桌会议；举办中非互联网发展与合作论坛，提出了"中非数字创新伙伴计划"；中国—南非新媒体圆桌会议、中坦（坦桑尼亚）网络文化交流会、中肯（肯尼亚）数字经济合作发展研讨会等活动加强了中非在新媒体、网络文化、数字经济等领域的交流合作；举办多届网上丝绸之路大会，在信息基础设施、跨境电子商务、智慧城市等领域与阿拉伯国家开展切实合作。

8.4.2　网络安全国际合作

中国企业、科研机构和高等院校等积极参与信息技术和网络安全领域的国际标准制定，推动新兴技术发展。中国机构持续加强与国际标准化组织（ISO）、国际电工委员会（IEC）等标准组织，以及国际自动识别与移动技术协会（AIM Global）、数据标识符管理委员会（DIMC）等产业组织的合作。全国网络安全标准化技术委员会承担ISO和IEC第一联合技术委员会信息安全分技术委员会（ISO/IEC JTC1 SC27，简称"SC27"）的技术业务工作，自2004年起连续多年参加SC27国际网络安全标准化工作会议，推动一批中国自主研制的网络安全标准转化为国际标准，多名中国专家担任SC27召集人和联络官，为网络安全国际标准的制定贡献中国智慧。

中国建立网络安全应急响应领域的国际渠道。国家计算机网络应急技术处理协调中心与全球主要国家级计算机应急响应组织、政府部门、国际组织和联盟、互联网服务提供商、域名注册机构、学术机构以及其他互联网相关公司和组织开展交流。截至2021年，已与81个国家和地区的274个计算机应急响应组织建立了"CNCERT国际合作伙伴"关系，与其中33个组织签订网络安全合作备忘录。中国还与东盟建立了"中国—东盟网络安全交流培训中心"，共同提升网络安全能力。

中国推动与特定地区组织、国家建立深层次的网络安全领域合作。2017年，金砖五国达成《金砖国家网络安全务实合作路线图》。2021年，上海合作组织信息安全专家组一致通过《上合组织成员国保障国际信息安全2022—2023年合作计划》。2021年，中国与印度尼西亚签署《关于发展网络安全能力建设和技术合作的谅解备忘录》。2022年，中国与泰国签署

《关于网络安全合作的谅解备忘录》。

8.4.3 合作打击网络犯罪

中国一贯支持打击网络犯罪国际合作。中国推动联合国网络犯罪政府间专家组于2011—2021年召开7次会议，为通过关于启动制订联合国打击网络犯罪全球性公约相关决议做出重要贡献。中国在上合组织框架下参与签署了《上海合作组织成员国元首关于共同打击国际恐怖主义的声明》等重要文件，共同打击包括网络恐怖主义在内的恐怖主义、分裂主义和极端主义。中国主办和积极参与金砖国家反恐工作组系列会议，就打击网络恐怖主义介绍中国具体实践，提出金砖国家加强网络反恐合作交流建议。

中国加强网络安全国际执法司法合作。中国与多国达成网络安全领域合作共识，在打击网络恐怖主义、电信网络诈骗等方面开展深层次务实合作。在打击网络恐怖主义方面，通过联合反恐演习、联合边防行动、警务合作、司法协助等多种形式，不断深化与相关国家交流合作，携手应对威胁挑战，共同维护世界和平和地区稳定。在打击电信网络诈骗方面，中国积极开展国际执法司法合作，与多国联合侦办跨境重大案件，取得明显成效。2022年3—6月，在国际刑警组织框架下，中国与其他75个成员国共同参与"曙光行动"，逮捕犯罪嫌疑人2 000余名，拦截非法资金5 000余万美元，有效遏制跨国电信网络诈骗活动。

中国与世界各国携手保护未成年人网络权益。中国积极与联合国儿童基金会、国际互联网举报热线联合会等国际组织以及英国、德国、阿联酋等国相关部门开展合作，治理线上未成年人色情问题；加入"WePROTECT 终结网络儿童性剥削全球联盟"，与全球200多个政府、企业和民间社会组织一道努力打击儿童网上性剥削及性虐待，为儿童创造更加安全的网络环境。

8.5 小   结

在当今数字化时代，全球网络空间发展面临诸多挑战。数字鸿沟不断扩大，广大发展中国家信息化建设步伐滞后，网络安全风险如影随形，数字贸易规则也有待健全。这些问题严重掣肘全球网络空间的健康有序发展，对各国网络安全和经济利益构成现实威胁，国际社会携手应对网络空间治理挑战已刻不容缓。在此背景下，推动全球数字经贸合作成为必然趋势。

中国始终秉持"人类命运共同体"这一理念，积极投身全球网络空间治理，为解决上述难题贡献中国智慧与中国方案。中国政府提出构建"网络空间命运共同体"的重要主张，并通过举办世界互联网大会等一系列高规格活动，向世界传递中国在网络治理方面的坚定决心和积极倡议，有力推动这一主张从愿景迈向实践。中国倡导构建发展、安全、责任、利益共同体，旨在促进各国在网络空间实现共同发展、协同维护安全、广泛参与治理、公平分享成果，为全球网络空间治理提供一套全面系统且富有建设性的框架，引领全球网络空间朝着更加公平、安全、繁荣的方向稳步前行。

在数字经济国际合作领域，中国展现出大国担当，发挥着不可替代的重要作用。在信息基础设施建设方面，中国深度参与互联网基础资源管理，积极投身国际信息基础设施建设项目，为全球互联互通贡献力量。在全球数字服务供给方面，中国凭借北斗卫星导航服务、云服务等优质数字服务，为世界各国提供了高效、可靠的技术支撑。同时，中国积极参与多边机制下的数字经济合作，大力推动跨境电商发展，与众多国家紧密合作，实现互利共赢，有力促进了全球数字经济的蓬勃发展，带动参与国实现经济增长和数字化转型。

在网络空间治理国际合作领域，中国同样发挥着关键引领作用。中国始终恪守《联合国宪章》，坚定支持联合国在网络空间国际治理中的主渠道地位，积极参与区域性网络治理规则制定，秉持平等、互信、合作的态度与各国开展广泛对话合作。在网络安全方面，中国积极参与国际标准制定，建立健全应急响应国际渠道。在打击网络犯罪方面，中国大力推动国际合作，并积极携手各国保护未成年人网络权益。中国的不懈努力为维护全球网络空间安全稳定、保障各国网络权益筑牢了坚实根基。

长期以来，中国坚持以联合国为主渠道，深度参与网络空间国际规则的制定，切实投身全球信息基础设施建设，全力推动全球互联网健康发展。中国还通过跨境电商等多种途径，与世界各国共享中国发展机遇。中国提出的一系列方案和采取的实际行动，为全球数字经济发展和网络空间治理注入了强大动力，充分展现了大国担当，有力促进了全球网络空间的和平、安全与繁荣，为构建更加美好的数字世界贡献了中国力量。

1 Basics of the ICT Industry

1.1 Brief History

Information is the representation of the movement and changes of things. From the invention of language and script by the ancients to written communication, and futher to the use of electronic technology to process and disseminate information, the history of human information exchange has spanned thousands of years. Human beings have experienced five innovations in information technology, and a corresponding information industry has been formed in its promotion and application.

1.1.1 Language and Script

The emergence and use of language and script are generally regarded as the beginning of human information technology innovations, which have promoted the development of ancient agriculture, handicrafts, and commerce. Human language is considered as the most primal and enduring conduit of information. It stands as the paramount instrument of interpersonal communication, and a symbolic medium through which expressions are conveyed. Script, as the written symbol carrying the mantle of language, is a tool used by humans to convey information, enabling the transmission of information to transcend the boundaries of time and space for posterity.

Modern *Homo sapiens*, endowed with robust linguistic communication abilities, embarked on a momentous journey "out of Africa", venturing into the vast expanse of the Eurasian continent. Over the course of millennia, diverse ethnic groups across the globe cultivated their unique languages, among which the four major ancient civilizations developed their own distinctive scripts, as shown in Table 1-1.

The shape of script is closely related to writing methods and record carriers, and gradually evolves with the development of social productivity. The following takes the evolution of Chinese script for case study. The earliest Chinese script with the characteristics of written symbols that can be traced back are the written symbols engraved on animal bones in the remains of the Longshan Culture around 2500 BC. This type of written symbol has the characteristics of hieroglyphic script. The oracle bone script that appeared in the Shang Dynasty around 1400 BC is regarded as the first form of Chinese script. It was engraved on tortoise shells and animal bones for the purpose of divination. The Chinese calligraphy brush pen that appeared in the Zhou Dynasty can be used to write characters on bamboo slips or textiles (such as silk). Different vassal states at that time had their own written scripts, which obviously hindered the cultural communication in ancient China.

Table 1-1　Overview of the four ancient civilizations

Civilizations	Appearance time	Geographic regions	Scripts	Examples
Egyptian Civilization	About 3000 BC	Nile River Basin in Africa	Hieroglyph	
Indus Valley Civilization	About 2500 BC	Indus Valley in Asia	Seal script	
Chinese Civilization	About 2070 BC	Yellow River Basin and Yangtze River Basin in Asia	Oracle bone script	
Babylonian Civilization	About 1800 BC	Tigris and Euphrates River Valleys in Asia	Cuneiform	

In 221 BC, China's first emperor Qin Shihuang unified China and declared "small seal script" as the standardized national script, marking the first formalization of Chinese script writing. During the Eastern Han Dynasty, around 105 AD, papermaking technology was improved and paper began to be used as the main writing material; at the same time, clerical script and standard script appeared, which were simpler and easier to recognize. After the development of the Han Dynasty, the Chinese script system reached maturity and the shapes almost ceased to evolve, so Chinese character is also called "Hanzi". The number of Chinese characters increased over time. By the Qing Dynasty, the *Kangxi Dictionary* had collected 47 035 Chinese characters.

Traditional Chinese characters have many strokes, which makes them difficult to read and remember. In 1956, the State Council of the People's Republic of China promulgated the "Scheme for Simplifying Chinese Characters". In 1964, the Chinese Script Reform

Committee officially compiled and printed the "General Table of Simplified Chinese Characters", which includes 2 238 simplified Chinese characters. They are the currently used Chinese characters. Table 1-2 takes three Chinese characters as examples, and lists the evolution processes of their form.

Table 1-2 Examples of Chinese character evolution

Fonts	Appearance periods	Recording methods	Example 1 (horse)	Example 2 (fish)	Example 3 (volume)
Oracle bone scrip	About 1400 BC	Engraved on tortoise shells or animal bones			
Bronze inscription	About 1300 BC	Cast or engraved on bronze			
Small seal script	221 BC	Written on bamboo slips			
Clerical script	About 150 AD	Written on paper			
Standard script	About 220 AD	Written on paper			
Simplified Chinese Character	1955	Written or printed on paper			

The emergence of script makes it possible to record knowledge and history. All dynasties of China attached great importance to the recording of history. The *Records of the Grand Historian*, written between 104 BC and 91 BC, documents Chinese history from ancient times up to the Han Dynasty. Among the four ancient civilizations in the world, Chinese Civilization is the only one that has continued to this day without interruption and has complete written historical records.

1.1.2　Printing and Postal Service

There have been many kinds of carriers for recording texts in human history, and paper is the most convenient and widely used carrier. Before the emergence of printing, humans recorded texts by hand-written transcription, with limited scope and scale of application. In the Northern Song Dynasty, around 1040 AD, movable type printing emerged, making it possible to reproduce books on a large scale. One example is as shown in Figure 1-1. Movable type printing was spread to Korea Peninsula, Japan and Central Asia, and then to Europe through Arabia and other regions, promoting the development of world civilization.

Figure 1-1　Fragments of an ancient book printed by movable type printing (Northern Song Dynasty, about 1100 AD)[①]
Image Source: Wenzhou Museum

In ancient times, the exchange and dissemination of information mainly relied on the transportation of paper carriers. Ancient China established a system dedicated to the transportation of information carriers and materials, called "Youyi", in which "You" were the institutions dedicated to the delivery of official documents, and "Yi" were the transfer stations for the horses and vehicles that delivered those documents. Ancient dynasties usually set up specialized stations called "Yizhan" in major transportation towns, and the documents were relayed from one station to another. In the Han Dynasty, urgent documents could be delivered 400 miles (about 200 kilometers) in one day. Figure 1-2 shows a painted brick of a postman unearthed in Jiayuguan on the Silk Road in the Wei Jin Periods. The Youyi system was mainly for official services and was not abolished until the

---

①　Fragments of pages from the movable type printing of *The Sutra on the Contemplation of Amitabha Buddha*, dating back to the Northern Song Dynasty, are now in the collection of the Wenzhou Museum in China. They are the earliest movable type prints discovered so far.

establishment of the postal system in the Qing Dynasty in 1896, existing for about 2 000 years.

Figure 1-2　The image of a postman in Youyi system (Wei Jin Periods, about 220-420 AD)
Image Source: Gansu Provincial Museum

With the development of society, an industry that specializes in providing letter and parcel transportation services, namely the postal industry, emerged. In the Ming and Qing Dynasties in China, there were "Xinju" that provided mailing services to the people; however, the delivery services of various Xinju were not interoperable. The modern postal industry was born in the United Kingdom (UK). In 1840, the UK issued the world's first stamp, the "Penny Black", and promoted the development of the postal industry through prepaid postage. In 1874, the "General Postal Union" (now the Universal Postal Union) was established, and sending letters through the postal system became the main way for countries around the world to exchange information at that time.

1.1.3　Telecommunications and Broadcasting

From the mid-19th century to the mid-20th century, electromagnetic theory gradually matured, and it was possible to make electrical signals as a carrier for communication. This brought fundamental and great evolution for the communication in human lives. The transmission of information can break away from conventional audio-visual method and use metal wires, or even rely on invisible and intangible electromagnetic waves.

American scientist Morse invented the telegraph, which transmitted English letters and other texts as a combination of dots and dashes. By sending a combination of electrical signals of different lengths, telegraph realized the transmission of text information. American inventor Bell invented the telephone, which could convert voice into electrical signals through microphones and speakers, thus realizing the transmission of language information through cables. Italian scientist Marconi invented the wireless telegraph, using air as the medium. The radios and televisions developed by British and American scientists can receive broadcasting signals from radio and television stations, then demodulate, recover and play the audio and video signals. The birth of telegraph, telephone, radio and television have changed the traditional way of communications that relied on paper media, and realized cross-regional long-distance communications. Table 1-3 lists the major inventions in the fields of telecommunications and broadcasting.

Table 1-3 Major inventions in the fields of telecommunications and broadcasting

Fields	Inventions	Representative events
Telecommunications	Cable telegraph	In 1837, American scientist Morse successfully developed the electromagnetic telegraph based on wired cables; in 1858, the submarine telegraph cable connecting Europe and America across the Atlantic Ocean was successfully laid
	Wireless telegraph	In 1896, Italian scientist Marconi successfully developed the wireless telegraph, and in 1901, transatlantic radio communication was realized
	Wired telephone	In 1876, American inventor Bell applied for a patent for the telephone he invented; in 1878, the long-distance telephone call experiment between Boston and New York was successfully done
	Telephone exchange	In 1926, the world's first large-scale crossbar automatic telephone exchange was put into use in Sweden; in 1938, the United States (US) deployed a crossbar automatic telephone switching system
Broadcasting	Electron tube	In 1904, British scientist Fleming invented the vacuum diode; in 1906, American inventor Lee de Forest invented the vacuum triode; in the late 1930s, electron tube became the mainstream electronic component
	Radio	In 1906, American scientist Fessenden conducted a broadcasting experiment using modulated radio waves to send music and speech; in 1910, Americans Dunwoody and Piccard successfully developed the crystal radio based on electron tubes
	Television	In 1933, American scientist Zoelkin successfully developed the camera tube and image tube for television; in 1954, the US successfully produced the world's first color TV

Telegraph, telephone and other communications technologies have also given birth to modern telecommunications services, with companies such as the American Telephone and Telegraph Company (AT&T) serving as examples. Meanwhile, radio broadcasting and television have given rise to modern media services, exemplified by orgnizations like the British Broadcasting Corporation (BBC). The United Nations (UN) first formulated the "International Standard Industrial Classification of All Economic Activities" in 1949, using code 73 to refer to communications, which includes not only the traditional postal industry, but also the information transmission services based on wired and wireless technologies, as well as the related information exchange, storage and recording services.

1.1.4　Computer and Internet

During the more than 50 years from the mid-20th century to the early 21st century, breakthroughs were made in technologies such as semiconductors, computers, the Internet, and mobile communications, setting off a wave of information technology revolution.

The development of microelectronics provides a theoretical basis for the technological upgrading of electronic components, devices and circuits. In 1958, the invention of integrated circuit (IC) put the development of semiconductor technology on the fast track. In 1965, Gordon Moore predicted that the number of transistors on a chip would double every 18 months in the future. The rapid development of the semiconductor industry and technology has laid a matarial foundation for the production and manufacturing of various electronic information products. Table 1-4 lists the major technological advances in the field of microelectronics.

Table 1-4　Major technological advances in the field of microelectronics

Achievements	Representative events
Transistor	In June 1948, the solid-state physics research group at Bell Laboratories invented the transistor; in 1953, Shockley and others from the research group successfully developed the silicon junction field-effect transistor; with its small size and stable performance, the transistor began to replace the electron tube as the basic device of electronic information products
Integrated circuit	In September 1958, Kilby of Texas Instruments developed the world's first germanium integrated circuit board containing transistors, resistors and capacitors; in 1959, Noyce of Fairchild Semiconductor used planar technology to produce silicon integrated circuits, truly realizing monolithic integrated circuits

Continued

Achievements	Representative events
Large scale integrated circuit (LSIC)	In 1967, Bell Laboratories in the US produced the world's first large-scale integrated circuit (integrating 1 000 components on a single chip), which was soon promoted to industrial production and practical applications

Theoretical breakthroughs have been made in the principles and architecture of modern computers. In 1945, scientist John von Neumann proposed the scheme of general-purpose electronic computer with binary storage program. In 1946, the first electronic computer was successfully created in the US. With the development of microelectronics, computers have entered the era of integrated circuit from the era of electron tubes and transistors, and computing power has been greatly improved with the improvement of the production process of central processing unit (CPU). Computers have changed from large equipment that only a few institutions have the opportunity to use to consumer electronic devices that have entered thousands of households. Table 1-5 lists the major technological advances in the field of computer industry.

Table 1-5　Major technological advances in the field of computer industry

Technologies	Representative events
Vacuum tube computer	In February 1946, Professors Mauchly and Eckert of the University of Pennsylvania successfully developed the computer ENIAC, which was the world's first general-purpose computer, using about 18 000 electron tubes, and was used for national defense and scientific calculations; in 1951, the computer UNIVAC developed by Remington Rand Corporation was used in the US census, and computers began to serve civilians
Transistor computer	In 1954, Bell Laboratories in the US developed the world's first transistor computer, TRADIC, while at the same time, operating systems and algorithmic languages were born, and high-level languages such as COBOL and LISP entered the practical stage
Integrated circuit computer	In April 1964, the International Business Machines Corporation (IBM) launched the world's first computer series, the IBM System/360 using integrated circuits; in 1968, IBM released the world's first commercial database system, the Information Management System (IMS); in 1981, IBM launched the world's first personal computer, the IBM 5150, and proposed an architecture standard for using microprocessors

Continued

Technologies	Representative events
Computer CPU	In 1971, Intel Corporation of the US released the world's first 4-bit microprocessor 4004 (containing more than 2 000 transistors and produced with a 10-micron process); in 1979, Intel Corporation launched the 8-bit microprocessor Intel 8088 (containing about 29 000 transistors); in 1985, Intel Corporation launched the 32-bit microprocessor 80386 (containing about 275 000 transistors); in 1993, Intel Corporation launched the Pentium processor (containing about 3 million transistors and produced with a 0.8-micron process); in 1999, Intel Corporation launched the Pentium III processor (containing about 9.5 million transistors and produced with a 0.25-micron process); in 2006, Intel Corporation launched the Itanium processor (containing 1.72 billion transistors and produced with a 90-nanometer process)
Computer software	In 1970, Bell Laboratories in the US launched the Unix operating system; in 1970, Edgar Frank Codd of IBM proposed the relational database theory; in 1984, Apple Computer launched the computer Macintosh (Mac for short), which provided a graphical operating system interface; in 1991, an university student from Finnish, Linus Torvalds, developed the open source Linux operating system; in 1995, Microsoft Corporation of the United States released the Windows 95 operating system and the office software Microsoft Office 95, which became the mainstream computer software

The global Internet for computer interconnection has been verified and applied. With the funding of the Defense Advanced Research Projects Agency (DARPA) of the US Department of Defense, major scientific research institutions in the United States gradually connected to the ARPANET (also known as the Advanced Research Projects Agency Network) during a period of 20 years, and explored solutions suitable for large-scale heterogeneous network interconnection. In 1995, after the Internet began commercial operation, it quickly became popular around the world and became the most mainstream communication network. Internet information services such as the World Wide Web, search engines, online e-commerce, and social networks have brought the world into the Internet age. Table 1-6 lists the major technological advances in the field of Internet.

Table 1-6　Major technological advances in the field of Internet

Technologies	Representative events
ARPANET	In 1966, the Defense Advanced Research Projects Agency of the US Department of Defense launched the ARPANET research project; in 1969, the University of California, Los Angeles and the Stanford Research Institute achieved the first long-distance communication on a packet switching network; in 1974, the first version of the Transmission Control Protocol (TCP) for heterogeneous network computer networking communications was officially released; in 1983, TCP was decomposed into the TCP/IP protocol suite and used by the ARPANET
Internet	In 1989, Web services based on Hypertext Markup Language (HTML) and Hypertext Transfer Protocol (HTTP) were released; in 1995, the US Department of Commerce took over the Internet Assigned Numbers Authority from the Department of Defense, and the Internet began its commercialization process; in 1998, the Internet Corporation for Assigned Names and Numbers (ICANN) was established
Internet services	In 1994, Yahoo Inc. was founded and began providing search engine services, and Amazon was founded and began providing online book sales services; in 1998, Google Inc. was founded and began providing search engine services; in 2004, Facebook (later renamed Meta) was founded and began providing social network services

Public cellular mobile communications networks provide global roaming wireless services. In the 1980s, the world began to deploy personal mobile communications networks based on cellular base stations. The demand for mobile communications gradually shifted from voice services to data services, and mobile phones were widely used to send and receive text messages and emails. In 2007, Apple Inc. launched the iPhone, marking the arrival of the era of touch-based smartphone. Mobile phones began to gradually replace personal computer (PC) as the main electronic device for personal Internet access, and applications running on mobile phones became the main form of personal software. Table 1-7 lists the major technological advances in the field of mobile communications.

Table 1-7　Major technological advances in the field of mobile communications

Technologies	Representative events
1st-Generation Mobile Communications (1G)	In 1978, Bell Laboratories successfully developed the Advanced Mobile Phone System (AMPS), marking the official entry of the 1G system, which is mainly characterized by analog cellular networks, into the historical stage; the capacity of the 1G analog cellular system is very limited, supporting only voice calls and not providing data and roaming services

Continued

Technologies	Representative events
2nd-Generation Mobile Communication (2G)	In 1990, 2G systems characterized by digitalization began to be widely deployed around the world; 2G systems mainly include the Global System for Mobile Communications (GSM) proposed by Europe and the interim standard-95 (IS-95) system proposed by the US; 2G systems have seen significant improvements in performance and capacity, with improved voice quality and confidentiality, and have transmission rates approaching 1 Mbps (megabits per second)
3rd-Generation Mobile Communication (3G)	Around 2000, 3G systems began to be used commercially on a large scale; 3G systems are centered on data services and realize real mobile multimedia communications with transmission rates of about 3 Mbps; the time division-synchronous code division multiple access (TD-SCDMA) system proposed by China is listed as one of the three major international standards for 3G
4th-Generation Mobile Communication (4G)	Around 2010, 4G systems began to be put into commercial use; 4G systems have greatly improved transmission speeds and can meet the needs of applications such as games, high-definition mobile TV, and video conferencing, the maximum transmission rate can reach 100 Mbps; the time division-long term evolution-advanced (TD-LTE-Advanced) proposed by China is listed as one of the international standards for 4G

Information and communications technology (ICT) is represented by semiconductors, computers, the Internet, mobile communications and other technologies. It is based on microelectronic and optoelectronic technologies, supported by computers and communications technologies, and covers the acquisition, transmission, storage, processing, display, and distribution of information. These technologies influence each other and iterate rapidly, having a huge impact on human society and bringing about the fourth information technology revolution.

Many new industries and categories have emerged around the processing of information. In 2006, the UN published the revised 4th edition of the "International Standard Industrial Classification of All Economic Activities", which newly established Category J "Information and Communications", including publishing activities (category 58), production of films, videos and television programs, and publishing of sound recordings and musical works (category 59), radio and television broadcasting (category 60), telecommunications (category 61), computer programming, consulting and related activities (category 62), information service activities (category 63), and other subcategories. In addition, in Category C "Manufacturing", the manufacturing of computers, electronic products and optical products (category 26) was established.

1.2   Features of ICT Industry

1.2.1   Scope of ICT Industry

China divides the industries of the entire society into three major sectors. The primary industry includes agriculture, planting, animal husbandry, fishery and other industries. The secondary industry includes mining, construction, machinery manufacturing and other industries. The tertiary industry includes education, health, finance, transportation and other service industries. Although the economic activities of the information industry have long appeared, they are still attached to other industries. For example, the information equipment manufacturing industry initially belonged to the secondary industry, and the consulting service industry initially belonged to the tertiary industry. With the widespread application of information technology in various fields of economy and society, the economic activity process of the information industry has gradually separated from the corresponding process of other industries and formed an independent industry. The US Department of Commerce gave the definition of the information industry in the *Digital Economy* 2000 in accordance with the Standard Industrial Classification (SIC) issued by the US in 1987: the information industry should be composed of hardware industry, software industry, service industry, communication equipment manufacturing industry and communication service industry. Table 1-8 lists the basic classification of ICT industry.

Table 1-8   Basic classification of ICT industry

Subclass names	Scopes
Basic telecommunications industry	It provides basic communications and transmission services for the public, including traditional telegraph, telephone and other services, wired broadband data communications services for the Internet, and mobile communications services for individuals
Information services industry	It includes traditional information services and new information services: traditional information services include publishing, postal services, document information, radio and television, etc.; new information services, also known as electronic information services, are information services that use electronic information technologies such as computers and modern communications as the main processing means, providing services such as information production and supply, information consulting, network operations and network value-added services, etc.
Information development industry	It includes software industry, database development industry, electronic publishing (including games, animation, etc.), application program development and other information development businesses, etc.

Continued

Subclass names	Scopes
Information manufacturing industry	With electronic computers and communications equipment manufacturing as its main content, it includes the electronics industry (electronic components, devices, complete machine manufacturing), communications and network equipment manufacturing, other information equipment manufacturing, etc.

1.2.2　Position of ICT Industry

The ICT industry is a basic industry. Basic industries refer to industries that support and carry the national economy and social development. Their development scale and level restrict the development speed and quality of the entire national economy. A World Bank research report shows that the higher the level of ICT development of an economy, the faster its economic growth rate. Statistical laws show that for every 10% increase in the penetration rate of high-speed broadband Internet, the per capita GDP (gross domestic product) in developing economies will increase by 1.38%, and for every 10% increase in the penetration rate of mobile phones, the per capita GDP in developing economies will increase by 0.81%.

The ICT industry is a leading industry. Leading industries refer to industries that have a guiding role and a significant role in promoting effect in the development of other industries in the national economy. The input-output ratio of information technology in the transformation of traditional industries can reach more than 1 : 10 in developed countries. The combination of ICT with machinery, energy, transportation, construction, textiles, metallurgy and other industries has continuously spawned new industrial categories and broader technological fields. The ICT industry has spawned and driven the development of emerging industries, such as the digital content industries (e.g., online publishing, online games, digital music, and mobile media), and the new Internet service industries (e.g., e-commerce, modern logistics, software and service outsourcing).

The ICT industry is a strategic industry. It has become a strategic industry for countries to compete for technological, economic, talent and military dominance and commanding heights. In the field of ICT, the intensity of competition in technical standards is far greater than in other industries. If a country or a company can control the standards, it will have a competitive advantage that other countries or companies cannot surpass. Additionally, the manufacturing of electronic information products and the software industry are also strategic sectors vital to national security, serving as the fundamental guarantee for a country's network and information security.

1.2.3　Features of ICT Industry

The ICT industry is an intellectually intensive industry. It is an industry that collects, produces and manages information. It is characterized by the substantial development of knowledge and technology, with a focus on intellectual labor. It is also an industry with the most concentrated and fierce competition for international patent technology. The top three high-patent-intensive industries in the US are the computer industry, the communications industry, and the electronics industry. For example, in order to seize the source and entrance of mobile Internet and big data, Google has launched patent acquisitions around intelligent terminals, and it acquired 17 000 patents from Motorola for 12.5 billion USD.

The ICT industry is a highly innovative industry. It is based on scientific research and exhibits characteristics of high innovation and a rapid pace of updates. The innovation speed of the ICT industry is also unmatched by other industries: the number of information technology doubles every three years, more than 300 000 new patents are added annually, and the effective lifespan of research data averages only five years. The rapid development of information technology has resulted in a shortened product lifecycle for information products, leading to increasingly frequent product updates. As Bill Gates, the former president of Microsoft, reminded his employees: Microsoft is always 18 months away from bankruptcy.

The ICT industry is an industry characterized by high risk and high returns. Researching and developing information products require substantial capital, and due to the uncertainty of the success probability in creating inventions, substantial investments may end up yielding no returns. The research and development of information products entails high fixed costs and low marginal costs. However, when it reaches the stage of mass production with standardized scales, the investment costs tend to be relatively lower. Information products often benefit from economies of scale, allowing manufacturers to reap much higher profit margins than those of traditional industries once they achieve significant sales volumes.

1.2.4　Development Laws of ICT Industry

Compared with traditional industries, the ICT industry has its own development laws, development paths, and development models. Among development laws, the most famous and far-reaching ones are Moore's Law, Metcalfe's Law, and "smiling curve".

1.2.4.1　Moore's Law

Moore's Law was proposed by Gordon Moore, one of the founders of Intel. In 1965, Moore was invited to write a review report entitled "Cramming More Components onto Integrated Circuits" for the 35th anniversary special issue of the journal *Electronics*. When Moore plotted the data, he found that the number of transistors that each generation of chips could accommodate was about twice that of the previous generation of chips, and the time interval between two generations of chips was within 18 to 24 months. If chip capacity develops according to this trend, computing power will increase exponentially relative to the time period.

Moore's Law summarizes the law of the speed of information technology development. It points out that the performance of integrated circuit chips has indeed been greatly improved in the past 30 years. When looking forward to the future of integrated circuit chips, information technology experts believe that Moore's Law may still apply. However, as transistor circuits gradually approach the performance limit, Moore's Law will come to an end in this specified area.

1.2.4.2 Metcalfe's Law

Metcalfe's Law was proposed by Robert Metcalfe, the founder of the American network equipment company 3Com Corporation. Its basic content is that the value of a network is equal to the square of the number of network nodes, that is, the commercial value of a network is proportional to the square of the number of the connected users. Metcalfe's Law reveals that the commercial value of a network grows quadratically with the growth of the number of the connected users.

Metcalfe's Law states that when a technology has established a necessary user scale, its value will explode. Since the 1990s, the Internet has not only shown this extraordinary growth trend, but has also widely penetrated and expanded into various fields of the economy and society. As the number of Internet users increases, network resources grow exponentially. Currently, with the widespread application of mobile Internet and social media, Metcalfe's Law has been fully confirmed.

1.2.4.3 Smiling Curve

Mr. Shi Zhenrong, the founder of Acer Group, proposed the famous "smiling curve" theory (see Figure 1-3) in 1992 in order to "rebuild Acer". The "smiling curve" divides the industrial chain of the manufacturing industry into three stages, namely research and development (R&D), manufacturing, and marketing. It believes that the added value of the industry is more reflected at the two ends, namely R&D and marketing, while the added value of the manufacturing stage in the middle is the lowest. Researches on the modern industrial value chain also show that the profit margins of enterprises at the two ends of the industrial chain are 20% to 25%, while the profit margins of processing and production enterprises in the middle are only about 5%. This form with the two ends facing up and the middle facing down is like a smile logo.

From a global perspective, developed countries and regions dominate the development trend and pattern of the ICT industry and are at the high end of the value chain. With its strong economic strength, large-scale basic research, and perfect venture capital mechanism, the US is committed to the research, development and application of information technology, constantly launching new technologies, and maintaining its leading position in the world. European countries such as the UK and Germany are also committed to R&D and standard setting in some areas of the ICT industry, and are at the high end of the value chain. South Korea, Singapore, and other countries and regions are

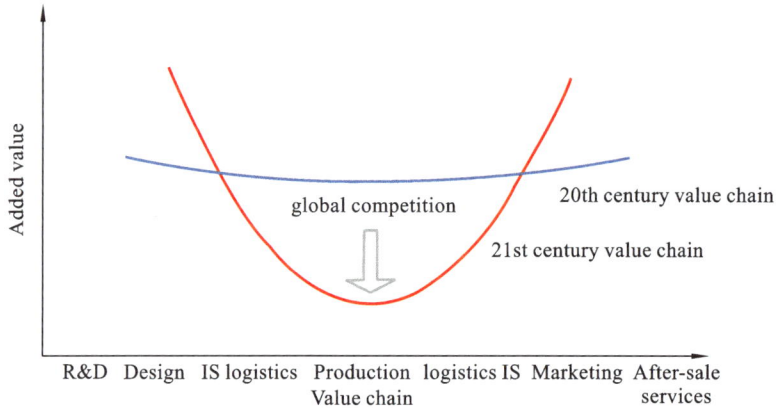

Figure 1-3 Smiling curve

Image Source: Shi Zhenrong, *Acer's Century of Change*, 2005

in the middle of the ICT industry value chain based on production technology.

1.3 Revolution of Technology and Industry

1.3.1 New-Generation ICT

After 2010, ICT ushered in a new round of development boom. Artificial intelligence (AI), the Internet of Things (IoT), and the new generation of mobile communications technologies are considered to be another major round of changes in the ICT industry. These new technologies will subvert traditional communications and computing models, and drive the ICT industry to a higher level. These new technologies support each other, evolve in groups, accelerate breakthroughs, and have been widely used. The representative new-generation ICT are shown in Table 1-9.

Table 1-9 The representative new-generation ICT

Fields	Content of technologies
5th-Generation Mobile Communications Technology (5G)	The 5th-Generation Mobile Communications Technology referred to as 5G, is a new generation of mobile communications technology with the characteristics of high speed, low latency and large connection, and the three major application scenarios of 5G defined by the International Telecommunication Union (ITU) are enhanced mobile broadband (eMBB), ultra-reliable and low-latency communication (uRLLC) and massive machine type communication (mMTC)

Continued

Fields	Content of technologies
Industrial Internet	The Industrial Internet is a new type of infrastructure, application model and industrial ecology that deeply integrates the new-generation ICT with the industrial economy; through the comprehensive connection of people, machines, objects, systems, etc., it builds a new manufacturing and service system covering the entire industrial chain and the entire value chain, and its network system includes three parts: network interconnection, data interoperability, and identity resolution
IoT	The IoT is a network and its application system with various sensor devices as nodes; it can realize the identification of physical objects, the perception of the environment, the control of equipment, etc., and improve the level of automation in production and life; its representative technologies include radio frequency identification (RFID), sensor networks, machine-to-machine (M2M), etc.
Cloud computing	Cloud computing is a model that provides computing resources (servers, databases, storage, etc.) and software services (platforms, architectures, applications, etc.) to users on demand through the Internet, and cloud computing service providers use distributed computing, virtualization and other technologies to achieve automated management, sharing and allocation of computing resources
Big data	Big data refers to the technology of processing, storing, analyzing and managing high-speed, large-scale and diverse data sets; with the huge amount of data accumulated by the Internet technology, big data technology needs to process a large amount of structured, semi-structured and unstructured data, which is often achieved by cloud computing
Blockchain	Blockchain is a distributed storage system based on the Internet; it uses technologies such as point-to-point transmission, consensus mechanism, and encryption algorithm, so it is anonymous and tamper-proof, and provides a secure and reliable decentralized storage solution
Metaverse	The metaverse is a virtual world system that is linked and created by scientific and technological means, and maps and interacts with the real world; it involves technologies such as virtual reality, augmented reality, digital twins, and human-computer interaction, and can form a digital living space with a new social system

Continued

Fields	Content of technologies
AI	AI is a technology that uses computers to simulate certain human thinking processes and intelligent behaviors (such as learning, reasoning, thinking, planning, etc.), involving fields such as robotics, language recognition, image recognition, natural language processing, computer vision, machine learning and expert systems; in recent years, large AI models have adopted machine learning models with ultra-large-scale parameters (usually more than 1 billion) and ultra-powerful computing resources, which have excellent performance in natural language processing, image processing, etc.

The new generation of ICT is accelerating its horizontal spread to other economic sectors and interpenetrating and integrating with the physical world. The fundamental and leading role played by ICT in high-tech industries is becoming more and more significant.

First, the connotation of information space is continuously enriched and profound, and it has become an important carrier to realize the control of matter and energy. The deep integration of information and physics has profoundly changed the perception, analysis, decision-making and execution process in the traditional control loop, and the control system has taken a substantial step towards intelligence. Artificial intelligence technology can achieve autonomous cognition and learning, thereby optimizing and reconstructing the production and industrial operation mode, and creating greater incremental value.

Second, the systematic development of information technology has become an important form of technological competition in the field of electronic information. The technologies of key links such as perception, transmission, storage, and computing are constantly cross-integrating, and the systematic development model is becoming increasingly obvious. The Internet and big data have given rise to a new paradigm of data-driven engineering technology development, triggering profound changes in scientific research methods and organizational methods.

Third, as a general technology, ICT is combined with various fields and generates new technical directions. For example, information technology is accelerating the cross-integration with manufacturing, materials, energy, biology and other technologies, giving rise to new technical directions such as intelligent manufacturing, new materials, and bioinformatics, and creating new industrial forms and business models such as the Industrial Internet, "Internet Plus", and the sharing economy.

1.3.2 Fourth Industrial Revolution

Science and technology are the main driving force for social and economic development. Every rapid economic growth is closely linked to a large-scale industrial revolution. The industrial revolution is based on new scientific discoveries and marked by the outbreak of technological revolution. New technologies are widely used in human production and life, thus triggering changes in industrial structure, economic situation, social division of labor system, global political and economic structure, and changing social and cultural values and the psychological state of social members.

The First Industrial Revolution was marked by the invention of the steam engine, led by the UK, and characterized by the replacement of human and animal power with mechanical power, which led to large-scale factory production and triggered the mechanization of the textile industry and the transformation of the metallurgical industry. The Second Industrial revolution was mainly marked by the invention and application of internal combustion engines and electric power technology, led by the US and Germany, and realized the electrification of production and life with electric power as the power, gave birth to the automobile manufacturing industry and petrochemical industry, and promoted the development of innovative industries such as railway transportation and shipbuilding. The Third Industrial Revolution was the information technology revolution, represented by the development and application of electronic computer technology, and continued to be led by the US, realizing the automation, informatization and modernization of production and life.

At present, a new technological revolution represented by AI, big data, the IoT, space technology, biotechnology, and quantum technology is underway. Ulrich Sendler, the author of *Industry 4. 0: The Coming Fourth Industrial Revolution*, calls this technological revolution the Fourth Industrial Revolution. The impact of various new technologies adopted in this technological revolution on human beings is systematic and holistic. Various emerging technologies are highly integrated and mutually infiltrated to form a complete technological system, which has the characteristics of synchronization, systematicity, and integrity in the transformation of human society, and has created new products, new formats, and new models that cross the boundaries of traditional industries. The Fourth Industrial Revolution is an intelligent revolution, represented by genetic engineering, quantum computing, new material technology, new energy technology, virtual reality, etc., to achieve comprehensive intelligence of production and living systems, and bring about major changes in the development mode of the economy and society. For example, the Internet is gradually moving towards the IoT, traditional enterprises are also evolving into digital enterprises, traditional manufacturing is transforming into "intelligent manufacturing", and intelligent robots will appear in all areas of human production and life. Figure 1-4 shows the history of technology innovations and industrial revolutions.

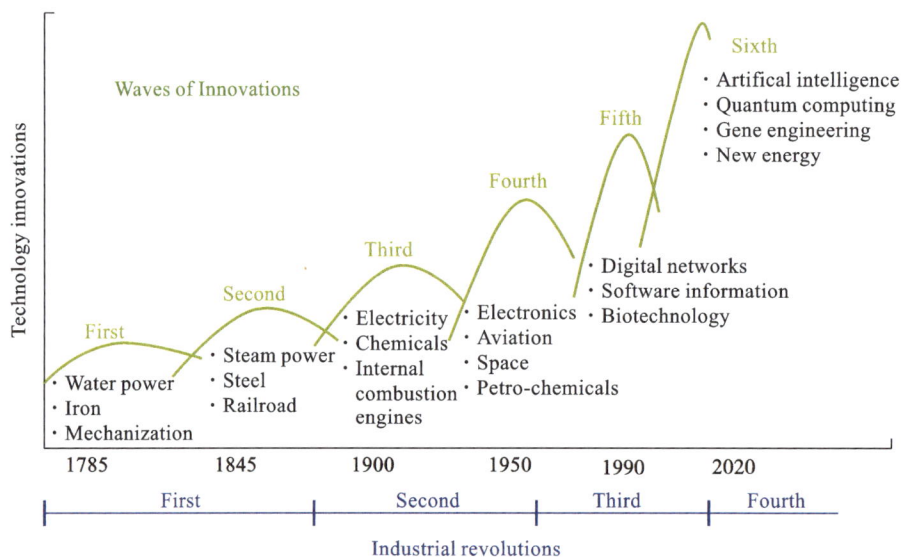

Figure 1-4　Technology innovations and industrial revolutions

1.4　New Digital Economy

1.4.1　Scope of Digital Economy

From the perspective of industrial revolution history, the digital economy can be traced back to the emergence of electronic computers in the 1950s. The early manifestation of the digital economy is the Internet economy. In 1994, the concept of "digital economy" appeared. The book *Digital Economy* by the famous economist Don Tapscott was also published in this year. This is the first book on digital economy, which predicts the new form of economic development in the Internet era, such as the emergence of e-commerce community. Nicholas Negroponte also described the social life scenes in the digital age in his book *Being Digital*.

With the promotion and application of the Internet and various information technologies, data has become a key factor of production fully embedded in the economic system. Due to its characteristics of being replicable, easy to spread, and able to transcend time and space, data has unprecedented application potential in various sectors, and data resources are called "the new oil of the 21st century". Data can effectively drive the network sharing, collaborative development, and efficient utilization of factors such as labor, capital, and technology, improve total factor productivity, and provide new impetus for economic and social development.

The digital economy is the main economic form after the agricultural economy and the industrial economy. The digital transformation is driving profound changes in production methods, lifestyles and governance methods, and has a great impact on the world's economic, political and technological landscape. Regarding the definition of the digital economy, many international institutions and organizations have made generalizations. The most representative definition is drawn in the "G20 Digital Economy Development and Cooperation Initiative" issued by the G20 Hangzhou Summit in 2016: "The digital economy refers to a broad range of economic activities that includes using digitized knowledge and information as the key factor of production, modern information networks as the important activity space, and the effective use of ICT as an important driver for efficiency-enhancing and economic structural optimization." The digital economy represents the sum of a series of economic activities of production, circulation and consumption around data, which serves as the key factor of production.

In the digital economy era, the process of gradually transforming traditional information industries into digital industries with digital as the main factor of production to promote the development of a new generation of information industries is called "digital industrialization", which refers to the industrialization, commercialization and marketization of data elements. The informatization and digital transformation of traditional industries is called "industrial digitization", which means using modern digital information technologies, like the Internet and AI to transform traditional industries in all perspectives, directions, and chains, so that digital technology can be deeply integrated into and develop with all walks of life in the real economy.

In May 2021, the National Bureau of Statistics of the People's Republic of China released the "Statistical Classification of Digital Economy and Its Core Industries (2021)", which for the first time defined the industrial scope of the digital economy: digital product manufacturing industry, digital product service industry, digital technology application industry, digital element-driven industry, and digital efficiency improvement industry. These five categories can be grouped into two aspects: digital industrialization and industrial digitization.

Digital industrialization: The first four categories above are the digital industrialization part, namely the core industries of the digital economy, which refer to the various economic activities that provide digital technologies, products, services, infrastructure and solutions for the digital development of industries, as well as all kinds of economic activities that are completely dependent on digital technologies and data elements. They correspond to the 26 major categories, 68 medium categories and 126 small categories in the "National Economic Industry Classification" and are the foundation for the development of the digital economy. The scope of digital industrialization is basically the same as that of the traditional ICT industry, including basic telecommunications industry, Internet industry, information service industry and electronic information manufacturing industry.

Industrial digitalization: The fifth major category of "digital efficiency improvement industry", namely the industrial digitalization part, refers to the application of digital technologies and data resources to traditional industries to increase output and improve efficiency. It is the integration of digital technologies and the real economy. This part covers digital application scenarios such as intelligent manufacturing, smart agriculture, and smart transportation, corresponding to 91 major categories, 431 medium categories, and 1 256 small categories of the "National Economic Industry Classification". This reflects that digital technologies have been and will be further integrated into various industries of the national economy.

1.4.2　Global Digital Strategies

The role of data in promoting the economy is becoming increasingly prominent, and using ICT to promote the digital transformation of traditional industries has become a consensus among countries. In recent years, the value of data elements has been released in some countries and regions, such as the EU, the UK, the US, Brazil, Japan, etc. The value of data market has continued to increase, and relevant data indicators such as data professionals and data companies have been rapidly developed. In 2020, the value of the data economy in the 27 EU countries reached approximately 355.1 billion euros, an increase of 9.3% over 2019. In order to further promote the development of the ICT industry and the digital economy, more and more countries have taken various positive measures to protect and develop their own ICT industries. The *Digital Economy Outlook 2020* published by the Organization for Economic Cooperation and Development (OECD) shows that, in the digital economic policy survey conducted in 37 countries, 34 countries had formulated national overall digital strategies.

In order to maintain its absolute global leadership in the field of electronics information, the US has continuously strengthened the government's guidance on the development direction of information technology and released relevant development plans or strategies in a timely manner. In 1998, the US Department of Commerce released the "Emerging Digital Economy" series of reports; in recent years, it has successively released the "Initiative on the Digital Economy", the "Federal Data Strategy 2020 Action Plan", and the US Innovation and Competition Act of 2021, repeatedly emphasizing the important role of the digital economy in the development of the national economy. In October 2020, the US released the "National Strategy for Critical and Emerging Technologies", redefining 20 key and emerging technologies, and proposing to fully maintain the global leadership of the US in cutting-edge technologies such as quantum physics and AI.

In order to rebuild Europe's international competitive advantage in the field of ICT, the EU has actively laid out the innovative development of information technology. The "Horizon 2020" scientific research plan was implemented from 2014 to 2020, strengthening the innovation and application of information technology, of which investment in the field of ICT accounts for 46% of the total investment. After the EU proposed the European data strategy in 2014, it successively launched the "Digitising European Industry Initiative", the

European Artificial Intelligence Act, and other documents, and released the "Shaping Europe's Digital Future" in February 2020, as well as the "2030 Digital Compass: the European Way for the Digital Decade" in March 2021, which comprehensively planned the EU's digital development path from 2021 to 2030.

1.5 Summary

The level of information technology has an important impact on social and economic life. Papermaking and printing techniques in ancient China provided a carrier for the recording and communication of traditional information, and promoted the development and communication of ancient world civilizations. Benefiting from the development of modern science and technology, various technologies were invented based on the electronic devices and radio waves, including telegraphs, telephones, and televisions, bringing human society into an era of global communication and exchange. Over the past half century, information technologies such as integrated circuits, computers, the Internet, and mobile communications have developed rapidly, driving the rapid progress and development of human society and profoundly affecting people's work and life. The development history of ICT industry shows that ICT, as a general technology, has a strong driving role and radiation effect on the development of other industries and the society, and is an economic growth "multiplier", a development mode "converter", and an industrial upgrading "booster".

At present, a new generation of ICT, which is represented by cloud computing, big data, 5G, Industrial Internet, artificial intelligence, blockchain, etc. is developing rapidly, and is also promoting the Fourth Industrial Revolution on a global scale. The widespread application of ICT in all walks of life has promoted the arrival of a digital society. Data has become an important factor of production and strategic resource, and is a new driving force for optimizing resource allocation, promoting the continuous upgrading of traditional industries, and improving social labor productivity. Developing a digital economy with data as the core element has become a consensus around the world. Meanwhile, formulating corresponding ICT development plans and digital economic development strategies has also become a consensus among major industrialized countries.

2　Overview of Digital China

2.1　Brief History

2.1.1　Self-reliance: Initial Establishment of China's ICT industry (1949-1978)

On October 1, 1949, Chinese President Mao Zedong announced the founding of the People's Republic of China at Tian'anmen Square in Beijing. China put an end to more than a century of suffering under oppression and aggression, finally gaining the opportunity for independent development. At that time, China had just emerged from decades of war, leaving the country war-torn and in a state of ruin, with everything needing to be rebuilt. It was a backward agricultural country with almost no industrial foundation, being unable to produce even steel gasoline barrels. Electronic products were mainly dependent on imports. Only a few major cities had telephones, with just 260 000 telephone users nationwide and a wired telephone penetration rate of only 0.05%. There were fewer than 50 000 scientific and technical personnel across the country, and very few experts in electronic technology.

China built an independent electronics industry from scratch. Starting from 1952, China established a number of electronic manufacturing enterprises through transformations and new constructions (see Table 2-1). Among them, Nanjing Radio Factory successfully developed China's first fully domestically produced electronic tube radio, the "Red Star" Model 502 in 1953, ending the history of relying on foreign components for radio assembly; Beijing Electron Tube Factory, with assistance from the Soviet Union, established an electron tube production line and became the largest electron tube factory in Asia during the 1960s. In 1963, the Fourth Ministry of Machine Industry (later renamed the Ministry of Electronics Industry in 1982) was founded to coordinate the national electronics industry, marking the establishment of China's information and communications technology (ICT) industry as an independent industrial sector.

China also built a scientific research team and talent cultivation system for the electronics industry from nothing. In November 1949, the Chinese Academy of Sciences

(CAS) was established, forming a strategic scientific and technological backbone of China. In electronics-related fields, CAS successively established the Institute of Applied Physics (1950), Institute of Electronics (1956), Institute of Computing Technology (1959), and Institute of Semiconductors (1960), initially forming a national research team covering electronic information-related disciplines. In 1952, China began to restructure its higher education system to meet national economic development needs. Electronic and communications-related departments were newly established in comprehensive universities, such as the Department of Radio Engineering at Tsinghua University in 1952, and the Department of Radio Electronics at Peking University in 1958. Specialized engineering colleges in telecommunications were also founded, including Beijing Post and Telecommunications Institute (now Beijing University of Posts and Telecommunications) in 1955 and Chengdu Institute of Radio Engineering (now University of Electronic Science and Technology of China) in 1956.

Under the complex and ever-changing international situation, Chinahas long relied on self-reliance and hard work. Over the past three decades, it has built a scientific and development team to develop electronic technology, communications technology, and semiconductor technology from scratch, established an independent electronics industrial system, and developed the ability to produce basic electronic devices such as simple electron tubes and transistors, as well as the ability to develop electronic products and computers.

Table 2-1 Development history of electronic manufacturing in China (1950s-1970s)

Fields	Representative developments
Semiconductor	In 1952, Nanjing Electric Factory successfully developed China's first radio tube; In 1956, the Institute of Applied Physics of the Chinese Academy of Sciences developed China's first triode; In 1957, the Beijing Electron Tube Factory produced China's first germanium single crystal; In 1968, Shanghai Radio 14th Factory manufactured PMOS integrated circuits
Electronic product	In 1953, Nanjing Radio Factory successfully developed the first domestically produced electronic tube radio; In 1958, China's first black-and-white TV was born and named "Beijing"; In 1960, China independently developed the first 1 000-door crossbar automatic telephone exchange equipment; In 1970, China's first artificial satellite "Dongfanghong-1" was successfully launched
Computer	In 1958, the Institute of Computing Technology of the Chinese Academy of Sciences successfully developed China's first small-scale general-purpose computer, the 103; In 1965, the Institute of Computing Technology of the Chinese Academy of Sciences successfully developed the first large-scale transistor computer, the 109B; In 1974, Tsinghua University and other units jointly developed the DJS-130 small multi-purpose computer using integrated circuits

However, due to limited overall national strength at the time, China's telecommunications infrastructure remained weak. By 1978, the national telephone network had not yet deployed automatic exchanges, and the manual exchanges were still used in many counties and rural areas. Long-distance transmission mainly relied on wires and analog microwaves. The national telephone capacity was 3.59 million lines, with 2.14 million users, and the telephone penetration rate was only 0.38%. Less than 1 in every 200 people had a telephone, which was less than 1/10 of the world average level at the time.

2.1.2   Reform and Opening-up: Rapid Development of China's ICT Industry (1978-2010)

In the late 1970s, significant changes occurred in the international landscape. In the 1980s, peace and development gradually became the themes of the era. At the end of 1978, China began to implement the national policy of "Reform and Opening-Up"[①]and shifted its focus to economic development, ushering in a period of rapid development for its ICT industry. Since 1986, China has carried out a strategic plan for the development of the postal and telecommunications industry and the electronics industry in the form of five-year plans. In 1993, China established a new group, named National Economic Informatization Joint Conference, to plan the countrywide informatization construction, especially the national information network infrastructure. In 1998, the State Council of China merged the Ministry of Posts and Telecommunications and the Ministry of Electronics Industry into the Ministry of Electronics Industry to reorganize it into the Ministry of Information Industry (MII). In 2006, China formulated the 15-year "National Informatization Development Strategy 2006-2020" to implement the guiding ideology of the new industrialization road of "driving industrialization with informatization and promoting informatization with industria-lization". In 2008, the MII and the State Council Informatization Office were integrated and reorganized to form the Ministry of Industry and Information Technology (MIIT).

In all previous five-year plans, the electronics industry and the information industry were the focus of industrial development, and promoting the penetration of the national telephone network and data communications network was the focus of information infrastructure layout. With the rapid development of China's information industry and the continuous improvement of information infrastructure, the information industry has gradually become an important driving force for promoting industrial upgrading and the overall economy. Table 2-2 lists the plans of China's information industry development

---

① At the end of 1978, China began to carry out the national policy of internal reform and opening-up to the outside world, transforming the planned economic system into the socialist market economic system, and actively participating in international economic cooperation and competition under economic globalization.

from 1986 to 2010.

Table 2-2 Plans of China's information industry development (1986-2010)

Planning period	Representative plans
During the 7th Five-Year Plan period (1986-1990)	In December 1986, the General Office of the State Council forwarded the "Report Outline on Doing a Good Job in the Promotion and Application of Computers in China" by the Electronic Revitalization Leading Group, and the outline proposed that the electronics industry should quickly shift to a track based on microelectronics technology and with computers and communications equipment as the main body; In March 1986, the "7th Five-Year Plan for National Economic and Social Development of the People's Republic of China" proposed to give priority to the development of transportation and communications
During the 8th Five-Year Plan period (1991-1995)	In April 1991, the "Ten-Year Programme of the People's Republic of China for National Socio-Economic Development and the Outline of the 8th Five-Year Plan" proposed to give prominence to the development of the electronics industry and make it a leading industry in promoting the modernization of the industrial structure and the entire national economy
During the 9th Five-Year Plan period (1996-2000)	In March 1996, the "9th Five-Year Plan for National Socio-Economic Development of the People's Republic of China and the Programme for the Long-Term Objectives by 2010" proposed that the postal and telecommunications industries should be developed with emphasis to form a unified national communications network system; In April 1997, the National Informatization Work Conference adopted the "Outline of National Informatization 9th Five-Year Plan and Long-Term Goals for 2010", proposing to establish a national Internet information center and an Internet exchange center, and include the Internet in the national information infrastructure
During the 10th Five-Year Plan period (2001-2005)	In March 2001, the "Outline of the 10th Five-Year Plan for National Economic and Social Development of the People's Republic of China" proposed to drive industrialization with informatization, accelerate the promotion of informatization, and increase the proportion of the information industry in the national economy; In October 2002, the "10th Five-Year Plan for National Economic and Social Development Informatization Development Key Special Plan" proposed to promote the application of information technology, enhance the level of informatization, and strengthen the construction of modern information infrastructure

Continued

Planning period	Representative plans
During the 11th Five-Year Plan period (2006-2010)	In March 2006, the "Outline of the 11th Five-Year Plan for National Economic and Social Development of the People's Republic of China" proposed to vigorously develop core industries such as integrated circuits, software and new components in the electronic information manufacturing industry, and focus on cultivating information industry clusters such as optoelectronic communications, wireless communications, high-performance computing and network equipment; In May 2006, the "National Informatization Development Strategy 2006-2020" was released, further emphasizing "promoting industrialization with informatization and driving informatization with industrialization" and proposing strategic actions such as the key information technology independent innovation plan

The ICT industry had gradually become a pillar industry of China's national economy. In 2010, the sales revenue of China's above-scale electronic information manufacturing industry reached 6 394.5 billion yuan, double the amount compared to 2005 (3 101 billion yuan), with a compound annual growth rate of more than 15% in the past five years; the export of electronic information products accounted for more than 30% of the country's foreign trade exports. Colorful TVs, microcomputers, mobile phones and other major output of fully-assembled products reached 120 million units, 250 million units and 1 billion units respectively, all accounting for more than 40% of the global total output. Industrial concentration has been significantly improved, and the competitiveness of key enterprises represented by the top 100 enterprises has been significantly enhanced. From 2005 to 2010, the main business revenue of the top 100 electronic information enterprises increased from 964.3 billion yuan to 1 535.4 billion yuan, and the sales revenue of Huawei, Lenovo, Haier and other companies exceeded 100 billion yuan.

The innovation system with enterprises as the main body has gradually formed. Significant progress has been made in the large-scale production technologies of thin-film transistor liquid crystal display (TFT-LCD) and plasma display panels (PDP). A number of mid-to-high-end integrated circuit products, such as central processing unit (CPU) and mobile communications chip, have made breakthroughs. Some special technologies, such as 65-nanometer advanced processes and high-voltage processes, have achieved mass production. Three-dimensional packaging and other new packaging technologies have been developed and applied. A complete industrial chain system for time division-synchronous code division multiple access (TD-SCDMA) technology has been established, and technological breakthroughs have been achieved in the field of 40 Gbps ultra-large-capacity optical transmission systems. Digital TV terrestrial transmission technology and digital audio and video encoding and decoding technology have reached international advanced levels. Table 2-3 lists China's achievements in communication infrastructure from 1978 to 2010.

Table 2-3 China's achievements in communication infrastructure (1978-2010)

Fields	Representative events
Optical fiber communications	In 1982, China built its first optical fiber communications system project, with a total length of 13.3 kilometers, a speed of 8.448 Mbps, and the ability to transmit 120 telephone lines, ushering in a new era of digital communications in China; In 1998, China's "eight vertical and eight horizontal" grid-shaped optical cable backbone network was completed two years ahead of schedule, covering cities above provincial capitals and 70% of prefecture-level cities nationwide, the national long-distance optical cable reached 200 000 kilometers, and China formed a long-distance backbone communications network with optical cables as the main medium and satellites and digital microwaves as the auxiliary components; In 2006, the first terabit-class, 10 Gbps submarine optical cable system, the Trans-Pacific Direct Cable System, between China and the United States was completed
Mobile communications	In 1993, China's first GSM digital mobile phone communications network (2G) was launched; In 2001, the number of mobile communications users in China exceeded 120 million, surpassing the United States to become the largest country in terms of mobile phone users; In 2003, China had 255 million fixed-line telephone users and 257 million mobile phone users, with mobile phone users exceeding fixed-line telephone users for the first time; In 2009, China issued three 3G licenses (CDMA2000, WCDMA, and TD-SCDMA)
Satellite communications	In 1984, China's first geostationary orbit experimental communications satellite, the Dongfanghong-2, was successfully launched, opening the history of satellite communications in China; In 1986, China's domestic satellite communications network was officially completed, including five communications satellites; In 1997, China successfully launched the Dongfanghong-3 satellite, which was equipped with 24 C-band transponders and reached the advanced level of similar communications satellites internationally; In 2000, China successfully launched the first two geostationary orbit satellites of the BeiDou Navigation Satellite System-1 (BDS-1), providing positioning services for China

Continued

Fields	Representative events
Internet	In 1994, the national computing and networking facility of China was officially connected to the Internet through a 64 Kbps (kilobits per second) international dedicated line, ushering in China's Internet era; In 1997, China included the Internet in its national information infrastructure construction plan, gradually built four backbone networks with international export capabilities, and established the operation and management system of China's national top-level domain name (.CN); In 2008, the number of Chinese Internet users reached 298 million, and the Internet penetration rate exceeded the global average

In terms of basic communications facilities, China has accelerated the construction of basic communications networks, covering optical fiber, mobile, and satellite communications, and established state-owned communications operators such as China Telecom, China Mobile, China Unicom, and China Satcom. In 2010, the basic telecommunications operators had the optical cable lines with a length of 9.962 million kilometers, 188 million Internet broadband access ports, and 620 000 3G network base stations. They had 1.6 Tbps (terabit per second) of total international communication business export bandwidth, with 7 land-submarine optical cables and 20 terrestrial cables. In 2010, the total number of telephone users in China reached 1.153 billion, with a penetration rate of 86.5 per 100 people; the number of Internet users reached 457 million, with a penetration rate of 34.3%. Besides the users of fixed-line telephone and mobile phones, the total number of Internet users and broadband access users in China jumped to the first place in the world in 2008.

In terms of the Internet, the number of Internet websites increased from 694 000 at the end of 2005 to 1.91 million in 2010, with a capacity of nearly 1 800 TB. In 2010, the scale of Internet service market exceeded 200 billion yuan, forming a group of backbone enterprises with international influence. In 2010, the scale of China's online retail users reached 161 million, and the transaction value reached 513.1 billion yuan, accounting for 3.3% of the total retail sales of social consumer goods. The growth rate of online retail value was 5.7 times that of the retail sales of social consumer goods in the same period. New payment services, such as online payment, mobile payment, and telephone payment, developed rapidly, and the scale of third-party electronic payment increased rapidly, reaching 1.01 trillion yuan in 2010. The rapid development of modern logistics industry and online retail drove the rapid development of express delivery services. In 2010, the business volume of express delivery service enterprises above designated size in China reached 2.34 billion pieces, and the business revenue reached 57.46 billion yuan.

2.1.3 Towards a New Era: Leapfrog Advancement of China's ICT Industry (2011 to present)

After 2010, the world once again set off a wave of accelerating informatization development. The rapid popularization of ICT technology represented by the Internet had a profound impact on international politics, economy, society, and culture. Various countries accelerated the development and application of information technology, and the integrated information network evolved towards broadband, convergence and ubiquity. ICT technology, products, content, networks and platforms had accelerated their integration and development.

In 2017, the report of the 19th National Congress of the Communist Party of China (hereinafter referred to as the 19th CPC National Congress) clearly proposed the development strategy of building a "Cyber Power", a "Digital China", and a "Smart Society". Since the 12th Five-Year Plan, China has gradually formed a wide-ranging and multi-layered planning system for national informatization. In addition to the regular plans established every five years, it has proposed different plans specifically for national information infrastructure construction, economic transformation and upgrading, and new technology development. The typical development plans of China's ICT industry from 2011 to 2020 are shown in Table 2-4.

Table 2-4 Typical development plans for China's ICT industry (2011-2020)

Planning period	Representative plans
During the 12th Five-Year period (2011-2015)	In March 2011, "the Outline of the 12th Five-Year Plan for National Economic and Social Development of the People's Republic of China" was released, proposing to cultivate and develop strategic emerging industries such as the "new generation of information technology industry"; In August 2013, the State Council issued the "'Broadband China' Strategy and Implementation Plan", proposing that by 2020, the fixed broadband household penetration rate will reach 70%, the proportion of administrative villages with broadband access will exceed 98%, and the broadband access capacity of urban and rural households will reach 50 Mbps and 12 Mbps, respectively; In March 2015, the "Guiding Opinions of the State Council on Actively Promoting the 'Internet Plus' Action" was issued, proposing eleven special actions to promote "Internet Plus" innovation and entrepreneurship, collaborative manufacturing, modern agriculture, smart energy, inclusive finance, public welfare services, efficient logistics, e-commerce, smart transportation, green ecology, and artificial intelligence (AI) to support China's economic transformation

Continued

Planning period	Representative plans
During the 13th Five-Year Plan period (2016-2020)	In March 2016, the "Outline of the 13th Five-Year Plan for National Economic and Social Development of the People's Republic of China" was released, which once again emphasized the support for the development of strategic emerging industries, proposed to expand the space of the network economy, develop a modern Internet industry system, implement the national big data strategy, and strengthen information security protection; In July 2016, the General Office of the Communist Party of China Central Committee and the General Office of the State Council issued the "Outline of the National Informatization Development Strategy", proposing to build a "Cyber Power", and by 2025, the household penetration rate of fixed broadband will be close to the international advanced level, an internationally leading mobile communications network will be built, and seamless broadband network coverage will be achieved; In March 2017, the State Council issued the "New-Generation Artificial Intelligence Development Plan", pointing out that the artificial intelligence industry has become a new important economic growth point, and proposed to making China the world's major AI innovation center by 2030, and that the intelligent economy and intelligent society will achieve significant results

The scale of the digital economy grows rapidly. From 2017 to 2021, the scale of China's digital economy increased from 27.2 trillion yuan to 45.5 trillion yuan, ranking second in the world, with a compound annual growth rate of 13.7%, and its share of GDP increased from 32.9% to 39.8%, becoming one of the main engines driving economic growth (see Figure 2-1).

The scale of digital industry grows rapidly. From 2017 to 2021, the revenue of above-scale computer, communications and other electronic equipment manufacturing industries increased from 10.6 trillion yuan to 14.1 trillion yuan; the revenue of large-scale enterprises in software industry increased from 5.5 trillion yuan to 9.5 trillion yuan; the revenue of above-scale enterprises in Internet and related service industries increased from 0.7 trillion yuan to 1.6 trillion yuan (see Figure 2-2). From 2015 to 2020, the transaction volume of China's e-commerce increased from 21.8 trillion yuan to 37.2 trillion yuan. From 2015 to 2020, the information consumption of China experienced rapid growth, and the scale of China's information consumption increased from 3.4 trillion yuan to 5.8 trillion yuan. In 2016, the scale of the big data industry was 0.34 trillion yuan, and by 2020 it had exceeded 1 trillion yuan.

The network infrastructure is world-leading. By 2020, all prefecture-level cities in China had been built into optical network cities, and the access bandwidth of optical fiber networks in China had achieved exponential growth from 10 Mbps to 100 Mbps and then to

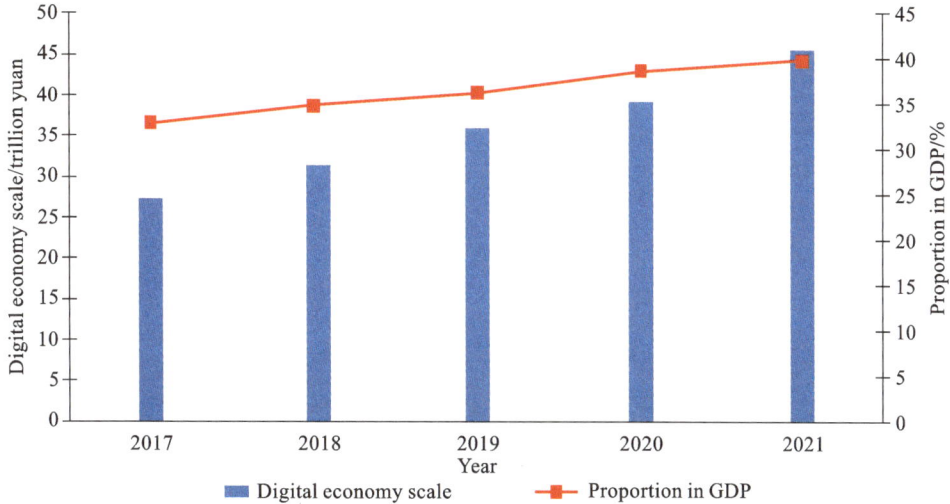

Figure 2-1   The scale of China's digital economy and its proportion in GDP (2017-2021)

Data Source: China Academy of Information and Communications Technology

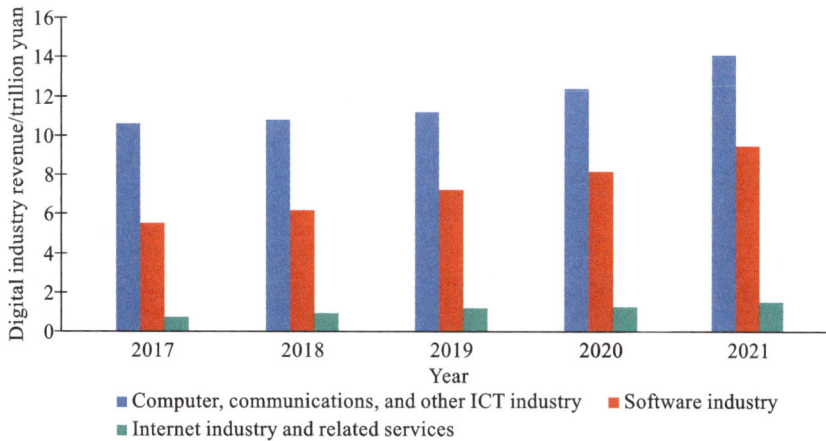

Figure 2-2   Revenue growth of China's digital industry (2017-2021)

Data Source: Ministry of Industry and Information Technology of the People's Republic of China

1 Gbps. The technical level and scale of China's mobile network had achieved a leap from "breakthrough in 3G" to "synchronization in 4G" and then to "leading in 5G" in the world. By the end of August 2022, the total number of 5G base stations in China had reached 2.102 million, and all prefecture-level cities and county towns had achieved full 5G coverage. The realization of "broadband access to every administrative village" had contributed to the completion of the historic goal of poverty alleviation[①] in China. The network infrastructure fully supported the Internet Protocol version 6 (IPv6). The number

---

①   The "poverty alleviation" campaign is a large-scale and systematic strategic initiative implemented by China to improve the living conditions of poverty-stricken areas and impoverished people, and to promote economic development and social progress. On February 25, 2021, General Secretary of the CPC Central Committee Xi Jinping announced that China had accomplished the arduous task of eradicating absolute poverty. This is a great achievement in human history.

of national Internet backbone direct connection points had increased to 19, and the scale of data centers had exceeded 5.2 million standard racks. The BDS-3 had been launched, with a global positioning accuracy of less than 10 meters. China's achievements in network infrastructure construction from 2011 to the present are shown in Table 2-5.

Table 2-5   China's achievements in network infrastructure construction (2011 to present)

Fields	Representative events
Optical fiber communications	In 2015, the number of fixed broadband users exceeded 200 million, ranking first in the world in terms of broadband user scale; In 2021, optical fiber broadband gigabit optical networks covered more than 120 million households, and the end-to-end broadband user experience speed reached 51.2 Mbps, ranking 18th among 176 countries and regions in the world
Mobile communications	In 2013, 4G commercial licenses were issued, ushering in China's 4G era; In 2015, the number of 4G users exceeded 380 million, and the scale of mobile broadband users (3G/4G) accounted for 60.1% of the total number of mobile users in China; In 2019, 5G commercial licenses were issued, ushering in China's 5G era
Satellite communications	In 2012, the BDS-2 was completed, including 14 satellites (5 geostationary orbit satellites, 5 inclined geosynchronous orbit satellites, and 4 medium earth orbit satellites), providing positioning services for the Asia-Pacific region; In 2017, ChinaSat 16 was launched, using a Ka-band multi-beam broadband communications system with a total capacity of 20 Gbps (Gigabit per second); In 2020, the BDS-3 was completed, with a total of 55 satellites, providing global positioning services
Internet	In 2012, mobile phones surpassed desktop computers to become the preferred terminal for Chinese netizens to access the Internet; In 2015, the number of Internet users reached 688 million, 90.1% of whom accessed the Internet via mobile phones, and the number of mobile Internet users reached 620 million; In 2015, online retail value ranked first in the world, reaching 3.88 trillion yuan; In 2020, e-commerce transaction value reached 37.2 trillion yuan

The number of Chinese Internet users increased from 688 million at the end of 2015 to 989 million at the end of 2020, the Internet penetration rate increased from 50.3% to 70.4%, and the number of mobile phone users increased from 1.11 billion to 1.643 billion, with the number of the users of 5G network growing from 0 to 355 million. Efforts to increase broadband speed and reduce fees have been continuously strengthened. In 2020, the average tariff level of fixed broadband and mobile data traffic dropped by more than

95% compared with 2015, and the average network speed increased by more than 7 times. The household penetration rate of fixed broadband increased from 52.6% at the end of 2015 to 96% at the end of 2020, the penetration rate of mobile broadband users increased from 57.4% at the end of 2015 to 108% at the end of 2020, and the proportion of administrative villages with optical fiber and 4G access had exceeded 98% nationwide. From the perspective of the proportion of broadband cost expenditure to per capita GDP, China's fixed broadband price index had risen from 71st in the world in 2017 to third in 2021, and the mobile broadband price index was lower than the global average for five consecutive years (see Figure 2-3).

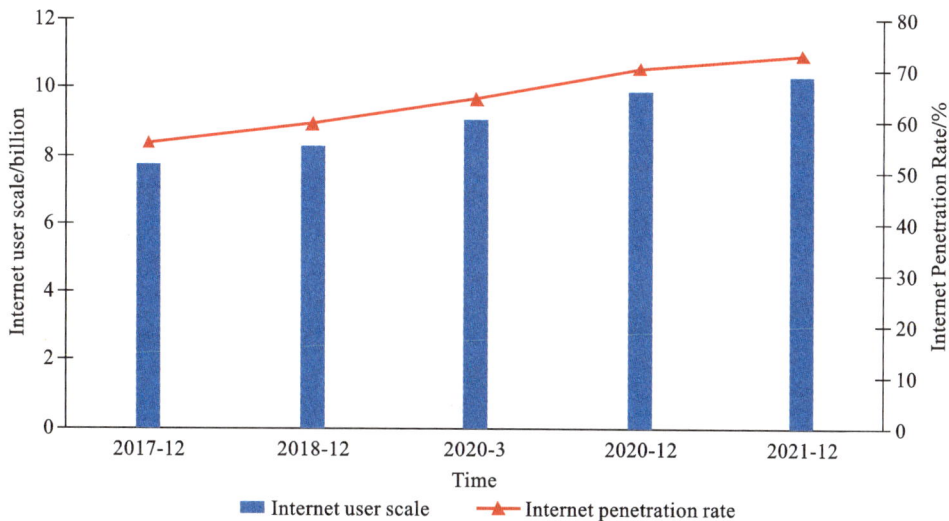

Figure 2-3 The changing trend of China's Internet user scale and Internet penetration rate (2017-2021)

Data Source: China Internet Network Information Center

2.2 Current Scale and Level

After more than 40 years of reform and opening-up, China has made great achievements in the traditional economic sectors. From 2012 to 2021, the added value of the manufacturing industry increased from 16.98 trillion yuan to 31.4 trillion yuan, and its share of the world's total increased from 22.5% to nearly 30%, continuing to maintain China's position as the world's largest manufacturing country. From 2012 to 2021, calculated at constant prices, China's total industrial added value grew by an average of 6.3% per year, far higher than the global average annual growth rate of about 2% in the same period. Among the 500 major industrial products, China ranked first in the world in the output of over 40% of them. As to some important electronic products, such as personal computers, air conditioners, solar panels, and mobile phones, China's output accounted for more than half of the world's output.

In terms of digital economy, China also occupied a prominent position in the world, and the growth of China's digital economy was significantly higher than that of other major economies. In 2020, the digital economy of the United States (US), China, Germany, Japan, and the United Kingdom (UK) accounted for 79% of the world's total; the US digital economy ranked first in the world, with a scale of 13.6 trillion USD, accounting for 41.7% of the world; China's digital economy ranked second in the world, with a scale of 5.4 trillion USD; Germany, Japan, and the UK ranked third to fifth, and the scales were 2.54 trillion USD, 2.48 trillion USD, and 1.79 trillion USD respectively. In 2020, the added value of China's core digital economy industries accounted for 7.8% of GDP. The "Global Digital Economy Competitiveness Development Report (2020)" released by the Shanghai Academy of Social Sciences showed that the competitiveness of China's digital economy ranked third in the world, following the US and Singapore, and the gap to the US was shrinking year by year. Among the various sub-indicators, China's score in the digital industry ranked first in the world, and its leading advantage was expanding year by year. The evaluation results and ranking of global digital economy national competitiveness in 2020 are shown in Table 2-6.

Table 2-6　Evaluation results and ranking of global digital economy competitiveness in 2020

Ranking	Nations	Digital industry	Digital innovation	Digital facility	Digital governance	Total score
1	the US	46.76	80.18	69.89	86.54	70.84
2	Singapore	27.55	82.18	50.53	67.43	56.92
3	China	65.31	51.52	46.07	49.65	53.14
4	South Korea	12.85	68.48	46.33	65.40	48.27
5	the UK	20.32	65.37	33.42	72.80	47.98
6	Japan	12.66	73.45	39.09	63.40	47.15
7	Finland	3.07	85.54	33.51	63.77	46.47
8	Sweden	9.32	69.71	38.18	62.82	45.01

In terms of digital infrastructure, China has built the world's largest, most widespread and technologically advanced information infrastructure. In terms of network facilities, mobile communications networks and optical fiber networks are the world's largest, with extensive coverage and leading technologies. In terms of computing power facilities, the scale of Internet data centers continues to grow rapidly, and a number of high-performance public computing platforms and intelligent computing centers dedicated to artificial intelligence are gradually taking shape. In terms of perception facilities, a pattern of coordinated development of narrowband Internet of Things (NB-IoT), 4G, and 5G networks has been formed, and network coverage capabilities continue to improve. The scale and level of China's information infrastructure in recent years are shown in Table 2-7.

Table 2-7 The scale and level of China's information infrastructure in recent years

Types of infrastructure	Indicator	Scale and level
Network facilities	Broadband fixed network coverage level	All prefecture-level cities have been fully built into optical network cities, and by the end of October 2022, users with access bandwidth of 100 Mbps and above accounted for 93.8%, and users with access bandwidth of 1 000 Mbps exceeded 80 million households
	Mobile communications network coverage level	The world's largest 5G network has been built, and by the end of September 2022, China had 2.22 million 5G base stations, accounting for more than half of the world's total, and 5G mobile phone users reached 510 million
	Satellite positioning and navigation service coverage level	In July 2020, the BDS-3 was officially launched, and one year later, high-precision services were launched in more than 20 countries, with a total number of users exceeding 2 billion
	IPv6 address resource scale	The network infrastructure has been fully evolved and upgraded to IPv6, and as of June 2022, the total amount of IPv6 address resources ranked first in the world, and the number of active IPv6 users reached 683 million
	Internet access level of residential users	As of June 2022, the number of Internet users in China reached 1.051 billion, with an Internet penetration rate of 74.4%, especially in rural areas, where the Internet penetration rate increased to 58.8%
	Internet access level in primary and secondary schools	By the end of 2021, the Internet access rate of primary and secondary schools reached 100%, the proportion of schools with export bandwidth of more than 100 Mbps reached 99.95%, and more than 210 000 schools had access to wireless networks
Computing facilities	Data center server scale	By the end of 2020, China had about 4.4 million standard data center racks in use, and the scale of cloud computing was close to 43 million cores, with an average shelf-load rate of about 50%, and a storage capacity of 800 EB (exabyte)
	Data center computing power level	By the end of 2021, China's total computing power scale exceeded 140 EFLOPS, with an average annual growth rate of more than 30% in the past five years, ranking second in the world in terms of computing power scale

Continued

Types of infrastructure	Indicator	Scale and level
Perception facilities	NB-IoT coverage scale	China has built the world's largest NB-IoT, and deployed millions of NB-IoT base stations, basically achieving continuous coverage above the county level; as of December 2022, the number of mobile Internet of Things (IoT) connections reached 1.845 billion, and the scale of cellular IoT terminal users was rapidly approaching that of mobile phone users
	Number of IoT applications	By the end of 2022, four 10 million-level applications had been developed, including water meters, gas meters, smoke sensors, and tracking, and seven million-level applications had been developed, including white goods, street lights, parking, and agriculture

China's e-commerce ranked first in the world in terms of online retail volume and number of online shoppers. From 2013 to 2022, the scale of China's online retail market ranked first in the world for nine consecutive years consecutive. Calculated by the proportion of e-commerce sales in the entire national retail market, China reached 55.6% in 2022, ranking first in the world, while South Korea ranked second at 31.6 %, the UK ranked third at 28.5 %, the US was only 16.3 %, and the average of Western European countries was 14.8 % (see Figure 2-4). China's online retail volume increased from 1.31 trillion yuan in 2012 to 13.1 trillion yuan in 2021, with an average annual growth rate of 29.15%; the e-commerce transaction value increased from 8 trillion yuan in 2012 to 42.3 trillion yuan in 2021, with an average compound annual growth rate of 20.3%. Relying on online e-commerce and mobile payments, the market scale of online car-hailing, online food delivery, digital culture, smart tourism, and other industries continually expanded.

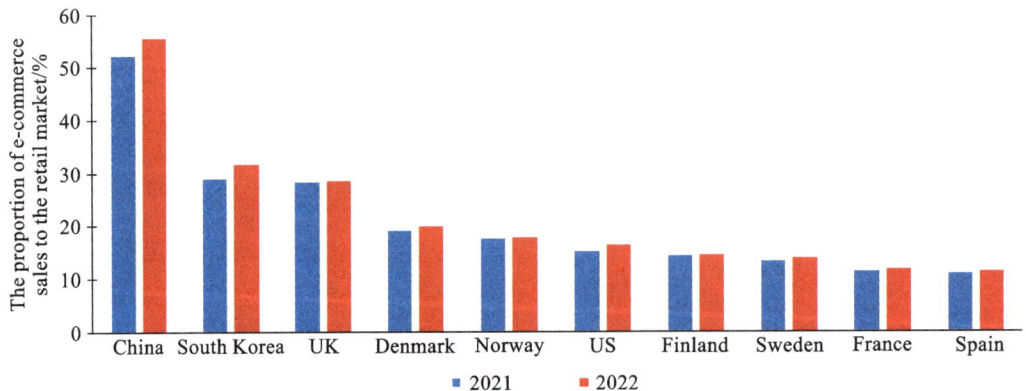

Figure 2-4　The proportion of e-commerce sales in the retail market for various countries (2021-2022)

Data Source: eMarketer

2.3 Macro Strategy and Industrial Planning

2.3.1 National Development Strategy

The CPC is the core force leading China's reform and development. The overall strategy formed at the important meetings of the CPC will be reviewed by the National People's Congress and implemented by the governments at all levels. The 19th CPC National Congress (2017) and the 20th CPC National Congress (2022) formed the overall national informatization strategy, including the "Cyber Power" strategy for the development of the information industry, the "Smart Society" strategy for people's livelihood services and social governance, and the "Digital China" strategy for the overall digitalization of the national economy and society.

2.3.1.1 Cyber Power

In February 2014, Xi Jinping, General Secretary of the CPC Central Committee, proposed to proceed from the international and domestic trends, make an overall layout, coordinate all parties, innovate and develop, and strive to build China into a "Cyber Power". In 2017, the report of the 19th CPC National Congress clearly proposed building a "Cyber Power". In 2022, the report of the 20th CPC National Congress further proposed to build a "Cyber Power". The strategic deployment of building a "Cyber Power" should be advanced in synchronization with the "Two Centenary Goals"[①]. Efforts should be following directions: the basic popularization of network infrastructure, significant enhancement of independent innovation capabilities, comprehensive development of the information economy, strong cybersecurity guarantees, and balanced network offensive and defensive capabilities. Main tasks of building a cyberpower include:

(1) Reaching a world-leading level in Internet-related information infrastructure. The network scale and broadband penetration rate, the competitiveness of the network-related information industry, and cybersecurity capabilities will be at the world's leading level, and the construction and application of cloud computing, mobile Internet, big data, and the IoT will also be at the world's leading level.

(2) Achieving independent control in key technologies related to the Internet. Fundamentally changing the situation where key technologies will be controlled by others requires major breakthroughs in key technology areas such as chip, operating system, and CPU.

---

① The "Two Centenary Goals" are, to build a moderately prosperous society in all respects by the 100th anniversary of the founding of the Communist Party of China (2021), and to build China into a great modern socialist country that is prosperous, strong, democratic, culturally advanced, harmonious, and beautiful by the 100th anniversary of the founding of the People's Republic of China (2049).

(3) Reaching a world-leading level in Internet applications. The Industrial Internet and the consumer Internet will be at a relatively high level as a whole, and e-commerce and e-government will be widely popularized and applied.

2.3.1.2　Smart Society

"Smart Society" was originally proposed by the European Union(EU) to explore how to use contemporary technological trends to solve the challenges facing modern society. The International Telecommunication Union Telecommunication Development Sector proposed that "Smart Society" refers to using the power and potential of technologies to improve human productivity, focus resources on important activities and relationships, and ultimately improve health, well-being and quality of life.

In 2017, the report of the 19th CPC National Congress clearly proposed to build a "Smart Society". It aimed to ensure people's livelihood, fully relying on information and intelligent means to provide the people with diversified, inclusive and equal public services. The main tasks of building a smart society include:

(1) Intelligent infrastructure. Carry out intelligent transformation of public social infrastructure that involves the lives of the broad masses of the people, including transportation, power grids, water services, and logistics.

(2) Informatization of planning and management. Through the comprehensive application of technologies such as City Information Model (CIM) and Geographic Information System (GIS), the digitization and precision of urban and rural infrastructure management such as urban and rural planning, land use, urban and rural pipe network, landscaping, and environmental protection will be promoted.

(3) Universalization of public services. Promote the informatization and intelligence of medical care, education, culture, tourism and other fields, promote the sharing and flow of high-quality medical and educational resources, and promote the digitization of public welfare venues such as libraries and museums.

2.3.1.3　Digital China

With the continuous acceleration of the digitalization process in various fields of economy and society, data elements will play a greater role in economic operation efficiency and total factor productivity. All countries in the world regard digitalization as the focus of economic development, and adopt policies and increase investment.

In 2017, the report of the 19th CPC National Congress clearly proposed to build "Digital China". In 2022, the report of the 20th CPC National Congress further proposed to accelerate the development of the digital economy, promote the deep integration of the digital economy and the real economy, and create a digital industry cluster with international competitiveness. The main tasks of building "Digital China" include:

(1) Create new advantages in the digital economy. The first is to strengthen the innovative application of key digital technologies. Accelerate the advancement of research and development (R&D) breakthroughs and iterative applications in the fields of high-end

chips, operating systems, key algorithms for AI, sensors, and general-purpose processors. The second is to accelerate the promotion of digital industrialization. Cultivate and expand emerging digital industries, and improve the industrial level of communication equipment, core electronic components, and key software. The third is to promote industrial digital transformation. Implement the action of "Using Data to Empower Wisdom on the Cloud" to promote the coordinated transformation of the entire industrial chain empowered by data. Deeply promote the digital transformation of the service industry, and cultivate new growth points such as crowdsourcing design, smart logistics, and new retail.

(2) Accelerate the new pace of digital society construction. The first is to provide smart and convenient public services. Promote the digitalization of resources in public service institutions such as schools, hospitals, and nursing homes, and increase the intensity of resource sharing and sharing services. Actively develop online classrooms, Internet hospitals, smart libraries, etc. The second is to build smart cities and digital villages. Promote the construction of new smart cities by class and classification, incorporate IoT sensing facilities and communication systems into the unified planning and construction of public infrastructure, promote the intelligent transformation of municipal public facilities, and promote the construction of urban data brains. The third is to build a new picture of a better digital life. Promote the construction of smart communities, and develop online and offline integrated community life services and community governance.

(3) Create a new ecosystem for digital development. The first is to establish and improve market rules for data elements. Cultivate standardized data trading platforms and market entities, promote basic legislation in the fields of data security and personal information protection, and promote the safe and orderly flow of data across borders. The second is to create a standardized and orderly policy environment. Improve the management norms of the sharing economy, platform economy and new individual economy, and improve the statistical monitoring system of the digital economy. The third is to strengthen cybersecurity protection. Establish and improve the key information infrastructure protection system, and strengthen cybersecurity risk assessment and review. The fourth is to promote the construction of a community with a shared future in cyberspace. Promote the formulation of international rules for digital and cyberspace with the United Nations as the main channel and the United Nations Charter as the basis, and promote the establishment of a multilateral, democratic, and transparent global Internet governance system.

2.3.2 Government Planning Hierarchy

At present, China has established a planning system for the ICT industry and national informatization, covering all levels of government departments and all industries (see Table 2-8). Among them, the national plans mainly include:

(1) Medium- and long-term development plans. These plans of about 15 years were made for the long-term development of national informatization. They could be the macro-overall planning, such as the "National Informatization Development Strategy 2006-2020" issued in 2006 and the "Outline of the National Informatization Development Strategy" issued in 2016. They could also be the special plans for certain fields, such as big data, AI, and 5G.

(2) Five-year plans. These plans were designed based on the overall five-year plan for national economic and social development. They specified the requirements for ICT development from various industry sectors, covering strategic emerging industries, electronic information manufacturing industries, digital transformation of traditional industries, social informatization and other fields. The competent departments of various industries would then formulate five-year information technology sub-item plans for each field based on the five-year plans.

(3) Short-term plans. These plans were designed by the relevant national ministries and commissions in response to the development needs of a certain field. They lasted about three years, and were designed to organize and coordinate major national projects and key projects, and make special adjustments and improvements to related supporting policies, measures, and environment.

Table 2-8 Relevant plans for ICT industry and informatization during the 14th Five-Year Plan period

Planning types	Sub-item types	Issuing authorities	Plans
Medium-and long-term plans	Macro plans	General Office of the CPC Central Committee, Office of the State Council	Outline of the National Informatization Development Strategy
			Outline of the 14th Five-Year Plan for National Economic and Social Development and the Long-Range Objectives Through the Year 2035 of the People's Republic of China
	Special plans	State Council	Next-Generation Artificial Intelligence Development Plan
Five-year plans	Macro-specific plans	Central Cyberspace Affairs Commission	14th Five-Year Plan for National Informatization
		State Council	14th Five-Year Plan for the Development of Digital Economy
		Office of the State Council	14th Five-Year Plan for the Modern Logistics Development

Continued

Planning types	Sub-item types	Issuing authorities	Plans
Five-Year plans	Information industry plans	Ministry of Industry and Information Technology	14th Five-Year Plan for Information and Communications Industry Development 14th Five-Year Plan for the Development of the Big Data Industry 14th Five-Year Plan for the Development of Software and Information Technology Services
	Industry informatization plans	Ministry of Industry and Information Technology, etc.	14th Five-Year Plan For the Development of Intelligent Manufacturing 14th Five-Year Plan for the Deep Integration Development of Informatization and Industrialization
		Ministry of Agriculture and Rural Affairs	14th Five-Year Plan for National Agricultural and Rural Informatization Development
		National Radio and Television Administration	14th Five-Year Plan for the Development of Radio, Television and Online Audiovisual
		Ministry of Commerce, etc.	14th Five-Year Plan for E-commerce Development
		Ministry of Transportation	14th Five-Year Plan for Digital Transportation
		Ministry of Housing and Urban-Rural Development, etc.	14th Five-Year Plan for National Urban Infrastructure Construction
		Ministry of Civil Affairs	14th Five-Year Plan for Development of Civil Affairs Informatization
		National Health Commission, etc.	14th Five-Year National Health Informatization Plan
		National Development and Reform Commission	14th Five-Year Plan for Promoting National Government Informatization

Continued

Planning types	Sub-item types	Issuing authorities	Plans
Short-term plans	Industry informatization plans	Ministry of Industry and Information Technology, etc.	Three‐Year Action Plan for the Construction of New Infrastructure for the Internet of Things (2021-2023) "Dual Gigabit" Network Collaborative Development Action Plan (2021-2023) Three‐Year Action Plan for the Development of New Data Centers (2021-2023) Action Plan for Green and Low-Carbon Development of the Information and Communication Industry (2022-2025) Action Plan for the Development of Basic Electronic Components Industry (2021-2023)
		Industrial Internet Special Working Group	Industrial Internet Innovation and Development Action Plan (2021-2023)
	Informatization application plans	Ministry of Industry and Information Technology, etc.	Action Plan for the Integrated Development of Virtual Reality and Industry Applications (2022-2026) 5G Application "Sailing" Action Plan (2021-2023)
		Central Cyberspace Affairs Commission, etc	Digital Rural Development Action Plan (2022-2025)

China had formed a complete planning system of "research-planning-execution-evaluation". In the process of developing plans, the central government and ministries will seek the opinions of relevant industry organizations and experts to ensure the scientific nature and feasibility of the plans. Major national plans, such as the five-year plans for national economic and social development, need to be reviewed by the National People's Congress and other legislative bodies. After the national plan is released, governments at all levels will develop corresponding plans at their level based on their spirit and in light of local realities, and submit them to the People's Congress at their level for deliberation and approval. Governments at all levels will list the goals in the plan as part of their annual work reports and summaries, report the progress of implementation to the People's Congress at the relevant level, and accept supervision.

China's hierarchical planning system can ensure that the central government's policies and plans can be effectively implemented throughout the country. As shown in Table 2-9, taking Hubei Province and Wuhan City as examples, after the State Council formulated the national five-year plan, Hubei Province and Wuhan City also formulated the relevant plans for their respective governments. After the national ministries and commissions formulated the five-year plan for one specified industry (such as the big data industry), the relevant industry authorities in Hubei Province further formulated the five-year plan for the industry in the province.

Table 2-9 Decomposition of China's information industry planning
(taking Wuhan, Hubei as an example)

Planning types	Issuing authorities	Layer	Planning	Release date
Decomposition of macro development plan		National	Outline of the 14th Five-Year Plan for National Economic and Social Development and the Long-Range Objectives Through the Year 2035 of the People's Republic of China	March 2021
		Provincial	Outline of the 14th Five-Year Plan for National Economic and Social Development and the Long-Range Objectives Through the Year 2035 of Hubei Province	April 2021
		Municipal	Outline of the 14th Five-Year Plan for National Economic and Social Development and the Long-Range Objectives Through the Year 2035 of Wuhan City	April 2021
Decomposition industry development plan	Ministry of Industry and Information Technology	National	14th Five-Year Plan for the Develop-ment of the Big Data Industry	October 2021
	Hubei Provincial Department of Economy and Information Technology	Provincial	14th Five-Year Plan for the Development of the Big Data Industry of Hubei Province	March 2022

2.3.3 Planning Policy Tools

The Chinese government adopted a variety of policy tools to promote and facilitate the development of relevant information industries. Taking the ICT related plans released from

2011 to 2020 as examples, total 90 plans or policy documents were collected and analyzed. Those documents were released by the General Office of the State Council, the MIIT, the National Development and Reform Commission (NDRC), the Ministry of Science and Technology (MST), and other departments. The commonly used policy tools were classified and counted according to the three aspects of supply, environment, and demand. The results are shown in Table 2-10.

Table 2-10 Statistics on the policy tools adopted in China's ICT related plans (2011-2020)

Tool types	Policy tools	Examples	Count in the selected set	Proportion of all tools
Supply-oriented	Talent development	Cultivate urgently needed specialized talents in R&D in key areas such as information technology	36	13.8%
	Infrastructure construction	Support the construction of electronic information industry engineering research centers, engineering laboratories, and enterprise technology centers	5	2.0%
	Public service	Support the construction of public R&D service platforms such as innovation knowledge centers, data centers, inspection and testing, and quality certification for the electronic information industry	32	12.3%
	Technology investment	Make full use of policy funds such as the National Integrated Circuit Industry Investment Fund to guide social capital investment and support the development of major industrialization projects	26	10.0%
Environment-oriented	Goal Planning	The construction of China's famous software city and national new industrialization industry demonstration base (software and information services) has reached a higher level, and the number of cities with industrial revenue exceeding 100 billion yuan has reached more than 20	47	18.0%

Continued

Tool types	Policy tools	Examples	Count in the selected set	Proportion of all tools
Environment-oriented	Regulatory Control	Accelerate the establishment of industry standards and important product technical standards systems that are conducive to the development of the new generation of information technology industries, and optimize the approval and management procedures for market access	24	9.2%
	Open to the outside world	Encourage domestic integrated circuit enterprises to expand international cooperation, integrate international resources, and expand international markets	16	6.1%
	Financial support	Actively support qualified software and integrated circuit enterprises to raise funds through issuing stocks, bonds and other means to expand direct financing channels	11	4.2%
	Tax incentives	The VAT credits at the end of the period incurred by relevant integrated circuit enterprises due to the purchase of equipment will be refunded	15	5.7%
	Intellectual property protection	Actively develop and apply network copyright protection technology for genuine software to effectively protect software and integrated circuit intellectual property rights	17	6.5%
Demand-oriented	Government procurement	Implement a new generation of information technology industry innovative products and services promotion plan, and increase the government's first purchase and ordering efforts for software and other products	6	2.3%
	Transformation of scientific and technological achievements	Establish a benign interaction mechanism among enterprises, research institutes, and universities to provide full-process services to promote technology transfer and achievement transformation in the new generation of information technology industries	23	8.8%

Continued

Tool types	Policy tools	Examples	Count in the selected set	Proportion of all tools
Demand-oriented	Trade controls	Support software exports and service outsourcing through export subsidies and other means	3	1.1%

The policy tools for the new generation of ICT industries were mainly supply-oriented and environment-oriented ones. During the 12th Five-Year Plan period, some subdivided policy tools were not activated, such as infrastructure construction within supply-oriented policy tools, and trade control within demand-oriented policy tools. Since the 13th Five-Year period, various types of policy tools have been enriched and expanded to a certain extent. In the supply-oriented policy tools, the talent development, public service, and technology investment were the main supporting tools, and their support increased significantly in 2016, while the support for infrastructure construction was relatively weak. In the environment-oriented policy tools, the government mainly promoted industrial development by formulating guiding policies like development goals and plans, followed by policies related to property rights protection and those related to financial support. In the demand-oriented policy tools, the most supportive tool was transformation of scientific and technological achievements, which grew rapidly after 2015, and had different trend compared with the supply-oriented policy tools. Now the Chinese government is actively exploring the application of different types of policy tools for industrial incentives and promotion methods, and promoting the development and progress of the industry considering the pains and shortcomings troubling various industries.

2.4　Development Goals and Key Areas

In February 2023, the CPC Central Committee and the State Council issued the "Overall Layout Plan for the Construction of Digital China". The plan pointed out that building "Digital China" is an important engine for promoting Chinese modernization in the digital era and a strong support for building new national competitive advantages. The construction of "Digital China" was laid out in accordance with the overall framework of "2522", namely, consolidating the "two foundations" of digital infrastructure and data resource system, and promoting the deep integration of digital technology and the Five-Sphere Integrated Plan for economic, political, cultural, social and ecological civilization construction, strengthening the "two major capabilities" of digital technology innovation system and digital security barrier, and optimizing the "two environments" (see Figure 2-5) of domestic and international digital development.

"Two environments" for Digital China

Domestic: digital
governance ecosystem

International: cooperation
in digital field

Digital
technology
innovation
system

Two major capabilities for Digital China

Digital
security
barrier

Deep integration of digital technology in five areas

| Digital economy | Digital government | Digital culture | Digital society | Digital ecological civilization |

"Two foundations" for Digital China

Digital infrastructure

Data resource system

Figure 2-5   Content framework of "Overall Layout Plan for the Construction of Digital China"
Image Source: China Netcom

The overall goal of "Digital China" is: by 2025, decisive progress will be made in the construction of "Digital China", the level of ICT development will be significantly upgraded, the digital infrastructure will be fully consolidated, the innovation ability of digital technology will be significantly enhanced, the value of data elements will be fully utilized, the digital economy will be developed in a high-quality way, and the efficiency of digital governance will be improved as a whole.

2.4.1   Digital Infrastructure

In March 2020, the Standing Committee of the Political Bureau of the CPC Central Committee clearly proposed to accelerate the construction of the new infrastructures such as 5G networks and data centers. The new infrastructures are those strategic and network-based infrastructures with a multiplier effect, which are fit for the new generation of technological revolution and industrial transformation, and provide underlying support for the innovative, coordinated, green, open and shared development of the economy and society. There are three categories of new infrastructures. The first category is information infrastructure, which mainly refers to the infrastructure generated by the new-generation information technologies, such as the communications network infrastructures (e.g., 5G, IoT, Industrial Internet, and Satellite Internet), the computing power infrastructures (e.g., data centers and intelligent computing centers), and the new technology infrastructures (e.g., AI, cloud computing, and blockchain). The second category is integrated infrastructure, which mainly refers to the integrated infrastructure formed by deeply applying information and communication technologies like the Internet, big data, and AI to support the transformation and upgrading of traditional infrastructure. Examples of this category are the smart transportation infrastructure and smart energy infrastructure. The third category is innovative infrastructure, which mainly refers to public welfare infrastructure that supports scientific research, technology development, and product development. This category includes the major scientific and technological infrastructure, scientific and educational infrastructure, and industrial technology innovation infrastructure. With the technological revolution and industrial transformation, the connotation and extension of new infrastructures will not remain unchanged, but will continue to evolve and change. The main contents of China's new infrastructure are shown in Table 2-11.

Table 2-11   Main contents of China's new infrastructure

Categories	Sub-categories	Scopes
Information infrastructure	Communications network infrastructure	5G, IoT, Industrial Internet, Satellite Internet, etc.
	Computing power infrastructure	Data centers, intelligent computing centers, etc.
	New technology infrastructure	AI, cloud computing, blockchain, etc.
Integrated infrastructure	Smart transportation infrastructure	Intercity high-speed railway, urban rail transit
	Smart energy infrastructure	Ultra-high voltage transmission and transformation network, new energy vehicle charging piles
Innovative infrastructure	Public welfare infrastructure supporting the development of science and technology	Major scientific and technological infrastructure, scientific and educational infrastructure, industrial technology innovation infrastructure, etc.

In the "Overall Layout Plan for the Construction of Digital China" issued in February 2023, the "information infrastructure" in the "new infrastructures" was referred to "digital infrastructure". This document also presented the recent construction priorities. In terms of network infrastructure, accelerate the coordinated construction of 5G networks and gigabit optical networks, deepen the large-scale deployment and application of IPv6, promote the comprehensive development of mobile IoT, and vigorously promote the large-scale application of BDS. In terms of computing power infrastructure, systematically optimize the layout of countrywide computing infrastructure, promote efficient complementarity and coordinated linkage of computing power in the east and west of China, and guide the reasonable deployment of data centers, supercomputing centers, intelligent computing centers, edge data centers, etc. In terms of application infrastructure, strengthen the digitalization and intelligent transformation of traditional infrastructure, and improve the intelligence level of social general infrastructure, such as electricity, transportation, and logistics. The development goals of China's communications network infrastructure in the 14th Five-Year Plan period are shown in Table 2-12.

Table 2-12 The development goals of China's communications network infrastructure in the 14th Five-Year Plan period

Metrics	2020	2025
Internet user scale	989 million	1.2 billion
5G user penetration rate	15%	56%
Number of optical fiber users with 1 000 Mbps or higher access bandwidth	6.4 million	60 million
Number of active IPv6 users	462 million	800 million

2.4.2　Digital Economy

Since entering the 14th Five-Year Plan period, China has intensively released a number of important plans related to the digital economy, including the "Outline of the 14th Five-Year Plan for National Economic and Social Development and the Long-Range Objectives Through the Year 2035 of the People's Republic of China", the "14th Five-Year Plan for Digital Economy Development", and the "14th Five-Year Plan for the Deep Integration of Informatization and Industrialization". The national 14th Five-Year Plan has established a systematic framework for promoting digital development. In terms of overall goals, it is proposed that by 2025, the added value of China's core industries in the digital economy will account for 10% of GDP, up from 7.8% in 2020. See Table 2-13 for China's digital economy development goals in the 14th Five-Year Plan period.

Table 2-13 The development goals of China's digital economy in the 14th Five-Year Plan period

Metrics	2020	2025
The added value of core industries in the digital economy as a percentage of GDP	7.8%	10%
In terms of digital industrialization, the scale of information consumption	5.8 trillion yuan	7.5 trillion yuan
In terms of digital industrialization, online retail value	11.76 trillion yuan	17 trillion yuan
In terms of industrial digitalization, the ratio of enterprise industrial equipment going cloud-ward	13.1%	30%
In terms of industrial digitalization, the proportion of enterprises with comprehensive digitalization of key business links	48.3%	60%

2.4.2.1　Digital Industrialization

Accelerate the promotion of digital industrialization. Cultivate and strengthen emerging digital industries such as AI, big data, blockchain, cloud computing, and cybersecurity, and improve the industrial level of communications equipment, core electronic components, and key software. Encourage enterprises to open up search, e-commerce, social and other data, and develop third-party big data service industries.

Promote the sound development of sharing economy and platform economy. The key industries and development goals of China's digital industrialization in the 14th Five-Year Plan period are shown in Table 2-14.

Table 2-14 The key industries and development goals of China's digital industrialization in the 14th Five-Year Plan period

Fields	Development goals
Cloud computing	Accelerate the iteration and upgrading of cloud operating systems, promote technological innovations such as ultra-large-scale distributed storage, elastic computing, and data virtual isolation, and improve cloud security levels; focus on hybrid cloud to cultivate cloud service industries such as industry solutions, system integration, and operation and maintenance management
Big data	Promote technological innovations in big data collection, cleaning, storage, mining, analysis, and visualization algorithms, cultivate a full life cycle industry system for data collection, labeling, storage, transmission, management, and application, and improve the big data standard system
IoT	Promote technological innovations such as sensors, network slicing, and high-precision positioning, coordinate the development of cloud services and edge computing services, and foster the Internet of Vehicles (IoV), medical IoT, and home IoT industries
Industrial Internet	Build an independent and controllable identification resolution system, standard system, and security management system, strengthen the research and development and application of industrial software, cultivate and form an Industrial Internet platform with international influence, and promote the construction of the "Industrial Internet plus Intelligent Manufacturing" industrial ecosystem
Blockchain	Promote innovation in blockchain technologies such as intelligent contracts, consensus algorithms, encryption algorithms, and distributed systems, focus on developing blockchain service platforms and application solutions in the fields of financial technology, supply chain management, and government services with alliance chains as the key point, and improve regulatory mechanisms
AI	Build AI data sets for key industries, develop algorithm reasoning training scenarios, promote the design and manufacturing of intelligent products such as intelligent medical equipment, intelligent vehicles, and intelligent recognition systems, and promote the construction of general and industry-wide artificial intelligent open platforms

2.4.2.2 Industrial Digitalization

Promote the transformation of industrial digitalization. Accelerate the integration and application of the new-generation ICT and the real economy, implement the "Using Data to Empower Wisdom on the Cloud" action, and create a smart supply chain system supported by big data, networked sharing, and intelligent collaboration. Build smart agriculture, accelerate the digitalization and intelligent upgrading of all links in the agricultural production, processing, sales, logistics and other industrial chains. Build an agricultural basic data resource system, and accelerate the informatization of agricultural science and technology services. Accelerate the digital transformation of the manufacturing industry, develop a multi-level systematic Industrial Internet platform system and innovative applications, strengthen the development of standard system for informatization and industrialization, and deeply implement the intelligent manufacturing projects. Deepen the digital transformation of the service industry and cultivate new growth points such as crowdsourcing design, smart logistics, and new retail. The typical industry development goals of China's industrial digitalization during the 14th Five-Year Plan period are shown in Table 2-15.

Table 2-15 The typical development goals for industrial digitalization in the 14th Five-Year Plan period

Industrial sectors	Development goals
Intelligent manufacturing	Promote equipment networking, digital connection of production links and coordinated response of supply chain, promote the integration of production data, flexible manufacturing, personalized products and intelligent management
Smart agriculture	Promote precision sowing, fertilization and pesticide application, and harvesting of field crops, and promote the intelligent application of facility horticulture, livestock and poultry aquaculture; build a smart water conservancy system, and improve water situation monitoring and intelligent scheduling capabilities based on river basins
Smart energy	Promote the intelligent upgrading of coal mines, oil and gas fields, power plants, etc., carry out extensive collection of energy consumption information and online analysis of energy efficiency, and realize the interaction of source, grid, load and storage, multi-energy synergy and complementarity, and intelligent regulation of energy demand
Intelligent transportation	Develop autonomous driving and vehicle-road collaborative travel services, promote intelligent highway management, traffic signal linkage, and public transportation priority control, and build smart railways, smart civil aviation, smart ports, digital waterways, and smart parking lots

2.4.3　Digital Society

The "14th Five-Year Plan for National Informatization" proposed to steadily advance the construction of a digital society. Cultivate new business models driven by digital technology and data resources. Encourage intelligent upgrading and business model innovation in the fields of travel, catering, accommodation, culture, tourism, sports, logistics, and housekeeping, promote brand consumption and quality consumption, and cultivate a high-quality digital life service market. The public service system should be more convenient and beneficial to the people, and the role of informatization in supporting basic livelihood security and basic social services should be effectively enhanced. The level of equalization of digital public services should be significantly improved, and the gap in service levels between urban and rural areas should be significantly narrowed. The development goals for typical fields of digital public services in China in the 14th Five-Year Plan period are shown in Table 2-16.

Table 2-16　The development goals for typical fields of digital public services in the 14th Five-Year Plan period

Typical fields	Development goals
Smart education	Promote the inclusion of high-quality social online course resources into the public teaching system, promote the online radiation of high-quality educational resources to weak schools in rural and remote areas, and develop scenario-based, experiential learning and intelligent education management and evaluation
Smart healthcare	Improve electronic health records, medical records, electronic prescriptions and other databases, and accelerate data sharing among medical and health institutions; promote telemedicine, advance the application of medical image-assisted interpretation, clinical-assisted diagnosis, etc; use big data to enhance the supervision of medical institutions and medical behaviors
Smart culture and tourism	Promote scenic spots, museums, etc. to develop online digital experience products, build scenic spot monitoring facilities and big data platforms, and develop new cultural and tourism services such as immersive experience, virtual exhibition halls, and high-definition live broadcasts
Smart community	Promote the interconnection of government service platforms, community sensing facilities and household terminals, develop community welfare services such as intelligent early warning, emergency rescue and smart elderly care, and establish an unmanned logistics distribution system
Smart home	Apply induction control, voice control, remote control and other technical means to develop smart home appliances, smart lighting, smart security monitoring, smart speakers, wearable devices, service robots, etc.

2.5 Summary

Under the leadership of the Communist Party of China, China has developed from a poor and backward agricultural country into a prosperous and progressive industrial country after more than 70 years of development. Earth-shaking changes have taken place across China, and the Chinese people are enjoying prosperous and peaceful life.

China has not only built globally leading information infrastructure but also built a technologically advanced and comprehensively covered industrial chain, ranking at the forefront of the world in many application fields such as mobile Internet, e-commerce, and mobile payment. Currently, China's digital economy scale ranks second in the world in scale, and the proportion of added value from core digital economy industries in GDP has been gradually increasing. China's independent innovation capabilities in ICT have significantly improved, with scientific and technological strength and international competitiveness growing day by day.

As a socialist country, China demonstrates institutional advantages in industrial planning and development. The government has established an ICT industry and informatization planning system covering all industries, including multi-level layouts such as medium- and long-term plans, five-year plans, and short-term plans. It comprehensively uses policy tools such as supply-oriented, environment-oriented, and demand-oriented measures to accurately promote the development of the ICT industry. At present, China has established macro strategies such as "Cyber Power", "Smart Society", and "Digital China". "Cyber Power" focuses on infrastructure, key technologies, and application innovation; "Smart Society" promotes intelligent infrastructure and inclusive public services; "Digital China" emphasizes creating new advantages in the digital economy and fostering a new ecosystem for digital development.

The Chinese government attaches great importance to the transformative role of ICT in industries and society. Telecommunications infrastructure construction has been listed as a key task in several five-year plans, serving as the foundation to drive digital transformation and industrial upgrading across all industries. China is advancing steadily toward the goal of building a "Digital China", demonstrating strong momentum and a bright future in the global informatization.

3　ICT Innovations

3.1　Scientific Research Innovation System

Deng Xiaoping, the chief architect of China's reform and opening-up, pointed out that science and technology are the primary productive forces. Information and communications technology (ICT) innovation is the core element in the development of the ICT industry. Due to the highly innovative and high-risk characteristics of the ICT industry, conducting organized scientific research has become a characteristic way for China to catch up with and surpass the world's advanced scientific and technological levels. This chapter first introduces China's existing scientific research innovation system, as well as the science and technology development plans. Then it focuses on China's major science and technology projects and industrial technology breakthrough achievements in the field of ICT in recent years.

When the People's Republic of China was founded in 1949, there were only around 30 institutions engaged in scientific and technological research nationwide, and there were almost no scientific research teams specializing in ICT. Since then, China gradually established ICT teaching, research and production bases from scratch. After about 70 years of development, China has established a relatively complete research and development system for ICT, including colleges and universities, scientific research institutions, industrial clusters and so on.

3.1.1　Strategic Scientific Research Force

In the 1950s, China initially established an independent ICT research and development team. In 1956, the Ministry of Education (MOE) gathered teachers and students from five universities to the Department of Physics of Peking University to establish the first semiconductor major in China. In 1956, the Institute of Computing Technology of the Chinese Academy of Sciences was established, and in 1960, the Institute of Semiconductors of the Chinese Academy of Sciences was established. After the reform and opening-up, the national strategic scientific and technological force system has been gradually improved, covering state key laboratories for basic research, and innovation bases for market applications such as the national engineering research centers and national technology innovation center.

3.1.1.1 State Key Laboratory

The state key laboratories are important scientific and technological innovation bases where China organizes basic research, applied basic research and cutting-edge technology research, gathers and cultivates leading innovative talents, conducts high-level innovative cooperation, and produces major original achievements. The state key laboratories that began to be established in 1984 had reached a total of 265 by 2021. The main supporting units are China's key universities and major scientific research institutions in related fields. The state key laboratories actively participated in international big science programs and big science projects, and promoted China's breakthroughs in basic theoretical research and major key technologies. By 2021, there were 26 state key laboratories in the field of ICT, involving semiconductors, electromagnetism, communications, computers, networks and other fields.

According to the "Outline of the 14th Five-Year Plan for National Economic and Social Development and the Long-Range Objectives Through the Year 2035 of the People's Republic of China", China will strengthen national strategic scientific and technological strength, promote the optimization and combination of innovation systems guided by national strategic needs, and accelerate the construction of strategic scientific and technological strength led by national laboratories. Focus on major innovation fields such as quantum information, photonics and micro-nano electronics, network communications, and artificial intelligence (AI) to establish a number of state laboratories, reorganize state key laboratories, and form a laboratory system with a reasonable structure and efficient operation. Optimize and upgrade innovation bases such as the national engineering research centers and the national technology innovation centers, carry out in-depth industry-university-institute cooperation, and promote the radiation and driving effect of basic theories and key technologies on the industry.

The Law on Scientific and Technological Progress of the People's Republic of China implemented in January 2022 proposed to "establish and improve a laboratory system led by state laboratories and supported by national key laboratories". National key laboratories have replaced state key laboratories to become important strategic scientific and technological forces. In July 2022, the Ministry of Science and Technology (MOST) organized a meeting to promote the optimization and reorganization of state key laboratories. After reorganization, recommendation and evaluation, the first batch of 20 benchmark national key laboratories were selected and approved for construction. Among them, there were 9 national key laboratories in the field of ICT, covering sub-fields such as AI, integrated circuits, and micro-nanoelectronics (see Table 3-1).

Table 3-1   Benchmark national key laboratories in the field of ICT (July 2022)

National key laboratories	Supporting institutions
National Key Laboratory of Micro-Nano Electronic Devices and Integrated Technology	Peking University
National Key Laboratory of Virtual Reality Technology and Systems	Beihang University
National Key Laboratory of Integrated Chips and Systems	Fudan University
National Key Laboratory of Brain-Computer Intelligence	Zhejiang University
National Key Laboratory of Autonomous Intelligent Unmanned Systems	Beijing Institute of Technology, Tongji University
National Key Laboratory of Cognitive Intelligence	iFLYTEK Co., Ltd., University of Science and Technology of China
National Key Laboratory of Processors	Institute of Computing Technology of the Chinese Academy of Sciences
National Key Laboratory of Integrated Circuit Materials	Shanghai Institute of Microsystem and Information Technology of the Chinese Academy of Sciences
National Key Laboratory of Multimodal Artificial Intelligence Systems	Institute of Automation of the Chinese Academy of Sciences

3.1.1.2   National Engineering Research Centers

The national engineering research centers (NERCs) are research and development entities organized by the National Development and Reform Commission (NDRC). These centers are established by institutions with strong research and development (R&D) capabilities and comprehensive strengths, including universities, scientific research institutes, and enterprises. They are an integral part of the national innovation system. In response to the needs of national major strategic missions and key construction projects, efforts are made to tackle key technologies and conduct experimental research, develop major equipment, and carry out engineering experimental verification of significant scientific and technological achievements, in order to break through the constraints of key technologies and core equipment.

As of the end of 2022, there were 191 national engineering research centers, and 50 of them were in the fields of ICT. The categories of supporting institutions are relatively wide, including well-known universities and scientific research institutions, major telecommunications service operators (such as China Telecom, China Mobile, China

Unicom, etc.), major information technology companies (such as Baidu, iFLYTEK, etc.), major electronic manufacturing companies (such as BOE, Haier, etc.), and scientific and technological major forces which carry out informatization in various industrial sectors (such as China UnionPay, PetroChina, etc.). Table 3-2 lists 12 national engineering research centers in the fields of ICT.

Table 3-2 Typical national engineering research centers in the fields of ICT

National engineering research centers	Supporting institutions
NERC for Next Generation Internet Core Technologies	Tsinghua University
NERC for Mobile Private Networks	Beijing Jiaotong University
NERC for Mobile Internet Security Technology	Beijing University of Posts and Telecommunications
NERC for Next Generation Internet Access System	Huazhong University of Science and Technology
NERC for Optical Fiber Sensing Technology and Network	Wuhan University of Technology
NERC for New-Generation Mobile Communications Test and Verification	China Academy of Information and Communications Technology
NERC for Cybersecurity Emergency	National Computer Network and Information Security Management Center
NERC for Cloud Network Infrastructure Security	China Telecom Global Limited
NERC for Next-Generation Internet Broadband Service Application	China Unicom Network Technology Research Institute
NERC for New-Generation Mobile Communications Technology	China Mobile Communications Group Co., Ltd.
NERC for Mobile Communications and Internet of Vehicles	Datang Telecom Technology Co., Ltd.
NERC for Digital Home Network	Haier Group Co., Ltd.

According to the "Outline of the 14th Five-Year Plan for National Economic and Social Development and the Long-Range Objectives Through the Year 2035 of the People's Republic of China", China will concentrate on integrating and upgrading a number of key common technology platforms, and support leading enterprises in the industry to cooperate with universities, scientific research institutes and upstream and downstream enterprises in the industry to jointly build national industrial innovation centers, which will undertake the major national scientific and technological projects. China will support qualified enterprises to transform into scientific research institutes, and provide public welfare and common technical services. Some common technology platforms will be set up to solve key common technical problems across industries and fields.

3.1.2　High-tech Industrial Development Zones

High-tech industrial development zones (HIDZs) are specific areas established with the approval of governments at all levels for the purpose of developing high-tech. They mainly rely on the advantages of being knowledge-intensive and technology-intensive, as well as their regional economic strength, geographical location and openness to the outside world, and focus on the development of high-tech industries supported and encouraged by national policies. Enterprises settled in the HIDZs can enjoy preferential policies such as income tax preferential tax rate, export tariff exemption, and plant construction tax exemption. By the end of 2020, the total number of national high-tech industrial development zones (NHIDZs) had reached 169, including 70 in the east, 44 in the central region, 39 in the west, and 16 in the northeast; 21 national independent innovation demonstration zones (NIIDZs) had been established and become important carriers for implementing the innovation-driven development strategy. These zones had become the "leaders" of local innovation and development. From 2015 to 2020, the GDP of HIDZs increased from 8.1 trillion yuan to 12.2 trillion yuan, an increase of more than 50% in five years. The number of high-tech enterprises increased from 79 000 to 225 000.

The HIDZs have become an important scientific and technological force for breakthroughs in key technologies and enhancement of original innovation capabilities. In 2021, the NHIDZs gathered 84% of the state key laboratories and 78% of the national technology innovation centers. Enterprise R&D spending was 3.3 times that of 2012, accounting for 50% of the country's total; "Patent Cooperation Treaty" (PCT) international patent applications accounted for about 50% of the country's total. By the end of 2022, there had been 128 innovative industrial clusters in the NHIDZs. The scale of information technology industry in Beijing Zhongguancun NHIDZ accounted for 17% of the country's total; the scale of optoelectronic information industry in Wuhan East Lake NHIDZ accounted for 50% of the country's total; the scale of integrated circuit industry in Shanghai Zhangjiang NHIDZ accounted for 35% of the country's total. The HIDZs had cultivated and gathered 36.2% of the country's high-tech enterprises, 67.1% of the companies listed on the Science and Technology Innovation Stock Board, and 35.9% of the technology-based small and medium-sized enterprises. A number of world-class enterprises had also emerged.

3.1.3　Innovative Industrial Clusters

Since the founding of the People's Republic of China, China has preliminarily established an independent ICT industry chain, covering upstream and downstream links from raw materials to manufacturing of devices, instruments, and system equipment, and formed a regional industrial cluster with national information security industry bases and national information industry parks as the main body, mainly concentrated in the three major regions of the Bohai Rim Region (Beijing / Tianjin), the Yangtze River Delta Region (Shanghai /Hangzhou), and the Pearl River Delta (Guangzhou / Shenzhen).

In recent years, China has regarded ICT industry as one of the strategic emerging industries, and promoted it in combination with industrial cluster policies. In 2010, the "Decision of the State Council on Accelerating the Fostering and Development of Strategic Emerging Industries" was issued, and the new-generation information technology was listed as one of the strategic emerging industries. In 2019, the "Notice of the National Development and Reform Commission on Accelerating the Construction of Strategic Emerging Industry Clusters" was issued, announcing the first batch of national strategic emerging industry cluster construction lists in 12 key fields, involving 66 clusters in 22 provinces, autonomous regions, and municipalities, of which 23 industrial clusters were established in the field of new-generation information technology, as shown in Table 3-3. In order to promote the balanced development of the information technology industry in various regions, Shanghai located in the eastern China, Wuhan and Hefei located in the central China, each has three industrial clusters on the list, becoming the two cities with the most strategic emerging industry clusters in the field of new-generation information technology.

Table 3-3 Industrial clusters established by China in the field of new-generation information technology

Subfields	Names
Integrated circuit	Shanghai Pudong New Area Integrated Circuit Industry Cluster
	Xi'an Integrated Circuit Industry Cluster
	Beijing Economic-Technological Development Area Integrated Circuit Industry Cluster
	Wuhan Integrated Circuit Industry Cluster
	Hefei Integrated Circuit Industry Cluster
New display device	Hefei New Display Device Industrial Cluster
	Shenzhen New Display Device Industrial Cluster
	Wuhan New Display Device Industrial Cluster
Next-generation information network	Wuhan Next-Generation Information Network Industry Cluster
	Yingtan Next-Generation Information Network Industry Cluster
	Zhengzhou Next-Generation Information Network Industry Cluster
Information technology services	Hangzhou Information Technology Service Industry Cluster
	Jinan Information Technology Service Industry Cluster
	Guiyang Information Technology Service Industry Cluster
	Dalian Information Technology Service Industry Cluster
	Shanghai's Yangpu District Information Technology Service Industry Cluster
	Chengmai Information Technology Service Industry Cluster
	Zhengzhou Information Technology Service Industry Cluster

Continued

Subfields	Names
Network information security products and services	Tianjin Binhai High-Tech Industrial Development Area Network Information Security Product and Service Industry Cluster
Artificial intelligence	Beijing Haidian District Artificial Intelligence Industry Cluster
	Hefei Artificial Intelligence Industry Cluster
	Shanghai Xuhui District Artificial Intelligence Industry Cluster
	Shenzhen Artificial Intelligence Industry Cluster

The industrial cluster has the characteristics of network organization and flexible manufacturing, which is conducive to the realization of continuous technological innovation and the promotion of regional economic development. The "Outline of the 14th Five-Year Plan for National Economic and Social Development and the Long-Range Objectives Through the Year 2035 of the People's Republic of China" and the "14th Five-Year Digital Economy Development Plan" clearly stated that localities with conditions are encouraged to establish mixed-ownership industrial technology research institutes based on industrial clusters to serve the research and development of key common technologies in the region, actively explore the joint operation mode of platform enterprises and industrial parks, and explore the establishment of a new mechanism for cross-regional and cross-platform collaboration of various industrial clusters.

3.1.4　Technology Innovation Capability

According to the *Global Innovation Index 2021* released by the World Intellectual Property Organization (WIPO), China ranked 12th in the world, went up two places from 2020, and was the only middle-income economy in the top 30 of the world, ranking higher than the developed economies such as Japan, Israel, and Canada. In the world's top 100 science and technology clusters of 2021, China had 19 clusters on the list, only 5 fewer than the United States (US), ranking second. Among them, the cluster of Shenzhen-Hong Kong-Guangzhou ranked second, and that of Beijing rose to third. In 2021, China's total number of PCT international patent applications was 69 540, ranking first in the world for three consecutive years; the number of PCT international patent applications in the field of ICT exceeded 30 000, an increase of 60% from 2017, accounting for 37.80% of the world's total (see Figure 3-1).

In 2021, China ranked first in the world in the number of PCT international patent applications in the fields of computer technology and digital communications, accounting for more than one-third of the world; the two fields with the fastest growth in the effective number of domestic invention patents in China were information technology management methods and computer technology, with a year-on-year increase of 100.3% and 32.7% respectively; the innovative vitality of enterprises had been further stimulated, 13 Chinese

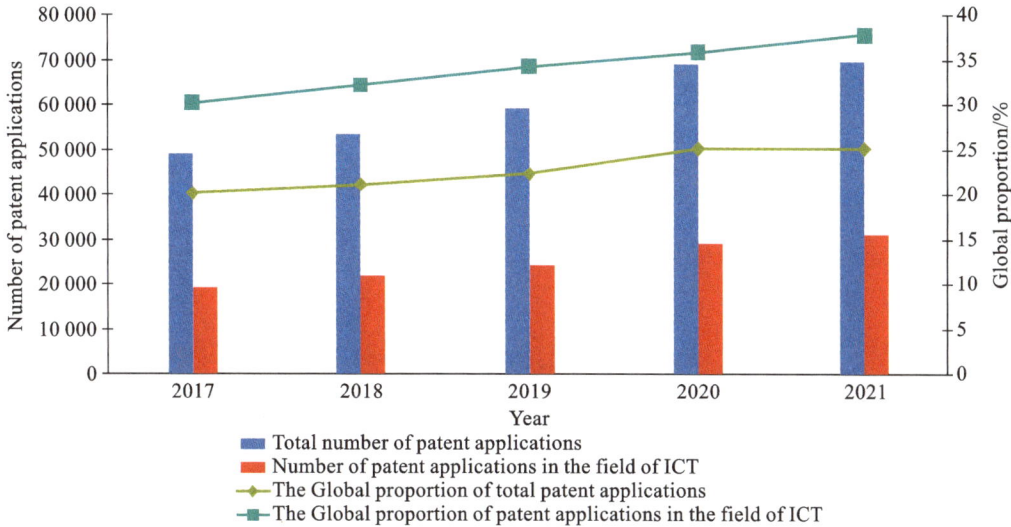

Figure 3-1 Growth of China's PCT international patent applications (2017-2021)

Data Source: World Intellectual Property Organization

enterprises had entered the top 50 list of PCT international patent applicants in the world, and Huawei had topped the list for five consecutive years. The number of high-level papers in the field of digital technology had further increased. As of September 2021, the number of highly cited papers in China was 42 900, accounting for 24.8% of the global share, among which the number of international citations of papers in the field of computer science had risen to the first place in the world.

China has made great strides in fields of 5G, AI, and other technologies. As of October 2020, China had declared a total of 13 282 5G standard essential patents, accounting for 37% of the global total. Huawei and ZTE ranked among the top 3 in the world in the 5G standard-essential patent declarations ranking published by the European Telecommunications Standards Institute (ETSI). China had become the second largest AI innovation center in the world after the US Among the top 100 highly cited papers in the direction of AI in the world from 2015 to 2020, China produced 21 papers, ranking second. From 2011 to 2020, China's patent applications in the field of AI accounted for 74.7% of the global total, 8.2 times that of the US.

In addition, China has made new progress in many core technologies in the fields of ICT. The development of key basic software has been accelerating, the ecological compatibility of desktop operating systems has continued to improve, the distributed operating system for all scenarios has entered the stage of industrialization, and some technical indicators of cloud databases are leading the world. The chip design capabilities in some fields have reached the internation top tier, the development of three dimensions non-volatile flash memory (3D NAND flash memory), dynamic random access memory (DRAM), and other memory technologies has been accelerating, and tens of millions of gate-level field programmable gate array (FPGA) products have been successfully mass-produced. The new display industry has made new breakthroughs. In 2020, the TFT-LCD production capacity in Chinese mainland ranked first in the world, and domestic flexible active matrix organic light emitting diode (AMOLED) entered the supply chain of international first-tier brands. The key technical capabilities of optical communications continue to improve, and some high-end optoelectronic chips such as laser chips, detector chips, and supporting electrical chips above 25G have been mass-produced.

3.2　Science and Technology Development Planning

3.2.1　National Science and Technology Plans

Since China introduced its first national science and technology plan in 1982, there have been more than 30 science and technology plans that support the national economy and social development and the advancement of science and technology from different angles. These plans complemented each other and formed an organic whole. China's current national science and technology plan system can be divided into five categories, namely the National Natural Science Foundation of China (NSFC), the National Science and Technology Major Project, the National Key Research and Development Program, the Technological Innovation Guidance Project, the Base and the Talent Project. Among them, the first three categories are the main traction plans for scientific and technological innovation.

(1) National Natural Science Foundation of China. This is a nationwide natural science foundation established to promote the reform of China's science and technology system and change the way of scientific research funding, aiming to support national basic research. During its development, the NSFC gradually formed a funding structure consisting of three series of projects, namely research projects, talent projects and environmental conditions projects, promoting the development of China's natural science research and promoting the construction of basic disciplines, and discovering and cultivating outstanding scientific and technological talents.

(2) National Science and Technology Major Project. To achieve national goals, these major projects were designed to produce major strategic products and key common technologies through core technology breakthroughs and resource integration, in certain time limit. By giving full play to the advantages of the socialist system in concentrating forces on major tasks and the role of market mechanisms, national science and technology major projects strive to make breakthroughs, achieve leapfrog development of productivity driven by partial leaps in technological developments and fill in the gaps in national strategies.

(3) National Key Research and Development Program. Facing the world's scientific and technological frontiers, the main battlefield of the economy, and major national needs, these programs focus on funding major social public welfare researches that require long-term evolution in the fields related to the national economy and people's livelihood, such as agriculture, energy resources, ecological environment, and health, and strategic, fundamental and forward-looking major scientific issues, major common key technologies and products, and significant international scientific cooperation related to the core competitiveness of industries, overall independent innovation capabilities and national security.

The ICT related fields are the key areas supported by the national science and technology plans. The ICT related projects currently supported by the National Natural Science Foundation of China, the National Science and Technology Major Project, and the National Key Research and Development Program are shown in Table 3-4.

Table 3-4   Representative ICT projects supported by national science and technology plans of China (2020-2022)

National science and technology plans	Representative projects
National Natural Science Foundation of China	Major Research Plan "Basic Theory and Key Technology Research of Inclusive Robots", Major Research Plan "Basic Theory and Key Technology of Future Industrial Internet", Major Research Plan "Construction and Manipulation of the Second-Generation Quantum System"
National Science and Technology Major Project	Core Electronic Devices, High-end General Chips and Basic Software Products, Very Large-Scale Integrated Circuit Manufacturing Technology and Complete Sets of Processes, New-Generation Wireless Mobile Communications
National Key Research and Development Program	New-Generation Artificial Intelligence, Advanced Computing and Emerging Software, Social Governance and Smart Society Technology Supports Intelligent Sensors, Intelligent Robots, Cyberspace Security Governance, Information Photon Technology, Micro-Nano Electronic Technology, Multi-Modal Network and Communications, Blockchain, New Display and Strategic Electronic Materials, Quantum Control and Quantum Information

3.2.2   National Digitization Projects

According to the "14th Five-Year Plan for National Informatization", China divided the construction goals of Digital China into multiple goals, including digital infrastructure system, data element resource system, digital productivity innovation and development system, digital industry system, industry digital transformation and development system, digital social governance system, etc. The plan set up 17 national key informatization projects, as shown in Table 3-5.

Table 3-5 National key informatization projects in the 14th Five-Year Plan period

Fields	Project Names
Digital infrastructure	5G Innovative Application Engineering
	"Intelligent Network Connection" Facility Construction and Application Promotion Project
	National Integrated Big Data Center System Construction Project
	Three-dimensional Network Construction and Application Demonstration Project of Space, Sky, Land and Sea
Digital technology innovation system	Core Technology Breakthrough Project in the Field of Information
	Information Technology Intellectual Property and Standardization Innovation Project
Digital economy	Data Element Market Cultivation Project
	Big Data Application Improvement Project
	Information Technology Industry Ecological Cultivation Project
	Manufacturing Digital Transformation Engineering
	Information Consumption Expansion and Quality Improvement Project
Digital society	Smart Public Security Development and Improvement Project
	Artificial Intelligence Social Governance Experimental Project
	Emergency Management Modernization Capacity Improvement Project
Digital government	National Integrated Government Service Improvement Project
Digital livelihood	Digital Public Service Optimization and Upgrading Project
International cooperation in the digital field	"Digital Silk Road" Joint Construction and Shared Use Project

3.2.3 R&D Investment

Since surpassing Japan in 2009 and the European Union (EU) in 2013, China has been the world's second-largest R&D investment spender after the US. In 2019, China's R&D investment exceeded the 2 trillion yuan mark for the first time; in 2020, R&D investment reached 2.4 trillion yuan, and the R&D investment intensity (ratio to GDP) was 2.4%. Calculated in 2019 purchasing power parity dollars, China's R&D investment accounted for about 25% of the total R&D investment of 37 countries counted by the Organization for Economic Cooperation and Development (OECD), second only to the US (about 30%).

According to the "Outline of the 14th Five-Year Plan for National Economic and Social Development and the Long-Range Objectives Through the Year 2035 of the People's Republic of China", during the 14th Five-Year Plan period, China will increase fiscal investment in basic research, optimize the investment structure, implement tax incentives for enterprises to invest in basic research, encourage the society to invest in multiple channels such as donations and the establishment of funds, and form a sustained and stable investment mechanism. The proportion of basic research investment in R&D investment will increase to more than 8%.

In addition to the national investment in basic research and public information facilities, industry enterprises also invested a huge amount of R&D funds. The ICT industry is a typical technology-intensive industry with rapid technology iteration and rapid market changes. Enterprises often need to invest higher R&D costs to quickly iterate related technologies and seize technological opportunities and commanding heights. From 2017 to 2021, the R&D investment of listed Internet enterprises in China increased by 227%. Among the global top 2500 industry enterprises in R&D investment released by the European Commission in 2021, 597 Chinese enterprises were selected, including 210 enterprises in the fields of information technology software services and hardware equipment. For example, Huawei's R&D investment in 2012 was 30.1 billion yuan, with an intensity of 13.7%, and its R&D investment in 2021 increased to 142.7 billion yuan, with an intensity of 22.4%; ZTE's R&D investment in 2012 was 8.829 billion yuan, with an intensity of 10.5%, and its R&D investment in 2021 was 18.8 billion yuan, with an intensity of 16.4%. The overall R&D investments of these enterprises are much higher than those of traditional enterprises and general manufacturing enterprises, laying the foundation for the rapid development of ICT.

3.3 Major Science and Technology Project

When a nation faces major opportunities and challenges in its development, it is essential to prioritize national interests, follow the guidance of national will, and accurately grasp strategic objectives. This requires pooling the nation's top scientific, technological, and management talents to undertake foundational major science and technology projects. Such a whole-nation system has been widely adopted globally for technological innovation, exemplified by the US Manhattan Project and Apollo Program, Japan's Fifth Generation Computer System (FGCS) project and Very Large Scale Integration (VLSI) project. This section highlights China's advancements in basic research and critical infrastructure through three case studies: supercomputers, communications and quantum computing, and the BeiDou Navigation Satellite System (BDS).

3.3.1 Supercomputer

A supercomputer refers to a computer that could perform a large number of high-speed calculations that ordinary personal computers cannot handle. High-performance computing has become the evolution direction of data-intensive research disciplines such as high-energy nuclear physics, space science, material science, life science, and AI. It is the core infrastructure that supports industrial scale growth and application model innovation. It is the strategic high ground that major developed countries in the world are vying for. The US, the EU and Japan have successively formulated national-level plans such as open science network, high-performance infrastructure, and advanced computing partners.

China's supercomputer research started in the 1970s. In October 1972, the development of supercomputers was listed into the national key projects. In December 1983, China developed the first exascale supercomputer "Galaxy". It became the computer system with the fastest computing speed, the largest storage capacity, and the most powerful functions in China at that time, breaking the technological monopoly of developed countries in this field. China became the country that could independently design and manufacture supercomputers after the US, Japan, France, Britain, and Germany. After the "Galaxy-I", China has developed a series of "Galaxy" supercomputers of different sizes.

In 2006, the MOST of China listed high-performance computers as part of the national science and technology plan. "Tianhe-1", as a major project of China's "High-tech Research and Development Plan" (863 Plan), was developed on the basis of the "Galaxy" series of supercomputers of the National University of Defense Technology (NUDT). On October 29, 2009, the NUDT successfully developed the "Tianhe-1" supercomputer with a peak performance of 1 206 trillion calculations per second, making China the second country in the world capable of developing petaflop supercomputers after the US. On June 20, 2016, the International Supercomputing Conference was held in Frankfurt, Germany. During the conference, the 47th list of the International TOP 500 Organizations was officially released. China's "Sunway Taihu-Light" replaced "Tianhe-2" to top the list (see Figure 3-2). In the top 10 of the 2022 International TOP 500 list, China had two supercomputers, namely "Sunway Taihu-Light" ranked sixth and "Tianhe-2" ranked ninth. The former had a peak computing power of 125.44 quadrillion times per second, and the latter had a peak computing power of 100.68 quadrillion times per second. In the 2022 International TOP 500 list, China continued to lead the world with 186 supercomputers, and the US ranked second in the world with 123 supercomputers.

"Sunway Taihu-Light" used the chips with China's independent intellectual property rights, which are faster and more energy-efficient. A "chip" of about five square centimeters integrates 260 computing cores, billions of transistors, and has a computing power of more than 3 trillion operations per second. The computing power of the "Sunway

Figure 3-2 "Sunway Taihu-Light" supercomputer (2016)
Image Source: *Shenzhen Special Zone Daily*

Taihu-Light" supercomputer for 1 minute is about 32 years of non-stop calculations by more than 7 billion people around the world at the same time. At present, China's supercomputer applications involve weather and climate, earth science, marine environment, material design, biopharmaceuticals, aerospace, graph computing, quantum computing, life science, astrophysics and many other areas(see Figure 3-3). For example, by using supercomputers to calculate the high-resolution China Sea regional atmosphere-ocean coupling model, forecasts of three-dimensional ocean currents, waves, sea temperature, salinity, sea surface height and other marine environmental elements for the next 10 days can be completed within 25 minutes.

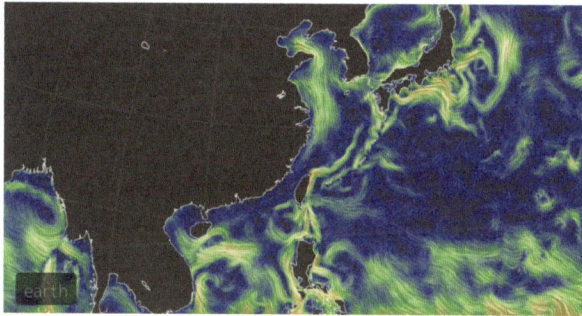

Figure 3-3 Using supercomputers to forecast marine environmental elements
Image Source: National Supercomputer Center in Guangzhou

3.3.2 Quantum Communications and Quantum Computer

Quantum computer was first proposed by American physicist Feynman in 1982. It is a physical device that uses the principles of quantum mechanics to perform high-speed mathematical and logical operations, and store and process quantum information. The natural parallel characteristics of quantum computing will play a huge role in processing certain large-scale parallel operations, and play a key role in the fields of massive information processing and research on major scientific issues. It will have a significant impact on one country's economy, science and technology, and military and information security, and has become one of the scientific and technological focuses of common concern and exploration by the global human race. In 2018, Google Inc. released a 72-bit superconducting quantum chip. In 2019, IBM of the US released the IBM **Q** System One quantum computer. In 2020, the US announced the construction of five quantum science joint research centers, including the Next Generation Quantum Science and Engineering (Q-NEXT), to continue to promote the development of quantum technology.

In 2005, China listed "Quantum Control Research" as one of the national basic research program of China in the "Outline of National Medium-and Long-Term Science and Technology Development Plan (2006-2020)". In 2017, China listed "Quantum Communications and Quantum Computer" in the "Science and Technology Innovation 2030-Major Project" and provided strong support. In August 2016, China successfully launched the world's first quantum science experiment satellite "Mozi" into space with the Long March 2D carrier rocket at the Jiuquan Satellite Launch Center. The research team of the University of Science and Technology of China (USTC) established quantum entanglement and secure communications between two ground stations more than 1 120 kilometers apart through "Mozi" (see Figure 3-4), and published a research paper titled "Entanglement-based secure quantum cryptography over 1 120 kilometers" online in the journal *Nature* in June 2020. According to China's quantum communications development plan, after the launch of the quantum satellite, China will build a "quantum communications trunk line between Beijing and Shanghai", and a wide-area quantum communications system will initially be formed in the country. By around 2030, China will take the lead in building a global quantum communications network.

Figure 3-4 China's quantum science experimental satellite "Mozi" achieves long-distance ground quantum communications

Image Source: University of Science and Technology of China

In 2017, Prof. Pan Jianwei's team at USTC built the world's first optical quantum computing prototype that surpasses early classical computers, and gradually demonstrated the superiority of quantum computing through experiments. In 2020, the team successfully built a Gaussian boson sampling quantum computing prototype named "Jiuzhang" with 76 photons and 100 modes. The output quantum state space scale of "Jiuzhang" reached 10^{30}, and its speed of processing Gaussian boson sampling was 100 trillion times faster than the supercomputer "Fugaku". In 2021, the number of photons detected by "Jiuzhang-2" (see

Figure 3-5) increased to 113, and the output state space dimension reached 10^{43}. It completed the rapid solution of the Gaussian boson sampling task used to demonstrate the "superiority of quantum computing", and the processing speed is 10^{24} times faster than the fastest supercomputer currently.

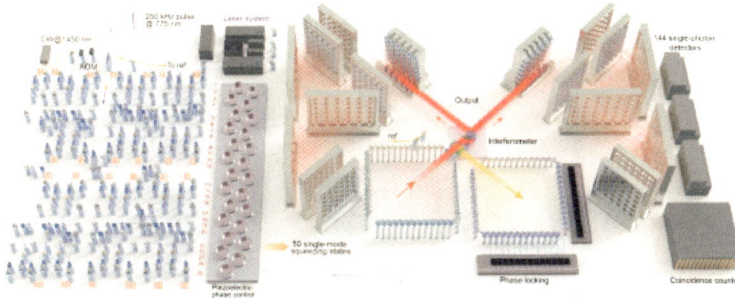

Figure 3-5 China's quantum computing prototype "Jiuzhang-2" was successfully developed

Image Source: University of Science and Technology of China

3.3.3 BeiDou Navigation Satellite System

The global navigation satellite system (GNSS) can provide users with all-weather air-based radio navigation and positioning services with three-dimensional coordinates, speed, and time information at any location on the earth's surface or in near-Earth space. In the 1970s, the US Department of Defense began to develop the "Global Positioning System for Navigation Satellite Timing and Ranging", referred to as the global positioning system (GPS). The GPS plays an important basic role in military, disaster prevention and mitigation, and surveying and mapping.

In 1994, China initiated the construction of the BDS. In 2003, the BDS-1 was built, consisting of three geostationary orbit satellites and related ground systems, which solved the problem of the existence of China's satellite navigation system and realized the active positioning of China and surrounding areas. China also became the third country in the world to have an independent satellite navigation system after the US and Russia.

In 2004, China launched the construction of the BDS-2 system with the goal of establishing a regional satellite navigation system. In December 2011, the BDS started to trial operation services, and provided services to China and parts of the Asia-Pacific region. The BDS adopted a hybrid constellation solution consisting of geostationary orbit, inclined geosynchronous orbit, and medium earth orbit satellites, realizing the integrated active and passive navigation multifunctional services.

In 2012, China launched the construction of the BDS-3 system. The research team conquered the constellation inter-satellite link technology, adopted an integrated design of inter-satellite and satellite-to-ground transmission functions, and realized the link interconnection between satellites and satellites, and between satellites and ground stations. On June 23, 2020, the 55th BeiDou navigation satellite was successfully launched, and the constellation deployment of the BDS-3 GNSS was fully completed. On July 31, 2020, Chinese President Xi Jinping announced the official commissioning of the BDS-3 GNSS system. The BDS is shown in Figure 3-6.

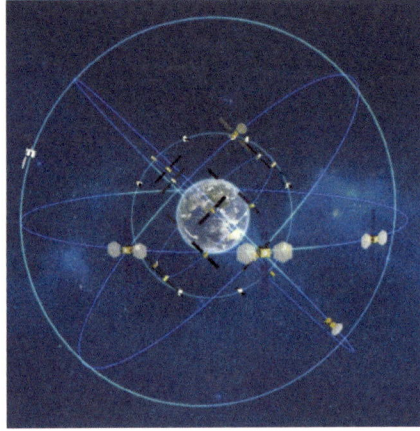

Figure 3-6 Schematic diagram of BDS

Image Sources: *Guangming Daily*

The "White Paper on the Development of China's Satellite Navigation and Location Services Industry (2022)" showed that in 2021, the core output value of BeiDou-related industries, including chips, devices, and algorithms. directly related to the research and development and application of satellite navigation technology, reached 145.4 billion yuan, and the associated output value driven by satellite navigation applications and services reached 323.6 billion yuan. The total number of enterprises and institutions in the field of satellite navigation and location services reached 14 000, and the number of employees exceeded 500 000. As of January 2023, the global cumulative number of intelligent device accessing to BeiDou space-time intelligent services exceeded 1.5 billion; BeiDou high-precision space-time services were called more than 170 billion times per month, and the service covered more than 230 countries and regions around the world; BeiDou had become the standard configuration of Chinese demestic smartphones. For example, the mobile APP of AutoNavi Maps called the positioning services of BeiDou satellites for more than 300 billion times per day.

3.4　**Industrial Technology Innovation**

The development of many key technologies in the ICT industry requires not only huge capital investment, but also clear market returns. China integrates the power of universities, scientific research institutions and enterprises in various ways to jointly break through the technical bottleneck of the information industry and promote industrial progress and development. This section selects some typical industries such as ultra-HD video, mobile communications, and integrated circuits to introduce China's progress in technological breakthroughs in the ICT industry.

3.4.1 Ultra-HD Video Industry

High-definition television (abbreviated as HDTV) was firstly developed and tested in 1968. The Japan Broadcasting Corporation (NHK) completed the research and development of the HDTV system and the MUSE satellite transmission system around 1980, and released the first HDTV video signal standard—1125/60 standard. In 1996, the Advanced Television Systems Committee (ATSC) of the US released the HDTV standard based on terrestrial transmission of the all-digital system.

China's attention to HDTV began during the 8th Five-Year Plan period. In 1993, the National Science and Technology Commission organized and established the "HDTV Development Strategy Expert Group". In 1998, China's first terrestrial digital HDTV prototype was successfully developed. In October 2003, the NDRC established a terrestrial digital television transmission standard research and development project. Tsinghua University, Shanghai Jiao Tong University, Academy of Broadcasting Science and other eight universities and research institutions established a special working group on the national standard for terrestrial transmission of digital television, aiming to develop a new solution based on the three standard solutions of Tsinghua University's DMB-T, Shanghai Jiao Tong University's ADTB-T, and the Academy of Broadcasting Science's TiMi. In August 2006, "Framing Structure, Channel Coding and Modulation for Digital Television Terrestrial Broadcasting System" became a mandatory national standard, with the standard number "GB 20600—2006", which was officially implemented on August 1, 2007.

At 9:00 a.m. on January 1, 2008, the China Central Television (CCTV) launched free service of terrestrial digital HDTV broadcasting, marking the substantive launch of China's national standard for terrestrial digital television. On May 1, 2008, Beijing Television launched the Olympic HD Channel(see Figure 3-7). The core equipment used in this batch of HD channels was all domestically produced, and basically all adopted the terrestrial digital TV single-carrier mode and related equipment. The development of HDTV in China took advantage of the opportunity of the Olympic Games and achieved good results. By the end of 2008, China had 45.28 million digital TV users, a year-on-year increase of nearly 70% over 2007, of which more than 500 000 were HDTV users, and Beijing users accounted for more than 60%. By March 2009, 229 cities in China had completed the overall digital conversion of cable TV.

HDTV technical standards have promoted the upgrading of the TV industry. In June 2012, the starting meeting of the 12th Five-Year Plan 863 Program "Research and Verification of New-Generation Digital TV Key Technologies" was held in Beijing to promote "synergy between content and network", "interaction between broadcasting network and Internet", "new wireless overlay network design" and other technological

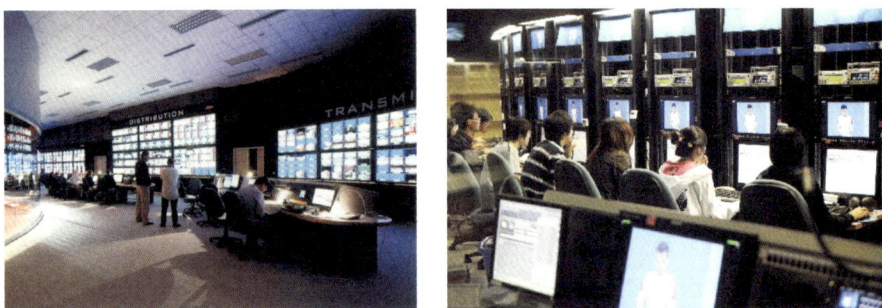

Figure 3-7 The HD broadcasting studio of Beijing Television during the 2008 Beijing Olympic Games
Image Source: CCTV. com

breakthroughs. In February 2019, the Ministry of Industry and Information Technology (MIIT), the National Radio and Television Administration, and CCTV jointly issued the "Ultra-HD Video Industry Development Action Plan (2019-2022)", which clarified the overall requirements, development goals, key tasks and safeguards for the development of the Ultra-HD video industry. In 2019, China's Ultra-HD video display technology gradually matured, mainly including memory chips, high-performance display driver chips, TV main control chips, Ultra-HD set-top box chips, 4K/8K image processing chips, etc. The sales of 4K TVs in China were gradually increasing, occupying a dominant position in the Ultra-HD video industry.

The development of the 4K TV industry has promoted the gradual maturity of the 4K Ultra-HD video industry ecosystem. The market share and international influence of well-known Chinese companies (such as TCL, Hisense, Skyworth, etc.) continue to increase. In 2019, the new set-top boxes of China's three major telecommunications operators fully supported 4K 60 frames/HDR/BT. 2020/10bit video decoding capabilities. In 2020, the global shipment of 4K set-top boxes exceeded 120 million units, and China became the world's largest market for 4K set-top boxes.

3.4.2 Mobile Communications Industry

The mobile communications technology involves the information infrastructure of various countries, and the competition for the new generation of 5G mobile communications technology is fierce. Internationally, South Korea launched the formulation of South Korea's national 5G standards in 2017 and launched 5G commercial services in 2019; the EU issued the "5G Action Plan" in 2016, and announced in 2017 that it would allocate 700 million euros in the "Horizon 2020" scientific research plan to support the development of 5G; the US released the 24 GHz high-frequency band of 5G in July 2016, and planned to invest 400 million USD to support 5G trials and research and development.

China's mobile communications industry experienced the development process of "following in 2G", "breakthrough in 3G", and "synchronization in 4G", and are striving to achieve the new goal of "leading in 5G". In the 2G era, China introduced foreign 2G technical standards such as the global system for mobile communications (GSM) and code division multiple access (CDMA), and gradually realized independent research and development of equipment and products. In the 3G era, China's time division-synchronous code division multiple access (TD-SCDMA) standard was approved by the International Telecommunication Union (ITU) in May 2000 as one of the 3G international standards, and was successfully commercialized in 2009. In the 4G era, the time division-long term evolution-advanced (TD-LTE-Advanced) standard led by China became the 4G international standard in January 2012.

With the technical accumulation and industrial achievements of 3G and 4G, China fully launched the work of 5G research and development and standardization. In February 2013, the MIIT, the NDRC, and the MOST jointly promoted the establishment of the IMT-2020 (5G) Promotion Group to coordinate China's 5G technology research, standard formulation, R&D trials, and industrial promotion. In October 2015, the ITU's 2015 World Radiocommunication Conference was held in Geneva, Switzerland. At this conference, eight of the nine technical indicators of the "Flower of 5G" proposed by China were adopted by the ITU (see Figure 3-8). Since then, key technologies such as flexible system design, polarization codes, large-scale antennas and new network architecture proposed by Chinese enterprises have become the focus of international standards. Chinese technical experts have began to hold multiple important positions in international standard organizations such as the ITU and the Third Generation Partnership Project (3GPP), and preside over related work on key projects.

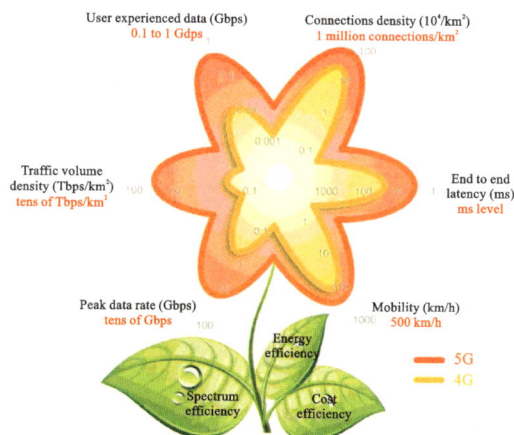

Figure 3-8　"5G Flower" standard proposed by China

Image Source: IMT-2020 (5G) Promotion Group, 5G Vision and Requirements White Paper, 2014

In the field of 5G technology research and development, China's scientific research teams and enterprises have made significant breakthroughs. In terms of 5G baseband chips, Huawei's multi-mode commercial 5G baseband chip Balong 5000 supports 2G/3G/

4G/5G networks, Sub-6 GHz, millimeter wave, 5G non-standalone networking (NSA) and 5G standalone networking (SA). In the field of 5G air interface technology, Huawei and ZTE are leaders in Massive MIMO technology, and Huawei released the world's first 5G base station core chip. In the field of channel coding, the Polar code launched by Huawei and other companies is currently the channel coding method that has been strictly proved to reach the Shannon limit, and it has determined the channel coding technology solution for the 5G eMBB (enhanced mobile broadband) scenario. In the core network field, China Mobile took the lead and jointly proposed service-based architecture with 14 global operators and 12 network equipment vendors including Huawei, which was officially confirmed by 3GPP as the only infrastructure standard for the 5G core network.

Some core technologies of the 5G standard are also protected by patents, and the relevant patents are called 5G standard essential patents. The technical directions of 5G standard essential patents include wireless resource management, access technology, multi-carrier transmission, channel coding, core network, and next-generation access network. The current 5G communications standards R15, R16 and R17 have all completed the "frozen version", and the corresponding standard essential patent layout has basically become a foregone conclusion. The database search results of the German patent database company IPlytics showed that as of February 2022, the number of 5G standard essential patents owned by Chinese enterprises had ranked second among the relevant countries/regions in the world, accounting for 38.4% (see Figure 3-9). As of December 2022, the number of 5G standard essential patents declared worldwide had exceeded 84 900, of which the top 10 enterprises contributed 75% of the total number of patent families; the number of effective global patent families of Chinese enterprise Huawei accounted for 14.6%, ranking first among global enterprises, and the number of effective global patent families of other Chinese enterprises such as ZTE, Datang, OPPO, and Xiaomi also ranked among the top ten in the world.

In terms of 5G commercial use, China launched a commercial 5G technology research and development test in 2016. In December 2018, the MIIT issued 5G system low-and medium-band test frequency use licenses to China Telecom, China Mobile, and China Unicom. In order to reduce the investment in 5G construction, under the leadership of the government, China Telecom and China Unicom achieved the co-construction and sharing of 5G network base stations through China Tower Corporation, sharing more than 300 000 5G base stations, and saving more than 60 billion yuan in construction investment. By the end of 2023, China had built and opened more than 3.377 million 5G base stations, achieving full coverage of cities at or above the prefecture level across the country, with 805 million 5G mobile phone users and 47% of 5G network access traffic. From January to December 2023, China's domestic 5G mobile phone shipments reached 240 million units, an annual increase of 11.9%, accounting for 82.8% of mobile phone shipments in the same period. China has become the country with the largest scale of 5G applications in the world.

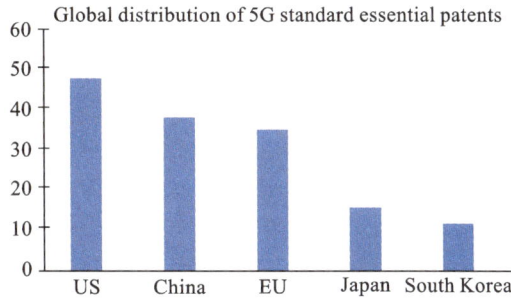

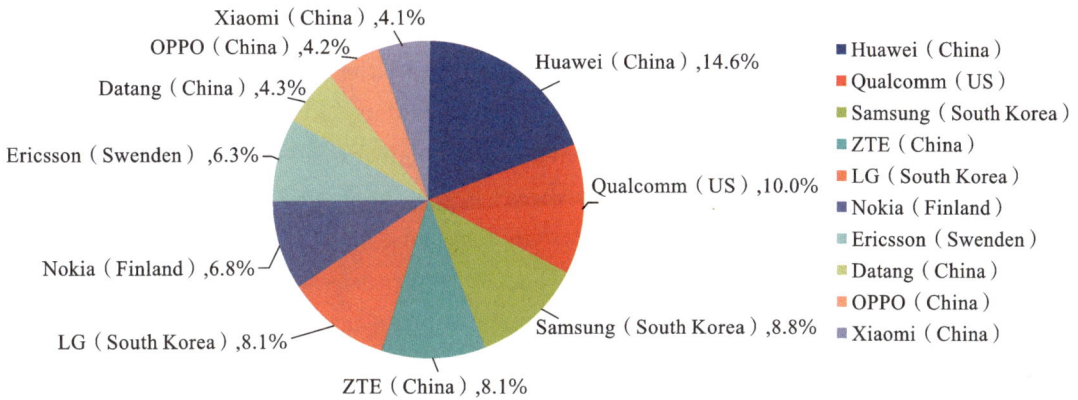

Figure 3-9　Global distribution of 5G standard essential patents (February 2022)

Data Sources: China National Intellectual Property Administration (top), China Academy of Information and Communications Technology(bottom)

With the advancement of commercial use, 5G, a new engine for the development of the digital economy, will not only open up new development space for the ICT industry, but will also be deeply integrated with the real economy. Commercial 5G professional modules have also been launched, which can support 5G 8K TVs, 5G industrial production lines, smart transportation and other industry applications. A related report from the China Academy of Information and Communications Technology predicted that in 2025, 5G will drive China's economic added value by about 1.1 trillion yuan, contributing 3.2% to the GDP growth of that year, and indirectly driving GDP by 2.1 trillion yuan; in 2030, 5G is expected to contribute more than 2.9 trillion yuan to China's economic added value, with a compound annual growth rate of 41% over the past 10 years.

3.4.3　Integrated Circuit Industry

Integrated circuits are known as the foundation of the ICT industry. The integrated circuit industry is a strategic industry that affects the comprehensive competitiveness of a country's economy, politics, and national defense. Its technical level and industrial scale have become an important sign to measure a country's industrial competitiveness and comprehensive national strength.

Integrated circuits include multiple fields, the most representative of which is the field of memory chips. Data showed that the global semiconductor market scale exceeded 180 billion USD in 2022, with memory chips accounting for about 35%. The memory chip market could be further divided into the memory (DRAM) market and the flash memory (NAND) market, of which the memory market scale accounted for about 61% of the global storage market scale, while the flash memory market scale accounted for about 36%. A few years ago, the international semiconductor memory field was mainly monopolized by several enterprises such as Samsung and Hynix in South Korea, Micron in the US, and Toshiba in Japan. China's annual chip imports amounted to nearly 2.8 trillion yuan, of which the import value of memory chips was about 700 billion yuan.

In order to solve the common technical problems of the integrated circuit industry, China launched the National Science and Technology Major Project "Very Large Scale Integrated Circuit Manufacturing Equipment and Complete Process" in 2008. The overall goal of this project was to carry out research on integrated circuit manufacturing equipment, complete process and material technology, and master core technologies. Since the implementation of this project, more than 200 enterprises and institutions and more than 20 000 scientific researchers have participated in technical research. Before 2008, the most advanced mass production process of integrated circuit manufacturing in China was 130 nanometers, and the process level of research and development was 90 nanometers; after the implementation of this project, by 2017, the mainstream process level had been improved by 5 generations, and the three generations of complete process of 55 nanometers, 40 nanometers and 28 nanometers had been successfully developed and mass-produced, and the research and development of 22 nanometers and 14 nanometers leading technologies had made breakthroughs and formed independent intellectual property rights. China has successfully developed more than 30 high-end equipment such as 14 nanometer etcher and thin film deposition, and hundreds of material products such as target materials and polishing liquids, with performance reaching international advanced levels.

In order to solve the financing support problem of the integrated circuit industry, the State Council of China issued the "National Outline of Promoting the Development of Integrated Circuit Industry" in June 2014. In the same year, the National Integrated Circuit Industry Investment Fund Co., Ltd. (hereinafter referred to as the "National Big Fund") was established. In 2019, the National Integrated Circuit Industry Investment Fund Phase Ⅱ Co., Ltd. (hereinafter referred to as the "National Big Fund Phase Ⅱ") was established. As of December 2021, the National Big Fund and the National Big Fund Phase Ⅱ had completed investments in 83 integrated circuit entity companies, covering the backbone enterprises in the industrial chain, such as SMIC, Huahong Group, and China Resources Microelectronics in the wafer manufacturing industry, Yangtze Memory, Changxin Storage, and GigaDevice in the storage industry, Changdian Technology, Tongfu Microelectronics, and Huatian Technology in the packaging and testing industry,

Guowei and Huada Jiutian in the electronic design automation tool industry, Unisoc, and Zhixin Microelectronics in the design industry, North Huachuang, and China Microelectronics in the equipment and parts industry, and Yak Technology and ANJI in the materials industry.

By taking the above measures, many problems of Chinese semiconductor enterprises in technology, capital and other aspects have been solved, and domestic enterprises have made breakthroughs in multiple semiconductor fields.

In terms of memory chips, Changxin Storage was jointly established in Hefei in May 2016 by the Hefei Municipal Government, GigaDevice, and the National Big Fund. It is China's first independent memory chip manufacturing project, with a total investment of over 200 billion yuan. Changxin Storage purchased the memory technology of the German company Qimonda and completed the original technology accumulation. Later, Changxin Storage invested 2.5 billion USD in research and development expenses for upgrading. In the first quarter of 2018, Changxin Storage completed the equipment installation of the first 12-inch (30.48 cm) wafer factory, and developed China's first 8 Gb DDR4 chip in the same year. In the third quarter of 2019, Changxin Storage successfully mass-produced DDR4 memory (see Figure 3-10) and LPDDR4 memory using the 19-nanometer process technology, achieving a yield of 70% to 75%, and the maximum speed can reach 3 200 Mbps, becoming the world's fourth manufacturer that can mass-produce memory chips below 20 nanometers. Changxin Storage had achieved a memory chip production capacity of 60 000 pieces/month in 2021, and the future goal was to achieve a production capacity of 300 000 pieces/month.

Figure 3-10　DDR4 memory module launched by Changxin Storage
Image Source: Changxin Storage

In terms of flash memory chips, Yangtze Memory was established in Wuhan in July 2016. Investors include Tsinghua Unigroup, Hubei Integrated Circuit Industry Investment Fund, China Development Fund, and National Big Fund. Yangtze Memory and Phison Semiconductor completed the accumulation of basic technologies in cooperation, and then jointly developed with the Institute of Microelectronics of the Chinese Academy of Sciences. In February 2017, the Institute of Microelectronics of the Chinese Academy of Sciences announced that the domestically produced 32-layer 3D NAND flash memory chip passed various tests, including those for electrical characteristics. In August 2018,

Yangtze Memory released Xtacking technology at the Flash Memory World (FMW). This technology processes storage units and logic circuits separately on two wafers, and then connects the two wafers together through millions of metal channels, increasing the maximum access speed of flash memory chips to the level of DDR4 memory. In September 2019, Yangtze Memory created the world's first 64-layer TLC 3D NAND flash memory chip based on the Xtacking architecture and achieved mass production(see Figure 3-11). In April 2020, Yangtze Memory launched the world's first 128-layer QLC 3D NAND flash memory chip, which has the largest storage capacity and the highest I/O interface transmission speed. At the end of 2021, Yangtze Memory reached a production capacity of 100 000 wafers per month. In November 2022, Yangtze Memory achieved mass production of 232-layer 3D NAND flash memory chips, becoming the first NAND storage manufacturer in the world to achieve mass production of NAND flash memory chips with more than 200 layers. The I/O speed of the NAND flash X3-9070 reached 2 400 MT/s (million transfers per second), with a 50% performance improvement and a 25% reduction in power consumption.

After nearly six years, China's semiconductor storage enterprises represented by Changxin Storage and Yangtze Memory integrated the achievements of China's scientific and technological projects, actively forged ahead, aggressively innovated, and made pioneering breakthroughs in the storage field. According to statistics, the market share of Chinese manufacturers in the global memory chip market was still 0 in 2015, but by 2022, their combined market share in the global DRAM＋NAND flash memory chip market was close to 5%. The rapid growth of these enterprises was inseparable from the support of national policies, the sharing of scientific and technological achievements of state-owned scientific research institutes, and the backing of the National Big Fund.

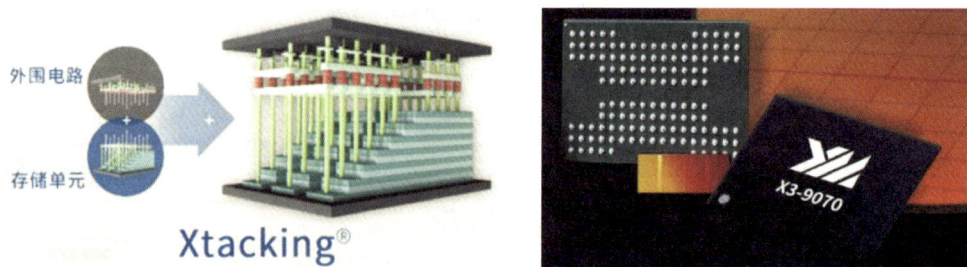

Figure 3-11　Xtacking-based NAND flash memory launched by Yangtze Memory
Image Source: Yangtze Memory

3.5　Summary

At the beginning of the founding of the People's Republic of China, the foundation for

ICT research and development was extremely weak. After more than seven decades of development, China has gradually established a complete system for scientific research and technological development. China has established a strategic scientific and technological force system, and institutions such as national key laboratories and NERCs are responsible for undertaking research in basic theories and key technologies. At the same time, China has established various types of industrial innovation bases, including HIDZs and innovative industrial clusters, to encourage enterprises to carry out technological research and innovation. Currently, China has achieved breakthrough progress in fields such as integrated circuits and new display technologies.

China has established comprehensive science and technology development planning systems. Through different levels of plans, such as the National Natural Science Foundation of China, National Science and Technology Major Project, and National Key Research and Development Programs of China, China guides domestic scientific research institutions and enterprises to conduct research in key fields. China has also deployed a number of national key projects for "Digital China" construction, covering areas such as digital infrastructure and the digital economy, and laying the foundation for the digital transformation and upgrading of various industries. China has established a multi-dimensional mechanism for R&D investment. The state's investment in basic theoretical research has been continuously increasing, and enterprises' investment in product development has also been gradually enhanced.

In terms of major scientific and technological projects, China has achieved a number of world-renowned achievements. The development of supercomputers has been remarkable, progressing from the "Yinhe" series to the "Tianhe" series, and then to the "Sunway Taihu-Light", computing power has been continuously increasing, with applications spanning multiple fields including scientific computing. China has made outstanding achievements in the fields of quantum communications and quantum computers. The "Micius" satellite has achieved long-distance quantum communications, and the "Jiuzhang" quantum computing prototype has demonstrated super-strong computing power, with related technologies at the forefront of the world. After three rounds of construction, the BDS project has achieved global networking and provided advanced civil global navigation services.

In terms of tackling key problems in information industry technologies, China has also made remarkable progress. The Ultra-HD video industry has established digital television standards, and the industrial ecosystem has gradually been improved, leading the development of 4K Ultra-HD technology. The mobile communications industry has achieved a leap from following to leading. China has made breakthroughs in aspects such as 5G baseband chips and air interface technologies. China leads globally in the number of essential patents for the 5G standard of the new-generation mobile communications, and boasts the world's largest commercial scale. With the support of national special projects and funds, the IC industry has achieved major breakthroughs in the field of memory chips, gradually overcoming the technical bottlenecks.

China has achieved all-round development and progress in ICT innovation. The national education system established by China over the years has developed a well-structured engineer workforce for ICT industry. The strategic scientific research forces have provided a crucial support for solving theoretical problems in information science. The science and technology development planning systems established have formed an efficient scientific research organization model, and completed major scientific infrastructure projects such as supercomputers and quantum computers. Through measures such as establishing HIDZs, innovative industrial clusters, and industrial development funds, the Chinese government encourages enterprises to carry out technological innovation and has achieved breakthroughs in multiple industrial technologies.

4　Digital Industrialization

Digital industrialization, that is, the industrialization of digital technology, refers to the transformation of digital technology into marketable goods and services, thereby forming industries with economic scale and market competitiveness. The content of digital industrialization involves aspects such as digital product manufacturing, digital product services, digital technology applications, and etc. Its scope includes traditional information industries and emerging digital application industries. For the convenience of readers, this chapter is organized according to the classification of traditional information industries (fundamental telecommunications industry, Internet industry, software and information technology services industry, and electronic information manufacturing industry) to present the development achievements China has made in recent years.

4.1　Fundamental Telecommunications Industry

From 2012 to 2021, China's information and communications technology (ICT) industry grasped the opportunities of global development, and quickly integrated into the international industrial division of labor system. The modern ICT business, represented by the telecommunications sector, rose rapidly. In around 10 years, the average growth rate of China's telecom business reached more than 20%, far exceeding the average GDP growth rate during the same period. Especially in 2017 and 2018, the growth rate of total telecom business was as high as 76.7% and 137.5% respectively. In 2021, the total business of China Telecom reached 1.7 trillion yuan.

4.1.1　Internet Infrastructure

4.1.1.1　Optical Fiber Backbone Network

In 1994, China established several high-performance backbone networks covering all cities nationwide. After 2000, a hierarchical architecture of interconnected backbone networks emerged, with Beijing, Shanghai, and Guangzhou as the main backbone direct connection points, supplemented by exchange centers. In 2013, seven new backbone direct connection points were added in the city of Chengdu, Wuhan, Xi'an, Shenyang, Nanjing, Chongqing, and Zhengzhou. The activation of these new backbone direct connection points resulted in a performance enhancement of over 60%, significantly enhancing the backbone network intercommunication efficiency and forming a balanced regional structure.

The construction of the optical fiber backbone network made remarkable achievements. China has built the world's largest optical fiber broadband network, occupying about half of the global optical fiber market demand since 2014. By the end of 2021, the total length of optical fiber cable lines in China had reached 54.81 million kilometers, an increase of approximately 2.7 times compared with that of 2012. Concurrently, backbone transmission had evolved towards ultra-high-speed, high-capacity networks, fully establishing a national single-wave 100 Gbps backbone network; the transmission speed of the backbone network had entered the 200 Gbps era, with 400 Gbps transmission systems piloted in some cities. The trends of the total length of optical cable lines and the length of trunk lines in China from 2016 to June 2021 are shown in Figure 4-1.

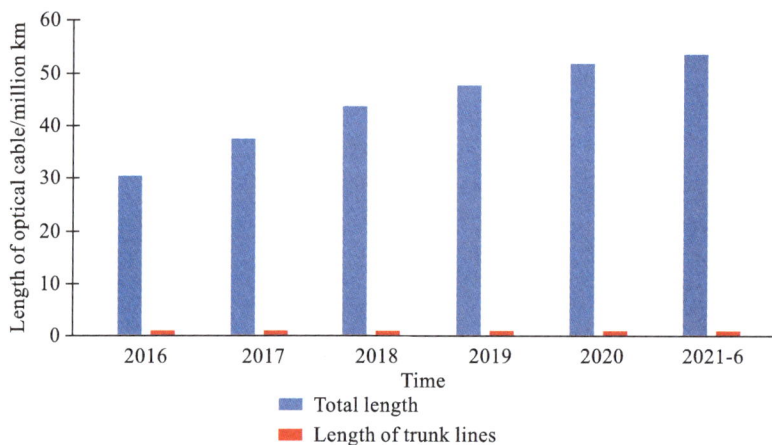

Figure 4-1 The Trends of the total length of optical cable lines and the length of trunk lines in China(2016-June 2021)

Data Source: Ministry of Industry and Information Technology of the People's Republic of China

The comprehensive transmission capacity of the network has been continuously improved. As of June 2021, a total of 14 backbone direct connection points had been built in China. Taking the National (Hangzhou) Novel Internet Exchange as an example, its total access bandwidth reaches 2 Tbps, the comprehensive, multi-level, and three-dimensional network interconnection architecture has been further optimized, and the performance of inter-network communications has continued to improve. As of the end of June 2021, China's internation Internet bandwidth reached 8.6 Tbps, representing a year-on-year increase of 31.6%.

The network infrastructure fully supports IPv6. China has built the world's largest IPv6 network infrastructure. As of December 2021, the number of IPv6 addresses in China had reached 60 059 (/32), ranking first in the world; the number of active IPv6 users in China had reached 608 million, accounting for 60.11% of the total number of Internet users; IPv6 network traffic had grown rapidly, with mobile network IPv6 traffic accounting for 35.15% of the total mobile network traffic.

The international interconnection facilities have been further upgraded. The pace of the related construction such as submarine optical cables and cross-border terrestrial cables has been accelerated, and the interconnection level with countries jointly building the "Belt and Road" has been steadily improved. By the end of June 2021, China's Internet international import and export bandwidth had reached 8.6 Tbps, a year-on-year increase of 31.6%. By the end of 2020, China Telecom, China Mobile, and China Unicom had built more than 400 overseas Internet points of presence (POPs).

4.1.1.2 Optical Fiber Access Network

The broadband access network continues to be upgraded. In March 2021, the Ministry of Industry and Information Technology (MIIT) released the "Action Plan for the Coordinated Development of 'Dual-Gigabit' Internet (2021-2023)". The "dual-gigabit" Internet, represented by gigabit optical network and 5G network, can provide a single user with gigabit access capability of fixed and mobile networks. It has the characteristics of super-large bandwidth, ultra-low delay, and advanced reliability, and is an important component and carrying base of new infrastructure.

Gigabit optical fiber has covered one-third of China's households. By the end of June 2021, the total number of optical fiber to the home/office (FTTH/O) ports in China had reached 920 million, accounting for 93.5% of all broadband access ports, an increase of 1.4 percentage points from the same period last year. The optical fiber access capacity generally exceeds 100M, and is further upgraded to a speed of more than 1 000 M. As of June 2021, 36 provincial-level operators across China had released fiber-to-the-room (FTTR) packages, and the pilot program-basically covered the whole country. Home and enterprise ultra-high-speed LAN networking solutions were gradually promoted and applied. In December 2021, 29 cities in China became the first batch of gigabit cities, having built 7.86 million 10 Gigabit Passive Optical Network (10 G-PON) ports, with gigabit optical networks capable of covering over 300 million households. The trends of the number and proportion of FTTH/O ports in China from 2016 to June 2021 are shown in Figure 4-2.

The users' actual Internet access experience has been greatly improved. In 2012, China's average access network speed was only about 2 Mbps, ranking in the middle and lower levels among major countries in the world. In 2021, the average download speed of China's mobile network had reached 59.34 Mbps, and the average download speed of fixed networks had exceeded 62.55 Mbps, ranking among the top in the world; the average download speed of rural optical fibers had also exceeded 100 Mbps, and infrastructure construction had achieved improvements in both network coverage and network speed. According to the monitoring data released by the network speed test and statistics company Ookla, in September 2021, the average download speed of China's fixed broadband ranked 15th among 181 countries.

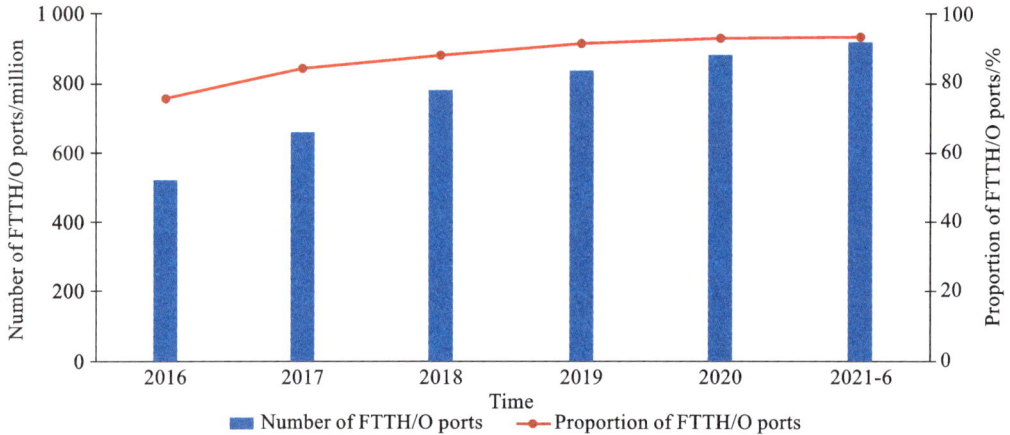

Figure 4-2 The trends of the number and proportion of FTTH/O

ports in China(2016-June 2021)

Data Source: Ministry of Industry and Information Technology of the People's Republic of China

4.1.1.3 Mobile Communications Network

In the 10 years from 2012 to 2021, the mobile communications sector in China had successfully achieved several technological breakthroughs, progressing from "breakthrough in 3G", "synchronization in 4G" to "leading in 5G". In 2013, China realized the commercialization of 4G; in 2019, China realized the commercialization of 5G. In 2021, China's 5G patent applications exploded, and the number of mobile communications patents accounted for more than 30% of the world's total. China has become the world's primary producer of 5G patents and a standard-setting country, realizing the leadership of mobile communications technology.

In parallel with technological breakthroughs, the base station construction are advancing rapidly. By the end of 2019, China had built 8.41 million mobile communications base stations, with 5.44 million 4G base stations. By the end of 2021, over two years into the 5G era, China had 9.96 million mobile communications base stations, an 18.4% increase from 2019, with 5.9 million 4G base stations and 1.425 million 5G base stations; the 5G network had already covered all urban areas of prefecture-level cities, over 98% of county-level urban areas, and 80% of township-level urban areas; over 99% of the administrative villages had 4G coverage. Internationally, in the 5G era, China took the lead in 5G base station construction, with over 60% of the world's 5G base stations located in China, making it a global leader in 5G network construction. Figure 4-3 shows the trends of the number and proportion of 5G base stations in China from March 2020 to June 2021.

Mobile terminals are becoming increasingly widespread. According to the statistics of the MIIT and the Global System for Mobile Communications Association (GSMA), by 2021, the number of mobile users in China had reached 1.64 billion, with a penetration rate of 116.3 per one hundred people. The number of 5G mobile phone terminal connections in China had rapidly increased, exceeding 490 million. As 4G users gradually

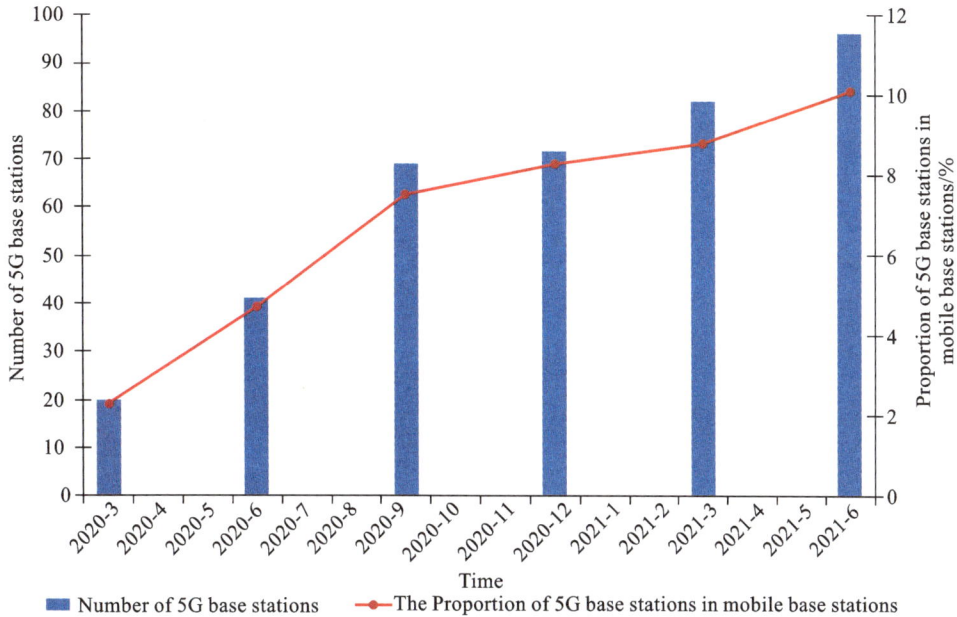

Figure 4-3 The trends of the number and proportion of 5G base stations
in China(March 2020 - June 2021)

Data Source: Ministry of Industry and Information Technology of the People's Republic of China

migrated to 5G, the number of 4G users in 2021 decreased by 12% compared with 2020, totaling approximately 1. 13 billion, with a penetration rate of 68. 8%. In 2021, China's mobile data traffic continued to grow, with the average monthly mobile Internet access traffic (discharge of usage, DOU) per user in October being 14. 32 GB, about 23. 7% higher than the global average.

Mobile data tariffs continue to decline. In the first half of 2021, the average mobile data tariff in China fell to 3. 2 yuan/GB, a 24. 6% decrease from the previous year; and the average monthly mobile data usage per user was 12. 6 GB, a year-on-year increase of 32.6%. The substantial growth in mobile data consumption led to a year-on-year increase of 4. 8% in average revenue per user (ARPU), reaching 49. 9 yuan. From an international comparison perspective, according to the GSMA statistics, in the fourth quarter of 2020, China's mobile communications tariffs were among the lowest globally, with the average monthly expenditure of mobile communication users ranking 93rd out of 237 countries and regions from low to high in terms of price, significantly lower than that of the United States (US), Canada, and South Korea. Figure 4-4 shows the average mobile data traffic tariff and cumulative average monthly mobile data usage per user in China from March 2020 to June 2021.

4.1.2 Satellite Internet

Satellite communications will be an effective solution for achieving ubiquitous

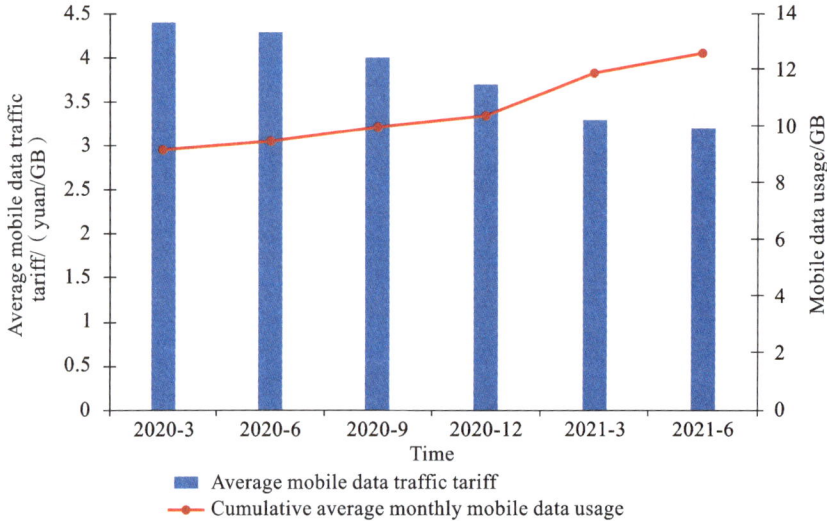

Figure 4-4 The average mobile data traffic tariff and cumulative average monthly mobile data usage per user in China (March 2020 - June 2021)

Data Source: Ministry of Industry and Information Technology of the People's Republic of China

communications in the future. Satellites are classified into five types based on their orbits: low earth orbit (LEO), medium earth orbit (MEO), geostationary earth orbit (GEO), sun-synchronous orbit (SSO), and inclined geo-synchronization orbit (IGSO). Due to the unique requirements of the space environment, the construction and maintenance costs for each satellite are tens to hundreds of times higher than those for wireless base stations, resulting in higher satellite communications tariffs compared with terrestrial mobile communications. Currently, satellite communications serves as a supplement to traditional optical fiber and 5G coverage, primarily targeting remote areas that optical fiber cannot reach, as well as specific regions such as oceans, deserts, and polar regions. This approach shifts network coverage focus from population centers to territorial expanses.

In recent years, LEO broadband communications satellites have garnered significant industry attention. These satellites offer lower launch costs and shorter round-trip times, making them a primary means for achieving satellite Internet and a key consideration for next-generation 6G mobile communications standards. LEO broadband communications satellites use the inter-satellite link technology to create a space backbone network via laser or microwave links. Satellite communications terminals can transmit data via orbital satellite constellations, through the space backbone network or directly through gateway stations, facilitating international Internet communications. SpaceX's Starlink project has launched numerous LEO broadband communications satellites, and by August 2021, it had covered all regions of the Earth except the Antarctic and Arctic, and related services have been deployed in the US, Canada, and Europe, with a planned deployment of 12 000 satellites by 2027.

In terms of high-throughput satellites, China has established a satellite network composed of three high-throughput satellites. In April 2017, China launched its first high-throughput satellite, Zhongxing-16, with a Ka-band multi-beam broadband communications capacity of 20 Gbps, covering most parts of China. By July 2020, it passed commercial flight network tests, achieving an access speed of over 150 Mbps. In November 2022, China launched the Zhongxing-19 high-throughput satellite to cover the Pacific region. In February 2023, China launched the Zhongxing-26 high-throughput satellite, covering China and its surrounding areas. At present, the Zhongxing-26 satellite is China's most advanced civil and commercial communications satellite, boasting a communications capacity of over 100 Gbps, equipped with 94 user beams and 11 gateway beams, and offering a terminal communications speed up to 450 Mbps. Together, these three high-throughput satellites provide high-speed network communications services and satellite Internet access to users.

In terms of GEO satellite mobile communications systems, China has launched three "Tiantong-1" satellites. In August 2016, China launched the Tiantong-1 01 satellite, which was the first satellite of China's satellite mobile communications system; subsequently, in November 2020 and January 2021, China launched the Tiantong-1 02 and Tiantong-1 03 satellites, respectively. These satellites, together with China's terrestrial mobile communications system, have formed an integrated space-ground mobile communications network, providing all-weather, all-time, stable, and reliable mobile communications services for users in China, neighboring Asian regions, and parts of the Pacific and Indian Oceans. In August 2023, Huawei released the smart phone of Mate 60 Pro, which supports access to the Tiantong-1 satellite mobile communications system. It is the world's first regular commercial mobile phone that supports satellite mobile communications, allowing users to make and receive satellite calls in areas where mobile communications networks are difficult to cover, such as mountains, deserts, and islands.

In terms of LEO satellite communications networks, China's two major aerospace groups, China Aerospace Science and Technology Corporation Limited, and China Aerospace Science and Industry Corporation, have initiated their own LEO network projects: the "Hongyan Satellite Constellation" planning to launch 300 small satellites, and the "Hongyun Project" planning to launch 156 satellites. Both projects completed their first satellite launches in 2018. In April 2020, satellite Internet was designated as one of China's "New infrastructure", marking 2020 as the inaugural year for satellite Internet construction in China. The "Outline of the 14th Five-Year Plan for National Economic and Social Development and the Long-Range Objectives Through the Year 2035 of the People's Republic of China" released in March 2021, called for the construction of high-speed, ubiquitous, integrated, interconnected secure, and efficient space-ground information infrastructure. In April 2021, China Satellite Network Group Co., Ltd (China SatNet) was established to specialize in the design, construction, and operation of satellite Internet. China has submitted network application to the International Telecommunication

Union (ITU) for LEO constellation orbits and frequencies, totaling 12 992 satellites in orbits ranging from 590 to 1 145 kilometers above the Earth. China SatNet plans to launch about 10% of these satellites within five years, supporting the deployment of the 6G mobile communications network by 2035.

4.1.3 Internet of Things

The Internet of Things (IoT) is a digital information infrastructure that uses a collaborative multi-network cellular mobile communications network to achieve ubiquitous connectivity and the interconnection of all things. International communications standardization organizations have successively completed various IoT-related technical standards, ranging from narrowband and low-speed to high-speed and low-latency. Among them, narrowband IoT (NB-IoT) meets most low-speed IoT requirements, 4G Cat. 1 (a 4G network with speed category 1, including LTE-Cat. 1) meets medium IoT and voice requirements, 5G RedCap meets mediums to high-speed requirements, and 5G NR meets high-speed and low-latency IoT requirements.

In scenarios with wide coverage, low sensitivity to latency, and low data rates, such as intelligent metering, tracking and positioning, intelligent smoke detection, and smart parking, NB-IoT technology is suitable. For scenarios where requirements for data rates are moderate but power consumption and transmission stability is critical, such as Quick Response (QR) code payments and charging stations, 4G Cat. 1 technology is ideal. For applications requiring higher data rates along with specific constraints on size, cost, and power consumption, such as video surveillance, industrial sensing, medical monitoring, and high-end wearable devices, 5G RedCap technology is appropriate. In scenarios demanding ultra-high bandwidth, low latency, and high mobility, such as industrial IoT, smart healthcare, intelligent transportation, and entertainment, 5G NR technology is the best fit.

China places significant emphasis on mobile IoT, continuously driving its development. In May 2020, the "Notice of the General Office of the Ministry of Industry and Information Technology on Deeply Advancing the Comprehensive Development of Mobile Internet of Things" was issued, which proposed migrating 2G/3G IoT services and creating an integrated mobile IoT ecosystem that facilitates coordinated development of NB-IoT, 4G, and 5G. Chinese telecom operators are promoting the adoption of NB-IoT terminals through subsidies. According to the 2021 "China Narrowband IoT (NB-IoT) Industry Market Research" report, since 2017, China Mobile had allocated 1 billion yuan in subsidies for NB-IoT modules, with the maximum subsidy rate for a single module reaching up to 80%; China Telecom increased its subsidy rate for a single module to 50%, with a maximum subsidy of 30 yuan. The price of NB-IoT modules had fallen to around 15 yuan, nearly matching the cost of 2G IoT modules. NB-IoT had achieved millions of connections across various industries, and the large-scale implementation helps narrow the gap between revenue and connectivity.

China has established the world's largest mobile IoT, with 1.845 billion connections, representing over 70% of the global total. This makes China the first major economy to achieve "more connected devices than connected people". NB-IoT has formed millions to tens of millions of connections in sectors such as water management, gas, firefighting, tracking and positioning, door locks, and electric vehicle theft prevention. Mobile IoT has seen large-scale applications in digital city construction, intelligent manufacturing, smart transportation, mobile payments, and other fields, profoundly transforming people's lifestyle.

4.1.4　Internet of Vehicles

The Internet of Vehicles (IoV) uses new-generation ICT to achieve comprehensive network connections among vehicles, within vehicles, between vehicles and roads, between vehicles and people, and between vehicles and service platforms. IoV can enhance vehicle intelligence and autonomous driving capabilities, fostering new business models for automotive and transportation services. Regarding vehicle-to-vehicle networking standards and technologies, the 3GPP began the standardization of long term evolution-vehicle to everything (LTE-V2X) in early 2015, with China playing a leading role in international standardization efforts.

China has developed a complete industry chain based on LTE-V2X technology, with chips, modules, on-board units (OBUs), and roadside units (RSUs) that are mature and have undergone extensive testing, ready for commercial deployment. Regarding IoV standards and technologies based on 5G cellular networks, the 5G Automotive Association (5GAA) and Europe's 5GCroCo project conducted research on remote control driving scenarios; in 2019, China's IMT-2020 (5G) Promotion Group supported the establishment of the first testbeds integrating mobile edge computing and cellar-vehicle to everything (C-V2X).

In October 2018, the MIIT became the first globally to release the frequence regulation on IoV, titled "Interim Provisions on Managing the 5905-5925MHz Frequency Band for Direct Communications of the Internet of Vehicles (Intelligent Connected Vehicles)", designating this frequency band for LTE-V2X-based IoV direct communications. In February 2020, the National Development and Reform Commission (NDRC) and 10 other ministries issued the "Intelligent Vehicle Innovation Development Strategy", aiming for regional coverage of in-vehicle wireless communications networks (such as LTE-V2X) by 2025 and gradual application of 5G-V2X in some cities and highways, along with full coverage of high-precision space-time benchmark service networks. In March 2020, the MIIT issued the "Notice on Promoting the Accelerated Development of 5G", advocating for the coordinated development of "5G + IoV". In November 2020, the State Council issued the "New Energy Vehicle Industry Development Plan (2021-2035)", which further emphasized the deep integration of new energy vehicles with energy, transportation, and information communications sectors, and the coordinated advancement of intelligent road network infrastructure.

China has rapidly implemented new IoV infrastructure, yielding initial results. From

2019 to 2023, the MIIT successively approved seven national IoV pilot zones in Jiangsu (Wuxi), Tianjin (Xiqing), Hunan (Changsha), Chongqing (Liangjiang New Area), Hubei (Xiangyang), Zhejiang (Deqing), and Guangxi (Liuzhou). These zones actively promoted the construction of IoV infrastructure, interoperability testing, and large-scale pilot demonstrations.

In 2021, the Ministry of Housing and Urban-Rural Development (MHURD) and the MIIT designated 16 cities as pilot sites for the collaborative development of smart city infrastructure and intelligent connected vehicles. These cities are allowed to conduct demonstration applications of various levels of intelligent connected vehicles in specific scenarios. By October 2021, more than 20 cities and several highways in China had deployed over 4 000 RSUs supporting direct communications, with over 3 500 on urban roads and more than 500 on highways, covering a total road length of more than 3 500 kilometers.

4.1.5 Computing Infrastructure

In the digital economy era, computing power is emerging as a new form of productivity, providing essential support for the digital transformation of numerous industries. Data centers, as the physical hosts of computing power, are crucial infrastructure for digital development. With the widespread adoption of the Internet and ICT applications in China, the scale of data centers and servers has rapidly expanded. In 2021, the number of data center racks in use in China reached 5.2 million, with large and above data center racks accounting for 4.2 million, about 80% of the total. Data centers housed 19 million servers, with a storage capacity of 800 EB. Figure 4-5 shows the scale of data center racks in use in China from 2017 to 2023.

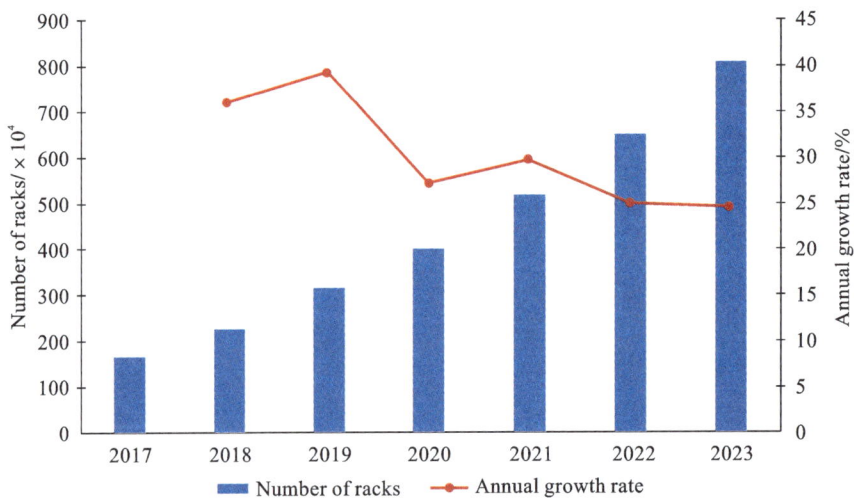

Figure 4-5　The scale of data center racks in use in China (2017-2023)

Data Source: Ministry of Industry and Information Technology of the People's Republic of China

However, the high energy consumption of large data centers is becoming a significant issue. For instance, in 2020, China had over 3 million data center racks in use, consuming more than 200 billion kilowatt-hours annually (based on a standard rack power density of 2.5 kilowatts). This consumption is nearly equivalent to the output of two Three Gorges hydropower station[①] and accounts for 2.7% of the country's total electricity use. Therefore, the energy conservation and consumption reduction of data centers have become the focus of attention for data center enterprises. Chinese enterprises have carried out active explorations. Take Alibaba Cloud as an example, it is the cloud service arm of Alibaba Group, has established five super data centers in Hangzhou, Nantong, Zhangbei, Ulanqab, and Heyuan in China. These data centers utilizes proprietary technologies to reduce energy consumption. For example, the Hangzhou data center uses the world's largest immersion liquid cooling server cluster, the Ulanqab data center relies on renewable sources of energy such as wind and solar power with natural wind cooling, and the Heyuan data center uses deep lake water for natural cooling.

From a broader geographical perspective, the contradiction between the computing power demands and energy supplies in various regions of China is becoming increasingly prominent. On the one hand, the economically developed eastern coastal regions of China have strong demands for computing power, but face a large electricity gap. On the other hand, the western regions of China are rich in various types of clean power generation resources, but have relatively lagging economic development with few demands for computing power. By building national systems for big data centers, a new type of computing power network system that integrates data centers, cloud computing, and big data can be constructed, and the computing power demand in eastern China can be guided to western China in an orderly manner. The green energy in the west can be consumed locally, solving long-standing problems such as high energy consumption of data centers and low utilization efficiency of data resources.

The "Outline of the 14th Five-Year Plan for National Economic and Social Development and the Long-Range Objectives Through the Year 2035 of the People's Republic of China" explicitly called for accelerating the construction of a national integrated big data center system, enhancing the unified and intelligent scheduling of computing power, and building several national hub nodes and big data center clusters. In May 2021, the NDRC, the MIIT, and other units jointly issued the "Implementation Plan for the Computing Hub of the National Integrated Big Data Center Collaborative Innovation System", proposing to carry out the "Eastern Data, Western Computing" demonstration project. It is an integrated layout super project adjusting and allocating national computing

---

① The Three Gorges hydropower station is the largest hydroelectric power station in the world and also the largest engineering project ever constructed in China. It officially started construction in 1994 and was completed in 2009. In 2023, it has completed a power generation of 802.71 billion kilowatt hours.

resources from a national perspective. The project included eight computing hub nodes, ten national data center clusters, and an all-optical interconnected high-speed network between these nodes and clusters. Data center clusters would be built in the four major economic regions of Beijing-Tianjin-Hebei, the Yangtze River Delta, the Guangdong-Hong Kong-Macao Greater Bay Area, and Chengdu-Chongqing, and computing hub nodes would be built in the four western regions of Inner Mongolia, Guizhou, Gansu, and Ningxia. The latter would take over the computing power needs of the former, and the computing power would be integrated and dispatched within the national system to realize western computing for eastern data.

The "Eastern Data, Western Computing" project can not only alleviate the pressure of China's rapidly growing computing power demand every year, but also alleviate the problem of unbalanced economic development between eastern and western China. The annual investment volume of this project will reach hundreds of billions of yuan, and the driving effect on related industries will reach 1 : 8. The data center industry chain includes traditional civil engineering projects as well as information technology equipment manufacturing, information and communications, basic software, green energy supply and other industries. It is long, covers a wide range of categories, and has a strong driving effect. The construction of computing power hubs and data center clusters will effectively drive upstream and downstream investment in industries in western China and promote social and economic growth.

4.2　Internet Industry

China's Internet industry has grown from scratch, from weak to strong, and now China has become a powerful Internet country in the world. China's top Internet enterprises include Alibaba, Tencent, Ant Douyin, Pinduoduo, and JD. com. (see Table 4-1) As of July 2022, the number of telecommunications business licensed enterprises across the country had surpassed 130 000, 4.9 times that of 2012, and the market players were more diversified; 10 enterprises ranked among the top 30 global Internet enterprises by market value, and their core competitiveness continues to improve.

Table 4-1　Representative Internet enterprises in China in 2022

Abbreviation	Full names	Business and brands	Locations
Tencent	Shenzhen Tencent Computer Systems Co., Ltd.	WeChat, QQ, Tencent Cloud	Guangdong
Alibaba	Alibaba (China) Co., Ltd.	Taobao, Alibaba Cloud, Youku, ele. me	Zhejiang

Continued

Abbreviation	Full names	Business and brands	Locations
Meituan	Beijing Sankuai Online Technology Co., Ltd.	Meituan, Dianping, Meituan Waimai	Beijing
Ant Technology	Ant Technology Co., Ltd.	Alipay, AntChain, OceanBase Database	Zhejiang
Douyin	Beijing Douyin Information Service Co., Ltd.	TikTok, Today's Headlines, Xigua Video	Beijing
JD. com	JD.com, Inc.	JD.com, JD Logistics, JD Technology	Beijing
Baidu	Baidu, Online Network Technology (Beijing)Co.,Ltd.	Baidu Search, Baidu Cloud, Baidu Apollo	Beijing
Pinduoduo	Shanghai Xunmeng Information Technology Co., Ltd.	Pinduoduo	Shanghai
Kuaishou	Beijing Kuaishou Technology Co., Ltd.	Kuaishou, Kuaishou Express, AC-Fun	Beijing
Trip	Trip.com Group Limited	Trip.com, Qunar, Skyscanner	Shanghai

Data Source: Internet Society of China

In the domains of e-commerce, social media, entertainment media, and finance, the applications produced by China are globally dominant. In e-commerce, China's transaction value and market scale have consistently been the largest in the world. In social media, WeChat and **QQ** boast nearly 1 billion monthly active users. In entertainment media, Chinese-developed apps like TikTok have become global sensations. In finance, third-party payment tools such as Alipay and WeChat led the world in application scale.

In the first half of 2022, various personal Internet applications in China continued to grow. Short videos experienced the most significant increase, with 28.05 million new users added since December 2021, a growth rate of 3.0%, pushing the usage rate of online videos to 94.6%. Instant messaging retained the highest user base, with 20.42 million new users since December 2021, reaching a usage rate of 97.7%. Online news and live streaming saw user increases of 16.98 million and 12.90 million with growth rates of 2.2% and 1.8%, respectively. Table 4-2 shows the user scale and usage rates of various Internet applications in China for the first half of 2022.

Table 4-2   User scale and usage rates of Internet applications in China, first half of 2022

Application types	Applications	December 2021		June 2022		Growth rate/%
		User scale /×10⁴	Usage rate/%	User scale /×10⁴	Usage rate/%	
Instant messaging	Instant messaging	100 666	97.5	102 708	97.7	2.0

Continued

Application types	Applications	December 2021		June 2022		Growth rate/%
		User scale /×10⁴	Usage rate/%	User scale /×10⁴	Usage rate/%	
Content services	Online video (including short videos)	97 471	94.5	99 488	94.6	2.1
	Short video	93 415	90.5	96 220	91.5	3.0
	Search engine	82 884	80.3	82 147	78.2	−0.9
	Online news	77 109	74.7	78 807	75.0	2.2
	Online music	72 946	70.7	72 789	69.2	−0.2
	Live streaming	70 337	68.2	71 627	68.1	1.8
	Online gaming	55 354	53.6	55 239	52.6	−0.2
	Online literature	50 159	48.6	49 322	46.9	−1.7
E-commerce	Online payment	90 363	87.6	90 444	86.0	0.1
	Online shopping	84 210	81.6	84 057	80.0	−0.2
Online to offline (O2O) services	Online office	46 884	45.4	46 066	43.8	−1.7
	Ride-hailing	45 261	43.9	40 507	38.5	−10.5
	Online travel booking	39 710	38.5	33 250	31.6	−16.3
	Online healthcare	29 788	28.9	29 984	28.5	0.7

4.2.1　Instant Messaging

From 1994 to 2009, the primary means of accessing the Internet was through personal computer (PC) terminals. In December 2009, the proportion of mobile phone Internet users in China surpassed 50% for the first time. In June 2012, the number of Internet users accessing the Internet via mobile phones reached 388 million, making mobile phones the most common Internet access terminal in China. Since 2010, with the rapid development of mobile Internet, the proportion of mobile phone Internet users among all Chinese Internet users rose from 66.2% in December 2010 to 99.6% in June 2022. Figure 4-6 shows the user scale of various Internet terminals in China from June 2002 to June 2022.

Instant messaging is the most frequently used Internet application among Chinese Internet users, with popular apps including WeChat and QQ. As of June 2022, the number of instant messaging users in China had reached 1.027 billion, an increase of 20.42 million since December 2021, accounting for 97.7% of all Internet users. Mobile Internet traffic grew rapidly, reaching 124.1 billion GB in the first half of 2022, a year-on-year increase of

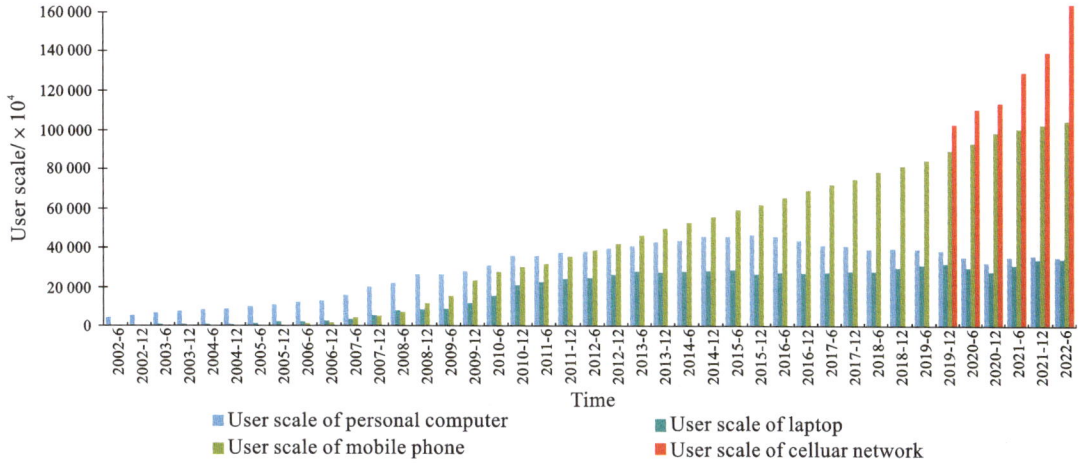

Figure 4-6　The user scale of various Internet terminals in China (June 2002-June 2022)

Data Source: China Internet Network Information Center

20.2%.

WeChat has become an essential instant messaging tool for Chinese Internet users. Different from traditional instant messaging apps, WeChat integrates public accounts and mini-programs, allowing seamless access to third-party apps and creating a vast software ecosystem. It has become the primary gateway for users to various mobile apps, maintaining over a billion monthly active users. In August 2021, the popular WeChat mini-programs (with over 100 million monthly active users) included various categories, such as city services (including health codes), utility payments, office documents, online shopping, and ride-hailing, covering essential daily activities of general Chinese Internet users. Figure 4-7 illustrates WeChat's monthly active user scale and WeChat mini-program penetration rate from 2020 to 2021.

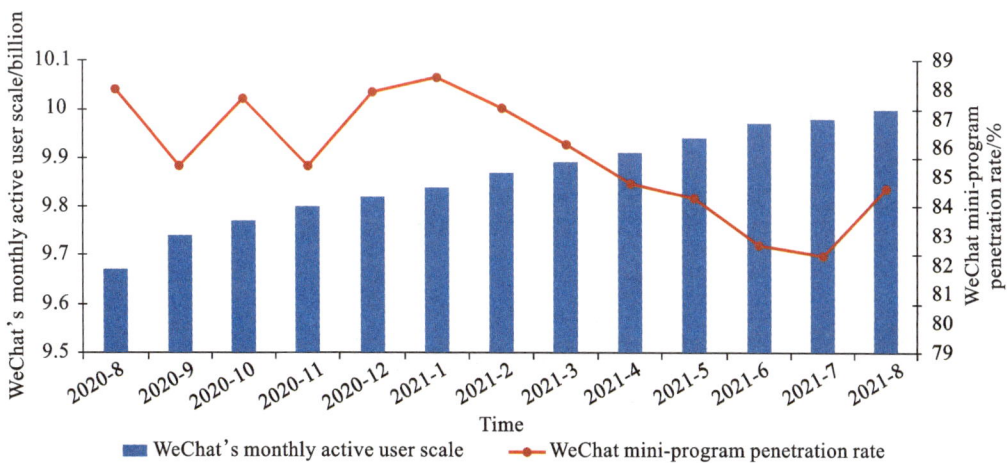

Figure 4-7　WeChat's monthly active user scale and WeChat mini-program penetration rate (2020-2021)

Data Source: QuestMobile

4.2.2　E-commerce

E-commerce involves conducting business activities through the Internet and other information networks, such as selling goods or providing services. It is a crucial part of both the digital and real economies. China has long held the number one position globally in e-commerce transaction volume and market scale. E-commerce in China has become deeply integrated into all aspects of production and daily life, playing a pivotal role in the digital transformation of the economy and society.

According to the National Bureau of Statistics (NBS), the national e-commerce transaction volume reached 42.3 trillion yuan in 2021, with an annual growth rate of 19.6%. By transaction type, the goods transaction volume of 2021 was 31.3 trillion yuan, with an annual growth rate of 16.6%, while the transaction volume of services reached 11 trillion yuan, with an annual growth rate of 28.9%. By region, the eastern region's e-commerce volume of 2021 was 27.4 trillion yuan, with an annual growth rate of 18.2%; the central region's was 7.1 trillion yuan, with an annual growth rate of 22.6%; the western region's was 6.5 trillion yuan, with an annual growth rate of 24.2%; the northeastern region's was 1.3 trillion yuan, with an annual growth rate of 11.8%. Figure 4-8 shows China's e-commerce transaction value and annual growth rate from 2011 to 2021.

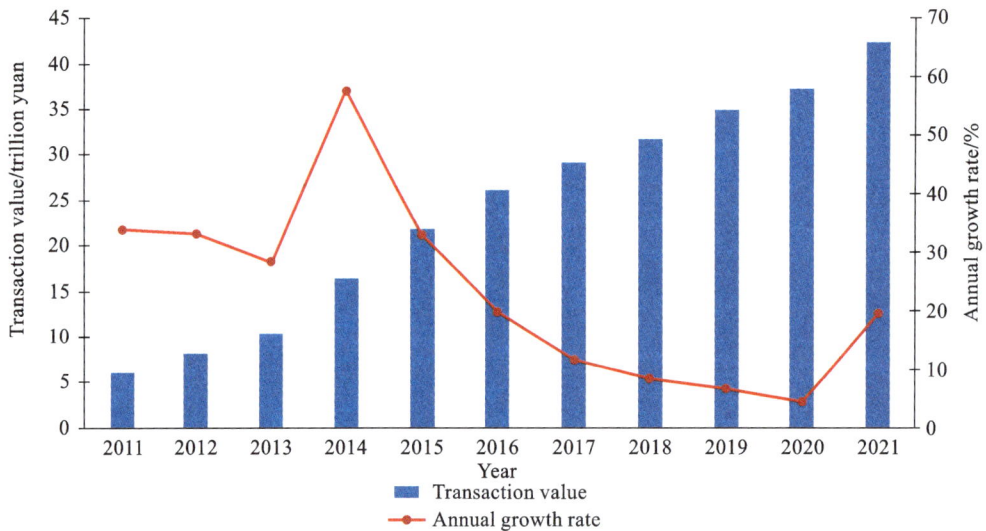

Figure 4-8　China's e-commerce transaction value and annual growth rate (2011-2021)

Data Source: National Bureau of Statistics

Various new forms of e-commerce such as live streaming and community group buying have developed rapidly, accelerating the integration of e-commerce with the real economy and attracting more people to the e-commerce industry. According to the National Engineering Laboratory for E-commerce Transaction Technology, in 2021, the number of e-commerce practitioners in China reached 67.278 million, representing an 11.8% year-on-year increase. Among them, 41.2632 million were directly employed or started businesses in e-commerce, while 26.0148 million were in information technology, related services, and supporting industries driven by e-commerce. Figure 4-9 shows China's e-commerce employment scale and annual growth rate from 2014 to 2021.

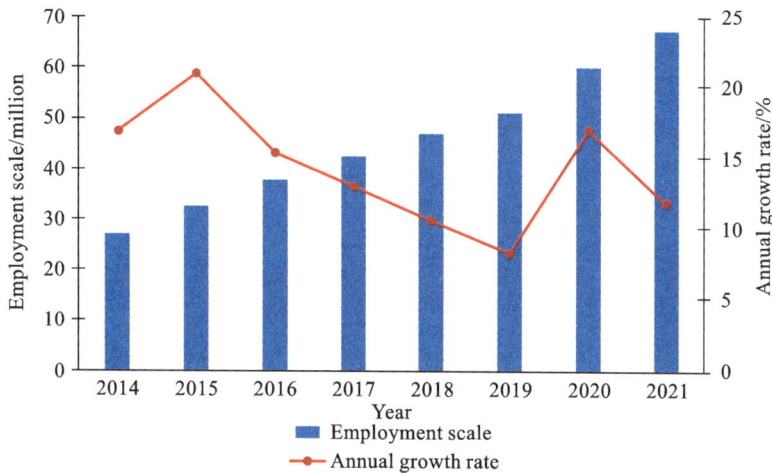

Figure 4-9　China's e-commerce employment scale and annual growth rate (2014-2021)

Data Source: National Engineering Laboratory for E-commerce Transaction Technology

4.2.2.1　Industrial E-commerce

Industrial e-commerce involves transactions between enterprises through third-party and self-operated B2B platforms. This includes bulk e-commerce for commodity trading, industrial products e-commerce for maintenance, repair and operations (MRO) and bill of material (BOM) services, wholesale e-commerce for consumer goods, enterprise procurement e-commerce for office supplies and business services, and related service providers. Key players in the industrial e-commerce in China include Alibaba, Beijing United Information Technology Co., Ltd., Netsun, HC Group, Focus Technology, Wangku Group, and Yiwu Purchase. Statistics showed that the scale of China's industrial e-commerce market grew from 6.25 trillion yuan in 2012 to 25.19 trillion yuan in 2021, a 3.03-fold increase over 10 years. Figure 4-10 illustrates the market scale and annual growth rate of China's industrial e-commerce from 2015 to 2023.

4.2.2.2　Online Retail

According to the China Internet Network Information Center (CNNIC), as of December 2021, there had been 842 million online shopping users in China, accounting for 81.6% of all Internet users. Data from the NBS showed that in 2021, China's online retail value reached 13.09 trillion yuan, with an annual growth rate of 14.1%, maintaining the position of the world's largest online retail market for nine years. Online retail value of physical goods amounted to 10.8 trillion yuan, with an annual growth rate of 12.0%, representing 24.5% of total retail sales of consumer goods. In online retail value of physical goods, food, clothing, and daily necessities grew by 17.8%, 8.3%, and 12.5%, respectively. In terms of categories of goods, the top three were apparel, daily necessities, and household appliances and

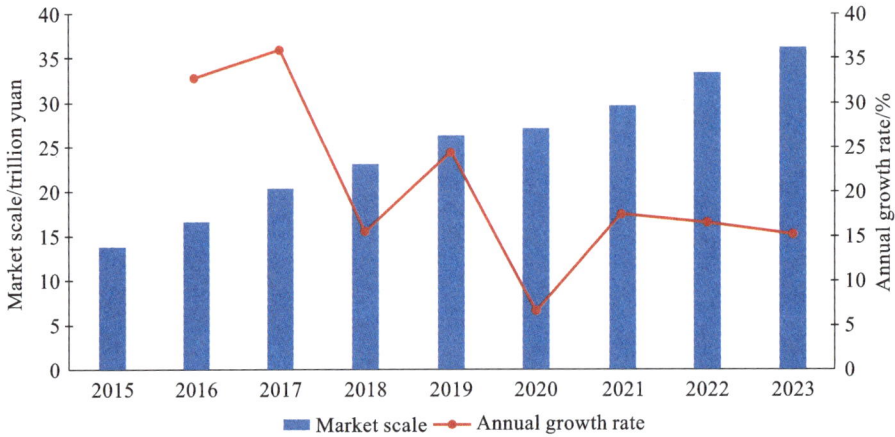

Figure 4-10　The market scale and annual growth rate of China's industrial e-commerce (2015-2023)

Data Source: www.chyxx.com

audio-visual equipment, accounting for 22.94%, 15.23%, and 10.43% of physical goods online retail value, respectively. Figure 4-11 shows China's online retail value and annual growth rate from 2011 to 2021.

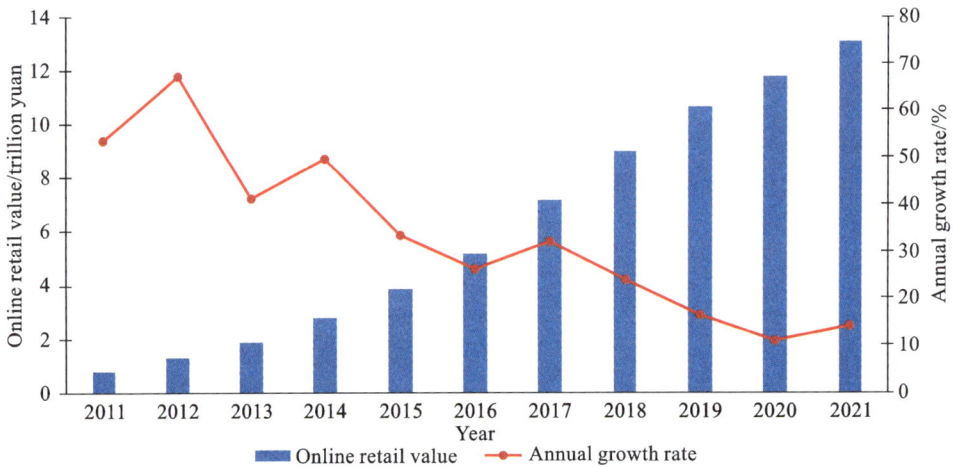

Figure 4-11　China's online retail value and annual growth rate (2011-2021)

Data Source: National Bureau of Statistics

The "Double 11" shopping festival is a hallmark of China's online retail market. In November 2009, Tmall leveraged "Singles' Day" to establish a special shopping day. In 2019, Tmall's "Double 11" shopping festival set a sales record of 268.4 billion yuan, five times the transaction value of the Western "Black Friday" shopping festival that year.

Nowadays, the "Double 11" shopping festival is not only a major sales event for China's leading e-commerce platforms (Taobao, Tmall, JD.com, etc.), but also an annual global festival. Many international brands actively participate through national pavilions, overseas shopping, and direct brand sales. Data shows that from 2009 to 2021, the total transaction value of the "Double 11" shopping festival on Chinese e-commerce platforms increased annually, rising from 52 million yuan in 2009 to 965.12 billion yuan in 2021.

Figure 4-12 shows the transaction value and annual growth rate of China's e-commerce platforms during the "Double 11" shopping festival from 2013 to 2021.

As more and more Internet platforms enter the e-commerce space, online shoppers are increasingly diversifying their consumption channels from traditional platforms like Taobao and JD.com to short video platforms, community group buying, and social media. Estimates from January to June 2022 indicate that 27.3% of online shoppers only used traditional e-commerce platforms, while 49.7% shopped on short video live streaming platforms, 37.2% on fresh food e-commerce, 32.4% on community group buying, and 19.6% on WeChat.

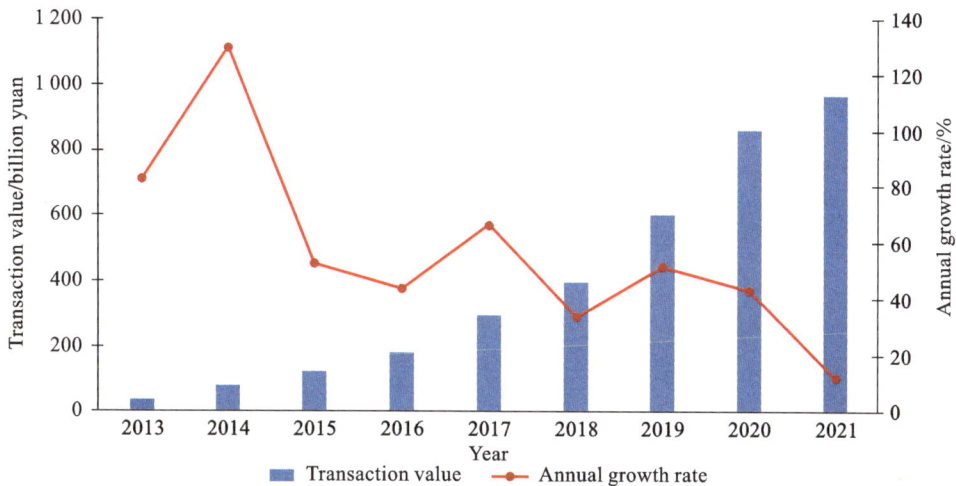

Figure 4-12　China's e-commerce platform transaction value and annual growth rate during the "Double 11" shopping festival (2013-2021)

Data Source: data.iimedia.cn

4.2.2.3　Express Logistics

Online shopping has become a key consumption channel for Chinese residents, spurring rapid growth in related markets. In 2021, China's express delivery industry saw significant increases in both business volume and operating revenue. Specifically, according to the State Post Bureau of China, China's total business volume of express service enterprises reached 108.3 billion pieces, with an annual growth rate of 29.9%, while the total operating revenue hit 1 033.23 billion yuan, with an annual growth rate of 17.5%. Intracity deliveries totaled 14.11 billion pieces, with an annual growth rate of 16.0%; intercity deliveries totaled 92.08 billion pieces, with an annual growth rate of 32.8%. Figure 4-13 shows China's express service enterprises business volume and annual growth rate from 2011 to 2021.

Various automated and unmanned systems have been integrated into logistics processes. In November 2016, the Nanjing Suning Super Cloud Warehouse, covering approximately 200 000 square meters, became Asia's largest intelligent logistics base. By 2019, it had been upgraded to a "next-generation unmanned warehouse", featuring various

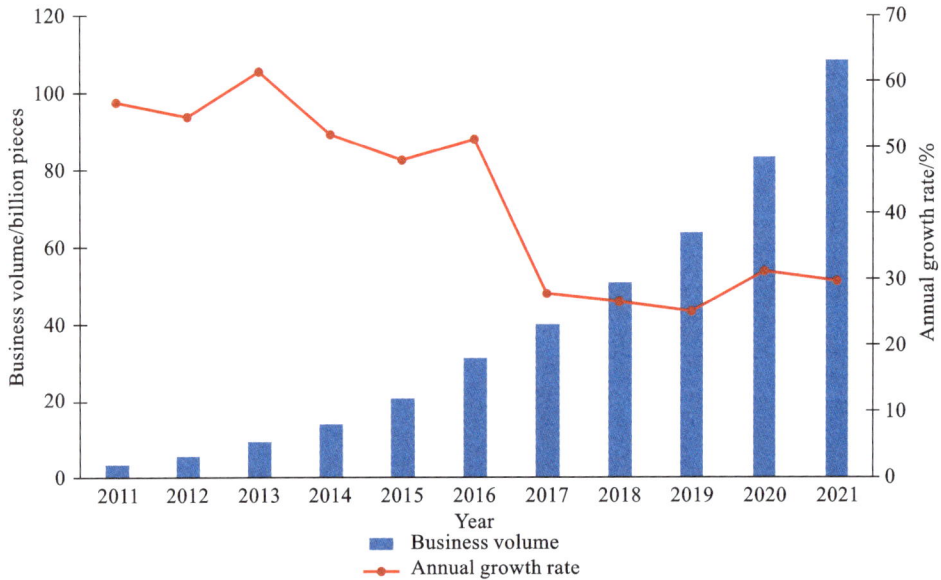

Figure 4-13 China's express service enterprises business volume and annual growth rate（2011-2021）

Data Source：State Post Bureau of China

technical devices such as unmanned vehicles, fully automated transport robots, robotic arms, and automatic packaging machines, enabling fully unmanned operations. In 2018, the super robot sorting center jointly built by Cainiao and YTO Express was officially put into operation at the YTO Express Hangzhou Transit Center, with 350 robots capable of sorting over 500 000 parcels daily. In 2019, the number of China's intelligent express delivering cabinets reached 406 000, with an annual growth rate of 49.3%, and nearly 26 times that of 2014.

4.2.3 Content Services

Content services are the major applications of the Internet. Initially, search engines dominated Internet content services. Recently, to meet the fragmented and multi-scenario reading needs of mobile Internet users, news-pushing applications using "algorithm editing plus intelligent distribution", such as Toutiao, have emerged. As of June 2022, the number of search engine users in China had reached 821 million, a decrease of 7.37 million from December 2021, representing 78.2% of all Internet users; the number of online news users had reached 788 million, an increase of 16.98 million from December 2021, accounting for 75.0% of all Internet users.

The entertainment industry, including music, video, live streaming, and gaming, is also a significant part in Internet content services. As of June 2022, online video users in China had numbered 995 million, an increase of 20.17 million from December 2021, making up 94.6% of all Internet users. Major online video platforms focused on vertical markets by producing original and custom dramas to attract and retain paid members, thus boosting membership revenue. Membership revenue had become a primary revenue source for these platforms, alongside advertising. For instance, in the first quarter of 2022, Bilibili had 20.1 million paid members, with an annual growth rate of 25%, of which nearly 80% were annual or auto-renewal subscribers. iQIYI's membership service revenue reached 4.5 billion yuan, with an annual growth rate of 4%. Figure 4-14 shows the user scale and usage rate of various categories in China's online content (entertainment industry) in December 2020 and December 2021.

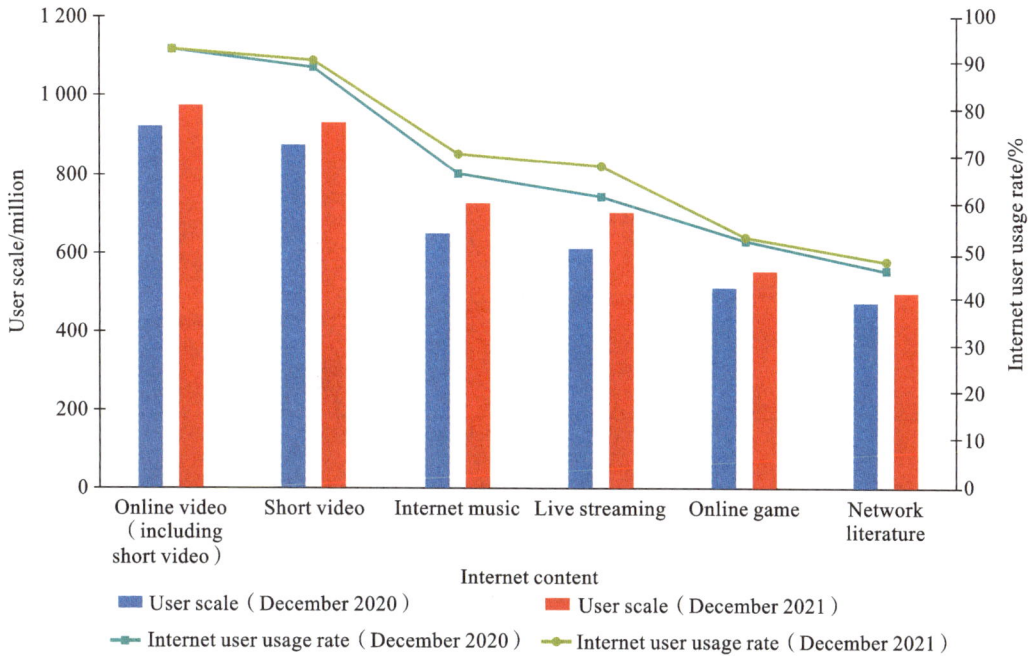

Figure 4-14　The user scale and usage rate of various categories in China's online content (entertainment industry)

Data Source: China Internet Network Information Center

4.2.3.1　Short Video

The short video industry emerged in 2011, initially centered on personal users creating and sharing homemade videos. This new form of communication suits the fragmented and decentralized nature of mobile Internet, offering diverse content types and enhanced social features. It fulfills users' varied content and social needs, becoming a key and rapidly growing sector in the Internet industry.

According to statistics from the CNNIC, by December 2021, the number of short video users in China had reached 934 million, with an annual growth rate of 7%, representing 90.5% of all Internet users. Data from QuestMobile shows that in December 2021, Douyin[①] and Kuaishou had 672 million and 411 million monthly active users, respectively. In December 2021, the average monthly usage time for short videos increased to 53.2 hours per person,

---

①　The TikTok mobile application (released in 2017) is the English international version of the Douyin application (released in 2016).

with total short video usage time accounting for 25.7% of total Internet usage time, surpassing instant messaging as the most time-consuming activity for Internet users. The number of short video users far exceeded that of music, live streaming, gaming, and other entertainment forms, with Internet user penetration rate still rising. Short videos have become a crucial form of online social interaction and entertainment. Figure 4-15 shows the user scale of major short video platforms in China in December 2020 and December 2021.

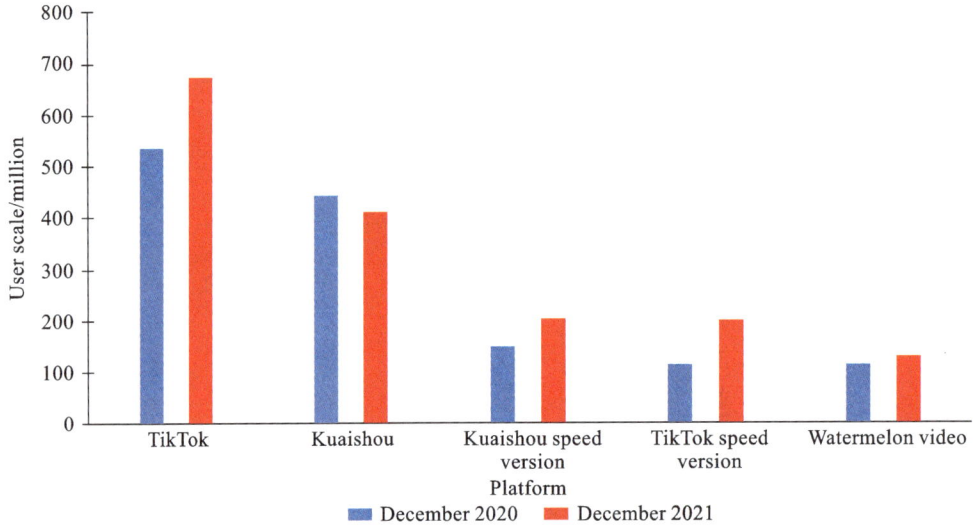

Figure 4-15 User scale of major short video platforms in China (December 2020 and December 2021)

Data Source: QuestMobile

Short video platforms have a large user base and high active penetration rate, with users spending significant amounts of time on these platforms, accumulating extensive user data. This broadens the audience for advertisements and allows personalized recommendation algorithms to precisely target advertisements, improving conversion rates. Short video advertising leads the online advertising market and has become a crucial channel for digital marketing. In the Chinese Internet advertising market, short video advertising overtook search engine advertising in 2020 with a market share of 17.4%, making it the second largest advertising type after e-commerce advertising.

Short videos have shifted China's e-commerce user behavior from search-based to recommendation-based consumption. Traditionally, online shoppers search for product and service information, but with advancements in big data and artificial intelligence (AI), personalized recommendations based on algorithm have become mainstream. From May 2021 to April 2022, TikTok hosted over 9 million live streams each month, selling more than 10 billion items, with the total transaction value increasing by 2.2 times year-on-year.

4.2.3.2 Live Streaming

The live streaming industry in China began in 2005, initially focusing on vertical and pan-entertainment categories. It has since expanded to include e-commerce, gaming events, pan-entertainment, education, and travel live streaming. In 2016, the women's e-commerce platform MOGU and the comprehensive e-commerce platform Taobao launched live streaming for selling products. Between 2016 and 2018, the major short video platforms Douyin and Kuaishou also quickly entered the live streaming e-commerce space. As of June 2022, China had 716 million online live streaming users, an increase of 12.9 million since December 2021, representing 68.1% of all Internet users.

Live streaming e-commerce offers consumers an immersive experience with real-time interaction, allowing hosts to quickly understand viewer preferences and adjust marketing strategies. A wide range of Internet celebrities, stars, and industry professionals have joined this trend, creating an environment where anything and anyone can be streamed. Online live streaming and social networking have fueled the rise of social media marketing, leveraging word-of-mouth to drive consumption, and giving rise to new economic models like the Internet celebrity economy and the trust economy.

From June 2020 to June 2022, the number of live streaming e-commerce users in China grew from 309 million to 469 million, with a compound annual growth rate of 23.2%. The usage rate among Internet users increased from 32.9% to 44.6%, rising by 11.7 percentage points over two years. According to CNNIC, as of June 2022, the number of live streaming e-commerce users in China had reached 469 million, up 5.33 million from December 2021, representing 44.6% of all Internet users. In April 2020, the China Consumers Association released the "Outline Survey Report on Consumer Satisfaction with Live Streaming E-commerce Shopping", which indicated that 68.5% of consumers used Taobao Live, with 46.3% frequently using it. Figure 4-16 shows the market share of consumers on China's live streaming e-commerce shopping platforms from January 2020 to March 2020.

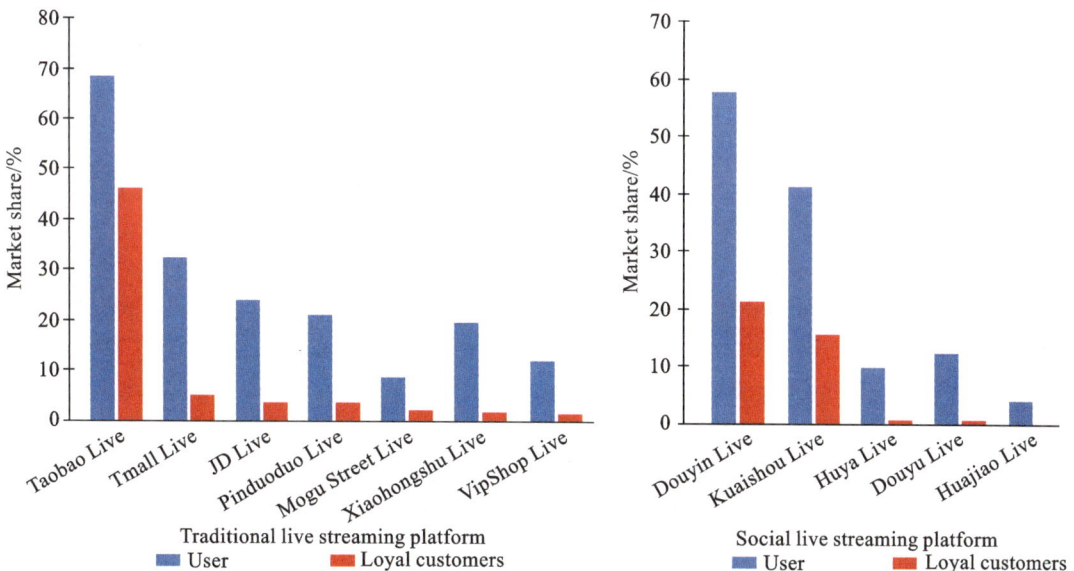

Figure 4-16 The market share of consumers on China's live streaming e-commerce shopping platforms (January 2020-March 2020)

Data Source: China Consumers Association

4.2.4 Life Services

The digitization of the service industry has accelerated evolving in China, with the O2O (online-to-offline) interaction model becoming increasingly vibrant, driving the integration and innovation of the Internet and the service sector. Mobile Internet and other new technologies continuously foster online-offline interaction, offering consumers more service options and delivery convenience. By deeply analyzing user data, enterprises can better match goods and services with user needs, promoting the integration of industry chain resources, the transformation of physical stores, the improvement of operational efficiency, and innovation in business models. O2O is currently one of the most active fields for mass entrepreneurship and innovation. In service sectors such as tourism, car rental and ride-hailing, food delivery, domestic services, beauty and health, education and training, and vehicle maintenance, the variety of products and service models based on the O2O model continue to expand.

Digital technology is rapidly integrating with various industries, driving the recovery of the consumer market by shifting offline advantages in dining, tourism, and shopping to online platforms. As of December 2021, China had 469 million users of online office services, 298 million users of online medical services, and 544 million users of online food delivery, with annual growth rates of 35.7%, 38.7%, and 29.9%, respectively. New business models such as online tourism, adoptive agriculture, and creative homestays are flourishing. By June 2022, the number of online travel booking users in China had decreased to 333 million, a drop of 64.6 million from December 2021, accounting for 31.6% of all Internet users. The number of online medical service users had increased to 300 million, up by 1.96 million from December 2021, making up 28.5% of all Internet users.

4.2.5 Payment Service

4.2.5.1 Online Payment

China is a leader in online payment. As of December 2015, the number of online payment users in China had reached 416 million, surpassing online shopping users for the first time, which indicated the Internet's growing penetration into offline consumption scenarios and the emerging habit of going out "wallet-free" and spending "cashless". By June 2022, the number of online payment users in China had reached 904 million, with an increase of 810 000 from December 2021, accounting for 86.0% of all Internet users.

Since 2020, online payment and contactless payment methods have become deeply integrated, making online payment the third largest online application after instant messaging and online video (including short videos) in China. The integration of online and offline consumption has essentially formed. According to the "2020 Mobile Payment User Survey Report" by the Payment & Clearing Association of China, nearly 75% of users used mobile payment daily. Data showed that in the first quarter of 2022, banks processed 23.57 billion online payment transactions, totaling 585.16 trillion yuan, with annual growth rates of 4.60% and 5.72%, respectively. Mobile payment transactions reached 34.653 billion, totaling 131.58 trillion yuan, with annual growth rates of 6.24% and 1.11%, respectively.

Alipay began its global expansion in 2007. As of June 2019, Alipay and its overseas partners had provided mobile payment and inclusive financial services to over 1.2 billion users worldwide, making it the world's largest non-social application. Alipay offers three main financial services to global merchants and consumers: online payment channels through Global Pay, offline payment for outbound tourism, and global digital inclusive financial services.

Global Pay involves Alipay collaborating with financial institutions and third-party partners worldwide to facilitate online payment channels worldwide, allowing global consumers to complete cross-border payments using localized methods. Nowadays, Alipay partners with over 250 financial institutions globally, facilitating online payment in more than 220 countries and regions and supporting transactions in 27 currencies. Global Pay makes global buying and selling possible. Figure 4-17 shows the user scale of China's online shopping and online payment from June 2007 to June 2022.

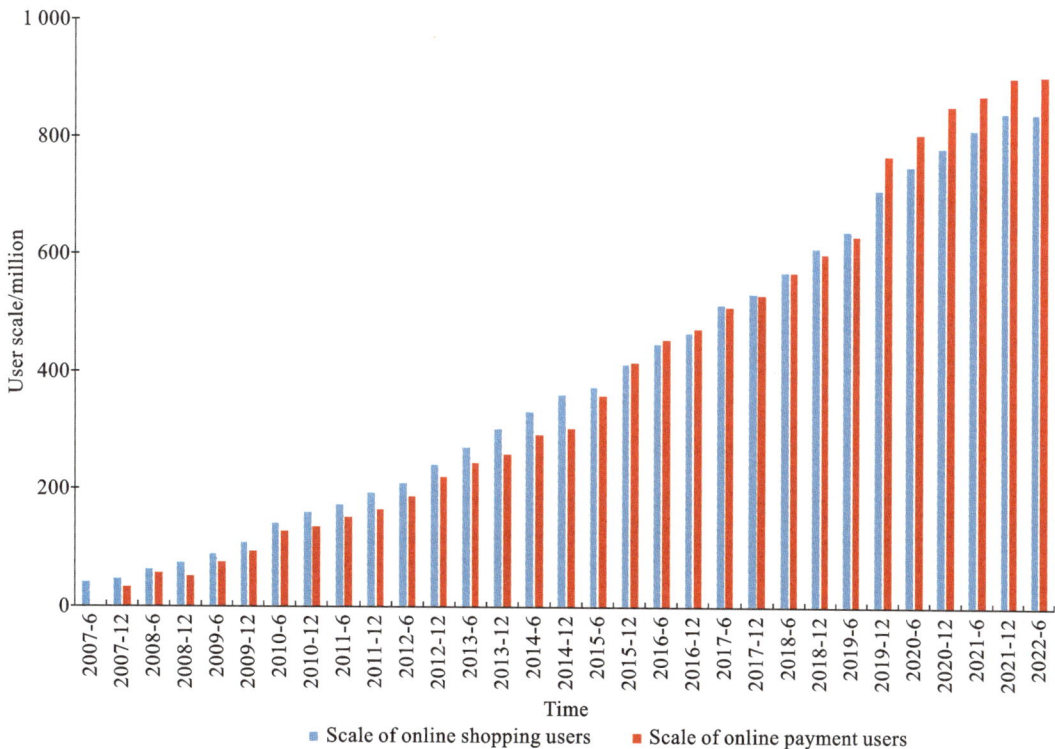

Figure 4-17 The user scale of China's online shopping and online payment (June 2007- June 2022)

Data Source: China Internet Network Information Center

4.2.5.2 **Unmanned Economy**

The unmanned economy is a result of advanced ICT, based on the Internet, utilizing big data, Radio Frequency Identification (RFID), IoT, and other sensing technologies to reduce labor output. Unmanned supermarkets, vending machines, and unmanned shelves are the key examples of unmanned economic terminals. China's unmanned retail economy has developed rapidly, with the market scale growing from approximately 1.7 billion yuan in 2014 to about 19.8 billion yuan in 2018, and over 40 billion yuan in 2023. It is expected to surpass 80 billion yuan by 2026, becoming prominent in retail channels. Vending machines remain the dominant channel, holding the largest market share. In 2015, the sales volume of vending machines in China reached 128 200 units, mainly in economic developed areas such as Beijing, Shanghai, Guangzhou, and Shenzhen. The service types have expanded from traditional food vending machines to include self-service coffee machines, beverage machines, and KTV sing-along machines. Figure 4-18 shows China's unmanned retail market scale and annual growth rate from 2016 to 2022.

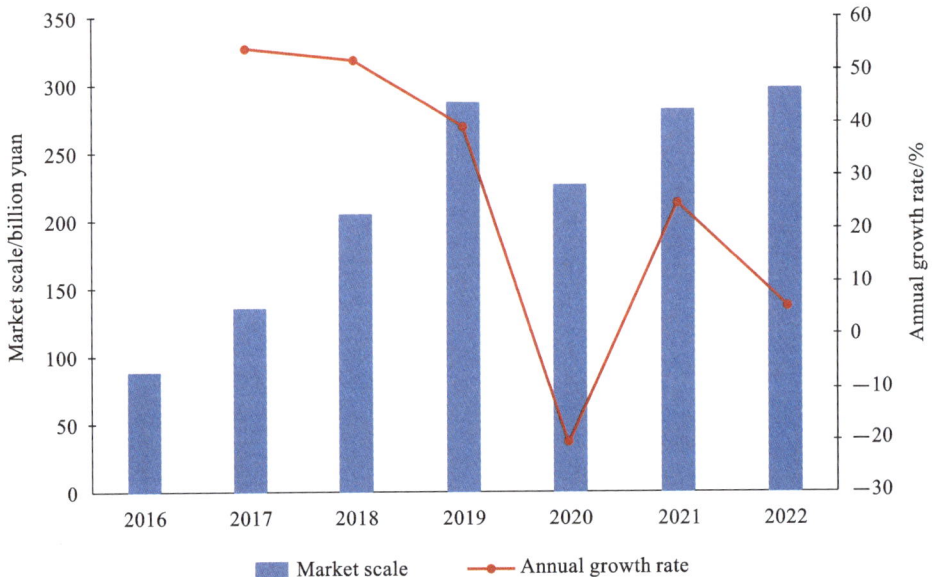

Figure 4-18   China's unmanned retail market and annual growth rate (2016-2022)

Data Source: Compiled by Insight and Info

4.3   **Software and Information Technology Services Industry**

China's software and information technology services industry has seen rapid development, with significant growth in scale and benefits. From 2012 to 2021, the scale of the software industry grew approximately 2.8 times, from 2.479 4 trillion yuan in 2012 to 9.499 4 trillion yuan in 2021, with a compound annual growth rate of 16.1%, ranking among the top industries in the national economy. With its proportion within the ICT industry increasing from 23.4% in 2012 to 33.0% in 2021, the software and information technology services industry has become a key driver for expanding the ICT industry. Figure 4-19 shows the revenue growth of China's software and information technology services industry from 2013 to 2020.

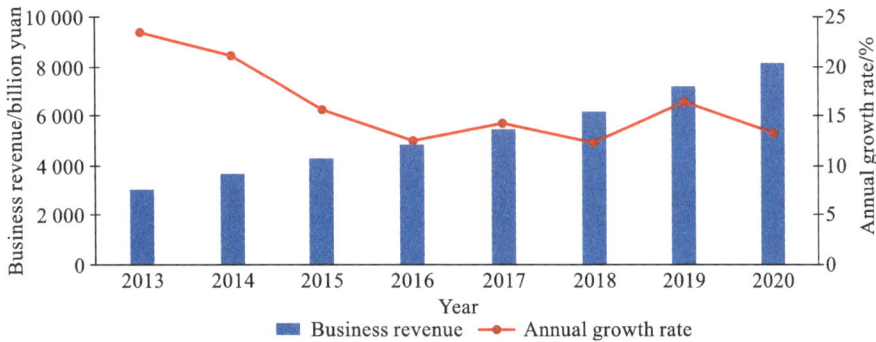

Figure 4-19   The revenue growth of China's software and information technology service industry (2013-2020)

Data Source: Ministry of Industry and Information Technology of the People's Republic of China

The innovation system for the software and information technology services industry has been established, with significant breakthroughs in basic software such as operating systems, databases, middleware, and office software, achieving a series of landmark achievements. Innovative applications like remote office and collaborative research and development software strongly support various industries. In 2022, China registered 1.835 million computer software copyrights, maintaining over one million registrations annually for five consecutive years. Compared with 2012, the annual number of registrations of software increased 12-fold.

The integration of applications is deepening, significantly enhancing their impact. In 2022, the number of registration of AI and big data software applications exceeded 35 000, respecting a 32-fold and 45-fold increase compared with their initial registration numbers, respectively. By the end of 2020, nearly 100 influential industrial Internet platforms had been established, connecting over 70 million devices and hosting more than 350 000 industrial applications, effectively promoting the transformation and upgrading of the manufacturing industry; over one million enterprises had adopted cloud services, and software and information technology services consumption accounted for more than 50% of the total information consumption.

The strength of key enterprises has grown, and their international competitiveness has been significantly improved. In 2020, China's software and information technology services industry had over 40 000 large-scale enterprises, employing 7.047 million people; the top 100 enterprises generated more than 25% of the industry's total revenue, up five percentage points from 2015, with research and development investment accounting for

27.9% of the industry total; 10 enterprises had revenues exceeding 100 billion yuan, and 2 ranked among the top 10 global enterprises by market value.

The industrial clustering effect has become prominent, and the overall service system for this industry has been more complete. In 2020, 268 software industrial parks contributed over 75% of the total software revenue in China, and 13 renowned software cities accounted for 77.5%. During the 13th Five-Year Plan period, 269 national software standards and 43 industry standards were established, policies benefiting enterprises, such as tax incentives, were further improved, and public service systems for investment and financing, intellectual property, and talent cultivation were continuously optimized.

4.3.1　Fundamental Software

4.3.1.1　Operating System

The operating system is the most critical and fundamental software in a computer, situated above hardware components like the central processing unit (CPU) and memory and beneath various application software, making it the closest software to the hardware layer. Operating systems are classified by the kernel code into open-source systems, such as Linux, and closed-source systems, such as Windows and MacOS. They can also be categorized by the terminal device type into desktop, server, and mobile operating systems. Globally, Linux and Windows dominate the server operating system market. In 2021, of the 13.54 million servers shipped worldwide, 63.47% ran Linux, 36.25% ran Windows, and only 0.28% ran Unix or other systems. In 2022, Linux led China's server operating system market with a market share of 79.1%, followed by Windows with a market share of 20.1%.

The "ZTE Incident"[1] in 2018 underscored the need for China to develop its independent digital ecosystem. As the fundamental layer of computer software, domestic operating systems are vital to creating a secure and independent digital ecosystem for China. Developing these systems is essential. China's domestic operating systems have progressed significantly, moving from being merely "usable" to "user-friendly".

For desktop computers, China has developed over 30 domestic operating systems, most of which are secondary developments based on the Linux kernel. Major manufacturers include Kylin, UnionTech, iSoft, and Euler. These domestic operating systems have been implemented in various sectors, such as party and government, finance, transportation, energy, and telecommunications, and are gradually penetrating core business areas.

For servers, Huawei has developed the Euler open-source operating system

---

[1]　On the evening of April 16, 2018, the US Department of Commerce announced that the US government would prohibit ZTE from purchasing sensitive products from the US companies for the next seven years. From then on, more and more Chinese high-tech companies, such as Huawei, were prohibited to purchase electrical and related products and parts from the US.

(openEuler) tailored for digital infrastructure. OpenEuler is designed for enterprise-level applications such as databases, big data, cloud computing, and AI, supporting Kunpeng and various other processors. As of November 2022, openEuler had been installed on 2.45 million systems, with over 750 000 community users and more than 12 000 contributors in the Euler community.

For mobile terminal devices, Huawei has developed the Harmony operating system (HarmonyOS), which can run on smartphones, computers, tablets, TVs, smartwatches, and other consumer electronic devices and household appliances. According to the globally renowned market research institution Strategy Analytics, HarmonyOS held a 2% market share in global mobile operating systems in 2022, ranking third after iOS and Android. By July 2022, HarmonyOS Connect had over 2 000 partners, and more than 320 million Huawei devices were equipped with the HarmonyOS.

4.3.1.2 Database

The database is the collection of related data. A database management system (DBMS) is system software responsible for building, using, and maintaining databases. It provides key functions such as data definition, organization, storage, management, operation, and maintenance through organizing, indexing, querying, and modifying database files. Based on the deployment method, databases can be categorized into traditional private databases (deployed within enterprises or platforms) and cloud databases (deployed on public clouds). According to iResearch, the total market scale of databases in China reached 28.68 billion yuan in 2021, a 16.1% increase from 2020. From 2021 to 2026, the compound annual growth rate is expected to reach 13.4%.

The areas of China's domestic market feature databases in enterprises like Dameng, KingbaseES, GBASE, and Shenzhou General. These databases can also be deployed on the cloud to serve users. With the rise of cloud computing, cloud-native databases have emerged, offering advantages in leveraging cloud environments, such as Alibaba Cloud's PolarDB and Huawei Cloud's GaussDB. According to iResearch, in 2020, databases deployed on public clouds accounted for 32.7% of the market share by revenue in China. In 2021, Alibaba Cloud's distributed database PolarDB entered Gartner's global database leader quadrant for the first time, ranking third in global cloud database market share.

With the explosive growth of data and increasing application loads, distributed database solutions have become popular for enhancing database access performance. Notable self-developed databases in China include OceanBase and TiDB. OceanBase, a self-developed distributed database initially developed by Alibaba, replaced Oracle in 2014 to support Alipay's core transaction system. OceanBase handled all transaction traffic for the 2015 "Double 11" shopping festival and supported Alipay's core accounting and payment systems in 2016, achieving peaks of 120 000 transactions per second and 175 000 transactions per second. In 2019, OceanBase broke Oracle's nine-year world record in the TPC-C test with 60.88 million tpmC (transations per minute, Concurrent) and set a peak record of 61 million transactions per second during the "Double 11" shopping festival. In 2020, it achieved 707 million tpmC in the TPC-C test.

4.3.2 Cloud Computing

Cloud computing is a kind of pay-by-use model that allows users to access a shared pool of configurable computing resources (including networks, servers, storage, applications, services, etc.) via convenient and on-demand network access. In 2006, Google officially introduced the concept of "cloud computing", with focuses on data services and server infrastructure. Since then, more and more developers and enterprises have adopted cloud computing, leading to the growth of the cloud service industry, primarily centered around IaaS (Infrastructure as a Service), PaaS (Platform as a Service), and SaaS (Software as a Service) delivery models.

The year 2015 marked the beginning of China's cloud computing policy initiatives. China successively issued three policy documents related to cloud computing, covering industry development, industry promotion, application infrastructure, and security management. In April 2022, the MIIT began drafting the "Cloud Adoption Implementation Guide (2022)", aiming to continuously deepen enterprise cloud adoption, further enhance the capabilities and effectiveness of cloud computing applications, and promote high-quality cloud adoption amd application among enterprises.

China's cloud computing market has been growing rapidly. In 2021, the market developed rapidly, with a market scale of 322.9 billion yuan, an increase of 54.4% from 2020. Specifically, the public cloud market scale surged by 70.8% to 218.1 billion yuan, and is expected to drive market growth in the coming years; the private cloud market also surpassed 100 billion yuan, growing by 28.7% to 104.8 billion yuan. China's public cloud IaaS and PaaS segments saw high growth, while SaaS developed steadily. In 2021, the public cloud IaaS market reached 161.47 billion yuan, an 80.4% increase, accounting for nearly 75% of the total market scale. PaaS had the highest annual growth rate at 90.7%, reaching 19.6 billion yuan. The SaaS market grew steadily to 37.04 billion yuan. Figure 4-20 shows China's public cloud market scale and annual growth rate from 2017 to 2021.

The cloud services provided by Chinese enterprises have witnessed rapid development. By 2021, Alibaba Cloud had deployed hundreds of cloud data centers across 25 global regions, with a total of 80 availability zones. Alibaba Cloud's self-developed cloud operating system, Feitian, manages millions of servers worldwide, covering major overseas markets such as Southeast Asia, Japan, Australia, the US, Europe, and the Middle East. According to the Internet Data Corporation (IDC), Alibaba Cloud ranked third in the global public cloud IaaS market in 2020, following Amazon and Microsoft. Gartner's data indicated that Alibaba Cloud was the leader in the Asia-Pacific region in 2020, with a market share equal to the combined shares of Amazon and Microsoft.

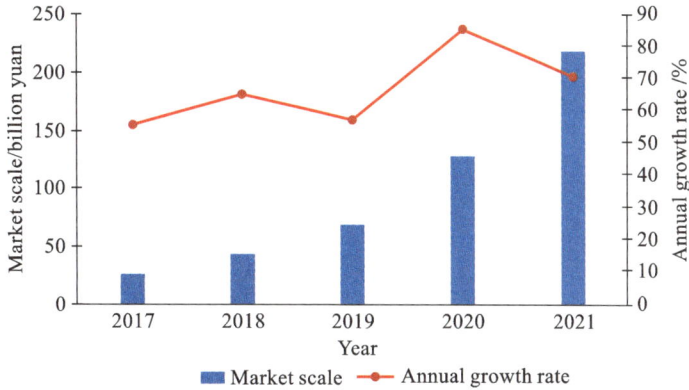

Figure 4-20　China's public cloud market scale and annual growth rate (2017-2021)

Data Source: China Academy of Information and Communications Technology

4.3.3　Big Data

Big data refers to the technologies for processing large volumes of data characterized by volume, variety, velocity, and value. The big data industry, which focuses on data generation, collection, storage, processing, analysis, and services, is a strategically emerging industry. In August 2015, the State Council issued the "Action Outline for Promoting the Development of Big Data", elevating big data to a national development strategy. In 2016, the MIIT released the "Development of the Big Data Industry(2016-2020)", leading to a peak in the development of the big data industry. In recent years, the Chinese government has strategically focused on the digital economy, data element market, and the layout of national integrated big data centers, relevant ministries have issued over 20 big data policy documents, local governments have introduced more than 300 related policies, and big data management institutions have been established in 23 provinces, 14 municipalities with independent planning status and sub-provincial cities, creating a collaborative framework for big data development at both the central and local levels.

It should be specifically pointed out that the Chinese government actively explores the integrated development of the information industry and regional economies. Taking Guizhou Province as an example, it is one of the economically underdeveloped provinces in southwest China. This province is located on the Yunnan-Guizhou Plateau, with 92.5% of the area covered by mountains and hills, and the per capita arable land area in Guizhou Province was only 1.35 mu (1 mu≈666.67 square meters). It was a key province for poverty alleviation by the Chinese government. Guizhou's alpine landform provides an environment with cool climate, sufficient electricity, and low seismic activity, which is suitable for the development of computing power infrastructure such as large-scale data centers. To this end, China proposed the development of Guizhou's big poverty alleviation and big data strategy, and promoted the migration of the domestic big data industry to Guizhou.

The National Big Data Comprehensive Experimental Zone has been carrying out experiments and explorations in areas such as big data system innovation, public data open sharing, big data innovative applications, and big data industry aggregation. In September 2015, Guizhou Province launched the construction of China's first National Big Data Comprehensive Experimental Zone. As of 2022, there had been 11 super-large data centers. In 2017, the People's Government of Guizhou Province signed an agreement with Apple, under which the operation of Apple's iCloud service in Chinese mainland would be undertaken by Yunshang Guizhou Company. At the same time, the construction of Huawei, Tencent, and Apple data centers was initiated one after another. In Guizhou Province, Guizhou Gui'an New District became one of the regions with the largest number of super-large data centers in the world. Big data has become an important tool for Guizhou's economic development. In 2021, the revenue of Guizhou's software and information technology services industry saw a year-on-year increase of 59.3%, the fastest growth rate in China. Notably, cloud services became Guizhou's veritable "first industry", accounting for 46.4% of the revenue of software and information technology services industry from 23.1% in 2020. In 2021, the growth rate of Guizhou's digital economy reached 20.6%, 4.4 percentage points higher than the national average growth rate of China's digital economy. As of 2022, Guizhou had gathered more than 9 000 big data enterprises with an output value of more than 100 billion yuan, attracting tens of thousands of big data talents every year.

In October 2016, the second batch of big data comprehensive experimental zones was approved, including 2 cross-regional zones (Beijing-Tianjin-Hebei region, Pearl River Delta), 4 regional demonstration zones (Shanghai, Henan, Chongqing, Shenyang), and 1 infrastructure coordinated development zone (Inner Mongolia). Additionally, 11 national new industrialization industry demonstration bases in the field of big data were organized. Local governments and enterprises had also been actively promoting the development of the big data industry, establishing over 100 big data industrial parks.

From 2017 to 2021, China's data production increased from 2.3 ZB to 6.6 ZB, accounting for 10.5% of the global total and ranking second worldwide in 2021. The big data industry in China grew rapidly, expanding from 340 billion yuan in 2016 to 1.57 trillion yuan in 2022, with a compound annual growth rate of over 30%. The number of provincial public data open platforms increased from 5 in 2017 to 24 in 2021, and the number of open, valid data sets grew from 8 398 to nearly 250 000. By 2022, 208 provincial and municipal governments had launched government data open platforms, and the national integrated government data sharing hub had released 15 000 types of data resources, supporting over 500 billion sharing calls. The application scope of big data in China was rapidly expanding, with the industry scale achieving significant growth. Figure 4-21 shows China's big data industry scale and annual growth rate from 2016 to 2022.

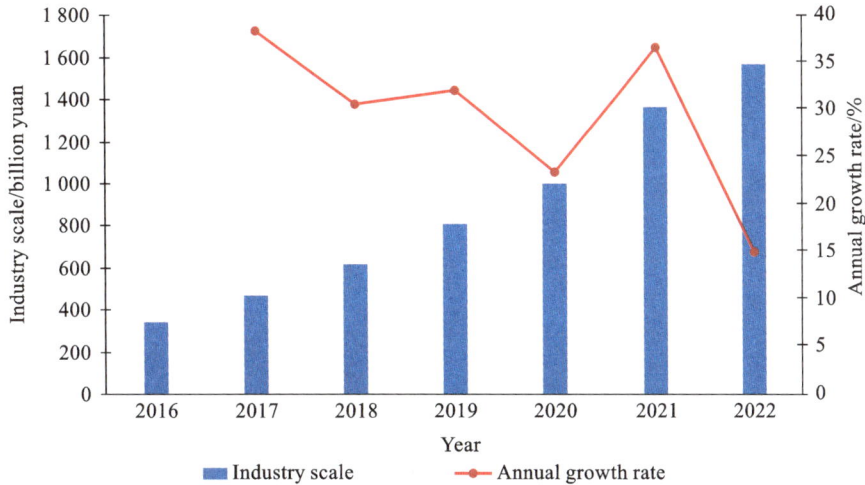

Figure 4-21　China's big data industry scale and annual growth rate (2016-2022)

Data sources: Cyberspace Administration of China, National Data Bureau of China

4.3.4　Artificial Intelligence

AI is a strategic emerging technology that drives the new wave of technological revolution and industrial transformation. The "Guideline of the State Council on Actively Promoting the Internet Plus Action", issued in July 2015, first listed AI development as a key task. In July 2017, the State Council released the "New-Generation Artificial Intelligence Development Plan", elevating the development of AI to a national strategy. In 2019, the seventh meeting of the Central Committee for Deepening Overall Reform approved the "Guideline on Promoting the Deep Integration of Artificial Intelligence and the Real Economy", aiming to leverage AI's integrative nature to advance industrial upgrading. The MIIT issued the "Three-Year Action Plan for Promoting the Development of a New Generation of Artificial Intelligence Industry (2018-2020)" and other policy documents. Additionally, more than 20 provinces, autonomous regions, and municipalities have issued over 60 special plans for AI.

China's innovation capability on AI technology continues to improve. China has a relatively high entry rate in global competitions for intelligent tasks such as computer vision and speech, and has repeatedly refreshed the accuracy record for SOTA model (state-of-the-art model, the best model on one task) of intelligent tasks in global competitions, such as conversational question and answer, reading comprehension, and face recognition. The total number of AI papers, the number of highly cited papers, and the number of invention patents from China are in the first echelon. The AI patents from China increased from 7 968 in 2012 to 80 785 in 2021, accounting for 70.9% of the world's total, ranking first in the world. The published papers on AI technologies in China had increased from 3 423 in 2012 to 26 000 in 2021, accounting for 26.5% of the world's total and ranking first in the world. From the perspective of the subdivision of papers, the themes of China's AI papers are mainly concentrated in the fields of decision-making systems, computer vision, deep learning, intelligent robots, expert systems, fault diagnosis, and neural networks.

The scale of the AI industry in China has been continuously expanding. The industrial ecology has been basically formed, and the overall strength of the industry has been significantly enhanced. As of 2020, the scale of China's AI industry, the number of key enterprises (including the number of unicorn enterprises) were both second only to the US, ranking second in the world, and a relatively complete industrial chain had been established.

In terms of AI computing power infrastructure , China has built the world's largest AI computing power network cluster. Several AI computing centers have been established and put into operation : Pengcheng Cloud Brain Ⅱ , Hengqin Advanced Intelligent Computing Center, Wuhan AI Computing Center, Nanjing AI Computing Center, Nanjing Kunpeng/Shengteng AI Computing Center, Xi'an Future AI Computing Center, Central Plains AI Computing Center, and Chengdu AI Computing Center, etc. Among these centers, the Hengqin Advanced Intelligent Computing Center, built in Zhuhai, Guangdong Province in 2019, is the world's largest AI computing center. The "Intelligent Computing Network", jointly developed by Pengcheng Laboratory and Huawei in June 2022, is a core segment of the first phase of the China's first AI computing power network, marking the full launch of the "China Computing NET" plan. The world's largest integrated AI computing power network has gradually taken shape.

In terms of core AI technologies, several Internet enterprises in China have conducted research on a variety of AI technologies. They have established deep learning institutes, AI labs, and intelligent driving teams, focusing on machine learning, deep learning, image recognition, speech recognition, autonomous driving, etc. Over the past decade, Baidu has launched AI products such as "Intelligent Cloud" and "Baidu Brain". Alibaba began building its AI research institute in 2012 and launched the visual AI platform DT-PAI that integrates its core AI algorithms in 2015. Alibaba also introduced the virtual assistant "Ali Xiaomi" and the ET robot. Additionally, Alibaba has integrated AI with its existing e-commerce, big data, cloud computing businesses and other original businesses, creating intelligent products like warehouse robots, City Brain, E-commerce Brain, Industrial Brain, Alibaba Green Net, and Medical Brain.

In terms of industrial innovation of AI, as of 2022, China had established 8 National New-Generation Artificial Intelligence Innovation Application Pilot Zones and 18 National New-Generation Artificial Intelligence Innovation Development Experimental Zones. The development of AI industry in China has been continuously deepening, showing initial success in integrating with the primary, secondary, and tertiary industries. AI has been expanded from the leading sectors (like healthcare, transportation, and education) to the traditional sectors of manufacturing and agriculture. Intelligent finance, healthcare, security, and transportation have become key application areas for accelerating the AI industrialization. New intelligent products, business models, and format are continuously emerging. Figure 4-22 shows the scale of China's AI industry from 2020 to 2023 and the share of different AI modalities in 2023.

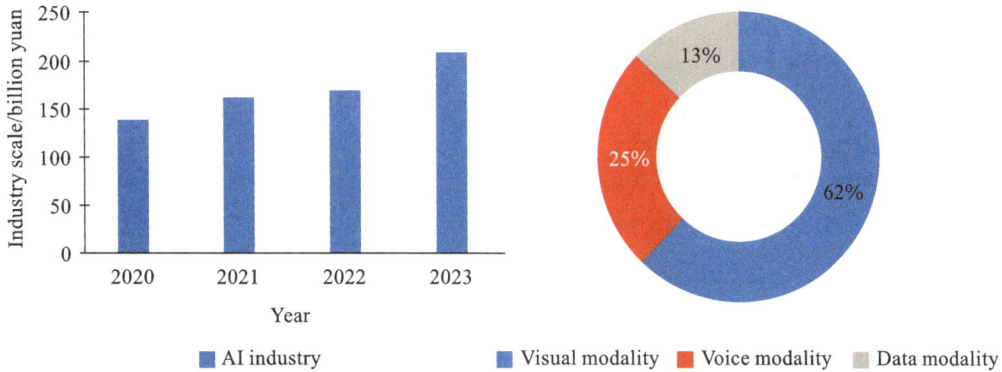

Figure 4-22   The scale of China's AI industry (2020-2023) and the share of different AI modalities in 2023

Data Source: iResearch

4.3.5   Blockchain

Blockchain is a distributed digital ledger that records information and data, stored across multiple participants in a peer-to-peer network. Participants use cryptographic signatures to add new transactions to the existing chain, creating a secure, continuous, and immutable data structure. Blockchain ensures multi-node consensus, transparency, and tamper-proofing, making it an essential technology for protecting data assets. Developing blockchain technology can promote data element rights confirmation, innovate data sharing and openness methods, and establish a robust data regulatory governance system.

Since China listed the development of blockchain in the "Outline of the 13th Five-Year Plan for National Economic and Social Development of the People's Republic of China" in 2016, the country has continuously introduced policies to support the blockchain industry and encourage the application of blockchain technology across various sectors. In the "Outline of the 14th Five-Year Plan for National Economic and Social Development and the Long-Range Objectives Through the Year 2035 of the People's Republic of China", blockchain was listed as one of the seven key industries in the digital economy. The blockchain related research in China has been in the leading position in the world. According to the list of Top 50 Blockchain Papers and Scholars of 2018 presented by the Silicon Valley Insight Research, 30% of the scholars on the list were from the US, and 28% were from China. In 2018, the global blockchain patent applications reached 2 966, with China accounting for 2 435, representing 82.1% of the global total.

The scale of the blockchain industry in China has been steadily growing. Since 2020, provincial governments have been actively promoting blockchain technology, initiating over 90 blockchain projects primarily in government services, justice, traceability, and trade finance, with the application scale continuing to expand. In 2021, the industry scale continued to rise, reaching an annual industry size of approximately 6.5 billion yuan, with an annual growth rate of 34.9%. For example, Hainan Province's blockchain-based "financial electronic invoice" application platform ensures that invoices are trustworthy, verifiable, secure, and supervisable. These invoices enhance tracking and auditing of financial expenditures in public services, preventing duplicate reimbursements. By October 2021, Hainan Province had issued 26.61 million blockchain financial electronic invoices, amounting to over 40 billion yuan, with 2 795 units online, covering 14 fields such as justice, real estate, education, and healthcare. Figure 4-23 shows China's blockchain industry scale and annual growth rate from 2018 to 2021.

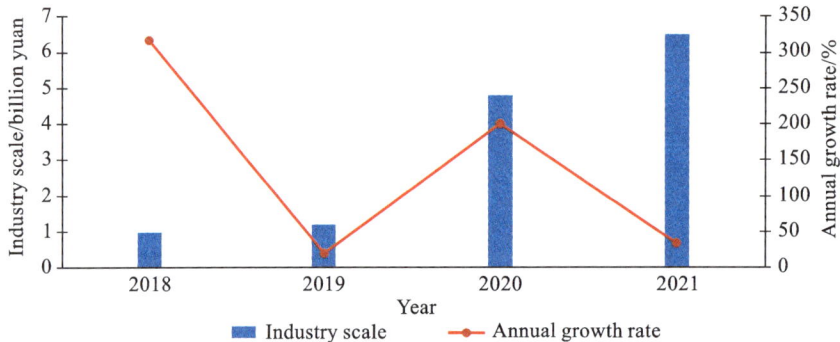

Figure 4-23　China's blockchain industry scale and annual growth rate (2018-2021)
Data Source: China Center for Information Industry Development

4.4　Electronic Information Manufacturing Industry

From 2012 to 2021, the profits of China's electronic information manufacturing enterprises saw remarkable growth, with the annual growth rate increasing from 7.9% in 2012 to 38.9% in 2021; the operating revenue of China's large-scale electronic information manufacturing enterprises increased from 10.7 trillion yuan to 14.1 trillion yuan, surpassing the average growth rate of China's industrial sector. The contribution of this industry to China's industrial production has been significantly strengthened.

From the perspective of electronic product research and development (R&D), China's electronic information manufacturing industry has made continuous breakthroughs in key components and core technologies, with some areas reaching advanced levels in the industry. In the chip sector, the Loongson 3A5000's performance has approaching that of mainstream desktop CPUs. In the storage sector, a production line for the first-generation

10-nanometer 8GB DDR4 product has been established, keeping pace with international DRAM products. In the printer sector, significant progress has been made in laser printing engine core technology, and printing equipment based on Loongson and Phytium chips has been mass-produced and widely used.

From the perspective of technical innovation, the number of invention patent applications of China in the electronic information manufacturing industry has increased rapidly, far exceeding other manufacturing industries. In 2020, it accounted for 27.4% of the number of invention patent applications in the country, which was 14 percentage points higher than that of the second-ranked electrical machinery and equipment manufacturing industry. In the 2021 TOP 10 list of global international patent application enterprises released by the World Intellectual Property Organization (WIPO), Chinese enterprises Huawei, OPPO and BOE were on the list, all of which are electronic information manufacturing enterprises.

From the perspective of industrial cooperation platforms, the Chinese innovative platforms such as new displays and integrated circuits play an important role in tackling key technology problems. At present, China has established institutions such as the National Printing and Flexible Display Innovation Center, the National Integrated Circuit Innovation Center, the National Intelligent Sensor Innovation Center, the National Center of Technology Innovation for Display, and the National Third-Generation Semiconductor Technology Innovation Center. These institutions have rallied the "China Power" in key industrial segments, promoting the innovation of core technologies of integrated circuit (IC) design in China.

4.4.1 Semiconductor Sector

Since 2015, China has intensified its support for the semiconductor industry, with policies and funding being gradually implemented. The "National Outline of Promoting the Development of Integrated Circuit Industry" set policy goals for various segments of the semiconductor industry, including the market scale, materials and equipment, design, manufacturing, and packaging, and offered policy support and tax incentives. The 14th Five-Year Plan emphasized that high-end chips are a "national urgent need and long-term demand", and that integrated circuits are a "fundamental core field crucial to overall development and national security".

According to the NBS, China's semiconductor IC production reached 359.4 billion units in 2021, a 33.3% increase from the previous year. According to the data of the Semiconductor Industry Association of America, Chinese enterprises' market share in the global semiconductor market was 15% in 2021. In 2021, the market scale of China's semiconductor industry was 192.5 billion USD (1.39 trillion yuan), with an annual growth rate of 27.1%. Figure 4-24 shows the market scale and annual growth rate of China's semiconductor industry from 2015 to 2021.

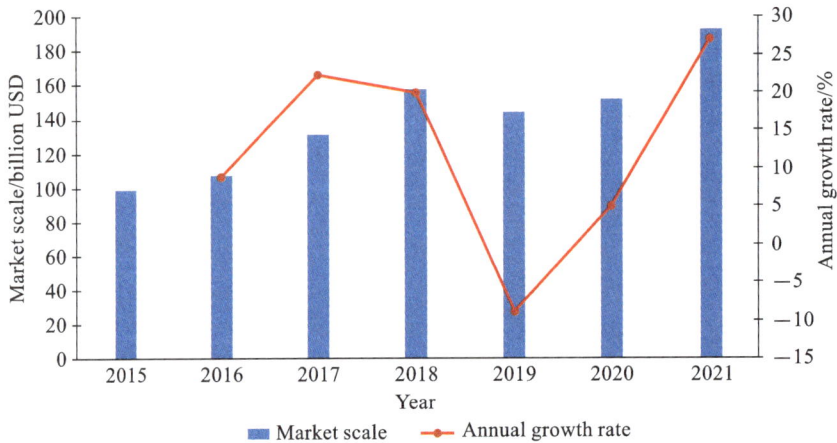

Figure 4-24　China's semiconductor industry market scale and annual growth rate(2015-2021)

Data Source: Insight and Info

4.4.1.1　Semiconductor Material

Semiconductor materials refer to special electronic functional materials, interconnection and packaging materials, processes and auxiliary materials used in the preparation of electronic components, modules and systems. These materials are essential throughout the semiconductor manufacturing process. In wafer manufacturing, significant quantities of silicon wafers, electronic specialty gases, photomasks, and polishing materials are used, while packaging and testing primarily involve packaging substrates and lead frames. Semiconductor materials are crucial in the production of electronic information products, with their process level and quality directly determining the performance of components.

In 2020, the NDRC and other departments issued the "Guiding Opinions on Expanding Investment in Strategic Emerging Industries, Fostering New Growth Areas", aiming to accelerate breakthroughs in high-strength and high-conductivity heat-resistant materials, corrosion-resistant materials, large-size silicon wafers, and electronic packaging materials. China's share of the global semiconductor material market increased annually from 2012 to 2019, rising from 12.28% to 16.67%, ranking third globally. According to the National Bureau of Statistics, the revenue of China's electronic specialty material manufacturing industry grew steadily from 2018 to 2020, reaching 160.94 billion yuan in 2020, with an annual growth rate of 39.39%.

Semiconductor silicon wafers are one of the main materials for wafer manufacturing, and the finished product is called "silicon wafers", which are crucial for manufacturing semiconductors such as integrated circuits. From 2016 to 2018, the market sale of Chinese mainland's semiconductor silicon wafer industry grew from 500 million USD to 996 million USD. China is the largest producer of small and medium-sized silicon single crystals and has led the world in the production of printed circuit boards, copper-clad laminates, magnetic materials, and organic films for three consecutive years. From 2017 to 2020, China invested in silicon wafer production projects and expanded silicon wafer production capacity, with wafer plant capacity growing at a compound annual growth rate of 13%. China's wafer production increased from 2.3 million wafers per month in 2015 to 4.717 million per month in 2020, with an expected 8.583 million wafers per month by 2035. According to Knometa Research, in 2021, Chinese mainland's wafer capacity accounted for 16% of the global total, with the expansion speed of wafer plants in Chinese mainland significantly higher than that of other countries and regions. Figure 4-25 shows China's semiconductor material market scale and annual growth rate from 2015 to 2021.

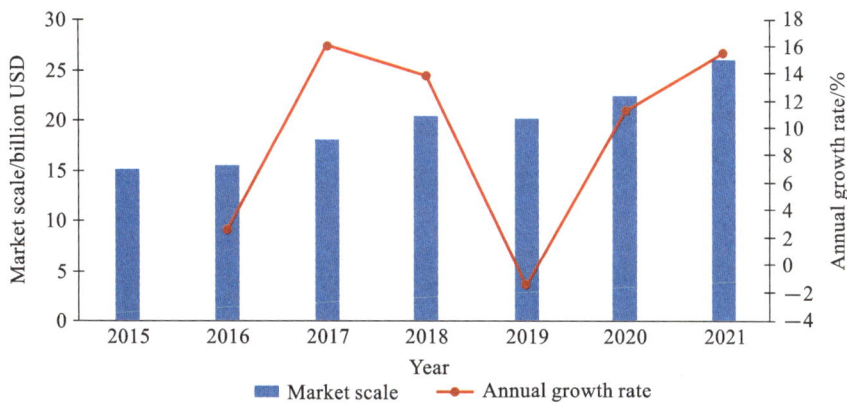

Figure 4-25　China's semiconductor material market scale and annual growth rate (2015-2021)

Data Sources: International Semiconductor Industry Association, qianzhan.com

4.4.1.2　Semiconductor Equipment

Semiconductor equipment, used in the manufacturing and testing processes of chips, encompasses various types of devices, including lithography machines, etching machines, thin-film deposition equipment, ion implantation machines, testing machines, sorting machines, probe stations, and more. Semiconductor equipment needs to stay ahead of semiconductor product manufacturing development. With each new generation of product, there is a need for a more advanced generation of process equipment. Currently, the global semiconductor equipment market has a high level of concentration, with the top 10 enterprises, primarily from the US, the Netherlands, and Japan, monopolizing over 90% of the global market share.

China places significant emphasis on developing semiconductor equipment. The Ministry of Science and Technology (MOST) launched a major project, "Manufacturing Equipment and Complete Process for Very Large Scale Integrated Circuits", bringing together over 200 entities, including upstream and downstream enterprises, research institutions, and universities involved in manufacturing process, equipment, related components, and materials, to collaboratively advance industries, universities, and research institutions. Domestically produced equipment now covers all stages of semiconductor manufacturing, excelling particularly in etching, cleaning, and thin film equipment. Chinese enterprises NAURA Technology Group Co., Ltd ranks among the Top 10 global semiconductor equipment enterprises. According to the International Semiconductor Industry Association, Chinese mainland's semiconductor equipment market scale reached 29.6 billion USD in 2021, representing 29% of the global market, making it the largest market worldwide. The localization rate of semiconductor equipment in China increased from 17% in 2020 to 20% in 2021. The China Electronic Production Equipment Industry Association reported that in 2021, major domestic semiconductor equipment market scale in Chinese mainland reached 38.6 billion yuan, with a localization rate of 20.2%. Figure 4-26 shows China's semiconductor equipment market scale and annual growth rate from 2016 to 2022.

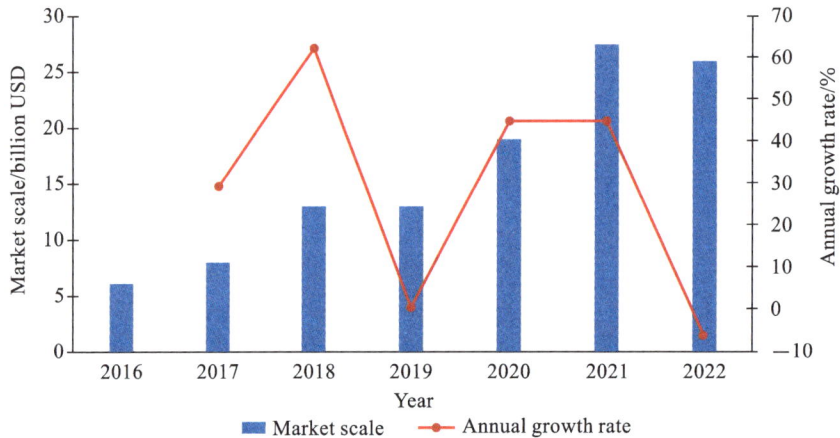

Figure 4-26   China's semiconductor equipment market scale and annual growth rate (2016-2022)
Data source: huaon. com

4.4.1.3 Electronic Components

Electronic components are essential parts of electronic devices and small machines and instruments, and are the general term for electronic devices such as capacitors, transistors, hairsprings, and springs. Electronic components are the cornerstone that supports the development of the information technology industry, and are crucial for ensuring the safety and stability of the industrial chain and supply chain. Taking multilayer ceramic capacitor (MLCC) as an example, the average number of MLCC used per smartphone exceeds 1 000, and each new energy vehicle uses more than 10 000.

China has developed the world's largest and most comprehensive electronic component industrial system, with a nearly complete industrial chain. It leads globally in the production of various electronic components, including electroacoustic devices, magnetic material components, and optoelectronic cables. The industry's overall scale has exceeded two trillion yuan. In December 2019, the annual growth rate of the added value of China's electronic device and electronic specialty material manufacturing industry was 20.7%, while the annual export delivery value decreased by 2.3%. Among the main products, the annual growth rate of the output of electronic devices was 26.9%. In 2019, the annual growth rate of the operating revenue of this industry was 0.3%, while the annual profit declined by 2.1%. Figure 4-27 shows the output scale and annual growth rate of semiconductor discrete devices in China from 2015 to 2020.

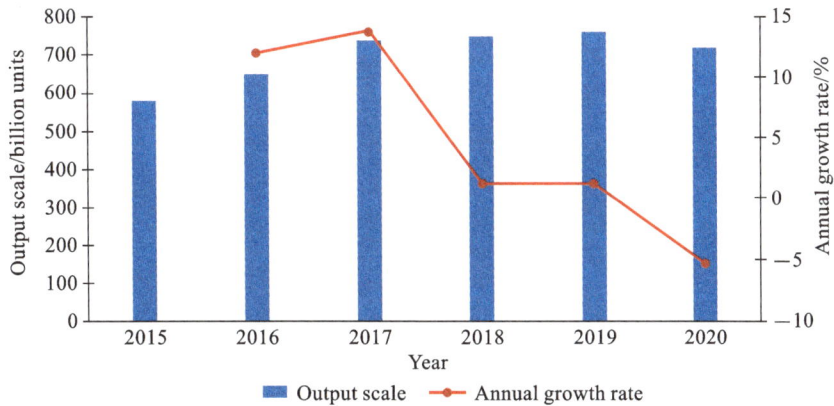

Figure 4-27 China's semiconductor discrete devices output scale and annual growth rate (2015-2020)

Data Sources: National Bureau of Statistics of the People's Republic of China, qianzhan.com

4.4.1.4 Integrated Circuit and Chip

Semiconductors are typically classified into four categories: ICs, discrete devices, optoelectronic devices, and sensors. ICs are miniature electronic circuits integrated onto a small semiconductor chip through specific design techniques and semiconductor processing technology. IC accounts for about 80% of the global semiconductor sales, as the "industrial food", they are the core of the modern information technology industry. The IC industry mainly comprises design, manufacturing, and packaging and testing sectors.

In 2014, the State Council issued the "National Outline of Promoting the Development of Integrated Circuit Industry", making the development of the IC industry a national strategy. In September of the same year, the National Integrated Circuit Industry Investment Fund was established with an initial capital of over 130 billion yuan. In 2020, the State Council released the "Policies for Promoting the High-Quality Development of the Integrated Circuit Industry and Software Industry in the New Era".

Although China's IC industry started relatively late, it has become a key player in the global IC market. According to the China Semiconductor Industry Association, as of the first half of 2020, sales in China's IC industry reached 353.9 billion yuan, with an annual growth rate of 16.1%. From 2018 to 2021, the compound annual growth rate was 17%, over three times the global growth rate during the same period. In 2020, China's IC output reached 261.26 billion units, with an annual growth rate of 29.45%. Figure 4-28 shows China's IC output scale and annual growth rate from 2015 to 2021.

China has made significant strides in enhancing its independent capabilities. With the implementation of national science and technology major projects, the localization

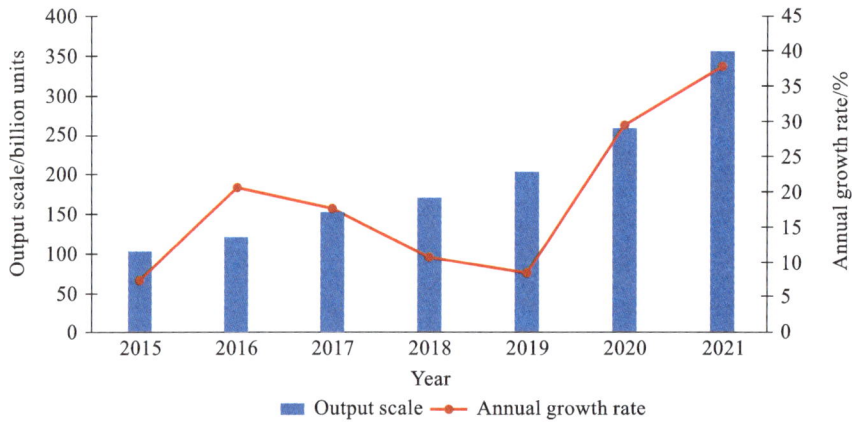

Figure 4-28　China's IC output scale and annual growth rate (2015-2021)

Data Source: National Bureau of Statistics of the People's Republic of China, qianzhan.com

verification efficiency of key IC equipment for mainstream process nodes has increased fourfold. Major equipment such as chemical mechanical polishing machines, dielectric etching machines, and cleaning machines has entered the verification stage for advanced process nodes. The proportion of domestically sourced advanced packaging equipment has reached 79%, saving over 30% in procurement costs. The variety coverage of hundreds of key process materials across seven categories has exceeded 25%, with a localization rate of over 20%.

China's chip design capabilities and innovation levels have also been steadily advancing. As of December 2021, the number of chip design enterprises in Chinese mainland had grown from 2 218 in 2020 to 2 810, with an annual growth rate of 26.7%. In 2020, high-performance processors were widely used in the party, government, and military markets, and China achieved significant breakthroughs in developing large-capacity, high-density 3D NAND flash memory and fourth-generation DDR4 memory products.

In the sector of high-end chips, China has made substantial advancements. Over the past decade, China's domestically produced general-purpose CPUs have evolved from "barely usable" to "fully functional". Domestic embedded CPUs competed directly with foreign products, achieving annual sales of several hundred million units. Domestic 3D flash memory and DRAM have entered mass production, approaching international advanced technology levels. Additionally, domestic FPGA chips have been fully integrated into the communications and entire machine markets. In the field of domestic electronic design automation tools, significant progress have been made, with the development of a series of key tools for both analog and digital circuit design processes.

In the sector of mid-and low-end chips, China have successfully achieved import substitution, fully replacing European and American products. For instance, Jiangsu

Runshi, after four to five years of development, has made significant strides in analog chips. Its products, such as operational amplifiers, comparators, analog switches, and level shifters, can replace those from enterprises like Texas Instruments Inc. (TI), Analog Devices, Inc. (ADI), Microchip Technology Inc. (MICROCHIP), and ON Semiconductor.

4.4.2　New Display Industry

The new display industry is a pioneering and foundational sector. "The 12th Five-Year Plan for National Strategic Emerging Industries" elevated it to a national strategic industry. The NDRC, the MOST, the MIIT, and other ministries have supported the industry with special plans, highlighting key development areas and technological breakthroughs. As the world's largest consumer electronics market, China has also provided momentum for the development of this industry. From 2012 to 2021, China's new display industry transformed from "following" and "running alongside" to "leading", solving the long-standing "few screens" issue. The industry scale and TFT-LCD capacity have both reached global leadership. Figure 4-29 shows China's new display industry scale and annual growth rate from 2017 to 2022.

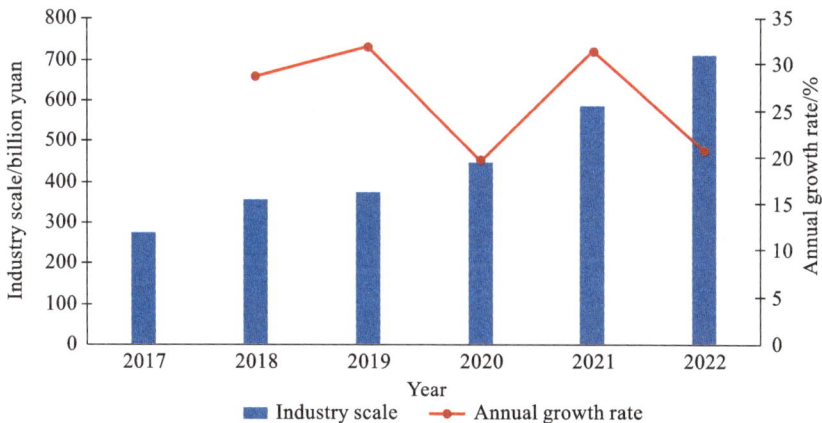

Figure 4-29　China's new display industry scale and annual growth rate (2017-2022)
Data Source: China Optics and Optoelectronics Manufactures Association

China has developed a complete new display industry chain centered on panel manufacturing. The industry's total revenue grew from 74 billion yuan in 2012 to approximately 510 billion yuan in 2021, with a compound annual growth rate of over 20% over the past decade. In 2021, the overall revenue from China's display support field surpassed 100 billion yuan, ensuring a secure and stable supply chain for the new display industry. China leads the global market in five major panel applications: mobile phones, televisions, tablets, laptops, and monitors. From 2013 to 2022, China's average annual shipments of smartphones, tablets, and television reached 391 million units, 22.03 million units, and 45.95 million units, respectively.

Significant breakthroughs have been made across various technical routes in the new display industry. In terms of intelligent property rights, China has become the largest source of panel technologies, and as of 2021, the number of applications of China's panel patents had accounted for 35% of the global total. Enterprises like BOE, Wuhan CSOT, and Shenzhen CSOT were in the top 50 global international patent applicants in 2021. Technological innovations such as mini-LED and Dual Cell backlight adjustment, and quantum dot color solutions have achieved large-scale production in large-size LCD products. Technologies like low-power adaptive frequency modulation, under-screen fingerprint recognition, under-screen cameras, and Pol-less display have been successfully integrated into medium-and small-size OLED products. Domestically produced flexible OLED screens have entered the supply chains of several global high-end flagship brands.

4.4.3　Electronic Manufacturing Industry

4.4.3.1　Computer

Electronic computer manufacturing industry produces various computer systems, peripheral equipment, terminal equipment and other related devices. As physical components and devices have evolved, not only have computer mainframes been updated and replaced, but their external devices have also continually evolved.

China is the world's largest producer of computer products. In 2021, China's electronic computer output was 485.464 million units, with an annual growth rate of 19.8%. The southwest China produced 219.2221 million units, accounting for 45.05% of the national total. The output included approximately 230 million laptops, 70 million desktops, and many other devices such as tablets, workstations, and industrial control terminals. According to the International Data Corporation, the top 5 vendors in China's electronic computer market in 2021 were Lenovo (32.8%), HP (15.6%), Dell (14.0%), Huawei (10.4%), and Apple (7.3%). Figure 4-30 shows China's electronic computers output scale and annual growth rate from 2016 to 2021.

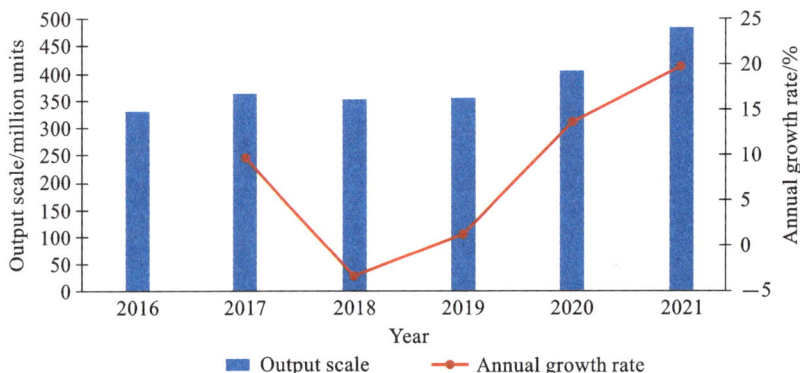

Figure 4-30　China's electronic computers output scale and annual growth rate (2016-2021)

Data Source: National Bureau of Statistics of the People's Republic of China

In the server market, China's server shipments have been steadily increasing, reaching an estimated 3.91 million units in 2021, which was 28.9% of the global total, with an annual growth rate of 11.7%. Inspur, Lenovo, and Huawei are the leading server manufacturers in China. Inspur has become a core member and standard advocate of the three major global open computings organizations: ODCC, OCP, and OPEN19 Fundation. With a business presence in 120 countries and regions, Inspur held a 9.4% share of the global server market in 2021, ranking second worldwide.

4.4.3.2 Communications Equipment

The communications system equipment manufacturing industry involves producing equipment necessary for constructing communications systems, including fixed and mobile communications access, transmission, and switching equipment. This includes providing transmission, access, and bearer network solutions for operators and enterprise customers. Communications terminal equipment includes audio, graphic image, video, data, and multimedia communications terminals.

In terms of communications system equipment, several government departments have issued policies to support and regulate the development of the communications equipment manufacturing industry in recent years. These policies address 5G network construction, terminal IPv6 upgrades, "double gigabit" network infrastructure, and industrial Internet construction. According to the "China Electronic Information Industry Statistical Yearbook 2019", from 2014 to 2019, the operating revenue of China's large-scale communications equipment manufacturing industry continuously grew. The MIIT reported that in 2020, the operating revenue of China's communications equipment manufacturing industry grew by 4.7% year-on-year.

In terms of communications terminals, China has the world's most complete mobile phone industry chain. Over the decade from 2012 to 2021, Chinese enterprises focused on terminal equipment manufacturing, leading to the rapid rise of domestic mobile phone brands. In 2012, China produced 1.18 billion mobile phones, primarily using a low-price strategy. By 2021, this number grew to 1.66 billion, making China the world's largest producer of information and communications terminals. According to Counterpoint Research, China accounted for 67% of the global mobile phone production in 2021. Xiaomi ranked third globally with shipments of 1.903 million units, capturing a global market share of over 14% and capturing three of the top five positions in the global smartphone market along with OPPO and Vivo. According to the International Data Corporation, China's smartphone shipments reached 340 million units in 2021, with an annual growth rate of 13.33%. The China Academy of Information and Communications Technology reported that domestic brand shipments totaled 304 million units, with an annual growth rate of 12.6%, and 5G phones accounted for 266 million units, with an annual growth rate of 63.5% in the same period, making up 75.9% of total shipments. Figure 4-31 shows China's smartphone shipments and annual growth rate from 2011 to 2021.

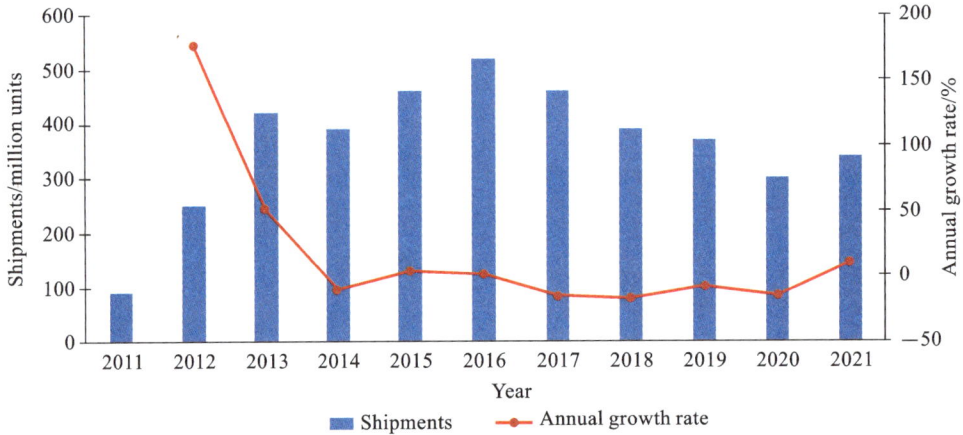

Figure 4-31　China's smartphone shipments and annual growth rate (2011-2021)

Data Sources: Ministry of Industry and Information Technology of the People's Republic of China, International Data Corporation

Huawei (including Honor) used to hold a market share of 46%; however, affected by the trade war initiated by the US in 2018, Huawei's smartphone market share was significantly impacted. The brand of Honor was then forced to be independent. In response to the US chip supply cut-off, Chinese smartphone manufacturers began to strengthen technological innovation and started developing their own chips. Vivo introduced the V1 imaging chip, OPPO launched a 6nm NPU chip for imaging, and Xiaomi released the Surge C1 and Surge P1 to enhance imaging and charging performance. According to International Data Corporation, the top five smartphone vendors in China by shipments in 2021 were Vivo, OPPO, Xiaomi, Apple, and Honor.

4.4.3.3　Consumer Electronics

From 2017 to 2022, China held the position of the world's largest goods trading nation for six consecutive years, leading the world in the production of over a hundred types of products. In 2021, China's home appliance industry generated prime operating revenue of 1.73 trillion yuan, with an annual growth rate of 15.5%, and profits of 121.8 billion yuan, with an annual growth rate of 4.5%. Sub-sectors such as refrigeration products, air conditioners, and kitchen appliances all saw double-digit growth in prime operating revenue. In 2021, China's home appliance export value exceeded 100 billion USD, with products sold in over 160 countries and regions, reaching more than 2 billion households worldwide. The global market share of Chinese-made refrigerators, air conditioners, washing machines, televisions, and small home appliances popular among young people all exceed 50%.

The home appliance industry's development trend was shifting from single-product intelligence to whole-house intelligence. From 2012 to 2021, the market scale of China's smart small appliances grew from 262.1 billion yuan to 379.3 billion yuan, with an annual growth rate of 45%. Wearable device shipments soared from 2.3 million units to 140 million units, a 60-fold increase. In 2020, China's smart home market shipped about 201 million units, and in the first half of 2021, smart home device shipments reached approximately 100 million units, with an annual growth rate of 13.7%. The International Data Corporation predicted that China's smart home device market would continue to grow, with shipments reaching 540 million units by 2025. Figure 4-32 shows China's home appliance retail sales and annual growth rate from 2012 to 2021.

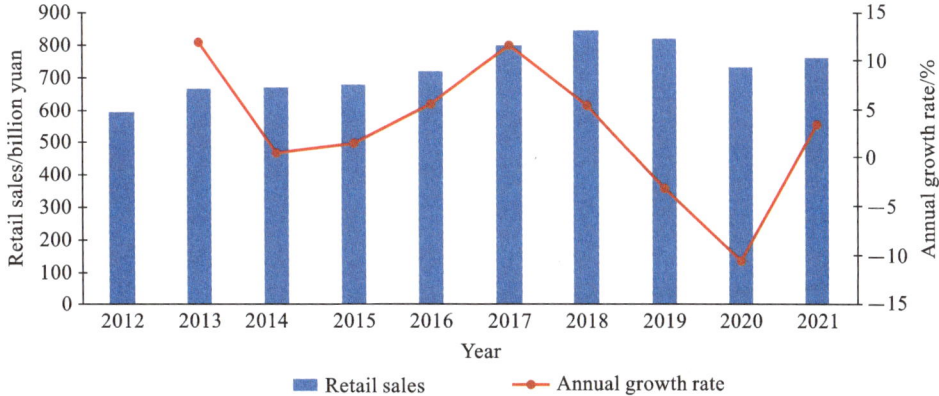

Figure 4-32　China's home appliance retail sales and annual growth rate (2012-2021)

Data Source: All View Cloud

China has the world's largest home appliance manufacturing base. In 2020, Haier operated 14 R&D centers, 122 manufacturing centers, and 108 marketing centers globally, forming an extensive R&D resource-sharing network that includes shared modules, reusable technologies, and some shared patents. Haier Smart Home topped the 2020 "Global Smart Home Invention Patent Rankings" with 2 034 patents, holding the global first place for the fourth consecutive time. In 2020, Midea had around 200 subsidiaries, 28 R&D centers, and 34 major production bases worldwide, including 18 overseas R&D centers, employing over 15 000 R&D personnel. By the end of 2020, Midea's cumulative patent applications exceeded 160 000, with over 62 000 granted patents.

4.5　Summary

In the era of the booming digital economy, the traditional ICT industry is accelerating its transformation and upgrading, deeply integrating into the digital economy wave, and gradually developing into a key industry covering new digital products and cutting-edge digital technologies. China uses the concept of "digital industrialization" to summarize the development connotation of the ICT industry in the new situation of the digital economy. It involves multiple fields, including fundamental telecommunications industry, the Internet industry, software and information technology services industry, and electronic information manufacturing industry.

In the field of fundamental telecommunications industry, China gives full play to the guiding role of policies and the demonstration and leading role of state-owned enterprises, and continuously promotes the optimization and upgrading of the national communications network infrastructure. In the construction of Internet infrastructure, China has built the world's largest optical fiber broadband network, ranking first in the world in the number of IPv6 addresses and active users. In the field of mobile communications, China took the lead in breaking through 5G technology and built the world's largest 5G mobile network. The number of 5G base stations in China accounts for more than 60% of the global total. The construction of the satellite Internet is advancing steadily. Many types of satellites have been successfully launched and networked, and low-orbit satellite network projects are being carried out as planned. At the same time, China has also made significant progress in the IoT and the IoV. It has built the world's largest mobile IoT and established many IoV application demonstration bases. The advanced and cost-effective communications network infrastructure has not only greatly improved the quality of people's daily lives but also laid a solid foundation for the widespread and in-depth promotion of various information-based applications.

The Internet industry is regarded by China as an important engine for promoting high-quality economic development and transformation and upgrading. The Chinese government actively creates a favorable policy environment, encourages various market players to carry out Internet innovation activities, and vigorously promotes the in-depth application of the "Internet ＋" strategy in various fields. At the level of Internet applications, China shows strong competitiveness in fields such as e-commerce, social entertainment, and fintech. China's online retail value has ranked first in the world for many years. The instant messaging has a large user base, with over one billion monthly active users. The short-video industry is developing rapidly, with a user scale of more than one billion. Short-video platforms have become a new and important channel for digital marketing. In addition, China leads the world in online payment application scale. Mobile payment, with its convenience and efficiency, has profoundly changed people's payment habits. Alipay actively expands its global business and provides high-quality financial services to over 1.2 billion users worldwide. Relying on the booming Internet industry, new business forms and models such as the sharing economy, short-video platforms, and live-streaming e-commerce have emerged in an endless stream, strongly promoting the prosperous development of China's real economy.

As a strategic emerging industry, the software and information technology services industry has received high attention and strong support from the Chinese government. Through a series of industrial policies, China fully promotes the independent and controllable development of this industry and continuously improves the software innovation system. In the field of basic software, China has made a series of key breakthroughs, successfully developing many basic software products with independent intellectual property rights. These products cover areas such as server, personal computer, mobile terminal operating systems, as well as distributed databases, and have achieved large-scale applications in many industries. In emerging information technology fields such as cloud computing, big data, AI, and blockchain, Chinese enterprises are actively innovating and have launched a series of advanced technologies and products. The cloud computing market maintains rapid growth, and the competitiveness of public cloud services in the international market is constantly increasing. The big data industry is booming, and China's data sharing level ranks among the top in the world. The AI field has rich innovation achievements, and the industry scale continues to expand. Blockchain technology R&D is at the world-leading level and has already seen large-scale adoption in many fields such as finance. The rapid development of the new software and information technology services industry has injected continuous innovation vitality into the informatization construction of various industries.

As an important pillar of China's manufacturing industry, the electronic information manufacturing industry, with its complete industrial system, produces a large number of electronic devices and products globally. At the same time, China actively promotes the industrial upgrading of high-end manufacturing industries such as IC. In the semiconductor field, Chinese enterprises have faced difficulties and continuously overcome key technological "bottleneck" problems. They have made significant breakthroughs in semiconductor materials, equipment, IC, etc., and achieved the import substitution of most mid- to low-end products. In the field of new displays, Chinese enterprises have achieved a leap from following to leading in technology, built a complete industrial chain, and ranked among the top in the world in terms of industry scale and the number of technical patents. In the manufacturing fields of computers, communications equipment, and consumer electronics, China not only has strong manufacturing advantages but also continuously improves its technological innovation ability. China's electronic information products and technologies are widely exported around the world, providing global consumers with a wide variety of product choices.

In recent years, China has achieved remarkable development achievements in the fields of fundamental telecommunications industry, the Internet industry, software and information technology services industry, and electronic information manufacturing industry. The advanced network infrastructure has a wide coverage, building a high-speed channel for information circulation. Innovative applications in the Internet field emerge in an endless stream, shaping a convenient and efficient lifestyle and consumption pattern. The technological breakthroughs and product innovations in the software and information technology services industry provide strong support for the digital transformation of various industries. The industrial upgrading and technological progress in the electronic information manufacturing industry have enhanced China's position in the global industrial chain. These achievements have significantly improved China's social outlook: convenient network communications allow people to enjoy instant access to information anytime and anywhere; applications such as mobile payment and e-commerce simplify the consumption process; short-videos and instant messaging enrich people's social and entertainment lives. At the same time, these achievements have also played a crucial role in promoting China's overall economic development. They have given birth to a large number of new business forms and models, created numerous job opportunities, promoted the transformation and upgrading of the real economy, and driven the coordinated development of related industries, thereby serving as an important engine for promoting high-quality economic development in China, and serving an advantage for China in the global digital economy competition.

5　Industrial Digitalization

Industrial digitalization refers to the application of information and communications technology (ICT) and data resources to increase output and improve efficiency in traditional industries. Over the past decade, China has actively promoted the digitalization process of various industries and facilitated industrial upgrading through digital transformation. This chapter focuses on the current status and achievements of China's digital development in industries such as manufacturing, agriculture, energy, and transportation.

5.1　Intelligent Manufacturing

China is a manufacturing powerhouse and has maintained the title of the "world's factory". From 2012 to 2021, the value-added by China's manufacturing industry increased from 16.98 trillion yuan to 31.4 trillion yuan, with its global share rising from 22.5% to nearly 30%. China consistently holds the position of the world's leading manufacturing nation. The number of industrial and information technology brands from China entering "The World's 500 Most Influential Brands" increased from 10 to 24 during this period.

China's manufacturing industry is comprehensive, comprising 31 major categories, 179 subcategories, and 609 minor categories, making it the most complete and integrated manufacturing sector globally. In May 2015, the State Council released the "Made in China 2025" plan, aiming to promote the integrated development of industrialization and informatization through the "Internet Plus" initiative. In April 2021, the Ministry of Industry and Information Technology (MIIT) issued the "14th Five-Year Plan for the Development of Intelligent Manufacturing", outlining goals of achieving comprehensive digitalization and networking for large-scale manufacturing enterprises by 2035, with key industry leaders achieving basic intelligence.

5.1.1　Industrial Internet

Industrial Internet, as an emerging industry pattern and application model resulting from the deep integration of new-generation information technology and the manufacturing industry, is a crucial foundation for achieving the digital transformation of industries. With the convergence of ICT and the industrial sector, industrial equipment becomes increasingly networked, industrial software becomes more intelligent, and industrial manufacturing becomes more collaborative, leading to the emergence of various new applications in industrial manufacturing. In November 2017, the State Council launched the "Guidance on Deepening the Development of 'Internet Plus Advanced Manufacturing' to Promote the Development of the Industrial Internet". In December 2020, the MIIT issued the "Industrial Internet Innovation and Development Action Plan (2021-2023)", proposing 5 aspects, 11 key actions, and 10 major projects to address deep-seated issues in the development of the Industrial Internet.

The depth and scope of the Industrial Internet platform system continues to expand. Currently, China's comprehensive, distinctive, and professional Industrial Internet platform system is continuously improving. As of December 2021, China had over 150 influential Industrial Internet platforms and a total of over 76 million connected devices; benchmark comprehensive Industrial Internet platforms had significantly led the way, with 15 enterprises accelerating the construction of cross-industry, cross-domain platforms to support the development of industrial enterprises. Specialized Industrial Internet platforms focuses on in-depth industry cultivation, forming a differentiated development pattern. Professional Industrial Internet platforms are accelerating their development, covering specific areas such as digital twins, industrial intelligence, industrial big data analytics, edge computing, and remote monitoring.

In terms of the industrial Internet identification and resolution system, in June 2020, the China Academy of Information and Communications Technology (CAICT) was authorized by the International Association for Automatic Identification and Mobile Technology (AIM Global), and became an international code issuer alongside large international organizations such as the International Article Numbering Association, the Institute of Electrical and Electronics Engineers, and the Universal Postal Union. It was assigned the code "VAA" and has the capability to issue global identification codes. In January 2021, the Data Identifier Management Committee (DIMC), the sole global management organization of the data identifier list, formally approved the exclusive international data identifier "15N" for the Industrial Internet identification and granted it to the CAICT for management and maintenance, which has a significant impact on the international promotion of the Industrial Internet identification.

Efforts have been made to implement the digital transformation of the manufacturing industry and the intelligent manufacturing project , creating an upgraded version of the integration standardization of industrialization and informatization. As of October 2022, over 57 000 enterprises in China had participated in the integrated management system standardization , with over 1 500 pilot demonstration projects in digitalized, networked, and intelligent manufacturing; the number of industrial apps had reached 283 200; over 300 national standards and 42 international standards for intelligent manufacturing had been released; nearly 100 suppliers with prime operating revenue exceeding one billion yuan had been nurtured, covering over 90% of manufacturing sectors such as automobiles, textiles, and pharmaceuticals.

5.1.2　Industrial Robot

The robotics industry in China is experiencing vigorous growth, injecting robust momentum into economic and social development. During the 13th Five-Year Plan period, China's robotics industry has demonstrated a positive trend through continuous innovation and deepened applications. The industry's scale has rapidly expanded, with a compound annual growth rate of approximately 15%. In 2020, the operating revenue of the robotics industry surpassed 100 billion yuan, production of industrial robots reached 212 000 units; and the robot density in the manufacturing industry reached 246 units per 10 000 employees, nearly double the global average.

The core competitiveness of the robotics industry continues to improve. China has overcome some technical challenges in core components such as reducers, controllers, servo systems, and the core components have been gradually localized. Taking the reducer as an example, the Y series harmonic reducer made by Leader Harmonious Drive Systems Co., Ltd., based on the principle of triple harmonic reduction, has significantly enhanced torsional rigidity and transmission accuracy. The application of machine vision technology has significantly improved the degree of flexibility and automation in industrial production. For example, Zhongke Xinsong Co., Ltd. combines machine vision with collaborative robots to provide stable and continuous three dimensions (3D) vision flexible positioning for collaborative robot operations.

Industrial robots have penetrated into complex and precise scenes. They are more flexible after integrating the flexible force control characteristics, realizing the application of higher precision and stronger sensitivity, and their popularization and application in complex and precise scenes such as assembly, grinding, and riveting have been accelerated. Chongqing Huashu Robot Co., Ltd., targeting computer, communications, and consumer electronic products (3C products), has introduced precision processing robots equipped with independently developed high-performance servo motors and control technology. These robots focus on breaking through typical processes in the entire production of notebook computers, achieving full-process robot production, and applying a complete set of automated factory systems.

5.1.3　Intelligent Factory

5.1.3.1　Electronics Manufacturing

Realizing flexible production and manufacturing to improve production capacity. Huawei, in cooperation with China Mobile, has realized flexible production and manufacturing using 5G technology at the Huawei South Factory in Songshan Lake,

Guangdong Province (see Figure 5-1). The original mobile phone production workshop required 90 000 meters of wiring, with an average of 186 devices per production line. The production line is upgraded and adjusted every six months with the update of new mobile phone models, and all the network wires in the workshop are rearranged, with each adjustment requiring a two-week work stoppage. Through the integration of 5G and the Industrial Internet, Huawei South Factory has realized wireless connection of the existing machines, reflow ovens and dispensing machines of the production line through the 5G network, and shortened the adjustment time of each production line from two weeks to two days.

Figure 5-1　Huawei: Songshan Lake mobile phone production base

Image Source: Huawei

Implementing on-site assisted assembly to accelerate assembly efficiency. Haier, in cooperation with China Mobile, utilized 5G technology to realize on-site assisted assembly of precision industrial equipment in Qingdao City, Shandong Province. Haier's Qingdao Washing Machine Factory built a connected factory based on 5G MEC (mobile edge computing) and carried out 5G remote-assisted assembly based on augmented reality (AR) glasses. Workers collect on-site videos of key industrial equipment by wearing AR glasses, and at the same time retrieve product installation instructions from the back-office system and push them to the AR glasses to realize efficient assembly. Workers can also contact remote experts through the 5G network to realize remote guidance.

Deploying machine vision for quality inspection to enhance automated detection. Gree, in collaboration with China Unicom, utilized 5G technology in Guangdong Province to implement machine vision quality inspection. Gree established an industrial virtual private network in its assembly workshops to realize the integration of the production control network with the production management network. By utilizing 5G network, the content to be inspected is automatically photographed, and the photo and video streams can be uploaded to the machine vision quality inspection application deployed on the MEC platform; by leveraging graphics processing unit (GPU) arithmetic resources and data models, real-time comparison and analysis inspections can be conducted, realizing the automatic identification of equipment; the quality inspection system then performs the operation of separating defective products (see Figure 5-2).

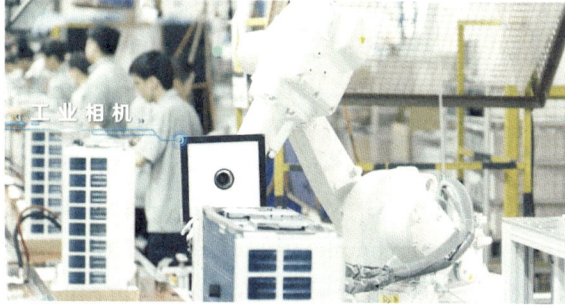

Figure 5-2   Gree: machine vision quality inspection application

Image Source: Gree

5.1.3.2 Equipment Manufacturing

Creating factory-area smart logistics to promote logistics development. Foton Motor, in cooperation with China Unicom, built a super truck factory in Zhucheng of Weifang City, Shandong Province, and realized factory-area smart logistics using 5G networks. In the scheduling link of inbound vehicles, Foton Motor developed an inbound synergy system integrating virtual electronic fences, automatic vehicle recognition, vehicle detection and other technologies, and used 5G technology to transfer real-time information such as the status of vehicle parking in the factory to a variety of intelligent display terminals and information systems, realizing paperless receipt of goods.

Collaborating on research and development (R&D) and design to accelerate the R&D process. Commercial Aircraft Corporation of China, Ltd. (COMAC) cooperated with China Unicom to carry out the construction of the project of "5G Plus Industrial Internet Enabling Intelligent Manufacturing of Large Aircraft" in Shanghai Pudong New Area. Based on 5G network services, COMAC supports cross-region, real-time online collaboration and remote diagnosis during the R&D and experimental phases of products through real-time uploading of AR data (see Figure 5-3), which has realized issue identification in R&D and design and compressed the time cost of R&D experiments.

Figure 5-3   COMAC: AR glasses assisted assembly remote diagnosis

Image Source: Xinhua News Agency

Facilitating collaborative equipment operations to enhance scheduling efficiency. Sany Heavy Industry, in cooperation with China Telecom and Huawei, carried out the construction of "5G plus Industrial Internet" private network project in Beijing, and 5G technology has been deeply integrated with the production process of machinery manufacturing to realize the cooperative equipment operation. The workshop network has been built through 5G technology, and the 3D images and status information of the automated guided vehicle (AGV) are transmitted based on the 5G network with large bandwidth and low latency; the 5G MEC platform and GPU arithmetic integration capability are utilized to reduce the complexity and cost of the single-machine function of the automatic guided vehicle and improve the efficiency of production scheduling.

5.1.3.3　Steel Production

Realizing remote equipment control and improving operational efficiency. Hunan Valin Steel Group Co., Ltd. (Valin Steel) cooperated with China Mobile to realize the remote control for overhead cranes and slag-adding robotic arms based on 5G technology in Hunan Province (see Figure 5-4). By utilizing 5G's large uplink and download speed, operators can control the unloading of overhead cranes, lifting and loading slots, and overhauling operations in the remote control room in real time, ensuring the accuracy and real-time nature of remote control and improving operational efficiency.

Figure 5-4　Valin Steel: remote control of overhead cranes and robotic arms
Image Source: China News Network

Implementing machine vision quality inspection to improve monitoring efficiency. Anshan Iron and Steel Group Co., Ltd. (Ansteel) cooperated with China Mobile to carry out the constructing of the project of "R&D and Application of 5G-based Machine Vision Strip Steel Surface Inspection Platform" in Liaoning Province (see Figure 5-5). The 5G network is deployed to transmit the collected high-definition image data from the cold rolling site to the platform in the operation room, and then the platform's visual AI analysis capability is leveraged to process and analyze the images, realizing the real-time detection of surface defects on strip steel. After the deployment of the program, the detection rate of conventional defects in strip steel has been improved, reducing the downtime of strip breakage and injured roll change caused by defects in strip steel.

Conducting equipment fault diagnosis to enhance predictive accuracy. Baoshan Iron & Steel Co., Ltd. (Baosteel) cooperated with China Unicom to carry out the construction of

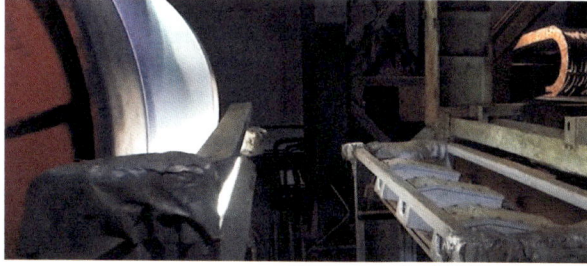

Figure 5-5 Ansteel: machine vision strip steel surface defect detection
Image Source: *Ansteel Daily*

the project of "5G Plus Industrial Internet High-Quality Network and Public Service Platform for Process Industry" in Zhanjiang City, Guangdong Province, and realized the fault diagnosis of continuous casting rolls, fans, and other equipment by utilizing 5G technology (see Figure 5-6). Through the 5G network, equipment data are transmitted in real time to relevant systems for equipment fault diagnosis. Utilizing artificial intelligence (AI) and big data technology, the project can predict equipment lifespans, reducing the workload associated with on-site wiring and improving the predictive accuracy of equipment lifespans.

Figure 5-6 Baosteel: remote industrial control
Image Source: *Zhanjiang Daily*

5.2 Smart Agriculture

China, as a prominent agricultural powerhouse, ranks among the world leaders in agricultural production. Despite this, the per capita agricultural resource of China is relatively scarce. At the end of 2019, China's arable land area was 1.918 billion mu, while the per capita arable land area was only 1.36 mu, which is less than 40% of the world average. At the same time, the spatial distribution of China's arable land resources is uneven, the overall quality is not high, and more than half of China's arable land relies on the natural conditions.

Since 1949, China has elevated its agricultural development through scientific breeding, water conservancy projects, and the widespread adoption of agricultural machinery, achieving self-sufficiency in the three staple foods. With less than 9% of the world's arable land, China produces approximately 25% of the world's grain output, sustaining nearly 20% of the global population and garnering remarkable achievements.

In recent years, China has implemented various policies to promote the modernization of agricultural science and technology, including the "14th Five-Year Plan for National Agricultural and Rural Informatization Development", the "13th Five-Year Plan for Agricultural Science and Technology Development", and the "Digital Agriculture and Rural Development Plan (2019-2025)". Starting from 2011, the Chinese government has allocated funds from the central fiscal budget to support the implementation of the National Internet of Things Application Demonstration Project's smart agriculture initiatives at the local level.

In February 2021, the "Opinions of the Central Committee of the Communist Party of China and the State Council on Comprehensively Advancing Rural Revitalization and Accelerating Agricultural and Rural Modernization" was issued, emphasizing the development of smart agriculture. Smart agriculture involves the deep integration of modern information technologies such as the Internet, the Internet of Things (IoT), big data, cloud computing, and artificial intelligence with agriculture. This integration facilitates a new agricultural production model characterized by agricultural information perception, quantitative decision-making, intelligent control, precise input, and personalized services. Smart agriculture relies on the support of information technology, utilizing high-tech solutions and scientific management to maximize resource efficiency.

5.2.1　Agricultural Big Data

China has successfully established a comprehensive agricultural geographic big data platform. The Ministry of Agriculture and Rural Affairs (MARA) has built platforms for geographic information public services, government data sharing, and agricultural and rural big data. The national three-dimensional "One Map" of natural resources continues to be improved, and results of delineations for arable land and permanent basic farmland, ecological protection redlines, and urban development boundaries (the "Three Lines") have been mapped and stored (see Figure 5-7). Various business data layers related to agriculture and rural areas have been constructed, forming a "One Base Map ＋ N Agricultural Special Application Maps" model. This enables hierarchical presentation, intuitive comparison, and dynamic tracking of data with fine granularity and visualization. A three-dimensional investigation system for new types of crops, covering "space, sky, and land", has been initially established. This system allows for the accurate acquisition of data on major crops' sowing areas, spatial distribution, and crop growth conditions, etc.

Efforts have been made to enhance the early warning and monitoring of significant natural disasters in agriculture. The meteorological information warning and agricultural

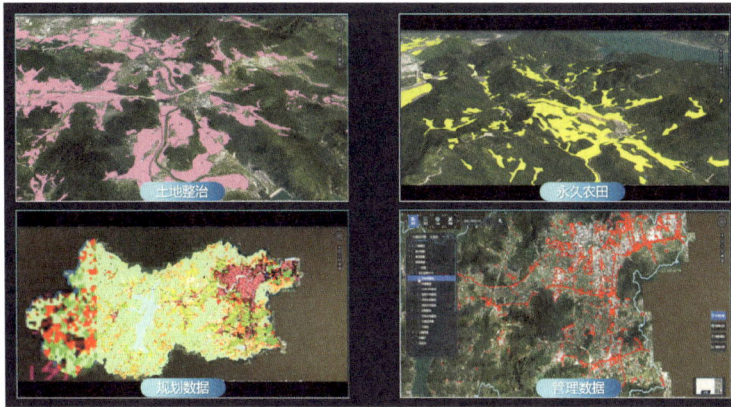

Figure 5-7　Three-dimensional display of natural resources (land remediation, permanent farmland, planned data, etc.)

Image Source: Taizhou Bureau of Natural Resources and Planning

situation dispatch system played a crucial role in addressing the flood disaster during the 2021 autumn-winter planting season and the meteorological drought in the Yangtze River Basin in 2022. Monitoring of agricultural non-point source pollution and irrigation water usage has been comprehensively strengthened, with a total of 3 882 monitoring points for agricultural non-point source pollution control sections as of June 2022. The national digital monitoring and early warning system for major crop diseases and pests has been continuously improved, with integration into 22 provincial platforms and more than 4 000 IoT devices. This system provides robust support for the effective detection and control of major crop diseases and pests such as wheat stripe rust, rice brown planthopper, and fall armyworm.

China has initiated agricultural product market monitoring and early warning systems. A series of big data analysis application centers for the whole industrial chain of single agricultural products have been established. Efforts have been intensified in constructing an agricultural monitoring and early warning system, improving the analysis system for the balance between agricultural product supply and demand, and guiding various market entities to explore and innovate the application of agricultural and rural big data. Pilot projects for the whole industrial chain big data construction of 15 varieties in eight categories, including soybeans and apples, are steadily progressing. The information data platform for hog products has gone online, providing data for the whole pork industry chain. A data channel has been established on the MARA website, issuing the Agricultural Product Wholesale Price 200 Index. The analytical and judgment capabilities for the agricultural product market have significantly improved.

China has implemented traceability systems for the quality and safety of agricultural products and agricultural supplies. The National Agriculture Food Quality Safety Traceability Management Information Platform has achieved connectivity with 31 provincial platforms and agricultural reclamation platforms. The "Compliance and Qualification

Certificate plus Traceability Code" model has been promoted, enabling full-process traceability from field to table. As of June 2022, 465 000 production and operation entities had completed registration on that platform. The "Sunshine Agriculture Safety" pilot program was underway in five provinces, contributing to the continuous improvement of the agricultural product quality and safety traceability system. The informatization management of agricultural supplies such as pesticides, veterinary drugs, and fertilizers have been comprehensively promoted. As of August 2022, the Pesticide Digital Supervision & Management Platform of China had achieved 100% traceability with a "one bottle, one code" system for pesticide products nationwide.

5.2.2 Smart Cultivation

Guided by the MARA, modern ICT is rapidly applied in the field of crop cultivation, witnessing widespread adoption of technologies and equipment such as precision sowing, variable-rate fertilization, smart irrigation, environmental control, and agricultural unmanned aerial vehicle (UAV). By the end of 2021, China had established nine agricultural IoT demonstration provinces, implemented 100 digital agriculture pilot projects, and collected and released 426 agricultural IoT application achievements and models of reducing costs and increasing efficiency.

Agricultural UAV has gained extensive application in agriculture. Compared with manual labor or traditional machinery, UAV demonstrates significant advantages in tasks such as crop seeding (pollination), pesticide spraying, fertilization, as well as monitoring crop growth and detecting pests and diseases. China has become the world's largest user of agricultural UAV. In 2020, approximately 150 million mu of arable land in China utilized crop protection and remote sensing UAV operations, accounting for 8.3% of the country's arable land area, surpassing Japan's UAV-operated area by 100 times. According to data from the MARA, over 30 000 UAVs were put into use during the spring planting season in 2021. As of 2022, the national inventory of crop protection UAV reached 121 000 units, with an annual operation of 1.07 billion mu. Figure 5-8 shows the application of a 5G network-connected crop protection UAV developed by Chongqing Academy of Agricultural Sciences.

Unmanned agricultural machinery and equipment have achieved widespread application. As of 2022, the accuracy of the BeiDou Navigation Satellite System (BDS) terminal for agricultural machinery has been improved to two meters; over 600 000 tractors and combine harvesters had been equipped with BDS-based operation monitoring and intelligent control terminals, with more than 100 000 tractors featuring auxiliary autopilot systems; the data platform had aggregated 20 billion agricultural machinery comprehensive data from 490 000 agricultural machinery BDS terminals, enabling real-time collection and dynamic display of national agricultural machinery operation data. In 2021, the operation area served by BDS in China exceeded 60 million mu. Specifically, Heilongjiang Reclamation Area built six smart (unmanned) farm clusters, and had modified and

Figure 5-8   5G network-connected crop protection UAV developed by Chongqing Academy of Agricultural Sciences

Image Source: Red Star News(left), Xinhua net(right)

upgraded a cumulative total of 6 288 unmanned and assisted driving machinery in paddy and dry fields, with a demonstration operation area of 6.08 million mu, and an average yield increase of 3% to 5% per mu. Figure 5-9 shows the scenes of BDS-assisted unmanned rice transplanter and unmanned harvester in Hongwei Farm of Beidahuang Group.

Figure 5-9   BDS-assisted unmanned rice transplanter and unmanned harvester used in Hongwei Farm of Beidahuang Group

Image Source: *Heilongjiang Daily*

The IoT-assisted precision farming has also been applied on a large scale. In the Smart "Wuhu Rice" Production Demonstration Base in Wuhu City, Anhui Province, the rice production process is divided into 13 stages, including sowing, transplanting, tillering, etc. Additionally, 49 smart decision points, such as variety selection, land leveling, and nitrogen fertilizer usage, are identified. The base has established a dual-drive technology system with "smart agronomy + intelligent agricultural machinery", enabling information perception, quantitative decision-making, and intelligent operations throughout the entire cultivation cycle (see Figure 5-10). In 2022, the test area expanded to 150 000 mu, and the test results showed an average annual increase of 14.3% per mu, nitrogen fertilizer savings of 32.5%, phosphorus fertilizer savings of 16.8%, medicine reduction of 38.0%, and an average income increase of about 500 yuan per mu. According to statistics, in 2021, the informatization rate of China's field cultivation was 21.8%, of which the production informatization rates of wheat, rice, cotton and corn were 39.6%, 37.7%, 36.3% and 26.9%, respectively.

Figure 5-10 Paddy field sensors and its automatic irrigation system used in the Smart "Wuhu Rice"
Production Demonstration Base in Wuhu City, Anhui Province
Image Sources: *Wuhu News* (left), Wanjiang Pearl Network (right)

5.2.3 Smart Farming

Modern ICT has been widely used in the whole process of livestock and poultry farming. In 2021, the informatization rate of livestock and poultry farming in China reached 34.0%, with the informatization rates for hog and poultry farming being 36.9% and 36.4%, respectively. Comprehensive information platforms for animal husbandry and feed and fresh milk quality supervision systems had achieved comprehensive supervision over more than 180 000 large-scale pig farms, more than 4 200 fresh milk acquisition stations, over 5 800 transportation vehicles, 300 or so ranches, and approximately 13 000 feed production enterprises holding licenses. Various types of farms had increased labor productivity by over 30% through the application of unmanned environmental control platforms, automatic inspection and alarm systems, intelligent feeding systems, etc., reducing costs by approximately 150 yuan per head of slaughtered hog.

Smart farms has realized intelligent monitoring of farming environments and individual behaviors of livestock and poultry. For instance, in the fully automated unmanned "future pig farm", 5G-enabled mobile patrol robots scan pig pens back and forth, displaying real-time data such as pig body temperature and pen temperature on a large screen. The "future pig farm" has achieved intelligent, digital, and unmanned management throughout the entire process of hog farming. The average annual production of market pigs per sow increased from 18.5 heads in conventional farming methods to 26.5 heads, achieving an efficiency increase of 43.2%. The labor requirement for 2 500 hogs decreases from 4 people to 0.8 people, saving 80% of labor. The total water consumption of the farm has been reduced by 60%. Figure 5-11 shows the "future pig farm" in Shimen Town, Tongxiang City, Zhejiang Province.

The fishery industry has been promoting factory farming, rice-shrimp farming, and aquaponics models based on digital technology. In 2021, the informatization rate of China's aquaculture was 16.6%, of which the production informatization rates of crabs, shrimps, fishes, and shellfishes were 23.6%, 21.6%, 20.9%, and 6.0%, respectively. Coastal

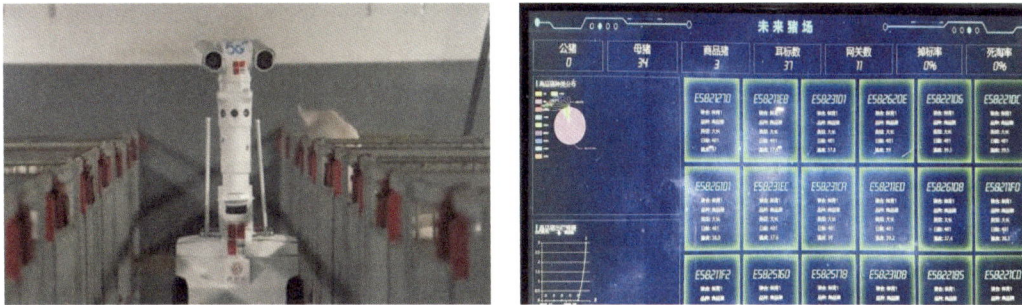

Figure 5-11 The "future pig farm" in Shimen Town, Tongxiang City, Zhejiang Province

Image Source: Guangming Net

provinces have been continuously carrying out the deployment of equipment such as BeiDou and Tiantong satellite terminals for marine fishing vessels. Leveraging the dynamic monitoring management system for fishing vessels, China has built a comprehensive "one map" of national marine fishing vessel dynamic positions, creating a complete database for "fishing vessels + ports + crew, nearshore + offshore" fishing activities, providing strong support for off-season fishing bans and fishing vessel supervision.

In Pukou District, Nanjing City, Jiangsu Province, the entire process from production to distribution, and then to consumption of freshwater shrimp has been digitized to create an industry system based on order production, transparent supply, and trusted consumption. A digital freshwater shrimp farming system has been established to achieve online perception of farming environments, real-time regulation of water dissolved oxygen, and precise feeding. This has improved water quality, increased stocking density from 100 000 to 120 000 per mu, raised production by 20%, reduced labor input by 150 yuan per mu, and saved 200 yuan per mu in inputs. The survival time of freshwater shrimp during storage and transportation has increased from 1 hour to 10 hours, with a survival rate of over 98%. The entire system has reduced more than 15% of labor costs in farming, saved more than 20% in storage, processing, and logistics distribution costs, and increased farming income by more than 15%. Figure 5-12 shows the digital fishery in Pukou District, Nanjing City, Jiangsu Province.

Figure 5-12 The digital fishery in Pukou District, Nanjing City, Jiangsu Province

Image Sources: njdaily. cn (left), Media Center of Pukou District (right)

5.3 Smart Energy

China stands as a significant player in both energy production and consumption. It has fundamentally established a multi-faceted energy production system propelled by coal, oil, gas, electricity, nuclear power, new energy, and renewable energy. In 2019, China's primary energy production reached a substantial 3.97 billion tons of standard coal, making it the world's leading energy producer. The cumulative installed capacity of hydropower, wind power, and photovoltaic power ranked first globally, while the capacity of nuclear power plants in operation and under construction ranked second worldwide. During the 13th Five-Year Plan period, China continually optimized its energy structure, achieving remarkable success in the low-carbon transformation. The proportion of coal consumption decreased to 56.8%, with installed capacities for conventional hydropower, wind power, solar power, and nuclear power reaching 340 million kilowatts, 280 million kilowatts, 250 million kilowatts, and 50 million kilowatts, respectively.

In response to environmental challenges such as global warming, the world's 178 contracting parties signed the Paris Agreement in 2016. On September 22, 2020, Chinese President Xi Jinping declared at the General Debate of the 75th United Nations General Assembly that China would enhance its nationally determined contributions, adopt more robust policies and measures, and strive to peak its carbon dioxide emissions before 2030 and achieve carbon neutrality by 2060. Driving the digitalization and intelligence of the energy industry has been regarded as a pivotal strategy to guarantee China's carbon peaking and neutrality goals. In 2020, China introduced the new infrastructure initiative, encompassing ultra high-voltage power transmission lines, new energy charging stations, and other energy infrastructure, and emphasized the establishment of smart energy infrastructure. The "14th Five-Year Plan for Modern Energy System", released by the National Development and Reform Commission (NDRC) and the National Energy Administration (NEA) in January 2022, advocates for the digitalization of energy infrastructure, promoting the digital transformation of the energy industry and enhancing the application of new information technologies, including next-generation ICT, AI, cloud computing, blockchain, the IoT, and big data, in the field of energy.

5.3.1 Intelligent Coal Mine

In February 2020, eight ministries of the Chinese government jointly issued the "Guiding Opinions on Accelerating the Intelligent Development of Coal Mines", which emphasized the need to leverage ICT to establish intelligent systems with comprehensive perception, real-time interconnection, analytical decision-making, autonomous learning, dynamic prediction, and collaborative control. The objective was to achieve the intelligent operation of various processes in coal mining, including exploration, excavation, transportation, ventilation, washing and selection, safety assurance, and business management, in order to enhance coal mine safety production levels and ensure stable coal supply. By 2035, it envisioned the comprehensive implementation of intelligence across various coal mines, constructing integrated intelligent systems across multiple industry chains and systems, ultimately establishing intelligent coal mine systems characterized by intelligent perception, intelligent decision-making, and automatic execution.

The level of information infrastructure in the coal industry has significantly advanced. Operational networks in factory areas has transitioned from hundred-megabit and gigabit industrial Ethernet Ring to networks exceeding 10 gigabits, even reaching 100 000 gigabits. Underground wireless communications systems has evolved from the deployment of 3G and 4G networks to the integration of 5G, Wi-Fi 6, F5G (fifth-generation fixed network), and other converged network communications. Personnel positioning systems underground has upgraded from radio-frequency identification (RFID) interval positioning to ultra-wideband sub-meter precision positioning. In June 2020, the first 5G intelligent coal mine in the country was completed at Shanxi Xinyuan Coal Mine. In 2023, over one hundred coal mines nationwide had implemented 5G networking and applications, continuously deepening applications such as remote control of coal mining and driving face, panoramic video stitching, open-pit coal mine autonomous driving, AR intelligent inspections, and remote diagnostic.

Autonomous driving technology has been deployed in open-pit coal mines. The Inner Mongolia Dayan Coal Industry Co., Ltd. conducted the "Demonstration Project of 5G plus Autonomous Trucks in Open-pit Coal Mines under Extremely Cold and Complex Climate Environment". The operating speed reached an industry-leading 40 kilometers per hour, with an autonomous system availability exceeding 96.7%, and the comprehensive efficiency of autonomous transport not lower than that of manned driving. This project marked the first 5G network unmanned driving project in China's open-pit coal mines, the first project for unmanned transformation of over 200-ton-level vehicles, and the first project to achieve all-weather three-shift unmanned formation operation. As of the end of 2021, China had 146 unmanned driving vehicles in open-pit coal mines. Figure 5-13 shows the "unmanned mining truck" of the Inner Mongolia Dayan Coal Industry Co., Ltd.

Progress has been made in the connected transformation of mining equipment. In 2021, the China Energy Investment Co., Ltd. and Huawei released MineHarmony, the first Industrial Internet operating system in the mining sector, in Beijing. As of November 2022, more than 3 300 sets of equipment had been deployed in 13 coal mines and 1 coal washing plant, and the applications supported include intelligent control of equipment, unmanned inspection of fixed places, and online upgrading of equipment. The MineHarmony system utilized 5G＋AI video splicing technology to achieve remote control; it also utilized 5G to send back images of the main transport belt in real time, with AI

Figure 5-13　The "unmanned mining truck" of the Inner Mongolia Dayan Coal Industry Co.,Ltd.

Image Source：ccoalnews.com

algorithms identifying anomalies such as lumps of coal and anchors, so as to achieve full-time monitoring, which could reduce the number of inspection personnel in the underground by 20%. Figure 5-14 shows the scene of MineHarmony system assisting coal mines to realize intelligent inspection.

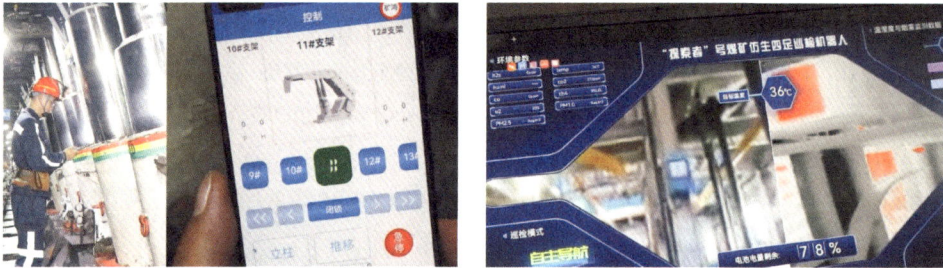

Figure 5-14　Huawei's Industrial Internet operating system "MineHarmony" assists coal mines in realizing intelligent inspection

Image Source：Wisdom Valley Trend

5.3.2　Smart Power Plant

In March 2023, the "Opinions of the National Energy Administration on Accelerating the Digitalization and Intelligence Development of Energy" was released, outlining the acceleration of clean and low-carbon transformation in power generation through the application of digital and intelligent technologies. The document emphasized expediting the digital design, construction, and intelligent upgrading of traditional power sources such as thermal power and hydropower, along with promoting the development and application of intelligent decentralized control systems. The concept of the "smart power plant" was introduced, where a new type of power plant is formed by integrating various systems with information technology, intelligent control technology, and power generation industry technology, based on the physical power plant.

Significant progress has been achieved in the intelligent transformation of thermal power plants. Traditional coal-fired thermal power remains a cornerstone of power generation in China, contributing approximately 71.13% to the country's total electricity generation in 2021, with a year-on-year growth of 8.4%. The Guodian Inner Mongolia Dongsheng Co-generation Power Co., Ltd. deployed a coal-piling robot in July 2019. The 3D laser unmanned coal-piling robot, equipped with a flexible guide rail system on the coal bin ceiling, created a 3D model of the coal pile in the coal yard. This achieved unmanned, intelligent patrolling through 3D laser unmanned coal-piling, requiring only five minutes for inventorying an entire coal yard. In 2020, the plant established a plant-level 5G network, achieving downstream rates of 350 Mbps, upstream rates of 160 Mbps, and bidirectional latency of less than 15 ms within the thermal power plant area, utilizing unmanned robots to enable comprehensive coverage of production and high-risk sites, providing a versatile inspection operation with multiple business and operation mode functionalities. Figure 5-15 shows the "intelligent thermal power plant" of Dongsheng Co-generation Power.

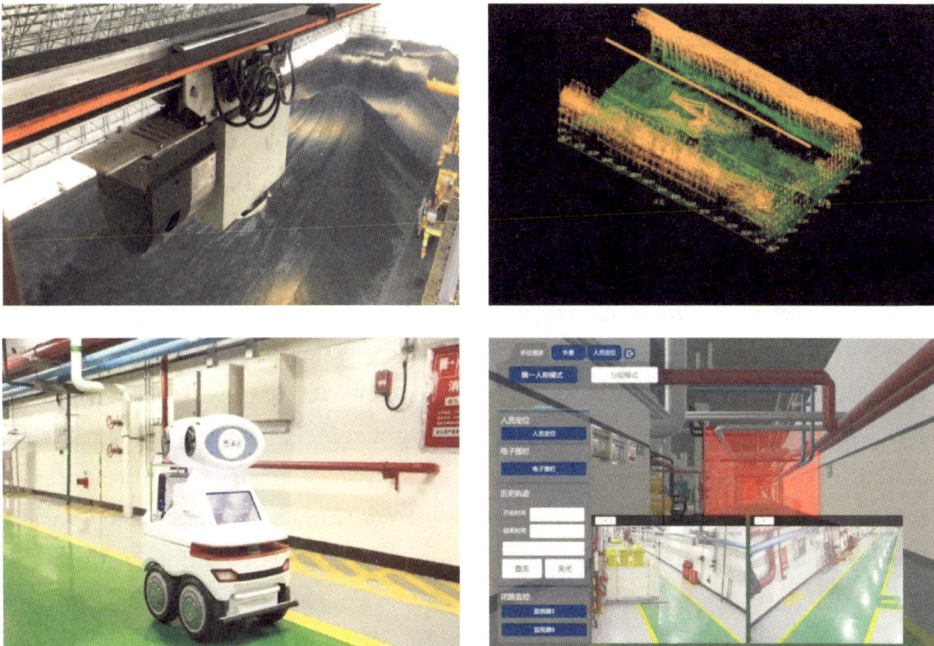

Figure 5-15 Dongsheng Co-generation Power's "intelligent thermal power plant"
Image Sources: National Energy Investment Group (top), National Energy Voice (bottom)

Substantial progress has been made in the digitization of offshore wind farms. Typically located 20-120 kilometers offshore, offshore wind farms cannot be adequately covered by onshore mobile communications base stations. Previous communications in offshore areas primarily relied on satellite or narrowband private network communications, supporting only basic voice and simple data collection business requirements. In December 2022, State Power Investment Corporation Limited's Jieyang Shenquan II offshore wind power project in Jieyang, Guangdong Province, smoothly achieved full-capacity grid connection, boasting the world's largest single-unit capacity in a mass-applied offshore wind power project, with a total installed capacity of 502 MW. In collaboration with Huawei, China Mobile (Guangdong Province) deployed and activated two 5G base stations at the offshore booster station, 25 nautical miles from the coastline. This enabled network coverage for an area exceeding 1 000 square kilometers, approximately 20-50 kilometers offshore, with download speeds exceeding 100 Mbps and network latency below 40 ms. 5G technology facilitated high-definition video surveillance, offshore inspection, intelligent dispatching, and other applications in offshore wind farms. Figure 5-16 shows a 5G offshore wind farm in Jieyang City, Guangdong Province.

Figure 5-16   5G offshore wind farm in Jieyang City, Guangdong Province, China
Image Sources: *China Daily* (left), Huawei (right)

5.3.3   Smart Power Grid

There is a significant geographical imbalance between China's energy resources and demand. Over 80% of energy resources are concentrated in the western and northern regions, while over 70% of energy consumption is concentrated in the eastern and central regions, which necessitates large-scale, long-distance, and efficient electricity transmission. Long-distance and cross-regional electricity transmission requires precise regulation of the electric grid. The strategic goal of a "strong smart grid" was introduced in May 2009, with an emphasis on using ultra-high-voltage (UHV) grids as the backbone, coordinating the development of various levels of grids, and featuring characteristics of informatization, automation, and interaction. By the end of 2017, all planned UHV projects, known as "four crosses and four straights", were fully operational. These UHV projects, generally originating in resource-rich western and northern regions and terminating in the central and eastern regions, successfully met the growing electricity demand in load centers. By the end of 2020, China had essentially completed the construction of a strong smart grid, with technology and equipment reaching international advanced levels.

In March 2023, the "Opinions of National Energy Administration on Accelerating the Digitalization and Intelligence Development of Energy" was released, advocating for the use of digital and intelligent technologies to support the construction of new power systems. The document encouraged the digital presentation, simulation, and decision-making of physical power grids, explored the application of AI and digital twins in intelligent decision support and control of power grids, and enhanced the intelligent level of multi-energy complementary joint scheduling in the power system. Currently, China is accelerating the transformation from digitalizing the power grid towards evolving into an Internet of energy.

Visualization is a key aspect of planning and construction. The State Grid Corporation of China (State Grid) focuses on key areas such as production, operation, and service, melds various business systems and data, and realizes diagnosis of grid problems on the map, intelligent generation of planning, online review of projects, intelligent preference of plans, and automatic generation of reports. As of 2022, the production domain digitalization of China Southern Power Grid covered 933 application links in 68 application scenarios for four specialties of power generation, transmission, substation, and distribution (see Figure 5-17). In terms of power transmission, a 3D digital twin covering over 1.3 million kilometers had been constructed, achieving over 250 000 kilometers of autonomous flight routes and accumulating an AI training sample library of over 400 000 graphics cards, reducing defect analysis time from 15-30 days to a few hours. In terms of power transmission, remote automatic control of substations had been implemented, achieving "unmanned and remote operation" of substations and improving the operating efficiency of substation equipment by 30%.

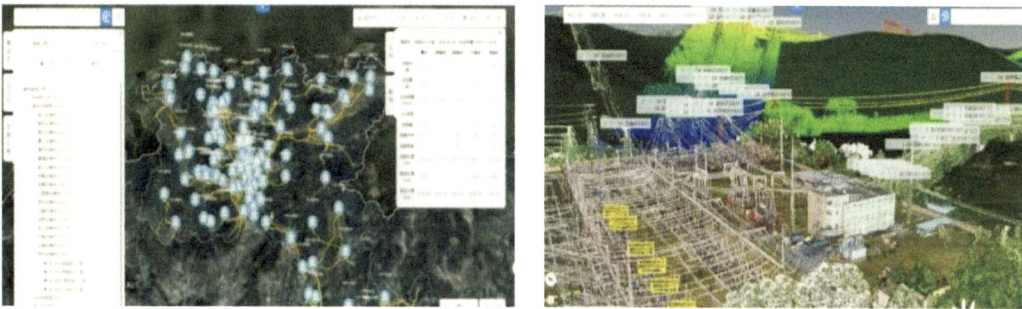

Figure 5-17 China Southern Power Grid: digital twin of the main 110 kV and above transmission network
Image Source: China Southern Power Grid

Production and operation have become increasingly intelligent. The State Grid has strengthened the digital control of grid scheduling and operation, and production and inspection. A new-generation scheduling technical support systems have been developed to achieve holographic perception of power grid operation status, observable and controllable generation-load resources, and efficient operation of scheduling tasks, supporting the safe operation of large power grids. In the field of operation and inspection, UAV for autonomous inspections have been widely promoted, enabling automatic identification of equipment inspection images, some regions have employed UAV with fire-extinguishing capabilities to clear foreign objects from power lines; intelligent inspections of substations (converter stations) have reduced the average inspection time in operational UAV substations (converter stations) from 120 minutes for human inspections to 40 minutes for machine inspections, forming a "machine-centric, human-assisted" inspection model (see Figure 5-18).

Figure 5-18   State Grid: UAV and unmanned vehicle involved in facility operation and inspection
Image Sources: The Paper(left), State Grid(right)

The autonomy of power equipment is emphasized. Power chips provide the underlying core support for the development of the power industry and are the most crucial components in power control systems. However, the domestication rate of core chips in equipment such as power transmission, transformation, and distribution remains relatively low. Since 2013, the level of domestic production of power hardware-level chips in China has been continuously improving. By the end of 2019, the "Fuxi" chip sample developed by the China Southern Power Grid was successfully delivered. It is based entirely on domestic instruction set architecture and domestic core, with comprehensive performance 1.5 times that of similar imported products. The "Fuxi" chip has been successfully applied in nearly 30 categories of devices, including power transmission, power distribution, new energy, and edge computing (see Figure 5-19). In 2021, Shenzhen deployed 340 pieces of power equipment across eight categories, including charging piles, energy meters, and concentrators, with the "Fuxi" chip.

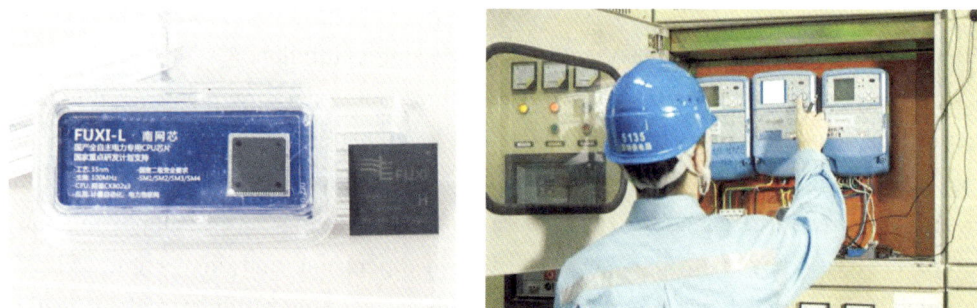

Figure 5-19   China Southern Power Grid deploys domestic power specialized master control chip "Fuxi" in power grids
Image Sources: *People's Daily* (left), *Yangcheng Evening News* (right)

Digitalization of electricity services has been promoted. The State Grid has built the world's largest new energy cloud platform, providing one-stop services for new energy planning and construction, trading and settlement, etc. It has also built the world's leading smart Internet of Vehicles (IoV) platform with the widest coverage, the largest number of accessed charging piles, and the collaborative development of vehicles, changing piles, and power grid, providing convenient and intelligent charging and exchanging services for the travel of new energy vehicle owners. Furthermore, it has built one-stop services for household photovoltaic (PV) power station construction, grid connection, and settlement in the whole process, relying on the online platforms such as the "Online State Grid" APP and the new energy cloud, thus enhancing its ability to serve customers (see Figure 5-20).

Figure 5-20　"Online State Grid" APP allows users to handle services such as household PV power generation and new energy meters

Image Sources: State Grid (left), Ningbo Publishing (center), *Zhejiang News* (right)

5.4　Intelligent Transportation

Since 1949, China has consistently prioritized and considered transportation infrastructure as the cornerstone and focal point of national economic development. It has constructed the world's largest transportation infrastructure. By the end of 2021, the total mileage of roads in China had reached 5. 28 million kilometers, with the national expressway[①] spanning 117 000 kilometers, ranking first globally. As of July 2022, the highway network, mainly composed of national expressways, has covered 98.8% of urban areas, cities with populations exceeding 200 000, and prefecture-level administrative centers, connecting approximately 88% of county-level administrative regions and about 95% of the population. By the end of 2022, the total operating mileage of the national railway reached 155 000 kilometers, with high-speed railway[②] covering 42 000 kilometers,

---

① Expressway refers to the multi-lane highways exclusively designed for vehicles to travel in separate directions and lanes, with fully controlled access. The speed limit is typically 60-120 km/h in China.

② High-speed railway refers to the closed rail transit system that supports the operation of high-speed trains and the operating speed is usually 250-350 km/h in China.

ranking first globally in high-speed railway mileage; a total of 53 cities had implemented urban rail transit projects, accumulating an operational mileage of 9 584 kilometers, with subways accounting for more than 8 000 kilometers, ranking first in the world; inland waterways had a navigable distance of 128 000 kilometers. In 2022, China's waterways completed a freight volume of about 8.55 billion tons, with the Yangtze River mainline exceeding 3 billion tons, maintaining its position as the world's leading inland water transportation for over a decade. China's ports handled a cargo throughput of 15.68 billion tons, with Chinese ports occupying 8 out of the top 10 global ports and 7 out of the top 10 container ports in the world.

Simultaneously, the informatization of China's transportation infrastructure has advanced rapidly. According to the "Digital China Development Report (2020)", by the end of 2021, 21 provinces, autonomous regions, and municipalities had implemented the construction of highway and waterway and transportation market credit information service systems, achieving interconnected operation of the nationwide expressway electronic toll collection (ETC) system; 42 vessel traffic management systems (VTMS) and the automatic identification system (AIS) covering coastal areas, the Yangtze River mainline, and other inland waterways had been established; interconnected and interoperable transportation smart cards had been realized in 303 cities at or above the prefecture level; urban rail transit vigorously promoted smart subway services, serving a population exceeding 390 million with a daily average passenger volume exceeding 45 million nationwide; the "one-click ride-hailing" function of ride-hailing services had covered nearly 300 cities, and over 200 ride-hailing platforms had been connected to the online ride-hailing supervision information exchange platform, with a daily average order volume reaching 21 million.

In December 2021, the Ministry of Transport (MOT) issued the "14th Five-Year Plan for Digital Transportation", proposing six major development goals to be achieved by 2025: digital perception of transportation infrastructure, extensive coverage of information networks, convenient and intelligent transport services, online collaboration in industry governance, vibrant innovation in technology application, and robust cybersecurity guarantees. In December 2021, the State Council issued the "14th Five-Year Plan for the Development of the Modern Comprehensive Transportation System", proposing to build a modern, high-quality national comprehensive transportation network that is convenient, cost-effective, green, intelligent, and safe by 2035.

5.4.1　Smart Road Transportation

5.4.1.1　Road Facility Management

Roads constitute the fundamental component of China's transportation system, serving as the vital arteries for the healthy operation of the national economy. According to the "Digital China Development Report (2020)", the level of digitalization in China's transportation infrastructure had significantly increased, with widespread application of road construction information models and accelerated promotion of intelligent maintenance systems; all the highways had achieved comprehensive coverage of toll collection, communications, and monitoring systems, providing comprehensive support for expressway operations, management, and vehicle safety services; dynamic monitoring had been implemented for 50% of the key sections of national and provincial main roads, as well as special large bridges and exceptionally long tunnels. By the end of 2021, the density of China's road network had reached 55 kilometers per 100 square kilometers.

In terms of road facility management, in 2019, toll stations at provincial borders on national expressways were eliminated, and the ETC system was fully integrated across the country. By the end of 2020, the number of ETC lanes on expressways had reached 66 000, with a total of 227 million ETC users; the utilization rate of ETC for passenger vehicles exceeded 70%, and for freight trucks, it surpassed 56%; the national expressway system had 28 000 ETC gantries, 250 000 sets of antennas and license plate recognition devices, accumulating over 1 petabyte of recorded data. In 2022, the Highway Monitoring and Response Center of the MOT issued the construction of the National High-speed Traffic Network's TraffiCatcher Integrated System. This system utilizes highway monitoring videos to detect traffic incidents, relay the information to the road network monitoring command center, and notify nearby ETC gantries and traffic information boards for timely traffic flow management.

In the realm of vehicle information management, the MOT leverages BDS to enhance the management of special vehicles. Since August 2011, newly manufactured "Two Passengers and One Hazardous" vehicles (where "Two Passengers" refer to tourist charter buses and scheduled passenger buses, and "One Hazardous" denotes vehicles transporting hazardous materials) are required to be equipped with BDS terminals before leaving the manufacturing factory. A nationwide intelligent monitoring platform for key "Two Passengers and One Hazardous" operational vehicles has been established, enabling dynamic monitoring and management of the operational status of key vehicles. By the end of 2021, more than 7.9 million operational vehicles had been installed with BDS terminals.

Taking Guangdong Province as an example, in February 2021, the "Two Passengers, One Hazardous, and One Heavy Cargo" Key Vehicle Intelligent Monitoring and Early Warning Convergence Platform (see Figure 5-21) was formally put online. An intelligent video monitoring system was installed free of charge on 405 000 key vehicles across the province. The system monitors the driver's driving behavior and the vehicle's trajectory (speed, geographic location, etc.), identifying and providing early warnings for various types of traffic hazards or violations of the law. After the deployment of this system, the number of traffic accidents and facilities in Guangdong Province in 2021 decreased by 62.87% and 59.26% respectively compared with the same period in 2020.

Figure 5-21   The application scenarios of "Two Passengers, One Hazardous and One Heavy Cargo" Key Vehicle Intelligent Monitoring and Early Warning Convergence Platform of Guangdong Province

Image Sources: *Yangcheng Evening News* (left), Southern News Network (right)

5.4.1.2   Intelligent Connected Vehicles

China has initiated research on autonomous driving since the 1980s, progressing through five levels (L1 to L5) based on the degree of automation. At L2, partial automation of functions, such as adaptive cruise control, lane-keeping assistance, automatic emergency braking, and automated parking, can be achieved under driver supervision. L4 represents highly autonomous driving, where the system handles all driving operations, and in specific scenarios, it requests the driver's response, allowing the driver to opt not to respond.

As of November 2022, China had witnessed sales of over 8 million vehicles equipped with L2 intelligent driving assistance functions, with a penetration rate of around 33%. The actual road test mileage for L4 autonomous driving had exceeded 40 million kilometers. In 2013, Baidu began embark on the development of autonomous vehicles. The autonomous vehicle solution of Baidu relies on the technologies of traffic scene object recognition and environmental perception, which can achieve high-precision detection, identification, tracking, distance and speed estimation, road segmentation, and lane detection. In December 2015, that solution achieved full autonomous driving in mixed road conditions, including urban streets, ring roads, and highways for the first time in China. In 2019, Baidu, in collaboration with the China First Automobile Group Co., Ltd. (short for FAW), produced China's first batch of mass-produced L4 autonomous passenger vehicles. Each vehicle was equipped with a LiDAR (LightLaser Detection and Ranging) sensor on the roof to sense the environment around it, with an effective detection range of up to 240 meters. In October 2020, Baidu's autonomous driving ride-hailing service was fully launched in Beijing.

The intelligent connected vehicle utilizes modern communications and network technologies, equipping the vehicle with sensors to perceive complex environments. If corresponding sensors and communications devices are installed on the roadside, the sharing of information between the vehicle and the infrastructure would be achieved. The onboard computing unit achieves information integration and intelligent decision-making, and the actuators execute actions according to the instructions issued by the computing unit, allowing the vehicle to travel safely in an efficiently energy-saving manner, realizing intelligent vehicle control.

In July 2021, the MIIT, the Ministry of Public Security (MPS), and the MOT jointly released the "Intelligent Connected Vehicle Road Test and Demonstration Application Management Regulations (Trial)". As of August 2021, China had established 16 intelligent connected vehicle test demonstration areas, providing access to over 3 500 kilometers of test roads, and more than 700 test licenses were issued, accumulating a total test mileage of over 7 million kilometers. Taking Wuhan as an example, the National Intelligent Connected Vehicle (Wuhan) Test Demonstration Zone (see Figure 5-22) was officially inaugurated in September 2019. The planned test roads cover 159 kilometers, encompassing residential areas, commercial areas, logistics zones, tourist scenic areas, and industrial zones. By adopting the "5G + BeiDou" vehicle-road cooperative network, the zone was developed into a national vehicle-to-everything (V2X) vehicle-road cooperative test area, achieving millisecond-level latency and centimeter-level positioning accuracy. Along the test roads, autonomous driving bus demonstration routes were launched and demonstration applications such as unmanned logistics delivery, unmanned sweeping, and smart parking were implemented.

Figure 5-22   National Intelligent Connected Vehicle (Wuhan) Test Demonstration Zone
Image Source: *Hubei Daily*

5.4.2 Smart Rail Transit

5.4.2.1 Smart High-speed Railway

The Chinese government considers high-speed railway as a crucial national public transportation infrastructure and has actively pursued its development. Given China's vast territory, when the coastal regions got developed first during the reform and opening-up, the other regions of China had uneven economic development, particularly the less developed central, western, and northeastern regions. As a high-capacity, long-distance mode of transportation, high-speed railway serves to reduce both temporal and spatial distances, facilitating effective connections between resources dispersed across regions and accelerating the integration of logistics, passenger flow, information flow, and capital flow.

China has built a huge "four longitudinal and four transverse" high-speed railway network, with the mileage of the high-speed railway ranking first in the world, reaching about 95% of the cities with a population of more than 500 000 people, and forming "hourly economic circles" around a number of major cities. In July 2016, the NDRC issued "Medium-and Long-Term Railway Network Plan", which explicitly proposed the construction of "eight longitudinal and eight transverse" high-speed railway main channels. It is expected to be completed by around 2026. In 2020, China proposed the new infrastructure initiative, which included high-speed railway and urban rail transit, aiming to establish the new intelligent transportation infrastructure. Alongside the development of China's high-speed railway network, significant progress has been made in the construction of rail supporting facilities and the intelligence of high-speed trains.

In terms of intelligent railway construction, the Beijing-Zhangjiakou high-speed railway is the first high-speed railway in the world designed with an intelligent approach (see Figure 5-23). This project is geared toward the needs of the 2020 Beijing Winter Olympics, connecting Beijing and Zhangjiakou. The project started construction in April 2016 and opened for operation in December 2019, with a mainline length of 174 kilometers and a maximum design speed of 350 km/h. It was a large-scale and complex systematic project, involving multiple professional disciplines and presenting significant challenges in coordination. For this reason, it adopted new-generation information technologies such as building information modeling (BIM), big data, AI, BDS, 5G, and carried out intelligent innovation on the construction, equipment and operation technologies. The project implemented a BIM-based multi-disciplinary collaborative design platform and independently developed various professional BIM collaborative design software for surveying, routing, bridges, tunnels, roadbeds, catenary systems, signals, etc., saving approximately 8% of coordination liaison time and 3% of material costs.

In the realm of high-speed train intelligence, the Beijing-Zhangjiakou high-speed railway has achieved the sophistication of its multiple-unit trains. The new-generation bullet train system integrates a suite of technologies such as intelligent composite sensors, real-time transmission of train-ground information, big data mining and analysis, automation control, intelligent information processing, fault prediction, and health management. This integration enables intelligent train operations, intelligent maintenance (with monitoring points reaching up to 2 718), intelligent services, and safety monitoring (introducing 168 new vibration monitoring points of the running gear). By adding automatic train operation (ATO) related equipment on the basis of the Chinese Train Control System, Level 3 (CTCS-3), the trains have achieved automatic driving (see Figure 5-24). Additionally, precise positioning responders have been installed on the track in station areas, facilitating the trains' automatic and precise alignment parking. This accomplishment encompasses automatic train departure at stations, automatic interval

Figure 5-23   Beijing-Zhangjiakou high-speed railway: intelligent construction of high-speed railway engineering

Image Source: WANG TJ, The intelligent Beijing-Zhangjiakou high-speed railway, *Engineering*, 2021, 7 (12): 1665-1672

running, automatic stopping, automatic door opening, and synchronized door operation with platform doors. The Beijing-Zhangjiakou high-speed railway had set the world record for the first 350 km/h multiple-unit bullet train automatic driving.

Figure 5-24   Beijing-Zhangjiakou high-speed railway: automatic driving of high-speed trains
Image Source: CCTV.com

5.4.2.2 Smart Metro

Along with the development of urbanization, China's urban population has been increasing, and the pressure on urban transportation has become increasingly significant. According to the results of the seventh national census in 2021, there were 21 megacities in China with a permanent resident population of more than five million, among which seven cities, including Beijing, Shanghai, and Guangzhou, have a population of more than 10 million. Cities with high population density in China are mainly concentrated in the Yangtze River Delta, Pearl River Delta, and Beijing-Tianjin region, with the population density of the top eight cities exceeding 2 000 people per square kilometer. Metro is an important part of the comprehensive 3D transportation system of cities and an important means to alleviate the traffic pressure of large cities. According to the MOT, by the end of 2022, 53 cities in China had opened and operated 290 urban rail transit lines, with a total operating mileage of about 9 584 kilometers. Along with the construction and development of metros, China has begun to explore the use of various types of information technology to improve the digitalization of metro operation and management.

Traditional metros are operated on a single line and managed manually. The smart station can break down the barriers between various specialties of the metro, realize the linkage between the equipment, and build an intelligent integrated control platform in the metro station. Taking the example of demonstration project by Beijing Metro, which was supported by the National Key Research and Development Plan "Key Technology for Efficient Transportation and Safe Service of Mega-City Rail Transit System", it relies on BDS, 5G, spatial digitization and other emerging technologies to build the Beijing Capital International Airport line into China's first full-scenario smart metro demonstration line. The system data in the station are connected to the meteorological data, which can receive real-time weather warning information, and the intelligent detection equipment in the station could monitor the rainfall and water level outside the station (see Figure 5-25), and automatically activate the corresponding equipment when encountering dangerous situations, so as to solve the emergency situation on the spot. Through the verification of BeiDou positioning and a multi-mode navigation system, passengers can enjoy accurate location query, path planning, and other services on the Beijing Capital International Airport line through the Beijing Metro APP and WeChat mini-programs in the future, shortening the time of entering the station and improving the travel efficiency.

Figure 5-25　Beijing Metro: weather awareness and customer flow scheduling

Image Source: *Beijing Youth Daily*

5.4.3　Smart Water Transportation

Compared with land transportation such as roads and railways, water transportation has the comparative advantages of high capacity, low cost, low energy consumption, and low pollution, and it is the main direction of China's efforts to accelerate the restructuring of transportation and promote the green and low-carbon transformation of transportation. As an important part of water transportation, ports and waterways are important hubs and channels of the national comprehensive transportation network.

China has established a water transportation infrastructure system with coastal shipping routes, the Yangtze River mainline, the West River shipping mainline, the Beijing-Hangzhou Grand Canal, and the Huai River main stream as the primary waterways. This system, centered around major ports, connects railways, highways, pipelines, and other modes of transportation, linking the world and forming a seamless connection between trunk and branch waterways. Water transportation handles a significant portion of cross-regional cargo transportation within China and is responsible for transporting about 95% of the country's foreign trade goods.

5.4.3.1 Digital Waterways

By the end of 2021, China's ports had 20 867 berths for production terminals, 2 659 berths of 10 000 tons and above, and the navigable mileage of inland waterways was 127 600 kilometers, of which the navigable mileage of Class III waterways and above was 14 500 kilometers, and there were 125 900 water transport vessels. The Yangtze River is the busiest waterway in China, and its freight volume has ranked first in the world for many consecutive years.

The construction of "Digital Yangtze River" has been advancing continuously, with initial gradually emerging. On September 30, 2019, the comprehensive connectivity of the digital navigation system along the Yangtze River officially commenced operation, enabling the dynamic monitoring of information such as navigation marks, water conditions, controlled river sections, and channel dimensions along the 2 687.8 kilometers main channel of the Yangtze River. The establishment of the navigation maintenance and management platform, navigation dynamic monitoring platform, and navigation emergency command platform, with the mobile application Electronic Channel Map of Yangtze River and the Yangtze River Navigation Comprehensive Service Information System (portal website) as the carriers, had marked the initial success of the "One Map, One Station, Three Platforms" approach (see Figure 5-26). The service model for managing the Yangtze River waterway is transitioning from a traditional manual mode to a digital mode, realizing the principles of "remote observation, precise management, and on-site utilization".

5.4.3.2 Smart Ports

China holds the distinction of being the country with the highest maritime connectivity globally, having established maritime routes with main ports in over 100 countries and regions. Its pivotal role in the global shipping and logistics system continues to rise. Among the top 10 ports worldwide in terms of cargo throughput and container throughput, China claims eight and seven positions, respectively. Shanghai Port, Ningbo-Zhoushan Port, and Shenzhen Port consistently ranked at the forefront in container throughput for multiple years. In 2021, ports in China handled a total cargo throughput of 15.55 billion

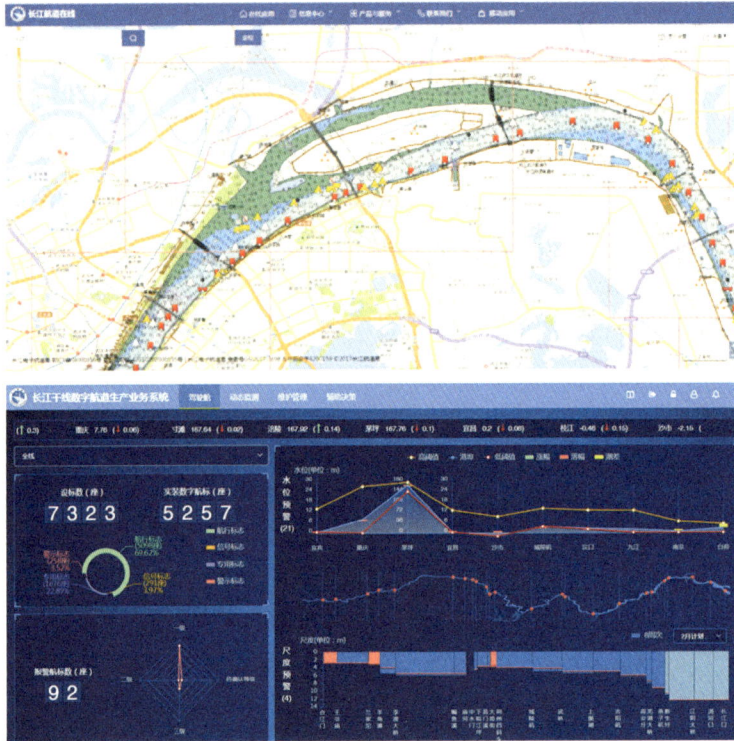

Figure 5-26 Water condition and shipping monitoring of digital waterways along the Yangtze River mainline

Image Sources: Changjiang Waterway Bureau (top), Yangtze River Waterway (bottom)

tons, marking a 6.8% increase from 2020 and ensuring the smooth flow of "outbound and inbound" goods.

Port logistics informatization continues to deepen. After years of construction and development, the efficiency of loading and unloading operations at specialized coastal terminals and the container throughput along hundred-meter shorelines are both at the forefront globally. China has essentially formed a port logistics operation system characterized by "one cargo manifest, one information network". The application of blockchain-based electronic container release platforms in port navigation has accelerated. The average processing time for container documents has been compressed from two days to within four hours. Information exchange on container vessels has been achieved among 19 major ports in China, Japan, and South Korea. The international maritime container transportation has fully implemented electronic data interchange (EDI) and been incorporated into the international trade "single window" system.

Significant achievements have been made in the automation of container ports. Several fully automatic container terminals, including Xiamen Yuanhai and Qingdao Qianwan, have been completed. Among them, the automatic terminals of Shanghai Yangshan Deepwater Port Phase Ⅳ (see Figure 5-27) is the world's most intelligent container terminal. The Intelligent Terminal Operating System independently developed by Shanghai International Port (Group) Co., Ltd. served as its "brain"; while the Equipment Control System independently produced Shanghai Zhenhua Heavy Industries Co., Ltd. served as its "nervous system". Battery-driven automated guided vehicle (AGV) have achieved unmanned driving, automatic navigation, and path optimization. The more than 100 rail-mounted cranes and over 160 AGVs at the terminal of Shanghai Yangshan Deepwater Port Phase Ⅳ Automated Terminal can load and unload cargo 24 hours a day without human intervention, achieving millimeter-level hoisting accuracy and significantly improving port operational efficiency. Shanghai Yangshan Deepwater Port Phase Ⅳ Automated Terminal handled a daily throughput of 20 823.25 ETUs, with a per capita labor productivity reaching 213% of that of traditional terminals.

Figure 5-27   Monitoring room and unmanned AGVs at the automatic terminal of Shanghai Yangshan Deepwater Port Phase Ⅳ Automated Terminal

Image Sources: *Shangguan News* (left), Xinhua News Agency (right)

5.5   Summary

For a long time, China has attached great importance to leveraging the driving effect of ICT on the development of traditional industries. It has successively put forward the development strategies such as "boosting industrialization with informatization" and "promoting the deep integration of informatization and industrialization". Since the 13th Five-Year Plan period, in line with national conditions and the development needs of the times, China has meticulously formulated scientific development plans and strategies, and actively promoted the digital transformation and upgrading of key industries such as manufacturing, agriculture, energy, and transportation.

In the field of manufacturing industry, as the "world's factory" with a complete industrial system, China occupies an important position in the global manufacturing landscape. At present, China is actively addressing the challenges of transforming into an environment-friendly high-end manufacturing industry, and vigorously promoting the implementation and application of new technologies such as the Industrial Internet, industrial robots, and 5G in manufacturing. In industries such as electronic device manufacturing, equipment manufacturing, and steel production, "smart factories" are emerging in an endless stream. These factories have effectively improved production efficiency and optimized product quality, providing a Chinese model for the transformation and upgrading of the global manufacturing industry.

In the field of agriculture, China has achieved self-sufficiency in staple food, effectively ensuring national food security. However, the relatively insufficient per capita agricultural resources remains a problem. In response to this challenge, China has established multiple big data systems for agriculture, realizing functions such as disaster early warning, market monitoring, and product traceability. In the field of cultivation, technologies such as unmanned aerial vehicles, unmanned agricultural machinery, and IoT are widely used. They can not only improve the operational efficiency of large-scale farms but also enhance the operational accuracy of small-scale farms. In the field of livestock and fishery sectors, the application of robot and IoT technologies has achieved intelligent monitoring and digital management, injecting new impetus into the development of agricultural modernization.

In the field of energy industry, China is the world's largest energy producer and consumer. It actively fulfills its responsibilities in addressing climate change and has announced its carbon peaking and carbon neutrality goals to the world. China is accelerating the digital and intelligent development of the energy industry. In the field of intelligent coal mining, the information infrastructure has been upgraded. Breakthroughs have been made in autonomous driving and equipment interconnection. The construction of smart power plants has promoted the intelligent transformation of fields such as thermal power and wind power. The construction of smart power grids has effectively alleviated the regional imbalance between energy supply and demand and has achieved excellent results in grid visualization, intelligent operation, and the localization of power equipment.

In the field of transportation industry, China has built the world's largest transportation infrastructure network. To further improve the quality and efficiency of transportation, China is vigorously developing intelligent transportation. In the field of intelligent road transportation, the digital management level of road facilities has been significantly improved, the ETC system has been fully popularized, and technologies such as intelligent connected vehicles and autonomous driving have been applied on a large scale, placing China in the global leading group. In the field of intelligent railway transportation, the intelligent construction of high-speed railways has made impressive achievements, and the digital operation management of metros is continuously advancing. In the field of intelligent water transportation, the construction of digital waterways and the intelligent development of ports have achieved remarkable results, improving water transportation efficiency and service quality.

The digital transformation and upgrading of traditional industries is a challenge faced by all countries in the world. In the process of industrial digitalization, China gives full play to the leading and driving role of state-owned enterprises. Through carrying out demonstration projects, China promotes the wide application of new technologies. At the same time, China continuously strengthens the construction of industrial digital infrastructure, builds advanced platforms, and improves the regulatory system. The achievements of China's digital transformation of traditional industries have not only promoted the high-quality development of its own economy, but also contribute Chinese wisdom and Chinese solutions to the digitalization of global industries.

6　Digital Society

The digital society is a new type of social formation characterized by the deep integration of digital technologies into social operation and lifestyle. According to the "Overall Layout Plan for the Construction of Digital China" released in 2023, the construction of the digital society includes the universalization of digital public services, the precision of digital social governance, the intelligentization of digital life, and so on. This chapter introduces China's achievements in smart cities, digital villages, smart education, and smart healthcare in recent years.

6.1　Smart City

China stands as the world's most populous nation, with its demographic concentration predominantly within urban centers. The urbanization rate of China embarked on an ascendant trajectory, crossing the 40% threshold in 2003 and surging to 51.27% by 2011. This milestone heralded the advent of an era where urban societies form the primary demographic paradigm. Presently, there exist over 300 cities in China boasting populations exceeding one million, and projections, based on an annual growth rate of 1.2%, foresee that over 70% of the population will live in by the year 2030. The aggregation of dense populations within urban locales poses formidable challenges to essential infrastructure such as urban transportation, municipal services, and power supply. Addressing these challenges necessitates the adoption of crucial measures, with the construction of a smart city through digitalization and informatization emerging as a pivotal solution.

China perceives the concept of smart cities as the advanced phase in the realm of urban informatization. In January 2013, the Ministry of Science and Technology (MOST) and the National Standardization Administration initiated 20 smart city pilot demonstration projects, paralleled by the Ministry of Housing and Urban-Rural Development (MOHURD) launching the first batch of 90 national smart city pilot projects. The year 2014 witnessed the issuance of the guideline titled "Guidance on Promoting the Healthy Development of Smart Cities", followed by the introduction of national standards in 2017, including the "Smart City Technical Reference Model" and the "Smart City Evaluation Model and Basic Evaluation Indicators". As of August 2018, all sub-provincial cities and above, along with over 76% of prefecture-level cities and 32% of county-level cities, totaling approximately 500 cities, had explicitly articulated their commitment to or were in the process of constructing innovative smart cities.

6.1.1　Urban Traffic Coordination

Urban transportation stands as a pivotal facet of municipal operational management. Over 400 cities in China have established intelligent traffic command and control centers, amalgamating functions such as emergency response, information gathering, and traffic control. These cities have also implemented oversaw key systems including traffic signal control, traffic guidance, traffic surveillance, and electronic law enforcement. Mega-cities such as Beijing, Shanghai, Guangzhou, and Shenzhen have erected transportation operations coordination centers (TOCC), which can intelligently monitor, coordinate, and command the integrated traffic operations, and achieved comprehensive coordination and management of urban road traffic, rail transit, civil aviation, as well as urban parking and public transportation services.

Significant achievements have been realized through the public transport comprehensive monitoring platform. Taking the city of Shenzhen as an example, since the reform and opening-up, Shenzhen has metamorphosed from a small border town with a permanent resident population of just around 30 000 into an expansive and densely populated city spanning 1 997 square kilometers, with a permanent resident population of 17.56 million. It boasts the highest vehicle density in the nation (over 500 vehicles per kilometer) and the third-highest container throughput at its ports nationwide. Shenzhen has pioneered the construction of TOCC in China, encompassing domains of sea, land, air, and rail (see Figure 6-1). The city's 2 700 signal-controlled intersections boast a 98% networking rate, resulting in a 70% reduction in personnel input through optimized timing and a decrease of over 30% in the workland for manual inspections. The deployment of intelligent traffic signal control at over 700 intersections citywide has significantly enhanced traffic management efficiency. In 2020, during the morning rush hour, the average road speed in Shenzhen reached 27.1 km/h, maintaining optimal traffic efficiency among first-tier cities, and the vehicular mortality rate plummeted to 0.62 people per 10 000 vehicles.

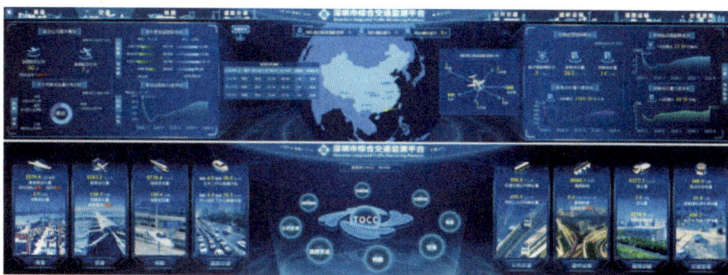

Figure 6-1　Urban traffic management in Shenzhen: TOCC

Image Source: Shenzhen Integrated Transportation Operations Command Center

Individual-oriented public transport data services become more and more popular. Leveraging extensive data from mobile terminal positioning, smartphone navigation applications can estimate real-time traffic conditions. For instance, Baidu Maps APP integrates data from five major data sources: enhanced location data, real-time satellite orbit data, road data, satellite signals, and mobile sensor data. This integration facilitates minute-level real-time updating of dynamic traffic data for over 380 cities nationwide, with a location accuracy reaching the lane level (see Figure 6-2). By the end of 2021, Baidu Maps averaged over 130 billion daily location service requests, covering over 11 million kilometers of roads, and serving more than 600 000 mobile applications.

Figure 6-2　Smart Eye function in the Baidu Maps: urban commuting big data and traffic flow migration trend awareness

Image Source: Baidu Maps

6.1.2　City Brain

The concept of the City Brain is an innovative initiative originating from China, representing a commendable exploration for urban development worldwide. The City Brain is a product that combines the architecture of the Internet Brain with the construction of smart cities, constituting a city-level and brain-like complex intelligent mega-system. Spearheaded by the municipal government of Hangzhou, the City Brain was initiated in March 2016, and the City Brain 1.0 was fully operational by October of the same year at the Yunqi Conference in Hangzhou. It can enhance urban operational efficiency and address the intricate challenges inherent in urban management. Presently, there exists a lack of unified understanding of the City Brain among the industrial sector, academia, and various sectors of economic and social development. Some approach it from the perspective of urban transportation, some from the standpoint of urban security, some delve into the realm of urban artificial intelligence hubs, and still, some from the perspective of the brain-like structure, resulting in a multitude of research angles and implementation outcomes.

In November 2020, the Department of Informatization and Industrial Development of the National Information Center proposed that the core of the City Brain was a data-driven artificial intelligence central platform based on ubiquitous sensing, comprehensive interconnection, and digital twinning at the Smart City Expo World Congress. In December 2020, the City Brain Global Standard Research Group, the Research Center on

Fictitious Economy & Data Science of the Chinese Academy of Sciences, and the Center for Digital Governance Studies of the China Institute for Innovation and Development Strategy jointly released the "City Brain Global Standard Research Report", outlining nine research directions for global standards related to the City Brain, and research on the "City Brain" continues to deepen. As of 2020, the City Brain had been implemented in over 10 cities, including Hangzhou, Suzhou, and Haikou, and nearly 500 cities nationwide has initiated City Brain construction projects, with an investment exceeding hundreds of billions of yuan.

Hangzhou, as the inaugural city to adopt the City Brain, began its collaboration with Alibaba Cloud in October 2016. The City Brain has been applied to urban transportation, emergency rescue, and public safety (see Figure 6-3). As of 2017, the City Brain had taken control of 128 signalized intersections in Hangzhou, resulting in a 15.3% reduction in travel time in pilot areas and a saving of 4.6 minutes on elevated road journeys in the main urban area; in the main urban area of Hangzhou, the City Brain generated over 500 daily event alerts with an accuracy rate of 92%; in Xiaoshan District, the arrival time of ambulances had been halved, with over 120 ambulances reaching the scene in record time.

Figure 6-3　City Brain in Hangzhou: urban transportation and public safety
Image Source: rmzxb.com.cn

6.1.3　**Digital Twin City**

The concept of "Digital Twin" involves mapping a physical entity into virtual space, creating a "Digital Counterpart". In the context of a digital twin city, Internet of Things (IoT) technology, geographic information technology, and intelligent building city models are employed to transform the physical city into a virtual digital city model, enabling functions such as prediction, analysis, and optimization through model simulating operations. Digital twin cities seamlessly integrate the virtual and the real, allowing for the overlap of physical entities and their corresponding twins, facilitating interaction between the digital and physical realms on the foundation of digitalization and informatization.

In June 2021, the MOHURD issued the "Technical Guidelines for the City Information Model (CIM) Foundation Platform" (Revised Edition), reinforcing guidelines for the construction of the "three-dimensional digital foundation" of digital twin cities from a technical implementation perspective. Regions such as Shanghai, Zhejiang Province, and Xiong'an New Area in Hebei Province, expedited the establishment of city-level CIM foundation platforms, exploring and deploying pilot applications for digital twin cities.

Shanghai has initiated the trial operation of a comprehensive city management system based on digital twin technology, achieving a preliminary realization of "an integrated network for urban operations" (see Figure 6-4). This system integrates access to public security, greening and urban appearance, housing and urban and rural development, transportation, emergency response, ecological environment, health, and other fields, and supports cross-departmental and cross-system joint operations to increase efficiency and empowerment. As of 2022, the Shanghai Urban Operation and Management Center had connected to 220 systems of 72 departments (units) and a number of digital twin application scenarios and continuously summarized and improved them, actively promoted the application of digital twins in infrastructure, historical buildings, communities, cultural tourism, education, healthcare, emergency response, fire protection, and other fields, and created a number of unique digital twin application scenarios in urban safety, urban operation, and innovation leadership. Shanghai has put forward the concept of urban agent, taking a building as the smallest management unit of the city, and has been exploring innovative practices in the transformation of urban digital governance.

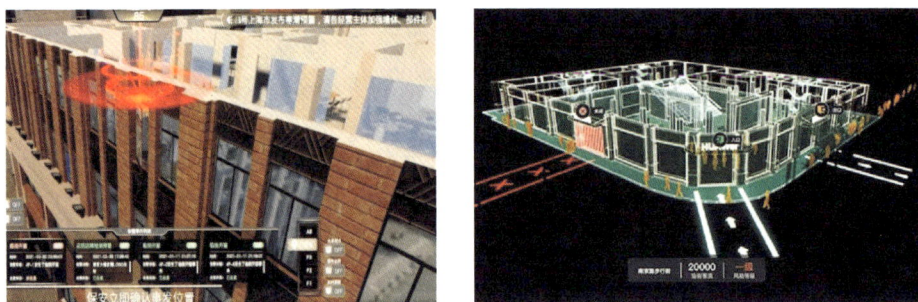

Figure 6-4   Digital twin city application in Shanghai: digital governance based on urban intelligence

Image Source: Shanghai Internet Information Office

6.2   Digital Village

From a historical perspective across various nations globally, the development of industrialization and urbanization has often been accompanied by a decline in rural populations and the deterioration of rural economies, leading to social upheaval. Rural areas, typically characterized by vast expanses and sparse populations, face high costs and slow returns in constructing essential infrastructure such as public transportation, information networks, and healthcare. As a socialist country, China places great emphasis on addressing the rural-urban relationship in the process of modernization. Drawing lessons from Western nations' experience in rural-urban development, China has formulated the strategic goal of "rural revitalization".

In the 14th Five-Year Plan, China articulated the strategy of "supporting agriculture with industry, promoting rural areas with urban development, fostering a new model of mutually reinforcing relationships between industry and agriculture, and urban and rural areas, characterized by coordinated development and shared prosperity and accelerating the modernization of agriculture and rural areas". China regards the construction of digital villages as an important way to promote rural revitalization and the integrated development of urban and rural areas.

6.2.1 Rural Network Infrastructure

6.2.1.1 Village-to-Village Project

Since the initiation of the reform and opening-up policy, China's ICT industry has made significant strides, yet the development disparities in communications, particularly in revolutionary base areas, ethnic minority areas, national border areas and impoverished areas, have become increasingly prominent. In 2003, nearly 80 000 out of 695 000 administrative villages still lacked telecommunications access. To address the challenges in rural communications development, the Ministry of Information Industry introduced the "Implementation Plan for Universal Service of Rural Communications—Village Connection Project" (abbreviated as the "Village-to-Village" project) in January 2004, requiring basic telecommunications operators to undertake the construction of communications networks in rural and remote areas through segmented contracting, self-raised funds, and self-operated maintenance. The project was implemented in three phases: the first phase (2004-2005) aimed to achieve "telecommunications access for over 95% of administrative villages", the second phase (2006-2010) aimed to achieve "telecommunications access for every village, and Internet access for every township", and the third phase (2011-2015) aimed to achieve "broadband access for every village" in administrative villages.

Constructing communications networks in remote rural areas presents numerous challenges. On the one hand, these areas are often characterized by remote geographical locations, harsh climatic conditions, and frequent natural disasters, leading to significant difficulties in construction projects and posing extreme challenges to human labor. On the other hand, rural areas, as a whole, exhibit relatively backward economic development and low population density, giving rise to high construction and ongoing operational costs for both optical fiber networks and mobile communications base stations. Furthermore, the number of users is limited, resulting in low market returns. According to estimates, the cost of connecting each administrative village by optical fiber networks in the "three areas and three prefectures"[①] is on average four times that of the eastern and central regions of the country; the construction cost of each base station is, on average, 3.3 times that of the eastern and central regions of the country; in some remote areas, this difference reaches approximately tenfold.

As the most populous developing country globally, China leverages its institutional advantages of concentrating efforts to address major issues. The state-owned telecom operators employ the "segmented contracting" method to advance the "Village-to-Village" project, allocating the funds needed for universal telecom services among the six telecom operators at that time, including China Telecom, China Netcom, China Mobile, China Unicom, China Satcom, and China Tietong. The allocation proportions for each operator are consistent with their respective shares of the total revenue and profits among all telecom operators, with revenue and profit weights each accounting for 50%.

After over a decade of implementation, the phased goals of the "Village-to-Village" project have been essentially achieved. The construction and service levels of rural communications have been significantly improved, with the scope of universal communications services gradually expanding from voice services to Internet services. By the end of 2014, the annual tasks of the "Village-to-Village" project had been exceeded, achieving new progress in the popularization of telecommunications services. Specifically, the proportion of administrative villages with broadband access nationwide reached 93.5%, the proportion of villages with more than 20 households having telecommunications access reached 95.8%, over 3 000 townships and villages and 150 000 administrative villages completed broadband construction, and 18 000 impoverished villages achieved Internet coverage, along with 6 400 rural schools and public institutions gaining broadband access.

6.2.1.2　Internet-based Poverty Alleviation Action Plan

In 2012, China initiated the poverty alleviation project, aiming to address the poverty issues affecting approximately 122 million rural residents nationwide. Following the "Village-to-Village" project, an unprecedented nationwide campaign for Internet-based poverty alleviation was launched across the country. Its goal is to bring advanced optical fiber broadband and 4G networks to impoverished villages, achieving parity in Internet access and speed between rural and urban areas.

On October 14, 2015, the State Council executive meeting decided to increase central financial investment, guide localities to strengthen policy and financial support, encourage telecom operators, broadcasting enterprises, and private capital to participate fairly in rural

---

① The "three areas" refer to the Tibet Autonomous Region, the Hotan, Aksu, Kashgar prefectures and the Kizilsu Kirgiz Autonomous Prefecture in southern Xinjiang, and prefectures and counties with large Tibetan populations in the provinces of Sichuan, Yunnan, Gansu and Qinghai. The "three prefectures" refer to the Liangshan Yi Autonomous Prefecture in Sichuan Province, the Nujiang Lisu Autonomous Prefecture in Yunnan Province, and the Linxia Hui Autonomous Prefecture in Gansu Province. These areas have harsh geographical conditions and lay behind in economic development, and are designated as national-level improverished regions.

broadband construction and operation and maintenance through competitive bidding and explore market-oriented approaches such as public-private-partnership (PPP) and entrusted operation to mobilize the participation of various entities.

In 2016, the Office of the Central Cyberspace Affairs Commission, the National Development and Reform Commission (NDRC), and the State Council Leading Group Office of Poverty Alleviation and Development jointly issued the "Action Plan for Internet-Based Poverty Alleviation", which proposed five major projects: network coverage project, rural e-commerce project, network-based intelligence support project, information service project, and network public welfare project. Among them, the network coverage project, that is, the pilot project of universal telecommunications services, mainly involves the most challenging construction tasks left by the "Village-to-Village" project, and are mainly distributed in remote areas with high mountains and valleys and few people (see Figure 6-5).

Figure 6-5   Internet-based poverty alleviation project: harsh conditions for laying out communications networks

Image Source: NI GN, *China's Road to Science and Technology · Information Volume · Intelligent Connection of Everything*, 2021

The state-owned telecom operators and other key industries spared no effort, with millions working day and night, creating a world miracle in rural communications coverage. As of 2020, China had implemented six batches of universal telecom service pilot projects, covering 27 provinces, autonomous regions, and municipalities nationwide, and completed the construction of optical fiber networks for 130 000 administrative villages and 4G base stations in 50 000 rural areas, including optical fiber networks in 43 000 impoverished villages and 4G base stations in 15 000 impoverished villages. The national coverage ratio of optical fiber networks and 4G networks in administrative villages exceeded 98%, and the average download speed of rural optical fiber broadband surpassed 100 Mbps, achieving parity in Internet access and speed between rural and urban areas. The goal of "broadband network coverage for over 90% of impoverished villages" proposed in the "13th Five-Year Plan for Poverty Alleviation" was achieved ahead of schedule and was surpassed. Information superhighways comparable to those in urban areas have been established in the once-isolated deep mountains, allowing more and more people in remote urban areas to share the digital dividends of the information era and embark on the path to prosperity and well-being.

In the Internet-based poverty alleviation action plan, China's state-owned telecom operators have made substantial investments in rural areas. As of 2019, China Telecom had invested more than 100 billion yuan in rural areas, achieving 100% 4G network coverage in townships nationwide, broadband access in more than 91% of administrative villages, and 90% optical fiber broadband coverage in townships and towns nationwide; China Mobile had invested more than 80 billion yuan, providing telephone access in 122 000 villages and broadband access in 840 000 administrative villages, with a 4G coverage rate of more than 98% in administrative villages nationwide; China Unicom had achieved 100% network coverage in more than 90 000 townships amd towns nationwide, and the total number of administrative villages covered had exceeded 460 000.

China Telecom, China Mobile, and China Unicom have launched large-scale initiatives to offer discounts, ensuring that residents in remote areas not only have access to broadband networks, but can also afford them and utilize them effectively. In 2020, China Telecom had launched poverty alleviation packages at 35 000 business outlets across the country, offering discounts totaling more than 1.9 billion yuan since 2019, built a big data management platform for targeted poverty alleviation, and served 39 million impoverished residents in 17 provinces, autonomous regions, and municipalities; China Mobile had launched heavily discounted exclusive "poverty alleviation packages" and mobile phone purchase subsidies for impoverished residents, benefiting more than 14 million registered poor households and offering profits of 3 billion yuan, and donated its own-brand mobile phones and other terminal devices to residents in poverty-stricken areas; China Unicom provided tariff discounts for poverty-stricken areas, launched more than 150 exclusive discount packages, and cumulatively reduced and exempted communications fees by 367 million yuan, helping more than 400 000 poor households to successfully get rid of poverty. The optical fiber network and 4G network coverage in China's administrative villages from 2016 to 2020 is shown in Figure 6-6.

Through a series of rural network infrastructure developments, China has progressively narrowed the digital divide between rural and urban areas. In 2021, broadband coverage was achieved in every administrative village, with a nationwide broadband coverage rate of 100%. Optical fiber network and 4G network coverage rate both exceeded 99%, essentially realizing the goal of "same network access and speed in rural and urban areas". The extension of 5G to rural areas has been expedited. As of 2022, China had established and activated a total of 1.968 million 5G base stations, and the 5G network had covered all prefecture-level city urban areas, county-level city urban areas,

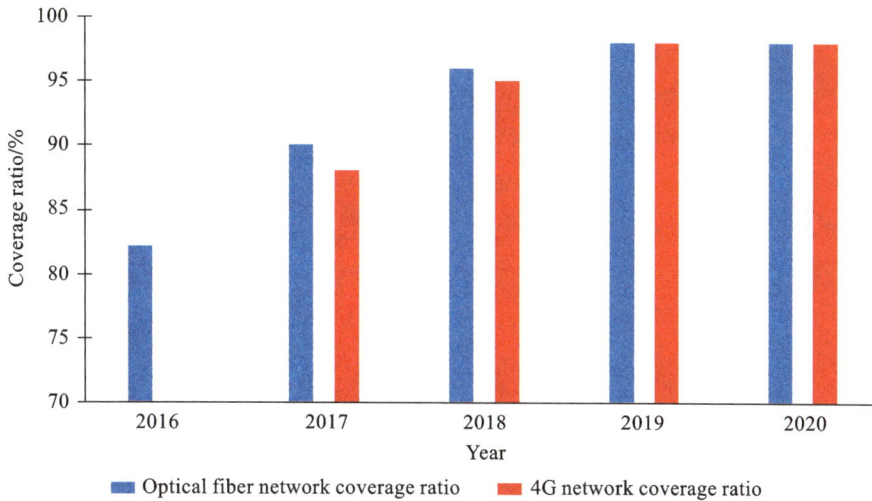

Figure 6-6　Optical fiber network and 4G network coverage in China's administrative villages (2016-2020)

Data Source: Ministry of Industry and Information Technology of the People's Republic of China

and 96% of township areas, achieving "5G coverage in every county". As of 2021, rural residents, on average, had 229 Internet-enabled mobile phones per 100 households, marking a 4.4% increase from the previous year. As of June 2022, the Internet users in rural areas had reached 293 million, with a rural Internet penetration rate of 58.8%, narrowing the urban-rural Internet penetration gap by nearly 15 percentage points compared to the 13th Five-Year Plan period.

6.2.2　Rural E-commerce

The Chinese government considers the development of rural e-commerce as a primary means to advance the digital economy in rural areas. Governments of various levels have initiated and organized diverse activities to promote rural e-commerce, such as the "Internet Plus" project for the online sale of agricultural products, the "Digital Business Empowers Agriculture" project, and the "Great Country Craftsman" National Farmers' Skills Competition. In recent years, the Ministry of Commerce (MOFCOM) and other departments have continued to promote rural e-commerce, achieving remarkable results. As of 2023, more than 20 billion yuan of central financial funds had been arranged to support a total of 1 489 counties, and construct more than 2 600 county-level public service centers for e-commerce and logistics distribution centers and more than 150 000 rural e-commerce and express delivery service sites. Express delivery services have continued to extend to primary rural areas. In 2021, more than 80% of villages were covered by the "Express Delivery to Villages" initiative, with the total volume of express parcels in rural areas reaching 37 billion.

By the end of 2021, 36.3% of key agricultural leading enterprises at or above the municipal level had engaged in sales through e-commerce. Agricultural processing enterprises utilizing e-commerce reported a 10.8% increase in operating revenue compared with the previous year. E-commerce plays a crucial role in facilitating the sales of agricultural products in poverty-stricken areas, contributing significantly to preventing a return to poverty on a large scale. In 2022, China's rural online retail volume reached 2.17 trillion yuan, marking a 3.6% increase from the previous year. China's rural online retail value from 2016 to 2022 is shown in Figure 6-7.

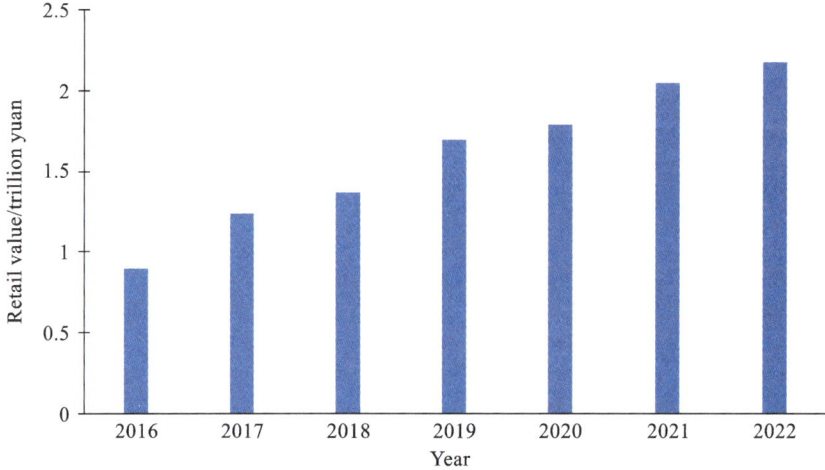

Figure 6-7 China's rural online retail value (2016-2022)

Data Source: Ministry of Commerce of the People's Republic of China

Live streaming for product promotion, known as "live commerce", has become a highlight in rural e-commerce. Under the coordination of relevant departments such as the Regional Revitalization Department of the NDRC and the Public Service Department of the National Radio and Television Administration, Alibaba Group's Taobao platform launched the "Village Live Streaming Program" in 2019, providing training for farmers in skills such as online live streaming and online traffic management. As of September 2021, the program had incubated over 110 000 farmer livestreamers, conducted more than 2.3 million live streaming sessions to assist farmers, covered over 2 000 counties in 31 provinces, autonomous regions, and municipalities, and driven agricultural product sales exceeding 5 billion yuan, creating employment opportunities for over 200 000 people.

The "Taobao village" develops rapidly. It is a term for rural e-commerce and regional agglomeration. There are three statistical standards for Taobao villages: (1) Business location. In rural areas, the administrative village is used as the unit. (2) Sales scale. The annual e-commerce sales of the whole village reaches 10 million yuan. (3) Online merchant scale. The number of active online stores in the village reaches 100, or the proportion of active online stores reaches 10% of the local households. Since the emergence of the first three Taobao villages in 2009, Taobao villages have achieved exponential growth. As of 2022, Taobao villages had covered 28 provinces, autonomous regions, and municipalities, and 180 cities (regions) across the country, with a total number of 7 780 (see Figure 6-8).

The emergence of Taobao villages and their increase in number represent the continuous improvement of the scale of grass-roots e-commerce operations based on administrative villages, attracting more and more talents to take root in rural areas and promote the prosperity of rural industries.

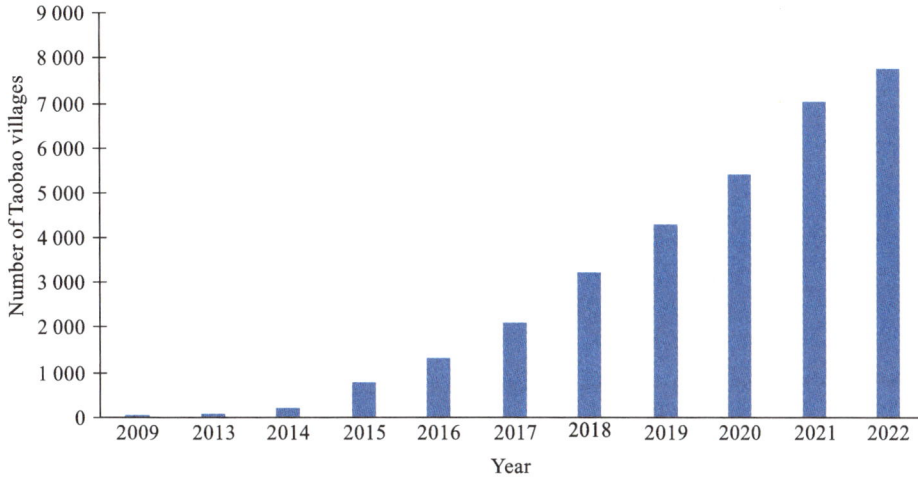

Figure 6-8　Number of Taobao villages in China (2009-2022)
Data source: Ministry of Commerce of the People's Republic of China

Rural e-commerce represented by Taobao villages has become one of the important ways for the Chinese government to eliminate poverty in rural areas. Taking Heze City, Shandong Province as an example, it promotes the "e-commerce poverty alleviation" model, deepens cooperation with e-commerce platforms such as Alibaba and JD.com, and carries out targeted training such as Taobao store operation skills improvement, new media operation, and live streaming. As of November 2018, Heze City had developed e-commerce in 563 poor villages, benefiting more than 25 000 impoverished residents, of which 43 poor villages have developed into Taobao villages and achieved poverty alleviation for the entire village. In October 2019, the Heze Poverty Alleviation and Development Office won the 2019 National Poverty Alleviation Award for Organization Innovation. In November 2019, the World Bank, Alibaba Group, and the China International Development Knowledge Center released the "E-commerce Development: Experience from China". The report affirmed that the pioneering spirit of online merchants is the most basic and fundamental driving force for the development of Taobao villages. It expected that the experience of Taobao villages will be more widely disseminated and applied in the central and western regions, so as to change the situation of more backward villages and towns, and it also expected that the experience of Taobao villages can be replicated and spread in the vast developing countries.

Internet-based informatization has helped accelerate the development of rural tourism, leisure agriculture, and homestay economy. As of September 2022, the Ministry of Agriculture and Rural Affairs (MARA) had released more than 70 promotions of rural leisure tourism boutique scenic spots and routes through its official website, covering 211 rural leisure tourism routes in 148 counties (cities, districts) of 31 provinces, autonomous regions, and municipalities across the country, and utilized the "Want to Go to the Countryside" mini-program to promote 681 rural leisure tourism boutique routes, covering over 2 500 high-quality scenic spots and other high-quality resources. The number of people returning to their hometowns to start businesses is growing rapidly. In 2021, that number reached 11.2 million in China, an increase of 10.9% over 2020.

6.2.3 Rural Public Services

The level of comprehensive rural grass-roots governance has been continuously improved. The "Internet ＋ Grass-roots Social Governance" action has been implemented in depth, and various regions have actively promoted the construction and open sharing of grass-roots social governance data resources. By the end of 2021, China had 483 000 village-level comprehensive service stations that use information technology to carry out basic public services and public utility services, with a coverage rate of 86.0 % of administrative villages. In 2021, the administrative village coverage of the Public Safety Video Application System reached 80.4%. Notably, critical water level alarm monitoring and panoramic surveillance were installed in rural water areas, effectively preventing water-related accidents. By leveraging the Child Welfare Management Information System, a comprehensive understanding of the care service recipients in rural areas has been obtained. From July 2021 to June 2022, information on 755 000 left-behind children was collected, further enhancing the precision of child welfare and protection of minors in rural areas.

Information services for agriculture, rural areas, and rural residents have become more accessible and profound. By the end of 2021, 467 000 beneficial agricultural information centers had been established and operated across the nation, collectively providing various information services to 980 million individuals. Agricultural technology services have transitioned from the fields to online platforms, with innovative services methods such as the 12316 hotline and the National Agricultural Science and Technology Service Cloud Platform Continuously evolving to serve farmers. As of August 2022, the registered users on the National Agricultural Science and Technology Service Cloud Platform had surpassed 13 million, accumulating over 3.5 billion visits, with a daily service engagement exceeding 4 million individuals, and the online question-answering response rate maintained over 92%. Notably, in 2021, the nationwide number of new agricultural business entities (including farmer cooperatives and family farms) receiving information technology-based agricultural technology promotion services reached 2.233 million.

The rural online cultural life is vibrant and diverse. The Internet has become an important channel for everyone to participate in and experience the Chinese farmers' harvest festival. In 2022, China Central Radio and Television Station created the first immersive online harvest festival gala "2022 Online Harvest Evening". "Internet Plus" mass cultural activities are booming. During the New Year's Day and Spring Festival in 2022, the National Public Culture Cloud Platform launched an online "Village Evening" special, live broadcasting 127 selected events from various places, with 148 million online participants. The "June 6th" Miao Chixin Festival basketball game spontaneously organized by the villagers of Taipan Village, Taijiang County, Guizhou Province has become a viral sensation, affectionately called Village Basketball Association (VBA) by netizens. The related online broadcasts and short videos garnered over 100 million online viewers (see Figures 6-9).

Figure 6-9 Live streaming of VBA in Taipan Village, Taijiang County, Guizhou Province
Image Sources: Tianyan News, Xinhua News Agency, CCTV News, CCTV Video

The continuous advancement of digital technology has facilitated the ongoing exploration and realization of the cultural, social, and economic values inherent in agricultural civilization. The digitalization of intangible cultural heritage resources within China's traditional villages is steadily progressing, incorporating rural cultural forms with significant value and distinctive characteristics into the overall protection scope of national pilot zones for ecological conservation. In 2021 and 2022, significant support was directed towards the digital preservation efforts of intangible cultural heritage resources in 364 traditional Chinese villages. As of June 2022, the digital museums for traditional Chinese villages had meticulously gathered and organized information on 6 819 such villages. The construction of 658 individual village exhibits had been completed, establishing a comprehensive database of traditional villages that encompasses various data types, including panoramic roaming, texts and images, audio-visual elements, and real-life models.

6.3 Smart Education

China has made great achievements in national education. Firstly, the level of education popularization has achieved a historic leap. By the end of 2021, there were

529 300 schools of all levels and types in China, with 291 million students enrolled. There were 207 000 schools in the compulsory education stage[①], with 158 million students enrolled, and the comprehensive popularization of compulsory education had been achieved; there were 22 000 high schools with 39.17 million students and a gross enrollment rate of 91.4%; there were 3 012 higher education schools with a total enrollment of 44.3 million people and a gross enrollment rate of 57.8%. Secondly, new achievements have been made in educational equity. As of 2022, 2 895 counties in China had achieved basic balance in compulsory education and established a student aid policy system covering "all educational stages, all schools, and all economically disadvantaged students" to ensure that "no student loses educational opportunities due to family economic difficulties".

Education informatization helps promote the sharing of high-quality educational resources, promote educational equity, and improve educational quality. The Ministry of Education (MOE) attaches great importance to education informatization and has carried out long-term and continuous construction of education informatization. In 2012, the MOE issued the "Ten Year Development Plan for Education Informatization (2011-2020)", setting the goal of achieving "Three Universal Accesses, and Two Internet-based Platforms", which includes "broadband network access for all schools, high-quality resources for all classes, and online learning space for everyone", as well as the educational resource public service platform and the educational management public service platform. In 2018, the MOE released the "Education Informatization 2.0 Action Plan", which proposed the development goal of "Three Coverages, Two Enhancements, and One Major Platform". "Three Coverages" means full coverage of teaching applications for all teachers, learning applications for all school-age students, and digital campus development for all schools. "Two Enhancements" means enhancing the application level of ICT in education and digital literacy among teachers and students. "One Major Platform" is to build a large-scale "Internet + Education" integrated platform.

After years of education informatization construction, China's education informatization development stage has shifted from application popularization to integrated innovation. Utilizing information technology to promote the digital transformation of Chinese education and achieve high-quality development has become a development task in the new era. In February 2019, China released the "China's Education Modernization 2035", which was the first medium-and long-term strategic plan with the theme of education modernization. It proposed to "accelerate the transformation of education in the information age", with a focus on the construction of intelligent campuses and the use of modern

---

① Since the promulgation of the "Compulsory Education Law of the People's Republic of China" in 1986, China has established a compulsory education system that spans nine years (primary and secondary education stages), all school-age children and adolescents to receive compulsory education.

technology to accelerate the reform of talent training models. In July 2021, the MOE and five other ministries issued the "Guidance on Promoting the Construction of New Education Infrastructure and Building a High-quality Education Support System", proposing a new education infrastructure system including information networks, platform systems, digital resources, smart campuses, innovative applications, and trustworthy security.

6.3.1 Digital Campus Facility

The network conditions of schools at all levels and types have improved significantly. In 2012, the MOE proposed the construction goal of "broadband network access for all schools". As of 2022, the Internet access rate of primary and secondary schools (including teaching points[①]) in China had reached 100% (see Figure 6-10), an increase of 75 percentage points from 2012; more than 75% of schools were covered by wireless networks, 99.5% of schools had multimedia classrooms, with a total number of more than 4 million, and the number of teacher and student terminals equipped in schools had exceeded 28 million; the number of digital terminals per 100 students in China's primary and junior high schools was 14.9 and 21.0 respectively, an increase of 8.4 and 10.6, respectively, compared with ten years ago; the digital teaching conditions in primary and secondary schools had been comprehensively upgraded, and a ubiquitous learning environment with complete network coverage and the integration of offline multimedia teaching space and online teaching space had basically been formed.

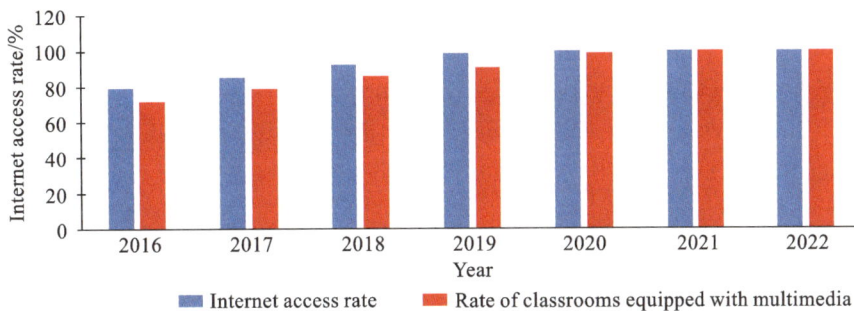

Figure 6-10 Campus network construction of China's primary and secondary schools (2016-2022)

Data Source: Ministry of Education of the People's Republic of China

With the improvement of campus network conditions, high-quality educational information resources can be effectively shared. Taking the Ningxia Hui Autonomous Region, which is located in the hinterland of northwest China as an example, the issues of unbalanced and insufficient education development there is relatively prominent. In 2018, Ningxia was approved to build a national "Internet + Education" demonstration zone. The

---

① Teaching points are small-scale, incomplete primary schools established in remote and educationally under-resourced areas, primarily utilizing multi-grade classes (combined grades in one classroom). They typically cover only lower grades, with fewer than 20 students per point.

whole region achieved 200M network broadband access in schools and built 29 000 digital classrooms. With the help of high-speed and complete network infrastructure, more than 500 schools in Ningxia had conducted online pairing-up[①] with high-quality schools in Beijing, Fujian, and other places, and all rural primary and secondary schools cooperated with urban schools online, effectively alleviating the problem of teachers shortages in under-resourced schools through cross-school collaborative teaching and online teaching assistance. The index of education informatization development in Ningxia rose from 15th in the whole country in 2017 to 6th in 2020. By 2023, the number of Ningxia users registered at the Smart Education of China platform had reached 1.25 million, covering 100% of teachers and 64.9% of students in primary and secondary schools in the region.

At present, China has established a complete digital campus standard system, covering the digital construction standards of different types of schools such as primary and secondary schools, vocational schools, and colleges and universities. The construction aspects of digital campus covers online education, education management, education evaluation, application services, cybersecurity and other aspects. In 2012, the Ministry of Education launched activities such as "100 Digital Campus Demonstration Schools" evaluation to further implement the standards; provincial education authorities also regularly carry out evaluation and assessment work on digital campus construction. The current focus of campus informatization construction has shifted from "digital campus" to "smart campus". For example, in 2023, the Beijing Municipal Education Commission issued the "Beijing Primary and Secondary School Smart Campus Construction Specifications (Trial)", proposing that the content of smart campus construction includes intelligent environment, application integration and innovation, school education data and applications, Internet services and applications, digital literacy and skills, security and operation services, etc., with a focus on co-construction and sharing and smart applications.

6.3.2 Digital Course Platform

China has established a national public service system for digital educational resources for primary and secondary schools. As of November 2020, the national public service system for digital educational resources had connected to 84 provincial and municipal educational resource platforms, providing educational teaching and management services for teachers and students; the total number of application visits had exceeded 300 million, the total number of resource sharing had exceeded 320 million, and the number of monthly

---

① Online pairing-up serves as a specific implementation of pairing assistance. China has established this mechanism between developed and underdeveloped provinces to deliver targeted support through cross-regional collaboration in funding, technology, and resource allocation, effectively narrowing regional development gaps. This approach leverages the institutional strengths of socialism with Chinese characteristics, achieving coordinated development across regions via government-led resource redistribution.

active users had reached over 60 million; more than 100 million teachers and students had created their online learning spaces, and nearly half of teachers used online learning spaces for teaching and research; to supply digital educational resources for rural schools and teaching points, a special project had been implemented to share 6 948 hours of digital resources in subjects such as English, music, and art, as well as a total of 50 million resources aligned with all subject textbooks in the basic education stage.

China has established a series of online course platforms for higher education. In 2013, Chinese universities began to build massive open online course (MOOC). Different kinds of online teaching modes, such as cross-school and cross-regional online teaching, "1 (MOOC) + M (universities) + N (students)"collaborative teaching and online and offline hybrid teaching, "MOOC + SPOC① + flipped classroom" have been realized in the university classrooms. In 2019, the Higher Education Department of the MOE issued a call for "MOOCs for the West", and a total of 172 900 MOOCs and customized course services have been provided to the under-resourced universities in the western China, helping the western region to carry out 3. 27 million blended teaching courses, with 376 million students participating in learning and 1.71 million teachers in the western region participating in application training.

In early 2020, the sudden outbreak of the COVID-19 pandemic triggered an unprecedented large-scale online teaching practice. The MOE launched the campaign of "suspension of classes but not learning", opening up a National Primary and Secondary School Network Cloud Platform to ensure home-based learning for students in areas without network or with slow network speeds through Classroom in the Air (TV version). Relying on the existing educational platforms and resources, teachers at all levels and types of schools actively carried out teaching activities (see Figure 6-11). In February 2020, the MOE's National Primary and Secondary School Network Cloud Platform was successfully launched, coordinating 7 000 servers and 90 T of bandwidth, capable of supporting simultaneous online access for 50 million students. As of May 2020, the National Primary and Secondary School network Cloud Platform had accumulated 2.07 billion views and 1.71 billion visits. Additionally, 27 provinces, autonomous regions, and municipalities opened provincial online learning platforms and guided certain cities, counties and schools with necessary infrastructure to make effective use of their local educational resources.

During the epidemic, 1 454 colleges and universities in China carried out online teaching, 1.03 million teachers taught 1.07 million courses online, and a total of 17.75 million students studied online. Supported by the Secretariat of the World MOOC and Online Education Alliance, Chinese universities have organized more than 10 global online education dialogues, opened 168 global integrated courses, implemented mutual

---

① Abbreviation for small private online course, a hybrid teaching model that combines physical classroom instruction with online learning.

recognition of credits with 13 world-renowned universities in 11 countries, and launched 8 English global open courses, attracting 7.3 million learners worldwide, with international online education cooperation and exchanges continuing to deepen. On March 13, 2020, United Nations Educational, Scientific and Cultural Organization (UNESCO) released a list of remote learning solutions to the world, recommending 27 learning applications and platforms that can be obtained freely worldwide, among which iCourse and Alibaba DingTalk from China were selected (see Figure 6-12).

Figure 6-11　During the epidemic, students learned online courses in various ways

Image Source: Wuhan Radio and Television Station

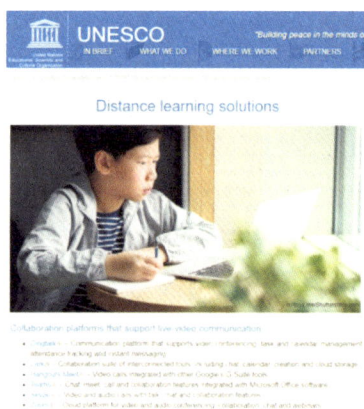

Figure 6-12　China's online course platform was included in the UNESCO recommended remote learning solutions

Image Source: UNESCO

In recent years, China has further integrated online digital education resources and platforms such as the National Digital Education Resource Public Service System and the National Primary and Secondary School Network Cloud Platform. In March 2022, the National Smart Education Public Service Platform for school students was officially launched, covering three major resource platforms: primary and secondary schools education, vocational education, and higher education, and providing 26 government services. The platform has brought together 44 000 basic education course resources, 6 628 high-quality online vocational education courses, and 27 000 quality courses in higher education. At the same time, public online course platforms opened to the public are also booming. As of November 2022, there were more than 61 900 MOOCs available online, with 402 million registered users and 979 million learners. China ranked first in the world in terms of the number of MOOCs and the number of learners, and maintains a rapid growth trend. Some MOOC platforms have introduced international versions targeting overseas learners, providing more than 900 multilingual course resources and necessary teaching services to learners from all over the world freely. Nearly a thousand online courses in 14 languages has been made available to college students and learners around the world, with a total of 670 000 learners worldwide.

6.3.3 Internet Education Application

The "three classrooms" are three types of online collaborative teaching proposed by the MOE for primary and secondary schools in educationally disadvantaged areas, including "special delivery classroom", "famous teacher classroom" and "online classroom from famous school" (see Table 6-1).

Table 6-1 Three types of online collaborative teaching for educationally disadvantaged areas

Applications	Objectives	Target users	Construction contents	Required facilities
Special delivery classroom	Solve the problem of teacher shortage in rural disvantaged schools and teaching points, and the inability to offer the national prescribed courses	Students in rural disvantaged schools and teaching points	Use online courses or synchronous classes to help them complete the national curriculum	Live streaming and recording system, remote multimedia display equipment, etc.
Famous teacher classroom	Assist skill development for teachers in rural areas	Teachers in rural disvantaged schools	Establish an online training community to improve the kills of ordinary teachers by leveraging the expertise of excellent teachers	Interactive recording and broadcasting system, online teacher training platforms, etc.
Online classroom from famous school	Narrow the disparity in education quality between regions, urban and rural areas, and schools	Teachers and students in rural disvantaged schools	Taking high-quality schools as the main body, promote the sharing of high-quality educational resources in the region through online schools, online courses, etc.	Smart classrooms, cross-school teaching platforms, etc.

In 2012, the MOE first proposed to develop "three classrooms" at the "Education Informatization Pilot Work Symposium", aiming to improve the quality of education in remote areas and promote the sharing of high-Quality teaching resources. In 2014, the MOE pointed out in the "Implementation Plan for Building an Effective Mechanism to Expand the Coverage of High-quality Education Resources by Informatization" that it was necessary to promote educational equity and improve the quality of education through various forms such as "three classrooms". In 2016, the "13th Five-Year Plan for Education Informatization" proposed actively promoting the construction of "special delivery classroom" to consolidate and deepen the "full coverage of digital teaching resources at teaching points". In March 2020, the MOE issued the "Guidance on Strengthening the Application of Three Classrooms", proposing the fully realization of "three classrooms" by 2022. In April 2022, the National Center for Educational Technology released innovative cases and shortlisted cases of the application of "three classrooms", promoted typical experiences and practices, and played a demonstration and leading role. The sample application of "three classrooms" is shown in Figure 6-13 to Figure 6-15.

Figure 6-13　Application of the "special delivery classroom": students at the teaching point in Ganzhou Economic Development Zone, Jiangxi Province interacted with students at the teaching end
Image Source: *China Education News*

Figure 6-14　Application of the "famous teacher classroom": Xinhu Primary School in Sanmen County, Zhejiang Province carried out teaching and research activities
Image Source: *China Education News*

Figure 6-15　Application of the "online classroom from famous school": exchange and training in
Three Schools Alliance in Jiangxi Province and Zhejiang Province

Image Source: *China Education News*

6.3.4　Smart Education Application

The era of artificial intelligence (AI) has brought all-round challenges to education. China attaches great importance to the impact of AI technology on education. In July 2017, the State Council issued the "New-Generation AI Development Plan", which clearly proposed the development of smart education. In April 2018, the MOE issued the "Innovation Action Plan for AI in Higher Education Institutions" and the "Action Plan for Education Informatization 2.0", which further clarified the integrated development of AI and education, and launched a pilot project to promote the construction of the teaching team with AI.

AI education is gradually entering school classrooms. The compulsory module of the "General High School Information Technology Curriculum Standards (2017 Edition, Revised in 2020)" compiled by the MOE has added basic knowledge of AI. Primary and secondary schools in various places are actively exploring the gradual popularization of information technology (IT) and AI technologies to lower-grade students. Schools have carried out the maker education and STEAM (science, technology, engineering, art and mathematics) education based on the facilities of intelligent robots. Some schools introduced the intelligent robot programming courses through IT courses and school-based elective courses established extracurricular interest groups, and offered AI popularization courses in some specified grades, bringing AI courses into the classrooms of primary and secondary school students (see Figure 6-16).

AI technology has also been applied to assist teaching in the school education. In 2016, iFLYTEK and the MOE Examination Center (now the National Education Examination Authority) jointly established a joint laboratory to explore and develop intelligent marking technology for oral English and composition in the college entrance examination. In the first half of 2017, intelligent marking technology was applied to the written examinations of the College English Test Band 4 and Band 6, as well as the high

Figure 6-16 AI course teaching and competition activities in secondary schools

Image Source: *China Education News*

school entrance examination, college entrance examination, and academic examination in 25 regions, covering nearly 7 million candidates. It can detect blank test papers, suspected duplicate test papers, and other problematic test papers, reducing the human labor workload by 20%. According to the "2022 Artificial Intelligence Education Blue Book" jointly released by East China Normal University, China Academy of Educational Sciences, Tencent Research Institute, and Tencent Education, among the 28 000 teacher samples in 25 provinces, autonomous regions, and municipalities across the country, 58% of teachers have used AI technology in the subjects they teach, 72% of teachers have adopted computer vision technology for graph recognition, and more than half of teachers have used related tools such as intelligent homework assignments, smart classrooms, and intelligent student performance analysis. Primary schools across the country have also carried out teaching explorations by introducing humanoid robots into the classroom to assist in the teaching process, as shown in Figure 6-17.

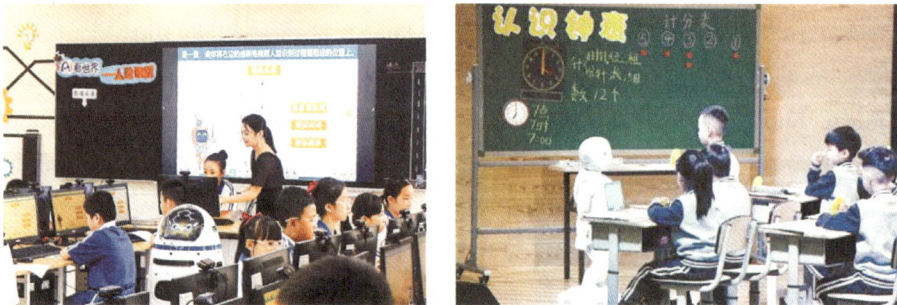

Figure 6-17 Primary schools introduced humanoid robots to assist classroom teaching

Image Sources: *China Education News* (left), *People's Daily* (right)

6.4　Smart Healthcare

China has made great achievements in national health. In 2019, the average life expectancy of Chinese residents reached 77.3 years, and the maternal mortality rate, infant mortality rate, and mortality rate of children under 5 dropped to 17.8/100 000, 5.6‰, and 7.8‰, respectively. The main health indicators were generally better than the average level of middle-and high-income countries. The framework of the basic medical and health system with Chinese characteristics has been established, and the accessibility of medical and health services has been continuously improving. As of 2020, the number of beds in medical and health institutions per thousand people had reached 6.46, 84% of county-level hospitals had reached the level of second grade hospitals and above[1], and nearly 90% of families were able to reach the nearest medical point within 15 minutes. The level of equalization of basic public health services in China has been further improved, with 14 major categories of national basic public health services provided free of charge to all urban and rural residents.

With the development of China's economy and society, the focus of China's health career in the new era has shifted from disease treatment to universal health. In October 2016, the CPC Central Committee and the State Council promulgated the "Outline of the Healthy China 2030 Plan", which established the new theme of shifting from "focusing on treating diseases" to "focusing on people's health". However, China faced the basic national conditions of uneven distribution of medical resources, large differences in service levels, and a continuously widening gap between supply and demand of medical and health services. The *2020 China Health Statistics Yearbook* showed that the number of hospitals, third grade hospitals, health technicians, and practicing physicians in the eastern region was significantly higher than that in the central and western regions. Promoting the informatization and intelligent upgrading of medical and health services is an important way to get rid of the dilemma of uneven distribution of medical resources. In November 2022, the National Health Commission (NHC), the National Administration of Traditional Chinese Medicine, and National Disease Control and Prevention Administration jointly promulgated the "14th Five-Year Plan for Universal Health Informatization", proposing that in the face of the opportunities and challenges brought about by digital transformation, it is necessary to further consolidate the new infrastructure of universal health informatization, cultivate new forms of health services, and enhance new momentum for the development of the health industry.

6.4.1 Digital Healthcare Infrastructure

China's hospital informatization has developed through several stages. It entered the

---

[1] According to the standards of the National Health Commission, the hospitals in China are classified into 3 grades and 10 levels, based on their scale, facility conditions, service scope, etc. In general, first-grade hospitals provide health services to local community residents; second-grade hospitals are regional hospitals that serve multiple communities; third-grade hospitals are cross-regional medical centers that can provide services to patients from local cities, provinces, or even across country.

initial stage in the 1990s. The focus of informatization during this period was on management informatization, computerizing traditional business management models (including hospital financial management, fee management systems, etc.) and realizing the application of computer technology in the medical and health system. In 2010, it entered the in-depth application stage. The focus then was to realize various clinical information systems with electronic medical record system as the core, including clinical examination information management system, medical imaging information management system, etc (see Figure 6-18). After 2015, it entered the stage of hospital integration platformization, that is, to realize information exchange within the hospitals and promote the in-depth application of electronic medical record.

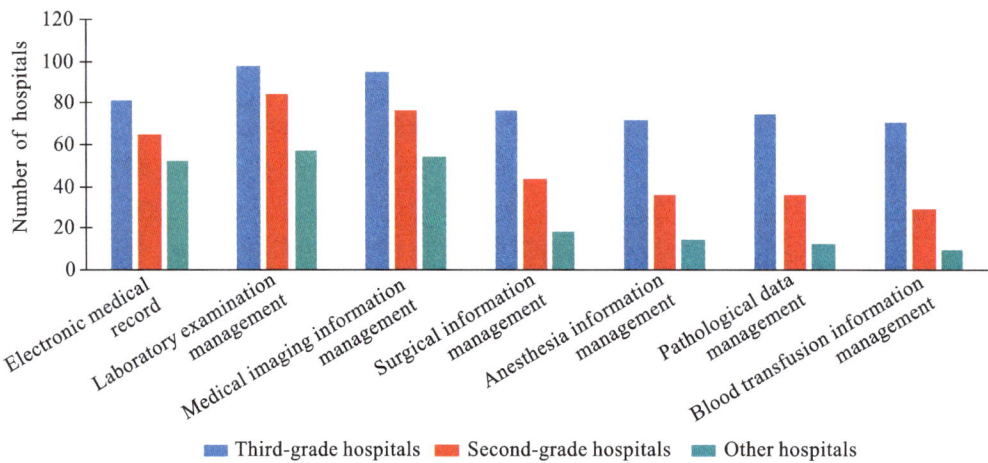

Figure 6-18　Development of clinical medical applications in hospitals at all grade in China

Data Source: Statistical Information Center of the National Health Commission, *Universal Health Informatization Survey Report—Regional Health Informatization and Hospital Informatization (2021)*, 2021

China has formulated a series of standards for the informatization construction of medical and health institutions across the country. From 2018 to 2019, the NHC successively issued the "Standards and Specifications for National Hospital Informatization Construction (Trial)", "Management Measures for the Grading Evaluation of the Application Level of Electronic Medical Record Systems (Trial)", "Grading Evaluation Standards for the Application Level of Electronic Medical Record Systems (Trial)", and "Standards and Specifications for National Basic Medical and Health Institutions Informatization Construction (Trial)", which clarified the construction content of informatization service standards for various business processes of primary medical and health institutions such as hospitals, community health service centers (stations), and township-level health centers (village health clinics). The NHC regarded the grading evaluation of the application level of electronic medical record systems as one of the iconic indicators of the informatization of medical and health institutions. As of July 2021, a total of 118 hospitals in China had participated in the electronic medical record evaluation and were rated as the fifth-level and above medical and health institutions; 153 regional competent units and 503 second-grade and above hospitals had passed the interconnection level evaluation.

At present, China has been actively promoting regional medical and health informatization, using tiered diagnosis and treatment and data sharing to provide data sharing services to institutions and individuals such as medical service providers, health management institutions, patients, medical payers, and pharmaceutical product suppliers within a certain geographical scope. For example, Jiangsu Province has built a universal health information platform covering the entire province. As of May 2022, this platform had connected to 13 municipal and 96 county-level (or district-level) health information platforms in Jiangsu Province, connecting more than 20 000 medical and health institutions, and formulated and issued nearly 40 local health information standards, achieving standardized data collection and gathering 41.8 billion pieces of data. Based on the universal health information platform, Jiangsu Province has built a one-stop people-friendly service system called "Jiangsu Health Pass", which has provided 10 million health records for residents across the province; more than 10 business applications have been carried out, including comprehensive supervision of medical services, primary health supervision, maternal and child health management, and infectious disease monitoring and early warning.

At the same time, China has also been promoting the informatization of medical insurance payment services. In 2022, China built a unified national medical insurance information platform, connecting to about 400 000 designated medical institutions and 400 000 designated retail pharmacies, effectively covering all insured persons. The national medical insurance service platform has 280 million real-name users, covering more than 100 service functions. New applications of digital technology in auxiliary diagnosis, rehabilitation, distribution and transportation, medical robots and other aspects have been rapidly popularizing, and new forms such as Internet live interactive family parenting, online infant and toddler raising courses, and parent classes have been constantly emerging.

6.4.2　Internet Medical Application

Internet medical applications have been widely deployed, with offline and online medical care showing trend toward collaborative development. As of October 2020, there were more than 900 Internet hospitals in China, the telemedicine collaboration network had covered all prefecture-level cities, and more than 5 500 hospitals at or above the second grade were able to provide online services. By the end of 2021, 64.6% of public hospitals at or above the second grade were able to provide telemedicine, and 54.5% had opened appointment diagnosis and treatment services. The service capacity of the health information platform of traditional Chinese medicine clinics continues to improve, and a total of 16 200 traditional Chinese medicine clinics have been connected to the platform. By the end of December 2020, the platform had received a total of 13 million patients, filled out nearly 1 million electronic medical records of traditional Chinese medicine, prescribed more than 870 000 prescriptions for treatment based on syndrome differentiation, and queried the knowledge base more than 1.03 million times. New health service models such as "Internet Plus" epidemic prevention science popularization, online consultation, remote consultation, and drug distribution have rapidly gained popularity.

During the COVID-19 pandemic in February 2020, more than 42 000 medical staff from all over the country rushed to Hubei Province to provide help. At the same time, more doctors took advantage of information technology to open up a "second battlefield" online, breaking through the bottleneck of medical service supply and effectively supporting the main battlefield in Hubei Province. For example, the medical team from Guangdong Province that provided pairing assistance[①] to Jingzhou City in Hubei Province collaborated with Jingzhou City to establish an Internet hospital. More than 1 300 doctors from 15 medical institutions in Guangdong Province volunteered to participate, and over 100 000 visits were made in 18 days, providing sustained medical support for Jingzhou City. "Internet + Medical Health" has broken the time and space limitations of the distribution of medical resources, and played an active role in the fight against the prevention and control of the COVID-19 pandemic by innovating service models, improving service efficiency, and reducing service costs.

5G smart emergency treatment has been deployed to improve the treatment efficiency. In March 2020, Hainan Province started the construction of 5G smart emergency platforms in Qionghai People's Hospital and Boao Central Hospital. From the first moment the emergency personnel receive the patient, the patient's basic vital signs data, condition assessment images, and emergency condition records are transmitted to the command center and emergency station in real time through the 5G network. Hospital experts can view patient testing and monitoring information and videos from the emergency ambulance, and provide remote guidance to the medical staff on the emergency ambulance through the remote consultation system and formulate rescue plans in advance (see Figure 6-19). In 2020, Hainan Province started the construction of the "Capacity Improvement Project for Primary Medical and Health Institutions Based on the 5G-assisted IoTs". By April 2021, the project had realized the 5G smart upgrade of seven third-grade and class A hospitals, 18 county-level hospitals in cities and counties, 340 township-level medical institutions and 2 693 village health clinics in the province.

5G remote surgery has begun operation. The 5G technology, characterized by high

---

① During the COVID-19 pandemic in 2020, China implemented a "pairing assistance" mechanism, where 16 provinces were designated by the State Council's joint prevention and control system to provide one-on-one support to prefecture-level cities in Hubei (excluding Wuhan), alleviating pressure on local medical resources.

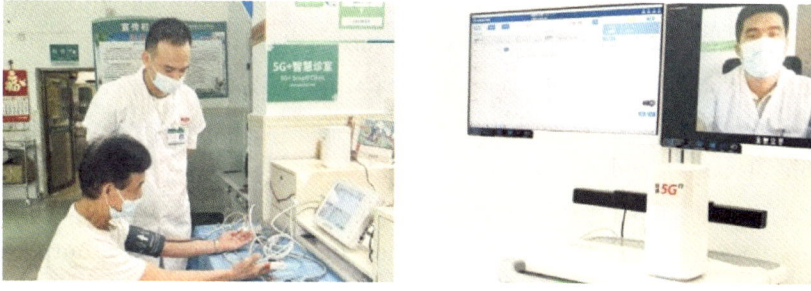

Figure 6-19 5G remote emergency: Hainan Province's 5G smart emergency platform

Image Source: *People's Daily*

bandwidth and low latency, shortens the network latency to 10 milliseconds, making remote surgery possible (see Figure 6-20). In January 2019, the world's first remote animal surgery based on 5G network was successfully implemented in Fuzhou City, Fujian Province. The doctor and the "patient" (piglet) were 50 kilometers apart. Through the 5G network environment built by China Unicom in Fujian Province, the doctor remotely controlled the surgical robot and successfully removed the piglet's liver lobule. In March 2019, China's first 5G-based remote human surgery—Parkinson disease "brain pacemaker" implantation surgery was completed in Beijing. This surgery was carried out through the 5G network, spanning nearly 3 000 kilometers, and successfully realized the Parkinson disease "brain pacemaker" implantation surgery between the First Medical Center of the Chinese People's Liberation Army General Hospital in Beijing and one hospital in Hainan Province, realizing 5G remote surgery control.

Figure 6-20 5G remote surgery

Image Sources: *People's Daily*

6.4.3 Smart Medical Application

AI technology has been introduced in the assistance of diagnosis. For a long time, China's rural primary medical resources had been in a relatively disadvantaged position. The use of AI technology can provide auxiliary diagnosis suggestions for primary doctors and improve their diagnostic and treatment capabilities. "Smart Medical Assistant" is an artificial intelligence application for medical and health institutions promoted by the Health

Commission of Anhui Province. Based on the medical knowledge graph, the application extracts and analyzes the electronic medical record information of the patient to provide doctors with a list of suspected diseases. "Smart Medical Assistant" has the monitoring and early warning capabilities for all 40 statutory communicable diseases, 15 key communicable diseases, and 6 syndromes. In 2017, this application passed the written examination of the national Medical Comprehensive Written Examination for Physician Qualification. "Smart Medical Assistant" also supports batch voice outbound calling, which can help primary doctors complete chronic disease follow-up, maternal and child health follow-up, notification, education, physical examination appointments and other tasks for contracted residents. As of October 2022, the "Smart Medical Assistant" had achieved full coverage and regular application in 104 districts and counties in Anhui Province, serving more than 30 000 primary doctors, assisting doctors in completion of more than 160 million electronic medical records, providing more than 430 million auxiliary diagnosis suggestions, and issuing more than 130 million rational drug quality inspection prescriptions.

AI also plays an increasingly important role in pathological diagnosis. According to the current medical standards in China, 1 to 2 pathologists are required for every 100 medical beds. Based on this calculation, there is a shortage of 80 000 to 100 000 pathologists in China. In general, it will take 30 to 40 minutes for a human pathologist to read each film manually, but the accuracy rate is only 60%. AI technology can help doctors improve the repeatability, accuracy and efficiency of diagnosis, and alleviate the shortage of pathologists to a certain extent. In November 2017, the MOST announced the first batch of national new-generation AI open innovation platforms, and specifically designated Tencent to build the "New-Generation AI Open Innovation Platform for Medical Imaging". In 2018, Tencent established an AI medical center, applied for more than 1 500 patents, and published more than 300 papers at top academic conferences. As of 2019, Tencent had cooperated with more than 100 third-grade and class A hospitals in China, processed more than 270 million images in medical imaging, and developed AI imaging products such as early esophageal cancer screening, early lung cancer screening, diabetic retinopathy detection, colorectal cancer screening, early breast cancer screening and early cervical cancer screening; the AI auxiliary/guidance system had been introduced into 300 hospitals and 4.7 million accurate guidance had been carried out.

6.5　Summary

The Chinese government attaches great importance to improving the living standards and quality of the people. In recent years, China has given full play to its advantages in informatization and established a comprehensive and multi-level digital social service system, which has greatly expanded the coverage of public services and significantly enhanced the level of equalization of basic public services. Through the construction of smart city and digital village, urban and rural public services have achieved coordinated optimization, making people's lives more convenient and better. The in-depth advancement of smart education and smart healthcare has effectively promoted educational equity and the rational distribution of medical resources.

China regards smart city as an advanced stage of urban informatization construction and actively uses informatization means to address development challenges in densely populated cities. In terms of urban traffic control, many cities, such as Shenzhen, have built intelligent traffic command and control centers, greatly improving traffic efficiency. In urban comprehensive governance, China pioneered the concept of the "City Brain". Practices in places like Hangzhou have achieved fruitful results and effectively solved urban operation problems. In terms of urban digital governance, cities such as Shanghai have explored the construction of digital twin city systems, making urban management more efficient and intelligent.

China attaches great importance to coordinated urban-rural development and regards the construction of digital villages as a key path to rural revitalization. In the construction of rural network infrastructure, China has maintained continuous investment over the years. Through projects such as the "Village-to-Village" project, the Internet-based Poverty Alleviation Action Plan, China has overcome numerous difficulties and achieved full coverage of rural network infrastructure, greatly narrowing the "digital divide" between urban and rural areas. As to the rural digital economy, the government actively promotes the development of rural e-commerce. Innovative models such as Taobao Villages have driven the sales of agricultural products and the employment of farmers, providing new ideas for global rural economic development and poverty reduction. In addition, China has also used digital methods to improve the level of rural public services, enhance the level of rural grass-roots comprehensive governance, and enrich the cultural lives of farmers.

China regards education informatization as an important way to address the imbalance of educational resources and actively promotes the digital transformation of education. In the construction of digital campus facilities, the network conditions of schools have been significantly improved, high-quality educational resources are being effectively shared, and a complete digital campus standard system has been established. Digital course platforms are constantly being improved, covering primary and secondary education as well as higher education. They played an important role during the pandemic, enabling continuous learning despite school closures. Internet-based education applications represented by the "Three Classrooms" have promoted educational equity in basic education and effectively addressed the shortage of educational resources in remote rural areas. AI general education, represented by IT education and robot innovation, is being gradually promoted in primary and secondary schools, providing support for cultivating a scientific research talent team for China in the future.

China takes medical informatization as an important means to address the uneven distribution of medical resources. In terms of digital medical infrastructure, China has established a basic medical security system covering the entire population, formulated standards for hospital informatization, and significantly improved the modernization level of medical institutions at all levels and of various types. In the application of Internet-based medical services, the ICT applications such as 5G have achieved breakthroughs in remote first aid and remote surgery, making up for the development gap in medical levels between regions. In the application of new technologies, the AI applications in auxiliary diagnosis and pathological diagnosis are becoming more and more mature. These measures improved the medical level at the grass-roots level, alleviated the healthcare workforce shortage of medical resources, and contributed Chinese wisdom to global medical development.

It is worth noting that during the construction of a "Smart Society", the advantages of socialism with Chinese characteristics have played a crucial role in the face of many difficulties and challenges. Take rural network construction as an example, although facing problems such as high construction investment, high maintenance costs, and low investment returns, Chinese state-owned enterprises, proceeding from national strategies and the interests of the people, have bravely taken on heavy responsibilities and made continuous investments. They have successfully extended information networks to every remote village, building the world's most extensive rural network infrastructure. This has provided solid support for China to win the battle against absolute poverty, demonstrating the strong advantage of the socialism with Chinese characteristics in pooling resources to accomplish major tasks and offering a successful example for the construction of a global digital society.

7 Cyberspace Governance

7.1 Demands and Challenges

7.1.1 Overview of Cyberspace

The concept of cyberspace was initially introduced by Western scholars and has gradually gained global recognition. In 1984, American science fiction writer William Gibson first proposed the concept of cyberspace in his novel *Neuromancer*, referring to the space formed by the global computer network. Major countries in the world have different definitions of cyberspace. For example, the United States (US) describes cyberspace as "an interdependent network of mutual trust composed of information technology infrastructure, including the Internet, telecommunications networks, computer systems, etc., as well as a virtual environment for information and human interaction"; Germany defines cyberspace as "including all information infrastructure that can be accessed through the Internet across territorial boundaries"; the United Kingdom (UK) defines cyberspace as "a human-computer interaction field composed of digital networks and used to store, modify, and transmit information, including the Internet and other information systems used to support business, infrastructure and services"; China's "National Cyberspace Security Strategy" points out that cyberspace is "composed of the Internet, communications networks, computer systems, automatic control systems, digital devices and the applications, services and data they carry".

Cyberspace has become the overarching term for the digital society constructed by information and network technologies and products. The omnipresence of the Internet makes a secure, stable, and prosperous cyberspace increasingly significant for national and global peace and development. Cyberspace governance encompasses various aspects, including cyberspace information security, legal construction in cyberspace, and regulation of the digital economy. In comparison to governance in traditional human societies, cyberspace governance exhibits four distinctive characteristics.

Firstly, cyberspace governance is fundamental. With the rapid development of global informatization, network information systems have become key platforms and nerve center for national politics, economy, culture, and society. Nearly all the activities in social production and life are increasingly inseparable from network information systems, including state organs and various enterprises and institutions fulfilling their social management responsibilities, providing social services, and maintaining their normal operations.

Secondly, cyberspace governance is open. The Internet is inherently open, and information exchange in cyberspace transcends geographical boundaries and is not constrained by space. This characteristic also means that cyberspace security has no obvious boundaries. In this sense, cyberspace security is not only the responsibility of a country, but also the common responsibility of the international community.

Thirdly, cyberspace governance is systematic. Cyberspace governance encompasses everything from the hardware of network construction and the software managing and controlling networks to network services and applications. The higher the degree of informatization, the greater the number of distributed nodes. Any node in the network can impact cyberspace security, akin to the weakest-link principle. Complex network systems require a focus on the security levels of the most vulnerable elements.

Finally, cyberspace governance is strategic. As cybersecurity and informatization continue to play an increasingly crucial role in national security and development, they have risen to the level of major national strategies. China needs to strengthen top-level design and strategic coordination. Cyberspace security represents a strategic mindset and deployment in the era of the Internet.

7.1.2　Cyberspace Security and Governance

Cyberspace security represents a novel form of societal security, encompassing the security of governments, social organizations, and individuals on a global scale. It primarily involves three aspects: the security of computer systems, the security of programs and data within the systems, and the security of network connections. The security of computer systems, forming the physical foundation of cyberspace security, not only supports the normal functioning of the network, but also accepts services, serving as a critical guarantee for the network's normal operation. The security of programs and data within the systems is essential for ensuring the stable and reliable operation of applications and protecting software data from damage and theft. The security of network connections refers to the protection of information during the process of network connection, such as protecting the transmission path and specific content from malicious alteration, defending against the intrusion of Trojans and viruses, and more.

Cyberspace has gradually become a crucial domain for social life, economic interactions, political maneuvering, and cultural integration. However, it has not fundamentally altered the basic legal order of human society. The actions of individuals and groups in both physical space and virtual cyberspace constitute their complete behavior in human society, requiring protection and supervision under the rule of law. The continuous interaction and collaboration of humans in the virtual cyberspace have promoted the formation of the cyber society. The concept and scope of cyber society governance are continuously evolving. Representative issues include the protection of user digital rights, governance of online behavior, technical algorithm governance, digital economic regulation, and more. Specifically:

First, the connotation of user digital rights is relatively broad, usually including the right of every citizen to access the Internet normally, the right to conduct relevant activities on the Internet, and the right to protect the privacy of personal digital information. Internet access services have become public services like ordinary postal services. Civil activities carried out by individuals on the Internet are also legally binding, such as payment and signature, which require a sound personal identity authentication system to ensure. Individuals' participation in online activities, such as online shopping and online medical consultation, also involves personal privacy and other sensitive information, which requires a sound personal information protection mechanism.

Second, there are also many illicit activities and illegal behaviors in cyberspace, which need to be governed in line with the existing laws and regulations. Typical illegal online behaviors involve the dissemination of illegal content, including editing and disseminating infringing digital content, disseminating violent and reactionary content, and disseminating false information. In addition, using the Internet to engage in illegal activities will also damage the rights and interests of the general public. For example, illegal activities such as online fraud, online gambling, online pyramid schemes, and online illegal fundraising will cause significant losses to the victim's property and affect the normal order of life.

Third, the technology and algorithm governance of cyberspace faces multi-dimensional challenges. Artifical intelligence (AI) technology, dominated by machine learning algorithms, has become the core driving force of major online platforms. However, its structural flaws in terms of fairness, transparency, and security have led to frequent occurrences of irregular algorithm applications. These technological risks have gradually evolved into complex challenges for cyber society governance, affecting many aspects such as social fairness and justice, the legitimate rights and interests of Internet users, and the security of virtual property.

Fourth, competition in the online market during the digital economy era has brought many new problems. For example, super platforms have become digital economic infrastructure formed in a highly digital market environment, and the operation and supervision of platforms are difficult to manage through traditional market supervision methods. For another example, online commodity transactions involve not only online links such as buying and selling, and after-sales service, but also offline links such as express logistics, which are difficult to track and supervise through traditional channels.

Cyberspace is not beyond the reach of the law. Safeguarding the lawful rights of individuals and groups in cyberspace and maintaining the normal operation of the cyberspace are new challenges for every government. Countries worldwide are taking measures, including legislative actions, to govern behaviors in the cyber society. Taking

2020 for instance, in January, the US released the "Guidance for Regulation of AI Applications", emphasizing flexible regulatory approaches to avoid hindering innovation; in February, the European Commission released the "White Paper on Artificial Intelligence: a European approach to excellence and trust" and proposed to build a "regulatory framework for AI"; in June, the European Commission assessed the "General Data Protection Regulation", and established a personal data usage model based on principle that "processing personal data is generally prohibited, unless it is expressly allowed by law"; in December, the European Commission unveiled drafts of the "Digital Services Act" and the "Digital Markets Act", requiring that technology companies must not utilize competitors' data to compete against them and should ensure fair product displays on their platforms.

7.2　Cyberspace Legal System

With the development of the Internet, China's cyber legislation has gone through a development process from nothing to something, from few to many, from points to lines, from lines to planes, and from planes to volumes.

The first stage ran from 1994 to 1999, which represented the access popularization of the Internet in China. The number of Internet users and devices increased steadily. The cyber legislation at this stage mainly focused on network infrastructure security, namely computer system security and cybersecurity.

The second stage ran from 2000 to 2011, marking the extensive application of the Internet, a period when personal computers served as the primary terminal devices for Interent access. As the number of computers gradually increased and Internet connection services became more affordable, Internet access became increasingly common, and network information services developed rapidly. During this stage, cyber legislation shifted its focus to network information services and content management.

The third stage began from 2012, which corresponded to the widespread adoption of mobile Internet, with smartphones becoming the predominant terminal devices for accessing the Internet. Cyber legislation at this stage gradually tends to comprehensively cover the network information services, information development, cybersecurity, and other aspects of comprehensive Internet governance.

As of 2023, China had established over 140 cyberspace-related laws, forming a comprehensive legislative framework for digital governance. Anchored in the Constitution and strengthened by multi-tiered legal instruments—including laws, administrative regulations, departmental rules and local regulations, and local administrative rules—this framework extends from the traditional legislation, addresses the special domains of cyberspace, such as online content construction and governance, cybersecurity and informatization development, and provides institutional bedrock for advancing China's strategic cyberpower objectives. The overview of China's cyber legislation is shown in Table 7-1.

Table 7-1   Overview of China's cyber legislation

Types	Examples
Laws	Electronic Commerce Law of the People's Republic of China Electronic Signature Law of the People's Republic of China Cybersecurity Law of the People's Republic of China Data Security Law of the People's Republic of China Personal Information Protection Law of the People's Republic of China Law on Combating Telecom and Online Fraud of the People's Republic of China
Administrative regulations	Regulations on the Protection of Computer Information Systems of the People's Republic of China Regulations on Computer Software Protection Administrative Measures on Internet Information Services Telecommunications Regulations of the People's Republic of China Regulations on the Administration of Foreign Investment in Chinese Telecommunications Businesses Regulations on the Protection of the Right of Communication Through Information Networks Regulations on the Security and Protection of Critical Information Infrastructure
Departmental rules	Regulations on the Protection of Children's Online Personal Information China Internet Domain Name Regulations Measures on the Supervision and Administration of Online Transactions Provisions on the Administration of Internet News and Information Services Regulations on the Governance of Internet Information Content Regulations on the Management of Algorithmic Recommendations for Internet Information Services
Local regulations	Guangdong Provincial Digital Economy Promotion Act Zhejiang Provincial Digital Economy Promotion Act Hebei Provincial Regulations on Information Technology Development Guizhou Provincial Regulations on Government Data Sharing Shanghai Municipal Data Regulations
Local administration rules	Measures of Guangdong Province on Public Data Management Measures of Anhui Province on the Management of Data and Resources for Government Affairs Measures of Jiangxi Province on the Protection of Computer Information System Security Interim Measures of Hangzhou City on the Administration of Online Transactions

7.2.1　Protection of Personal Rights

Safeguarding citizens' freedom and confidentiality of communications. The protection of freedom and confidentiality of communications is a prerequisite for ensuring that citizens can express their demands and ideas independently in cyberspace. As early as 1997, the State Council formulated the "Administrative Measures for the Security Protection of International Internet Connection of Computer Information Networks" to implement the protection of the basic rights of freedom and confidentiality of communications in the Constitution; the "Telecommunications Regulations of the People's Republic of China" promulgated in 2000 stipulates that the freedom of telecommunications users to use telecommunications in accordance with the law and the confidentiality of communications are protected by law; the "Radio Management Regulations of the People's Republic of China" revised in 2016 further strengthens the protection of confidentiality of communications in the field of radio, realizing the all-round protection of this basic right in cyberspace.

Protecting personal information rights and interests. Through civil law, criminal law, and special legislation, a legal barrier for the protection of the entire chain of personal information rights and interests has been established. The Amendment Ⅸ to the "Criminal Law of the People's Republic of China" adopted in 2015 makes more detailed provisions on the crime of illegally obtaining citizens' personal information and strengthens the criminal law protection of personal information. In the special network legislation, the "Decision of the Standing Committee of the National People's Congress on Strengthening the Protection of Network Information" adopted in 2012 clearly protects electronic information that can identify citizens' personal identities and involves citizens' personal privacy; the "Cybersecurity Law of the People's Republic of China" promulgated in 2016 has further improved the rules for personal information protection; the "Personal Information Protection Law of the People's Republic of China" promulgated in 2021 refines and improves the principles of personal information protection and the rules for personal information processing, regulates the activities of state organs in handling personal information in accordance with the law, grants personal information subjects a number of rights, and strengthens the obligations of personal information processors.

Preserving the property safety of citizens. China continues to increase legislative protection efforts to curb the use of the Internet to infringe on property rights and interests. The "Electronic Commerce Law of the People's Republic of China" promulgated in 2018 stipulates that "the goods sold or services provided by e-commerce operators shall comply with the requirements for protecting personal and property safety and environmental protection requirements, and shall not sell or provide goods or services prohibited by laws and administrative regulations". The "Civil Code of the People's Republic of China" clearly states that the use of the Internet to infringe on the property rights and interests of others shall bear corresponding legal responsibilities. The "Law on Combating Telecom and Online Fraud of the People's Republic of China" promulgated in 2022 provides strong legal support for combating telecom and online fraud activities and effectively safeguards the property rights and interests of the people.

Ensuring the digital rights for special groups. Through multi-level and multi-dimensional legislation, the digital divide of special groups such as minors, the elderly, and the disabled can be bridged, so that they can integrate into the digital society more equally and widely, and enjoy the dividends of the digital age. The "Cybersecurity Law of the People's Republic of China" stipulates that "the state supports the research and development of network products and services that are conducive to the healthy growth of minors, punishes the use of the Internet to engage in activities that endanger the physical and mental health of minors in accordance with the law, and provides a safe and healthy network environment for minors." The "Regulations on the Protection of Children's Online Personal Information" issued in 2019 gives priority to the protection of children's personal information rights and interests. The "Minors Protection Law of the People's Republic of China" revised in 2020 makes special provisions for strengthening the Internet literacy education of minors, strengthening the supervision of Internet content for minors, strengthening the protection of minors' personal information and the prevention and treatment of Internet addiction, etc., to protect the legitimate rights and interests of minors on the Internet. The "Data Security Law of the People's Republic of China" issued in 2021 requires that intelligent public services should fully consider the needs of the elderly and the disabled, and avoid obstacles to the daily lives of them.

7.2.2 Digital Economy Regulation

Continuously improving data infrastructure system. China maintains digital market order, and regulates new digital economic formats and models, providing a good institutional foundation for the healthy development of the digital economy and helping the economy shift from high-speed growth to high-quality development. China pays attention to the role of data as a basic resource and an innovation engine. The "Data Security Law of the People's Republic of China" makes relevant provisions for implementing the big data strategy, supporting data-related technology research and development and commercial innovation, promoting the construction of data-related standard systems, and cultivating data trading markets, so as to improve the level of data development and utilization and promote the development of the digital economy with data as the key element.

Clarifying operational systems for the digital market. China adheres to the legal and standardized development of the digital market, resolutely opposes monopoly and unfair competition, improves digital rules, and effectively maintains a fair and competitive market environment. The "Electronic Commerce Law of the People's Republic of China" comprehensively regulates e-commerce business operations, clarifies the responsibilities of e-commerce platform operators and operators within the platform, and requires e-commerce operators with market dominance not to abuse their market dominance to exclude or restrict competition, and maintain a fair market competition order. The "Law of the People's Republic of China on the Protection of Consumer Rights and Interests" revised in 2013 established systems such as "seven-day no-reason return" for online shopping, and strengthened the main responsibility of online operators for consumer rights protection. The "Anti-Unfair Competition Law of the People's Republic of China" revised in 2017 added a special article on the Internet, prohibiting the use of technical means for unfair competition. The "Measures on the Supervision and Administration of Online Transactions" formulated in 2021 refines the relevant provisions of the "Electronic Commerce Law of the People's Republic of China" and further improves the online transaction supervision system.

Regulating new business formats and models in the digital economy. New business formats and models of digital economy in China are emerging rapidly, bringing tremendous impetus and potential to economic and social development while also posing new challenges to social governance and industrial development. The "Civil Code of the People's Republic of China" improves the rules for the conclusion and performance of electronic contracts, brings data and network virtual property into the scope of legal protection, and promotes the development of digital economy. The "Interim Measures for the Administration of Online Taxi Booking Services", the "Regulations on the Management of Algorithmic Recommendations for Internet Information Services", the "Provisions on the Administration of Blockchain Information Services", the "Interim Measures for the Administration of Business Activities of Online Lending Information Intermediaries", and the "Interim Provisions on the Administration of Online Tourism Services" regulate new technologies and formats of business such as online taxis, algorithms, blockchain, Internet finance, and online tourism, and enrich the legal basis for the governance of various fields of "Internet Plus".

7.2.3 Network Information Security

Establishing cybersecurity rules. In 1994, China issued the "Regulations on the Protection of Computer Information Systems of the People's Republic of China", which established the protection system and security supervision system of the computer information system security; in 2000, the "Decision of the Standing Committee of the National People's Congress on Ensuring Internet Security" was passed, which divided Internet security into Internet operation security and Internet information security, and established a cybersecurity responsibility system framework of civil liability, administrative liability, and criminal liability; on November 7, 2016, the "Cybersecurity Law of the People's Republic of China" was passed, which is China's first basic law to comprehensively regulate issues related to cybersecurity management. The "Cybersecurity

Law of the People's Republic of China" clarifies the systems for ensuring network operation security, network products and services security, network data security, and network information security. Laws and regulations such as the "Measures on Cybersecurity Review" and the "Regulations on the Management of Security Loopholes of Network Products" further refine the relevant systems of the "Cybersecurity Law of the People's Republic of China". In May 2019, the "Information Security Technology—Basic Requirements for Cybersecurity Level Protection" was officially released, making the official entry of China's cybersecurity level protection work into the 2.0 era.

Ensuring security of critical information infrastructure. Critical information infrastructure is the nerve center of economic and social operations, and is of great significance for maintaining national cyber sovereignty and national security, ensuring the healthy development of the economy and society, and safeguarding public interests and the legitimate rights and interests of citizens. The "Regulations on the Security and Protection of Critical Information Infrastructure" passed in 2021 has improved the critical information infrastructure identification mechanism, and made specific provisions for operators of critical information infrastructure to implement cybersecurity responsibilities, establish and improve cybersecurity protection systems, set up special security management institutions, conduct security monitoring and risk assessments, and standardize network products and services procurement activities, providing a legal basis for accelerating the improvement of critical information infrastructure security protection capabilities.

Constructing a legal system for data security management. Based on the actual data security work and focusing on prominent issues in the field of data security, China has strengthened data security protection through legislation to enhance the country's data security protection capabilities. The "Data Security Law of the People's Republic of China" was officially issued in June 2021, achieving a "breakthrough" from scratch in the data governance system and becoming a basic law in the field of China's data security. The "Data Security Law of the People's Republic of China" clearly stipulates the establishment and improvement of systems such as data categorization and classification protection, risk monitoring and early warning, emergency response, and data security review; it also contains measures to facilitate data security and development and provisions for the security and openness of government data.

7.2.4 Network Ecosystem Norms

The cyberspace serves as a collective spiritual haven for hundreds of millions of people. A cyberspace characterized by a clear and pure atmosphere and a thriving ecosystem, embodies the aspirations of the populace for an ideal online home. Out of a strong sense of responsibility toward society and the people, China has introduced laws and regulations for cyberspace governance, focusing primarily on regulating online information content and persistently purifying the online environment.

Standardizing the order of online information dissemination. Facing with the global problem of online information governance, China has promulgated laws and regulations such as the "Civil Code of the People's Republic of China", the "Cybersecurity Law of the People's Republic of China", and the "Administrative Measures on Internet Information Services" to clarify the norms for the dissemination of online information content and the responsibilities of relevant entities, providing a legal basis for the governance of illegal acts that endanger national security, damage public interests, and infringe upon the legitimate rights and interests of others.

Building legal instruments to combat terrorism in cyberspace. China stands firm to against the threat of cyberterrorism in accordance with the law. The "Criminal Law of the People's Republic of China", the "Criminal Procedure Law of the People's Republic of China", the "Anti-Money Laundering Law of the People's Republic of China" and other laws have made provisions for the criminal liability of terrorist crimes, the litigation procedures for punishing terrorist crimes, and the monitoring of terrorist funds. The "Anti-Terrorism Law of the People's Republic of China", passed in 2015, has made special provisions on the objects, measures and mechanisms of cyberterrorism.

7.3 Cybersecurity Protection

7.3.1 Cybersecurity Technology Standards

China has strengthened research on new technologies, developed and deployed a series of security products and system platforms, and overcome a number of major technical challenges in the field of information security. China has independently developed the ZUC[①] stream cipher algorithm, which has encryption strength comparable to that of international mainstream cipher algorithms. Significant progress has been made in the joint efforts to tackle key problems in the field of secure and reliable basic software and hardware. Self-developed security operating systems have progressed from "basic availability" to "availability". Domestic databases are widely used in state organs and important fields. Domestic computers based on domestic basic software and hardware have been tried out in some party and government agencies and key fields. The industrialization of security protection systems for industrial control systems have made positive progress. In August 2010, the TePA (Tri-element Peer Authentication) proposed by China was officially approved by the International Organization for Standardization (ISO), becoming the first international standard approved in the field of basic common technologies for cybersecurity.

① ZUC is named after Zu Chongzhi, a renowned Chinese mathematician and astronomer of the 5th century AD.

China actively promotes cybersecurity standardization and builds a sound national cybersecurity standard system. In 2020, the National Technical Committee on Information Security Standardization promoted the release of 53 national cybersecurity standards and more than 10 international standards led and co-developed by China. In 2021, China made new breakthroughs in the international standardization of commercial cryptography. Its independently developed SM9 identification cipher algorithm was officially released as an ISO/IEC (International Organization for Standardization/International Electrotechnical Commission) international standard, and the SM4 block cipher algorithm entered the ISO/IEC official release stage. As of June 2021, China had issued a total of 323 national cybersecurity standards, which play a fundamental, normative and leading role in supporting national cybersecurity work and safeguarding the vital interests of the majority of Internet users.

7.3.2 Cybersecurity Protection Forces

China has established a number of professional cybersecurity institutions, which have effectively improved China's cybersecurity monitoring and emergency response capabilities. In 1996, the National Computer Virus Emergency Response Center was established to mobilize domestic anti-virus forces to quickly discover and deal with computer virus epidemics and network attacks, providing important technical support for the country to formulate computer virus prevention and control policies, regulations and standards. In 1998, the China Information Technology Security Evaluation Center was established to carry out security vulnerability analysis and information notification of information technology products and systems. In 2001, the National Computer Network Emergency Response Technical Team/Coordination Center of China (CNCERT/CC) was established to carry out prevention, discovery, early warning, and coordination and disposal of Internet cybersecurity incidents. In 2004, the National Cybersecurity and Information Security Notification Center was established as a national cybersecurity and information security notification outlet to report and notify information on China's network information security. In 2005, the National Information Technology Security Research Center was established to mainly conduct the security analysis of and research on information technology products and systems and provide the information security assurance of national basic information networks and important information systems.

At present, China has developed the technical capabilities for information content supervision, such as identifying harmful information on the Internet and early detection of emergencies, the technical capabilities for overall confrontation in cyberspace, such as emergency response and coordinated handling of cybersecurity incidents and in-depth protection of information systems, the technical capabilities for information resource protection, such as centralized network access for government departments and network identity authentication management, and the technical capabilities for security support in new technologies and new applications such as cloud computing and the Internet of Things (IoT), forming a relatively sound cybersecurity protection capability system.

In 2020, the CNCERT/CC coordinated and handled about 103 000 cybersecurity incidents of various types, a decrease of 4.2% compared with the previous year. From 2016 to 2020, the number of hosts infected with computer malicious programs in China continued to decline and remained at a low infection level, with an average annual decreasing rate of 25.1%. Through the China Cybersecurity Threat Governance Alliance, 10 domestic browser manufacturers has cooperated in a collaborative defense pilot to provide prompts and interception when users visit phishing websites. The number of prompts and interceptions reached 390 million times in 2020. The CNCERT/CC continues to carry out governance work on network resources used for distributed denial of service (DDoS) attacks. Consequently, such exploitable attack resources within China are continuously declining, and DDoS attacks have been curbed at the source. According to statistics, the annual decreasing rate of DDoS attacks in China in 2020 was 16.16%, the total attack traffic decreased by 19.67% year-on-year, and the global share of botnet control terminals in China steadily decreased to 2.05%.

7.3.3　Development of Cybersecurity Industry

China's cybersecurity industry has evolved from non-existence to establishment, and expanded from small-scale to large-scale. The industrial structure has gradually become complete, and the industrial agglomeration effect has begun to emerge, playing an important role in promoting the healthy development of the Internet. Projects such as the "Information Security Special Project" of the National Development and Reform Commission (NDRC), the "National Science and Technology Support Program" of the Ministry of Science and Technology (MOST), and the "Electronic Information Industry Development Fund Project" of the Ministry of Industry and Information Technology (MIIT) effectively promote the industrialization of cybersecurity. In September 2019, the MIIT publicly solicited opinions on the "Guidance on Promoting the Development of the Cybersecurity Industry (Draft for Comments)", which is committed to strengthening the emphasis on cybersecurity, increasing the application scale of cybersecurity products, and actively innovating cybersecurity services models.

China has developed cybersecurity products covering various fields, including physical security, communications security, data security, application security, security management platform, and new application security, forming a relatively complete information security industry chain from security chips, network and border security products, data security products, application security products to security services. A fully controllable system of independent research and development, production, upgrading and maintenance from basic software and hardware to application software has basically formed. In terms of basic hardware, domestic chip products such as processors, switching chips, and display chips have approached the level of mainstream foreign products, and have the conditions for systematic deployment. In terms of basic software, domestic operating systems and domestic database technologies have become mature and covered fields such as servers, desktops, mobile devices, and embedded systems. In terms of application software, China's independently controllable software for office automation, enterprise management, and industrial application system has been applied in communications, military, aviation, aerospace, and other fields with high-precision technologies and high real-time requirements.

In 2019, the scale of China's cybersecurity industry reached 156.36 billion yuan, with an annual growth rate of 17.1%, significantly higher than the international average growth rate of 9.11 %, maintaining a healthy development trend. By the end of November 2019, there were 23 listed cybersecurity enterprises in China, more than 100 venture capital institutions invested in the field of cybersecurity, and more than 150 innovative and entrepreneurial enterprises were gathered. According to the "2020 China Cybersecurity Industry Statistical Report" released by the Cyber Security Association of China in June 2020, the total revenue of China's cybersecurity technology, products and services in 2019 was about 52.31 billion yuan, with an annual growth rate of 25.37%; the number of employees in cybersecurity enterprises was about 100 000.

7.4 Cyberspace Governance

7.4.1 Public Environmental Governance

China has established and improved the basic legal environment for the Internet, and has successively issued a series of laws and regulations related to the Internet, covering the management of Internet infrastructure resources, information dissemination norms, market order norms, information security guarantee, and other aspects, and has made provisions for the responsibilities and obligations of Internet access service providers, Internet information service providers, government management departments, and Internet users. According to their duties, relevant departments have issued a series of departmental regulations and normative documents in the fields of Internet news and information services, news publishing, audio-visual programs, online games, online culture, online medicines, online copyrights, online transactions, electronic certification, network domain names, Internet access, and system security and confidentiality.

In terms of the management of Internet infrastructure resources, China has strengthened the management of domain names, IP addresses and website registration and filing, access services and others, in accordance with the law. On December 20, 2004, the "Regulations on the Administration of Internet Domain Names in China" was officially implemented, which ensured the safe and reliable operation of China's Internet domain name system and standardized the domain name related to registration and management. In February 2005, the Ministry of Information Industry launched the centralized filing of Internet sites nationwide, and gradually established three basic databases including Internet content provider (ICP) filing information, IP address usage information, and domain name information. As of 2015, the filing rate of Chinese websites had increased to 99.98%, and the accuracy rate of the filing subject information had reached 84.7%.

In terms of user account name management, China issued the "Regulations on the Administration of Business Premises of Internet Access Service" in September 2002 to strengthen the management of Internet access service business premises and regulate the business behavior of operators. In 2012, China began to authenticate the real identity information of users registering accounts for Internet information service; from September 1, 2013, new fixed-line phones and mobile phones (including wireless network cards) were required to register their real identity information. On January 22, 2021, the Cyberspace Administration of China (CAC) issued the revised "Regulations on the Management of Internet User Public Account Information Services", which made the management of public accounts more refined and precise.

7.4.2 Personal Privacy Protection

Data security is closely tied to personal safety. Once a large amount of personal privacy of citizens, such as personal identity, family, economic status, hobbies, and irreversible biometric information such as face, fingerprint, and DNA are maliciously leaked, the security risks cannot be underestimated. Based on this, China has successively formulated laws and regulations such as the "Cybersecurity Law of the People's Republic of China", the "Electronic Commerce Law of the People's Republic of China", and the "Civil Code of the People's Republic of China". The "Data Security Law of the People's Republic of China" implemented in September 2021 and the "Personal Information Protection Law of the People's Republic of China" implemented in November 2021 constitute the other two pillars of China's continuous efforts to strengthen personal information security and privacy protection.

Since 2020, China has widely promoted applications for epidemiological surveys and the protection of public health and safety. It is particularly important to protect the personal privacy data in these applications. On March 6, 2020, China issued a new version of the "Information Security Technology—Personal Information Security Specification", which clearly stated that "trajectory" belongs to "personal sensitive information", and the collection of such information must adhere to the "minimum necessary principle" and the "legitimacy principle", with authorization only waived in 11 exceptional situations "directly related to public safety, public health, and significant public interests".

7.4.3 Individual Rights Protection

Mobile Internet applications have become a focal point for the protection of personal information. In March 2021, the Cyberspace Administration of China and other departments jointly issued the "Regulations on the Scope of Necessary Personal Information for Common Types of Mobile Internet Applications", which clarified the basic functions of 39 basic types of applications and the specific types and usage requirements of personal information collected to ensure their normal operation. In April 2021, the MIIT, together with the Ministry of Public Security (MPS) and the State Administration for Market Regulation (SAMR), drafted and promulgated the "Interim Regulations on the Protection and Management of Personal Information of Mobile Internet Applications (Draft for Comments)", which detailed the identification standards of "informed consent" and "minimum necessary", and promoted the effective solution to the problem of collection and use of user's personal information in practice such as unclear rules, purpose, method, and scope.

In terms of the protection of minors' online content, the revised "Law of the People's Republic of China on the Protection of Minors" officially came into effect on June 1, 2021, opening a new chapter in the protection of minors' online content. Relevant departments have successively issued normative documents and deployed special actions related to the protection of minors' online content. A series of special actions have been jointly carried out across the country to combat pornography and obscenity on the Internet and mobile media, rectify vulgarity on the Internet, rectify cyberbullying and violence, rectify unlicensed Internet cafes, and clean up and rectify online games. News websites and commercial websites have been organized to self-examine and self-correct and clean up all kinds of illegal and harmful information, and the online environment has been continuously purified.

In terms of supporting the elderly in using the Internet, in December 2020, the MIIT issued the "Special Action Plan for Elderly-Oriented and Accessibility Renovation of Internet Application" to deploy relevant products and services measures. In April 2021, the MIIT issued the "General Design Specifications for Elderly-Oriented Mobile Internet Applications" and the "General Design Specifications for Elderly-Oriented Internet Websites", which clearly prohibit the inclusion of advertising content and plug-ins in the elderly-oriented interface misleading buttons that induce downloads and payments. In June 2021, the MIIT officially issued three standards, namely "Technical Requirements of Mobile Terminal Suitability for Elderly Person", "Test Methods of Mobile Terminal Suitability for Elderly Person", and "Technical Requirements for Elderly-Oriented Consideration of Smart Television", focusing on solving the various difficulties encountered by elderly person when using smart terminal products.

In terms of protecting the rights and interests of workers in the digital economy,

China pays attention to protecting the interests of the majority of workers, consumers and other groups, maintaining social fairness and justice, and ensuring the sustained, stable and healthy development of the digital economy. On July 26, 2021, the SAMR, the Cyberspace Administration of China (CAC) and five other departments jointly issued the "Guidelines on Implementing Responsibilities of Online Food Delivery Platforms and Effectively Safeguarding the Rights of Delivery Workers" in the form of a normative document, which puts forward comprehensive and specific requirements for protecting the legitimate rights and interests of delivery drivers, and requires that the legitimate rights and interests of delivery drivers be effectively protected from 10 aspects, including labor income, assessment system, dispatch mechanism, and labor safety.

7.4.4　Digital Content Regulation

In order to protect the rights of communication through information networks of copyright owners, performers, and authors of audio and video recordings, the right of communication through information networks was formally included in the revised "Copyright Law of the People's Republic of China" in October 2001; in May 2006, the "Regulations on the Protection of the Right of Communication Through Information Networks" was officially promulgated. In June 2014, the National Copyright Administration, together with the CAC, the MIIT, and the MPS, launched the "Sword Net 2014" special campaign, continuously carrying out special rectification of online infringement and piracy, cracking a number of key online infringement and piracy cases, and closing 200 websites suspected of infringement and piracy in accordance with the law.

China vigorously combats illegal activities such as telecommunications and online fraud and the infringement of citizens' personal information. It has launched the "Operation Clean Net" special campaign. The "Operation Qinglang" special campaign has been implemented in depth, effectively curbing the spread of Internet chaos. From 2019 to 2022, China had cleared 20. 49 billion pieces of illegal and harmful information and 1. 39 billion accounts, removed more than 67 000 illegal and irregular applications, and closed more than 42 000 illegal websites through nearly 30 special campaigns. China continues to strengthen the construction of online information content, actively create a good network ecosystem, and promote the formation of a clean and sound cyberspace.

7.4.5　Information Technology Governance

China has formulated specialized legal regulations for the management of AI algorithms. In August 2021, China issued the "Guidelines for the Construction of National New-Generation Artificial Intelligence Standard System" to regulate AI services and meet the requirements of traditional moral ethics and legal order. On August 27, 2021, the CAC issued a notice on soliciting public opinions on the "Regulations on the Management of Algorithmic Recommendations for Internet Information Services (Draft for Comments)", which specifically regulates the management of algorithm recommendation technology. In September 2021, the CAC and eight other ministries and commissions jointly issued the "Guiding Opinions on Strengthening the Comprehensive Governance of Internet Information Services Algorithms", which clearly requires enterprises using algorithms to bear the main responsibility for the results of algorithm application, establish an algorithm security responsibility system and a scientific and technological ethics review system, improve the algorithm security management organization, strengthen risk prevention and control and hidden danger investigation and governance, and improve the capability and level of responding to algorithm security emergencies.

China has also established regulations related to the security of Internet of Vehicles (IoV) and automotive data. In August 2021, the CAC and other departments jointly issued the "Several Provisions on the Administration of Automobile Data Security (Trial)", advocating the adherence to the principles of "in-vehicle processing", "non-collection by default", "applicable accuracy range", and "desensitization processing" to reduce the disorderly collection and illegal abuse of automobile data. On September 13, 2021, the MIIT issued the "Notice of the Ministry of Industry and Information Technology on Strengthening the Real-Name Registration Management of Internet of Vehicles SIM Cards", clarifying the requirements for real-name registration of IoV subscriber identity module (SIM) cards at different sales stages to prevent security risks in the IoV. On September 15, 2021, the MIIT issued the "Notice of the Ministry of Industry and Information Technology on Strengthening the Cybersecurity and Data Security of the Internet of Vehicles", which put forward basic requirements for the cybersecurity and data security of the IoV.

7.4.6　Digital Economy Regulation

In the early stages of the development of the platform economy of the digital economy, China adopted the development concept of "inclusiveness and prudence" and did not intervene too much or too early in corporate behavior. However, as platform enterprises reach a considerable scale and the industry becoming increasingly mature, strengthening supervision has become a necessary measure to maintain market competition and promote the survival of the fittest.

China has been actively building a digital development governance system to create a healthy and orderly development environment. It has formulated and implemented the "Electronic Commerce Law of the People's Republic of China", the "Anti-Unfair Competition Law of the People's Republic of China", the "Anti-Monopoly Law of the People's Republic of China", and the "Regulations on Optimizing the Business Environment". It has issued the "Guiding Opinions of the General Office of the State Council on Promoting the Standardized and Healthy Development of the Platform Economy" to promote the standardized and healthy development of the platform economy, as well as effectively safeguard the legitimate rights and interests of market entities and the people. In February 2021, the Anti-Monopoly Committee of the State Council issued the "Anti-Monopoly Guidelines of the Anti-Monopoly Committee of the State Council on the Platform Economy", clarifying the principles of anti-monopoly law enforcement in the field of platform economy. In March 2021, the SAMR issued the "Measures on the Supervision and Administration of Online Transactions" to further standardize online transaction activities, maintain online transaction order, and protect the legitimate rights and interests of all parties involved in online transactions.

China has formulated relevant regulations for new online marketing methods to keep pace with the times. In the field of online live streaming and marketing, at the end of 2020, relevant normative documents such as the "Guiding Opinions of the State Administration for Market Regulation on Strengthening the Supervision of Online Live Streaming Marketing Activities" and the "Notice of the State Administration of Radio and Television on Strengthening the Management of Online Show Live Streaming and E-commerce Live Streaming" were successively issued. On April 16, 2021, the CAC, the MPS, the Ministry of Commerce (MOFCOM), and other four ministries and commissions jointly issued the "Measures on the Management of Online Live Streaming Marketing (Trial)", which systematically and comprehensively solved the problems of e-commerce online live streaming marketing by issuing normative documents.

7.4.7　Collaborative Governance Model

The Chinese government has played a coordinating and leading role, actively involving various parties in the Internet governance. By employing a comprehensive approach that includes legal regulations, administrative management, industrial policies, technical standards, and public education, the government has mobilized efforts from all sides to collectively promote the Internet development. This has led to the establishment of an Internet governance model that not only aligns with global Internet norms but also embodies distinct characteristics tailored to China.

Internet enterprises conscientiously fulfill their principal responsibilities. In November 2004, Sina, Sohu, and NetEase announced the self-discipline details of the "Integrity Self-discipline Alliance" of the Chinese Internet industry, marking that China's Internet information service enterprises have taken the initiative to assume the principal responsibility for maintaining market order. In June 2013, 21 Internet enterprises including Alibaba, Tencent, Baidu, Sina, Shengda, and NetEase established the "Internet Anti-Fraud Committee" to promote the joint fight against online fraud across the network and jointly build a transaction security ecosystem. In 2013, search engine service enterprises like Baidu and Qihoo 360 successively launched plans to protect the rights and interests of Internet users, taking on greater social responsibilities.

Industry organizations have been effectively promoting the healthy development of the

Internet. China attaches great importance to the important role of social organizations in the field of Internet governance, strongly supports the construction of various industry associations and social organizations, and actively participates in Internet governance. In May 2001, the Internet Society of China, a national industry organization, was established. It formulated and issued a series of self-discipline norms, including the "Self-Discipline Convention of China's Internet Industry", "Self-Discipline Norms for Internet Sites to Prohibit the Spread of Obscene and Pornographic and Other Harmful Information", "Self-Discipline Convention for Resisting Malware", and "Copyright Self-Discipline Declaration of China's Internet Industry". In November 2002, the Internet Society of China established the Anti-Spam Coordination Group, which made outstanding contributions to the governance of spam.

7.5　Summary

The Internet and the cyberspace derived from it are the remarkable achievements of the development of human civilization. In cyberspace, all kinds of activities of individuals and groups need to be protected and supervised within the law framework of human society. The concept and scope of cyberspace governance are constantly evolving and developing. Governments around the world shoulder the important mission of protecting the legitimate rights and interests of individuals and groups in cyberspace and maintaining the normal order of cyberspace.

China has established a complete legal system for cyberspace. From the initial connection to the Internet to becoming a world-leading power in mobile Internet application innovation, China's cyber legislation has achieved a historic leap from no-existence to gradually being sound, and from a single norm to comprehensive coverage. By June 2024, China had established more than 150 pieces of legislation governing cyberspace. These legislation cover many key areas, such as the protection of personal digital rights and interests, the improvement of digital economy rules, the maintenance of network information security, and the optimization of the cyber-ecological norms. China's legal system for cyberspace not only ensures the orderly development of China's cyberspace, but also provides rich reference examples for global cyber legislation.

China has built a strong force for protecting cybersecurity. China has been committed to the independent research and development of a series of cybersecurity technologies, overcoming many key security technical problems, developing a series of advanced security technologies and algorithms, and constructing a complete security technology standard system. China has established professional protection institutions and high-quality teams covering key security fields. With the ability of regular network monitoring and efficient emergency response, China can respond to various cybersecurity threats timely and properly. China's cybersecurity industry is showing a good momentum of vigorous development, the industry scale continues to grow steadily, and products cover many key fields, forming a complete and mature industrial chain. China's cybersecurity technologies and industry not only ensure the healthy operation of domestic networks and information systems, but also can provide professional security services for other countries.

China has carried out all-round and multi-dimensional cyberspace governance practices. In the field of public environment governance, China continuously improves the Internet legal environment, strengthens the management of Internet infrastructure resources, and strictly standardizes user account management, maintaining a well-ordered cyberspace. In terms of personal rights and interests protection, the data collection process has been standardized, and the personal privacy protection has been strengthened, ensuring that groups such as teenagers and the elderly can access the Internet equally and conveniently, and effectively safeguarding the legitimate rights and interests of workers in the digital economy. In addition, China continues to make efforts in areas such as digital content supervision, information technology governance, and digital economy regulation. The Chinese government plays a leading and coordinating role, mobilizing all parties related to the Internet industry to participate in cyberspace governance, forming a collaborative, efficient, and sustainable development governance model.

The booming development of the Internet has brought rare opportunities as well as many challenges to the world. The rule of law is undoubtedly the core element in Internet governance. Since connecting to the international Internet, China has comprehensively promoted the rule of law in cyberspace, established a sound legal system, and effectively promoted the positive interaction between cybersecurity and development. The path of governing the Internet according to law taken by China, has not only significantly improved the domestic Internet governance level, but also provided a comprehensive, systematic, and reference-worthy governance model for other countries in the world, contributing Chinese wisdom to promoting the improvement and development of the global Internet governance system.

8 International Digital Cooperation

8.1 Demands and Challenges

Since the advent of the 21st century, the advancement of information and communications technology (ICT) has not only expanded the living space for humanity, but has also transformed the modes of societal production. However, it has not fundamentally altered the international political order. Various issues persist within the global governance of cyberspace, such as the disparities between the East and the West as well as the North-South divide. This urgently calls for nations across the globe to unite and collectively address these challenges.

8.1.1 Digital Divide in Internet Era

The Internet serves as the shared habitat of humanity, and its evolution reflects the level of a country's economic and technological development. Undoubtedly, the development of the global Internet exhibits disparities among nations and regions. This discrepancy is commonly referred to as the "digital divide".

The global digital divide persists and is widening. According to the data from the International Telecommunication Union, by the end of 2021, the number of global Internet users had reached 4.9 billion, approximately 63% of the global population, with an annual growth rate of 13.3% among Internet users in developing countries. Over the period from 2015 to 2021, the coverage of 4G networks doubled, encompassing 88% of the global population. In the Asia-Pacific region, Europe, and the Americas, 90% of the population can access to mobile broadband networks (3G or above). Between 2020 and 2021, Africa has witnessed a 21 percentage point increase in 4G network coverage. However, as of 2021, a significant gap still existed, with 18% of the population unable to access to mobile broadband networks, highlighting substantial disparities in coverage. Globally, in 2021, approximately 2.9 billion people still lack access to the Internet, with 96% located in developing countries, and around 390 million individuals residing in areas devoid of mobile broadband signal coverage. The global distribution and number of people who do not use the Internet in 2022 are shown in Figure 8-1.

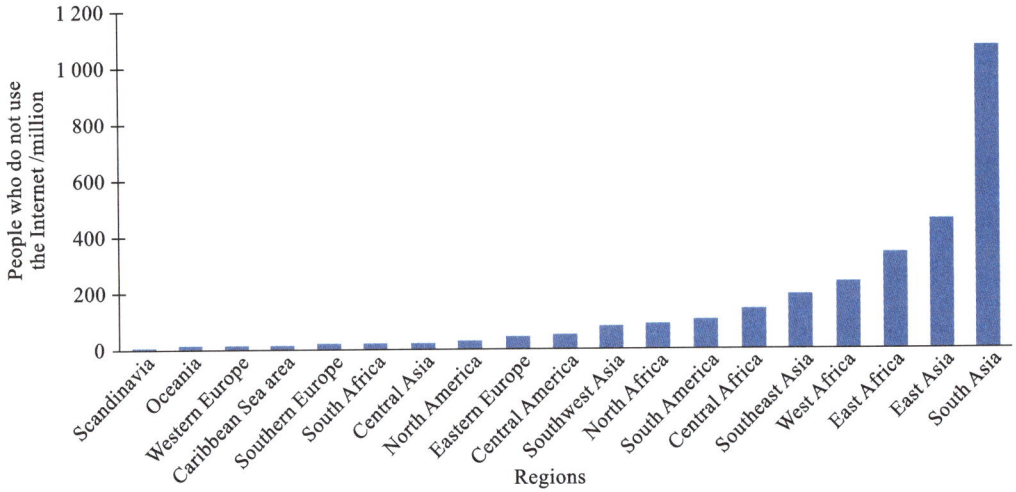

Figure 8-1 Global distribution and number of people who do not use the Internet (2022)
Data Source: Digital 2022: Global Overview Report

Developed nations, leveraging their technological advantages, have secured the authority to formulate rules and control the discourse within the realm of the Internet. It is difficult for the developing countries in the digital sphere to participate in an equal footing in various global cyberspace governance affairs. They are technologically subordinate and economically subjected to constraints and exploitation. This highlights the presence of imbalances and inadequacies in the development of cyberspace, calling for the establishment of just and equitable rules and mechanisms on a global scale. This initiative aims to safeguard the right of developing countries to participate equally in global cyberspace affairs and achieve sustainable development in the digital realm.

8.1.2 Global Cybersecurity Risk

In recent years, the global cybersecurity landscape has become increasingly perilous, marked by numerous significant incidents of cybersecurity threats, such as distributed denial of service (DDoS) attacks, ransomware attacks, telecommunications fraud, and malicious code attacks on mobile terminals. According to the "Global Risks Report 2024" released by the World Economic Forum, cyber insecurity ranks among the top 10 global risks of most concern over the next decade. In 2021, cyberattacks frequently triggered disruptions in Internet services and halted factory operations, profoundly affecting social stability and the daily lives of citizens.

For instance, in May 2021, Colonial Pipeline, the largest fuel pipeline operator in the United States (US), fell victim to a Darkside ransomware attack, severely impacting fuel supplies along the US East Coast. In July 2021, the automatic ticketing system of the Northern Railways in the United Kingdom (UK) experienced a ransomware attack, leading to the paralysis of the ticketing network. In September 2021, Vocus, a telecommunications enterprise in New Zealand, faced a DDoS attack, resulting in disruptions in network services in cities such as Auckland and Wellington.

Cyberterrorism proliferates unchecked in cyberspace, and traditional criminal activities are increasingly becoming networked. Consequently, many nations have elevated the importance of cybersecurity to the level of a national strategy. In 2014, the National Institute of Standards and Technology (NIST) in the US released the "Framework for Improving Critical Infrastructure Cybersecurity", defining cybersecurity as the "process of protecting information by preventing, detecting, and responding to attacks". In the same year, the Russian Federation, in its "Concept of the Russian Federation Cybersecurity Strategy", defined cybersecurity as the "sum of all the conditions to prevent potential threats and their consequences from affecting all components of cyberspace". In 2020, the European Union (EU) issued "The EU's Cybersecurity Strategy for the Digital Decade", encompassing relevant recommendations in terms of regulations, investments, and policy tools.

The continual iteration of new technologies and their widespread social applications pose novel governance obstacles and challenges for the international community. With the emergence and proliferation of technologies such as big data and artificial intelligence, cybersecurity faces unprecedented technical challenges. In November 2020, the World Economic Forum released a report titled "Future Series: Cybersecurity, Emerging Technologies and Systemic Risks". The report stated that with the development of emerging technologies, the scale, speed and connectivity of cyberspace are undergoing major changes, which brought about a series of new systemic risks and challenges. Therefore, it is necessary to establish cybersecurity norms that are generally recognized by all countries, put transnational cybercrime issues on the track of the rule of law, and safeguard the legitimate rights and interests of cyber actors in all countries.

8.1.3 Global Digital Trade Demands

The new generation of ICT is accelerating its extension into the international economic and trade sectors, giving rise to digital trade, which has profound impacts on trade methods, trade objects, trade rules, and trade landscape. From 2011 to 2020, global digital trade experienced rapid development, with a compound annual growth rate of 4.4% in digital services trade, significantly surpassing that of traditional international services trade (1.19%) and goods trade (−0.4%). The proportion of digital trade in global trade continues to rise. Since 2012, over 90% of services trade agreements have started to incorporate relevant clauses or dedicated chapters on digital trade (e-commerce). Simultaneously, international digital trade encounters numerous challenges. For example, the digitalization of trade objects and methods has led to the emergence of many new rule vacuums that urgently need to be addressed and perfected, and the existing trade rules and negotiation mechanisms also require modification and updates.

With the evolution of ICT, an increasing amount of goods trade is transforming into digitized, virtual services trade. While digital technology can benefit small and medium enterprises (SMEs) in developing countries by reducing trade costs and lowering entry barriers, these nations face greater challenges in engaging in digital trade due to the influence of technological industry development trends and super platforms. For instance, when SMEs in developing countries conduct international trade through online platforms, they may encounter unfair treatment from online platform services providers. Shortcomings in digital infrastructure and data management experience of developing countries can also result in losses. For example, due to a lack of appropriate technological regulatory measures, developing countries are at risk of erosion in tariff revenue from digital trade.

8.2 Community with a Shared Future in Cyberspace

The "community with a shared future in cyberspace" is an extension of the concept of "community with a shared future for humanity" into the realm of the Internet. In March 2013, Chinese President Xi Jinping first introduced the significant concept of "community with a shared future for humanity" during his visit to Russia. On November 23, 2020, the World Internet Conference·Internet Development Forum opened in Wuzhen City, Zhejiang Province. Chinese President Xi Jinping sent a congratulatory letter to the forum, in which he pointed out that China is willing to work with all countries in the world to seize the historical opportunities of the information revolution, cultivate new impetus for innovation and development, create a new situation for digital cooperation, foster a new landscape of cybersecurity, build a community with a shared future in cyberspace, and work together to create a better future for mankind.

8.2.1 China's Voice in Cyberspace Governance

Since 2014, China has consecutively hosted the World Internet Conference (WIC) in Wuzhen City, Zhejiang Province for 11 years. This conference serves as both establishing an international platform for connectivity and cooperation between China and the world in the field of the Internet and a Chinese platform for shared governance and collaboration in cyberspace. Representatives from various sectors, including governments, international organizations, Internet enterprises, think tanks, industry associations, and technical communities, have been invited to participate in the conference for exchanges.

The organizing committee of the conference has successively released a concept document named "Jointly Build a Community with a Shared Future in Cyberspace", as well as the "Initiative on Jointly Building a Community with a Shared Future in Cyberspace". It has also organized case presentations and demonstrations to elaborate on the implementation of the concept of constructing a community with a shared future in cyberspace. The successful hosting of the conference has significantly promoted close connections and in-depth communication in the global Internet, effectively advancing China's experience, solutions, and ideas in building a community with a shared future in cyberspace from conceptual consensus to concrete practices, and propelling the global Internet governance system toward a more just and equitable direction.

In August 2021, the China-Africa Internet Development and Cooperation Forum, themed "Seeking Development, Ensuring Security, and Building a Community with a Shared Future in Cyberspace", was conducted through video linkages. Representatives from 14 African countries and the African Union Commission attended the forum, engaging in extensive discussions on topics such as sharing the dividends of digital technology and jointly safeguarding cybersecurity. China initiated the "China-Africa Initiative for Building a Community with a Shared Future in Cyberspace", calling for the participation of governments, Internet enterprises, technical communities, social organizations, and individual citizens from both China and African countries to collaboratively build a more closely-knit community with a shared future in cyberspace.

China has been continuously promoting international exchanges and cooperation in cyberspace. By leveraging the United Nations (UN) as the primary channel and adhering to the United Nations Charter (UN Charter), China actively participates in the formulation of international rules in the digital and cyberspace realms. China also provides digital assistance, including technology, equipment, and services to less developed countries, enabling them to share the benefits of the digital age and supporting the realization of The 2030 Agenda for Sustainable Development.

8.2.2   Building a Community with a Shared Future in Cyberspace

China's advocacy for a community with a shared future in cyberspace is rich in connotations. China adheres to the global governance principle of achieving shared growth through consultation and collaboration, promoting the establishment of a multilateral, democratic, and transparent system of the international cyberspace governance. China proposes that the future international cyberspace should be characterized by innovation, security, order, equality, respect, openness, and sharing. All countries worldwide are encouraged to jointly promote development, collectively safeguard security, participate in governance, and share the achievements in cyberspace. The concept of a community with a shared future in cyberspace can be interpreted as a community in terms of development, security, responsibility, and interests.

Building a community of development. Addressing the imbalances in the development levels of different countries and regions in aspects such as Internet penetration, infrastructure construction, technological innovation, digital economic development, and digital literacy and skills is crucial, which affects and limits the informatization efforts and digital transformation of countries worldwide, particularly developing countries. The emphasis on building a community of development involves adopting more proactive, inclusive, coordinated, and beneficial policies. This aims to accelerate the global popularization of information infrastructure and provide affordable and quality network services for developing countries. It involves maximizing the role of the digital economy as an engine for global economic development and actively promoting the development of digital industries and the transformation of industrial digitalization.

Building a community of security. Security is considered a prerequisite for development, and a secure, stable, and prosperous cyberspace is of significant importance to all countries globally. Given that cybersecurity is a challenge of global scale, no country can remain unaffected or isolated. Building a community of security involves advocating an open and cooperative cybersecurity ideology, emphasizing the dual importance of security and development, and encouraging both encouragement and regulation. It entails strengthening the protection of critical information infrastructure and promoting international cooperation on data security. It also involves maintaining the neutrality of ICT and globalizing industrial security to jointly curb the misuse of ICT. Establishing strategic mutual trust, timely sharing information on cybersecurity threats, effectively coordinating major cybersecurity incidents, cooperating in combating cyberterrorism and cybercrime, and collectively safeguarding the peace and security of cyberspace are integral to this community.

Building a community of responsibility. Cyberspace is a common space for human activities, and the future and destiny of cyberspace should be jointly controlled by all countries in the world. Building a community of responsibility means adhering to multilateral participation and multi-party participation, and actively promoting the reform and construction of the global Internet governance system. It entails giving full play to the UN as the main channel for international governance in cyberspace, and utilizing the roles of various subjects such as governments, international organizations, Internet enterprises, technology communities, social organizations, and individual citizens to establish cooperation based on mutual trust and coordinated order. It also involves improving the dialogue and consultation mechanism, jointly studying and formulating cyberspace governance norms, reflecting the interests and concerns of all parties in a more balance manner, especially the interests of the vast number of developing countries, and making the governance system more fair and reasonable.

Building a community of interests. The achievements of cyberspace development and governance should be shared globally to ensure that different countries, different ethnic groups, and different populations have equal access to the benefits of cyberspace development. Building a community of interests involves facilitating the use of new-generation ICT by SMEs to promote innovation in products, services, processes, organizations, and business models. This ensures that SMEs can share more opportunities from digital economic development. The community emphasizes the protection of vulnerable groups in cyberspace, strengthens the development of cyber ethics, and fosters a civilized cyberspace. Enhancing the network development capabilities of developing countries, bridging the digital divide, and promoting a more inclusive global development are integral to this community.

8.3　International Cooperation on Digital Economy

China actively engages in international cooperation in the digital economy. It participates in the construction of Internet information infrastructure in various regions, promotes the internationalization of various new ICT and their applications, and contributes to the improvement of global digital connectivity. China also collaborates with various countries in the field of digital trade, fostering the integrated development of the global digital economy and the real economy.

8.3.1　Global ICT Infrastructure Development

8.3.1.1　Management of Internet Infrastructure Resources

The Internet infrastructure resources encompass IP addresses, domain names, and more. China places great emphasis on communications and collaboration with international Internet organizations, such as the Internet Corporation for Assigned Names and Numbers (ICANN), Asia-Pacific Network Information Centre (APNIC), World Wide Web Consortium (W3C), Internet Society (ISOC), Internet Architecture Board (IAB), and Internet Engineering Task Force (IETF). This effort aims to promote the rational allocation of critical Internet resources and the interconnection of basic Internet services, such as domain name service (DNS).

In 2002, the ICANN meeting was held in Shanghai, China for the first time. In 2003, Qian Hualin, a researcher from the Chinese Academy of Sciences, was elected as an ICANN director. In November 2020, Yao Jiankang, a technical expert from the China Internet Network Information Center (CNNIC), was elected as a new director of the Country Code Names Supporting Organization (ccNSO), playing an active role in the organization's relevant policy formulation, agenda setting, and international exchanges and cooperation, and enhancing China's activity and recognition in the international technology community.

The Asia Pacific Top level Domain Association (APTLD) is an organization of country code top-level domains (ccTLDs) in the Asia-Pacific region. Its purpose is to promote information exchange on the development of Internet domain name application technology among its members, and enhance the influence of these members in the global Internet field. As of 2021, APTLD had 50 formal institutional members and 19 associate members.

In February 2021, a CNNIC representative was elected as the member of the new APTLD board, making important contributions to further maintaining international community relations and deepening regional exchanges and cooperation.

APNIC is one of the five major regional Internet IP address registration and management institutions worldwide, responsible for the allocation and management of IP addresses in the Asia-Pacific region. All of China's IP address resources are obtained through APNIC. In March 2021, a CNNIC representative was elected as the member of the APNIC Executive Committee. China took this opportunity to deepen cooperation and exchanges with APNIC and promote cooperation with the countries along the Belt and Road.

8.3.1.2　African ICT Infrastructure Development

Over the years, China has been actively engaging in infrastructure development in Africa, aiding the implementation of numerous projects for both basic infrastructure and public welfare. From the establishment of the Forum on China-Africa Cooperation (FOCAC) in 2000 to 2021, China had added and upgraded more than 10 000 kilometers of railway networks, nearly 100 000 kilometers of roads, 120 million kilowatts of installed power capacity, and 150 000 kilometers of communications backbone networks in Africa. As of June 2019, about 80% of the backbone networks in Africa were invested by Chinese funded enterprises; among the 54 African countries, more than 40 countries have adopted Chinese products and technologies in communications network facilities.

In 2018, the Beijing Summit of the FOCAC was held in Beijing, and it released the "Forum on China-Africa Cooperation Beijing Action Plan (2019-2021)". China and African countries encourage and support their respective enterprises to cooperate in the construction of communications infrastructure such as optical cable backbone networks, cross-border interconnection, international submarine optical cables, new-generation mobile communications networks, and data centers in African countries. The two sides will actively explore and promote the application of new technologies such as cloud computing, big data, and mobile Internet, and enhance the role of ICT in maintaining social order, counter-terrorism, and combating crime.

With the participation of Chinese enterprises, the level of broadband network infrastructure in some African countries has been significantly improved. For example, Chinese enterprises had undertaken the construction of the Glo-2 submarine optical cable system of Nigerian telecom operator Globacom. The system will be laid along the coast of Nigeria, connecting Alpha Beach in Lagos to the southern region, with a total length of 850 kilometers and providing a transmission capacity of 12 Tbps.

With the help of Chinese enterprises, Africa is also accelerating into the 5G commercial era. In July 2020, South African telecom operator Rain successfully launched Africa's first 5G commercial network with the technical support of Huawei. In November 2022, Zambian mobile communications operator MTN launched the country's first 5G commercial network services with the support of Huawei. In April 2023, Chinese enterprises and partners such as Ugandan telecom operator MTN and HIMA Cement Company jointly launched the Ugandan's first 5G digital cement factory project supported by the Chinese-funded enterprise in Kampala, the capital of Uganda, to achieve real-time data transmission in the production area.

8.3.2 Provision of Global Digital Services

Besides the network infrastructure, China also actively participates in the digital industrialization processes of various countries, providing globally-oriented information technology services to nations worldwide. This includes services like the BeiDou Navigation Satellite System (BDS) and cloud services.

BDS has become an important global space-time infrastructure. China continues to carry out satellite navigation cooperation and exchanges with regions, countries, and regional organizations such as the League of Arab States (LAS), the Association of Southeast Asian Nations (ASEAN), Central Asia, and Africa. Beidou-related products have been exported to more than half of the countries and regions in the world. In 2021, at the first China-Africa BDS Cooperation Forum held in Beijing, the "10 Application Scenarios of BDS in Africa" was officially released, showing BDS's application cases and application solutions in the fields of road transportation, vehicle management, railway industry, precision agriculture, etc. in Africa.

The China-Arab BDS/GNSS Center was located in Tunis, the capital of Tunisia. It was China's first overseas BDS center, providing satellite navigation training, test evaluation, and technical research for African and Arab countries. The center's central screen can display the collected data in real time, and Tunisia can receive signals from more than 12 BeiDou satellites on average. In Mozambique, the China-Africa Saisai Agricultural Cooperation Project widely used drones with BDS positioning for field plant protection operations such as farmland mapping, rice sowing, and pesticide spraying. Compared with traditional manual spraying of only 3 to 4 mu per hour, plant protection drones can spray pesticides on hundreds of acres per hour, and the cumulative operation has exceeded 30 000 acres.

In addition, China's cloud computing platform has also begun to provide international services, especially for Africa, the Middle East, Southeast Asian countries and participating countries in the Belt and Road Initiative (BRI). The "Global Microbial Resource Data Sharing Platform", a global microbial big data platform infrastructure led by China, had gathered 520 000 microbial physical resource data from 141 partners in 51 countries as of 2021, forming an interconnected cooperation network, establishing a global microbial strain collection catalog, and promoting the effective use of global microbial data resources.

8.3.3　Cooperation on Global Digital Economy

China actively engages in international and regional multilateral mechanisms for cooperation on digital economic governance, advocating and advancing various initiatives and declarations. It puts forth proposals aligning with the interests and demands of the majority of countries worldwide, strengthened collaboration with specialized international organizations, and contributed to global digital economic governance.

Promoting the digital economy cooperation process of the Asia-Pacific Economic Cooperation (APEC). In 2014, as the host of APEC, China introduced the Internet economy into the APEC cooperation framework for the first time, initiating and promoting the adoption of the "APEC Initiative of Cooperation to Promote the Internet Economy". In 2019, after the establishment of the APEC Digital Economy Steering Group, China actively promoted the comprehensive and balanced implementation of the "APEC Internet and Digital Economy Roadmap". Since 2020, China has successively put forward initiatives such as "optimizing the digital business environment and activating the vitality of market entities", all of which have been unanimously adopted by APEC.

Actively participating in digital economy cooperation under the G20 framework. In 2016, the 11th G20 Summit was held in China. Driven by China, the meeting listed "digital economy" as an important topic in the G20 Innovation Growth Blueprint for the first time, and adopted the "G20 Digital Economy Development and Cooperation Initiative", which is the world's first digital economy policy document signed by leaders of many countries. Since then, digital economy has become one of the core topics of the G20. In recent years, China has actively participated in the G20 Digital Economy Ministerial Meeting and relevant consultations of the Digital Economy Task Force (DETF), and promoted the upgrade of the DETF to a working group to ensure that the achievements of digital economic development benefit people around the world.

Continuously expanding exchanges and cooperation in the digital economy among BRICS countries. In 2017, the ninth BRICS Leaders' Meeting was held in China. The "BRICS Leaders Xiamen Declaration" adopted at the meeting clearly proposed to deepen pragmatic cooperation in the fields of information and communications technology, e-commerce, and Internet space. In 2019, the China Branch of BRICS Institute of Future Networks was officially unveiled in Shenzhen. In 2022, the 14th BRICS Leaders' Meeting adopted the BRICS Digital Economy Partnership Framework. In addition, China held important events such as the BRICS Digital Economy Dialogue, opening a new process of BRICS digital economy cooperation.

Deepening digital economy cooperation with ASEAN. In 2020, the China-ASEAN Year of Digital Economy Cooperation was held, with the theme of "Combating COVID-19 through Joint Efforts, Embracing Cooperation through ICT and Digital Development" and a network affairs dialogue. The 23rd China-ASEAN Leaders' Meeting issued the "China-

ASEAN Initiative on Establishing a Digital Economy Cooperation Partnership", and agreed to further deepen cooperation in the field of digital economy.

Actively promoting digital economy cooperation in the World Trade Organization (WTO). In 2017, China officially announced its accession to the WTO's "Friends of E-commerce Development" and worked with developing members to support the WTO's e-commerce consultations. In 2019, China and other 75 WTO members including the US, the EU, Russia, Brazil, Singapore, Nigeria, and Myanmar, jointly issued a "Joint Statement on E-commerce" to launch negotiations on trade-related e-commerce issues. In 2022, China and other WTO members jointly issued the Ministerial Decision on the E-commerce Work Plan, supporting the exemption of tariffs on electronic transmissions and promoting the development of the global digital economy.

8.3.4 International Cross-Border E-commerce

China is a major exporter of cross-border e-commerce and the largest import market for cross-border e-commerce in the world. With the vigorous development of cross-border e-commerce, China is actively strengthening coordination and interaction with other countries in the field of international laws and regulations for cross-border e-commerce, and deepening cooperation with other developing countries and economically backward countries in the field of e-commerce, helping SMEs in various countries to narrow the digital divide and form a win-win development pattern of international cooperation. The development of China's cross-border e-commerce has developed from buying and selling globally to the stage of international ecological cooperation. The development of cross-border e-commerce not only sells products to end consumers in overseas markets, but also integrates various domestic and foreign resources, integrates market entities in different countries, forms a cross-border e-commerce ecological service system that transcends national boundaries, and promotes the development of global digital trade.

In October 2021, the Ministry of Commerce, the Office of the Central Cyberspace Affairs Commission, and the National Development and Reform Commission jointly issued the "14th Five-Year Plan for E-commerce Development", and put forward development goals in the relevant part of cross-border e-commerce, namely, to increase the transaction value of cross-border e-commerce from 1.69 trillion yuan in 2020 to 2.5 trillion yuan by 2025. In 2023, China's cross-border e-commerce imports and exports totaled 2.38 trillion yuan, with an annual growth rate of 15.6%; specially, exports were 1.83 trillion yuan, with an annual growth rate of 19.6%; imports were 548.3 billion yuan, with an annual growth rate of 3.9%. The number of Chinese consumers participating in cross-border e-commerce imports has been increasing year by year, reaching 163 million in 2023.

8.3.4.1 Policies for Cross-Border E-commerce Cooperation

China actively promotes international cooperation in cross-border e-commerce, participates in e-commerce consultations under multilateral and regional trade mechanisms such as the WTO, the G20, the APEC, the BRICS, and the Shanghai Cooperation Organization (SCO), jointly builds regional high-level digital economy rules with free trade partners, and has made breakthroughs in the construction of international e-commerce rules. The e-commerce chapter in the "Regional Comprehensive Economic Partnership (RCEP)" has become the international e-commerce rule with extensive coverage area, comprehensive content, and a high level of expertise. In 2022, the top 10 countries in terms of China's cross-border e-commerce exports are the US, Malaysia, Singapore, Australia, Vietnam, South Korea, Thailand, the Philippines, India, and Japan; the top 10 countries (regions) in terms of cross-border e-commerce imports are China's Hong Kong, South Korea, Japan, the US, Australia, the Netherlands, New Zealand, Germany, France, and the UK.

In conjunction with the BRI, China has proposed a bilateral international cooperation mechanism for "Silk Road E-commerce". By signing a bilateral e-commerce cooperation memorandum, China has formulated a cross-border e-commerce strategy based on the economic development characteristics of the partner countries, giving play to China's advantages in e-commerce technology application, model innovation, and market scale. On November 4, 2022, Chinese President Xi Jinping proposed in his speech at the opening ceremony of the fifth China International Import Expo (CIIE) to create a "Silk Road E-commerce" cooperation pilot zone and promote high-quality Belt and Road cooperation. As of September 2023, China had signed bilateral e-commerce cooperation memoranda with 30 countries. "Silk Road E-commerce" has become a new channel and new highlight of international economic and trade cooperation, and its partner countries are spread across the five continents of the world. In 2023, the cross-border e-commerce import and export value between China and the "Silk Road E-commerce" partner countries accounted for more than 30% of China's total cross-border e-commerce value.

The cooperation mechanism of "Silk Road E-commerce" is conducive to countries sharing the opportunities presented by the Chinese market. At previous CIIEs, the "Silk Road E-commerce" partner countries used the CIIE as a window to set up national pavilions to display their most distinctive and high-tech products, and quickly launch cross-border e-commerce platforms, obtaining huge Chinese orders. Hongqiao Pinhui is the Shanghai import commodity exhibition and trading center and the permanent exhibition center of the CIIE. In 2022, Hongqiao Pinhui built two important sub-platforms, Shanghai International Friendship City Port and Live E-commerce Base, attracting nearly 5 000 products from 36 partner countries. In 2023, Hongqiao Pinhui opened the "Silk Road E-commerce" online country pavilion to create convenience for high-quality enterprises and products from partner countries to enter the Chinese market. In the first half of 2023 alone, 42 suppliers from partner countries were introduced.

8.3.4.2　Measures for Cross-Border E-commerce Development

The management of cross-border e-commerce involves the management of multiple processes such as transactions, payments, logistics, customs clearance, tax refunds, and foreign exchange settlement. In order to promote the development of the cross-border e-commerce industry, China is actively exploring a more efficient cross-border e-commerce management mechanism. China has established cross-border e-commerce comprehensive pilot zones in many cities and regions, aiming to promote the pioneering trials of cross-border e-commerce technical standards, business processes, regulatory models, and informatization construction. Starting from the State Council's approvement to establish the China (Hangzhou) Cross-border E-commerce Comprehensive Pilot Zone in March 2015, as of November 2022, the number of China's cross-border e-commerce comprehensive pilot zones had reached 165, covering 31 provinces, autonomous regions, and municipalities. Taking the China (Hangzhou) Cross-border E-commerce Comprehensive Pilot Zone as an example, the region has carried out cross-border e-commerce "small package export", "direct mail import", "online shopping bonded import", as well as cross-border business-to-business (B2B) export, bonded export and other business pilots, and took the lead in exploring cross-border e-commerce return and exchange centers, "global central warehouses", fixed-point distribution, "bonded import + retail processing" and other initiatives. As of June 2023, the scale of cross-border e-commerce import and export in China (Hangzhou) Cross-border E-commerce Comprehensive Pilot Zone had expanded from 120 million yuan in the early stage of its establishment to more than 120 billion yuan, and the number of cross-border e-commerce enterprises had jumped from more than 200 to more than 55 000, gathering 2/3 of the country's cross-border e-commerce platforms. Additionally, cross-border payment institutions in Hangzhou had served 1.5 million sellers nationwide, and their transaction value accounting for 70% of the country's cross-border payment transaction value.

The implementation of cross-border e-commerce is inseparable from the construction of a cross-border international logistics system. "China Railway Express (CR Express)" and "Silk Road Maritime (SRM)" are important platforms for China to promote international comprehensive logistics services. CR Express is an international railway combined transport train for containers between China and Europe and countries along the Belt and Road. In March 2011, the first CR Express departed from Chongqing, China to Duisburg, Germany. After more than 10 years of development, CR Express has opened more than 70 operating routes, which can reach more than 160 cities in 22 European countries, becoming the backbone of international logistics land transportation. As of November 2023, a total of 77 000 CR Express train trips had been launched, with a total mileage of more than 700 million kilometers. SRM is an international shipping integrated service platform initiated by China to connect global ports and shipping, which can realize data sharing and information exchange among ports, shipping, logistics, trade, and other enterprises. In December 2018, the first container route named SRM was launched from Xiamen, China. By April 2024, there were already 122 SRM named routes, connecting 135 ports in 46 countries and regions around the world, including 106 ports in 37 countries and regions that jointly build the Belt and Road. Through sea-rail transport, the function of ports can be extended to inland cargo sources. Cross-border e-commerce goods in Jiangxi Province, Hunan Province, and other places can be directly shipped to the sea after arriving at the port through the "one container to the end" model, shortening the transportation time. Chinese enterprises are also accelerating the construction of overseas service networks, especially overseas warehouses. The so-called "overseas warehouse" refers to domestic enterprises transporting goods to the target country by sea, land, air and other means of transportation, building their own warehouses locally or cooperating with platform warehouses and third-party overseas warehouses to sort and ship goods in local warehouses according to sales orders, which is much more efficient than direct domestic delivery. As of May 2024, Chinese enterprises have built more than 2 500 overseas warehouses with an area of more than 30 million square meters, of which more than 1 800 overseas warehouses focus on serving cross-border e-commerce, with an area of more than 22 million square meters.

Relying on cross-border e-commerce comprehensive pilot zones, cross-border logistics platforms and other industrial promotion measures, various places of China have focused on developing characteristic cross-border e-commerce industries. Taking Xi'an City, Shaanxi Province, as an example, this city is located in inland China and is an important stop for CR Express in the northwest region. Xi'an International Port Station covers an area of about 500 football fields, with an annual designed container throughput of 5. 4 million twenty-foot equivalent units (TEUs) and a railway freight volume of 66 million tons. It operates 18 international trunk lines from Xi'an to Almaty in Kazakhstan, Tashkent in Uzbekistan, Hamburg in Germany, as well as lines crossing the Caspian Sea, covering the entire Eurasian continent. On average, a CR Express departs or arrives from Xi'an every 100 minutes. In 2015, Xi'an International Trade and Logistics Park was approved as a national e-commerce demonstration base, it vigorously developed the cross-border e-commerce industry, and approved for 15 national demonstration projects such as the cross-border e-commerce comprehensive pilot zone and the import trade promotion innovation demonstration zone. Additionally, it gradually built a complete cross-border e-commerce industry ecosystem led by various e-commerce leading enterprises such as Alibaba, JD. com, Amazon, eBay, and Douyin. By the end of 2023, Xi'an International Trade and Logistics Park had gathered 322 cross-border e-commerce and upstream and downstream enterprises, with the annual cross-border e-commerce transaction value exceeding 4 billion yuan.

8.3.4.3 Cross-Border E-commerce Exports

China's manufacturing industry ranks first in the world. In 2023, China exported 23.51 trillion yuan of manufacturing products, of which cross-border e-commerce transactions increased year by year. China's large e-commerce platforms have set up branches overseas. For example, JD.com has established an e-commerce platform for global consumers, JD Global Sales, through which merchants can sell products to more than 200 countries and regions. JD.com has established branches in the US, Indonesia, Latin America, Europe and other countries and regions, and has also established multiple sub-websites in Russian, Spanish, English and other languages. Additionally, JD.com has set up more than 110 overseas logistics warehouses on five continents to reduce unnecessary logistics costs for global shopping. While the scale of cross-border e-commerce is expanding, a group of new-generation cross-border e-commerce platforms are developing rapidly in overseas markets, becoming a "Chinese force" that cannot be ignored. Today, these cross-border e-commerce platforms have a growing share of the global market and have become a new shopping choice for global consumers. Among the cross-border e-commerce platforms, Shein, Temu, AliExpress, and TikTok Shop are the most eye-catching. According to statistics from the Shanghai Pudong International Airport Customs, the export declaration volume of the three e-commerce platforms—Temu, TikTok, and Shein—in 2023 saw a more than tenfold increase compared to 2022.

Relying on the successful experience of Chinese e-commerce, the new cross-border e-commerce platforms have integrated China's domestic supply chain and quickly occupied the e-commerce market in many countries. In September 2022, Temu went online in the US and put forward the slogan "Shop like a billionaire". On the one hand, Temu replicated the marketing model employed by its parent company Pinduoduo in China to acquire users, and implemented it in the US market, gathering and gathered a large number of user orders; on the other hand, Temu launched "full trusteeship" and "flexible supply" services for China's SMEs. For merchants and enterprises settled in, Temu launched a support policy of zero commission and zero deposit, and provided warehousing, logistics, after-sales and other infrastructure services. The special team of the "Duoduo Overseas Support Plan" has successively visited more than 100 small commodity industrial belts in more than 10 provinces in China, and organized the export of cost-effective goods overseas. Relevant data show that the prices of shoes, clothing, daily necessities and other supplies on Temu are usually 30% to 50% lower than those of its competitors. Duoduo Cross-border exports more than 400 000 parcels per day, with an average daily cargo weight of about 600 tons. As of December 2023, Temu's global unique visitors had reached 467 million, ranking second globally in cross-border e-commerce, after Amazon; about 18% of American households had shopped on Temu. In 2023, Temu brought Pinduoduo more than 25 billion yuan in revenue.

At the same time, Chinese entrepreneurs have expanded overseas markets. Founded in Kenya in 2014, Kilimall is an e-commerce platform that entered the African market early and has occupied and maintained a leading position. By referring to China's experience in developing e-commerce, the platform, based on the concept of taking root in Africa and coexisting and prospering with local African partners, has gradually built six major service systems, including Kilimall e-commerce transaction services, LipaPay payment services, KiliExpress logistics services, KiliShop community service stores, KiliWarehouse warehousing services, and KiliClick marketing services. Kilimall has a leading market share in Africa, especially in East Africa, where its market share remains above 50%. By the end of 2022, the platform had more than 10 million registered users, and more than 7.2 million annual active users, with an annual repurchase rate of more than 50%, making it an e-commerce platform with significant influence in Africa. Kilimall serves more than 8 000 enterprises, has opened more than 12 000 stores with more than 1 million products, and has created more than 5 000 jobs. It not only brings high-quality and low-priced Chinese products to the African people, but also promotes the online sales of local SMEs in Africa.

8.3.4.4　Cross-Border E-commerce Imports

China has a large middle-income group and is also one of the most promising markets in the world. In 2023, China imported more than 5 trillion yuan of bulk commodities, nearly 3 trillion yuan of electronic components and nearly 3 trillion yuan of consumer goods, providing a broad market space and cooperation opportunities for enterprises from all over the world. In 2023, China imported 1.95 trillion yuan of specialty foods, maternal and child products, digital home appliances and other consumer goods, an increase of 1.2%; among them, cross-border e-commerce imports was 548.3 billion yuan, representing an increase of 3.9%. The "White Paper on China's Cross-Border Import Consumption Trends in 2024" released by Nielsen IQ showed that the scale of China's cross-border import e-commerce increased from 444.1 billion yuan to 548.3 billion yuan from 2018 to 2023, and the number of users of China's cross-border import e-commerce increased at a compound annual growth rate of nearly 20% from 2017 to 2023, reaching 188 million people in 2023.

China's major e-commerce platforms such as Tmall and JD.com have opened international channels, specializing in cross-border e-commerce imports. Taking Tmall Global as an example, it was officially launched in February 2014. From the initial cooperation with 100 overseas brands, it has gradually grown into a cross-border e-commerce platform that includes more than 46 000 global brands from more than 90 countries and regions around the world, covering more than 7 000 product categories, and serving more than 100 million consumer groups. Tmall Global took the lead in launching a bonded warehouse network and related infrastructure construction. Overseas goods can be temporarily stored in bonded areas and supervised by customs and inspection and quarantine departments. After an order is generated, the goods are shipped from the bonded area and can be delivered to consumers in one to three days. By the end of 2023, Tmall Global had built six major procurement centers in overseas regions, and its supply chain logistics network had covered more than 100 overseas warehouses, 500 international transportation trunk lines by sea, land and air, 40 core ports, and more than 100 bonded warehouses. 80% of the goods shipped from Tmall Global bonded warehouses support door-to-door delivery services, covering more than 260 cities in China, and more than half of the orders in China can be delivered "next day"; among overseas direct mail products, more than half of the orders can be delivered within seven days.

The development of China's cross-border e-commerce has also driven the rapid development of related industries in the source countries. The most representative case is the Chilean cherry industry. Chile is located in the southern hemisphere, and its fruit supply period coincides with the winter market in China when fruits are scarce. In the past, the cost of transporting Chilean cherries to China was high, with challenges in the routes, storage, and preservation of bulk transportation. Driven by the demand for winter fruits in China, China's cross-border e-commerce and logistics platforms have actively adjusted and responded. China COSCO Shipping Corporation Limited and other freight enterprises have opened the "Cherry Express" connecting the Port of San Antonio in Chile and Shanghai in China, shortening the original 32-day voyage to 23 days, and increasing the supply of sea-borne cherries by 1.8 times. Cross-border e-commerce platforms such as JD. com and Tmall Global have deployed direct procurement in Chile, monitoring the entire supply chain, and minimizing the time it takes for cherries to arrive from the place of production to consumers. Under various measures, Chilean cherries have gradually become a hot-selling winter fruit on Chinese e-commerce platforms. According to statistics from the Chilean Fruit Exporters Association, Chile's cherry exports to China grew by an average of 29% annually from 2016 to 2023, with 92% of cherries shipped to China from the end of November to February of the following year. Data released by the Chilean Agricultural Research and Policy Office show that the planted area of cherry cultivation in Chile has grown rapidly from 3 241 hectares in 2000 to 67 570 hectares in 2023. The hot sales of cherries in the Chinese market have in turn promoted agricultural production in Chile.

The development of China's cross-border e-commerce has also explored new ways to eliminate poverty through cross-border trade. A typical case is Ethiopian coffee. In the past, Ethiopian coffee beans were mainly exported as raw beans in general trade. In addition, due to the restrictions of traditional trade rules, trade costs were high. The revenue from coffee planting and processing accounted for less than 10% of industrial chains total revenue, and majority of the profits were generated in the circulation and sales links. The electronic world trade platform initiated by Alibaba has carried out cooperation and innovation in customs clearance, payment, logistics, etc. with Malaysia, Ethiopia, Rwanda and other countries. With the help of the electronic world trade platform, sales through Tmall Global can effectively reduce trade costs, benefit local coffee farmers, and allow Chinese consumers to taste boutique coffee beans originating from Ethiopia at a more favorable price. At the same time, the rapid expansion of the Chinese market has also increased the willingness of Ethiopian coffee manufacturers to purchase fully automatic coffee roasting and packaging equipment from China, enabling them to produce roasted coffee beans locally, and further expand the market. In January 2022, the Ethiopian ambassador live-streamed the sale of coffee on a Chinese e-commerce platform, and four tons of Ethiopian coffee beans were sold out in five seconds. In recent years, the sales value of Ethiopian coffee beans in the Chinese market has grown rapidly at an annual rate of 27%. According to Chinese customs data, China imported 20 000 tons of raw coffee beans from Ethiopia from January to November 2023 alone. At the 2023 WIC, the project "Alibaba Digital County Partnering with International Trade Center to Support Digital Poverty Alleviation in Developing African Countries" was selected as one of the 2023 "Excellent Cases of Working Together to Build a Community with a Shared Future in Cyberspace". Pamela Kirk-Hamilton, Executive Director of the Untied Nations International Trade Center, said that the development of e-commerce is an important channel for SMEs to achieve growth, and the project provides new development opportunities for developing countries in Africa.

8.4　International Cooperation on Cyberspace Governance

Safeguarding cybersecurity is a shared responsibility of the international community. China staunchly upholds the international system centered around the UN, the international order grounded in international law, and the fundamental principles of international relations based on the objectives and principles of the UN Charter. Building on these foundations, China works to formulate internationally accepted rules for cyberspace. China deepens international cooperation in cybersecurity emergency response, and collaborates with the global community to enhance data security and personal information protection, jointly combating cybercrime and cyberterrorism.

8.4.1　International Collaboration on Internet Governance

China consistently adheres to the principles of sovereign equality, non-use or threat of force, and peaceful settlement of disputes established in the UN Charter, and respects the rights of all countries to independently choose their own path of network development, network management model, Internet public policy, and equal participation in international governance of cyberspace. China firmly believes that all countries, regardless of their size, strength, and wealth, are equal members and have the right to equally participate in the construction of international rules and order to ensure that the future development of cyberspace is jointly controlled by people of all countries. In September 2020, the "Position Paper of the People's Republic of China on the 75th Anniversary of the United Nations" was released, calling on the international community to strengthen dialogue and cooperation on the basis of mutual respect, equality and mutual benefit, use cyberspace to promote economic and social development, international peace and stability and human well-being, oppose cyber warfare and cyber arms race, and jointly build a peaceful, secure, open, cooperative, and orderly cyberspace.

China supports the UN as the main channel in the international governance of cyberspace. It supports the UN to formulate a global convention to combat cybercrime, and has jointly proposed and promoted the adoption of a resolution by the UN General Assembly to establish an ad hoc intergovernmental committee of experts, calling for the early conclusion of an authoritative and universal convention to provide a legal basis for the international community to cooperate in responding to the challenges of cybercrime. China attaches great importance to giving full play to the key role of the UN in responding to international information security threats and, in collaboration with other member states of the SCO, has submitted to the UN the draft update of the "International Code of Conduct for Information Security". China has expanded its cooperation with specialized institutions of the UN on cyber affairs, participated in the formulation of the United Nations Educational, Scientific and Cultural Organization's "Recommendations on the Ethics of Artificial Intelligence", and carried out extensive cooperation with the World Intellectual Property Organization (WIPO) in the fields of domain name rule-making and domain name dispute resolution.

In March 2017, China issued its first "International Strategy of Cooperation on Cyberspace", which comprehensively and systematically proposed China's propositions on promoting international exchanges and cooperation on cyberspace for the first time, sending a positive signal to the world that China is committed to the peaceful development and win-win cooperation in cyberspace. China actively participates in the formation of regional cyber governance rules. China signed the RCEP, which covers a high-level international e-commerce rules. China actively promotes the process of joining the "Comprehensive and Progressive Agreement for Trans-Pacific Partnership" and the "Digital Economy Partnership Agreement", and participates in the formulation of high-standard rules in the field of digital economy.

China conducts dialogue and exchanges with the US with an attitude of equality and mutual respect. China is committed to conducting dialogue and exchanges with the US in the field of Internet on the basis of respecting each other's core concerns and properly managing differences, creating a sound market environment for the development of enterprises from all over the world, including the US, in China, and promoting cooperation in the field of cyberspace between China and the US However, for some time, the US has adopted a wrong policy toward China, which has caused serious difficulties in China-US relations, but China will adhere to the principle of independence and unswervingly safeguard its national sovereignty, security and development interests in cyberspace.

China deepens high-level cooperation with Russia in the field of cyberspace. In 2015,

China and Russia signed the "Agreement on Cooperation between the Government of the People's Republic of China and the Government of the Russian Federation in the Field of Ensuring International Information Security", which set the direction for cooperation between the two countries in the field of information security. In 2021, on the occasion of the 20th anniversary of the signing of the "Treaty of Good-Neighborliness and Friendly Cooperation between the People's Republic of China and the Russian Federation", China and Russia issued a joint statement, in which the two sides reiterated that they would consolidate bilateral and multilateral cooperation in the field of international information security and continue to promote the construction of a global international information security system based on the principle of preventing conflicts in information space and encouraging the peaceful use of information technology.

China is committed to promoting China-EU cooperation in the field of cybersecurity with an open and inclusive attitude. It jointly established the China-EU Digital Economy and Cybersecurity Expert Working Group with the European Commission and held several meetings; in 2012, it established the China-EU Cyber Working Group mechanism, and the two sides continuously strengthened dialogue and cooperation in the cyberspace under the framework of the working group; it jointly issued the 2019 China-Germany Internet Economy Dialogue Outcome Document with Germany. China co-hosted several China-UK Internet Roundtables with the UK and reached a number of cooperation consensuses in the fields of digital economy, cybersecurity, child online protection, data and artificial intelligence.

China strengthens cooperation in the field of cybersecurity with its neighbors and other developing countries. The China-ASEAN Information Port Forum has been successfully held for consecutive years, continuously promoting cooperation between China and ASEAN countries in the digital field, and establishing a China-ASEAN network affairs dialogue mechanism; a China-Japan-South Korea trilateral network consultation mechanism has been established; the China-South Korea Internet Roundtable was co-hosted with South Korea; the China-Africa Internet Development and Cooperation Forum has been held the "China-Africa Digital Innovation Partnership Program" has been proposed; China-South Africa New Media Roundtable, China-Tanzania (Tanzania) Network Culture Exchange Conference, China-Kenya (Kenya) Digital Economy Cooperation and Development Seminar and other activities have strengthened exchanges and cooperation between China and Africa in the fields of new media, network culture, digital economy, etc.; multiple online Silk Road conferences were held to carry out pragmatic cooperation with Arab countries in the fields of information infrastructure, cross-border e-commerce, smart cities, etc.

8.4.2 International Cooperation on Cybersecurity

Chinese enterprises, scientific research institutions and universities actively participate in the formulation of international standards in the fields of ICT and cybersecurity, and promote the development of emerging technologies. Chinese institutions continue to strengthen cooperation with standard organizations such as the International Organization for Standardization (ISO) and the International Electrotechnical Commission (IEC), as well as industry organizations such as the International Association for Automatic Identification and Mobile Technology (AIM Global) and the Data Identifier Management Committee (DIMC). China's National Technical Committee for Cybersecurity Standardization is responsible for the technical business work of the Information Security Subcommittee of the First Joint Technical Committee of ISO and IEC (ISO/IEC JTC1 SC27, referred to as "SC27"). Since 2004, it has participated in the SC27 International Cybersecurity Standardization Working Conference for many consecutive years, promoting a number of China's independently developed cybersecurity standards to be transformed into international standards. Many Chinese experts serve as conveners and liaison officers of SC27, contributing Chinese wisdom to the formulation of international cybersecurity standards.

China has established international channels in the field of cybersecurity emergency response. The National Computer Network Emergency Response Technical Team/ Coordination Center (CNCERT/CC) engages in exchanges with major national computer emergency response organizations, government departments, international organizations and alliances, Internet service providers, domain name registries, academic institutions and other Internet-related companies and organizations around the world. As of 2021, it had established "CNCERT International Partnership" with 274 computer emergency response organizations in 81 countries and regions, and signed cybersecurity cooperation memoranda with 33 of them. China has also established the "China-ASEAN Cybersecurity Exchange and Training Center" with ASEAN to jointly enhance cybersecurity capabilities.

China promotes in-depth cybersecurity cooperation with specific regional organizations and countries. In 2017, the BRICS countries reached an agreement on the "BRICS Practical Cooperation Roadmap for Cybersecurity". In 2021, the SCO Information Security Experts Group unanimously adopted the "SCO Member States Cooperation Plan for Ensuring International Information Security 2022-2023". In 2021, China and Indonesia signed the "Memorandum of Understanding on the Development of Cybersecurity Capacity Building and Technical Cooperation". In 2022, China and Thailand signed the "Memorandum of Understanding on Cybersecurity Cooperation".

8.4.3 Cooperation Against Cybercrime

China has always supported international cooperation on combating cybercrime. China promoted the UN Intergovernmental Experts Group on Cybercrime to hold seven meetings from 2011 to 2021, and made important contributions to the adoption of relevant resolutions on launching the formulation of a UN global convention on combating cybercrime. China participated in the signing of important documents such as the

"Statement of the Heads of the SCO Member States on Jointly Combating International Terrorism" under the framework of the SCO, jointly combating terrorism, including cyberterrorism, as well as separatism and extremism. China hosted and actively participated in a series of meetings of the BRICS Counter-Terrorism Working Group, introduced China's specific practices in combating cyberterrorism, and put forward suggestions for BRICS countries to strengthen cooperation and exchanges on cyberterrorism.

China strengthens international law enforcement and judicial cooperation in cybersecurity. China has reached a consensus on cooperation in the field of cybersecurity with many countries, and carried out in-depth and pragmatic cooperation in combating cyberterrorism and telecommunications and cyber fraud. In combating cyberterrorism, through various forms such as joint counter-terrorism exercises, joint border defense operations, police cooperation, and judicial assistance, China has continuously deepened exchanges and cooperation with relevant countries, jointly responded to threats and challenges, and jointly maintained world peace and regional stability. In combating telecommunications and cyber fraud, China has actively carried out international law enforcement and judicial cooperation, and jointly investigated and handled major cross-border cases with many countries, achieving significant results. From March to June 2022, under the framework of International Criminal Police Organization (ICPO), China and other 75 member states jointly participated in the "Dawn Operation", arrested more than 2 000 criminal suspects, intercepted more than 50 million USD of illegal funds, and effectively curbed transnational telecommunications and cyber fraud activities.

China joins hands with countries around the world to protect the online rights and interests of minors. China actively cooperates with international organizations such as the UN Children's Fund and the International Association of Internet Hotlines, as well as relevant departments of the UK, Germany, the United Arab Emirates and other countries to address the problem of online pornography of minors; it has joined the "WePROTECT Global Alliance to End Online Child Sexual Exploitation", and worked with more than 200 governments, enterprises and civil society organizations around the world to combat online child sexual exploitation and abuse, and create a safer online environment for children.

8.5   Summary

In the contemporary digital era, the development of the global cyberspace confronts numerous challenges. The digital divide is steadily expanding. Developing countries are lagging behind in informatization construction. Cybersecurity risks loom large, and digital trade rules call for urgent improvement. These issues significantly impede the sound and orderly development of global cyberspace, posing tangible threats to the cybersecurity and economic interests of all countries. It is, therefore, of utmost urgency for the international community to jointly address the challenges in cyberspace governance. Against this backdrop, promoting global digital economic and trade cooperation has become an irresistible trend.

China has consistently championed the concept of a "community with a shared future for humanity" and actively engaged in global cyberspace governance, offering Chinese wisdom and Chinese solutions to tackle the aforesaid problems. The Chinese government has put forward the crucial proposition of building a "community with a shared future in cyberspace". Through a series of high-profile events like the WIC, China has communicated its firm resolve and proactive initiatives in cyberspace governance to the world, effectively facilitating the translation of this proposition from vision into practice. China advocates the construction of communities of shared development, security, responsibility, and interests. The aim is to foster common development, coordinated security safeguarding, extensive governance participation, and equitable achievement-sharing among countries in cyberspace. This provides a comprehensive, systematic, and constructive framework for global cyberspace governance, guiding the global cyberspace to evolve steadily towards a more equitable, secure, and prosperous future.

In the field of international cooperation in the digital economy, China has exhibited its responsibility as a major country and played an indispensable role. Regarding information infrastructure construction, China is deeply involved in the management of Internet infrastructure resources and actively participates in international ICT infrastructure construction projects, contributing to global connectivity. In the provision of global digital services, China offers high-quality digital services such as BDS and cloud services, providing efficient and reliable technical support to countries worldwide. Meanwhile, China actively participates in digital economic governance cooperation under multilateral mechanisms, vigorously promotes the development of cross-border e-commerce, and collaborates closely with numerous countries to achieve mutual benefit and win-win outcomes, effectively spurring the robust development of global digital economy and driving the economic growth and digital transformation of participating countries.

In the field of international cooperation in cyberspace governance, China also assumes a pivotal leading role. China has always strictly abided by the principles of the UN Charter, firmly supported the leading position of the UN in international cyberspace governance, and actively participated in the formulation of regional cyberspace governance rules. It conducts extensive dialogue and cooperation with other countries on the basis of equality, mutual trust, and cooperation. In the field of cybersecurity, China actively participates in the formulation of international standards and establishes international emergency response channels. In the fight against cybercrime, China vigorously promotes international cooperation and actively joins hands with other countries to protect the cyberspace rights and interests of minors. China's unremitting efforts have laid a solid foundation for maintaining the security and stability of global cyberspace and safeguarding the cyberspace rights and interests of all countries.

Over the years, China has adhered to the UN as the main channel, deeply participated in the formulation of international rules for the cyberspace, earnestly engaged in the construction of global information infrastructure, and made every endeavor to promote the healthy development of the global Internet. China also enables countries around the world to share China's development opportunities through various means, especially cross-border e-commerce. A series of plans proposed by China and its practical actions have injected strong impetus into the development of the global digital economy and cyberspace governance, which fully demonstrates China's responsibility as a major country, effectively promotes the peace, security, and prosperity of global cyberspace, and contributes China's strength to building a better digital world.

参 考 文 献
References

1 信息产业概述
Basics of the ICT Industry

[1]　周友兵.中国信息产业简史[M].北京:知识产权出版社,2017.

[2]　联合国经济和社会事务部统计司.所有经济活动的国际标准行业分类(修订本第 4 版)[M/OL].纽约:联合国,2009:192-215[2023-12-21].https://unstats.un.org/unsd/publication/SeriesM/seriesm_4rev_4.pdf.

[3]　张显龙.自主•可控:信息产业创新之中国力量[M].北京:清华大学出版社,2016.

[4]　Carlota Perez. Technological Revolutions and Financial Capital: The Dynamics of Bubbles and Golden Ages[M].Cheltenham:Edward Elgar Publishing,2003.

[5]　Chris Freeman. The Fronomics of Technical Change [J]. Cambridge Journal of Economics,1994(5): 463-514.

[6]　吴沅,朱敏.新一代信息技术产业[M].上海:上海科学技术文献出版社,2014.

[7]　王广宇.2049 智能崛起:新一代信息技术产业中长期发展战略[M].北京:中信出版社,2015.

[8]　中国信息与电子工程科技发展战略研究中心.中国电子信息工程科技发展研究(综合篇)[M].北京:科学出版社,2017.

[9]　高文,等.新一代信息产业发展重大行动计划研究[M].北京:科学出版社,2019.

[10]　(德)乌尔里希•森德勒.工业 4.0:即将来袭的第四次工业革命[M].邓敏,李现民,译.北京:机械工业出版社,2014.

[11]　(美)尼古拉•尼葛洛庞帝.数字化生存[M].胡泳,译.海口:海南出版社,1997.

[12]　国家统计局.数字经济及其核心产业统计分类(2021)[A/OL].(2021-05-27)[2023-12-21].https://www.gov.cn/gongbao/content/2021/content_5625996.htm.

[13]　中国信息通信研究院.数字经济概论:理论、实践与战略[M].北京:人民邮电出版社,2020.

[14]　中国信息通信研究院.全球数字经济白皮书(2022 年)[EB/OL].(2022-12-07)[2023-12-21].https://www.caict.ac.cn/kxyj/qwfb/bps/202212/P020221207397428021671.pdf.

2　数字中国概况
Overview of Digital China

[1]　叶秀敏.中国电子商务发展史[M].太原:山西经济出版社,2017.

[2]　中华人民共和国科学技术部.中国科技发展70年[M].北京:科学技术文献出版社,2019.

[3]　吕本富,等.网络强国发展战略研究[M].合肥:安徽教育出版社,2021.

[4]　中共中央党史和文献研究院.习近平关于网络强国论述摘编[M].北京:中央文献出版社,2021.

[5]　何伟,等.数字中国:洞察产业数字化发展新趋势[M].北京:人民邮电出版社,2022.

[6]　黄奇帆,等.数字上的中国[M].北京:中信出版社,2021.

[7]　刘如.我国新一代信息技术产业政策特点、问题与未来方向——基于2011—2020年政策文本的分析[J].全球科技经济瞭望,2022,6(37):5-10.

[8]　国家互联网信息办公室.数字中国发展报告(2020年)[R/OL].(2021-07-02)[2023-12-21].https://gxj.xm.gov.cn/xwzx/tzgg/202107/P020210712364847771519.pdf.

[9]　国家互联网信息办公室.数字中国发展报告(2021年)[R/OL].(2022-08-02)[2023-12-21].https://www.cac.gov.cn/2022-08/02/c_1661066515613920.htm.

[10]　中国互联网络信息中心.第49次中国互联网络发展状况统计报告[R/OL].(2022-02-25)[2023-12-21].https://www.cnnic.cn/NMediaFile/2023/0807/MAIN1691372884990HDTP1QOST8.pdf.

[11]　尹丽波.数字经济发展报告(2019—2020)[M].北京:电子工业出版社,2020.

[12]　赵岩.数字经济发展报告(2020—2021)[M].北京:电子工业出版社,2021.

[13]　中国通信企业协会.2021—2022中国信息通信业发展分析报告[M].北京:人民邮电出版社,2022.

[14]　前瞻产业研究院.2020年中国数字经济发展报告[R/OL].(2020-08-30)[2023-12-21].https://www.idcode.org.cn/UploadFiles/20210426160807200.pdf.

[15]　张立.2019—2020年中国电子信息产业发展蓝皮书[M].北京:电子工业出版社,2020.

[16]　中国信息通信研究院.2022年ICT深度观察[M].北京:人民邮电出版社,2022.

[17]　中国信息通信研究院.中国数字经济发展白皮书(2021年)[R/OL].(2021-04-23)[2023-12-21].https://www.caict.ac.cn/kxyj/qwfb/bps/202104/P020210424737615413306.pdf.

[18]　中国信息通信研究院.中国数字经济发展报告(2022年)[R/OL].(2022-07-08)[2023-12-21].https://www.caict.ac.cn/english/research/whitepapers/202208/P020220819505049573088.pdf.

[19]　中国社会科学院工业经济研究所未来产业研究组.中国新基建:未来布局与行动路线[M].北京:中信出版社,2020.

[20]　吴宁川.读懂新基建:数字技术带来全民机遇[M].北京:电子工业出版社,2021.

[21]　赛迪智库电子信息研究所."新基建"发展白皮书[R/OL].(2020-03-23)[2023-12-

21］．https://www.ccidgroup.com/info/1096/21559.htm.

［22］　杨裕民.新中国70年信息化发展的历程回顾与经验总结［J］.齐齐哈尔大学学报（哲学社会科学版），2019（9）：36-40＋44.

［23］　中华人民共和国国务院.中华人民共和国国民经济和社会发展第十四个五年规划和2035年远景目标纲要［EB/OL］.（2021-03-13）［2023-12-21］.https://www.gov.cn/xinwen/2021-03/13/content_5592681.htm.

［24］　中华人民共和国国务院.数字中国建设整体布局规划［EB/OL］.（2023-02-27）［2023-12-21］.https://www.gov.cn/xinwen/2023-02/27/content_5743484.htm.

［25］　中华人民共和国国务院.国务院关于印发"十四五"数字经济发展规划的通知：国发〔2021〕29号［A/OL］.（2021-12-12）［2023-12-21］.https://www.gov.cn/gongbao/content/2022/content_5671108.htm.

［26］　中央网络安全和信息化委员会."十四五"国家信息化规划［EB/OL］.（2021-12-28）［2023-12-21］.https://www.gov.cn/xinwen/2021-12/28/5664873/files/1760823a103e4d75ac681564fe481af4.pdf.

［27］　中华人民共和国工业和信息化部."十四五"信息通信行业发展规划［EB/OL］.（2021-11-01）［2023-12-21］.http://big5.www.gov.cn/gate/big5/www.gov.cn/zhengce/zhengceku/2021-11/16/5651262/files/96989dadf83a4302895cd17cbeec6600.pdf.

3　信息技术创新
ICT Innovations

［1］　杨新年，陈宏愚，等.当代中国科技史［M］.北京：知识产权出版社，2014.

［2］　中华人民共和国科学技术部.国家高新技术产业开发区名单［EB/OL］.［2023-12-21］.https://www.most.gov.cn/zxgz/gxjscykfq/gxjsgxqml/.

［3］　国家发展和改革委员会.国家发展改革委关于加快推进战略性新兴产业集群建设有关工作的通知：发改高技〔2019〕1473号［A］.2019-09.

［4］　World Intellectual Property Organization. Global Innovation Index 2021（14th Edition）［EB/OL］.（2021-09-20）［2023-12-21］.https://www.wipo.int/edocs/pubdocs/en/wipo_pub_gii_2021_exec.pdf.

［5］　World Intellectual Property Organization. World Intellectual Property Indicators 2021［EB/OL］.（2021-03-21）［2023-12-21］.https://www.wipo.int/edocs/pubdocs/en/wipo_pub_941_2021.pdf.

［6］　中华人民共和国科学技术部.中国科技发展70年［M］.北京：科学技术文献出版社，2019.

［7］　中华人民共和国国务院.中华人民共和国国民经济和社会发展第十四个五年规划和2035年远景目标纲要［EB/OL］.（2021-03-13）［2023-12-21］.https://www.gov.cn/xinwen/2021-03/13/content_5592681.htm.

［8］　中央网络安全和信息化委员会."十四五"国家信息化规划［EB/OL］.（2021-12-28）［2023-12-21］.https://www.gov.cn/xinwen/2021-12/28/5664873/files/1760823a10

3e4d75ac681564fe481af4.pdf.

[9]　杨玉良.中国科技之路·总览卷·科技强国[M].北京:科学出版社,2021.

[10]　杨元喜.中国科技之路·航天卷·北斗导航[M].北京:科学出版社,2022.

[11]　邵素宏,武聪,黄小红.中国科技之路·信息卷·智联万物[M].北京:人民邮电出版社,2021.

[12]　中国卫星导航定位协会.2022年中国卫星导航与位置服务产业发展白皮书[R/OL].(2022-05-18)[2023-12-21].https://fe.faisco.cn/pdfjs/web/viewer.html.

[13]　赛迪研究院电子信息研究所.量子计算发展白皮书(2019年)[EB/OL].(2019-09-11)[2023-12-21].https://www.ccidgroup.com/info/1207/42117.htm.

[14]　中国信息通信研究院.量子信息技术发展与应用研究报告[EB/OL].(2021-12-24)[2023-12-21].https://www.caict.ac.cn/kxyj/qwfb/bps/202112/P020211224561566573378.pdf.

[15]　中国电子信息产业发展研究院,中国超高清视频产业联盟政策工作组.超高清视频产业发展白皮书(2021年)[EB/OL].(2021-05-09)[2023-12-21].https://docs.qq.com/pdf/DWUtCWm1LZ1dnV1Fn?.

[16]　赛迪顾问股份有限公司,中国计算机用户协会数字经济分会(数字经济产业联盟).5G产业发展白皮书(2020)[EB/OL].(2020-09-22)[2023-12-21].https://www.ccidgroup.com/info/1096/21319.htm.

[17]　艾瑞咨询.2022年中国半导体IC产业研究报告[R/OL].(2022-09-01)[2023-12-21].https://report.iresearch.cn/report_pdf.aspx?id=4055.

4　数字产业化
Digital Industrialization

[1]　国家互联网信息办公室.数字中国发展报告(2020年)[R/OL].(2021-07-02)[2023-12-21].https://gxj.xm.gov.cn/xwzx/tzgg/202107/P020210712364847771519.pdf.

[2]　国家互联网信息办公室.数字中国发展报告(2021年)[R/OL].(2022-08-02)[2023-12-21].https://www.cac.gov.cn/2022-08/02/c_1661066515613920.htm.

[3]　中国信息通信研究院.2022年ICT深度观察[M].北京:人民邮电出版社,2022.

[4]　中华人民共和国工业和信息化部."十四五"信息通信行业发展规划[EB/OL].(2021-11-01)[2023-12-21].https://www.gov.cn/zhengce/zhengceku/2021-11/16/5651262/files/96989dadf83a4302895cd17cbeec6600.pdf.

[5]　中国通信企业协会.2021—2022中国信息通信业发展分析报告[M].北京:人民邮电出版社,2022.

[6]　中国信息通信研究院.2020数字中国产业发展报告(信息通信产业篇)[EB/OL].(2020-05-18)[2023-12-21].https://www.caict.ac.cn/kxyj/qwfb/bps/202005/P020200518608842463758.pdf.

[7]　张立.2019—2020年中国电子信息产业发展蓝皮书[M].北京:电子工业出版社,2020.

[8]　中国信息通信研究院.中国宽带发展白皮书(2021年)[EB/OL].(2021-09-01)[2023-

12-21]. https://www.caict.ac.cn/english/research/whitepapers/202112/P02021122
4524461536711.pdf.

［9］ 中华人民共和国工业和信息化部.工业和信息化部关于印发《"双千兆"网络协同发展行动计划(2021—2023 年)》的通知:工信部通信〔2021〕34 号［A/OL］.(2021-03-24)
［2023-12-21］. https://www. gov. cn/zhengce/zhengceku/2021-03/25/content _
5595693.htm.

［10］ 中华人民共和国国务院新闻办公室.2021 中国的航天［EB/OL］.(2022-01-28)［2023-
12-21］. http://www. scio. gov. cn/zfbps/ndhf/2022n/202207/t20220704 _130728.
html.

［11］ 赛迪智库无线电管理研究所.中国卫星通信产业发展白皮书［EB/OL］.(2019-07-10)
［2023-12-21］. https://mp. weixin. qq. com/s?＿＿biz＝MjM5MzM4MjQwMA＝＝
＆mid＝2657675197＆idx＝1＆sn＝89438b17c0ca6fca19b98afef165e828＆chksm＝
bd0baed28a7c27c4cd5fee1c6368726443f0d3e3a0b1e3c62362c8042decf21abc989df0289
d＆scene＝310♯wechat_redirect.

［12］ 前瞻产业研究院.2019 年物联网行业市场研究报告［R/OL］.(2019-08-19)［2023-12-
21］. https://bg. qianzhan. com/report/detail/1908191411410400. html♯read.

［13］ 中国信息通信研究院.物联网白皮书［R/OL］.(2020-12-15)［2023-12-21］. https://
www.caict.ac.cn/kxyj/qwfb/bps/202012/P020201215379753410419.pdf.

［14］ 艾瑞咨询.2022 年中国物联网行业研究报告［R/OL］.(2022-01-29)［2023-12-21］.
https://report. iresearch. cn/report_pdf.aspx?id＝3930.

［15］ 前瞻产业研究院.2019 年中国自动驾驶行业发展研究报告［R/OL］.(2019-08-12)
［2023-12-21］. https://bg. qianzhan. com/report/detail/1908121708491526. html♯
read.

［16］ 中国信息通信研究院.车联网白皮书(网联自动驾驶分册)［EB/OL］.(2021-12-15)
［2023-12-21］. https://www.caict.ac.cn/kxyj/qwfb/bps/202012/P0202012153829
68589778.pdf.

［17］ 中国信息通信研究院.中国算力发展指数白皮书［EB/OL］.(2021-09-18)［2023-12-
21］. https://www.caict.ac.cn/kxyj/qwfb/bps/202109/P020210918521091309950.
pdf.

［18］ 中国信息通信研究院.数据中心白皮书(2022 年)［EB/OL］.(2022-04)［2023-12-21］.
https://www.caict.ac.cn/kxyj/qwfb/bps/202204/P020220422707354529853.pdf.

［19］ 前瞻产业研究院.大国算力——2022 年东数西算机遇展望［EB/OL］.(2022-09-07)
［2023-12-21］. https://bg. qianzhan. com/report/detail/2209071416019696. html♯
read.

［20］ 中国电子信息产业发展研究院.2019—2020 年中国互联网产业发展蓝皮书［M］.北京:电子工业出版社,2020.

［21］ 中国互联网络信息中心.第 49 次《中国互联网络发展状况统计报告》［R/OL］.(2022-
02-25)［2023-12-21］. https://www.cnnic. net. cn/NMediaFile/2023/0807/MAIN16
91372884990HDTP1QOST8.pdf.

［22］ 尹丽.2019—2020 数字经济发展报告［M］.北京：电子工业出版社,2020.

［23］ 赵岩.2020—2021 数字经济发展报告［M］.北京：电子工业出版社,2021.

［24］ QuestMobile.2022 中国移动互联网年度大报告［R/OL］.（2023-02-21）［2023-12-21］.https://mp.weixin.qq.com/s/A30Al0z7yH7Ow690mKgVcw.

［25］ 前瞻产业研究院.2009—2019 年"双 11"购物节关键数据盘点与发展趋势分析报告［R/OL］.（2019-11-04）［2023-12-21］.https://bg.qianzhan.com/report/detail/1911041621381335.html♯read.

［26］ 中华人民共和国商务部.中国电子商务报告 2021［R/OL］.（2022-11-16）［2023-12-21］.https://dzswgf.mofcom.gov.cn/news_attachments/e15a638b133d52134e0b1393fc13fc8a92bdd5ab.pdf.

［27］ 前瞻产业研究院.2019 年中国短视频行业研究报告［R/OL］.（2019-09-09）［2023-12-21］.https://bg.qianzhan.com/report/detail/1909091648561802.html♯read.

［28］ 前瞻产业研究院.2020 年中国直播电商研究报告［R/OL］.（2020-05-12）［2023-12-21］.https://bg.qianzhan.com/report/detail/2005121533237188.html♯read.

［29］ 前瞻产业研究院.2020 年中国无人经济市场研究报告［R/OL］.（2020-08-01）［2023-12-21］.https://bg.qianzhan.com/report/detail/2008111448446736.html♯read.

［30］ 中华人民共和国工业和信息化部."十四五"软件和信息技术服务业发展规划［EB/OL］.（2020-07-06）［2023-12-21］.https://www.gov.cn/zhengce/zhengceku/2021-12/01/5655205/files/a44b507d67c74591ad4f5e55b98c4518.pdf.

［31］ 艾瑞咨询.2021 年中国数据库行业研究报告［R/OL］.（2021-05-28）［2023-12-21］.https://report.iresearch.cn/report_pdf.aspx?id＝3787.

［32］ 中国信息通信研究院.云计算白皮书［R/OL］.（2021-07-27）［2023-12-21］.https://www.caict.ac.cn/kxyj/qwfb/bps/202107/P020210727458966329996.pdf.

［33］ 中华人民共和国工业和信息化部."十四五"大数据产业发展规划［R/OL］.（2022-07-06）［2023-12-21］.http://big5.www.gov.cn/gate/big5/www.gov.cn/zhengce/zhengceku/2021-11/30/5655089/files/d1db3abb2dff4c859ee49850b63b07e2.pdf.

［34］ 中国信息通信研究院.大数据白皮书［R/OL］.（2021-12-20）［2023-12-21］.https://www.caict.ac.cn/kxyj/qwfb/bps/202112/P020211220495261830486.pdf.

［35］ 前瞻产业研究院.2019 年人工智能行业现状与发展趋势报告［R/OL］.（2019-10-08）［2023-12-21］.https://bg.qianzhan.com/report/detail/1910081709070618.html♯read.

［36］ 中国信息通信研究院.人工智能白皮书（2022 年）［R/OL］.（2022-04-12）［2023-12-21］.https://www.caict.ac.cn/kxyj/qwfb/bps/202204/P020220412613255124271.pdf.

［37］ 艾瑞咨询.2021 年中国人工智能产业研究报告［R/OL］.（2022-01-21）［2023-12-21］.https://report.iresearch.cn/report_pdf.aspx?id＝3925.

［38］ 前瞻产业研究院.2019 年区块链产业现状与技术应用分析报告［R/OL］.（2020-01-07）［2023-12-21］.https://bg.qianzhan.com/report/detail/2001071621583572.html♯read.

[39]　中国信息通信研究院.区块链白皮书[R/OL].(2021-12-22)[2023-12-21].https://www.caict.ac.cn/kxyj/qwfb/bps/202112/P020211224394830046624.pdf.

[40]　赛迪网络安全研究所,赛迪区块链研究所.区块链＋数字经济发展白皮书[EB/OL].(2021-03-18)[2023-12-21].https://baijiahao.baidu.com/s?id=1696891122897630389&wfr=spider&for=pc.

[41]　中国电子信息行业联合会.2021年中国电子信息行业经济运行报告[R/OL].(2022-02-15)[2023-12-21].https://lwzb.stats.gov.cn/pub/lwzb/tzgg/202205/W020220511403033781746.pdf.

[42]　前瞻产业研究院.2020年中国半导体材料行业发展报告[R/OL].(2020-11-05)[2023-12-21].https://bg.qianzhan.com/report/detail/2011051011220492.html♯read.

[43]　前瞻产业研究院.2020年中国半导体设备行业市场研究报告[R/OL].(2020-10-22)[2023-12-21].https://bg.qianzhan.com/report/detail/2010221109417456.html♯read.

[44]　艾瑞咨询.2022年中国半导体IC产业研究报告[R/OL].(2022-09-01)[2023-12-21].https://report.iresearch.cn/report_pdf.aspx?id=4055.

5　产业数字化
Industrial Digitalization

[1]　何伟,左铠瑞,张东,等.数字中国:洞察产业数字化发展新趋势[M].北京:人民邮电出版社,2022.

[2]　工业和信息化部新闻宣传中心.5G赋能 百业互联 智领未来:中国5G＋工业互联网应用示范案例集(2021)[M].北京:人民邮电出版社,2022.

[3]　中华人民共和国工业和信息化部,等."十四五"智能制造发展规划[EB/OL].(2021-12-21)[2023-12-21].https://www.gov.cn/zhengce/zhengceku/2021-12/28/5664996/files/a22270cdb0504e518a7630fa318dbcd8.pdf.

[4]　中华人民共和国工业和信息化部."十四五"信息化和工业化深度融合发展规划[EB/OL].(2021-11-17)[2023-12-21].https://www.gov.cn/zhengce/zhengceku/2021-12/01/5655208/files/c09d992d37384268a73a201ef284909e.pdf.

[5]　中华人民共和国工业和信息化部,等."十四五"机器人产业发展规划[EB/OL].(2021-12-21)[2023-12-21].https://www.gov.cn/zhengce/zhengceku/2021-12/28/5664988/files/7cee5d915efa463ab9e7be82228759fb.pdf.

[6]　前瞻产业研究院.2019年中国智能制造发展现状及趋势分析报告[R/OL].(2019-10-14)[2023-12-21].https://bg.qianzhan.com/report/detail/1910141608391476.html♯read.

[7]　中国信息通信研究院.中国"5G＋工业互联网"发展报告[R/OL].(2021-12-27)[2023-12-21].https://www.caict.ac.cn/kxyj/qwfb/bps/202112/P020211227607989259287.pdf.

[8]　中国信息通信研究院.工业互联网产业经济发展报告（2020年）[R/OL].（2020-03-24）
[2023-12-21].

[9]　中华人民共和国农业农村部信息中心."十四五"全国农业农村信息化发展规划[EB/
OL].（2022-06-07）[2023-12-21]. https://www.caict.ac.cn/kxyj/qwfb/bps/202003/
P020200324455621419748.pdf.

[10]　中华人民共和国农业农村部信息中心.中国数字乡村发展报告（2022年）[R/OL].
（2023-03-01）[2023-12-21]. https://www.cac.gov.cn/rootimages/uploadimg/
1679309718522950/1679309718522950.pdf.

[11]　中国信息通信研究院,中国人民大学.中国智慧农业发展研究报告——新一代信息技
术助力乡村振兴[R/OL].（2021-12-24）[2023-12-21]. https://pdf.dfcfw.com/pdf/
H3_AP202201061538808867_1.pdf?1641482951000.pdf.

[12]　中华人民共和国国家能源局."十四五"现代能源体系规划[EB/OL].（2022-03-22）
[2023-12-21]. https://www.nea.gov.cn/1310524241_16479412513081n.pdf.

[13]　中华人民共和国国家能源局.2022年度能源领域5G应用典型案例汇编[G].（2023-
04-20）[2023-12-21]. https://www.nea.gov.cn/download/nylydxalhb.pdf.

[14]　中华人民共和国交通运输部.数字交通"十四五"发展规划[R/OL].（2022-01-12）
[2023-12-21]. https://xxgk.mot.gov.cn/jigou/zhghs/202112/P0202112225496942
16970.pdf.

[15]　中华人民共和国交通运输部.交通运输领域新型基础设施建设行动方案（2021—2025
年）[EB/OL].（2021-09-23）[2023-12-21]. https://www.gov.cn/zhengce/zhengcek
u/2021-09/29/5639987/files/a2d1ca20cc0448cc9380c6f2f1f7c340.pdf.

[16]　中国信息通信研究院.智能网联汽车应用服务市场研究报告（2023年）[R/OL].
（2023-04-21）[2023-12-21]. https://www.caict.ac.cn/kxyj/qwfb/ztbg/202304/
P020230421601499344793.pdf.

[17]　全球移动通信系统协会,中国信息通信研究院.中国5G垂直行业应用案例（2020）
[R].2020-03-19.

[18]　北京软件和信息服务业协会.2021产业互联网实践案例汇编[G].2021-08-02.

[19]　中国电子学会.中国机器人产业发展报告（2022年）[R].2022-08-18.

6　数字社会
Digital Society

[1]　前瞻产业研究院.2020年中国智慧城市发展研究报告[R/OL].（2020-04-28）[2023-12-
21]. https://bg.qianzhan.com/report/detail/2004281427056927.html♯read.

[2]　中国信息通信研究院,中国互联网协会,中国通信标准化协会.数字孪生城市白皮书
（2022年）[R/OL].（2023-01-11）[2023-12-21]. https://www.caict.ac.cn/kxyj/
qwfb/bps/202301/P020230111662616392246.pdf.

[3]　艾瑞咨询.中国数字孪生城市行业研究报告[R/OL].（2023-01-17）[2023-12-21].
https://report.iresearch.cn/report_pdf.aspx?id＝4133.

[4]　中华人民共和国农业农村部信息中心."十四五"全国农业农村信息化发展规划［EB/OL］.(2022-02-22)［2023-12-21］. https://www. moa. gov. cn/zxfile/reader?file＝http://www. moa. gov. cn/govpublic/SCYJJXXS/202203/P020220309588817315386.ofd.

[5]　中华人民共和国农业农村部信息中心.中国数字乡村发展报告（2022 年）［R/OL］.(2023-03-01)［2023-12-21］. https://www. cac. gov. cn/2023-03/01/c_1679309718486615.htm.

[6]　中华人民共和国商务部.中国电子商务报告 2021［R］.2022-09-01.

[7]　前瞻产业研究院.2019 年中国智慧教育行业市场发展及趋势研究报告［R/OL］.(2019-07-22)［2023-12-21］. https://bg. qianzhan. com/report/detail/1907221621522510.html♯read.

[8]　中华人民共和国教育部.教育部关于印发《教育信息化"十三五"规划》的通知:教技〔2016〕2 号［A/OL］.(2016-06-07)［2023-12-21］. https://www. gov. cn/gongbao/content/2016/content_5133005.htm.

[9]　中华人民共和国教育部.教育部关于印发《教育信息化 2.0 行动计划》的通知:教技〔2018〕6 号［A/OL］.(2018-04-13)［2023-12-21］. http://www. moe. gov. cn/srcsite/A16/s3342/201804/t20180425_334188.html.

[10]　艾瑞咨询.2022 年中国中小学教育信息化行业研究报告［R/OL］.(2022-03-28)［2023-12-21］. https://report. iresearch. cn/report_pdf.aspx?id＝3959.

[11]　中华人民共和国国家卫生健康委员会,国家中医药管理局,国家疾病预防控制局.关于印发"十四五"全民健康信息化规划的通知:国卫规划发〔2022〕30 号［A/OL］.(2022-11-07)［2023-12-21］. http://www. nhc. gov. cn/guihuaxxs/s3585u/202211/49eb570ca79a42f688f9efac42e3c0f1.shtml.

[12]　艾瑞咨询.2022 年中国医疗信息化行业研究报告［R/OL］.(2022-03-04)［2023-12-21］. https://report. iresearch. cn/report_pdf.aspx?id＝3942.

[13]　中华人民共和国国家发展改革委."十四五"推进国家政务信息化规划［EB/OL］.(2021-12-24)［2023-12-21］. http://big5. www. gov. cn/gate/big5/www. gov. cn/zhengce/zhengceku/2022/01/06/5666746/files/cbff2937df654b44a04c6ef9d43549e9.pdf.

[14]　中国信息通信研究院.数字政府发展趋势与建设路径研究报告［R/OL］.(2022-11-23)［2023-12-21］. https://www. caict. ac. cn/kxyj/qwfb/ztbg/202211/P020221123496269315741.pdf.

[15]　中国信息通信研究院.数字政府典型案例汇编（2022 年）［R/OL］.(2023-02-15)［2023-12-21］. https://www. caict. ac. cn/kxyj/qwfb/ztbg/202302/P020230215518101160564.pdf.

7　网络空间治理
Cyberspace Governance

[1]　中国网络空间研究院.中国互联网 20 年发展报告［M］.北京:人民出版社,2017.

［2］ 中共中央党史和文献研究院.习近平关于网络强国论述摘编［M］.北京:中央文献出版社,2021.

［3］ 中华人民共和国国务院新闻办公室.携手构建网络空间命运共同体［M］.北京:外文出版社,2022.

［4］ 中华人民共和国国务院新闻办公室.新时代的中国网络法治建设［M］.北京:人民出版社,2023.

［5］ 国家互联网信息办公室.数字中国发展报告(2021 年)［R/OL］.(2022-08-02)［2023-12-21］.https://www.cac.gov.cn/2022-08/02/c_1661066515613920.htm.

［6］ 中国互联网络信息中心.第 49 次中国互联网络发展状况统计报告［R/OL］.(2022-02-25)［2023-12-21］.https://www.cnnic.cn/NMediaFile/2023/0807/MAIN1691372884990HDTP1QOST8.pdf.

［7］ 中国信息通信研究院.中国网络安全产业白皮书(2020 年)［R/OL］.(2020-09-16)［2023-12-21］.https://www.caict.ac.cn/kxyj/qwfb/bps/202009/P020200916482039993423.pdf.

［8］ 中国信息通信研究院.人工智能治理白皮书［R/OL］.(2020-09-28)［2023-12-21］.https://www.caict.ac.cn/kxyj/qwfb/bps/202009/P020200928368250504705.pdf.

［9］ 中国信息通信研究院."互联网＋行业"个人信息保护研究报告(2020 年)［R/OL］.(2020-03-01)［2023-12-21］.https://www.caict.ac.cn/kxyj/qwfb/bps/202003/P020200302576687898634.pdf.

［10］ 中国信息通信研究院.可信人工智能白皮书［R/OL］.(2021-07-08)［2023-12-21］.https://www.caict.ac.cn/kxyj/qwfb/bps/202107/P020210709319866413974.pdf.

［11］ 中国信息通信研究院."十三五"中国网络版权治理白皮书［R/OL］.(2021-09-26)［2023-12-21］.https://www.caict.ac.cn/kxyj/qwfb/bps/202109/P020210926498663209246.pdf.

［12］ 中国信息通信研究院.互联网法律白皮书(2021 年)［R/OL］.(2021-12-27)［2023-12-21］.https://www.caict.ac.cn/kxyj/qwfb/bps/202112/P020211217543290402526.pdf.

［13］ 中国信息通信研究院.移动互联网应用程序(APP)个人信息保护治理白皮书［R/OL］.(2021-11-19)［2023-12-21］.https://www.caict.ac.cn/kxyj/qwfb/bps/202111/P020211119513519660276.pdf.

［14］ 中国信息通信研究院.信息无障碍白皮书(2022 年)［R/OL］.(2022-05-18)［2023-12-21］.https://www.caict.ac.cn/kxyj/qwfb/bps/202205/P020220518510041281463.pdf.

［15］ 中国信息通信研究院.网络立法白皮书(2022 年)［R/OL］.(2023-01-12)［2023-12-21］.https://www.caict.ac.cn/kxyj/qwfb/bps/202301/P020230114499859875704.pdf.

8　国际数字合作
International Digital Cooperation

［1］ 中国网络空间研究院.中国互联网 20 年发展报告［M］.北京:人民出版社,2017.

［2］　中共中央党史和文献研究院.习近平关于网络强国论述摘编［M］.北京:中央文献出版社,2021.

［3］　中华人民共和国国务院新闻办公室.携手构建网络空间命运共同体［M］.北京:外文出版社,2022.

［4］　中国信息通信研究院.全球数字治理白皮书(2020)［R/OL］.(2020-12-15)［2023-12-21］.https://www.caict.ac.cn/kxyj/qwfb/bps/202012/P020201215465405492157.pdf.

［5］　中国信息通信研究院.数字贸易发展白皮书(2020 年)［R/OL］.(2020-12-16)［2023-12-21］.https://www.caict.ac.cn/kxyj/qwfb/bps/202012/P020201216506475945126.pdf.

［6］　艾瑞咨询.2021 年中国新跨境出口 B2B 电商行业研究报告［R/OL］.(2021-02-28)［2023-12-21］.https://report.iresearch.cn/report_pdf.aspx?id＝3737.

［7］　中国信息通信研究院.全球数字经济白皮书——疫情冲击下的复苏新曙光［R/OL］.(2021-08-02)［2023-12-21］.https://www.caict.ac.cn/kxyj/qwfb/bps/202108/P020210913403798893557.pdf.

［8］　中国信息通信研究院.全球数字治理白皮书［R/OL］.(2021-12-23)［2023-12-21］.https://www.caict.ac.cn/kxyj/qwfb/bps/202112/P020211223383085909153.pdf.

［9］　艾瑞咨询.2022 年中国跨境电商服务行业趋势报告［R/OL］.(2022-06-28)［2023-12-21］.https://report.iresearch.cn/report_pdf.aspx?id＝4014.

［10］　前瞻产业研究院.2022 年中国及全球数字贸易发展趋势研究报告［R/OL］.(2022-03-23)［2023-12-21］.https://bg.qianzhan.com/report/detail/2203231520200387.html♯read.

［11］　中国信息通信研究院.全球数字经济白皮书(2022 年)［EB/OL］.(2022-12-07)［2023-12-21］.https://www.caict.ac.cn/kxyj/qwfb/bps/202212/P020221207397428021671.pdf.